LIBRARY OF HEBREW BIBLE/ OLD TESTAMENT STUDIES

690

Formerly Journal for the Study of the Old Testament Supplement Series

Editors
Claudia V. Camp, Texas Christian University, USA
Andrew Mein, University of Durham, UK

Founding Editors
David J. A. Clines, Philip R. Davies and David M. Gunn

Editorial Board
Alan Cooper, Susan Gillingham, John Goldingay,
Norman K. Gottwald, James E. Harding, John Jarick, Carol Meyers,
Daniel L. Smith-Christopher, Francesca Stavrakopoulou,
James W. Watts

PERSIAN ROYAL–JUDAEAN ELITE ENGAGEMENTS IN THE EARLY TEISPID AND ACHAEMENID EMPIRE

The King's Acolytes

Jason M. Silverman

LONDON • NEW YORK • OXFORD • NEW DELHI • SYDNEY

T&T CLARK
Bloomsbury Publishing Plc
50 Bedford Square, London, WC1B 3DP, UK
1385 Broadway, New York, NY 10018, USA
29 Earlsfort Terrace, Dublin 2, Ireland

BLOOMSBURY, T&T CLARK and the T&T Clark logo
are trademarks of Bloomsbury Publishing Plc

First published in Great Britain 2020
Paperback edition first published 2021

Copyright © Jason M. Silverman, 2020

Jason M. Silverman has asserted his right under the Copyright,
Designs and Patents Act, 1988, to be identified as Author of this work.

For legal purposes the Acknowledgements on pp. xv-xvii constitute
an extension of this copyright page.

All rights reserved. No part of this publication may be reproduced or
transmitted in any form or by any means, electronic or mechanical,
including photocopying, recording, or any information storage or retrieval
system, without prior permission in writing from the publishers.

Bloomsbury Publishing Plc does not have any control over, or responsibility for,
any third-party websites referred to or in this book. All internet addresses given
in this book were correct at the time of going to press. The author and publisher
regret any inconvenience caused if addresses have changed or sites have
ceased to exist, but can accept no responsibility for any such changes.

A catalogue record for this book is available from the British Library.

Library of Congress Cataloging-in-Publication Data
Names: Silverman, Jason M., Author.
Title: Persian royal-Judaean elite engagements in the early Teispid and
Achaemenid empire: the king's acolytes / Jason M. Silverman.
Description: London; New York: T&T Clark, [2019] |
Series: Library of Hebrew Bible/Old Testament studies; Volume 690 |
Includes bibliographical references and index.
Identifiers: LCCN 2019020066 (print) | LCCN 2019022359 (ebook) |
ISBN 9780567688538 (hardback)
Subjects: LCSH: Achaemenid dynasty, 559 B.C.-330 B.C. | Bible. Isaiah, I-XXXIX–Criticism,
interpretation, etc. | Bible. Zechariah–Criticism, interpretation, etc. | Iran–Civilization–To 640.
Classification: LCC DS281.S55 2019 (print) | LCC DS281 (ebook) | DDC 224/.106–dc23
LC record available at https://lccn.loc.gov/2019020066
LC ebook record available at https://lccn.loc.gov/2019022359

ISBN: HB: 978-0-5676-8853-8
PB: 978-0-5677-0153-4
ePDF: 978-0-5676-8854-5

Series: Library of Hebrew Bible/Old Testament Studies, 2513-8758, volume 690

Typeset by: Forthcoming Publications Ltd

To find out more about our authors and books visit
www.bloomsbury.com and sign up for our newsletters.

[Ancient History] is a game with very few pieces where the skill of the player lies in complicating the rules. The isolated and ineloquent fact must be exhibited with a tissue of hypothesis subtle enough to make it speak…

—Iris Murdoch (*The Nice and the Good*, 1968)

    Yes, even were all Seven Seas turned ink
      still hopeless, infinitely incomplete!
    Cut down all gardens, groves, for pens; still we'd
      not come one word closer to definition—
    that mass of pen and ink would pass away
    the tale, unfathomed, would go on and on

—Rumi (*Masnavi* 2, trans. Franklin D. Lewis)

To the memory of Dr. Lidia D. Matassa (†2016)

Build me up of memory
loving and angry, tender and honest.
Let my loss build me a heart of wisdom,
compassion for the world's many losses.
Each hour is mortal
and each hour is eternal
and each hour is our testament.
May I create worthy memories
all the days of my life.

—Debra Cash
"Mourner's Kaddish for Everyday"

CONTENTS

List of Figures	xi
Preface	xiii
Acknowledgments	xv
Abbreviations	xix

Chapter 1
INTO THE WOODS:
JUDAEAN ENGAGEMENTS WITH THE EARLY PERSIAN EMPIRE ... 1
  Conceptualization of "Influence" ... 2
  The Historical Context of the Judaeans in the Early Persian Empire ... 5
  The Sources Selected and Goals of This Study ... 15
  Assumptions of the Study ... 16
  Excursus: Prophecy as a Medium for Negotiating Religion
    and Secular Authority ... 17
  Outline of the Book ... 23

PART I

Chapter 2
SECOND ISAIAH ... 27
  Introduction ... 27
  The Rhetoric and Message of Second Isaiah ... 28
  Coherence and the Formation of the Text ... 52
  Date of Second Isaiah ... 61
  Social Contexts of Second Isaiah ... 72
  Background Summary for Second Isaiah ... 87

Chapter 3
OLD PERSIAN CREATION THEOLOGY ... 89
  The Old Persian Inscriptions ... 90
  Comparative Cosmogony/Theologies of Creation ... 101
  Second Isaiah in an Early Persian Context ... 108

Part II

Chapter 4
FIRST ZECHARIAH, THE TEMPLE, AND THE GREAT KING   121
   The Dating Formulae   122
   The Rhetoric and Meaning of First Zechariah   125

Chapter 5
THE PHENOMENOLOGY OF
DREAMS AND VISIONS   164
   Dream Reports in the Ancient Near East and the Persian Empire   167
   First Zechariah as a Dream Report in Persian Yehud?   185
   Coherence and Formation of the Text   187
   Achaemenids and Temple-Building in the Empire   189
   First Zechariah in an Early Persian Context   193

Part III

Chapter 6
THE GREAT KING, LOCAL ELITES, TEMPLES,
AND PRIESTS IN THE EARLY EMPIRE   215
   Initial Negotiations and Imperial Narratives:
     The Teispid Foundation   215
   Teispid and Achaemenid Relations with Temples:
     A Synthetic Overview and Assessment   228
   Excursus: Josephus and the Tale of Rising Priestly Power   242

Chapter 7
THE GREAT KING AND LOCAL ELITES
IN EARLY PERSIAN PERIOD DISCOURSE   247
   Breviloquent Refresher   248
   Elite Judaean Discourses Concerning the Early Persian Kings:
     Comparison between Second Isaiah and First Zechariah   250
   Elites in the Persian Empire:
     Towards a More Sophisticated Model   253
   Achaemenid–Elite Interactions in the Early Persian Empire   259

Chapter 8
EXIT, PURSUED BY A BEAR   266

APPENDIX:
TABLE OF DATES   271

Bibliography   273
Index of Sources   331
Index of Authors   342

List of Figures

Image in the dedication. *Lidia Matassa on Ireland's Eye* — vii
  Photo by author.

Figure 1.1. *Map of the Achaemenid Empire* — 4
  Map by author, using Google Earth contour base from 2012.
  Most recent copyright © 2018 US Department of State Geographer,
  ORION-ME.

Figure 2.1. *Model of the Ishtar Gate* — 78
  Photo by Olaf M. Teßmer. © Museen zu Berlin –
  Vorderasiatisches Museum. Used by permission.

Figure 4.1a. *Myrtle Berries* — 132
  Photo by Javier Martin; public domain.

Figure 4.1b. *Myrtle Bush* — 132
  Photo by the Royal Botanic Gardens Sydney, Raffi Kojian.
  Used under CC-BY-SA 3.0 license.

Figure 4.2. *Rod and Ring on Stele of Hammurabi* — 139
  Photo by Milkau Oberer. Public Domain.

Figure 4.3. *Panel from Arch of Titus* — 144
  Photo by the author.

Figure 4.4. *Astarte Throne, with Mischwesen (Sphinx), Beirut (DGA 20567)* — 150
  Photo by author. Used by permission of Ministry of Culture/
  directorate General of Antiquities of Lebanon/
  National Museum of Beirut.

Figure 4.5a. *Stork in Flight* — 152
  Photo by Carlos Delgado. Used under CC-BY-SA license.

Figure 4.5b. *Flock of Migrating Storks (over Israel)* — 152
  Photo by Henrike Mühlichen. Used under CC-BY-SA-3.0 license.

List of Figures

Figure 4.6. *Example Votive Inscription, Beirut (DGA 13201)*   157
    Photo by author. © Ministry of Culture/Directorate General
    of Antiquities of Lebanon/National Museum of Beirut.
    Used by Permission.

Figure 6.1a. *Public Sign Claiming Achaemenid-Era Temple,
Grakliani Gora, Georgia*   237
    Photo by author. (Site is unpublished and still under excavation;
    temple remains themselves were covered at site visit).

Figure 6.1b. *Public Sign Showing Achaemenid-Era Pottery,
Grakliani Gora, Georgia*   237
    Photo by author. (Site is unpublished and still under excavation;
    temple remains themselves were covered at site visit).

Preface

This book is an exercise in the history of religion and in ancient social history. It attempts to reconstruct *some* of the social, political, and religious processes that occurred among the Judaean populations when they lived under the early Persian kings of kings. It is also an exercise in the social historiography of empire, tracing the ways ancient, local elites interacted with imperial elites. In order to do this, the author has attempted to seek, as much as possible, "empirical" criteria for the dating of source materials. Anyone who has worked with the texts of the Hebrew Bible knows just how vexed a question that is. The author has been increasingly dissatisfied with traditional methods of redaction and source criticism as used within biblical studies, with their competing claims and methodological assumptions appearing to him as overly subjective and lacking any empirical substance. Since historiography is impossible without datable sources, this is nearly a debilitating problem. Nevertheless, an attempt must be made if the origins of the Hebrew Bible and of Judaism and Christianity are to be understood in any historical way.

This book, therefore, attempts to base its analysis as much as possible on texts and contexts for which empirical dating criteria are available or demonstrable on external grounds. Much more evidence for the Persian period is available than is sometimes utilized within biblical scholarship, and this material is a constant reference point for this study of the more problematic biblical texts. The two primary texts upon which this study is based—first Zechariah (1Zech) and Second Isaiah (2Isa)—are nearly universally agreed to belong to the Persian period, though the details of their exact dates and redactional growth have received no real scholarly consensus. Moreover, there is a voluminous bibliography for both, especially so for 2Isa. Due to the above-mentioned skepticism of the *status quo*, the author has attempted to address both of these texts independently and assess their coherence and datability *before* consulting the scholarly literature. Though it is a truism that one can never wholly shed one's biases, the author sincerely attempted to look at each text with no pre-conceived ideas other than the driving research questions. For the most part, this means only studies that the author found useful after conducting a preliminary assessment are engaged with in any detail in the book. It also means that the questions which this book tries to answer in the course of the investigation are not always the same that have often exercised other scholars. You, the reader, must judge how far the study has actually strayed off the standard path and gotten lost in the historiographical woods.

The methodological assumptions undergirding this study are based on the author's previous work, *Persepolis and Jerusalem* (2012), and they are explicated at greater length in the introduction. In short, the perspective is one that attempts to understand religion as both a communicative and social phenomenon, and to understand the significance of the Persians and Iranians for the development of what would become the Judaic religions. Thus the social world behind and around the texts are the primary interest, rather than an understanding of the texts *per se*—though some literary analysis comes as collateral damage.

All translations from Hebrew and Old Persian in this study are the author's own unless otherwise indicated.

The spelling of the Iranian chief deity varies depending on the context of its use; this study uses Ahura Mazda in reference to Avestan sources, but Ahuramazda in reference to the OP inscriptions.

December 2017
Helsinki

Acknowledgments

This study was planned, outlined, and initial research conducted at Leiden University within the context of the ERC project "By the Rivers of Babylon: Perspectives on Second Temple Judaism from Cuneiform Texts," Principal Investigator Caroline Waerzeggers. This environment was instrumental to the development of the perspective here, and the author is grateful for the opportunity to learn from (and drink with!) the Assyriologists there. Discussions with Caroline Waerzeggers, Jonathan Stökl, Tero Alstola, and Bastian Still were invaluable for understanding Babylonia in the first millennium. The book manuscript itself was researched and written within the context of the Academy of Finland's Centre of Excellence in Changes in Sacred Texts and Traditions, Principal Investigator Martti Nissinen. The ultimate proof-reading and corrections took place while a part of the Centre of Excellence in Ancient Near Eastern Empires, Principal Investigator Saana Svärd. Helsinki is a wonderful place in which to engage in such comparative and historical questions, and the value of conducting research in a large community like a Centre of Excellence can hardly be overestimated. The author is grateful to all his colleagues there. In particular, this work has benefited from discussions with the archaeologists and Near Eastern historians in Helsinki—especially Tero Alstola, Helen Dixon, Izaak de Hulster, Raz Kletter, Martti Nissinen, Saana Svärd, and Kirsi Valkama. The final stages of the manuscript were greatly facilitated by the bibliographic reach of Helen Dixon, Sebastian Fink, and Gina Konstantopoulos. My thinking has also been greatly impacted by the "Judaeans in the Persian Empire" sessions held at the EABS in Cordoba, Leuven, and Berlin, and the conversations with Caroline Waerzeggers, Lindsay Allen, and Uzume Wijnsma, among others, that we have had there. I am also grateful to LHBOTS's reviewers and editors for their comments. For all errors of citation or judgment, however, the author remains fully culpable.

Several sections of this study have received previous public airing, and several have appeared in slightly modified form in print. The section "The Historical Context of the Judaeans in the Early Persian

Empire" contains material previously published in Finnish as "The *Pax Persica* and the Judaeans."[1] The excursus "Prophecy as Medium for Negotiating Religious and Secular Authority" was originally presented at the Göttingen Graduiertenschule für Geisteswissenschaften summer school.[2] The material on creation in chapter 2 was presented in concise form in Istanbul as "Achaemenid Creation and Second Isaiah" and published under the same name in 2017.[3] The material on 2Isa's genre was included in modified form in "Achaemenid Sources and the Question of Genre."[4] The analysis of Zech 3 in chapter 3 draws on "Vetting the Priest in Zech 3."[5] Versions of the material on the identity of צמח in chapter 5 and on Josephus in chapter 6 were presented in the annual meeting of SBL in Boston, 2017, and a modified version of the assessment of Persian interactions with temples in chapter 6 was presented in the EABS/ISBL meeting in Berlin in 2017.

During the writing of this manuscript, my good friend and colleague from Dublin, Dr. Lidia D. Matassa, passed away suddenly (†2016). Her lively banter and no-nonsense attitude have forever impacted me, and she is sorely missed. This book is dedicated to her memory. I would like to think she would have appreciated it (though probably have taken umbrage at the superficial analysis of archaeology).

The author and publisher gratefully acknowledge the permission granted to reproduce the copyright material in this book. Every effort has been made to trace copyright holders and to obtain their permission for the use of copyright material. Image permissions are included in the list of figures and captions.

Epigraph from Iris Murdoch, *The Nice and the Good*. Published by Chatto & Windus. Reprinted by permission of the Random House Group Limited © 1968 (UK). Reproduced with permission of Curtis Brown Group, Ltd, London, on behalf of the Estate of Iris Murdoch. © Iris Murdoch, 1968 (Rest of World).

---

1. First presented at the Finnish Exegetical Society in February 2016 in Helsinki, and again in an Achaemenid seminar series in Dublin (same month). Published as Silverman 2016a; an English version is forthcoming.

2. "Ideology, Power, and Religious Change in Antiquity," 20–24 July 2015.

3. First presented at the Association for the Study of Persianate Societies conference in Istanbul, September 2015; published as Silverman 2017.

4. First presented at the Melammu conference in Helsinki (2015), and is forthcoming in the conference volume (Silverman 2018).

5. First presented at the EABS in Leipzig, 2013; published as Silverman 2014a.

Epigraph from Franklin D. Lewis, *Rumi: Swallowing the Sun*, is © 2013 and reproduced with permission of the licensor through PLSClear, license 7294.

The dedication poem by Debra Cash, "Mourner's Kaddish for Everyday" is used by permission of the author.

The epigraph from *Casablanca* is used by permission from Warner Bros.

The epigraph from "Into the Woods" comes from the song "Any Moment," Words and Music by Stephen Sondheim, © 1986 Rilting Music Incorporated. All Rights Reserved. International Copyright Secured. Used by Kind Permission of Hal Leonard Europe Limited.

The epigraph from *Monty Python and the Holy Grail* is used courtesy of Python (Monty) Pictures Limited.

Silverman 2017 is © Koninklijke Brill, NV, Leiden, 2017 and adapted by permission.

Silverman 2018 contains a section that is similar to a section in chapter 2. First published by Ugarit-Verlag and reprinted by permission.

The publisher apologizes for any errors or omissions in the above list and would be grateful if notified of any corrections that should be incorporated in future reprints or editions of this book.

ABBREVIATIONS

Sigla for the OP inscriptions follow the standard format of king, place, and number of inscription, e.g., DPa is Darius I, Persepolis, inscription a. An appended subscript e or a indicate the Elamite or Akkadian version, respectively (e.g., XPh_e).

1Isa	First Isaiah (Isaiah 1–39)
1Zech	First Zechariah (Zechariah 1–8)
2Isa	Second Isaiah (Isaiah 40–55)
2Zech	Second Zechariah (Zechariah 9–14)
ANE	Ancient Near East
CAD	*The Assyrian Dictionary of the Oriental Institute of the University of Chicago.* (26 vols, 1956–2010). All volumes are now open access on the Oriental Institute's website.
DCH	Clines, ed. *Dictionary of Classical Hebrew* (9 vols, 1993–2016).
HAL	Koehler and Baumgartner, *Hebrew and Aramaic Lexicon of the Old Testament* (trans. Richardson, 2 vols, 2001).
HB	Hebrew Bible / Tanak
OAv	Old Avestan (language of the *Gāθās*)
OP	Old Persian
STJ	Second Temple Judaism (i.e., Persian–Roman periods, c. 539 BCE–70 CE)
YAv	Young Avestan (language of the majority of the *Avesta*)

Bibliographic Abbreviations

AAASH	*Acta Antiqua Academiae Scientaiarum Hungaricae*
AB	Anchor Bible
AchHist	Achaemenid History
AfO	*Archiv für Orientforschung*
AJ	*The Antiquaries Journal*
AMIE	Archäologische Mitteilungen aus Iran Ergänzungsband
AMIT	*Archäologische Mitteilungen aus Iran und Turan*
ANE	Ancient Near East(ern)
ANEM	Ancient Near Eastern Monographs
ANES	*Ancient Near Eastern Studies*
AOAT	Alter Orient und Altes Testament
AoF	*Altorientalische Forschungen*

AsJT	*Asia Journal of Theology*
ATD	Das alte Testament, Deutsch
AUSS	*Andrews University Seminary Studies*
BA	*Biblical Archaeologist*
BAI	*Bulletin of the Asia Institute*
Bib	*Biblica*
BibEnc	Biblical Encyclopedia
BibInt	*Biblical Interpretation*
BibInt	Biblical Interpretation Series
BibOr	Biblica et Orientalia
BibS(N)	Biblische Studien, Neukirchen
BICL	*Bulletin of the Institute of Classical Studies*
BKAT	Biblischer Kommentar, Altes Testament
BO	*Bibliotheca Orientalis*
BR	*Biblical Research*
BSac	*Bibliotheca Sacra*
BSOAS	*Bulletin of the School of Oriental and African Studies*
BZAW	Beihefte zur Zeitschrift für die alttestamentliche Wissenschaft
CBC	Cambridge Bible Commentary
CBQ	*Catholic Biblical Quarterly*
CBQMS	Catholic Biblical Quarterly Monograph Series
CHANE	Culture and History of the Ancient Near East
CII	Corpus Inscriptionum Iranicarum
CleO	Classica et Orientalia
CM	Cuneiform Monographs
CSSCA	Cambridge Studies in Social and Cultural Anthropology
EJL	Early Judaism and its Literature
EncIr	*Encyclopedia Iranica*
FAT	Forschungen zum alten Testament
FOTL	Forms of the Old Testament Literature
FRLANT	Forschungen zur Religion und Literatur des Alten und Neuen Testaments
GDNES	Gorgias Dissertations in Near Eastern Studies
HBT	*Horizons in Biblical Theology*
HCOT	Historical Commentary on the Old Testament
HdO	Handbuch der Orientalistik
HSS	Harvard Semitic Studies
HThKAT	Herder's Theologischer Kommentar zum Alten Testament
HTR	*Harvard Theological Review*
ICC	International Critical Commentary
IEJ	*Israel Exploration Journal*
INJ	*Israel Numismatic Journal*
IrAnt	*Iranica Antiqua*
JA	*Journal Asiatique*
JANER	*Journal of Near Eastern Religions*
JAOS	Journal of the American Oriental Society
JBL	*Journal of Biblical Literature*

JCS	*Journal of Cuneiform Studies*
JESHO	*Journal of the Economic and Social History of the Orient*
JHebS	*Journal of Hebrew Scriptures*
JJS	*Journal of Jewish Studies*
JNEH	*Journal of Near Eastern History*
JNES	*Journal of Near Eastern Studies*
JRAS	*Journal of the Royal Asiatic Society*
JSJ	*Journal for the Study of Judaism in the Persian, Hellenistic, and Roman Eras*
JSOT	*Journal for the Study of the Old Testament*
JSPSup	Journal for the Study of the Pseudepigrapha Supplement Series
JSS	*Journal of Semitic Studies*
JTS	*Journal of Theological Studies*
LAI	Library of Ancient Israel
LCL	Loeb Classical Library
LHBOTS	Library of Hebrew Bible/Old Testament Studies
LNTS	Library of New Testament Studies
LSTS	Library of Second Temple Studies
MC	Mesopotamian Civilizations
NICOT	New International Commentary on the Old Testament (Eerdmans)
NINO	Nederlands Instituut voor het Nabije Oosten
OBO	Orbis Biblica et Orientalis
OCM	Oxford Classical Monographs
OIP	Oriental Institute Publications
OLA	Orientalia Lovaniensia Analecta
ORA	Orientalische Religionen in der Antike
OTE	*Old Testament Essays*
OTG	Old Testament Guides
OTL	Old Testament Library
OWC	Oxford World Classics
RA	*Revue d'Assyriologie*
RB	*Revue Biblique*
RGRW	Religions in the Greco-Roman World
RIMA	Royal Inscriptions of Mesopotamia, Neo-Assyria
RIME	Royal Inscriptions of Mesopotamia, Early Periods
SAA	State Archives of Assyria
SANE	Sources of the Ancient Near East
SANER	Studies in Near Eastern Religion
SBE	Sacred Books of the East
SBLDS	SBL Dissertation Series
SBLMS	Society of Biblical Literature Monograph Series
SBLSBS	Sources for Biblical Study
SBLStBL	Society of Biblical Literature Studies in Biblical Literature
SBT	Studies in Biblical Theology
SHANE	Studies in the History of the Ancient Near East
SIr	*Studia Iranica*

SJOT	*Scandinavian Journal of the Old Testament*
SJSJ	Supplements to the Journal for the Study of Judaism
SOTSMS	Society for Old Testament Studies Monograph Series
StAn	*Studia Antiqua*
TSAJ	Texte und Studien zum antiken Judentum
VT	*Vetus Testamentum*
VTSup	Vetus Testamentum Supplement Series
WAW	Writings from the Ancient World
WBC	Word Bible Commentary
WestBC	Westminster Bible Companion
WO	*Die Welt des Orients*
WUNT	Wissenschaftliche Untersuchungen zum Neuen Testament
YNER	Yale Near Eastern Researches
YOS	Yale Oriental Series Texts
ZA	*Zeitschrift für Assyriologie*
ZAW	*Zeitschrift für die alttestamentliche Wissenschaft*
ZDPV	*Zeitschrift für des deutschen Palästina-Vereins*

Chapter 1

INTO THE WOODS:
JUDAEAN ENGAGEMENTS WITH THE EARLY
PERSIAN EMPIRE

The present study investigates how the Achaemenid kings[1] portrayed their rule to subject minorities, in what ways the minority elites reshaped this ideology for their own use, and how long the impact of such shaping lasted. It does this through analysis of some of the earliest Judaean literary reflexes around the change from Babylonian to Persian rule and the expectations this created for the community, particularly for the temple and for Jerusalem.[2] The interest, therefore, is in understanding the social and religious developments among the Judaeans that were impacted by the greater Persian context. Careful consideration can then use these results to understand the Achaemenid kings' self-presentations and practical negotiations with one of their less numerous subject peoples better, something that remains an important desideratum for Achaemenid Studies. On a broader level of analysis, this provides a case study in minority elite engagements with new imperial realities.

The goals of the present study require several different stages, working from the "bottom up" as it were. First, close readings of two Hebrew texts provide the basis for an attempt to reconstruct some of the social-economic and political-cultural history of the Judaeans. Though literary analysis is of course necessary, it is only a preliminary step in a larger

---

1. "Achaemenid" is used as the least ambiguous referent for the empire. For a more detailed discussion of the historical context and of Persian kingship, see below.
2. This study uses "Judaeans" to refer to those living in and deriving from Judah/Yehud. "Yahwists" is used to refer to all those from Judah and Israel, including Samerina.

goal. Once these analyses have established some of the relevant pieces of evidence, they can be analyzed for elite Judaean culture. A second level of analysis can then attempt to place the previous analyses in conversation with the Persian perspective. As such, this study is both an exercise in exploring "Iranian influence" on the Judaeans and in the Achaemenid imperial engagement with their subjects. To prepare for the body of study, this introduction presents (1) the working conceptualization of "influence" that is utilized; (2) a basic overview of the historical context of Judaeans in the early Persian Empire; (3) a description of the sources utilized and the hoped for goals of their analyses; (4) the assumptions undergirding the approach; (5) a proposal for understanding prophecy within the context of elite engagements with new imperial masters; and finally, (6) an outline of the book.

Conceptualization of "Influence"

As argued in a previous study,[3] human traditions—whether religions or cultures—are in a continuous process of change and reinterpretation. This process follows what Light has called the principle of religious change and the principle of cognitive integrity.[4] This means that while change is continuous, it must follow a pattern that makes sense within a tradition's own terms. Light has characterized this as conforming to symbols, categories, and organizational rules.[5] Thinking along these lines provides a fruitful way to think about engagements with other human traditions: any change due to external interaction must also make sense from inside the system. One way to describe this process is therefore a form of "social hermeneutics": influence is "changes in thought or action which are due to interaction with other peoples, religions, and cultures… [I]n more technical language, influence is a comparative perspective on hermeneutics."[6]

As Hinnells has pointed out, such processes can be either conscious/deliberate or unconscious/unintentional; they can be positive (adoption of new ideas) or negative (rejection of ideas).[7] Textual borrowings are only one epiphenomenon of such broader interactions. For these reasons,

---

3. Silverman 2012: 29–37; cf. Silverman 2010.
4. Light 2000: 180.
5. Light 2000: 163.
6. Silverman 2011: 2–3.
7. Hinnells 1976: 9–11.

this study understands influence to mean interpretive and structural change in the receiving tradition on account of interaction.[8] To analyze literary sources as evidence for historical influence, six criteria are necessary: (1) pre-dating of the source tradition; (2) plausible historical context for interaction; (3) more structural sense in the original context; (4) a "hook" for the integration of the new element within the receiving tradition; (5) discrete, distinctive elements; (6) interpretive change.[9]

The processes of "social hermeneutics" are obviously not limited to a single domain of human thought or action. The carving up of human experience into areas such as politics, religion, and culture can be helpful to reduce the complexity and size of relevant data and to provide focus. Nevertheless, when it places unnatural limits on scholarly theorizing, it can be distorting. This study primarily investigates texts that eventually became "sacred" for several traditions, but the goal of the analysis is not limited to the religious domain, however understood. Rather, the analysis attempts to investigate how the sacred interacted with contemporary political, social, economic, and even psychological phenomena.

To understand influence like this is to understand it as a social process, predicated on human communication that is much broader than just the written reflexes with which the historian must work. The present author built this paradigm to investigate the question of Iranian influence[10] on the appearance of the genre of apocalypse, but the present study applies it to a much earlier time frame and to different genres. Analogous to the previous study, where an "apocalyptic hermeneutic" was posited as a relevant social reality behind the phenomena of the apocalypse, apocalypticism, and millenarianism, this study seeks to understand the social history of Judaean engagements behind two early Persian period texts, and to tease out what this might mean for the question of Iranian influence. The results still, of course, have ramifications for the understanding of the "apocalyptic hermeneutic" and apocalypses.

---

8. Silverman 2012: 36.
9. Silverman 2012: 35–6; cf. Silverman 2010.
10. "Persian" refers specifically to an area in modern southwestern Iran (more or less the province of Fars). "Iranian" refers to a wider language family and group of traditions, of which Persia is only one portion.

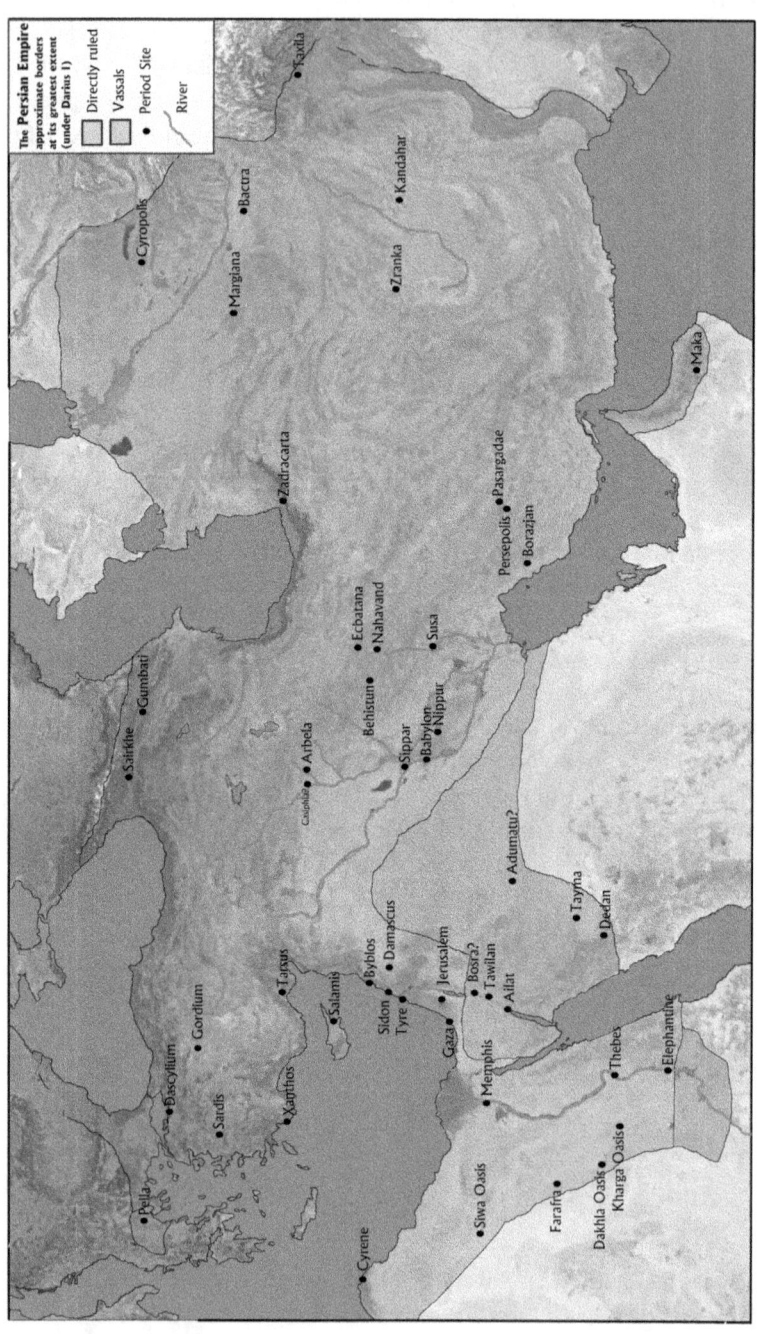

Figure 1.1. *Map of the Achaemenid Empire*

The Historical Context of the Judaeans in the Early Persian Empire[11]

When Cyrus II, son of Cambyses, conquered Babylon in 539 BCE, the Judaeans in Babylonia and in the southern Levant came under Persian control, at least nominally. The Judaeans in Egypt became fellow subjects when Cyrus's heir Cambyses II added Egypt to the empire between 525–522 BCE. With the periodic exception of those in Egypt, all Judaean communities would remain within this empire for two hundred years. These political changes also ushered in new, important social and economic realities in their wake, and it is difficult to overestimate the importance of this new context for the development of Early Judaism and the future shape of imperialism in the Near East more broadly.

Politically, two key dynamics shape this early period for the Judaeans. First is the relationship between the Teispid dynasty of Cyrus and the Achaemenid dynasty of Darius. The second is the exiled Davidic dynasty.

The pre-history of Anšan-cum-Persia (in southwest Iran, modern Fars) is murky. Nevertheless, there is little reason to doubt Cyrus's claim to be heir to an Anšanite dynasty.[12] Most likely, this dynasty was a Neo-Elamite dynasty that had successfully managed to negotiate the fracture of the Neo-Elamite state, the rise and fall of Neo-Assyrian imperialism, and the infiltration of Iranian-speaking nomads.[13] These events amalgamated Neo-Elamite and Iranian cultures and groups in the highlands to give birth to a new people calling themselves "Persians."[14] One of the power bases in the Iranian mix was likely a group of nobles or a clan called Achaemenids. A young noble from this group would serve Cambyses as a spearbearer during his conquest of Egypt (*arštibara*, δορυφόρος),[15] then murder Cambyses's brother Bardiya, and usurp the throne.[16] The political and social ramifications of this usurpation are a major element of the early Persian period.

---

11. Much of the material on Judaean social locations in this section were published in longer, earlier versions (Silverman 2016a [in Finnish]; Silverman forthcoming a [in English]).

12. Waters 2004; 2014: 35, 49–51; Stronach 2003: 137–8; Briant 2002: 17–18.

13. Waters 2004: 98; Stronach 1997b: 356.

14. On Persian ethnogenesis, see: Stronach 1997a; Henkelman 2003b, 2008; Waters 2014: 21.

15. Herod. III.139 (Herodotus 2000: 173); Aelian, *Varia Historia* XII.43 (Aelian 1997: 386–7, φαρετροφορον κύρου) states he was a quiverbearer for Cyrus. Cf. Briant 2002: 771, 108.

16. E.g., Balcer 1987; Briant 2002: 97–127; Zawadzki 1994; Tuplin 2005; Shayegan 2012; Waters 2014: 59–72.

Although Judah and Israel had ceased being independent monarchies before the Persian conquest, the Judaeans still likely had a Davidic court in exile in Babylon, whether an aging Jehoiachin or one of his sons.[17] Though probably devoid of any official positions of power, the continued existence of a dynasty with a political claim was a political and social issue for Judaean elites. In the uncertainty around the defeat of Nabonidus, the murder of Bardiya, and the accession of Darius, they would, of necessity, have had either to support or dismiss their claims.

Socially, an important fact to remember is that there was no single social location for Judaeans within the empire. Already by the time of Cyrus's conquests there were communities of Judaean and Israelite descent throughout the Near East. Unfortunately, the precise details cannot usually be delimited given the present available evidence. However, there were certainly communities in Egypt, Israel, Babylonia, Assyria, and probably Media and Susiana. Then, as now, none of these communities were likely homogenous in socio-economic status, either. Nevertheless, the old lachrymose narrative of slaves under the Babylonian yoke (and thus continuing on into the Persian Empire) cannot be held as universally true. While some Judaeans worked the land as semi-free farmers in the land-for-service sector, others became wealthy traders and still others rose in imperial service, under the Babylonians and under the Persians.[18] Some no doubt suffered under corvée labor and as slaves, while others would have been their masters.[19] Although legendary, the status of royal consort held by Esther was in of itself not an impossible social standing for a Judaean, even if unlikely.[20] The famous papyri from Elephantine come from a military colony: Judaeans working in the service to the Persian Empire at its south-western border. Thus, one needs to reckon with a wide variety of experiences and social settings, both synchronically and diachronically.

---

17. According to 2 Kgs 24:8, Jehoiachin was 18 years old when he was exiled in 597. That would make him 76 years old when Cyrus entered Babylon, an unlikely but not impossible age for a monarch in reasonably comfortable conditions (see chapter 2). According to 2 Kgs 25:27–30, he was released from prison by Nebuchadnezzar's briefly reigning son, Amēl-Marduk. For this issue, see Sack 1972.

18. E.g., Bloch 2014: 119–72; Alstola 2017a; Wunsch 2013: 247–60.

19. On the phenomenon of forced labor generally, see Silverman 2015b: 14–34. For an interesting discussion of the various complex social issues around the status of slave, cf. Wunsch and Magdalene 2012: 99–120.

20. Indeed, much much later there was a Jewish queen to another Persian king, the Sasanian Emperor Yazdegird I.

From an administrative perspective, Babylonia, Samerina, and Yehud were within the same satrapy, Babylon-and-Across-the-River, which was essentially the territories of the former Neo-Babylonian Empire. At some point, likely in the reign of Xerxes, the two were divided into separate satrapies, though the first satraps of Across the River were still drawn from Babylonia.[21] However, Babylonia was strategically and economically vital for the empire, while the importance of the southern Levant was mostly in its connections to Egypt and Arabia. Judaeans lived in several very small provinces in the southern Levant: Yehud, Samerina, Ammon, and eventually Idumea. Of these, Samerina was the richest, while Idumea became strategically important when the Persian hold on Egypt was troublesome or non-existent. Yehud was perpetually marginal, from the imperial perspective.[22]

The Judaeans who lived in Elephantine inhabited a key strategic position for the empire. They were "foreign" soldiers serving the emperor at the southwestern edge of the empire.[23] It is likely, however, that their role was more to police the Egyptian subjects, rather than guard against the Nubians. The soldiers' situations need to be considered an important part of the Judaean experience of the empire as a whole.[24]

Several Judaeans are attested within the imperial apparatus, at various places along the hierarchy: from low-level scribes to emissaries to governors of Yehud.[25] The marshaling of the various peoples within the empire is rather well attested, so this should come as no surprise.[26] One can therefore expect, despite the rather tiny size of Yehud, that Judaeans were well integrated into the imperial system, and were exposed to the various layers of administrative and cultural impacts that went along with it. Moreover, the intense Jerusalem and Yehud focus of the extant Hebrew corpus should not blind us to their relative status, even within the Judaean

---

21. Stolper 1989; Waerzeggers 2003/2004: 161; Jursa 2005: 54.

22. However, in this context, it is worth considering Brosius's argument that some regions with less advanced, pre-existing administrations may have been more directly integrated into the satrapal system as a result (Iberia, Colchis). See Brosius 2010.

23. The great kings periodically claim Nubia as a province, but it is uncertain how much beyond Aswan they controlled, or for how long. It seems likely any periods of control were mostly as vassals, like Cyprus and Arabia. See Strabo XVII.1.5 and Diodorus Sicculus (both in Kuhrt 2009: 116). See discussion in Tuplin 1991: 261–4.

24. For some recent studies, see Rohrmoser 2014; Granerød 2016; Siljanen 2017.

25. The most famous is probably Hananiah, attested at Elephantine. Even if one considers both Ezra and Nehemiah to be literary creations, Elnathan and Bagavahya were both probably Judaean governors of Yehud.

26. E.g., Henkelman and Stolper 2009.

community as a whole. The roles of Yahwists in Samerina and Babylonia (and beyond) have frequently been under-considered in scholarly discussions of this historical era.

The Judaeans in Babylonia and in Yehud had different minority statuses. In Babylonia, they were a small minority population among an imperial minority (local Babylonians).[27] In Yehud, they were presumably a majority, but in a tiny, marginal province. In neither instance would they have registered as particularly noteworthy by the Persians, nor deserving of unique treatment from the other peoples of the empire. Relations with Bactrians, Babylonians, and Egyptians would have ranked much higher in imperial priorities. However, the Judaean dispositions towards the Persians could have varied. For the Judaeans in Babylonia, imperial service would have provided one method of social advancement vis-à-vis their contemporaries. An analogous situation would be the Parsis in the British Raj, who were British loyalists against Hindu nationalists.[28] In Yehud, however, the Judaeans would have had incentives to compete with themselves in collaboration with the state, since they had the opportunity to be in positions of authority there. The same was potentially true for Samerina and Idumea, though in neither case were "Judaeans" likely the majority population.[29] In both cases, however, the local impact of imperial processes and changes should not be underestimated; Waerzegger's study of the career of Marduk-rēmanni brings this out very dramatically.[30]

Having no single location or social status, one cannot expect a single form of "Persian influence" on the Judaeans. This is especially true when one remembers that the period lasted over 200 years. Three different ways the new Persian context is relevant for the Hebrew literary texts are administrative locus, cultural horizons, and literary impetus.

While the Persian elite had a strongly oral culture,[31] the imperial administration itself shows signs of being highly bureaucratic, beyond

---

27. Though this itself was likely a fragmented identity. See, e.g., Waerzeggers 2015a.

28. On the Parsis, see Hinnells 2015.

29. There remains no truly satisfactory term for these groups. "Yahwists" as an over-arching category and "Samarians" for those in Samerina are perhaps the best options. In any case, the relations between Judaeans and Samarians requires further thought.

30. Waerzeggers 2015b.

31. For the functioning of orality in Iran generally and among the Achaemenids, see Boyce 1957; Huyse 1990; Lewis 1994; Skjærvø 2005–2006; Tavernier 2008; on the material implications of this system, see Allen 2013. On the issues around orality in Iran generally, see the collection of studies in Rubanovich 2015.

levels seen previously.[32] An efficient Aramaic chancellery operated across the empire; finds from Egypt and Bactria show a remarkably consistent system through time and space.[33] Administrative commands issued in Old Persian by the Great King, his satraps, and his nobles, were filtered through several layers of administration, mostly in Aramaic, until it reached local officials. The standardized Imperial Aramaic had widespread influence, and training in it would have been a career necessity for anyone not from the Persian elite interested in advancement.[34] This system facilitated the rapid dissemination of information, the movement of foodstuffs, armies, building supplies, and taxes. Important is the attestation of Judaeans within several layers of this system, and in various locations. There were several low-level Aramaic scribes in Babylonia, but the Yehud governors were also part of this system. Moreover, the military colony in Elephantine could not have been the only soldiers in imperial service, since the land-for-service system in Babylonia also entailed military service.

If Fried is right in extrapolating the potential for sub-satrapal governors to own estates outside their legal remit,[35] this highlights the benefits to local elites in supporting the Persian state. The discovery of what was probably a *paradise* at Ramat Raḥel dramatically brings home the administrative implications on Yehud.[36] The *paradise* was a material manifestation of the Persian ideology of the *Pax Persica*, put into practice by satraps and local governors. Here one likely has an instance of the governors of Yehud putting it into practice at home. This no doubt is the background for its use in the Song of Songs.[37] The *paradise* should be considered both in its administrative and social aspects. The political reality was that such practical engagement was a duty of the governor and his staff. The social reality was no doubt that there was potential social status to be gained by the display of Persian power in such a manner. The governor of Yehud could in no way rival the ostentatious displays of the satrap in Damascus

---

32. The classic study is Tuplin 1987a. On the administration as seen through the Persepolis finds, see Henkelman 2013; Briant, Henkelman, and Stolper 2008. For indications of relevance beyond the heartland itself, see Fisher and Stolper 2015.

33. See especially the Aršama and Bactrian archives: Porten and Yardeni 1986–99: 1:94–130; Naveh and Shaked 2012. On the system more generally, see Allen 2013: 21–36; Jacobs 2015.

34. See Folmer 2011; Tavernier 2008.

35. Fried 2003a.

36. Lipschits, Gadot, and Langgut 2012; Langgut et al. 2013; Lipschits et al. 2009; Lipschits et al. 2017.

37. See, e.g., the comments in Silverman 2015a.

or probably even the governor of Samaria, but he could still try to awe his local noble rivals.

The situation for other Judaean administrators was slightly different. The unprovenanced material from the rural Babylonian settlement "Judahtown" ([Āl-]Yāhūdu) and its neighbors is still being analyzed, but already it is clear that Judaeans were involved in the administration of these communities, beyond just being land-for-service holders.[38] As an example, one can note the individual named Yahu-šar-uṣur son of Nubâ, who appears to have been an administrator or at least seeking such a career by adopting a name type typical of royal administrators.[39] These officials would have been the day-to-day interface between the Judaean villages and the empire, facilitating taxes, corvée, and military duties. However, they would have done this in the context of a minority status. Unlike the old Babylonian families whose positions and prestige were threatened by the transfer of power to Iran from Babylon, the opportunity to work for the state offered them social and economic advancement, even if it potentially placed burdens on their fellow Judaeans. Another context was an urban one, such as Babylon, where King Jehoiachin and his entourage had been deported. Discoveries of some palace archives demonstrate that at least some of these Judaeans worked in governmental positions for the palace, and there are indications this continued into the Persian domination (see chapter 2).[40] Such officials would have been higher in the administrative hierarchy, and perhaps more committed to the imperial cause as a route to career advancement, especially after 484 BCE.

38. It is important to flag that these tablets are unprovenanced and most likely derive from illegal excavations or looting in Iraq, and thus their study raises serious ethical questions. At present there is no consensus within the Near Eastern guild on these matters, with the ASOR ethical guidelines for unprovenanced material making an exception for cuneiform (for current policy, see http://www.asor.org/news/documents/2014/ASOR_Policy_on_Professional_Conduct_PUBLICb.pdf). While it might seem clear that scholarly duty is not to publish such material, the issue becomes murkier for material that is already published and within the historiographical discourse. Since this corpus is already partially published and within the debate for this study's topic, the issue of provenance is flagged as a compromise solution.

The first volume of texts has been published as Pearce and Wunsch 2014. Another volume is expected as Wunsch forthcoming. For some early discussions of this material, see Pearce 2015; Waerzeggers 2014a, 2015c (on the ethical issues, see 187–8). A more thorough analysis of their context by Tero Alstola will be published in the near future.

39. In texts no. 2–4; see discussion in Pearce and Wunsch 2014: 29, 101.

40. The majority of these remain unpublished, though a few mentioning Judaeans were published by Weidner 1939: 923–35. See chapter 2.

One could introduce the culture of the empire through many different topics. Since the present study focuses on social issues around imperial kingship, the conceptualization of the *Pax Persica* is used here.[41] (For more on temples, see chapters 5 and 6).

The official royal presentation of imperial reality defined the meaning of "peace" with several nuances. Peace was not just an absence of conflict. It included a progressively fructifying and prosperous reality, one which invited all the peoples of the earth to voluntarily contribute their unique efforts and resources.[42] This was portrayed as the divine will, one accomplished through the efforts of the king and his ability to inspire the cooperation of his subjects. Aspects of this vision of peace have echoes throughout ANE culture in various forms. The ideas of fertility and divine blessing are well-worn. Older notions of fertility related to warrior themes and the defeat of chaos, however, are separated from it, and enter a separate discourse on royal and elite prowess.[43] These two discourses are somewhat at odds, reflecting the contradictions inherent in peace created and preserved through force. For those for whom the system was beneficial, this is a very attractive vision. The ancillary benefits of long-term stability in terms of trade and wealth accumulation should be remembered here. The cultural understanding of peace would likely carry similar connotations: the reality that allowed for cultural relations across a vast area. The empire-wide dissemination of at least aspects of elite culture (use of the well-known Achaemenid style bowls, etc.) should be seen within this context. In reality, of course, the "gifts" offered to the Great King "voluntarily" were not so freely given. The cultural appeal of the vision was probably not dimmed by this reality, however, any more than the rarity of the true rags-to-riches career in the US eliminates that narrative in the American dream. For the Judaeans in the empire, then, one should understand their engagements with the concept of peace in this light: one of very wide-ranging stability and prosperity, with an emphasis on voluntarism rather than force. They of course did not need to accept this understanding or definition, but it was within their cultural context.

The other aspect is the Persian nature of this vision. This should not be understood primarily as an ethnic delineation—though shades of ethnic identity existed. Rather, there is a threefold concentric circle: from the

---

41. A longer discussion of the *Pax Persica*, from which the material below is adapted, is published as Silverman 2016a/Silverman forthcoming a.

42. On such topics, see, e.g., Root 1979, 2000; Brosius 2005; Lincoln 2012a.

43. This is reflected particularly in the depictions of the king as hero and as archer. See particularly Garrison and Root 2001; Dusinberre 2013: 73–6.

Great King himself, to those in the king's favor, to the full extent of the Great King's rule. The (ideological) center and maintainer of the peace was of course the Persian king, who, at least from Darius I, did self-identify as Persian. While the Persians themselves did hold a special status, several other groups (Medes, Elamites, eastern Iranians) also held important esteem and functions in administration.[44] In practical terms, though, ethnicity appears not to have been a bar to participation even if it set the bar higher: high level Babylonians and Greeks are attested in Persian service, and several queens were Babylonian. The emphasis remained on the king and those in his favor. This is likely an instance where one needs to be nuanced in consideration of the role of ethnicity in this period. While the imperial elite was largely Persian, a more important criterion for social standing was royal favor, and this could fluctuate. Lastly, the Persian Peace was understood to be coterminous with the empire, which was implied to be coterminous with the entire known world. This was highlighted by Herrenschmidt who noted the use of the same OP word to denote both the world created by Ahuramazda and the empire itself (*būmi*).[45] The rhetorical identification of political control with the world is nothing new (cf. Assyrian and Babylonian claims to rule the four corners of the world). However, in practical terms, the well-protected and maintained roads and trade routes meant that the stability needed for long-term trade did indeed have a previously unparalleled extent. This must itself have had an impact on cultural imagination. The Persian nature of this, though, would likely invite two potential responses: either an identification with the Persians in an effort to participate in the benefits, or a rejection of the Persian nature in favor of another one—whether this was understood under "nationalist," local, or alternate religious umbrellas. This latter choice, however, is one which would be fraught with danger, and typically deadly until the arrival of Alexander. Both options were open to Judaeans, at least in a theoretical sense. Political actions designed to replace the Persian nature were not really open to them, though they were to bigger entities such as Egypt or Babylonia.[46] Lastly, one ought to remember that for the majority of the population across the ANE, Judaeans included, the identity of the rulers

---

44. For a discussion of the importance of the east, see Vogelsang 1992. For a useful collection of sources implying an especially important role for Bactria, see García Sánchez 2014.

45. Herrenschmidt 1976. This article has recently been republished in English translation as Herrenschmidt 2014.

46. The idea that local elites tended to compete with themselves within a larger imperial setting is argued by Fitzpatrick-McKinley 2015, esp. 79.

was likely to be unimportant—the pattern of subservience and extraction between peasants and elite remained similar whether the king was in a nearby city or another land.[47]

Since this study's two biggest pieces of evidence are literary, the literary contexts of the empire ought to be considered. At least three angles are helpful: the context of the written bureaucracy, the literature production around the empire, and scholarly narratives around the HB.

Imperial stability was maintained through an elaborate Aramaic bureaucracy, within which some Judaeans participated. Indeed, one would suspect that the majority, if not the entirety, of the literate Judaean population in this period was trained for this purpose.[48] This means that the Judaean scribes of this period were trained, and operating, in a system designed to perpetuate the empire. That this likely involved "indoctrination" in the official view of the world is suggested by the finds from the Judaean colony at Elephantine. Among the documentary material recovered were three pieces of literature: the Aramaic story of and proverbs attributed to *Ahiqar*, a Demotic *Tale of Ḥor*, and a translated version of Darius's Behistun inscription that included a section from his tomb on proper kingship.[49] The last one functions as a primer in maintaining the *Pax Persica* for the soldiers at the empire's frontier. It is reasonable to understand this as part of the scribal "curriculum" there.[50] Similar reflexes are expectable elsewhere as well. In any case, the very nature of their scribal education and administrative contacts no doubt familiarized them with the official narrative. Moreover, evidence for very long-distance travel along the Royal Road by individual messengers implies that some Judaeans may have had the opportunity to experience the imperial extent first hand.[51]

---

47. Cf. Boer 2015: 151, who characterizes the Persian Empire as simply being the most sophisticated in not extracting too much from its subjects; van der Steen 2011.

48. The estimation of literacy levels in antiquity is notoriously difficult, yet all but the most extreme scholars agree that it was a very low percentage of the population, certainly by modern standards. Niditch 1996: 39, gives an estimate of 10 percent for Greece and 1 percent for the ANE. Nissinen 2005: 158, favors under 10 percent for Yehud. Recently, Boer 2015: 130, favored only 1 percent literacy rate.

49. For the three texts, see Porten and Yardeni 1986–99: 3:21–71. For a discussion of the interpolation from DNb, see Sims-Williams 1981. For a discussion of some Judaean reception of this, see Granerød 2013 and Mitchell 2015. See also the comments on the genre in Silverman 2018.

50. Recently, on the basis of a renewed inspection of the papyrus, Mitchell has argued that the text was being continuously re-used. See Mitchell 2017.

51. For a traveling satrap, see Henkelman 2010: 704–13. For the system in general, see Graf 1994.

The production of "literature" itself, however, was unlikely to be part of any scribes' official duties, at least non-official genres. Indeed, beyond the official royal inscriptions and administrative texts, there is currently no evidence of the writing down of Iranian storytelling or religion. Yet it is known that some scholarly elites did indeed engage with, write, and transmit literature from their traditions. The most well-known and famous are the Babylonian scribes. There is also surviving Egyptian literature from the period of Persian control. The Achaemenid Empire is coterminous with much of the extant classical literature as well, partially written in reaction to it. The contexts of these comparators, however, are quite different from the Judaean ones. The elite Babylonians had lost an empire, and the Egyptians were in the process of permanently losing theirs. The Athenians were attempting to build their own sort of empire as a buffer to the Persians. The Judaeans were either in a post-collapse society (Yehud),[52] descendants of deportees (Babylonia, Assyria), military colonists (Elephantine), or long-term residents (Samerina). The reasons for writing were unlikely to be identical in all these areas.

In order to write literature, besides the requisite advanced literary skills, one must have sufficient wealth and leisure time to indulge in it, or a pressing incentive. This does not necessarily limit literary production to the highest classes, but it likely excludes the lowest. The reasons and implications of this production raise the question of the sociology of literature.[53] It has been fashionable recently to relate literary production (particularly within empires) to "identity formation."[54] This can indeed be an important element, though one should be aware that an explicit interest in "identity" as an issue is a modern lens. Identity is not the only reason for writing, however; the causes for writing literature are as varied and numerous as there are writers. In the present context, one must reckon with a situation in which a very small literate minority of a very small population took pains to write without a ready reading audience—thus even if identity proves a salient variable, it cannot exhaust the reasons.

A common discourse at present is to treat the origins of the HB as a response to crisis: the loss of independence and local kingship, and the formation of a new religious identity. At the same time, many scholars treat the collection as a product of the long period of Persian control over Palestine, if not in terms of writing, then at least in terms of collation and redaction. Persian control over Palestine entailed a remarkably

---

52. For the understanding of the Kingdom of Judah after 587 as a post-collapse society, see Faust 2007, 2012; Valkama 2013; the idea derives from Tainter 1994.

53. For an overview of some of the dynamics involved, see Wilson 2012.

54. E.g., Liss and Oeming 2010. Especially true for the HB, e.g., Ben Zvi 2011.

stable period. In one sense, this is an ideal setting for enabling efforts towards cultural pursuits like literature. In another sense, it is on first glance an unlikely cause for writing as a cure for crisis. This is a point that deserves some further thought. If the trauma of the Neo-Babylonian conquests, destruction, and deportations did not remain the impetus for some thoroughgoing tradition recovery, the Persian domination takes a particular hue. Either the overall collection was not the result of crisis, or the *Pax Persica* was perceived by those responsible for its collection as horribly oppressive. The present author suspects that subsuming writing or collecting under an umbrella of trauma is too reductionist. There is more at work in the dynamics around being a minority elite in an ancient empire. This study hopes to contribute towards delimiting some of the relevant dynamics.

The Sources Selected and Goals of This Study

The bulk of the present work is based on the analysis of two source texts: Second Isaiah (2Isa) and First Zechariah (1Zech). These texts were chosen as useful starting places, as each text is generally agreed to be relevant for the early Persian period, and as each addresses changing political and religious circumstances. Although decisions on their relationship to their current literary settings must be made (i.e., Isaiah and Zechariah), extensive consideration of redaction criticism falls outside the intended scope. Time and space have also not allowed, as originally intended, the inclusion of similarly extensive analyses of other texts relevant for the Persian era (e.g., Haggai, Ezra-Nehemiah, or the Elephantine corpus). Nevertheless, a wide variety of ANE texts are discussed along the way, as determined by questions raised in the first level of analysis. Other types of comparative questions, such as how these texts can be read in dialogue with other "canonical" Hebrew texts or with other theological "intertexts" is only of ancillary interest here. As indicated above, the controlling perspective for both 2Isa and 1Zech concerns reactions to the Persians in the reigns of Cyrus, Cambyses, Bardiya, and Darius I.

After the base analyses, this study tries to read the texts in light of the changing imperial contexts, again in dialogue with a broader array of ANE sources. The combined analyses of both texts can then provide a basis for a deeper consideration of how the Achaemenids interacted with local elites.

The goal with this procedure is to be able to pinpoint some of the ways the Judaeans reacted to the Persians, and some of the ways the Persians portrayed themselves to their subjects. Future studies can then build upon these results in dialogue with other Hebrew texts. The ultimate force of this study expands on the argument advanced in the present author's earlier work, *Persepolis and Jerusalem,* namely that the origins of "Iranian influence" belong in the Achaemenid Empire rather than in the Hellenistic or Roman Empires. Some arguments also continue the working thesis of the impact of Achaemenid imperial structures on Judaean conceptions of YHWH's heavens.

Assumptions of the Study

Both 2Isa and 1Zech derive from "prophetic" books, raising the question of what prophecy is. This study follows the studies of Wilson, Overholt, Pedersen, and Nissinen in understanding prophecy as a social phenomenon whereby an intermediary proclaims a supernatural message to a human audience, as an intuitive form of divination, with written reflexes an unnecessary epiphenomenon.[55] As such, the analysis of texts claiming to be prophetic involves consideration of the ways prophecy functioned, as well as the ways it became written down.

Although the initial analyses of this study focus on two literary texts from the Hebrew prophetic books, it is not *a priori* assumed that they share either the same genre or even the same literary origins. As Davies has noted, it is too simplistic to build a picture of a monolithic or teleological process in the prophetic collection's formation; each text must be analyzed on its own.[56] Thus 2Isa and 1Zech are scrutinized for their genre before using the genre to inform the historical analyses. To anticipate the later results, this study argues they are in fact entirely separate genres, 2Isa representing an oral dictated poem (chapter 2) and 1Zech a redacted vision report and oracle collection (chapter 5).

More broadly, this study assumes that literary texts cannot be understood in splendid isolation. Nor can they be understood only in relation to other literary texts. Rather, they are understood to be instances of human communication that must be analyzed—as far as possible—in line with other forms of communication. This means addressing not just questions of authors and audiences, but also questions of medium, genre, rhetoric, social and political contexts, material and imaginary cultures, and other structural features. Most of these aspects have their own disciplines and subfields within the academy. Therefore, where possible, this study seeks to dialogue with other disciplines when trying to answer questions

---

55. E.g., Wilson 1980; Overholt 1986, 1989; Nissinen 2000a, 2000b, 2003, 2014; Stökl 2012.

56. Davies 2000: 78.

raised by the textual analysis before seeking answers within the Hebrew "canon."[57] This study dialogues with oral theory and rhetorical theory, comparative mythology, sociology of forced migration, Assyriology, archaeology, psychology, iconography, and empire studies.

Excursus:
Prophecy as a Medium for Negotiating Religion and Secular Authority[58]

The Persian Empire incorporated, adapted, and superseded local forms of legitimacy and control, from the Danube to the Indus. Scattered evidence suggests the Great Kings made a concerted effort to disseminate their understanding of kingship. For this project to have been successful, local elites and communities had to have interacted with the process, both receptively and creatively. This excursus explores the role that the institutions of prophecy may have played within local negotiations of power and legitimacy vis-à-vis the Persians. Since prophecy had long local traditions in most areas of the empire, it offers a potentially effective but varied locus for such necessary negotiations.[59] In particular, it asks whether the Achaemenids made specific efforts to use or manipulate local prophets to bolster local approval, rewarded favorable oracles after the fact, or if local elites made use of the institution to justify their own collaborations with their new imperial lords. The present study explores these issues primarily with 2Isa and 1Zech, but this excursus tries to consider a broader ANE context.

The narrative of Herodotus contains a couple of references to various oracles that are suggestive in this perspective. One need not assume that these anecdotes are necessarily historically accurate; nevertheless, they are phenomenologically significant. Herodotus tells a few stories concerning the Persian conquest of western Anatolia; it is key to remember that Herodotus was retelling them with hindsight, after Xerxes's invasion of the Greek mainland. The fact that they are told well after the time period they describe is significant for how they were functioning when Herodotus heard them, regardless of their facticity.

The story of the Delphic oracle's ambiguous messages to Croesus is well known (Herod. I.50–6, 91).[60] Interesting in this story is the way that it maintains Croesus as a pious, albeit naïve, ruler while simultaneously supporting Cyrus's conquest and right

---

57. For reasons of methodological outlook, so-called intertextuality is not used in this study. For the present author's reservations, see Silverman 2016b.

58. The main idea of this excursus was first presented at the Graduiertenschule für Geisteswissenschaften Göttingen summer school in "Ideology, Power, and Religious Change in Antiquity," 20–24 July 2015.

59. Despite the title, the otherwise interesting collection of Lenzi and Stökl 2014 does not directly deal with this issue.

60. Available in Herodotus 2002: 57–63, 119.

to rule Lydia. By making his victory predicted by Apollo, the conquest by definition becomes divinely legitimated. Moreover, by being repeated after the fact with the notice of previous misinterpretation, it manages both to justify earlier resistance to the Persian army while supporting a present and continued legitimacy for the Persian supremacy. Indeed, the former Lydian monarch is himself depicted as accepting this transition of power as legitimate. The importance of Croesus's acceptance is strengthened when one considers that a pre-Herodotean tradition still held Croesus as having been pious[61]—in effect, handing Cyrus the same mantle.

This is not just a top-down form of propaganda; rather, it is a locally acceptable way for local elites to interact with and collaborate with the Persians. Through the medium of divine communication, they have their justification for participation with the new (legitimate) regime. The fact that Delphi was not within the relevant Anatolian territories makes it seem as if the above narrative was not a ploy on behalf of the sanctuary itself, but that it functioned more within the Greek-speaking communities that held the oracle in esteem. A few other examples, however, seem to evince more local machinations.

Also in Herodotus's narrative of the fall of Croesus, one of the local oracles is claimed to respond to a query by Croesus with the correct answer (i.e., that Cyrus would be victorious), but to arrive too late to Sardis to tell it to Croesus (Herod. I.78).[62] Though this of course fits Herodotus's general interest in fulfilled oracles, two details of this anecdote are suggestive: (1) the oracle comes from Telmessus in Lycia, a region that came under the Persian sway; (2) the answer never actually reached Croesus. A pro-Cyrus response was thus essentially synchronous with his victory or perhaps even *ex eventu*. In this light, the pro-Persian answer might have served as a way for the Lycians to negotiate their impending conquest, either by eliciting favor from Cyrus by having issued him a favorable oracle, or by justifying their own incorporation to themselves. A similar sort of dynamic could be considered for the oracle that ordered the Cnidians not to resist their capture by Cyrus's general Harpagus (I.174).[63] For a biblical scholar, the latter oracle is rather reminiscent of Jeremiah's exhortations to submit to the Babylonians.[64]

A last example from Herodotus comes from the oracle of Apollo at Miletus. Twice this oracle ordered the return of the rebel Pactyes to the Persians (I.158–9).[65] Briant has interpreted this episode as a sign of Cyrus's attempts to gain local sanctuaries' support.[66] No doubt there is truth in this. Indeed, Dusinberre sees the

61. In a verse by Bacchylides. Available in Kuhrt 2009: 65–6.
62. Available in Herodotus 2002: 99.
63. Available in Herodotus 2002: 219.
64. Thanks to Jonathan Stökl for reminding me of this parallel. Silver 2014 reads this rather as inverting Neo-Assyrian rhetoric.
65. Available in Herodotus 2002: 199–201.
66. Briant 2002: 38. Indeed, Kingsley 1995: 194 has seen deliberate Persian use of prophecy in the lead-up to Xerxes's invasion of the Greek mainland.

continued building works at the site as evidence of its Persian patronage.[67] However, this episode can equally be read as a ploy by the sanctuary and its supporters to negotiate their own positions in expectation of Persian rule.[68] For all the intricacies of the political situations, one way to understand the function of such oracles was to see them as providing the locals with a means of *self*-legitimation as much as for legitimation of the empire. Currying favor with the overlords therefore goes hand in hand with self-justification.

What is worth considering, therefore, is understanding certain instances of prophecy in this sort of social sense—from the "middle-up" as it were—as one mechanism whereby ANE elites could interact with new overlords in a way acceptable to *both* parties. Such an understanding somewhat collapses a distinction between imperial propaganda and local appropriation because it partakes of both. Dusinberre sees religion as a medium for local assertion of autonomy,[69] but it might be profitable to view it as more double-sided than that. This takes seriously two things: (1) the general sociological maxim that who can prophesy and what can be prophesied are socially determined,[70] so that, by definition, even novel prophecies are still utilizing aspects of inherited traditions, and (2) the obvious fact that local elites clearly *did* cooperate/collaborate/make use of Achaemenid hegemony, or the empire could not have lasted for over two centuries. This is a more positive and potentially useful way to think about such matters than the fashionable appeal to subversion and "hidden transcripts" based on the work of James C. Scott.[71] This "postcolonial" perspective is susceptible to a fourfold critique: (1) Scott's work was with lower classes versus upper classes rather than with local elites versus imperial elites, and thus the relations are quite different—it is fairly certain that our written sources from the ANE do not derive from the peasantry; (2) it is *a priori* prejudicial, viewing all things imperial as inherently bad, when there is no indication that such a view would have been a major

---

67. Dusinberre 2013: 221.

68. Briant 2002: 535 claims that this sanctuary's administration was so-pro-Persian that they had to seek protection from Xerxes, something he claims is in Ctesias §27 and Pausanias VIII.46.3. However, the present author cannot find this in Ctesias, and Pausanias rather claims that Xerxes confiscated their statue of Apollo. The story actually derives from Strabo 14.1.5.

69. Dusinberre 2013: 63.

70. E.g., Wilson 1980: 52–5; Overholt 1989: 17–25.

71. Scott 1985. For some examples of work appealing to his idea of the "hidden transcript," see, e.g., Mein 2001: 71; Smith-Christopher 2002: 24; 2011: 257; Carr 2011: 304; Portier-Young 2011; McKinlay 2013, esp. 89; Eidevall 2014: 110–11, 125; Finn 2017: 15–16. In general terms, discussions of "hidden transcripts" take a Hegelian view of "discourse," with a monolithic narrative creating its inevitable antithesis. All discourse is polyvalent, and traditions contain within themselves tools for their own critique—within limits. While Scott's work may very well be applicable to peasants, its applicability to the production of ancient elites (i.e., ANE literature)—is highly suspect.

or dominant view among ancient elites involved; (3) it often takes a Hegelian form of empire—resistance, as if either were monolithic entities with no shades of ambiguity or ambivalence; (4) the present author's suspicion that some of the enthusiasm within biblical studies for such postcolonial readings of (biblical) prophecy is to salvage them once again as modern ethical heroes, using the parlance of the twenty-first century—whereas the prophets were proto-Luthers for the ilk of Wellhausen, they are now proto-Marxes or Gandhis for the liberal West. Perhaps one should rather try to think about the phenomenon from a less ideologically charged starting point. Of course, such a critique does not imply either that resistance does not exist or was not important—merely that it cannot be assumed as a starting point; resistance is merely one option.

Unfortunately, the presently available evidence for ANE prophecy comes almost solely from royal contexts,[72] and thus it does not preserve any material from the kind of contexts that this excursus attempts to conceptualize. Incidental mentions of "lower class" prophecy appear through the cracks, making its existence without written preservation highly likely.[73] It must be assumed that prophecy continued to exist into the Persian Empire, however, even if it no longer would have had such close ties to monarchy. Sadly, the few hints of prophecy in the Persian Empire are dubious. Strabo mentions, in a discussion of oracles as divine laws which society formerly consulted, that among the Persians existed oracles from the Magi, necromancers, lecanomancers, and hydromancers (16.2.39).[74] However, the veracity of this list is dubious, given that he claims that the "Assyrian" oracles were called the "Chaldaeans." Similarly, Boyce's claim that the so-called Persian sibyl was a state-sponsored prophet in the late Achaemenid Empire cannot presently be corroborated.[75] Nevertheless, the phenomenon had not entirely disappeared by the Parthian era, as demonstrated by a reference in the astronomical diaries to a prophet of Nanaya in Babylon and Borsippa.[76] It is interesting to note, however, the scribe's dismissal of this prophet as a madman. In contrast, there are a few mentions of prophets operating in Persian Yehud within the HB.

The HB explicitly places four named prophets in Persian Yehud (Haggai, Zechariah, Shemaiah, Noadiah) and implies another in Babylon (within 2Isa, rather than the originator of the text of 2Isa itself, since the latter is only an inference from

---

72. The Mari texts derive from the palace before its conquest, and the same is true for the Neo-Assyrian examples. For a convenient collection, see Nissinen 2003. (There is soon to be an expanded, second edition.)

73. SAA 16 nos. 59–61 (Luukko and Van Buylaere 2002: 52–7, Nissinen 2003: nos. 115–17 [pp. 170–5]); cf. Stökl 2012: 105. Frahm 2010: 120–6 argues not lower class, but part of a counter-espionage attempt. Although the prophetess is called a "slave girl," she still prophesies in favor of a royal pretender.

74. Strabo 1930: 288–9.

75. Boyce 1989: 62.

76. Astronomical Diary -132b (Sachs and Hunger 1996: 210–21, see obv. line 29, rev. 25–36, and the left edge; Nissinen 2003: no. 134 [pp. 196–8]).

the text's current setting within a biblical prophetic book).[77] The first two appear in the books of their own name and in mentions in Ezra. (The prophecies attributed to Zechariah will be discussed in Part II). Nehemiah 6:10–14 mentions Shemaiah and Noadiah as prophets supposedly hired against Nehemiah by Sanballat and Tobiah. Moreover, Noadiah is said to have other prophets with her, giving an impression of a continued and typical social phenomenon. This story is an interesting instance of prophecy being used to foster Persian authority by local elites (indeed, neighboring governors), even if it is ahistorical. The potential for prophecy to bolster political stances is again reinforced in Neh 6:7, where Sanballat accuses Nehemiah of hiring (unnamed) prophets to call himself king. This would be prophecy used to justify a change in leadership, just like the supposed hiring of prophets by Sanballat and Tobiah to maintain the Persian *status quo*. Whatever one thinks of the narrator in Nehemiah, these mentions of prophets only make sense if the audience could have accepted the plausibility of prophets still functioning in such a manner.

Although chapter 2 argues that 2Isa was not originally prophecy (this designation only coming about as a result of its attachment to the book of Isaiah),[78] it still may contain some interesting evidence of prophecy functioning as local justifications for collaboration. In particular, there are the repeated mentions of previous prophecies whereby YHWH claims to have foretold Cyrus's success (e.g., 41:1–5; 48:14–16). No such predictions are extant. Their existence, however, would have been necessary for the rhetoric of 2Isa to have made any sense at all to its original audiences.[79] If this is granted, then one could consider these claims to be evidence that among the Babylonian Judaeans, (a) prophet(s) announced oracles favorable to Cyrus and that these would have been useful for some elites, such as the composer(s) of 2Isa itself. Indeed, the positive portrayal of Cyrus in this work is remarkable and is at least partially justified in this stance by these cited prophecies.

While we can assume that the book of Zechariah had a complex textual history, the present discussion focuses only on 1Zech, with the understanding that the dates are reasonably accurate indicators that the vision-oracles were pronounced on those days, even if the text which is extant is likely not identical to it.[80] Here the interest is in trying to explain some prophecy within Yehud as a mechanism for negotiating Persian rule rather than an understanding of the biblical book of Zechariah *per se*. Thus, the start is from the opposite angle taken by Blenkinsopp, though his methodological point is well-taken.[81]

---

77. The dates of the other minor prophets are debated and left out of discussion here. In any case, they are not explicitly named as prophets functioning in the Persian Empire. For a discussion of the genre of 2Isa, see chapter 2.

78. See chapter 2.

79. The present author does not find explanations of these as related to the present canonical book of Isaiah to be convincing.

80. See Part II.

81. Blenkinsopp 2001.

Therefore, one can consider the visions as if they were real visions and before their collection into the present books, and before they became "sacred scripture," whatever that actually means for STJ. While more traditional, theological readings are not necessarily contradicted by this reading, understanding these visions as prophecy mediating religious and secular concerns raises some new social and communicative understandings and questions. These latter are what this excursus explores. Taking this position would then mean that the analytical perspective changes to include pragmatic political considerations instead of the typical scholarly preoccupations with "eschatology" or "messianism."[82] Moreover, this perspective means that prophecy within Persian Yehud and even in Babylonia was still functioning in a similar manner to the way it had functioned in monarchic Judah, despite the lack of native monarchy. The social question it raises is for whom is it functioning as a useful medium: temple officials and/or priests? Governors? Local aristocrats/landowners? The scribal class? It also raises the vexed issue of the supposed "death of prophecy" and the appearance of the peculiar biblical genre of the prophetic book. The continued functioning of live prophets for at least a part of the early Persian period implies that an emphasis solely on the "literati" as is the wont of scholars such as Ben Zvi is likely too narrow and too focused on the extant biblical text to make much social sense.[83] At present two likely groups come to mind: the governor and his aristocratic allies and the temple administration. Both of these are groups that by necessity needed to cooperate with the Persian hegemony to retain their position, and thus would have been able to make use of the legitimizing potential of prophecy. The much discussed letter to Yehud and Samerina from Elephantine could be adduced as signs of ties between various such groups, the responding officials all being governors.[84] Moreover, the temple-centeredness of many presumably Persian-era biblical sources might indicate such was the case, i.e., that prophecy was functioning within the temple as part of the general administrative apparatus.

In previous work described above, a sociological model for understanding and investigating religious influence as it is detectable in texts was presented.[85] This effort produced six criteria for establishing influence in texts, but it left out a more social component. This present excursus tries to deal with similar sociological issues, but with more of a focus on the world outside of the textual reflexes. To use the terms used previously, this is discussing prophecy as a "hook" for interaction—in other words, a way for the new to be incorporated into the old. What is different is the positing of one particular kind of situation in which it would have been to the social

---

82. For some problematization of the use of these terms in scholarship, see Silverman 2014b.

83. This is the perspective he takes in most of his work. For a good representation of the way he discusses Persian Yehud, see, e.g., Ben Zvi 2004, 2011; cf. Wilson 2017.

84. AP 30/31 and its response in AP 32 from the governor of Yehud (Bagavahya) and the sons of the governor of Samerina (Shelemiah and Delayah). Available in Lindenberger 2003: 72–7; Porten and Yardeni 1986: 1:68–75 (A4.7).

85. Silverman 2012, chapter 1; an earlier version was published as Silverman 2010.

and political advantage of some elites to use a tradition (prophecy) deliberately to enable and establish their own positions, in relation to the Persians and in relation to their own positions locally. This does not mean that prophecy only functioned to parrot Persian ideology, nor that the way it functioned was entirely novel. Quite the contrary: prophecy continued to function, at least for a while, along the same lines as it had functioned in the monarchic era, as a medium for hearing from the divine and for ordering society accordingly. However, the social order had changed, and the need of society was no longer how to support the native monarchy or how to react properly to external imperial threat (the Neo-Assyrians and the Neo-Babylonians) but was now how to negotiate life as a province within the Persian Empire. This is one way to approach Haggai and Zechariah as prophets, and it perhaps raises a question whether prophecy played a role in this manner in Samerina and Babylonia as well as in Yehud. It is worth considering.

If prophecy in Yehud (and the empire in general) is considered along such lines, then strong prophetic support for the rebuilding of the temple in Jerusalem might be significant in terms of its function as interface with the empire. In particular, the temple may have been used to facilitate or organize labor (voluntary or forced) for the province—something raised elsewhere.[86] A temple with divine approval (certainly a necessity in ANE temple [re]building) was also one which could justify its own labor demands, making what could be viewed merely as secular, imperial demands become sacred obligations (e.g., work for the temple). From this perspective, the prophecies supporting rebuilding and the imperial interests could be mutually supportive. The local cultic tradition is revived and this enables local cooperation with imperial demands.

Outline of the Book

Both the research and the writing of this study attempt to be zetetic—starting from questions and the material and proceeding from there, with as few pre-conceived answers as possible. Thus the driving question is "how did the Achaemenid kings portray their rule to subject minorities, and in what ways did the minority elites reshape this ideology for their own use?" This is first pursued through the basic textual questions of content, rhetoric, forms, date, and audience. Since this study is intended for Achaemenid historians, Iranicists, Assyriologists, and biblical scholars, as few assumptions concerning the sources are taken as possible, and references to the editions of primary sources utilized are given in the footnotes.

Part I analyzes 2Isa. Chapter 2 provides a basic analysis of 2Isa. It discusses the text's message and rhetoric through the topics of creation, servanthood, cult, return, idolatry polemics, the rise of Cyrus, and the addressees. The chapter also tackles the issues of the text's coherence and formation, its date, and its social contexts.

86. Silverman 2015b.

Chapter 3 provides broader context for 2Isa by exploring creation in the OP inscriptions and briefly comparing these to other ANE creation traditions. It then analyzes 2Isa in light of the social and political context argued in chapter 2 (early Persian Babylon).

Part II analyzes 1Zech. Chapter 4 queries the reliability of the dates in 1Zech, then uses these for an analysis of the rhetoric and meaning of the text, following the order of the surviving visions.

To understand how to assess the genre of the material discussed in the previous chapter, chapter 5 explores the phenomenology of dreams and visions. This phenomenology then provides a basis for a discussion of 1Zech as a vision report in Persian Yehud, the text's coherence and formation, and the historical implications of the genre. The chapter concludes with further analysis of the implications of the Persian context.

Part III brings these texts into dialogue with broader imperial issues.

Chapter 6 discusses how Cyrus, Cambyses, and Darius interacted with local elites. This is done through discussion of the Babylonian *Akītu* festival, the policies during the conquest of Egypt, and an assessment of relations with temples between former imperial centers and the margins. The chapter concludes with an excursus on the usability of the end of Josephus's *Antiquities* 11 for the historiography of Persian Yehud.

Chapter 7 brings the above discussions together. After a brief recap of arguments made throughout the study, the relations of early Judaean elites is analyzed. The chapter then moves to problematizing how the concept of "elites" is utilized in discussions of interactions with the empire—including by this study itself. The chapter then concludes with an analysis of Achaemenid-elite engagements in light of the previous arguments.

The final chapter, chapter 8, concludes by clarifying the methodological limits and the scope of the arguments in this particular study, and it raises a few remaining desiderata. It is hoped this chapter might spur further work in related areas.

For the readers' convenience, an appendix with key dates around the early Persian Empire is included.

PART I

Chapter 2

SECOND ISAIAH*

> You'll excuse me, gentlemen. Your business
> is politics. Mine is running a saloon.
>
> —Rick, *Casablanca* (1942)

Introduction

Second Isaiah (2Isa) is a complex piece of poetry, containing numerous themes, sections, and interpretive difficulties, not to mention the theological and scholarly interpretations it has received. This chapter does not intend to give a comprehensive analysis of the text. Rather, it seeks to determine what the text can say about Judaean elite discourse in the early Persian period as it relates to the Persians. For this to be successful, consideration must begin with the evidence at hand, the text itself. Thus, this chapter begins with a rhetorical analysis of the text, with attention paid to the overall message of the text as well as the themes used in articulating that message. The present goal is historical; the meanings of the text in terms of later understandings are not directly of concern here. Attention is especially focused on how they impinge on topics of relevance to the social location and political ideology of the author(s) and audience(s). The goal is to read more for meaning than structure *per se*, except where structure influences the present reading. Once the given material is analyzed, the issues of origins/redactions, dating, and social context can be broached. These analyses will then allow for a historically grounded discussion of what the text says in a Persian context.

---

* Previous versions of various portions of the material on Isaiah were presented at the Melammu, EABS, ASPS, and SIE conferences in 2015. An earlier form of the material on genre is published as Silverman 2018; an earlier and adapted form of the material on creation is published as Silverman 2017.

A note on the choice of 2Isa as a historical document is warranted, given its status as a scholarly hypothesis and the lack of empirical support in the manuscripts. The formation of Isaiah is a minefield. Nevertheless, the consistency of the poetry, coherence, and distinctiveness from chs. 1–39 and 56–66 justify treating it as an object of historical analysis independently of the processes which created the canonical form of Isaiah. Even if it were composed to be part of an Isaianic collection,[1] it would be historically justified to treat that composition as one point in time. (The unity of 2Isa will be considered below.) The point that 2Isa presupposes the experience of exile, whereas the previous sections do not, is a reasonable place to begin.[2] While 2Isa may no doubt have known traditions related to Isa 1–39, there is no reason to assume a book form of them was pre-existing and for which 2Isa was created to continue. It is therefore legitimate to treat it as a source on its own, separately from considerations of relations with the remainder of the canonical book.

The Rhetoric and Message of Second Isaiah

Genre

The Jewish and Christian canons present 2Isa as an instance of prophecy, though the text itself gives no superscription specifying name, location, or situation, other than being included in the book of Isaiah.[3] If one follows the definition of Petersen, that means it would reflect some form of "intermediation,"[4] one presenting a message of YHWH requiring a response.[5] However, the move from oral prophecy to written oracles itself requires additional consideration.[6] 2Isa is usually considered to be poetry throughout.[7] A more precise genre, and one that might imply a more specific setting or origin, has not received any real consensus, despite the interpretive import. A number of scholars have called 2Isa a "drama"

---

1. As in Seitz 1991: 207.
2. E.g., Williamson 1994: 3; Davies 1998: 115.
3. Superscriptions are helpful starting points, whether or not they were "original" or "secondary" in any particular instance.
4. Petersen 2000: 37–8, 49; cf. Petersen 1997.
5. On the social phenomenon of prophecy in the ANE, see, e.g., Carroll 1979; Wilson 1980; Overholt 1989; Nissinen 2003; Doan and Giles 2005; Stökl 2012.
6. On this, see more below.
7. E.g., Korpel and de Moor 1998; Baltzer 2001: 7; Heffelfinger 2011: 1. Blenkinsopp 2002: 66–9 prefers "oratory" to poetry, despite the fact that the two are not mutually exclusive.

of some sort.⁸ Baltzer analyzed 2Isa as a "liturgical drama."⁹ Goulder analyzed all of Isaiah as a liturgical cycle for Tabernacles, with 2Isa being performed on days six and seven.¹⁰ He still considers the materials' origins, however, to derive from prophets continually re-updating Isaianic materials.¹¹ Tiemeyer argues it is a "reading drama," or a dialogic text that follows a "logical procedure of argumentation."¹² Heffelfinger objects to seeing the text as argumentative and rather argues it is lyric poetry.¹³ A key issue is whether the text that was originally oral pronouncement(s) and then subsequently written down, or whether it originated as literature and later disseminated via oral or written means.¹⁴ This latter issue bears on both the genre and social contexts; the question will be taken up further below. As an initial starting point, to be further refined, 2Isa is here considered to be rhetorical poetry, in the senses of being a unit and of attempting to persuade an audience, but without "rhetoric" being limited either to classical forms or conceptualizations or to rational discourse. Indeed, "speak to the heart of Jerusalem" (40:2) can be rendered "persuade Jerusalem."¹⁵

Message

The text opens with an announcement of comfort for Jerusalem, because it is forgiven and a theophany of YHWH is imminent (40:1–11).¹⁶ Since this YHWH created the world, he is greater than the nations (vv. 12–17) and the idols (vv. 18–20). He is creator and ruler of the earth (vv. 21–22),

---

8. Including Eaton 1979. Van der Woude 2005: 151–61 gives a helpful overview of these views. Nevertheless, her own conclusion that it is a not a drama but a "reading drama" is as perplexing as it is unjustified, ignoring the poetry of 2Isa and the potential for oral performance beyond theatre *per se*.

9. Baltzer 2001: 7–15.

10. Goulder 2004, days and sections pp. 4–7, cycle pp. 10–12.

11. Goulder 2004: 111–12.

12. Tiemeyer 2011a: 13, 47–50, cf. chapter 6. Berges 2008: 64–73 also defines 40–48 as a "reading drama."

13. Heffelfinger 2011: 17, 91 n. 36. She defines lyric poetry on pp. 37–42. She specifically notes that calling it prophetic is not sufficient to determine message or style (p. 14).

14. An important social and communicative question despite Gitay's claim that it makes no difference (Gitay 1980).

15. Rignell 1956: 9–10; Koole 1997: 52.

16. Scholars sometimes see this as a new exodus, e.g., Rignell 1956: 9. However, it is the coming of YHWH that is the topic, not the coming of the exiles.

and so is greater than the human rulers (vv. 23–24). The one who creates is also the one who sustains (vv. 25–31).

YHWH has called a victor from the east (41:1–4) who causes the nations to turn to their idols in fear (vv. 5–7). Yet Israel has nothing to fear as YHWH has chosen to protect and bless it (vv. 8–20). YHWH challenges the gods to predict the future (vv. 21–24) and announces that he called one from the north and told it in advance (vv. 25–29).

The creator of the nations calls his servant to teach them (42:1–9). The nations should glorify him for this (vv. 10–12). YHWH declares a holy war against idolaters (vv. 13–17), yet his servant does not notice despite punishment (vv. 18–25). Israel's punishment will transfer to the nations (43:1–8) and both the nations and Israel will be YHWH's witnesses (vv. 9–13). Babylon in particular will be punished (vv. 14–15). YHWH surpasses the old exodus (vv. 16–21). Although they and their ancestors failed to worship YHWH, he promises that their children will do so and will therefore be blessed (43:22–44:5).

YHWH is the god who fulfills promises (44:6–8), but idols delude those who make them (vv. 9–20). In contrast, the god who made Israel is able to act (vv. 21–23). It is Israel's creator, redeemer, and predictive God who says Cyrus will restore Jerusalem (vv. 24–28). Indeed, YHWH calls Cyrus, and Israel and the nations will know it is his doing (45:1–8). As creator, YHWH has the right to do as he wishes with his creations (Israel, Cyrus, and Jerusalem, vv. 9–13). The idolatrous nations will be ashamed, but Israel saved (vv. 14–17); indeed, this was foretold by YHWH to Israel (vv. 18–19). The unknowing nations will acknowledge YHWH's work (vv. 20–25).

Although gods need carrying, YHWH carries Israel (46:1–4), and unlike fabricated gods, YHWH completes his plans and thus Cyrus will do his will (vv. 5–13). Babylon will fall, deluded by its divination and thoughts of being divine (47:1–15). YHWH successfully foretold the exile in the past, and now he tells something new: his victor will defeat Babylon (48:1–16). Blessing will follow obedience (vv. 17–19). Leave Babylon and announce YHWH's works (vv. 20–22).

The servant then speaks of his commissioning (49:1–6) and announces the restoration of Israel and Israel's acknowledgment by the nations (vv. 7–13). Though Zion thinks it is abandoned, it is not (vv. 14–21). Indeed, the nations will submit to Israel, be punished, and acknowledge YHWH (vv. 22–26). Yes, YHWH can (50:1–3).

The servant suffers in order to announce this message to Israel (vv. 4–11). Return to YHWH, he is working as he has in the past (51:1–11), so do not fear, oppression is over (vv. 12–52:6). Good news, the restoration is here (vv. 7–12). The servant effects salvation through his suffering (52:13–53:12). Rejoice, for now there is restoration, forgiveness, and protection (54:1–17). Therefore, turn to YHWH and be blessed (55:1–8), YHWH's word will be effective (vv. 9–13).

The above is an elaborate, nuanced, and baroque[17] discourse, with a number of key arguments and themes embedded within it. Scholars have been divided over the overall meaning of the text, though this concern has sometimes been overshadowed by redactional questions and inflexible views of form/genre.[18] Westermann merely calls the message one of "salvation," as distinct from the judgment in 1Isa.[19] For Kapelrud the key issue is one of theodicy.[20] Blenkinsopp believes that the text's message is the validity of YHWH's word.[21] A major argument of the text *is* that YHWH's word is effective in two senses: that it imparts accurate knowledge of YHWH's purpose in advance and that his word is inherently effective in producing YHWH's purposes, the point on which the current text closes (55:9–13). While a key leitmotif, YHWH's word is only *one* of the arguments of the rhetoric, and it functions here to validate this particular utterance more than being the point of the discourse itself. Likewise, Baltzer appears to think the issue is the sovereignty of YHWH,[22] a theme belabored by the text but merely in service of a greater point. Whybray gives a threefold central message,[23] all elements of which are in fact here considered supporting arguments, while Goldingay and Payne are content with listing five foci within the text.[24] Wilson believes the goal is to give the exiles hope and purpose.[25] There is a real connection between this and sociological perspectives on migration and colonial peoples,[26] but this

---

17. Indeed, Brueggemann has called 2Isa an "oratorio" (Brueggemann 1998: 1).
18. Cf. comments by Heffelfinger 2011. This can also be seen in the useful overviews of form criticism by Merrill, which contain much discussion of genres but not of 2Isa as a whole (Merrill 1987a, 1987b).
19. Westermann 1969: 8–21.
20. Kapelrud 1982: 50–8.
21. Blenkinsopp 2002: 59.
22. Baltzer 2001: 44.
23. Whybray 1983: 45 (punishment over, YHWH about to act, word is guaranteed).
24. Goldingay and Payne 2006: 1:49–57.
25. Wilson 1986: 325–6; cf. Barstad 1997: 67, who thinks Judahite rather than exiles.
26. The major scholar in this area is Smith-Christopher. See, e.g., Smith 1989; Smith-Christopher 1997, 2002, 2011, 2012. For an introduction, see Silverman forthcoming b; see section below.

aspect is still subordinate to (or rather, the outcome of) a greater purpose. The same is true of Goldingay's similar suggestion that it prepares the people for a new exodus to Israel.[27]

Heffelfinger rejects a single message *per se*, seeing rather an "encounter" wrestling with the problematic of reconciliation between YHWH and Israel.[28] The multivocality she notes is true, but there remains an overall demand animating the text as a whole. Despite her pertinent points concerning the text's lyricism and complexity, these both function together to make a very strong rhetorical demand of the audience.[29] If one takes 2Isa seriously as a form of rhetoric—with the understanding that that is an utterance designed to evoke a response in its audience—the key message lies in the response that the text seeks to form in the implied audience.[30] From this perspective, *the key message in the text is that Israel should devote itself to YHWH*, a claim made explicit in two structurally key places (45:23–25; 55:1–8). This may seem a *passé* claim for a text in the HB, but it is important because it relativizes and contextualizes the other claims within the text of 2Isa.[31] The entire text gives reasons for and/or the results of Israel so doing. Why should Israel devote itself to YHWH? Because of YHWH's superiority and power—manifested in his creative work, in his control of the nations, in his effective word. He is superior to the gods who can do none of these. Further, he has not abandoned Israel and his plan to bless and restore it is in progress. Cyrus is the evidence and means for this. What will be the results? Israel will be served by the nations, it will receive a renewed land and renewed cult, it will again be in relation to YHWH, and its shame will be over. To make these points, a number of themes, sub-arguments, and even sub-genres appear, but all can be subordinated to this over-arching message: devote yourselves to YHWH. The implications for the implied and "original" audiences will be discussed below. If this is the basic, overall message of what the existing text says, a few rhetorical issues, arguments, and themes and still require closer examination.

---

27. Goldingay 2005: 7.
28. Heffelfinger 2011: 83, 275.
29. Conflict of assumptions is one form for achieving effects, according to Burke 1953: 161–3. See more below.
30. Similar in some respects to the thinking of Fisher, who argues that any work can be interpreted as rhetorical if the focus is placed on audience response (Fisher 1987: 161).
31. Not so different from Adams 2006: 91, though arrived at independently.

Rhetoric

The rhetorician Kenneth Burke provides two descriptions of possible rhetorical forms that are particularly useful for analyzing 2Isa's rhetoric as described above: the use of "repetitive form" and "qualitative progression."[32] What Burke means by "rhetorical form" in this context is the manner in which rhetoric is the "arousing and fulfillment of desires,"[33] or in other words, the way in which the structural and genre-related features combine to evoke emotional and ideational expectations within an audience and then fulfill them towards the rhetor's ends. Repetitive form is "the consistent maintaining of a principle under new guises" and is "basic to any work of art."[34] The use of repetition is a well-known, standard feature of Hebrew poetry on the scale of the verse (parallelism)[35] and a widely recognized feature of 2Isa on a larger, thematic scale (for discussion of some these, see below).[36] Repetition serves a number of functions within 2Isa. First, it provides a measure of coherence across the range of topics and arguments. The topics of creation, cult, and servanthood are important in this respect. Second, key arguments (such as YHWH is creator) receive strengthening through repetition. Third, the repetition of topoi such as idolatry or the responses of the nations provides a useful contrast to passages about YHWH or Israel. Fourth, the use of repetition to create a shock to expectations is evinced by the servant motif, which in the second major section of the text does not fulfill the rosy picture expected in the first half. The latter is also a pertinent example of qualitative progression. Burke understands this latter form to mean preparation for a new idea or theme in terms of emotion or mood more than logical progression.[37] Another example of this would be the oracle against Babylon in ch. 47, applying the critique of failed divination and of other cults in the previous chapters directly against Israel's imperial overlord; this no doubt builds on the audience's growing expectations for such a denunciation. Another example is likely the delay in the appearance of the name of Cyrus despite periodic allusions to him. The effectiveness of

---

32. In his essay "Lexicon Rhetoricæ," Burke 1953: 123–83.
33. Burke 1953: 124.
34. Burke 1953: 125. For Fisher, it is the primary way narrative works express their theses (Fisher 1987: 168). Niditch and Doran 1977: 183 also emphasize the role of repetitions in folkloric studies.
35. Alter 1987: 612–16; W. Watson 1984: 136–7; Berlin 1985; Korpel and de Moor 1998: 13; Hrushovski-Harshav 2007: 598–9. Cf. Schökel 1987: 174.
36. Korpel and de Moor 1998: 11, 15, 654; E.g., idol critiques or creation language.
37. Burke 1953: 125.

such rhetorical forms is highly linked to the existing belief structure of the author and the audience.[38] The import of this for 2Isa is made clear through the repeated appeals to the "former things" and its response to issues from previous traditions such as Lamentations or Proto-Isaiah.[39] In the final form of the text, 2Isa appears to evoke Israel's failure to heed former prophecy through the servant's current failure in prophecy, though all still couched in terms of comfort. To use the language of Bitzer, 2Isa seeks to remove the "exigence" of estrangement from YHWH, from the audience of Judaeans no longer devoted to his cult, under constraints including defeat by the Neo-Babylonians and pre-existing prophecies of punishment.[40]

Walter Fisher provides more tools for analyzing the values of the author and implied audience of 2Isa. In his theory of the narrative paradigm,[41] Fisher posits that the "logic of good reasons" (values) of a rhetorical utterance can be assessed through five questions: What does it take for granted ("facts")? To which values is appeal made ("relevance")? What are the effects of these values on life ("consequences")? What have the audiences' experiences already confirmed ("consistency")? And what is the ideal basis for the argument ("transcendent issue")?[42] Fisher insists that these criteria highlight the intersubjective, or social, element inherent in all rhetoric.[43] *Facts*. The text takes for granted a number of ancestor legends (e.g., Eden, 51:3; Noah, 54:9; Abraham and Sarah, 41:8; 51:2; the exodus, 43:16–17; 51:9–10; David, 55:3–4). Previous Yahwistic prophecies are assumed (e.g., 42:9; 44:26; 48:3–5). It presumes punishment for sin has occurred (e.g., 40:2; 43:27; 51:17–23). There is a presumption that some believe YHWH has abandoned Israel (e.g., 40:27; 43:22–26; 50:1). There is a lack of cult (e.g., 43:22–24; 44:28; 52:1–12). There is

38. Burke 1953: 161–4.

39. In general, see Willey 1997. On Lamentations, see, e.g., Gottwald 1954: 44–6, 115–6; Tiemeyer 2011a: 437–61; 2011b; Seitz 1991; Paul 2012: 50–59. The posited textual connections are often, however, very debatable and based on very vague connections, e.g., Sommer 1998 (despite his very illuminating methodological introduction). The use of "traditions" instead of "texts" within the body of the text above is therefore very deliberate.

40. E.g., Bitzer 1968: 6–8.

41. Fisher 1987. His theory argues that humans primarily communicate and assess communications through "good reasons," which are related to narrative and valuative criteria rather than rational ones. Though most of his book is concerned with rhetorical works such as speeches, he explicitly argues that his paradigm, specifically the "logic of good reasons," applies effectively to literature and drama (p. 158).

42. Fisher 1987: 109, 176.

43. Fisher 1987: 110–11.

familiarity with the material aspects of idol manufacture (e.g., 40:18–20; 44:6–20). There is knowledge of Cyrus's campaigns (e.g., 41:2, 25). There is an overall assumption that nations need gods for protection.

Relevance. The key values to which the text appeals are glory among the nations (e.g., 45:14–17; 49:6–7, 22–23; 52:10; 55:5) and life in the land of Israel (43:3–8; 44:26, 28; 49:19–23; 54). Another key value is צדק/צדקה, used in a number of senses throughout: used of what YHWH is bringing from the east (41:2); YHWH's right hand (41:10); what YHWH desires of his servant (42:21), and so on.[44] A key concept used mostly in parallel with this is ישע.[45] Used exclusively by 2Isa for YHWH, this term seems to connote the restoration of just, divine order.

Consequences. 2Isa posits a number of consequences that it sees as deriving from devotion to YHWH: comfort (e.g., 40:1), a restored land and rebuilt temple (e.g., 44:26, 28), blessing and security (e.g., 48:18; 49:18–23), recognition and glory (e.g., 45:14–17), as well as a right relation with their own god (frequently emphasized by use of epithets using Israel or Jacob, such as "Holy One of Israel").[46] Though technically these are all declared to be things YHWH is doing *already*, they are only comforting and effective if the audience does indeed accept the giver and the gifts, which implies renewed devotion.

Consistency. The text appeals primarily to two previous sets of experiences: the Babylonian destruction and YHWH's previous predictions concerning it. The sense of consistency is argued from the previously demonstrated reliability of YHWH's word, while the experience of defeat, destruction, and exile is a contrast to the new word of YHWH. The allusion and response to other Judaean traditions also serves this function.

Transcendent Issue. In line with the posited main message of the text, 2Isa posits the value of YHWH as a deity and thus the value of Israel's devotion to him. That these are clearly contested values requires 2Isa to bolster them and argue them from several different angles. The main alternative view would seem to be the view that other gods are more effective and thus more worthy of devotion.

The central argument as analyzed above utilizes a number of key sub-arguments, several already mentioned. The text argues that YHWH's word is effective and powerful, imparting accurate knowledge of his plans. It argues that YHWH is the creator of the world. It argues that YHWH is

---

44. Cf. Whitley 1972; Preuß 1976: 83–7; Ringgren and Johnson 2003: 239–63.

45. Used 36× in 2Isa according to *TDOT* 6 (1990): 446. Scheuer 2008, 135–6 thinks it is spiritual.

46. On the issue of "divine designations" in Isaiah as a whole, see Byrne 2006. For this epithet in particular, see pp. 39–43, 157–60.

superior to the nations, their gods, and their rulers. It argues that YHWH has not in fact abandoned Israel, despite its sin and punishment. It argues that Israel should worship YHWH, that it should return to Judah and Jerusalem, and that it should proclaim his cult to the nations. It argues that YHWH has a number of servants, including kings, prophets, and Israel.

To summarize the rhetorical material in 2Isa: Israel should devote itself to YHWH. This builds on past punitive actions against Judah, a wide array of Judaean traditions, the appearance of Cyrus on the historical scene, desires for international glory and blessings within Palestine, and the value of YHWH as a deity. It argues for YHWH as powerful, effective in word, creator of the world, superior to the nations, gracious in forgiving, and as utilizing all kinds of servants for his service.

The above argumentation weaves within in it six themes that are important to the present study: creation, servanthood, the cult of YHWH, a return to Judah, polemics against idolatry, and the rise of Cyrus.

Creation and YHWH as Creator[47]

2Isa represents one of the most sustained assertions of YHWH as creator in the HB.[48] As a theme, creation periodically appears throughout 2Isa from 40:12 to 54:16, thus the entire span of the work excluding the prologue and conclusion. The major passages, however, are clustered in the first main division (chs. 40–48). It appears as a subject on its own and in conjunction with the other themes considered here: servanthood, the cult, the return, idol polemics, and Cyrus. As such it participates in both repetitive form and qualitative progression. As a repetitive feature, it helps to provide coherence to the text. As part of the progression it serves a number of functions as argument and contrast. 2Isa is not interested so much in the mechanics of creation as in the proofs concerning the nature and ways of YHWH that it can derive from it. Though the idea that YHWH is creator is repeatedly stated to be something that the audience already knew (e.g., 40:21, "Do you not know, Have you not heard…"), the extent of the repetition (at least twenty-four times!)[49] implies at least some level of novelty or resistance to the idea.

---

47. An earlier version of the analysis of creation in relation to the Persians was presented at the Association for the Study of Persianate Societies's 2015 meeting in Istanbul and published as Silverman 2017.

48. Though less famous and narrative than Gen 1–2, 2Isa sustains the assertion longer. The only other comparable attention within the HB is Job.

49. As positing, discussing, or appealing to YHWH as creator, the author includes: 40:12–16, 21–22, 25–31; 41:4; 42:5–6; 43:1, 7, 10–13, 15, 21; 44:2, 21, 24; 45:7–12, 18; 46:4; 48:7, 8, 12–13, 16; 49:8; 51:13, 16; 54:16.

Creation plays a key role immediately after the introduction, in a sustained passage on the greatness of YHWH (40:12–31). 2Isa uses creation to assert YHWH's superiority over the cosmos (v. 12), his superior wisdom (vv. 13–14), and superiority to the nations (vv. 15–17). These assertions then form the basis for a twofold contrast between YHWH's creating abilities and the creative work of idol-manufacturers and of idols themselves (vv. 18–20). YHWH's creation is thus proof of his superiority to the inhabitants of the earth wholesale (vv. 21–22, mere "locusts" [חגבים]).[50] The corollary to this is his superiority to the nations (vv. 23–24). YHWH's creation and sustenance of the stars (vv. 25–26) then proves his ability to continue to sustain Israel through acts of continual recreation (vv. 27–31). This extended passage now sets the stage for YHWH's ability to awaken victory (צדק) from the east (41:2). The basis of this ability in creation is alluded to in 41:4 with the use of the phrase "primordial generations" (הדרות מראש).[51]

2Isa returns to creation in 42:5–7:

כה אמר האל יהוה	Thus says the god YHWH,
בורא השמים ונוטיהם	who creates the heavens and stretches them out
רקע הארץ וצאצאיה	who hammers out the earth and its produce
נתן נשמה לעם עליה	who gives breath to the people on it
ורוח להלכים בה	and spirit to ones walking on it:
אני יהוה קראתיך בצדק	I, YHWH, call you in victory
ואחזק בידך	and I grasp you by your hand
ואצרך ואתנך	and I form you and I give you
לברית עם	as a covenant for people,
לאור גוים	as a light for the nations
לפקח עינים עורות	for eyes of the blind to be opened
להוציא ממסגר אסיר	to bring prisoners from the dungeon
מבית כלא ישבי חשך	from the house of confinement those who dwell in darkness

---

50. This insect is allowed as food in Lev 11:22 and is a punishment in 2 Chr 7:13 (though not in Joel); the force of the term might be both complete domination as well as fitting into YHWH's control over nature, or perhaps with a nuance of complete interchangeability. Is it significant that locusts are a clean animal?

51. Usually translated as "generations from the beginning," but since דור means the time period in which a generation lives, "primordial generations" better renders the concept implied by the phrase, as well as keeping the appeal to the creation context in the text clear.

This pericope is noteworthy for the manner in which it predicates creation. First, it is given as a series of participles describing YHWH. Second, it is given in four stages, divided implicitly by time. YHWH creates heaven, earth, and humanity. These are implicitly primordial, despite the use of present participles. Then the text continues with the selection and fashioning of "you" (second person singular) in the present time (despite being in the imperfect tense). This "you" would appear to be YHWH's servant, as the servant is described in 42:1–4, 18–25, but there is an ambiguity to the specific referent (i.e., it could be Cyrus, or Israel, or even the narrator; see section on servant below). The function of creation here is threefold: it repeats the greatness of YHWH established previously; it makes service to YHWH part of a greater, cosmological plan; it justifies the servant's position and activities within the cosmos.

Creation occurs repeatedly in ch. 43. Four times YHWH claims to have created Israel (43:1, 7, 15, 21). Two of these (vv. 7, 21) explicitly state that this was for YHWH's glory/praise. The other two (vv. 1, 15) carry the force of ownership of Israel. The latter occurs with one of only three instances of the title "king" used for YHWH in 2Isa.[52] Since this is linked with the declared punishment of Babylon in v. 14, it is tempting to see it as an explicit refutation of Marduk, who was both creator and king in contemporaneous Babylonian mythology.[53] This impression might be reinforced by the oblique creation reference in v. 10, which denies any prior theogonies (לפני לא נוצר אל). The use of creation as a claim on Israel recurs in 44:2, 21. In both verses it is combined with Israel devoting itself to YHWH.

Chapter 44 ends in a cumulative passage combining five of the themes considered in this study (creation, servanthood, cult, return, Cyrus). Here creation begins a litany of aspects of YHWH guaranteeing the success of the project that 2Isa now announces: using Cyrus to rebuild Judah, Jerusalem, and the temple (creation, v. 24; restoration vv. 26–28). It functions to combine together the assertion of YHWH's ability with his attachment to Israel.

Perhaps the most discussed use of creation in 2Isa is 45:7:

יוצר אור ובורא חשך	who forms light and creates darkness
עשה שלם ובורא רע	who does peace and creates evil
אני יהוה עשה כל אלה	I am YHWH who does all these

---

52. E.g., Byrne 2006: 44–5, cf. 256–61.
53. On Babylonian creation mythology, see section below.

Interpreters often find this verse remarkable for predicating evil deeds of YHWH, and typically they either try to explain away the meaning of "evil" (רעה/חשך)[54] or argue that it is an explicitly anti-dualistic statement, with the usual implication that the rhetorical opponents are of course the Persians.[55] On first glance this seems to be a reasonable idea. However, this interpretation ignores both the rhetorical context in which this verse appears within 2Isa, as well as the history of prophetic announcements of YHWH's work. When these two contexts are taken into account, the surprising aspect of this statement is *not* that YHWH works evil, but rather that *he works good* (אור/שלום)![56] That the rhetoric of 2Isa works hard to "comfort" its audience and to predicate good of YHWH is widely acknowledged;[57] indeed, it is the first word of the text. This insistence suggests that this is not a foregone conclusion to the audience. Recall that the text puts negative ideas of YHWH in the audiences' mouth (e.g., 40:27; 49:14). Moreover, the text accepts the older prophetic insistence that YHWH brought evil (punishment) upon Israel, something that again is stated right at the beginning of the text (40:2) and very explicitly charged to YHWH's doing (e.g., 42:24–25). Within the prophetic tradition, the depiction of dark deeds by YHWH is widespread: it gets Jeremiah in political trouble, it makes Ezekiel use misogynistic language, it is the *raison d'être* of Habakkuk. More directly, Amos 5:18–20 characterized the Day of YHWH as darkness and not light. Even more broadly, within

54. E.g., Delitzsch [1877]: 2:174–5; Elliger 1978: 499–500; Koole 1997: 442; Paul 2012: 257–8.

55. E.g., Delitzsch 1881: 220 = Delitzsch [1877]: 2:174; Mills 1905–6: 276–7; Simcox 1937: 169; Carter 1970: 50–1; Bergman et al. 1975: 248; Otzen 1990: 264; Albertz 1994: 418; Ringgren 2001: 391; Smith 1990: 201; Boyce 2000: 283. Earlier, however, Boyce thought it was instead similar to Y. 44 (Boyce 1982: 44). Blenkinsopp 2002: 250 claims this interpretation cannot be ruled out, but he later rejects it (Blenkinsopp 2011: 499 n. 21, 506). It has become more common to reject a direct polemic; see, e.g., Elliger 1978: 501–2; Koole 1997: 441; Nilsen 2008: 22–25; 2013:6, all of whom reject any relevance of Zoroastrianism. Paul 2012: 257 notes that Saadya Gaon already saw an anti-Dualist polemic here (though Paul rejects it). A couple of critics still see it as anti-dualist, however, without specifying whose or which dualism they mean. Westermann 1969: 162 argues against all dualisms, as does Baltzer 2001: 227. Goldingay 2005: 269 only sees "latent" dualism here.

56. The inverse of this formulation appears in Job 2:10, though the underlying sentiment of evil deriving from YHWH remains the same.

57. E.g., Delitzsch [1877]: 1:10, 2:58; Carroll 1979: 151; Barstad 1997: 67. Brueggemann 1998: 8 titles 2Isa "God of All Comfort"; comfort also provides the title for Tiemeyer 2011a. For the interplay of comfort theme with more negative aspects, see Heffelfinger 2011: chapter 5.

the Neo-Babylonian discourse over Marduk, the chief deity's capacity for evil is taken for granted.[58] Within this greater context, the effort of the text is to engage the audience's attachment to YHWH by emphasizing his *positive* as well as negative works. What this means is that while such statements as this would indeed likely prove useful for later apologists attempting to refute Zoroastrianism and Manichaeism, such a rhetorical aim is a wholly unlikely understanding for its appearance here in the text, or its function in these verses. Rather, creation is here part of the text's attempt to demonstrate both YHWH's power and his continuing efforts to benefit Israel.

The chapter continues with five more verses on creation (vv. 9–12). Here creation is combined with its implications for YHWH's wisdom, to argue that his methods for dealing with Israel and the world should not be questioned. His workings are again specified to be a conqueror who will rebuild and end the exile. This use of creation also leads into two new ideas: that Israel will receive glory from the nations because they recognize YHWH's greatness (vv. 14–17) and the beneficent intent of his creation (v. 18). He did not create an abyss, but a place suitable for habitation. The latter amplifies the force of the good creation posited in 45:7. Here YHWH is clearly a creator god and not just an insignificant personal or local deity.

Several more uses of creation remain. Creation is again martialed to highlight the contrast between YHWH and the idols (46:4): he is able to save. As the first half of 2Isa culminates, creation returns to characterize YHWH's current activity. It is a new creation (48:7); it is a defining aspect of YHWH (48:12–13); it guarantees his ability to give Israel knowledge (48:16). It is linked to the restoration and servanthood of Israel (49:8). In ch. 51 creation carries a double, evaluative aspect: it serves as a rebuke to Israel (51:13) and as comfort to his servant (51:16). The last use of creation (54:16) serves to guarantee that YHWH can protect his servants against attacks.

Creation, therefore, plays a major role in the rhetorical strategy of 2Isa, although it is never described merely for its own sake: it serves to paint YHWH as a God who is able to act and to save, and deserving of Israel's devotion and loyalty. It also serves the function of legitimizing those who serve him. In a Neo-Babylonian context, several aspects of this rhetoric would appear as direct confrontations of Marduk, beyond the explicit mention of him and his son by name.

---

58. Pointed out as a significant element of the theology of *Ludlul Bēl Nēmeqi* by Lenzi 2012: 38.

Servanthood

A major literary and theological motif within 2Isa is that of the servant of YHWH, one that has attracted no shortage of scholarly attention. The majority of the latter, however, have attempted to *identify* this servant figure, either with an individual or collective identity, or to postulate various stages of reinterpretation of the identity of the figure.[59] While certainly relevant to the later reception history of this section of Isaiah,[60] such identifications bypass the rhetorical/literary and theological aspect of the idea of the "servant of YHWH" within the text. Indeed, it is more fruitful to see the servant of YHWH as, at least within the final form of 2Isa, a sophisticated theology of *what it means to serve YHWH*.[61] As such, the text depicts a variety of ways that a person or collective can function in the service of YHWH—with a corresponding variety of particular instances of "servant." Though the term "servant" (עבד) is indeed a key word for this theme, the poet also uses the language of choosing (בחר) and calling (קרא). The way in which these terms for servanthood are used and the way the theme is alternately applied to different types of service and particular servants mean that in any given instance it is often ambiguous to which specific servant the language applies. In this light, it is more profitable to discuss what the text asserts about servants of YHWH rather than beginning with their particular identities. In this understanding "the" servant is just one of the servants of YHWH.[62]

Perhaps obvious from the language used, the first claim 2Isa makes concerning servants of YHWH is that *servants are chosen by YHWH*. In fact, the two roots often appear in parallel (e.g., 41:8, 9; 42:1). This implies that it is a status conferred without regard to the servant's choice, and would appear to be a status from creation or birth (44:2). It also implies the active assistance of YHWH (e.g., 45:13) as well as a purpose for the calling. A reason for Cyrus's calling is to defeat Babylon (e.g., 48:14–15); a reason for Jacob's calling is for YHWH's glory (e.g., 43:21);

---

59. E.g., North 1956, who already in 1956 was able to list 16 historical individuals and two more interpretations posited by scholars just for the "suffering servant" in Isa 53. For some studies see Lindhagen 1950; McKenzie 1968: xxxix; Fohrer 1968: 379–81; Clines 1976; Wilcox and Paton-Williams 1988; Blenkinsopp 2002: 76–81; Sharp 2009: 168–74; Berges 2010; Paul 2012: 18.

60. For some studies, see Sawyer 1996; Bellinger and Farmer 1998; Janowski and Stuhlmacher 2004; Gignilliat 2004; Blenkinsopp 2006; McGinnis and Tull 2006.

61. Thus claiming for all of 2Isa something similar to what Clines argued for Isa 53, presenting a vision of "servanthood"; Clines 1976: 65.

62. Williamson 1998: 141 also notes this plurality.

the servant-speaking-in-first-person's purpose is to bring Israel to YHWH (e.g., 49:5). The corollary to this would be that as many purposes as YHWH has he also has servants for them. Despite the implication that servants should fulfill their chosen purpose, *servants can be recalcitrant*. This seemingly restores some of the agency lost in the idea of chosenness, albeit with a negative connotation. Within 2Isa, this recalcitrance is charged mostly against the servant Israel (e.g., 42:18–21; 44:21–2). While critique in this vein is well-precedented, 2Isa goes out of the way to argue that such failure does not, in fact, eliminate servant status. Rather, it highlights YHWH's attachment and mercy. YHWH is willing to go to great lengths to induce his servants to their purpose.

The greater workings of YHWH that break a strict sense of sin/punishment causality are emphasized with the idea that *servants can be unwitting*. The example which 2Isa uses for this is mostly Cyrus (45:4–5), though the idea that Israel is also unwitting despite all evidence available is continually present (though not usually within servant language contexts).

Beyond instrumental uses, *servants bring glory to YHWH and his knowledge to others*. In 2Isa the "others" in view is usually the nations (e.g., 42:1; 43:9;[63] 49:6). However, the servant can be sent to Israel as well (e.g., 49:5; 51:16), and servanthood appears to bring glory to YHWH simply by virtue of existing (e.g., 43:21). This function of the servant connects with the other themes used within 2Isa that emphasize YHWH's greatness.

Some servants can be obedient. The servants in chs. 42, 49, and 53 are positive examples of the servant of YHWH, sometimes despite significant opposition. Servanthood is not limited to unwitting usage or disobedience. YHWH's plans do come to fruition at times in more mutual ways, and this is a source of comfort.

However, 2Isa is unwilling to subscribe to a simple idea of service equating to automatic happiness—*servants can suffer*. This idea appears in chs. 49, 50, and 53. Unlike other passages in 2Isa that acknowledge Israel's sufferings due to its sins, in these cases YHWH's servants appear to suffer despite and because of doing as they ought. Most remarkable is the appearance of the idea of vicarious suffering in Isa 52:13–53:12. It is difficult to find pre-exilic precedence for the idea of redemptive suffering found here.[64] From a comparative sociological perspective, the idea of

---

63. Though this is not a servant passage *per se*, the connected witness passage just following it is.

64. Orlinsky 1964: 24; Blenkinsopp 2002: 119–20; Bailey 1998; Spieckermann 2004. Orlinsky 1964 and Whybray 1978 attempt to eliminate vicariousness from Isa 53,

vicarious suffering is in fact rather rare.[65] Moreover, the fact that those who later read this text as messianic usually dropped out or transferred to another figure the element of vicarious suffering[66] demonstrates the difficulty of the concept. In any case, in the context of 2Isa's elaboration of servanthood, it makes more sense to see this concept as a sophisticated attempt to deal with the complexities of sin, punishment, and forgiveness without simplistic recourse to an inflexible equivalence as in Chronicles. It certainly is *not* one of Messianic expectation.

More positively, *servants bring blessing to others*. This can either be as a direct move on YHWH's part (e.g., 44:3–4; 45:8), the actions of the servant (e.g., 42:1–4, 6–7; 49:5), or as a result of the servant's suffering (Isa 53). Like the idea of punishment, reward is expanded beyond simple correlation to behavior through the acting of YHWH through his servants. The anti-Babylonian *Schadenfreude* also receives a balancing perspective that sees a new way of relating to other peoples in a more positive, albeit perhaps patronizing, manner.

With all of these perspectives on how servanthood to YHWH can appear, the text posits servants with a number of different identities. They can be single people (prophets [e.g., 44:16], kings [e.g., Cyrus, 45:1]) or groups ("sects" [44:5], nations [Israel, e.g., 48:12]). As a complete text, 2Isa uses the servant as another instance of the power and effectiveness of YHWH in the world. Moreover, the status of being a servant appears to have different implications for different servants, the strongest distinction perhaps being made between the people of Israel-Judah and the "suffering servant" of Isa 53. Within the greater rhetorical context this serves to ask the audience which sort of servant they wish to be, singularly and collectively—in what manner will they attach themselves to YHWH and serve him.

For the purposes of this study, it is worth noting the place, status, and function of Cyrus as one form of servant (for a broader discussion of Cyrus see below). The most extended presentation of Cyrus as a servant

---

but this attempt has received little support. Rignell 1956: 81 tries to parallel this with the entirely different passages of Lev 16, Deut 21, and Exod 32. McKenzie 1968: liv thinks that it derives from the history of Israel.

65. The well-known attempts by Girard to ground all religion in a "scapegoat" mechanism is too tendentious to be useful in this regard; see Girard 1977, 1982, 1988. Neither does the substitute kingship ritual work, since suffering has no component in that context, nor is the issue guilt *per se*. For the ritual, see Nissinen 1998: 68–77. For an argument relating Isa 53, see Walton 2003. For a rejection, see Schipper 2013. Morrow 2004 has tried to relate the vicariousness to Post-Traumatic Stress Syndrome.

66. Hengel and Bailey 2004: 75–6, 145–46.

of YHWH falls in 44:26–45:13. In this context, Cyrus fulfills several purposes. He fulfills the prophetic word (44:26), he restores Judah, Jerusalem, and the temple (44:26, 28; 45:13, cf. 45:3–4, 8), he punishes the nations (45:1–2), he brings glory to YHWH (45:3, 6). He thus fulfills many of the functions of servanthood outlined above. Moreover, he is called YHWH's anointed one (משיחו; cf. "shepherd" in 44:28), taking an epithet of pre-exilic Judahite kings. However, this status is one applied without Cyrus's knowledge or consent. This choice on YHWH's part is not one automatically obvious to the audience, since this is immediately followed by asserting YHWH's right to do as he pleases (45:7–12). Later, also as servant, he is said to have an explicit purpose to punish Babylon (48:14–16). If one reads 42:1–7 as also referring to Cyrus as servant (a possible reading), then the text paints Cyrus in very rosy colors, with an almost evangelical mission on the behalf of YHWH.

Cult of YHWH

Though the worship of YHWH is very important to 2Isa, very little attention is paid to the details or mechanics thereof. The most elaborate depiction of Yahwistic worship comes in a passage accusing Israel of not fulfilling its created purpose to worship YHWH (43:21b–28), a failing which has existed the length of Israel's history from the patriarchs to the Babylonian destruction. The elements in view are burnt offerings, sacrifices, meal offerings, incense, and worship. These imply the desirability of blood cult such as had been offered in the Jerusalem temple previously, though the location (or numbers) of such cult is not specified. Elsewhere (52:11–12) this is envisioned as requiring purity and pure vessels; 52:1–2 is also concerned with purity.

For 2Isa Jerusalem is important, perhaps most important, as a cultic center. This can be seen in its predicted restoration (44:26–28) and in the idea that the holy city provides Israel with its identity (48:2). Indeed, YHWH calls Zion—presumably here the temple mount and surrounds—and her walls his un-abandoned children (49:14–18). However, in all of this there is no direct indication that this place is the only legitimate cultic center. One could even argue that the accusation concerning the lack of sacrifice in 43:21–28 implies the opposite: cult should still be happening, even if not in the destroyed Jerusalem.

However, 2Isa is more concerned with two other aspects of YHWH's cult: its ability to bring glory and praise to YHWH among the nations and its promulgation of teaching. The calling of the servant causes 2Isa to enjoin the praise of YHWH by the entire earth, and specifically by Edom (Kedar/Sela, 42:10–12). Egypt, Nubia, and Saba will honor Israel for honoring YHWH (45:14–15). More generally, YHWH will be worshipped by all for being the only source of צדק (45:23–25) and is a light to the nations (49:6). The cult is a source of identity (44:5; 48:2), teaching (תורה, משפט, 51:4; 54:13), peace, צדק, and security (54:14).

The cult, therefore, carries significance well beyond local concerns—it has cosmic (צדק, שלום) and international significance. It is also a locus for some form of "scholarship," since it creates disciples (למוד) and disseminates *torah* and *mišpaṭ*. There is also a connection between cultic activities and naming. The people will know YHWH's name (52:6), and the devoted descendants will be called Jacob and Israel, both parallels of "of the Lord" (44:5). "Jacob" and "Israel" here appear to be used in a cultic/religious sense more than in a national sense.

A key aspect of ANE cult is the concept of remembering, specifically in terms of leaving votive offerings to cause a deity to remember (for good) the dedicator.[67] The votive gift provides a twofold "ontological benefit": it causes the giver to be remembered as well as the deity's response to be remembered by future devotees.[68] The language of remembering appears in 2Isa in the accusation of Israel's cultic failures (43:21–28) and after a long passage condemning idolatry (44:21). In 2Isa, the remembering-relation of cult is reversed. Israel is exhorted to remember and to help YHWH remember. In this case, the deity's (YHWH) offering to Israel of forgiveness (43:25) and Cyrus's aid to Israel (in view in 44:21) cause Israel to remember YHWH and thus to increase Israel's glory. This action can, however, be aided by Israel (43:26). Presumably an active sacrificial cult would be useful for these ends, but it remains a response to a gift already given. Thus, ultimately, this would make a restored cult a votive offering to Israel of sorts—like the land itself (55:13). Moreover, one cannot forget the traditional role that temple-building played in royal legitimation discourses.

Return to Judah

The declaration and expectation of a return of exiles to Jerusalem is perhaps the largest reason for the discussion of 2Isa in the historiography of the Neo-Babylonian and Achaemenid period Judaeans; it is often seen as the message of the text wholesale.[69] The text is indeed concerned with a reversal of Judah's fortunes, but as discussed above, this idea serves as

---

67. Gudme 2012: 1–15; Gudme 2013.
68. Gudme 2012: 12–13.
69. E.g., Delitzsch [1877]: 2:59 (for 40–48); Middlemas 2007: 27, 95, 103; Carr 2011: 302; McKinlay 2013: 88; Chavel 2014: 47 (for 40–48).

an argument supporting the main goal of the text: it is proof of YHWH's power, goodwill, and continuing concern, and thus a reason for Israel to devote itself to him. It is *not*, however, a *demand* of the text towards the implied audience.

The expectations are fairly standard markers of blessing, although stated in a rather hyperbolic fashion.[70] A return of exiles from all over the compass is declared (43:5–8; 45:13; 48:20–1; 49:8–23; 51:11). As commonly noted, the exodus tradition is used as a way to describe this event (48:20–21: especially ch. 51).[71] Judah's towns, cities, and temple will be rebuilt by Cyrus (44:26–28). The new situation will be like Eden (51:3) with incredible prosperity (54:1–17; 55:12–13). The population will grow exponentially (49:8–23; 54:1–17), and cause joy (52:7–12). The nations will serve Israel (49:8–23) and know its renown (52:7–12). This renewed land will be pure and safe (52:7–12; 54:1–17). All this is expected to be well-planned and not hasty (52:12).

The promise of such blessing—life in the land, prosperity, multiple descendants, security—is nothing new. Indeed, it recalls the blessings of obedience as found in Deuteronomy.[72] Moreover, previous traditions provide the language of blessing here, most notably the appeals to the exodus and to Eden. Life in the land is assumed to be of relevance to the audience. The novelty in 2Isa is twofold: it reverses the contemporary state of punishment, and it is promised not only as a result of (future) obedience, but even *before* Israel repents. In the logic of the text it is a reason for, more than a result of, Israel's attachment to YHWH. In Fisher's terminology, the return functions to provide both relevance and consequences for devotion to YHWH. Thus, the return is not couched as a demand of Israel. The only command to leave Babylon is in the context of declaring to the nations the workings of YHWH, not of return to Judah (40:20–22). This is an important point to remember, and has sociological resonances (to be discussed below).

Idolatry Polemics

A major theme of 2Isa is the mockery of idols and of those who make and worship them, though the theme is almost entirely contained in

---

70. It is not "eschatological," contra Fohrer 1968: 383. For a discussion of the rhetoric of hyperbole, see Silverman 2014b.

71. E.g., Anderson 1962: 177–95; Ackroyd 1968: 129–31; Watts 1997; Goldingay 2005: 264; Tiemeyer 2011a: 155–204; Paul 2012: 45–6. Spencer 2000 argues this is overplayed, but that the resonance is still there.

72. E.g., Deut 11; 28; cf. Lundblom 2013: 52–4, 68–9.

chs. 40–48.[73] Like the theme of creation, the idolatry functions both as a repetitive form and in various instances of qualitative progression. Typically, the latter is in terms of contrasts, most significantly between YHWH and the idols and between the idolatrous nations and the people of YHWH. Creation, knowledge, and effective power are the primary loci of these contrasts.

The first appearance of this theme contrasts the work of idol manufacturers with the creation of YHWH (40:18–20), highlighting his superiority as creator. In the next appearance, these idols can do their worshippers no good (41:5–7), in contrast with the support YHWH provides to Israel. Again, though the nations' gods failed to predict the coming of Cyrus (41:21–24), YHWH not only predicted but called him. YHWH objects to idols being given his glory (42:8) and these idols will only cause shame (41:17). At great length, 2Isa then expounds on the making of idols to assert that they are not only unable to provide their makers with any knowledge, they are in fact deluding (44:6–20). This contrasts with YHWH's foreknowledge, and he mocks their diviners (v. 25). The idolaters will indeed discover this, and will turn to Israel when they realize his works (45:16, 20–25). In context this contrasts not only with contemporary non-Yahwistic theology, but with Israel's current ignorance of how YHWH is working. 2Isa then explicitly attacks the Neo-Babylonian system and the procession of Bel and Nebo, with YHWH carrying Israel instead of being carried (46:1–10).[74] All of this was predicted beforehand so that these things could not be credited to anyone but YHWH (48:5–6). The last mention of idolatry is an obscure condemnation of inappropriate worship among Israel (50:11).

Though it is not directly idol polemic, the oracle against Babylon in ch. 47 is qualitatively prepared for by it. Not only is Babylon one of the nations and the nation that the audience most likely would want to see receive come-uppance, but Babylonian divination was also famous and integral to the state superstructure. The previous argument against idols repeatedly claimed their inability to divine the future or the coming of Cyrus, thus preparing for the direct attack on Babylon's divination in the second half of the chapter. Moreover, the denial of the efficacy of these idols adds punch to the refutation of Babylon's claims to be divine (47:8d, 10f). The attentive audience could thus wallow in the complete impotence of their masters, whom the text now depicts as relying on empty power and empty knowledge.

---

73. Except 50:11.
74. The Babylonian context will be discussed more fully below.

The entire theme of idolatry presumes that gods exist and that they control human affairs. The debatable question for the audience is the identity of the responsible deity/ies. Lurking in the background must be the idea that the defeats of Jerusalem (and perhaps even the prior defeat of Samaria) demonstrated the impotence or at the very least the abandonment of YHWH. In such an interpretation the obvious alternate high god was Marduk, since he headed the pantheon of the victors. However, the advance of Persia could also lead to a preference for Ahura Mazda, Humban, or another Persian god. 2Isa wants to make clear that it is YHWH, and only YHWH, who is responsible. This answers the question of why he deserves Israel's continued/renewed devotion. Though the argumentation is largely predicated on ability and competence, the issue of national pride is also brought in, especially in places where the shame of idolaters is described. This latter aspect is well-calculated to appeal to defeated minority groups. Perhaps this is emphasized by the way this theme is mostly elaborated with a tone of mockery with the implied rhetorical response left only implicit: it enables the audience to choose to feel superior by siding with the mocking rhetor rather than the mocked idolaters. The desired end (attachment to YHWH) can thus feel like a satisfying form of resistance to the dominant culture.

Rise of Cyrus

Of central interest for this study is the widely discussed theme of the role of Cyrus, another motif restricted to chs. 40–48. Though mentioned by name only twice (44:28; 45:1), there are seven passages which likely treat his campaign (41:1–5, 25–27; 44:28; 45:1–8, 13; 46:11–13; 48:14–16) and another which could be read to include him as a referent (42:1–7).

Cyrus is first alluded to in a disputatious speech to the nations (41:1–5), describing a rapid and unrelenting succession of military victories.

החרישו אלי איים	Silence before me, O regions
ולאמים יחליפו כח	and peoples, discard[75] your power
יגשו אז ידברו	then present yourself and speak
יחדו למשפט נקרבה	Assemble for judgment, let us draw near
מי העיר ממזרח צדק	Who has awakened victory from the east
יקראהו לרגלו	called him to his feet
יתן לפניו גוים	given nations before him
ומלכים ירד	and subdued kings
יתן כעפר חרבו	bestowed his sword as dust
כקש נדף קשתו	dispersed his bow like chaff?

75. Taking חלף in sense of permanent removal rather than renewal.

ירדפם יעבור שלום	He pursues them and passes by unharmed
ארח ברגליו לא יבוא	a shackle[76] is not placed on his feet.
מי פעל ועשה	Who has worked and done (this)?
קרא הדרות מראש	One calling the primordial generations:
אני יהוה ראשון	I, YHWH, am the first
ואת אחרנים אני הוא	and with the last I am he
ראו איים וייראו	The regions look and fear
קצות הארץ יחרדו	The ends of the earth tremble…

In this passage Cyrus appears as receiving divine support for his rapid conquests of multiple kingdoms. The rhetoric continues, using this to show how the terrified nations turn to useless idols in fear. Here Cyrus serves to show YHWH's control over international affairs as well as superiority over the nations. The theme of creation is also alluded to. Worth noting is that Cyrus is referred to here with a key term of the text, here translated "victory" (צדק). Within the greater context of 2Isa this is a positive depiction, albeit the role is a rather limited one. Nevertheless, this passage prepares the way for the next mention of Cyrus (41:25–26), this time said to be both from the north and the east (ממזרח שמש, מצפון), and again summoned by YHWH (יקרא בשמי). One could either understand this to recall previous predictions of armies from the north[77] or a situation after Cyrus's victory over Lydia (c. 540s BCE). This mention repeats his victories and claims that YHWH is the only one who has predicted it. Again, though his name is not used, the audience would surely know about whom the text speaks. The rhetoric presupposes that the audience knows of a prediction of these events, even though no such prediction is extant.[78] In terms of argumentation, the claim that Cyrus is called and foreordained by YHWH is a key part of the claim of his continued effectiveness on the behalf of Israel.

The above passage leads into a much more expansive pericope, describing a servant of YHWH (42:1–7). The identity of the servant here is left unspecified, though the current context implies that it describes the

---

76. Following JPS in reading as "shackle" rather than "path." It has this meaning in Aramaic *Ahiqar* according to CAL; cf. Paul 2012: 43.

77. I.e., Silverman 2012: 136–7; this is not to imply an "enemy from the north" tradition, contra Childs 1959. It is too literal to read this as excluding a Babylonian location, à la Seitz 1991: 205. See more below.

78. Seitz 1996: 231 thinks these refer to Isa 1–39, even though Cyrus is definitely not predicted there; Goldstein 2002: 158 thinks it refers to Isa 13 and 21; appealing to the Nabonidus Sippar Cylinder, Blenkinsopp 2002: 207 thinks these refer to similar, non-extant Judaean prophecies about Cyrus, rather than previous HB texts.

rule of Cyrus.[79] Indeed, the phrase "I grasp you by the hand" (ואחזק בידך, v. 6b) is a common ANE phrase for accession to kingship, also appearing in the well-known Cyrus Cylinder.[80] When taken as a depiction of kingship, this passage presents a very idealized image. He is chosen and commissioned (v. 1); he will bring justice to the nations (vv. 1, 3, 4); he is unassuming (v. 2) and gentle (v. 3); he will teach the regions (v. 4). After describing his creation, YHWH appoints him as a blessing to peoples and as one releasing prisoners (vv. 6–7).[81] The exact force of the last two phrases of v. 6 are unclear (לאור גוים, לברית עם), but if taken according to the MT (4QIsa[h] provides a reading of לברית עולם)[82] it would seem to be expanding on the idea of YHWH's working through Cyrus: Cyrus is instituting a new way of dealing with the nations, one in which they will see his workings. It also seems to expand the idea of treaty beyond just the nation of Israel to all the nations.

The two mentions of Cyrus by name bring him into closer relationship with Judah (44:26–28; 45:1–8). Cyrus's victories are declared to be for the sake of Israel, and it is claimed that he will order the rebuilding of the temple and the repopulation of Jerusalem, though the ultimate agency is retained as YHWH's. Cyrus is declared to be a legitimate king, called shepherd (רעה), anointed one (משיח), and one grasped by the right hand (אשר החזקתי בימינו). Indeed, YHWH declares himself to be doing the fighting for Cyrus—as in the royal psalms. Nevertheless, it is claimed that Cyrus is ignorant of YHWH (45:4, 5). This is all about YHWH's glory and not Cyrus's. The next mention of Cyrus repeats the assertion that he will rebuild Jerusalem, and the released exiles in 42:6–7 are specified as YHWH's exiled people.

After mocking the idols, YHWH again declares himself to be responsible for Cyrus's rise (47:11–13). This time he is called a "bird of prey from the East" (ממזרח עיט) and called from a distant land (מארץ מרחק).

---

79. The ambiguity, or perhaps better, polyvalence, of the identity is likely intentional; cf. the discussion of the servanthood theme above. An "original" reference to Cyrus is supported by Blenkinsopp 2002: 210–11.

80. A similar phrase also occurs in 45:1, where it is "right hand." See the Cyrus Cylinder, line 12 (Kuhrt 2009: 70); cf. the *Verse Account of Nabonidus* Column ii, 9 and V, 18 (Kuhrt 2009: 76, 78) and the *Akītu* liturgy (Pongratz-Leisten 1994: 171–4; Bidmead 2002: 48–9, 154–62). In general, see Kittel 1898; Smith 1963.

81. The last two lines on the release of prisoners are very similar to the *Verse Account of Nabonidus*, col. iv. lines 26–7. For the translation, see Schaudig 2001: 563–78; Kuhrt 2009: 75–80. This makes the force of Albertz's arguments related to Darius's use of *aša* and *dāta* (Albertz 2003a: 382) rather unconvincing.

82. Skehan and Ulrich 1997: 118.

This repetition reinforces the claim that YHWH can and will do what he purposes, in this case the deliverance of Israel.

The last reference to Cyrus occurs in another assertion of YHWH's predictive abilities (48:14–16). This time the nation to be conquered is specified as Babylon/Chaldea. However, a closer relationship with YHWH is implied in this reference, with Cyrus referred to as "the one he loves" (אהבו, v. 14) and said to be sent with YHWH's spirit (רוחו, v. 16d). This claim leads to the conclusion of the first section of 2Isa, with a call for Israel to obey and to leave Babylon to announce YHWH's works to the world.

All of the above references or allusions to Cyrus are integrated into the main themes and arguments of 2Isa. He functions as a proof of YHWH's predictive abilities, his control of the nations, his concern for Israel, and his continued acts of creation. Despite some hints that the audience might be expected to object to this plan, 2Isa itself depicts Cyrus as a fully legitimate king, his non-Israelite and non-Yahwistic nature notwithstanding.

The Addressees (Jacob/Israel, Zion/Jerusalem)

The last issue to be discussed here is the manner in which the text refers to its audience. A wide variety of epithets and terms are used, in vocative and third person, most of which occur in parallelism. The most common is the use of the pair Jacob/Israel (40:27; 41:8, 14;[83] 43:1, 22, 28; 44:1, 21, 23; 45:4; 48:12; 49:5). This pair is also used with a few variants: with "the Lord's" (44:5); with "loins of Judah" (48:1);[84] with the added qualifications "tribes of Jacob"/"survivors of Israel" (49:6). These two names appear a few times alone (Jacob [48:20]; Israel [45:17]; Stock of Jacob [45:19]). Once Jacob is paired with Jeshurun instead (44:2).

The text also uses the name Zion, alone (49:14; 51:3; 52:2, 7, 8), with Israel (46:13), Jerusalem (51:16–17; 52:1), and once with Jerusalem and cities of Judah (40:9). Jerusalem/towns of Judah appears once (44:26), Jerusalem/temple once (44:28), and Jerusalem/my people twice (40:1–2; 52:9). Lastly, the audience is said to be named after the holy city once (48:2) and exiled people/my city once (45:13). In the later portions of 2Isa the audience is typically addressed in second person rather than with the above names.

---

83. With addition of "worm" and "maggot."

84. Emending "waters" to "loins." Several suggestions have been offered; *BHS* recommends וממעי for וממי following 1QIsa[a] 39:7; Baltzer 2001: 281, Blenkinsopp 2002: 285, and Paul 2012: 305 read "womb." Korpel and de Moor 1998: 362 n. 1 and Brueggemann 1998: 101 read "loins." Cf. Koole 1997: 556; Hermisson 2003: 202.

The specific concern with Jerusalem and its cult site would suggest that the text was envisioned as addressing a Judaean population largely derived from the Jerusalem environs. At the very least, Jerusalem is used as a useful metonym for the audience. No mention is made of any other specific sites in the land of Judah or Israel. This tallies with both the activities of First Isaiah and with the presumed origin of the majority of deportees to Babylonia. Nevertheless, the text's favorite way of referring to the audience is Jacob/Israel, a name more typically associated with the defunct northern kingdom. However, the use of these terms in parallel with an identity based on YHWH (e.g., 44:5), as well as the use of Jacob and Israel in titles of YHWH,[85] would seem to give these names a religious or cultic nuance more than an ethnic or national one.[86] This may be due to the overall message of devotion to YHWH; it is difficult to draw any real ethnic-identity conclusions from this aspect. In any case, the scattered and variegated usage of epithets for the audience does not suggest defined intra-groups within the perspective of 2Isa. The method the text uses to address its audience does not provide sufficient information on its own for clarifying a more specific implied or real audience.[87]

Summary of the Rhetoric of Second Isaiah

2Isa exhorts its audience to devote itself to YHWH. The poet offers a number of interlocking reasons for why this is desirable. YHWH is a powerful, effective, and forgiving deity. He will bring prosperity and security to Israel and will even inspire the nations to worship him. The punishment will soon be ended through the agency of Cyrus. A number of themes provide progression and unity to the overall text, and these include creation, the idea of servanthood, the cult of YHWH, the futility of idols, and the rise of Cyrus.

Coherence and the Formation of the Text[88]

The present text has a clear and rhetorically coherent twofold structure, often noted by scholars: chs. 40–48 and 49–54, with an introduction in 40:1–11 and conclusion in 55:1–13. Within the second section,

---

85. Byrne 2006: 39–48, 56–62, 163–7.
86. Davies 2007: 21 thinks this is true for the HB in general as well, but that is beyond the scope of this study.
87. Tiemeyer 2011a: 215–310 analyzes these more fully, but her conclusion that they mean Judahites is not at all clearly borne out.
88. An earlier form of some of this discussion was presented at the Melammu meeting in Helsinki, 2015, and is part of Silverman 2018.

52:13–53:12 functions as a sub-unit as well.[89] Two considerations show this large-scale section division between chs. 40–48 and 49–55: themes and rhetorical voice. In the first section, the themes of creation, idolatry, and Cyrus are prominent; in the second, Cyrus disappears while creation and idolatry are only referred to in passing. The second half instead elaborates on servanthood, return, and cult more than the first half. In terms of rhetorical voice, the first half tends to refer to the audience in vocative and third person, while the second more often in second person address. Together, however, they function as two stages in the appeal to attach to YHWH: the focus shifts from a more cosmological and international frame to one more closely focused upon the audience. The issue remains whether this coherence and unity through several sections (as well as all the potential sub-sections and forms, the traditional focus of form-criticism) mean that it represents an authorial unity in time, or whether this form developed over time, and, if the latter, what can be said concretely about such a process.[90] There is no shortage of scholarly opinions on this matter, ranging in a continuum from completely unified text to extensive levels of incremental growth.[91] The extant versions provide no empirical basis for deciding this: neither the Greek nor the Qumran texts show significant additions or deletions in comparison with the MT.[92]

This is an issue on which the exact type of medium and genre, something only mentioned in passing above, plays a decisive role: the type of coherence and types of textual growth to be expected vary

---

89. See overviews in Koole 1997: 13–18; Childs 2001: 189–91. Sadly, Korpel and de Moor 1998 do not comment on this level of the text, except by rejecting an introduction and conclusion (pp. 688–9) and rejecting a logical progression (pp. 659–62).

90. All of the presuppositions of source and form criticism as cited by Law 2012: 123–4, 163–4 are problematic and not shared by the present author.

91. A handy overview is available in Höffken 2004: 101–14. Williamson 1994: 26 treats it as a single text, but merely as a working hypothesis; Watts 2005: 71 rejects a separation of 2Isa from the remainder, thinking it is a single work throughout; Melugin 1976 thought the stages of growth were irrevocably lost; Chavel 2014: 6 has two stages; Westermann 1969: 28–30 argues it is all the work of 2Isa, but still brackets out the "Servant Songs," the idol polemics, and various other passages as additions; Albertz 2003b: 376–92 and 2014 argues for four stages; Kratz 1991 posits 5; Zapff 2001: 220–3 sees all sorts of additions.

92. Ulrich and Flint 2010: 2:40 notes that the Great Isaiah Scroll contains all of the book, though it marks a division after 33; 2:93–5 lists differences between the DSS manuscripts and the Old Greek, nothing more significant than several words. Cf. overview in Baltzer 2001: 2–4.

depending upon it. The importance goes beyond the implied author and audience—it fundamentally informs the appropriate interpretative import to be given to features (such as seams) observed within the text. Different genres imply that seams are more or less likely to be due to authorial or editorial work, thereby informing the discerning of the number of discrete historical units that are in play. There are at least four basic options for understanding 2Isa, each carrying with it implications for social setting, types of expected coherence, and manner of transmission and growth: (1) oral performance; (2) compiled and redacted oracles; (3) "drama" or "liturgy"; (4) scribal composition, whether for school-text, literature, or oral performance.

Oral Performance

By the medium of oral performance is intended the sort of communication as described by Albert Lord: the extemporaneous performance of traditional material that had been continually performed by oral poets, one performance of which, for whatever reason, was dictated and fossilized in writing.[93] This would imply (1) material that had been performed many times to a community; (2) a community that appreciated the content and the skills of the orator; as well as (3) some impetus for a performance to be recorded. This would mean that 2Isa would be merely a singular manifestation of a performance, fossilized as a text. Previous versions would be completely irrecoverable and largely irrelevant, but the present text would itself be a unity beyond secondary editing to fit into the Isaianic context; its relations to the formation of the book of Isaiah would then be secondary. Comparable texts in this understanding would be the epics of Homer.

A major obstacle to a comparison with Homer is the lack of narrative in 2Isa. In itself this need not obviate an origin in oral performance, if one alters the category from epic to lyric.[94] Both epic and lyric poetry are linked with music in elite and non-elite oral performances, thus the basic media context would likely be similar for epic and lyric poetry. The links with the psalms may suggest that such a musical context is appropriate. Though there is widespread evidence for musicians in the royal courts and major temples of Mesopotamia, the use of more popular forms is less

---

93. Lord 2000. It would fall in Lord's category of "oral dictated texts" (pp. 148–9). For a much more comprehensive discussion of issues of orality, see Silverman 2012: chapter 3.

94. The preferred designation of Heffelfinger 2011, discussed in terms of lack of narrative in pp. 45–53. See now also Dobbs-Allsopp 2015, especially 175–232.

well attested.⁹⁵ Though it appears that Mesopotamian scholars already had an advanced form of musicology, the actual praxis and transmission of music and songs appears to belong largely in a milieu similar to that adduced by Lord for Homer on the basis of Yugoslavic fieldwork.⁹⁶ The accomplished poetry of 2Isa would imply a skilled poet/musician, but our present knowledge of lyric poet in the ANE is likely insufficient to determine whether this would imply a context in the court of the Judaean king in exile in Babylon, the Judaean elite in the administration of Yehud in Mizpah, or the more rural communities in either Yehud or Babylonia. Modern anthropological studies of Middle Eastern tribal societies demonstrate the continued importance of oral poetry in a variety of genres and social settings, but this provides no more than a probability that the same had been true in the period of 2Isa.⁹⁷

To fit the (Parry-)Lord model of an oral poem 2Isa would need to display features consonant with that: formulas, patterns, themes, and ornamentation.⁹⁸ Watson argues that the equivalent of formulas in Hebrew poetry was rather the word pair, used for constructing parallelism.⁹⁹ There is no doubt that word-pairs are a significant feature of 2Isa.¹⁰⁰ However, the corpus of comparable material is much too small to assess the significance in terms of the originating poet.¹⁰¹ The thematic analysis above

---

95. On music in Mesopotamia—and its link to some attested forms of poetry such as hymns and laments—see Ziegler 2011. For evidence of musical instruments, see Kolyada 2009. For the appearance of instruments and performances in ANE art, see Perrot 1961: 297–312; King and Stager 2001: 287–98. For its regular use in the Achaemenid court during meals, e.g., Athenaeus IV.145d (Athenaeus 2007: 194–5), which mentions "concubines with harps" singing in unison (also cited Briant 2002: 293). This fits with later Iranian practice at the Parthian and Sasanian courts. On the latter, e.g., Boyce 1957.

96. On this oral aspect in the Mesopotamian context, see Ziegler 2011: 307–8. Also on the musicality of oral poetry in the ANE, see Dobbs-Allsopp 2015: 114–20.

97. For examples of some studies showing a variety of contexts and forms, see e.g., Caton 2009; Abu-Lughod 2009.

98. Lord 2000: 142–8.

99. W. Watson 2005: 81, 136–7; cf. Dobbs-Allsopp 2015: 272–6, although the latter underestimates the flexibility which Lord allows for the function of the formula in oral composition.

100. E.g., Korpel and de Moor 1998, who give an extensive index of parallel words (pp. 666–745).

101. Lord insists that proper comparison must be within the work of a single poet and of a significant corpus; his was based on years of collection. See Lord 2000. In a similar vein, Niditch also thinks the corpus is too small for the Psalms or the HB in general, Niditch 1996: 9.

adequately fulfills Lord's conception of thematic repetitions,[102] as one could also argue for the various forms adduced by earlier form critics. Given the length at which many of these themes are elaborated, it would be hard to deny a "grand scale of ornamentation" to the text, and thus one could reasonably insist that this fulfills an oral criterion for unity, rather than a "close-knit" one.[103] Korpel and de Moor have found a high degree of regularity in structures up to what they call "cantos" and "sub-cantos," but they deny overall coherence beyond catchphrases.[104] One could understand this as either conforming to the nature of oral poetry, or a secondary feature as in the next medium.

Compiled or Redacted Oracles

The medium of poetic oracle compilation would imply one or more instances of oral proclamation that were recorded and compiled. As above, the origins would remain oral to some sort of audience, but the expected unity and time frame would be different. The unity would be more combinational than "authorial," deriving from the reasons for compilation. Though analysis could treat it as a unity, there would be more scope for growth over time in the sense of a series of oracles given at various intervals, gradual collection, and/or supplementation. Moreover, one might suspect a greater scope for editorial activities than in the former option. The necessary appreciative audience for the oracles would also only need to be the one(s) responsible for the collection. Since the text would inherently be a combination of discrete sections, distinguishing between the first compilation and any additions would be nigh impossible without manuscript evidence, but the likelihood of additions would seem to increase.

This understanding of 2Isa would require two contexts: the one in which the poet-prophet(s) operated, and the one in which the collector(s) operated. In what context and for whom did the initial oracles belong, and how and why were they transcribed and collated? Perhaps biblical scholars are most inclined to answer this with recourse to an "Isaianic prophetic school" (thus one that conflates the prophets with the scribes),[105]

---

102. Lord 2000: 145.
103. Both quotations from Lord 2000: 148.
104. Korpel and de Moor 1998: see especially the summary tables in 656–7 and 659–62.
105. E.g., Mowinckel 2002: 60–4; Westermann 1969: 27; Michel 1981: 520–1; Wilson 1988: 54–5; Albertz 1994: 413–15; 2003a: 373 n. 7; in a different formulation, Baltzer 2001: 25–6.

but the present author is unaware of there being any comparable evidence in the ANE for such a context.[106] For this scenario to be plausible, one would need to assume that (1) the oracles were uttered or reported in some semi-official location, such as a temple or administrative center; and (2) someone literate at that location thought they were worth preserving. This would likely mean either in Babylon, perhaps around the "court" of the exiled king's sons, or in Mizpah or Ramat Raḥel, around the governor of Yehud.

The best comparative material for such collected oracles remains the Neo-Assyrian compilations.[107] The majority of the oracles within the collections end with the name and location of the prophet. The exception is the third collection, which seems to have been redacted for use within court ritual.[108] The Assyrian parallels show a lag in time from the individual oracles to their collection, and the handwriting appears to indicate the collections were the work of individual scribes.[109] They derive from a central institution (the royal archive) and seem to have been produced due to extenuating circumstances (the problematic accession of Esarhaddon).[110] The value of these two points for a genre decision on 2Isa are debatable. Perhaps the biggest objection to this medium is the complete lack of headings or colophons within 2Isa indicating the prophet, date, or location of the oracles.[111] Biblical scholars might be inclined to attribute such a lack to the editors responsible for the book of Isaiah, but as an argument from silence this is not particularly strong—depending as it does on this genre specification to begin with (i.e., it is a circular argument)—nor is it presently verifiable.

---

106. A lack of evidence is also the opinion of Nissinen 2008. More broadly, Nissinen 2014 notes the lack of comparisons for writing prophets. Rösel's attempt (2003: 118) to claim the Balaam inscription as evidence for schools of prophets would appear to be wholly predicated on biblical scholarship's predilection for such rather than any real evidence.

107. The standard edition of these is Parpola 1997; they are also available Nissinen 2003: 97–124. For a useful overview of the comparable ANE material, see Huffmon 2000. For an analysis discussing some implications of oracle collection, see van der Toorn 2000.

108. See SAA 9, no. 3, col. II 27–32 (Parpola 1997: 25; Nissinen 2003: 120)

109. Parpola 1997: lv; Nissinen 2003: 101.

110. Parpola 1997: lxviii.

111. As in oracle reports, e.g., K 1292 Rev. 6'–7' (Parpola 1997: 41; Nissinen 2003: 131).

Drama or Liturgy

Assigning the medium of 2Isa as either drama or liturgy likely inverts its relationship between oral and written media: presumably written in order to be performed.[112] Both forms would require a specific and regular performance for the text with some sort of "official" communal backing, either by "religious authorities" or community elders. Positing either drama or liturgy as the medium for 2Isa is distinct from positing its later re-use in either; anything can be re-used as part of a performance or ritual, but the relations between composition and audience are rather divergent. Accepting either liturgy or drama as the medium, however, would lead to the conclusion that while previous materials, perhaps even discrete texts, may have been used, the entire text would have been composed for a singular usage, and would thus would be best understood as a reflecting a single point in time, albeit one with continued resonance due to repeated performance and perhaps containing older materials.

The main objection to this understanding is the complete lack of either "stage directions" or ritual instructions in any extant manuscript. The first extant Greek tragedy, Aeschylus's *The Persians*, might have included markings separating speakers, albeit almost no stage directions *per se*.[113] However, the genre of this performance (as well as its date!) is known, a tradition of scholarship (*scholia*) has preserved some stage directions,[114] and the format of the text indicates changes in speakers and in action through the use of different verse-styles and direct indications in dialogue, enabling reconstruction.[115] The first (partially) extant example of a Judaean play is Ezekiel's *Exagoge*, and the available fragments suggest it belonged to the Hellenistic tragic tradition.[116] Though this text is several centuries later, the differences with 2Isa are significant. The best-known exemplar of an ANE liturgy is the *Akītu* festival, known in a number of local variations over an extended geographic and time period.[117] The available material includes not only ritual texts, but specific indications of the activities, offerings, and processions to accompany said texts. At best such a comparison would allow 2Isa to have been a text composed to

---

112. See nn. 8–12 above.
113. Rosenmeyer 1982: 20–1, 64.
114. Rosenmeyer 1982: 46–9.
115. E.g., Michelini 1982: 6–19.
116. Jacobson 1983: 23–8.
117. For some studies, see Cohen 1993: 400–53; Pongratz-Leisten 1994; Bidmead 2002; Zgoll 2006; cf. Ambos 2013. Of this, the most famous aspect is the *Enūma Eliš*, which was recited as part of the liturgy.

be used within a greater liturgy, rather than the liturgy itself. This would further raise the question of where and for what purpose such a liturgy or drama was designed and used.

"Scribal" Composition

This last medium is perhaps the one most likely favored by biblical scholars, one that eliminates the oral altogether and treats the text *qua* text, written to be read. This medium would allow for any number of compositional models: "monograph," collation, collection growing through time—in itself not necessarily solving any issues related to the unity or plurality of 2Isa. The written nature, however, would raise expectations for coherence and logical structure, allow for a broader array of written amendments and additions, and reduce the expected audience size to minimal numbers. The social context for such a text could include other Judaean "scholars" or use in scribal training as a school text. One might also posit that the text was also meant to be read out to groups, implying some sort of religious or instructional setting. In this sort of model, the unity of the text could be considerably devalued in favor of gradual growth over time, although raising the question of the reasons and contexts for such. The rarified social context such an origin requires likely would imply the text originated within a milieu nigh a center of administration, perhaps somewhere like Babylon, Mizpah, or Ramat Raḥel.

Which Model Best Describes Second Isaiah?

On purely formal criteria, the media of drama or liturgy have little to commend them: 2Isa does not have any of the markers of speakers or action that attested ANE examples contain. If it were composed for use within such a context, it was only as a single portion and has left no discernible trace in the received text.[118] A similarly formal evaluation speaks against an oracle collection. Not only the lack of distinct headings or colophonic information, but the sheer length of the various coherent sections and the variety of thematic material makes it a poor match for the closest ANE parallels.[119] This does not alone eliminate the possibility. 2Isa, however, would represent a uniquely uniform, coherent, and unmarked collection. Moreover, in the oracle collection model, the consistent message would have required such an extensive redaction that the "final form" genre would no longer be usefully called an oracle collection.

---

118. Wilks 2003 rejects on slightly different grounds.

119. Contra Weippert 2001. While his parallels with prophetic formulas are interesting as far as they go, they are insufficient to fit the genre of oracle collection.

Perhaps of use in considering this issue are the phenomena of *Sibylline Oracles*, known primarily through a very late compilation in Greek Hexameter purporting to go back to a series of famous female oracles, the Sibyls.[120] At first the length and poetic nature of the surviving texts make them an attractive parallel, but the issues are perhaps even more manifold than 2Isa. Though a tradition of an individual Sibyl making oral pronouncements in poetic verse goes back at least to the Persian period,[121] the idea of Sibylline oracles became a well-known literary genre with no real link to oral prophecy. One could thus use the Sibyl as an analogue for *either* oral poetic prophecy or for poetic prophetic literature.

Since the extant text has a very performative nature,[122] it seems that there are two best options: oral performance that was recorded, or poetry written for oral performance. Though certainty is impossible, 2Isa is here considered to be an "oral dictated text" as defined by Albert Lord, and thus a fossilized performance, analogous to *The Odyssey* and *The Iliad*.[123] The performative nature, consistent poetry, repetition, and rhetorical structure support this genre decision. It also easily fits into a context of forced migration. Just as with these texts, the exact circumstances and reasons for the writing down of an oral performance are forever lost and unknowable. The social context and expectations for this medium and genre decision, nevertheless, have important ramifications for understanding what 2Isa represents. These will be more fully explicated below, but a few preliminary arguments and observations should be stated here. First, for the early Persian Period 2Isa should be treated as a single unit, without direct reference to the remainder of the book of Isaiah, into which it was later redacted for whatever reasons. Any redaction of the performance, if such existed, is largely untraceable, and probably mostly

---

120. Walde 2001; Parke 1988; Collins 1997: part III. Convenient introductions and translations are available in Collins 1983 and Lightfoot 2007 (only first two oracles).

121. Aristophanes, *Knights* 61 has a character impersonating a Sibyl by singing oracles; Plato in *Phaedrus* 244 mentions the Sibyl as one example of ecstatic prophecy and in *Theages* 124d as a prophet. (Sources consulted through Perseus.) In the words of Lightfoot, "The Sibylline Oracles are a corpus of hexameters, a metre used both in historical oracle centres at Delphi and Asia Minor, and also for the literary depiction of legendary prophecy" (Lightfoot 2007: 16).

122. "Performative" here is not meant in the sense used by Sign Act Theory, but merely as designed for and reflecting live performance. Thus this is different from Adams 2006.

123. Dobbs-Allsopp 2015: 215–26 inclines towards reading the Song of Songs in a similar way, although p. 317 he calls 2Isa a late prophetic collection.

connected with the formation of the entire book of Isaiah, something beyond the present study's scope. Second, its relations to previous Judaean traditions should be seen as primarily *oral* rather than *scribal*. It presumably represents performances that had been repeated over time. Third, there are key parallels to the importance of oral poetry for refugee and forced migrant groups.[124] Moreover, oral poetry has been an important element of culture for both marginalized, illiterate groups as well as for elite circles, especially kings.[125] These connections aid in reconstructing the earliest social location of 2Isa. The balance of probability means it was likely performed within an elite context among its immediate community of origin. Fourth, as oral poetry 2Isa would represent, if not the "opinion" or "worldview" of a group, then at least it must have been considered an acceptable and important performance by a master poet by its original community.

Date of Second Isaiah

There is general agreement, in all but the most conservative circles, that 2Isa has a *terminus post quem* of c. 550 BCE, the year in which Cyrus defeated the army of Astyages, the king of Media.[126] This date derives from the mention of Cyrus by name, and the presumption that this victory marks the first time Cyrus would have been widely known among his contemporaries. This *terminus* is shared even by those who consider the name of Cyrus to be a later editorial addition.[127] A *terminus ante quem*, however, holds less universal agreement. The versions provide only a little help: the earliest Hebrew manuscript is 1QIsa^a, from the late second century BCE;[128] the translation to Greek is usually dated to the middle of the second century BCE,[129] though no manuscripts of Greek Isaiah exist so early. Presuming the Hebrew text was complete before translation into Greek and that therefore 2Isa was redacted into the book of Isaiah before

---

124. E.g., Siddiq 1995; Olden 1999; MacPherson 2001; Olszewska 2007.

125. E.g., Slings 1990–2; Zumthor 1990; Finnegan 1992; Foley 2002.

126. The date derives from *Nabonidus Chronicle* ii.1–4 (6th of Nabonidus, Glassner 2004: 235); the episode also appears in Sippar Cylinder of Nabonidus (in year 3; Schaudig 2001: 436–7) and Herod. I.127–30. Cf. the Harran Cylinder (Schaudig 2001: 473). All available in Kuhrt 2009: 50, 56–7.

127. E.g., Kratz 1991: 184–5, who prefers a date under Darius; Albertz 2003a.

128. Ulrich and Flint 2010: 2:61.

129. On the basis of historical allusions in the translation Seeligmann dated the translation to c. 170–150 BCE; see Seeligmann 1948: 76–94; cf. Blenkinsopp 2002: 122; Dines 2004: 22; Höffken 2004: 15–18; Paul 2012: 66.

that, these provide a comfortable *ante quem* of at least c. 200 BCE. Ben Sira's mention of Isaiah in 48:23–25, which might reference all three sections of the book, points in a similar direction.[130] Can this 350-year time span be narrowed?

Thematic parallels are a methodologically flawed angle for dating texts. Besides the circularity often caused by such procedures (whereby a text is deemed to fit a period due to themes, and then the period is characterized according to said themes), ideas and themes recur repeatedly over time and are thus resistant to dating. It is safer to base dating on other criteria, and then allow the achieved date to inform the context and understanding of ideas and themes within the text. This section will therefore eschew appealing to broad theological concepts and consider more specific potential data.

Another method for (at least relative) dating sometimes employed is the use of textual citations or "intertextuality."[131] This method depends on not only the (uncertain) dating of the proposed cited texts, it also often creates a problem of the direction of the quotation. For the purposes of establishing a date for 2Isa, this argumentation will not be utilized.

References to Babylon

Explicit references to Babylon would on first glance offer some historical anchors for the text. In 43:14 YHWH promises to release (his conqueror) to Babylon, paralleled with the Chaldeans. The reference to the Chaldeans is consonant with the Neo-Babylonian Empire, since the dynasty appears to have derived from the Chaldean tribes.[132] This merely corresponds with the previously assumed dating, though perhaps inclining towards the earlier end of the spectrum. The same is true for Lemaire's suggestion of an allusion to Nabonidus's sojourn in Teima.[133] The pair Babylon/Chaldea reappears in 48:14. However, if this text refers to the public performance of the Babylonian *Akītu* festival (see below), then it *may* imply a likely *ante quem*.

---

130. So Beentjes 1989.

131. E.g., Willey 1997: 117–8 sees Isa 52:7 cite Nah 2:1. This is possible should Nahum really pre-date 2Isa; even if it did, it would do no more than fit with the already posited basic date. In any case, many so-called citations and allusions are merely a few similar words, and thus not particularly compelling, e.g., almost all the relations with Jeremiah posited by Sommer 1998.

132. E.g., Arnold 2003.

133. Lemaire 2003: 286–7.

Isaiah 46:1–2 has Bēl and Nebo going into captivity (בשבי). This clearly must refer to the capture of Babylon, but it could be understood either as a prediction or description of current reality. The same is true of the defeat in 48:14, which merely mentions Babylon being in Cyrus's full control, something that could be predicted or descriptive.

After describing the sorry state of Zion's children, the text promises to pour wrath on their tormentors (51:22–23). This very vague statement cannot be taken as indicative of any specific time.

In 52:4–5 Assyria is accused of carrying off and robbing YHWH's people. This might be a cipher for Babylon, or perhaps referencing continued Judaean populations in places where they were settled by the Assyrians. Nothing can be inferred for dating.

A return of someone with pure cultic vessels from "there" is envisioned in 52:11–12. The most natural assumption is to see an expected return of cultic vessels from Babylon to Yehud, but this is mere surmise, nor can it provide a secure dating datum—not only is the date of the rebuilding(s) of the Jerusalem temple unknown for certain, it is not known when any vessels would have been returned, if ever.

The longest discussion of Babylon is in ch 47. This chapter mocks Babylon as it falls from an imperial center to a conquered province. It depicts widowhood and loss of children (v. 9), evil, ruin, disaster (v. 11), and a lack of fuel for fires (v. 14). This passage could be read as a prediction of the fall of the city (perhaps after the sacking of Opis?), or it could be read as an expectation for reprisals against the city after it fell peacefully. In principle, this chapter could also reflect any of the situations of expected warfare and reprisal against Babylon: Cyrus's invasion, the defeats of Nebuchadnezzars III and IV, or Xerxes's suppression of Bel-šimanni and Šamaš-erība. Thus, despite initial appearances, the allusions to Babylon provide little concrete chronological data.

One aspect potentially providing an *ante quem*,[134] however, are relations with the Babylonian *Akītu*.

Second Isaiah, Idol Polemics, and the Akītu

The extended idol polemics within 2Isa likely provide clues concerning the social location of the implied audience (and thus of what was socially understandable for the real audience). One may contend that the text has within its view not just generalized foreign cults, but specifically the *Akītu* festival as it was practiced in the city of Babylon. The first indication is

---

134. See the argument below: i.e., before the likely end of the living memory of the festival as a performance.

the specification of Bēl and Nebo in 46:1–2. These two were the main protagonists in the Babylonian version of the *Akītu*, though the festival had different ones in other times and cities.[135] While the festival liturgy as it survives involves twelve days of rituals, many within the closed precinct of the temple, 2Isa appears to be aware of the more public aspects of the festival: procession, transport by ship, manufacture of two new idols, and the widespread use of divination within and around the festival.

The first clue is in the otherwise obscure 43:14:

למענכם שלחתי בבלה	For your sakes I release towards Babylon,
והורדתי בריחים כלם	and I sink all their writhing,[136]
וכשדים באניות רנתם	and the Chaldeans in the ships of their shouting

Many commentators and translators either emend this or follow the Greek, assuming it to be corrupt.[137] However, the Hebrew of this verse makes sense if understood to be predicating the violent ending of the *Akītu* festival.[138] On two days of the festival, statues of the gods were processed through Babylon—gods visiting Marduk within Esagila, and the gods processing to the *Akītu* house outside of the city precincts.[139] The trip included a cruise for the statues on the Euphrates on an elaborately decorated barge.[140] This procession included prayers and hymns, and one would imagine the excitement and shouting by the crowds watching the procession; there was at least a ritual shout.[141] "Ships of shouting" makes perfect sense in this context. Further, this was a popular public

---

135. Especially emphasized by Pongratz-Leisten 1994; Cohen 1993: 427; Bidmead 2002: 32–8; cf. the festival in Borsippa, see Waerzeggers 2010b: 119–29; an alternate, autumnal festival is discussed in Ambos 2013. Vanderhooft 1999: 177 thinks these verses alone indicate a link with the *Akītu*.

136. Following the meaning as found in Job 26:13 and Isa 27:1, where it is used of the movement of the sea-dragon Leviathan. Day 1998: 435 notes this epithet is found for the dragon in Ugarit as well.

137. Elliger 1978: 331–2, 335–9; Koole 1997: 319–22; Brueggemann 1998: 57; Baltzer 2001: 169; Blenkinsopp 2002: 226; Childs 2001: 336 emends pointing; Westermann 1969: 125 calls it "difficult"; Korpel and de Moor 1998: 161 n. 6 claims all exegetes are simply "guessing"; Paul 2012: 214–15.

138. Already Rignell 1956: 38 suggested a link with processions of the gods, but he did not note a connection with בריחים.

139. Bidmead 2002: 86, 94 claims these are days 6 and 9; Zgoll 2006: 30–1, 42 on days 8 and 11. Cf. Waerzeggers 2011b: 731.

140. Pongratz-Leisten 1994: 196–7, 244–5.

141. Zgoll 2006: 33.

event.[142] The event lasted several days, involving six days of gift-giving.[143] Significantly, this barge was decorated with the god's emblems and was thought to signify Marduk's defeat of Tiamat and his glory as creator.[144] Since the word translated "writhing" above is used of Leviathan or the sea-dragon in its other appearances within the HB, this is a significant linkage—especially in light of the creation language in 2Isa generally. This makes the description in this verse highly sarcastic: the barges are to YHWH's conqueror (Cyrus) what Tiamat was to Marduk. Moreover, the movements of this barge were the objects of divinatory expectations.[145] If these connections appear too indeterminate, there are several other similarities to the *Akītu* demonstrable in 2Isa.

On day three of the festival, a metal worker, a carpenter, and a goldsmith use tamarisk and cedar to make two figures (either gods or human effigies).[146] This collaborative effort is similar to some of the descriptions of idol manufacturing by 2Isa. Isaiah 41:6–7 has a series of workers involved, including carpenter and smiths. 40:20 has a woodworker and a smith, using a wood called מסכן (perhaps Indian redwood).[147] Exotic woods are specified by 44:14, though one is a *hapax* (תרזה): cedar, oak, and *tirzah*. The passage is difficult, but whatever the exact interpretation, the use of aromatic and precious wood for idols still fits within an *Akītu* setting.[148]

---

142. Kuhrt 1987: 40; Bidmead 2002: 98. In this respect it is worth noting the ship models which were excavated in the so-called Merkes Quarter of Babylon (the wealthy residential neighborhood) and which the excavator interpreted as related to the *Akītu*. See Koldeway 1913: 251–2.

143. Zgoll 2006: 29.

144. Pongratz-Leisten 1994: 90, 245 (No. 13, line 13'–14'); cf. Schaudig 2008: 559.

145. Pongratz-Leisten 1994: 263–4 (No. 18, lines 37–46).

146. Bidmead 2002: 54–55; Zgoll 2006: 22–3.

147. Jerome takes it as "mulberry," from Akkadian *musukkannu* (Blenkinsopp 2002: 189 n. k.); if one were to take it from the Akkadian, one could also suggest a pun on Akkadian *musukku*, "impure person" (Black, George, and Postgate 2000: 220). Gerschevitch 1957 argued that the word actually refers to the Indian redwood (Sissoo), attested in use in Darius's palace at Susa and as being imported from Carmania. This identification is accepted by Dick 1999: 22 n. g., Vanderhooft 1999: 173, and Goldingay and Payne 2006: 1:115.

148. Sherwin 2003 gives a helpful overview of the various tree species potentially related to this verse, though his conclusion that the location of some species are native to the Mediterranean coast has little bearing on the context of the passage, since the coast was part of both the Neo-Babylonian and Persian Empires and that rare materials were deliberately shipped around both. Indeed, the above link with an

Specifically, on day six the two effigies are burned, and 2Isa likens the idols to ashes (44:20).[149]

It was noted above that 2Isa is rather consistent in mocking idolaters' failures in prediction, specifically professional diviners (44:25; 45:20; 47:13). Divination was a particularly important aspect of Mesopotamian administrations and scholarly tradition generally. However, it was also a key component of the *Akītu*, playing an especially important role due to its nature as a new year festival.[150] Schaudig has argued that behind Isa 46:1–2 are the processional omens of the *Akītu*, in which the movements of the statues were objects of interpretation.[151] He argues that these omena were ones that would have been "plainly seen and easily understood" by ordinary observers of the festival.[152] One need not take such a direct correlation between 46:1–2 and the omena to find the overall point pertinent—the *Akītu* was a time in which the Babylonian traditions of divination were prominently and publicly visible. The determination of the year's fortunes occurred twice as part of the festivities.[153]

In the context of deliberate mocking of the *Akītu*, the recollection of the exodus through the terms of the *Chaoskampf* tradition in Isa 51 is significant. It takes on the color of an explicit refutation of the mythology of Marduk as slayer of Tiamat. It is certain that the text of the *Enūma Eliš* played a major role within the festival.[154] Blenkinsopp analyzes 2Isa in respect to the *Akītu*, with his departure point being this ritual text.[155] The recognition of the *festival* context, however, obviates the need to appeal to the text *per se*—only to its representation through the ritual and procession itself. Access to the ritual text or even ability to understand its verbal recitation would not have been necessary for the audience to appreciate the overall narrative and ideological components.

Indian tree makes such an argument very tenuous. Moreover, Potts 1997: 107 lists these trees as attested archaeologically within Mesopotamia, and he argues some of them were likely deliberately grown in local plantations. Williamson 2015: 263 supports it as evidence for a Babylonian setting.

149. Link noted by Sherwin 2003: 517, but he does not see this significance; a description is given in Zgoll 2006: 28–9.

150. On the *Akītu* as new year festival, see Bidmead 2002: 39–45; Zgoll 2006: 13–14, 24, 27–8, 65–6, emphasizing the import of determination of the year's good fortunes (2×).

151. Schaudig 2008.

152. Schaudig 2008: 568.

153. Zgoll 2006: especially 65–6.

154. Zgoll 2006; cf. the section below on creation mythologies.

155. Blenkinsopp 2002: 105–8.

Lastly, the links of the *Akītu* with themes of creation and the kingship of Marduk serve as a broader comparison with 2Isa (43:15, 10). Moreover, since the entire festival has close ties with Babylon's claims for imperial sovereignty, it makes sense to see it as a useful, direct foil for 2Isa. If a symbolic target for a critique of the reigning imperial power were needed, the *Akītu* was a suitable choice. The festival celebrated the ascendancy of Marduk and of his city Babylon, two of the ideas under attack within 2Isa.

If the idol polemic is seen as a direct challenge to the *Akītu*, then this would imply that the text must derive from a context in which this festival had contemporary currency for its audience. Indeed, it solves the problem of Judaean access to rarified Babylonian theological discourse, since it relies on a public performance.[156] Although often assumed to continue unabated throughout the first millennium, there is actually no certain evidence of it ever being performed between one instance in the reign of Cyrus and the Seleucid-era texts of the ritual.[157] Due to the paucity of sources, particularly as the Persian period progresses, this might merely be the result of chance and not reflect the actual state of affairs. However, it

---

156. Which is a problem if the source is posited as the ritual text itself or sources such as the *mīs pî* ritual, as argued by Dick 1999: 26. This is the objection presented by Tiemeyer 2011a: 84, 95 (written source and ability to read Akkadian).

157. This observation belongs to Caroline Waerzeggers (personal communication; Waerzeggers 2015a: 201). Contra Glassner 2004: 82, who claims the Persians (and Macedonians) were "scrupulous" in observing it. Kuhrt (1987: 52; 2014: 165) notes the evidence for its celebration is scant, though she thinks its celebration in the Hellenistic period makes continuity probable, albeit without the Great King's participation. The Nabonidus Chronicle (Grayson's Chronicle 7) breaks off in Cyrus's first year, with the participation of Cambyses in some ritual, normally believed to be the *Akītu* (Grayson 1975: 111; Glassner 2004: 239). According to a reinterpretation of the *Verse Account*, Waerzeggers argues the *Akītu* mentioned there was performed in 538 BCE, so parallel to the Chronicle (Waerzeggers 2012: 318). The so-called *Akītu* and Religious Chronicles (Grayson's Chronicles 16 and 17) do not survive into the Persian period. Tolini 2011: 145 suggests that by 537 the Babylonian priesthood had accepted the king could not be around to participate any longer. A badly broken Chronicle 8 mentions a Festival of Bēl, with the name "Darius" also appearing in the text, but not enough is extant to know for certain if this indicates a performance of the *Akītu*. Grayson thinks it mentions Darius I and thus belongs under Xerxes, though the name is not extant (Grayson 1975: 112–13). However, van der Spek has re-edited this chronicle and sees it as firmly dealing with Darius III, and thus the festival in question as occurring under Alexander (van der Spek 2003: 301–10, his text 3). The first certain attestation of the festival again is in Chronicle 13a, under Seleucus III (Grayson 1975: 283; Glassner 2004: 252–5; Bidmead 2002: 144 [called 13b]). Zgoll 2006: 15, dates the tablets of the ritual to the Seleucid and Parthian eras.

seems the traditional Babylonian city priesthood largely lost its positions in the aftermath of the 484 rebellions against Xerxes;[158] therefore, it seems highly unlikely that any Persian king would have participated in the festival from that point on. The balance of probability then is that this would provide a reasonable *ante quem* of 484 BCE. If one assumes the practice was not continued beyond Cyrus (with Cambyses most likely away due to preparations for the campaign against Egypt),[159] then the end-point would be c. 530 BCE.

Other Potential Chronological Indications

Flogging and the plucking of beards is mentioned in Isa 50:6. Heltzer argues, on the basis of Plutarch's *Regum et imperatorum apophthegmata*, 173d, that Artaxerxes I banned the use of flogging and beard-plucking as punishments for elites (and sees this as a reason for dating Nehemiah to the first Artaxerxes's reign).[160] If one accepts this anecdote as reliable—which is rather dubious—then it would favor a date earlier than Artaxerxes I (c. before 424 BCE). Nevertheless, a text from the *Murašu* archive demonstrates the continued usage of both as a punishment under Darius II, so this detail cannot provide a chronological datum of any kind.[161]

Garbini has taken references to Egypt as indicative of a date in or after the reign of Cambyses.[162] In 43:3 YHWH promises to give Egypt, Ethiopia, and Saba as a ransom for Israel. One could understand these as either a stereotypical collection of far-away, southern peoples, or a direct reference to an expected campaign. If one prefers the latter, the obvious expected campaign would be that by Cambyses, though several subsequent kings also campaigned in Egypt, including Darius and Xerxes. Moreover, Saba was never part of the Achaemenid Empire. These three countries reappear as a set in 45:14, this time bringing tribute for YHWH's worship. A link to conquest would be rather tendentious in this reference,

158. The basis for this is not the Greek sources critiqued in Kuhrt and Sherwin-White 1987. See Waerzeggers 2003/2004; George 2005/2006; Jursa 2014a: 113, 116, 130; George 2010; Kuhrt 2010; cf. Waerzeggers and Seire 2019.

159. Tolini 2011 has reconstructed a journey of Cambyses from Uruk to Sippar in 528–7 BCE, but he does not appear to have been in Babylon during Nisan (summary, pp. 173, 175). On the basis of Camb 276 it would seem he was in Susa in XI of his fifth year preparing for the Egyptian campaign (p. 203).

160. Heltzer 1995–6; see Plutarch 1931: 17–19; cf. Brown 2001: 102.

161. CBS 5213, cited by Fried 2004: 219. The issue as official punishment is also used by Tiemeyer 2011a: 318 to argue for the plausibility of a Neo-Babylonian official within Yehud.

162. Garbini 1988: 95.

reinforcing the suspicion that the set is merely a conventional one without a particular, historical referent. Lastly, the appearance of the Sinim in 49:12 in the MT is replaced in 1QIsa^a with the Syenians, which one could take as a reference to Elephantine.[163] However, the date of this community is uncertain (perhaps with Cambyses, despite their claim to precede him)[164] as is the certainty of this textual version.[165] If these references can be taken to reflect anything at all, then perhaps they relate to a time in which Egypt was part of the Achaemenid Empire, or was expected to be—but this provides little definitive dating either. Surely once Babylon fell Egypt would have been considered the next likely target;[166] the Persian kings certainly never accepted its independence, despite their interregnum.

Sometimes a datum used for assigning a date to the text of 2Isa is its references to the Jerusalem cult.[167] However, as noted above, the accusation in 43:22–28 implies that cult ought to be happening somewhere and is not. To make much rhetorical sense this would imply the audience had reasonable access to some sort of shrine at least, a situation conceivable before or after the Jerusalem temple was rebuilt, in Yehud or Babylonia. The typical assumption that the Judaeans practiced no Yahwistic cult outside of Jerusalem is untenable.[168] The text does proclaim the restoration of the temple in 45:28, but since the actual date of the temple's rebuilding is unknown, this does not provide much. Since it is linked to Cyrus, it *perhaps* makes a time before his death more likely. A reference to the glory of Jerusalem in 52:1–2 is much vaguer. The call for the vessels to return in 52:11–12 at present cannot imply anything, since their return is otherwise un-datable (and dubious), and could have happened before or after the temple was rebuilt in any case.

163. Ulrich and Flint 2010: 1:82, 2:172.
164. In AP 30 and 31 (Cowley 1967: 108–22; Lindenberger 2003: 72–6; A4.7 and 4.8 in Porten and Yardeni 1986–99: 1:68–75).
165. The Greek has "land of Persians." Seeligmann 1948: 232, 235 [2004 edition] sees this as a sign of the Hellenistic era. Delitzsch [1877]: 2:230 thought the Sinim was China. Most commentators appear to accept the Qumran reading, Syene: Westermann 1969: 216; Koole 1998: 545–6; Hermisson 2003: 322–3.
166. Certainly the alliances made by Amasis in advance of the invasion implies that he expected it. Cf. the comments by Briant 2002: 51.
167. E.g., Fried 2002: 379; Albertz 2003b: 399–400.
168. Besides the later attested Yahwistic temples in Elephantine, Gerizim, and Leontopolis, one may surmise that cult had never stopped in Bethel. Moreover, it would be highly irregular for the Babylonian exiles to have had no religious provision, if only a local street shrine. Chong 1996 strongly argues that they did, though his bases are mainly Ezek 11:16, Ezra 8:17, and Zech 5:5–11.

Economic Context

A potentially useful consideration is the economic situation envisioned by the text. Though the rhetorical nature of the text must be taken into account, one might suspect that the basic nature of the contemporary economic system could be at least partially refracted in the text. Ignoring expressions of hyperbolic expectations for prosperity, only a few hints at economic issues are present in the text. They are implied to be poor and needy (41:17–19). The implied audience is addressed as oppressed and afflicted, sometimes with the implication of having been plundered (42:22–25; 49; 51:13–14). They are depicted as lying in the streets, "drunk" with punishment and a contrast with their lords (51:20–13). Most of these, however, seem to refer more to the state of military defeat and punishment—and the resulting morale deficiencies—than the general socio-economic status of the implied audience. They seem to perceive themselves as oppressed, but much more cannot be said. The greater economic context is only briefly alluded to; Babylon is called "pampered" (47:8) and as losing its trading partners (47:15). It is responsible for the sorry state of the audience (51:20–23).

According to Jursa's analysis of the economy of Babylonia in the "long sixth century," the Neo-Babylonian hegemony represented an unprecedented period of prosperity for the heartland, visible in terms of increased population, crop yields, and labor specialization.[169] Though prices rose through the period, they began to drop around 510/500, possibly related the end of Darius's construction works at Susa, which had demanded much Babylonian labor.[170] The structure of the Neo-Babylonian economy decisively changed in Northern Babylonia in 484, as a result of the suppression of the revolts against Xerxes.[171]

It would be difficult to describe the Judaeans in Babylonia as a whole as poor and oppressed during the Neo-Babylonian and early Persian periods, though it might fit the communities in Yehud and Samerina for a long time. Present analysis of the attested Judaean communities is not yet advanced enough to assess the relative differences between the various Judaean

---

169. His analysis is helpfully summarized in Jursa 2014a. Pages 129–30 give his criteria for establishing prosperity (stature, nutrition, mortality, life expectancy, disease patterns, material culture, housing). See his more detailed work in Jursa 2010; cf. Jursa and Waerzeggers 2009; Jursa 2014b. However, the critique of Jursa's economic model by Boer 2015 (esp. p. 11) should be noted.

170. Jursa 2014a: 126–7 gives tables for staple prices; he relates the rise in prices in part to Persian demands for labor, 128; he notes the demand for forced labor highest under Darius I, 124.

171. Jursa 2014a: 116, 130–5.

groups, urban and rural, but it is unlikely that they were quantitatively worse off economically than they had been in Palestine. Spencer argues that 2Isa encourages a return to Yehud despite expected detrimental effects on the returnees' economic situation.[172] His argumentation is at several points unconvincing, but the overall perspective still fits with the analysis here. The description of Babylon as "pampered" would be very ill-fitting after 484, and plausibly even under Darius, given the heavy labor demands. The mention of (military?) labor in 40:2 (צבא), however, is equally applicable to Yehud or Babylonia in both the Neo-Babylonian and Achaemenid regimes. Thus, the economic refractions in the text are not determinative, though they favor an *ante quem* by 484, possibly favoring earlier than later.

Conclusions for Dating

No conclusive evidence can be adduced at present from the text of 2Isa for a precise dating. The argument of Albertz that predictions of destruction of Babylon were only fulfilled by Darius over-interprets the oracles against Babylon: they expect humiliation and hardship and thus are consonant with more than just military conquest.[173] A date in the reign of Darius is not impossible, but it is not required, either. The best clue comes from the attacks on the *Akītu* festival. While itself indeterminate, it suggests that the likelihood decreases the further into the Persian period one progresses, with a date after 484 *prima facie* rather unlikely. On balance, a date somewhere in the decade between c. 545 and 530 BCE seems the most fitting, though the relevance of the material would remain for subsequent periods—indicated by its preservation and redaction into Isaiah if by nothing else. The attempts by Balzer and Watts to date it to the reigns of Artaxerxes I or Darius II (c. 450–400 BCE) would seem much too late, quite apart from any theories of parallels with the situation of Nehemiah.[174] This means that 2Isa should be read within a context of Judaeans' very early engagements with the Persians; it should probably also be read as a background for later expectations and attitudes towards the empire as it progressed. In any case, being an oral poem as argued above also means that the performance would likely have continued over a period of time, even if the form which is extant derives from an unknown particular recitation of it.

---

172. Spencer 2000.
173. Contra the argument in Albertz 2003a; cf. Albertz 2003b: 399–404.
174. Baltzer 2001: 30–2; Watts 2005: xxv, 71.

Social Contexts of Second Isaiah

Understanding the social context of 2Isa is fundamental for evaluating its evidence for Judaean interactions with the Persians. This means not just the likely geographical location of the "first" real audience, but also their social statuses and situations, whether elite or common, urban or rural. The genre, implied audience, and dating are key factors in evaluating this. Above it is argued that 2Isa represents a single textual reflex of an oral poem, one with strong rhetorical features, and dating somewhere between 545–484 BCE, with the earlier part of this period more likely than later. Where was this poem first composed and performed (and presumably recorded)?

Biblical scholarship has traditionally favored a Babylonian setting for 2Isa, though much recent scholarship has reacted against this and either directly argues for a setting within Yehud, or posits multiple stages, the later ones of which belong in Yehud/Jerusalem.[175]

Seitz presents five objections to placing 2Isa in Babylonia.[176] First, he notes the depiction of exiles returning from the north, east, south, and west.[177] This objection reads poetic and parallelistic language far too literally. Unless one has evidence that Judaeans in a particular geographical setting could not imagine groups in multiple directions, this objection lacks force. Second, he objects to the depiction of Cyrus as coming from the north and from afar. However, these also carry no force for the same reason given above. Moreover, if one assumes a dating after the Lydian campaign, then one can believe a depiction as coming from the north to be a reasonably accurate depiction, even for Babylonia. "Afar" is also no issue, as Anšan is rather far from Babylon, almost the same

---

175. For scholars arguing a setting in Babylon, e.g., Berquist 1995: 30; Vanderhooft 1999: 169–71; Snyman 2011: 255; Blenkinsopp 2002: 102–4 thinks Babylonia is "marginally preferable." For an overview of scholarship on location, see Barstad 1997: 17–58. Though Barstad is often cited as demonstrating a Palestinian origin, his argument in this book is more a critique of earlier scholarship and the idea of the "Myth of the Empty Land" than an argument for a Palestinian location. For various scholars arguing for Palestine as a setting, see Seitz 1991: 205–8; Davies 1995: 213–15; Albertz 2003a: 372–3; Tiemeyer 2011a. A number of scholars place 40–48 in Babylon and 49–55 in Yehud, though one might suspect this view to be predicated more on Ezra than 2Isa itself. E.g., Middlemas 2007: 96; Rom-Shiloni 2013: 11; Chavel 2014: 6.

176. Seitz 1991: 205.

177. Also noted by Tiemeyer 2011a: 135–8.

distance as from Jerusalem.[178] Third, he assumes the complaint about lack of sacrifice obviates distance from Jerusalem, but this is merely an assumption, already stated above to be insecure. Fourth, he objects to the focus on Zion. However, Zion is a symbol more than just a location. Moreover, it is the nature of expatriate communities to be concerned with their perceived homeland (see below). This objection therefore also lacks force. He also argues that the depiction of the land as ruined implies a setting there, but this is an invalid inference. Not only are the descriptions fairly vague, such situation would likely be presumed by exiles. The only cogent objection is his fourth one, whereby the text refers to Babylon as "there" (52:11). This text, however, immediately refers to the (unknown) location of the temple vessels, and so can hardly be used to exclude a setting in Babylonia.

Tiemeyer, and Barstad before her, are right to object to many of the simplistic assumptions and arguments which have been used to advance a setting in Babylonia. However, neither succeeds in positing positive evidence for adducing a Judaean setting. Tiemeyer's strongest point—the link with Lamentations—presumes both a literate acquaintance with the book of Lamentations as well as an inability for such laments to travel throughout the Judaean social network. Neither of these can be assumed. McKinley's objection that a "subversive" text like 2Isa would have been dangerous in Babylonia ignores the fact that at the same time Yehud was also in the Babylonian Empire, with administrators equally beholden to the Babylonian king.[179] The same critique applies to arguments from accessibility of building materials.[180] Since the text lacks clear geographical markers or indicators of implied audience, the best way to infer the setting is to ask for what implied audience would the rhetoric make sense and perhaps have been persuasive, and then see if that implied audience matches any real, historic audience that might be described more fully.

The main thrust of the text—attach yourselves to YHWH—is one which applies to any audience which identified itself with Yahwistic traditions. This in principle includes, potentially, any of the communities originating in Israel and Judah: those in Egypt, Samaria, and Assyria included. The use of "Israel" and "Jacob" as "religious" references to the audience emphasizes this. However, the concern for Zion implies

---

178. It is 530 miles from Babylon to Tall-i Malyan as the crow flies, using Google Earth. The distance (also in a straight line) between Babylon and Jerusalem is 540 miles.

179. McKinlay 2013: 89.

180. E.g., Sherwin 2003. Indeed, Potts 1997: 107 lists all of the supposedly Palestinian trees as attested archaeologically within Mesopotamia.

a group which considered the cult there of particular importance. One may suspect this means a group of Judaeans, but Northerners are not necessarily excluded. This still potentially includes groups in Egypt (note their interaction with the Jerusalem high priest), Assyria and Media (the deportees from Lachish), and Babylonia, as well as Yehud, Samerina, and Idumea. The close concern for Jerusalem does, however, suggest a more specifically Jerusalemite derivation for the implied audience—though this still potentially applies to descendants of the 597 deportations to Babylonia, deportees or refugees from 587, or perhaps even the Elephantine colonists, if they in fact derive from Babylonia.[181] The concern with Babylon and its gods, however, suggests a context within the Neo-Babylonian Empire, making Elephantine and Egypt unlikely. General condemnation would be of rhetorical relevance to any community within the empire. However, the specific mockery of the Babylonian form of the *Akītu* argued above only makes rhetorical sense within a context in which the implied audience is expected to be socially familiar with its significance (and details of the ideological import). The interlocking ways in which 2Isa uses the imperial and Babylon-city specific aspects of the festival—public procession, creation, kingship ideology, prediction—implies an immediate social relevance. This festival was a major social event within the city of Babylon and its immediate surroundings. It was a period to see and be seen, a day for the elite of Babylon to express their ancient heritage and political dominance. Moreover, it was the time for seeing what the new year was to hold. 2Isa appears to speak directly into such a context. The most relevant implied audience, therefore, would be one expected to have actually experienced this festival: thus, living in or near the city of Babylon itself, an urban community of Judaeans. The lack of concern with agriculture and the references to city streets supports such a view, as does the occasional use of loans from Akkadian which were apparently forgotten in transmission.[182] Can the implied audience reflect the social situation of the *real* audience?

It is a truism that the implied audience is not the same as the real audience—whether the first or the subsequent ones. One must ask, however, what real community would have likely been receptive to an implied urban, Babylonian setting? The extension to rural and more distant communities is quite reasonable, especially as the rhetorical aim is so conducive to the overall thrust of the HB in general. Nevertheless, an investigation of the sociology of urban "exiles" suggests that the intended

---

181. Becking 2011a: 405 suggests the possibility they come from Babylonia or Persian Yehud.

182. Cf. Berquist 1995: 30; on the loans, see Williamson 2015.

"real" and first audiences of the call to attach themselves to YHWH were urbanites, settled in the city of Babylon. This community had the reason and the cause to find the rhetoric compelling and engaging—and thus to preserve and transmit it. Moreover, this community is one most likely to have preserved monarchic, Jerusalemite traditions—having originally included the Judaean monarch, his family, and his retainers in 597. This is also a sociologically likely setting for the use of oral poetry in maintaining and reformulating traditions and identities. To explore this as a setting, it is necessary to discuss some of the evidence of communities within Babylonia (both Babylon and the region of Nippur), some aspects of the sociology of forced migrations and of minorities within empires, and the issues of "cosmopolitanism" and the collection of traditions.

Evidence for the Judaean Community in Babylon

Evidence for the very early Neo-Babylonian community of Judaean exiles in Babylon has been known since 1939, when Weidner published a few texts from a Babylonian archive mentioning King Jehoiachin and his sons.[183] Though these are part of a larger archive, this archive remains unpublished. Nevertheless, the few that are available so far show Jehoiachin, his five sons, and eight other Judaeans receiving royal rations and living within the Neo-Babylonian court. The published texts show them receiving sesame oil, and the quantities do not suggest deprivation. These individuals, moreover, appear in a context including, apparently, both ambassadors and foreign mercenaries.[184] Thus, this is an elite, cosmopolitan setting. A late Babylonian chronicle mentions the deportation of Sidonians to Babylon (and Susa) by Artaxerxes III.[185] This chronicle mentions Phoenician women being placed within the Achaemenid palace at that time, and it is reasonable to assume a similar pattern had been followed by Nebuchadnezzar, though the biblical sources are silent on the fate of exiled women. Sadly, there is no indication of how many lived in Babylon, or for how long past the date of the last document (569 BCE) the king's retinue remained within the court. Moreover, it must be assumed that not all the 597 exiles were part of the Judaean-court-in-exile, but still lived within the city on other terms. Though the book of Ezekiel portrays the eponymous prophet as settled in the rural hinterland,

---

183. Weidner 1939; Oded 1995: 210–11; Pedersén 2005; Avishur and Heltzer 2007; Cogan 2013: 141–4.
184. Pedersén 2005.
185. Chronicle 9, dated 13/?/Artaxerxes III 14 (Grayson 1975: 114; Glassner 2004: 240–1).

there is no real reason to assume that this was the fate of all the 597 exiles. Biblical sources (2 Kgs 25 and Jer 52) claim Jehoiachin was released from "prison" in 562 BCE by Nebuchadnezzar's son, Amēl-Marduk.[186] Whatever the reality behind this story, it likely indicates a continued circle of Judaeans in the city. There are other reasons to believe, however, that urban Babylon continued to house a Judaean community into and past the likely era of 2Isa. First, Judaean royal merchants in another northern Babylonian city, Sippar, are attested.[187] This family is attested in the reign of Nabonidus, and it operated within a milieu with links to the city of Babylon. If the political, business, and social climate allowed for this in other regional cities, there is no reason to exclude Babylon, especially since it was an original location of settlement. Second, two of the recently published texts from [Āl-]Yāhūdu were actually written in Babylon (nos. 61, 45). Both record business transactions that took place within the city. One is dated to Cyrus, the other to Darius I.[188] It is possible these transactions imply broader business arrangements—and thus Judaean businessmen resident still in Babylon. Outside of this collection, there are six more attested citations of Judaeans in Babylon.[189] One comes from Neriglissar, four come from the reign of Darius I, and one from Darius II (8/II/year 1, i.e. 19 May 423). One Judaean functions as a guarantor, one as a witness, and—interesting for present purposes—two are working within the imperial, Aramaic administration. These attestations, though few, still show the Babylonian Judaeans doing business with the three major Babylonian business houses (Egibis, Ilias, Murašu),[190] as well as serving within the administration as Aramaic scribes. This, combined with the reasonably large business venture in text 61 above (30 shekels of silver), implies that at least some of this community were relatively

---

186. For discussion of the evidence, see Sack 1972; Avishur and Heltzer 2007.

187. These were discussed by Alstola 2014. Alstola's PhD dissertation is currently being prepared for publication. The tablets have recently been published by Bloch 2014; cf. Zadok 2002; Jursa 2007a; Pearce 2016; Alstola 2017a. For a stimulating analysis of the implication of the social location of these merchant Sippareans, see Waerzeggers 2014a.

188. Pearce and Wunsch 2014: 196, 170–3.

189. The author is grateful to Tero Alstola for pointing out four texts, and providing the citation information for them. The four texts are Dar 310 (Abraham 2004: 410–11), BM 26553 (available in ORACC), BM 74554 (Stolper 1989), PBS 2/1 005 (oracc.museum.upenn.edu/ctij/P263898/html); Zadok 2014 nos. 1 and 5 are also from Babylon.

190. Archives from these families have been studied by Abraham 2004; Wunsch 2000a (Egibi), Stolper 1985 (Murašu), and Waerzeggers 2010b: 342, 434 (Ilias).

well-connected and wealthy, and that they remained within the city of Babylon. The function of witness implies a local status. Thirdly, though later and literary, the stories in Daniel 1–6 also presuppose the idea that at least some of the deported Judaean elite were deported to Babylon and trained for governmental service. The well-attested use of West Semites as royal merchants also supports such a rarified scenario for some.[191] It is worth remembering that by the arrival of Cyrus at least some of the Judaeans in Babylon would already have been third-generation residents (for more on immigrant generations, see below).

The evidence from [Āl-]Yāhūdu, Bīt-Avram, and Bīt-Našar show that the rural Judaeans retained a strong attachment to YHWH in terms of naming practices, at least.[192] Of course the use of these names is the primary method scholars use to identify individuals as Judaeans (thus carrying a risk of being a circular argument), and there is no discernible avoidance of "pagan" theophoric names. The interesting case of an individual using a Babylonian name with alternate theophorics (Bēl/Yāhu-šar-uṣur[193]) certainly raises questions concerning how the Judaeans understood YHWH, but it plausibly demonstrates that attachment to YHWH in some form remained important. This means that the message of 2Isa to attach to YHWH would have been "preaching to the choir" in the rural settlements. Perhaps it was the same in Babylon, or perhaps the attachment there was perceived as less. In this context it may be worth raising the question of the differences between learned, priestly Marduk-theologies and more popular forms. Though it was argued above that 2Isa shows close familiarity with the *Akītu* festival, the idol polemic still largely consists of caricatures of Mesopotamian theology as it exists within the Akkadian material.[194] It may be more useful to understand this discourse within a more "populist" understanding of Mesopotamian ritual and worship. Such would no doubt be the understandings within the context of the rural Judaeans. Perhaps it is also a relevant context for the urban ones.[195]

---

191. Dandamaev 1995; Jursa 2001, 2004; Alstola 2014, 2017a. Cf. Vanderhooft 1999: 113–14.

192. Cf. the discussion of Yahwistic names in Pearce and Wunsch 2014: 14–29.

193. Both names used for the son of Nubâ in texts 2–3; see Pearce and Wunsch 2014: 100–3.

194. Which is often noted, e.g., Dick 1999, especially from 32; Smith 2001: 186–8.

195. Gudme 2010 problematizes a distinction between "official" and "popular" religion, which is well-taken. However, a distinction between the understandings of elite theologians and "lay" worshippers would still seem relevant.

Figure 2.1. *Model of the Ishtar Gate*

Though unfortunately not as full as the material now available for the Judaeans in rural Babylonia, the above pieces of evidence make urban Babylon an important social and economic context for the Judaeans in Babylonia in general and for 2Isa in particular. Quite a few details of this context can be reconstructed.[196] Jursa has documented immense changes in the overall economy of Babylonia in the first millennium, first as a result of being an imperial center and then as a gradual result of its demotion to a province, in terms of overall wealth.[197] The city of Babylon itself also experienced dramatic changes, with massive monumental building works constructed by the Neo-Babylonian kings (though the basic topographical features appear to have remained relatively constant).[198] It must have been a major construction site for most of the relevant period: Nebuchadnezzar alone appears to have rebuilt the Ištar Gate three

---

196. For the reconstruction of Neo-Babylonian and Persian Babylon the author has relied on Koldeway 1913; George 1992; Boiy 2004; van de Mieroop 2003; van de Mieroop 2004; Pedersén et al. 2010; Gates 2011: 180–6; Baker 2011; Bergamini 2011; Lippolis, Monopoli, and Baggio 2011; Pedersén 2011; Baker 2014; Gasche 2013; Pedersén 2014. The material and economic depiction is based on Potts 1997; Baker and Jursa 2005, 2014; Jursa 2010, 2011a, 2014a; Baker 2015.

197. As discussed above.

198. The monumental building work (palace, temple, walls) was the primary interest of the excavators of the early twentieth century; see Koldeway 1913. On the general layout remaining the same from the Kassite to the Hellenistic period, see George 1992: 13, cf. 141 (fig. 7); Boiy 2004: 55, 72. In the interpretation of Gasche 2013, palatial building at least was continued by the Persian kings.

times.¹⁹⁹ Some evidence for continued construction is the famous Cyrus Cylinder, itself originally part of a construction project. Moreover, the city was in practice a new foundation of Nebuchadnezzar II, imprinted with the glory of his achievements.²⁰⁰ The labor and logistics for such efforts would have had great social and economic impact on the city's population. The military campaigns brought into the city wealth, building materials, and a wide variety of foreigners, some of whom are visible in the same context as the Judaeans noted above. The walls, monumental avenues and gates, the massive Esagila temple complex, and the three large palaces must have been awe-inspiring to ancient observers. Indeed, the grossly exaggerated size of the city in the classical authors is no doubt partially a reflex of this.²⁰¹ The impact on the Judaean exiles upon first arrival can be imagined: Babylon dwarfed even Iron Age Jerusalem in size and splendor—the inner city of Babylon occupied 400 hectares (900 hectares including the outer walls), while Jerusalem only 100 hectares.²⁰² Those exiles who arrived after 587 would have been impacted even more. A very useful description of the built monumental environment is given by van de Mieroop.²⁰³ The impact of the city's imposing ziggurat on Judaean tradition needs no rehearsal, but the resident would also have been overwhelmed by the pomp of the gates, walls, palaces, and paved processional streets. However, the power and prosperity of the city is also reflected (though much less well known) by the residential quarters, an aspect highlighted by Baker.²⁰⁴ As is typical in periods of growth, unprecedented wealth (visible in larger housing size averages) went hand in hand with increased social inequality. Baker gives a spectrum of house sizes ranging from 73.5 m² to the palace of 44,000 m².²⁰⁵ Only the wealthy, elite quarter (so-called Merkes Quarter) has been excavated to date.²⁰⁶ This was an exclusive area for the very wealthy, unsurprisingly located adjacent to the central Esagila and palace compounds.²⁰⁷

199. Van de Mieroop 2003: 267; cf. Koldeway 1913: 32–8.
200. Van de Mieroop 2003: 260.
201. E.g., van de Mieroop 2003: 261–2; Heinsch and Kuntner 2011.
202. For the size of Neo-Babylonian Babylon, Boiy 2004: 56–7; Pedersén 2011: 11 gives the size of the outer city as 800 hectares; for Jerusalem, Geva 2014: 139 (who gives 1000 dunams). For rough visual comparison, the old city center of Leiden is roughly 315 hectares, and the city center of contemporary Helsinki is roughly 500.
203. Van de Mieroop 2003.
204. Baker 2011, 2014, 2015.
205. Baker 2011: 541; 2014: 19.
206. For this sector generally, see Koldeway 1913: 233–88.
207. Baker 2011: 541–2 on this area.

Though largely unexcavated,[208] the general topography of the city is known. This includes the names and locations of the inner city's ten quarters, some of the main street names, and the location of many smaller temples. The inner city straddled the Euphrates River, with four quarters on the west bank (Kumar, Bab-Lugalirra, Tuba, and Nu[-]) and six on the east (Eridu, Šuanna, Kadingirra, Kullab, Newtown, and TE.E). Each half had four gates, and these were connected by 20 processional roads; the most important of the latter was the white and red paved *Ay-ibūr-šabû*, "May the Arrogant not Flourish," commonly called Babylon Street, which connected the Ištar Gate, Esangila, and the bridge over the Euphrates River.[209] Baker thinks that some of these neighborhoods were socially segregated while some were mixed.[210] The physical layout of the streets made some neighborhoods particular communities.[211] Though most attention has been paid to the massive Marduk complex in the center of the city, a large number of smaller temples to an array of deities are attested throughout the city, with more than one present in each quarter. Among these were at least three temples dedicated to Nabu, several to Gula, and one to Ištar of Nineveh.[212] Baker thinks that in addition to these other temples, there were street altars and local shrines that served local, neighborhood-level cohesion.[213] While the Marduk priesthood and the very rich appear to have lived in segregated quarters, the remainder of the residential areas must have been socially and ethnically diverse. The responsibility of the Esagila complex for the administration of some of the smaller temples, however, likely would have maintained at least some interconnections between the areas.[214] The area between the walls of the inner city and the outer walls is unexcavated, so the density and

208. According to Pedersén, the Germans excavated only 12 hectares of the city (Pedersén 2011: 11).

209. Boiy 2004: 57–8 on names of quarters and streets; Pedersén 2011: 19 on color of the paving; George 1992: 24 (fig. 4), 25, 64 line 64, 359.

210. Baker 2011: 544.

211. Van de Mieroop 2004: 79, cf. 112.

212. Boiy 2004: 85–92 lists the evidence for the continuance of these temples into the Hellenistic period. For the Nabu temples, see p. 90; for Gula and for Ištar of Nineveh see p. 91. Tablet IV of Tintir lists 43 "major" cult centers in Babylon (George 1992: 11).

213. Baker 2011: 546.

214. Jursa discusses the attested archives of some of the minor clergy from the smaller cult sites (Jursa 2010: 393–5), but also notes the responsibilities that Esagila had for other temples, even in Uruk and Sippar (2010: 68–73). Waerzeggers 2010b: 22 (BM 25849, no. 215) on distinct priests, 26–9 on overlaps.

nature of the city here is currently unknown, though apparently the Egibi family managed at least some gardens in this area.²¹⁵ In any case, the city's population was large enough to require large importation of grain from throughout Babylonia.²¹⁶ Van de Mieroop also emphasizes the important roles of the nearby city harbor, suburbs, and fields.²¹⁷

The exact location of the Judaeans' homes in Babylon is unknown, but the possibility of very comfortable situations for some (the royal hostages and successful Judaean merchants) and poorer, mixed residential settings must be considered.²¹⁸ The vast area added to the city by Nebuchadnezzar would seem a likely location for many of the newer groups brought to the capital during the campaigns. Yet since two to three generations had likely elapsed since the initial migrations had passed, one cannot assume all would have remained here, even if their initial settlements had been. Administrative, mercantile, and artisanal trades may have characterized many of these Judaeans, likely locating some of them in the harbor or suburban areas.²¹⁹ Some may have worked small gardens or as laborers in the monumental building projects. According to Baker, the average family was nuclear, with roughly five individuals.²²⁰ It is clear that in this situation, the old familial-clan affiliations and communal structures as had obtained in Judah/Jerusalem could not have been sustained without major alteration.²²¹ It is also clear that Babylon as the center of the world would have been an immediate reality, and its two rows of walls and 30 meter moats must have made the city appear more impregnable than Jerusalem ever had. Moreover, despite clear opportunities in royal service and in economic activities supporting the bustling capital economy, the Judaeans would nevertheless not have been part of the traditional, socially empowered groups (whether the priesthood, *kadinnu*, or aristocrats/ elders).²²²

---

215. Wunsch 2000 1:23, 127–33; 2:143–8. These fields are listed as "between the walls" or by similar expressions.

216. Pedersén et al. 2010: 134; Pedersén 2011: 16.

217. Van de Mieroop 2004: 65.

218. Baker 2011: 544.

219. Van de Mieroop 2004: 65–70.

220. Baker 2014: 14; van de Mieroop 2004: 15. He emphasizes fictional, professional kinship groups pp. 109–10.

221. Kessler 2006: 126, 133 also sees a shift in kinship relations in Babylonia. In his case he sees it as the creation of written genealogies in place of existential common knowledge, and the separation of the בת אבות from local ties.

222. On social structure, see van de Mieroop 2004: 109–39; on restrictions around the priesthood, see Waerzeggers 2010b: 357; cf. Waerzeggers 2011a; Jursa 2013.

Besides this general picture of the city of Babylon, the context of the Judaeans there can and should be strongly informed by the sociology of forced migration and minorities.

The Sociology of Forced Migration and Minorities in Empire

Any attempt to understand the social reality of the Judaeans in Babylon and Babylonia must grapple with the sociology of migration and minorities. This is a massive topic demanding monographs on its own; only a few aspects deemed relevant for the current discussion of 2Isa within urban Babylon are discussed here.[223]

In his pioneering work on forced migration, Smith-Christopher notes that typical phenomena include structural change of the community, often with a split in leadership.[224] This follows from the loss of the institutions and "social goods" which had supported previous systems. The change in communal structure can actually be quite radical, both eliminating and creating new intra-group divisions and hierarchies.[225] The experience of exiled elites (as were the primary exiles in 597 and presumably those settled in Babylon) is ambivalent: while the mental distress of their lost positions is greater than for lower social groups, their typically higher education means they can often better integrate into their new surroundings.[226] The attestation of later Judaeans working within the imperial administration suggests that at least some of this community did indeed find ways of integrating rather successfully into the new environment. Sadly, at present it is impossible to know whether these individuals came from formerly elite circles or not; examples of both are to be expected.

For a group which included an exiled monarch and his retainers, the above implies very significant changes and a likely identity crisis for his retainers. In fact, royal exiles are an often overlooked manifestation of forced migration, and a brief consideration of comparable situations to the one of Jehoiachin is instructive.[227] Mansel and Riotte offer a number of studies of European exiled monarchs.[228] In their overview of the material,

---

223. For other discussions, see, e.g., Alstola et al. forthcoming and the references cited there, and Alstola 2017b.

224. Smith 1989: 10–11.

225. E.g., Malkki 1995: 111, 161; Tweed 1997: 57; Adam 2008: 229, 235; Kiste 1974: 85, 107, 124, 188, 192–3.

226. See especially Scudder and Colson 1982: 280; McSpadden 1999. Lemos 2012: 96–8 emphasizes the traumatic aspects as they relate to Ezekiel. Cf. Mein 2001.

227. Kessler 2006: 120, 125 briefly characterizes Jehoiachin's court as a "government in exile," but does not discuss the implications.

228. Mansel and Riotte 2011b.

they point out that the task of an exiled monarch is to attempt to maintain royal status. This requires others to continue to accept their royal status as well as a situation in which restoration would appear plausible.[229] This situation is one in which legitimacy is an open question and in which new patterns of relation (e.g., increased importance of wives or roles as representative of a nation) develop.[230] Moreover, in an effort to maintain their royal status, the monarchs often patronize theatre and historiography.[231] These cultural productions are means for negotiating legitimacy, relevancy, and perpetuation of cultural memory. Though monarchs and their supporters would tend to emphasize the (royal) past, structural change is inherent in this process. This latter aspect is particularly suggestive for the situation of the Judaeans and the collection of Judaean traditions and perhaps even texts in the wake of the exile. The circles around Jehoiachin would have needed to grapple with ways to understand his new situation, both before and after the events of 587. Moreover, given the common ancient patronage of oral poets by kings, one potential location for the sort of poetry found in 2Isa would be in the court-in-exile. Two examples of former "kings" taking on new roles can be mentioned in passing. Though it fits one of his literary tropes, Herodotus describes the ex-king Croesus as a communal advisor for Cyrus,[232] and the (supposedly) Davidic exilarch functions so towards the Sasanians.[233] Similar sorts of dynamics would make sense among the Judaeans in Babylon, at least for the first few generations, or as long as a Davidic heir was able to claim royal status. The explicit transfer of all political prerogatives to Cyrus by 2Isa must be analyzed as significant in this light (see the analysis below).

Oral poetry's importance among refugees generally has a number of parallels, even outside any potential court in exile.[234] One reason for this is simply that oral poetry had previously been an important element of the culture; this is true for modern societies that had largely functioned orally (Palestinians, Somalis). Oral poetry is often a key element of such cultures wholesale. But another reason this is important especially for refugees or forced migrants is that it is non-material and thus remains available to the migrants regardless of their material circumstances.

229. Mansel and Riotte 2011a: 8.
230. Several studies note the increased role of royal women within the exiled courts. The Stuart court in Rome ended up functioning as an alternate British embassy.
231. Mansel and Riotte 2011a: 8.
232. Herod. I.155–6 (Herodotus 2002: 195–7); III.36 (Herodotus 2000: 47–9).
233. See Goodblatt 1994: 272–311; Herman 2012.
234. E.g., Siddiq 1995; Olden 1999; MacPherson 2001; Olszewska 2007; generally, cf. Foley 2002.

Thus, it is able to provide an element of continuity regardless of the vagaries of specific locations. Oral poetry is a form of continuity that simultaneously enables negotiation of the new context and reformulation of received tradition. In an interesting study of Afghani poets in Iran, Olszewska notes how poetry (both oral and written forms) was a medium for evaluating Afghani history as well as for incorporating elements of Iranian poetics.[235] Most interesting was a distinctive change between the initial immigrant poets and the next generation: their focus shifted from one on the ancestral land to their new context within Iran, although their interest in Afghanistan remained. If the genre of 2Isa is accepted as oral poetry, then this aspect of refugee studies provides an important element to the social context.

The experience of the "Babylonian Exile" is often considered an important impetus for the collection and redaction of some of the Judaean traditions which later became the HB. A study of forced migration can also be used to emphasize the way such experiences force cultural reappraisal, both in the drive to conserve the past as well as in formulation new solutions. The two above-mentioned phenomena—exiled monarchs and oral poetry—add some new elements to this claim. First, the collection of traditions derives from more than one impetus and accordingly can take multiple forms. A response to trauma is only one of these. Legitimation of new social structures or of continued claims for older ones is another. The processes which motivate exiled leaders to patronize older traditions are very different from those of migrants in general. The feature of structural change in leadership must be considered crucial in this respect: old elites finding their leadership lost, ignored, or contested and new leaders rising. Second, this process does not necessarily or always imply a textual medium. It may at some point utilize writing or be recorded, but codification and transmission in oral forms can happen on all social levels, elite and non-elites alike. When one considers the (non-)accessibility of the temple or palace archives of Jerusalem within Babylon, this oral medium is an important consideration.

A very stimulating comparator for the Judaean expatriates in Babylonia is the study of Burundian Hutu refugees by Malkki.[236] She found two very distinct reactions among the refugees, depending on their physical location. Those that were placed in homogenous refugee camps by the Tanzanian government strongly emphasized their Hutu ethnicity, a narrative of exile, and the importance of purity. However, those who settled

---

235. Olszewska 2007.
236. Malkki 1995.

within the urban environs of Kagoma city were much more pragmatic in their self-identifications. They chose a broader, national identity (Burudian instead of Hutu) or adopted labels as suited the needs of the moment. Moreover, these refugees lacked any historical narrative of exile and avoided the designation of "refugee." Their attitude to returning to Burundi was ambivalent. Though such a strong dichotomy is not always attested between refugee groupings, the importance of the nature of exilic life is.[237] The relevance of such considerations for the Judaeans in Babylonia is striking in terms of a clear differentiation between those settled in more or less homogenous, rural settings (i.e., [Āl-]Yāhūdu) and those settled in cosmopolitan, urban settings (i.e., Babylon). While a focus on purity, ethnicity, and narrative might be predicable for those in rural environs, such responses are much less likely for those in the city. Indeed, a "cosmopolitan," pragmatic response to the social setting is to be expected. This is indeed a good characterization of 2Isa: what is often called, in theological terms, "universalism" perhaps ought to be called, in sociological terms, "cosmopolitanism."[238] A concern with origins remains, but it is not held exclusively of other formulations. The openness of the Yahwistic cult to the nations fits such a social context. Moreover, the adoption of the titles "Israel" and "Jacob" in addition to Zion could be explained as part of a similar reflex. As old traditions were reorganized in terms of group boundaries and significations, interests and identifications broadened to more than just "Judacan" while retaining the local interest.

One of the most common phenomena associated with dislocation is a marked concern with "home" both as a concrete point of origin and as a metaphor for belonging.[239] This feature persists as "exile" morphs into "diaspora," or in other words, across the generations. The longer the experience lingers, the smaller the likelihood and desire for return to the "home" becomes, even though its use and appeal in rhetoric and social identity does not disappear.[240] Very small numbers of second- and third-generation migrants ever "return" to their ancestors' "homelands," even though the homeland will remain emotive and valuable within discourse.

237. E.g., Utas 1997; Adam 2008.
238. For some discussions of "universalism" in 2Isa, see, e.g., Vorländer 1981: 108–10; Blenkinsopp 1988; Milbank 1992; Kaminsky 2006.
239. E.g., Stock 2010; Taylor 2013.
240. On the generational aspect, see Agosino 2000; Southwood 2015. Cf. Ahn 2011: 28, 35, who emphasizes the different characters of the generations (on p. 160 he argues 2Isa was second generation).

Once again, this is very redolent of 2Isa. Zion and Jerusalem are incredibly prominent in the text, but demands for return migration are not. In fact, the main driving feature (attach to YHWH) is achievable *without* return. Given that the audience of 2Isa must have been second- to third-generation Judaeans, this makes eminent sense. A few may have actually desired to return to the land of their (grand-)parents, but the majority clearly did not. "Home" is a significant trope for 2Isa, but it refrains from demanding a return, clearly a rhetorically appealing element in its generational context.

Already mentioned several times above, the consolidation of traditions typically accompanies exilic groups, including royal exiles. This is also something which has prompted biblical scholarship to see the "Babylonian Exile" as a key point in the formation of the HB. However, this process need not always, primarily, or exclusively involve the collecting and redacting of texts. Such activities are plausible, but so are attempts to cultivate oral, musical, religious, and other traditions. Moreover, the practicalities of forced migrants being able to bring extensive documentation must also be queried. In this context, the development and later recording of oral poetry which recalled previous Judaean traditions makes eminent sense. 2Isa should be seen in this light.

It is a truism to say "self" needs an "other." "Minority" identity can in some ways be seen to be defined by a dialectic between its own identity and that of its "host" culture. Even while adjusting to local norms, to maintain distinctiveness, particular elements ("identity markers," "sites of memory," "traditions") will become important as signs. The harsh polemic against Babylon and its gods in 2Isa clearly fits into this kind of context. Such a dialectic makes sense of the combination of cosmopolitanism and anti-Babylon sentiment within 2Isa. Not only is Babylon an awe-inspiring and economically beneficial place to live, it threatens to eliminate Judaean particularity through this positivity. Besides its agency in forced migration to begin with, Babylon is thus the natural "other" for discourse, even for those otherwise quite content with their rarified Babylonian setting. However, this dynamic would likely have changed with the arrival of Cyrus. Like the Parsis in British India,[241] the Judaeans would have found themselves a minority among a local majority which was simultaneously an imperial minority. Perhaps like the Parsis and their British lords, the Judaeans may have seen the Persians as useful allies in social competition with their neighbors.

241. On the Parsis in general, see Firby 1988: 87–94; Hinnells 2000, especially 117–40, 175–200; 2002, 2015; For modern Zoroastrian history, see Stausberg 2002–4: vol. 2.

The last elements of the sociology of forced migration to be mentioned here is the advantage of Judaean elites who were exiled and their descendants' situations. At least some of the 597 exiles were educated already, probably in Aramaic and maybe even in Akkadian, before deportation to Babylon. Despite the initial trauma of moving and loss of social position, these were well-placed to adapt well to an urban setting where such skills could find gainful employment. Some studies of migrants have shown that the children of such parents sometimes do more poorly than the children of poorer migrants.[242] This suggests that by the period of 2Isa (second and third generations), some Judaeans would likely have improved their status vis-à-vis the Babylonians and others lost it: a perfect situation for new understandings of communal identity, leadership, and resentments. 2Isa's Judaeans on the street could well be referencing such struggling descendants. Moreover, the third generation tends to be the generation which tries to redefine the concept of "home" in a more metaphysical way,[243] fitting into the issues discussed above.

Conclusions on Social Context

Though very cursory, the above social contexts sketched for 2Isa are a fuller basis for assessing its relationships with the Persians and for Judaean interactions with the Persians at the very beginning of the empire. 2Isa comes from an urban, Babylonian context, addressing a second- and third-generation immigrant audience, one which was re-defining its social structure, understandings of home and tradition, and part of a local cosmopolitan setting while still resisting assimilation to it. This community had awareness and proximity to, though perhaps varying degrees of seclusion from, a very elite political and economic setting.

Background Summary for Second Isaiah

The above argued the following for 2Isa. It is a rhetorical unity, representing a recorded performance of oral poetry. Its central message is to attach oneself to YHWH, a message utilizing a number of subthemes, including creation, the appearance of Cyrus, and idol polemics. The performance was deemed to date to c. 545–484 BCE and from the city of

---

242. Noted by Ahn 2011: 161. However, it is important to note that rather than being a rule, the success of the second generation is highly dependent upon the position of the ethnic group and the culture of the host society. See Portes and Zhou 1993; Zhou 1997.

243. Kivisto and Blanck 1990: 3; Archdeacon 1990; cf. Ahn 2011: 223–6.

Babylon. The first audiences were second- to third-generation migrants in Babylon, who had the task of reformulating Judaean traditions and identities in the face of a new political context.

Before moving on to the goal analysis of this part, a lengthy discussion on creation in the Achaemenid inscriptions and the ANE is necessary.

Chapter 3

OLD PERSIAN CREATION THEOLOGY

A major component of Achaemenid ideology as attested in the royal inscriptions is creation, but the import of this for Persian-period Judaeans has largely gone unnoticed within biblical scholarship—and, indeed, even little noticed within comparative religion.¹ This section will demonstrate the importance and uniqueness of creation within Persian royal ideology, placed within a broader ANE context. The analysis in this section will follow four steps. First, a selection of the relevant Old Persian inscriptions is presented and analyzed.² The textual analysis presented here is then supplemented with some of the scholarship on Achaemenid ideology. Second, the phenomenon of a chief creator god is placed in comparative perspective, focusing on ANE and Indo-European mythologies. Third, the diffusion of Achaemenid creation is contextualized within Achaemenid discourse. Lastly, these data are placed within a broader discussion of Iranian traditions relating to creation.

---

1. The exception is Mitchell 2014: 305–8. Smith 1963: 420, citing oral communications with Bickermann, briefly noted the appearance of creation in an inscription of Xerxes, but failed either to take it into account or to note that it in fact appears in Darius's inscriptions. Blenkinsopp 2011: 503 briefly notes its appearance but makes no use of it in the article. Bianchi 2013: 89–90 also briefly notices the parallel, but discusses Y. 44 instead, like Smith had.

2. The transcriptions are based on those given by Schmitt 2000 and Schmitt 2009. The translations are the present author's own, with reference to the editions in Kent 1961, Lecoq 1997, and Schmitt 2009, and the OP Grammar of Skjærvø 2002. Any errors of transcription or translation are my own.

The Old Persian Inscriptions

Twenty-one OP inscriptions begin with a creation prologue,[3] including the first half of the inscription on Darius I's tomb at Naqš-ī Rustam (DNa), roughly 6 kilometers north of the Persepolis platform. According to the excavators and due to artistic considerations, the relief is generally dated to the early portion of Darius's reign, circa the last decade of the sixth century BCE.[4] The royal Persian concept of creation, then, has a clear *terminus ante quem*. Its currency for Achaemenid ideology must be considered to last at least through the reign of Artaxerxes III (359–338) due to A³Pa, thus practically to the end of the Achaemenid Empire. The importance of the prologue is underscored by its frequent repetition within the otherwise terse OP corpus.[5] Moreover, its wider use in distribution to Achaemenid subjects is perhaps suggested by the appearance of a portion of DNb and the Behistun inscription appearing at Elephantine.[6]

The terseness of this account might incline one to see little import in it. However, the precise vocabulary, its structure, and its placement at the beginning of so many (relatively short) royal texts reveal a very distinct concept of the world, and one which must have played a central role in the worldview presented by the dynasty, at least from Darius the Great onwards. First, the standard version as it appears on DNa will be discussed, and then two variants of this formula (DNb and DSs) will be addressed.[7]

---

3. Lincoln 2012a: 10 cites 23, though only 21 in OP. These are DEa, DNa, DNb, DPd, DSe, DSf, DSt, DSab, DZc, XEa, XPa, XPb, XPc, XPd, XPf, XPh, XPl, XVa, D²Ha, A²Hc, A³Pa, cf. DSi.

4. The text is in OP, Elamite, and Akkadian versions. Schmidt 1970: 80 says "soon after 520"; Root 1979: 45, 75–6; Lincoln 2012a: 137 is less specific, claiming either after 512 or 500; Garrison 2013: 577 implies the last decade of the sixth century; Herrenschmidt 1977: 34–47 tries to date DNa–b last in her relative dating, but gives no absolute dating.

5. Both Lincoln and de Jong rightly emphasize the import of this repetition; see, e.g., Lincoln 2007: 51; 2012a: 10, 173; Jong 2010: 87.

6. For the Aramaic of DB, see Greenfield, Porten, and Yardeni 1982. On the portion from DNb, see Sims-Williams 1981. Though neither of these contain the creation prologue in their preserved portions, they demonstrate that the content of the inscriptions were disseminated more widely than just within Fars itself, and therefore part of a broader ideological program. For a discussion of this, albeit without mention of the section from DNb, see Granerød 2013; cf. Mitchell 2015.

7. The primary textual analysis presented here is the present author's own, though points of agreement and disagreement with previous scholarship are noted where appropriate.

3. Old Persian Creation Theology

DNa §§1–2 (lines 1–15)[8]

baga **vazṛka** Auramazdā	A great god (is) Ahuramazda
haya imām **būmim** *adā*	who created this earth
haya avam asmānam *adā*[9]	who created that sky
haya martiyam *adā*	who created humankind
haya šiyātim *adā* martiyahạyā	who created the happiness of humankind[11]
haya Dārayavaum xšāyaθiyam *akunauš*	who made Darius king
aivam parūvnām xšāyaθiyam	One king of many
aivam parūvām framātāram[10]	one commander/coordinator of many
adam Dārayavauš xšāyaθiya	I (am) Darius, great king
vazṛka	king of kings
xšāyaθiya xšāyaθiyānām	king of peoples of all kinds
xšayaθiya dahyūnām vispazanānām	king in this earth, great and far-reaching
xšāyaθiya *ahạyāyā* **būmiyā**	Son of Hystaspes, an Achaemenid, a Persian,
vazṛkāyā dūraiy apiy	Son of a Persian, Aryan,[12] of Aryan seed
Vištāspahayā puça Haxāmanišiya	
Pārsa	
Pārsahayā puça Ariya Ariya čiça	

8. This prologue has several other identical or near-identical incarnations: DSt lines 1–6 = DNa lines 1–6; DE = DNa lines 1–13 with the change of "all kinds" to "containing many men" (*paruzanānām*); DZc lines 1–7 = DNa 1–13 with minor changes; DSe lines 1–14 = DNa lines 1–15. The prologue also begins the inscriptions of Xerxes, with the appropriate change of royal name (e.g., XPa, XPb, XPd, XPf, XPh, XE, XV) and all three Artaxerxeses that left inscriptions (Artaxerxes I [A¹Pa], Artaxerxes II [A²Hc], and Artaxerxes III [A³Pa]). Some iterations of the prologue add the epithet "greatest of gods" to Ahuramazda (*maθišta bagānām*). Herrenschmidt treated §§1–2 separately (Herrenschmidt 1976, 1977), though it is useful to consider them together, as done here.

9. Lecoq 1997: 219 notes that the Babylonian version inverts this order and reads "qui a créé la ciel et la terre." Further, he notes the Akkadian leaves out the creation of humankind (ibid).

10. Lecoq 1997: 219 notes the Elamite here transcribes a different OP word **dainām dātar*, which he gives as "donneur de *dainā*"—"giver of religion?" (cf. Av. *daēna-*).

11. *martiyahạyā* is in the genitive-dative; also translated as "for humankind."

12. "Aryan" is etymologically the same as "Iranian," although it is unclear whether here it is meant to be an ethnonym or a class, meaning something like "noble." For some discussions, see Gnoli 1989: 1–102; Sharma 1993; Briant 2002: 180–1.

The "creation" section proper is §1, though as is evident, there are important links between it and §2. Creation is described as an attribute of Ahuramazda, told through a series of relative clauses defining just what sort of god Ahuramazda is.[13] It is orderly and regular, almost rhythmic, culminating in the appearance of Darius as king.[14] There is no mention or interest in the mechanics or process of creation, just the bare elements of it. The seemingly banal first two terms (earth, heaven) disguise some significant elements. A subtle distinction is made between four proper creative acts and the act which makes kingship, a semantic distinction often noted: the verb *dā-*, "create" is used for the primordial creations, while the more prosaic *kar-*, "do, make," is used for Darius.[15] The OP verb *dā-* is unattested for any subject other than Ahuramazda, and this strengthens the impression of Ahuramazda being solely responsible for creation.[16] In this, it parallels the semantic distinction which Hebrew has between ברא and עשה/ישר.[17] The change in verb subtly informs the audience of two things: first, Ahuramazda's creation was beneficent—a *primordial* creation was "happiness of humankind," a term discussed more below. Ahuramazda did not create an ambiguous material world from a human perspective, but one in which happiness plays an integral part. Moreover, this happiness is not for divine beings, but for humanity. This is strongly emphasized by the placement of "of humankind" after the verb.[18] Second, despite being listed in the same syntactical manner as the previous four items of Ahuramazda's activity—as an attribute of Ahuramazda—King Darius is an activity of a different order, one in "historical time" to use Lincoln's phrasing.[19] Although clearly possessing

13. Herrenschmidt 1977: 29, 41 also notes the phenomenon of being listed as an aspect of Ahuramazda.

14. Herrenschmidt 1977: 29, 52 even thinks this makes it a fragment from a hymn or prayer, but this is not necessary.

15. Lincoln 2012a: 10, 447; Pompeo 2012. Kellens 1989 argues that in OAv. *dā-* does not signify "create" but "put in place," but refrains from certainty in terms of OP (228 n. 20). Even if this is true for OP as well, the semantic distinction remains. Cf. Bartholomae 1904: 444–8, 714 and the different meanings given in Kellens 1995b: 29–30, 79.

16. Bartholomae 1904: 716 (*dā-* V); Lincoln 2012a: 447; Pompeo 2012: 170–3.

17. Bergman et al. 1975; Otzen 1990; Ringgren 2001; Koch 2007: 224.

18. Hale 1988: 29; Skjærvø 2009: 96–8. Kent 1961 §310 (p. 96) does not comment on this. Pompeo 2012: 166–9 thinks rather that this placement disambiguates between "give" and "create" for the root *dā-*.

19. Lincoln 2012a: 15, Table 1.1, distinguishes between cosmogonic, historic, and eschatological time, but he sees Darius as placed in eschatological time.

a unique relationship with the creator god, Darius is not depicted as primordial; his rise to power is evidence of Ahuramazda's *continuing* creative activity.

The second section of the prologue dwells on the last item of activity, the king. Though at first glance merely a listing of royal titulature and basic genealogy, §2 in fact has important links with the first section. Besides continuing the rhythmic list-cadence, the first title of Darius in the opening line, "Great King," directly parallels the opening line of creation and Ahuramazda's title, "Great god."[20] He is king of all kinds of people, picking up on the emphasis on plurality in the last lines of §1. As noticed by Herrenschmidt, most important is the claim to be king "in this earth," using the same word (again with demonstrative pronoun) which was Ahuramazda's very first creation.[21] A parallel between the earth and the Achaemenid Empire is the inescapable implication. The last portion then places Darius within concentric sets of relations: from lineage, to clan (Achaemenid), to nation (Persian), and finally to either ethnicity or class (Aryan). This corresponds to the way §1 culminates in the person of the king, being one among many.[22] Lastly, it is worth noting the change in voice from third to first person between §§1 and 2.

A key term already noted is "joy, happiness" (*šiyāti-*), an atypical inclusion in a list of creation items, particularly one so brief as here (with only four items).[23] The import of this inclusion merits a brief overview of the term's attestation in OP and in Avestan. Kent lists the word as occurring 22 times in the corpus (including all creation prologues), in both nominative and adjectival forms, as well as an element in the name of royal queens (*Paru-šiyātiš, Greek Parysatis).[24] Including the subsequently

---

20. Also noted albeit in a different way by Herrenschmidt 1977: 44; Ahn 1992: 181–2, 187.

21. Herrenschmidt 1976, reprinted in English in Herrenschmidt 2014: 24; cf. Herrenschmidt 1977. Though the precise argumentation Herrenschmidt uses to reach this conclusion is unconvincing, the parallelism and usages confirm the basic insight.

22. One could also parallel the *ratus* in *Y.* 19:19 and the emanations of Mithra in the *Shahburāgān* (see Bivar 1988: 12–13).

23. Emphasized rightly by Herrenschmidt 1991; Lincoln 2012a: 11, 406, 477; cf. 258–64. For the present author's earlier discussion of this term, see Silverman 2016c: 186–7.

24. Daughter of Artaxerxes I/wife of Darius II and a daughter of Artaxerxes III. See Kent 1961: 210–11; in passing Balcer 1993: 167; Schmitt 2005: §12; Tavernier 2007: 266, 274 (cf. the other attested names with the same element 317–19). On her role in succession, influence, and wealth, see Brosius 1998: 65–7, 112–16, 123, 127–8; on her political and economic power, see Stolper 2006.

discovered DSab and the restored end of DNb (without counting the Akkadian DPg) brings the count to 24 times.[25] It is also attested in the name of a *paradise* near Persepolis, *Vispa-šiyātiš*.[26] Excluding the uses as one of the primordial creations leaves a few illuminating instances. DPe §3 links "enduring, unbroken happiness" for the royal house (*duvaištam šiyātiš axšatā*) to the protection of the Persian people/army (*kara-*). In a reconstructed section at the end of DNb §3, *šiyāti-* is enjoined to the "young man" as an object of striving.[27] In XPh, the so-called Daiva Inscription, *šiyāti-* appears in two contexts, in the creation prologue at the beginning, and twice in §6.[28] This section bristles with interpretive cruxes;[29] here only the use of *šiyāti-* will be discussed.

XPh §6 (OP)

Tuvam kā haya apara yadimaniyāiy **šiyāta** ahaniy jīva utā marta artāvā ahaniy avanā dātā parīdiy taya Auramazdā niyaštāya Auramazdām yadaišā artāčā[30] brazmaniya[31] martiya haya avanā dātā pariyaita taya Auramazdā nīštāya utā Auramazdām yadataiy artāčā brazmaniya hauv utā jīva **šiyāta** bavatiy utā marta artāvā bavatiy.	You who come afterwards, if you would think "I will be joyous alive and will be blessed when dead," perform this law which Ahuramazada established, worship Ahuramazda and Arta in the right fashion. The man who performs this law which Ahuramazda bestowed and worships Ahuramazda and Arta in the right fashion, he will become joyous (while) alive and will become blessed (when) dead.

25. Lincoln 2012a: 258 n. 2, 263, convenient table on p. 264; Vallat 2013b: 281–2.
26. Skjærvø 1994 (the author is grateful to Skjærvø for sending a copy of this article); Henkelman 2008: 430 n. 990 gives the Elamite as Mišbašiyatiš; cf. Lincoln 2012a: 211.
27. Lincoln 2012a: 262–5; Sims-Williams 1981: 6 retroverts the attested Aramaic טובד to *šiyātiyā*; he is followed by Schmitt 2009: 111 (here §12).
28. Kent calls this §4d; Schmitt §6.
29. On the find itself, see Schmidt 1953: 209. For some variant discussions of XPh, see, e.g., Abdi 2006, 2010; Ahn 1992: 111–22; Boyce 1982: 175–7; Briant 1986: 425–9; 2002: 550–3; Gnoli 1989: 88–92; Henkelman 2011b: 102–3; Kuhrt 2009: 304–6 (with notes); Lincoln 2012a: 417 n. 31; Vallat 2013a: 34, 46–7. For an overview, see Knäpper 2011: 101–5.
30. This word is variously understood as either Arta with an enclitic "and" (*ča*) or a contraction of Arta and relative pronoun (*hača*).
31. The meaning of this word in conjunction with Arta has been heavily debated. E.g., Bailey 1971: xliii; Wüst 1966: 221; Boyce 1982: 175; Schmitt 2009: 168; Knäpper 2011: 100–101; Lincoln 2012a: 417 n. 31.

In this passage, *šiyāti-* while living appears twice in parallel with *artāvan* while dead. This latter word, derived from *arta-*, "truth, order," is a principle of Ahuramazda and a term which has engendered considerable debate.[32] The key for present purposes though is that both terms are intimately associated here with Ahuramazda, his law (*dāta-*), and his worship (in conjunction with the worship of Arta). Moreover, *šiyāti-* is a condition of this *present* life, not of the one after death. In conjunction with its use in the same inscription as part of Ahuramazda's creation, this confirms the idea of happiness as a key component of Ahuramazda's creation, though with the implication that it is only achievable for those who worship Ahuramazda properly. It is perhaps worth noting that the Elamite version of XPh appears to have borrowed *šiyāti-* rather than translate it.[33]

The link between happiness and the worship of Ahura Mazda is also discernible in the Avestan cognate,[34] but it does not appear as one of the primordial creations of Ahura Mazda. However one wishes to construe the relations between the Achaemenids and the Avesta, this suggests that, at the very least, the Achaemenid king took an active role in shaping the concept of creation. The creation formula was specifically designed to highlight the aspect of benevolence, and it should not be seen as a slavish appropriation of previous Iranian religious tradition. There are hints that the formulation seen here continues some earlier traditions (such as the pair this earth/those heavens, which also appears in *Yt.* 13:153), but it departs from others (such as the seemingly older primordial pair of humans and cattle in *Vend.* 7:3).[35]

Turning back to the creation prologue, two variants of the standard prologue have also survived, DNb and DSs.

---

32. Normally translated as "blessed"; e.g., Kent 1961: 152 translates it as "blessed," as does Boyce 1982: 176–7; Schmitt 2009: 168 translates it as "selig sein"; Gnoli 1989: 88–91; Kellens 1995a: 29–37.

33. According to Cameron 1954–9: 471; Henkelman 2008: 368 agrees on the high incidence of loanwords. Vallat 2013a: 34 oddly thinks that XPh_e predates the OP, but this would only highlight the importance of the significance of *šiyāti-*.

34. See Bartholomae 1904: 1716. It is attested in *Yasna* 51:8 (*šiiātō*, Kellens and Pirart 1988, 1990, 1991: I:82, II:324), *Yasna* 60:11 = 71:29 (Mills 1988: 312, 320); *Vend* 3.1 (5×, Skjærvø 1999: 38; Darmesteter 1992: 22–4).

35. Out of date translations of these two passages are available in Darmesteter 1988: 229 and Mills 1988: 346, respectively. A newer translation for Yt 13:153 is available in Malandra 1977: 152; 1983: 116; Skjaervo 1999: 38.

DNb §1 (lines 1–5)[36]

baga vazṛka Auramazdā	A great god (is) Ahuramazda
haya adadā[37] ima frašam taya	who [gave/created] this excellence
vainataiy	which is seen
haya adadā šiyātim martiyahạyā	who [gave/created] the happiness of
haya xraθum utā aruvastam upariy	humankind
Dārayavaum xšāyaθiyam nīyasaya	who understanding and prowess upon
	Darius the King bestowed

Beginning the second major inscription on Darius's tomb (where the standard prologue was also found, in DNa), this version replaces earth and heaven with "this excellence which is seen." The term "excellence" (*fraša-*) is another key term in OP. It appears in several inscriptions at Susa to describe Darius's work there;[38] it is an eschatological term in the Avesta.[39] In the context of DNb, "this excellence" would seem to refer directly to Darius's building in the area, i.e., his tomb and the surrounding area.[40] Moreover, since this replaces earth and heaven in the standard formula, the phrase would appear to equate Ahuramazda's good creation directly with Darius's good imperial project. This comes before "joy of mankind," again likely insinuating the close link between the imperial project and the maintenance of *šiyāti-*, joy as well as protection. Lastly, kingship is replaced here by "understanding and prowess" (*xraθum utā aruvastam*), qualities which Darius later elaborates in the same inscription. This version also alters the use of *adā* to *adadā*.[41] This stresses the

---

36. Also XPl §1.
37. Lecoq 1997: 221 translates the OP as "créé," but notes that the Babylonian version uses "donné" in both instances. The OP can be understood as imperfect of one of the roots of *dā-* or of *dada-*. See Herrenschmidt 1977: 21; Skjærvø 2002: 64, 78–9 notes a formal distinction between aorist and imperfect, but no discernible difference in meaning (thanks to Professor Skjærvø for permission to cite this); Lincoln 2012a: 258 n. 2; Wüst 1966: 184 n. 24; Cheung 2007: 45.
38. DSa, DSf, DSi, DSo, DSz. Cf. Lincoln 2012a: 50–1.
39. Y. 30:7–9 (Kellens and Pirart 1988, 1990, 1991: 111–12; Mills 1988: 32–4; West 2011: 146–7); Yt. 19:11 (Darmesteter 1988: 290; Hintze 1994: 15); cf. Bailey 1971: viii–xvi.
40. The area includes Darius's tomb, the *Ka'bah*, a cistern, altars, and various (cultic?) buildings. See Schmidt 1970: 10–12; Razmjou and Roaf 2013: 421. Unfortunately, the present author had been unable to access Tilia 1972–78. This is preferable to reading it as replacing heaven, earth, and humankind, as in Herrenschmidt 1977: 30–1 and Lincoln 2012a: 370.
41. See n. 37 above.

goodness and beneficent nature of Ahuramazda's creation.[42] Although considerably shorter than the standard prologue, this iteration maintains all of the key elements already seen, though perhaps heightening the connection between creation and the empire.

A much less certain instance is the very fragmentary DSs, which was reconstructed by Scheil.[43] Schmitt refrains from reconstructing most of it,[44] and so the analysis will pass it over.[45]

Lastly, one can note that DPg_a expands the standard creation account by elaborating the nature of the earth over which Darius rules.[46] This version, in Akkadian, has a closer focus on the participation of the imperial subjects with the construction of Persepolis, but the key elements of the OP iteration remain: the particular creations, a linguistic distinction between primordial and kingly creative acts. The emphasis on the plurality of peoples and their comprehensive nature eliminates the parallelisms between §§1–2 of DPg_a, but the conceptualization of creation remains the same. Similarly, DPd condenses the formula to the creation of Darius as king.

To summarize the above discussion of the royal creation prologue, a few key elements are apparent. Creation is a feature of Ahuramazda, and Ahuramazda alone. Other gods are occasionally referenced as existing, but they have no creative import. Creation is regular and ordered—earth, heaven, humanity, and happiness for humanity—and there is no hint of a struggle. It is a *joyful* thing for humans. Lastly, despite the strong links to kingship, the king is an analogous and continuing aspect of Ahuramazda's creative activity, but he is not a primordial creation. This is the only distinction made between creation and forming/shaping.

42. E.g., Pompeo 2012: 172.
43. Scheil 1929: 66.
44. Schmitt 2009: 140.
45. The text as reconstructed is: DSs

[baga vazạrka Auramazdā	A great god (is) Ahuramazda
haya frašam ahạyāyā būmiyā kunautiy	who made excellence in this earth
haya martiyam ahạyāyā būmiyā kunautiy	who made humankind in this earth
haya šiyātim kunautiy martiyahạyā	who made the happiness of mankind
haya uvaspā uraθācā kunautiy	who made good horses and good chariots
manā haudiš frābara]	to me [them?] he gave
mām Auramazdā pātuv utā tayamaiy kartam	May Ahuramazda protect me and that which I built

46. As noted by Lincoln 2012a: 174–5. Text and translation in Weissbach 1911: 85–7; translation, Lecoq 1997: 229–30; Kuhrt 2009: 483.

There is no hint of separate acts or gods as creator/progenitor and demiurge. Nevertheless, despite the significant linkages created between Ahuramazda/his creation and Darius/his empire in the inscriptions, Ahuramazda is never called a king. He is "great" (*vazạrka*), "greatest of the gods" (*maθišta bagānām*), and creator, but not king. Only Darius (or his heirs) is king. Moreover, the overall rhetorical function of the creation prologue before the titulature is to establish Ahuramazda's ability to make Darius king as well as to create a parallel between the earth and the empire.[47] It also strongly implies that Darius intends to promote *šiyāti* just as Ahuramazda created it.

Achaemenid Royal Ideology in Recent Scholarship

Achaemenid ideology and religion have generated significant debate, though the import of the above prologue has not played as significant a role as it deserves.[48] A brief discussion of some scholarship on creation and on Achaemenid concepts will prepare the way for better understanding this prologue in its Persian context.

Despite her monumental achievement in writing a history of Zoroastrianism, Mary Boyce is often caricatured as uncritically reading the Sasanians back into the Achaemenids. While her interpretations are often strongly controlled by her sense of Zoroastrian orthodoxy, she did take Achaemenid religion seriously, and her views remain a useful resource. Perhaps her most known argument is her firm conviction that Cyrus was an "orthodox" Zoroastrian, and that it was a propagandist of his who introduced 2Isa to monotheism and creation theology.[49] This is an issue that will be dealt with in another section. For present purposes it is worth noting her opinion that Ahura Mazda appropriated the creative functions of the Indo-Iranian deity *Vouruna/Varuna,[50] that this creation was wholly good,[51] and that the significance of Ahura Mazda as creator is shown by four days in the Zoroastrian calendar being dedicated to

---

47. Similar to the "bottom line" of Herrenschmidt 1977: 52, though emphasizing the ability rather than the domain.

48. Ahn 1992: 299 discounts the importance of creation; Koch 2002 does not discuss creation; Knäpper 2011 passes over its importance. Even Cohn 1995, who makes a big point on the importance of creation in Iran only discusses the Avestan and Pahlavi materials (81–6), and his discussion of 2Isa makes no notice of the imperial connection in this regard (151–7).

49. Boyce 1982: 45–7, 66, 120; 2000: 282–3. In this she was largely following the argument of Smith 1963.

50. Boyce 1975: 62; 1982: 17; 1986: 149.

51. Boyce 1982: 120, 194.

him as creator, an event she argues happened during the Achaemenid era.⁵² She also thought that in the late Achaemenid period, under Darius II and Artaxerxes II, the "monotheistic" form of creation was modified to a "Zurvanite" belief in a *"deus otiosus* and an inferior creator-god," as in Babylonian traditions.⁵³ Oddly, although she noted the occurrence of creation motifs in the Achaemenid inscriptions, she never discusses them in any detail, preferring to refer to Avestan sources.⁵⁴ Though her reasoning and argumentation in respect of the relationship of the early Persian kings to creation ideas is suspect, Cyrus's use of the *paradise* system is something that will need to be considered further later.

The most sustained attention to the role of creation within the OP royal inscriptions is by Bruce Lincoln.⁵⁵ Lincoln takes the creation prologue as central to the Achaemenid self-presentation, and via a wide-ranging discussion of parallels with Avestan, Pahlavi, and Greek sources, sees it as undergirding an Achaemenid "soteriological" program to eliminate the Lie from the world.⁵⁶ As already noted, he is right to emphasize the import of the creation prologues and their inclusion of "joy" as a primordial element. He further points out the "subtle" phrasings and allusions apparent in the OP motifs—particularly *šiyāti* and *frašā*—and his appeal to the system of Achaemenid *paradises* is a pertinent reminder that Achaemenid ideology was no doubt played out in pragmatic ways beyond just the textual. Whatever one may think of his systematic reconstructions of the imperial "theology," Lincoln enables a better understanding of the religious implications in these texts often treated as if devoid of any religion.

Herrenschmidt has paid close attention to the OP inscriptions of Darius, and has made a few key advances in their meaning and implications (many of which are the starting points for Lincoln's analysis). She offers two "formal" analyses which highlight the importance of the creation prologue for Darius's ideology and the links between it and his titulature.⁵⁷ Although at times the specific argumentation is unconvincing or based on the authenticity of AsH and AmH, the role of *būmī* as "earth-empire" and the consequent linkage between the two sections are important. She also drew attention to the use of *šiyāti-*, arguing that

---

52. Boyce 1982: 247, 249; 2000: 305.
53. Boyce 1982: 233–9, quote 239; 2000: 306–7.
54. Boyce 1982: 120; 2000: 289.
55. Lincoln 2007, 2012a. He has discussed creation themes in broader Iranian and Indo-European contexts as well: Lincoln 1975, 1986, 1997, 2012b.
56. As conveniently summarized, Lincoln 2012a: 477–8.
57. Herrenschmidt 1976 (= Herrenschmidt 2014); 1977.

it is the positive counterpart of the three negative threats listed in DPd.[58] Moreover, she thinks this term demonstrates how distinct the Achaemenid and Zoroastrian worldviews were.

Although he only mentions creation in passing in his useful 1997 work,[59] de Jong has offered a crucial observation on the *Achaemenid* impact on Zoroastrian creation.[60] In this presentation he notes that kings tend to be influential on the formation of their "state" religions. Noting the uniqueness of the creation prologue within a broader ANE context, he highlights how this fits with the Zoroastrian myth *par excellence* of creation to *eschaton*.[61] He implies that the importance of creation within later Zoroastrianism might actually be a legacy of the Achaemenids' shaping of the tradition.[62]

Root strongly emphasizes the deliberate and unique use and transformation of ANE visuals and themes by the Achaemenids, especially starting with Darius.[63] She even argues that in iconography and in architecture the new synthesis presents the king as divine and the imperial as divine.[64] She has not focused specifically on the role of creation within this context, though she has noted in passing that Ahuramazda's creation in the inscription DPg$_a$ serves the same constitutive function for the empire as the military achievements did for Sargon in one of his.[65]

Skjærvø has argued at length the various ways in which the Avesta connects with the OP inscriptions.[66] He places both the Avestan concept of creation and the use of it by Darius within the context of successful sacrifice.[67] For him, this means that not only does it place the king and god in mutual dependence, but that it also implies that Darius is presented as a new Zoroaster, or in other words, as the epitome of the three Indo-European traditional functions (warrior, priest, husband).[68] While the importance of sacrifice to the Avesta generally and Avestan creation-eschatology is clear, the direct relevance of it to the OP creation prologue is less so.

58. Herrenschmidt 1991; as counterpart, see p. 16.
59. Jong 1997: 62–3, 248, 254.
60. Jong 2010.
61. Jong 2010: 87, 88, respectively.
62. Jong 2010: 89.
63. Root 1979, 2000, 2010.
64. See Root 2010 and 2013, respectively.
65. Root 2000: 21–2.
66. Especially Skjærvø 1999, 2005.
67. Skjærvø 2005: 54–8.
68. Skjærvø 2005: 76–9; 2014: 178.

Overall, it is clear that Achaemenid creation has not received much attention until recently, mostly in the work of Lincoln and de Jong. It can be seen, however, to be an element which integrates several of the known factors of Achaemenid ideology, has links with the Avesta, and is an aspect clearly datable. With de Jong one should take seriously the agency of the Persian kings in its formulation and importance.

Comparative Cosmogony/Theologies of Creation

Creation (or perhaps better, cosmogony) is an almost universal element of mythological traditions across the world,[69] and the various traditions of the ANE are no exception to this. The presence of creation in a Persian worldview is therefore to be expected. However, when viewed against the general pattern of other creation accounts within the ANE, the version given by the Achaemenid kings stands rather unique in the manner of its formulation and emphases. Discussing the distinctiveness of the Achaemenid theology of creation serves to clarify its intent and formulation; moreover, it will prove particularly pertinent when viewing 2Isa. Unfortunately, it is not possible to give an exhaustive comparative account of ANE cosmogonies here;[70] rather, the purpose is to place both the royal Achaemenid creation prologues and 2Isa's use of creation rhetoric within a broader frame of reference. To these ends, the summaries focus on texts dealing with formation of the cosmos and of humankind.

Assyria and Babylonia

Perhaps the most well-known Mesopotamian cosmogony to modern scholars is the *Enūma Eliš*.[71] Not the only or "original" conceptualization

---

69. E.g., Thompson 1955–58: types A0–2899, especially A600–870 (all volume 1). For a brief introduction with a sixfold typology, see Long 1987; with a different fivefold typology, Friedli 2007. An out-of-date overview which includes Iran (but without much noticing the Achaemenids) is Brandon 1963. The classic study within biblical scholarship is that of Gunkel and Zimmern 2006, an assessment of which is given in Scurlock and Beal 2013. For more recent overviews in the context of the ANE and ancient Mediterranean, see Clifford and Collins 1992b: 2–10; Clifford 1994: 11–134; Merkt et al. 2002; Batto 2013: 7–53. It is worth noting that none of the latter include Iran in their overviews of ANE cosmogonies. For the present author's views on "myth" as an analytical category, see Silverman 2012: 239; 2013b: 2–15.

70. A comprehensive, comparative study of ANE cosmogonies and creation theologies would be a valuable but would require a large study of its own.

71. For English translations, see Foster 1993: 350–401 (also in Hallo 1997: 390–402 [#1.111]; Dalley 2008: 228–77; transcription, transliteration, and translation

of creation in Babylonia or Assyria, it was most likely the most prominent version in both the Neo-Assyrian and Neo-Babylonian Empires.[72] The focus of this ritual narrative is the final ordering of the cosmos by a sixth-generation deity via combat. It demonstrates the kingship and warrior prowess of the new head of the pantheon as well as the primacy of his central shrine. In the Babylonian version this hero deity is Marduk, but some Assyrian versions gave the role to Aššur.[73] Although various elements of the creation are the result of several different deities largely in the language of begetting, the deity in focus—whether Marduk or Aššur—receives praise as the creator for fashioning the current cosmos from the bodies of his vanquished foes: the heavens and earth from Tiamat and humanity from Tiamat's general, Qingu.[74] This latter act, associated with the "black-headed people" (i.e., the Babylonians), brings joy to the gods, as humanity is envisioned as "setting the gods free" from their labors.[75] Both the cultic and political natures of the two versions of this text are readily apparent even upon a superficial reading, an aspect reinforced by its ritual use during the re-enactment of the establishment of divine kingship in a particular location (Babylon and Assur, respectively).[76] For the present purposes, several aspects are noteworthy. The deity praised as creator is not solely responsible for everything in world, but more for its ordering. Other gods or entities participate in the evolution of the cosmos as well, in varying capacities. This process involves various forms of destruction and violence rather than just creation. The use of creation functions to demonstrate the kingship of the god in question.[77] Lastly, the creation of mankind is to serve the gods.

Though the most extensive and perhaps contemporary version, several other conceptions of creation existed in Mesopotamia, many of which provided antecedents for elements in the *Enūma Eliš*. An earlier text

---

into French available in Talon 2005; Lambert 2013: part I). Judging by surviving testimonies, this version was also transmitted by Berossus. See Burstein 1978: 14–15. For a very useful analysis of creation in this text, see Seri 2012.

72. Clifford 1994: 83 dates *Enūma Eliš* to c. 1400–1104 BCE; Horowitz 2011: 108 to the late second millennium; Lambert 2013: 442–3 to Nebuchadnezzar I's reign (c. 1100 BCE). That this text was used in Assur, both with Marduk and Assur as protagonists highlights its influential nature.

73. Dalley 2008: 228, 275 n. 21; Foster 1993: 350 notes not all Assyrian versions replace Marduk, however.

74. Dalley 2008: 254–7, 261.

75. Dalley 2008: 261, 268; Clifford 1994: 92.

76. Cf. Dalley 2008: 232; Seri 2012: 7, 26.

77. Seri 2012: 12, 24, 26.

also associated with the *Akītu* festival has a series of divine generations repeating a pattern of incest and parricide in the origins of the world.[78] The idea of humanity as fashioned from a rebellious deity in order to serve the gods also appears in a version of the famous flood story, *Atraḫasīs*.[79]

An aspect of the various extant creation myths worth noting is that they very often are connected to the temple and the cults, perhaps related to the priestly and temple-related origin of many of the texts. Mesopotamian "creation prologues" are known in the context of temple construction inscriptions.[80] These vary greatly, though all involve multiple creator deities and all focus ultimately on the temple as the reason for creation. This temple-centric focus subsumed even humankind and kingship to temple-building in a Seleucid-era foundation text.[81]

A common theme in the traditions collected by Horowitz is the separation of heaven and earth, though the details and responsible gods vary greatly.[82] A text known as "the Song of the Hoe" has Enlil separate heaven and earth, and create humans by planting a brick mold in the earth. Again, the humans are required to work for the gods.[83] What Klein calls the "earliest composition dealing with the theme of man's creation," "Enki and Ninmaḫ," has Enki order several goddesses to form humankind from clay and give birth to them, to serve as laborers in place of the gods.[84] Lambert notes similarities to *Atraḫasīs* and thinks the basic idea was quite old.[85]

Striking in comparison with the OP version is the multiplicity of gods, the violence of the processes, and the subordination of humanity to the gods in all of these versions. It should also be noted that humanity is created for the gods' happiness.

Egypt

There was no single Egyptian creation myth.[86] In Clifford's characterization, all the accounts nevertheless involved the self-differentiation of

---

78. "Theogony of Dunnu," translated in Hallo 1997: 402–3 (#1.112); Dalley 2008: 278–81; Clifford 1994: 96–7 emphasizes the uniqueness of this text.

79. Cf. Dalley 2008: 15–16; Foster 1993: 168, cf. 384; Clifford 1994: 79–80; cf. Batto 2013: 28–30.

80. Clifford 1994: 59–61.

81. Clifford 1994: 62–5.

82. Horowitz 2011: 134–50.

83. Text translated in Hallo 1997: 511–13 (#1.157), relevant passage lines 18–34.

84. Text translated in Hallo 1997: 516–18 (#1.159), relevant lines 1–40; see the comments by the translator, Klein, on antiquity on p. 516; Lambert 2013: 330–45.

85. Lambert 2013: 334.

86. Clifford 1994: 99–116.

an *ur*-god into all the gods and then all of the created world.⁸⁷ This is described as occurring either via physical emanation, by the divine word, or by divine building.⁸⁸ The various "cosmic" elements are described as the begetting of divinities, typically starting with the atmosphere, earth, and/or sky. All of these are associated with a primal mound, one which is coterminous with a cult center.⁸⁹ The purpose of humankind does not appear to have played much of a role in creation in the extant Egyptian texts.

Elam

Despite the obvious relevance of Elamite mythic traditions for the Achaemenids, no narrative mythology from Elam is currently known.⁹⁰ A mysterious deity with a name or epithet Ruhuratir, "creator of man," sometimes with "the creator gods" appears in uniformative contexts,⁹¹ but nothing further is presently known. As far as the present author is currently aware, nothing further can be said about Elamite ideas of creation.

Greece

The most widely known Greek cosmogony—and one very influential—is Hesiod's *Theogony*.⁹² This poem describes a lengthy process by which the world was ordered, beginning with a series of cosmogonic spontaneous births and a variety of divine unions.⁹³ The process culminates in a series of divine coups and parricides, until Zeus is in place as the king of the gods. In this version, the goodness available to humankind comes as a secondary event (due to the trickery of another god, Prometheus). The similarities of this myth to Hurrian-Hittite myth is well-known and heavily discussed.⁹⁴ Rather different from the known Mesopotamian

---

87. Clifford 1994: 104.
88. Clifford 1994: 106–7.
89. Clifford 1994: 105–6.
90. For a useful overview, see Vallat 1998.
91. For attestations, see Steve 1967: 40–2, 78–80; Nasrabaid 2005; Scheil 1930: nos. 52, 71–6, 81, 132, 162; Vallat 1997: 37; Henkelman 2007 notes that one of these cult centers is attested as still functioning as a sacrificial site in the PFT but the god's title does not appear. Thanks to Wouter Henkelman for pointing out this epithet to the author.
92. For text and translation, see Evelyn-White 1998: 78–153 or Hesiod 2006. For a useful summary and discussion, see Woodard 2008: 84–165.
93. Cf. Sonik 2013: 8–9.
94. Discussed by Woodard 2007: 92–8, cf. 103–150; cf. West 1997. For the Kumbarbi myth, see Hoffner 1998: 42–6; López-Ruiz 2014: 135–62.

versions, however, creation is not cult-focused, nor are humans given a *raison d'être*.

As in the other areas discussed, there was not a singular creation tradition in Greece, either. A hint of other myths which circulated roughly contemporaneously with the Achaemenid Empire is available in the so-called Derveni Papyrus. This papyrus was found in a tomb near Thessaloniki that can be roughly dated to the fourth century BCE, or in the period when Macedon was transitioning from a vassal state of Persia to its conqueror.[95] This text is very fragmentary, but it appears to be a sophisticated attempt to reconcile traditional Greek theogonic and cosmogonic myths with a pantheistic and monistic understanding of Zeus.[96] The hermeneutic and philosophical character of this treatise makes it quite different from the other traditions so far discussed. For present purposes, the remaining basis in combat is noteworthy.[97]

Ugarit

An important background for understanding HB mythology is of course the preserved material from Ugarit, despite its long distance in time. Debate exists over whether the attested Ba'al Cycle is cosmogonic or not.[98] Although apparently doubled, the existing evidence suggests that the story of a defeat of a primal dragon or serpent is cosmogonic, just as it was in Babylonia, Greece, and among the Hittites. The apparently *deus otiosus* nature of 'El would seem to make his title as creator merely one of remote origins, with Ba'al the true creator of interest. The entire cycle, though, is intimately connected with his kingship, as was Marduk's.[99] The precariousness of Ba'al's position is noteworthy, as is his status as at least a second-generation deity.[100]

Urartu/Armenia

Though the mythology of Urartu is largely lost at present, the chief god of the royal pantheon (Haldi) would appear to have been a warrior deity similar to others known throughout the ANE.[101] It is impossible at present

95. Betegh 2004: 56–9.
96. Betegh 2004: 221.
97. Also see the discussions in Kouremenos, Parássoglou, and Tsantsanoglou 2006; López-Ruiz 2014: 48–50.
98. E.g., Wyatt 2007: 123 thinks it is; Koch 2007: 211–16 thinks it is not.
99. Smith 1997: 83.
100. For a translation of the cycle, see Smith 1997.
101. See the evidence discussed in Kroll et al. 2012, especially the contributions by Çilingiroğlu and Roaf.

to know whether Haldi was part of a creation narrative or not. Some hints of some of the local traditions are refracted through the work of Moses of Choren, though his narrative is strongly influenced by the Bible.[102] Sadly, for the present purposes, his creation account only reprises the biblical story of Adam.

Ancient Israel

Ancient Israel's mythology of creation would appear to have been very similar to that of Ugarit, with YHWH defeating a serpent as part of creation. Mostly attested in brief allusions in poetic texts (Job, Psalms), this version would seem to have originally been as equally violent and fit the pattern of a younger deity.[103] This myth later formed a model for the exodus tradition (Exodus, 2Isa) and was downplayed by Genesis. Though containing its own distinctive elements, the polytheistic, younger martial deity pattern would appear to have been the original Yahwistic creation myth.

Summary

While no region has preserved a systematic cosmology and the creator gods vary even by city, all of the above offer interesting contrasts to the Achaemenid creation prologue. The common features one can note in the attested examples is that creation is typically a violent affair and thus it is rarely if ever the work of a single deity. The nature of the plurality can vary between theogony and the carving up of primordial enemies, but this pattern holds true. Moreover, the creation of the cosmos would appear to be either something which just happened, or which the gods create for their own reasons. These observations hold true without making recourse to Lincoln's more sweeping appeal to "Eurasian cosmogony" for Darius's first inscription.[104]

These common features offer a striking contrast with the OP creation narrative.[105] Ahuramazda is not part of a theogony or battle. He is not a young, martial deity. The surprisingly anthropocentric nature of creation

---

102. For a translation, see Khorenats'i 1978.

103. The connections between these reflexes and the Ugarit material is of course much discussed in the literature, but this martial nature is widely accepted. For some discussions, see Cross 1973: 112–20; Day 1985, 2000; Yarbro Collins 2001; R. Watson 2005; cf. Clifford and Collins 1992a.

104. Lincoln 2012a: 380–7.

105. Hooker 2013: 119 has noted the contrast of 2Isa's "non-conflictual" model with ANE creation conflicts, but is ignorant of the Achaemenid version.

is particularly noticeable: only in the Achaemenid version is creation *for humanity* rather than humanity *for the gods*. From a comparative religious or mythological perspective, this observation is very significant. Something new is going on in the Achaemenid creation prologues.

Achaemenid Creation within Persian Discourse

The foregoing survey places the Achaemenid creation prologue within a particularly interesting discourse. Darius and his heirs chose to articulate a vision of creation that was rather distinctive, despite their overall debt to previous ANE forms of kingship and in contrast to the common kingly use of creation ideas. This vision is one of creation as peaceful, ordered, beneficent to humanity, purposeful, and tied directly to the authority of the Great King himself. Creation narratives typically justify temples, cults, cities, and kingships, but the way that the Achaemenid prologue does this is different. The choice of Darius as king by Ahuramazda becomes one aspect of the continuing and unfolding nature of Ahuramazda's beneficial, creative acts. It is not the outcome of violence and war; it is not accidental, capricious, nor threatened by rival gods or forces. Certainly theological language such as "creatio ex nihilo" or "monotheism" are anachronistic here; nevertheless, this shaping of the discourse is striking. It fits rather well with the image of the *pax Persica* which Darius also had inscribed visually in the iconography of Persepolis.[106] One might argue that this creation prologue also manages to redefine the categories of "god" and "king." Creation has become the characteristic quality of ultimate divinity, to the extent that Ahuramazda outshines all others. So too, the Great King has become more than just a temporary agent of the divine administration of his human servants, now being an integral part of his beneficial creative plans. This is a subtle yet profound change in the way of conceptualizing kingship as much as of conceptualizing the divine.

Achaemenid Creation within an Iranian Trajectory

From an Iranian perspective, this discourse is interesting in two respects. De Jong must be right that this emphasis on Ahuramazda as creator was partially a royal decision, and thus was a fundamental shaper of the subsequent trajectory of Iranian traditions. Second, the issue of the relationship between the Teispid and Achaemenid lines and their understandings of kingship come into play here. In particular, the issue which comes to mind is the *paradise* system. The origins of this must have been at least partially (Neo-)Elamite, founded by Cyrus, but it clearly became infused

---

106. E.g., Root 1979, 2000.

with "teleological" meanings similar to those inscribed in the Achaemenid Creation Prologue: a parallel between the Great God and the Great King, between the Good Cosmos and the Good Empire, the emphasis on variety and goodness. Avoidance of the title "king" for Ahuramazda in this context is also interesting.

To summarize this discussion of the Old Persian Creation, it was a feature of Ahuramazda, carried a teleological message, justified the Great King, was non-conflictual, beneficial for humans, and separated divine kingship from creatorship, though it tied human kingship with creation. The depiction of creation in this unique manner was the deliberate choice of the great king.

Second Isaiah in an Early Persian Context

Having explored the text of 2Isa, its message, rhetoric, genre, and social setting, as well as the appearance of creation in the Achaemenid inscriptions and the ANE, this study can now return to the analysis of 2Isa in an early Persian context. What does this source say about Judaean discourse concerning the Persians?

One can dispense at once with any simplistic notion of Judaean "conversion" to Iranian religion in 2Isa. As is argued above, the message of 2Isa was to attach oneself to YHWH. This attachment is depicted as something both rooted in the Judaean past as well as something new. It has expanded in importance and relevance to include the whole empire, but there can be no way to call it an adoption of Teispid, Achaemenid, or "Zoroastrian" religion, as older studies were wont to do. Nor can it be seen as in polemical relation to the Persian religion; in fact, Persian religion is entirely bracketed out of the discourse. At this point, the religious status of the Persian king is a non-issue for 2Isa.[107]

Nevertheless, the new context of being Persian rather than Babylonian subjects infuses the entire discourse of 2Isa, and thus it is improper to eschew the relevance of all things Persian. In fact, one of the big themes of the utterance, the nature of YHWH, cannot be satisfactorily considered without this context. Debates over the so-called monotheism in 2Isa entirely miss this point.[108] As should now be amply evident, this context ought to be seen rather in the theology of creation.

In 2Isa, creation plays a key role. It serves as one of the prime aspects predicated of YHWH: he is a *creator* god more than a warrior or dynastic

---

107. In this respect, Nilsen 2008 and 2013 are correct.
108. As rightly stated by Davies 1995: 222.

deity. His quality as creator is not just one of remote theoretical or philosophical origins, either. It is creatorship which 2Isa adduces as the proof of his control over the cosmos and his ability to achieve his purposes, and thus a key reason for attachment to YHWH as deity. 2Isa falls short of making creation itself teleological (though servanthood surely is), but creation is planned and benevolent. This discourse enables 2Isa to assert YHWH's superior wisdom, his superior strength, his ability to support his servants. It also provides a convenient weapon with which to attack Marduk and Babylon. This use of creation thus has three relevant contexts that must be considered to be simultaneously significant: older Judaean traditions of a conflictual creator, Babylonian traditions of Marduk as creator, and the Achaemenid Creation prologues. With creation, 2Isa manages to select and adapt Judaean tradition in such a way that not only provides a point of contrast with the surrounding Babylonian society—as often noted by scholars—but *also* in a way that is remarkably similar to imperial presentations of the same. Unlike the general conflictual pattern whereby a younger, martial deity shapes the cosmos from an opponent, creation is predicated as an inherent aspect of YHWH. By so doing 2Isa has reformulated received tradition—indeed, something new. This reformulation then offers a strong contrast to Marduk theology and the Neo-Babylonian Empire generally, but most specifically to the immediate, surrounding society of the initial implied audience (the urban Babylonian Judaeans). The Judaeans can be proud of their tradition and of their choice to attach to YHWH because their god *creates*, as part of his nature, and not simply as the side-effect of a battle for dominance amongst the gods. This contrast is obviously one likely to be immediately appealing to its Babylonian context. However, it receives strong support—perhaps necessary given its novelty—from the broader context: Marduk has, in fact, been defeated by another god, or, rather, his political seat has lost its position. 2Isa posits this is YHWH's doing via Cyrus, while the heirs of Cyrus position their right to rule over Babylon and Yehud in terms of Ahuramazda's creative attributes. In fact, the method of use of creation in 2Isa is remarkably similar to that in the Achaemenid Creation prologue. Isaiah 42:5–7 not only makes creation a divine attribute, it functions as a justification of YHWH's servant. As noted above, the Achaemenid creation prologue also primarily functions as a justification of Darius (and his heirs) as the agents of Ahuramazda. There is no question of borrowing of the text of the OP inscriptions here.[109] However, 2Isa is formulated in

---

109. Thus it is not a question of direct, textual dependency as posited by Smith 1963 for the Avesta.

such a way that it argues in line with Persian ideology and against the Babylonians. The Great King would seem to be allied with 2Isa against their local opponents.

In this respect, the dating of 2Isa must be raised again. The similarity between creation in 2Isa and the Achaemenid creation prologue cannot be mere coincidence, especially in light of the contrast with other ANE myths. Nonetheless, it was noted above that it was uncertain when 2Isa was composed, beyond a vague period between 545–484 BCE. The Achaemenid creation prologue is a creation of Darius I and thus would be too late to be a direct comparator for 2Isa should it indeed date to the reign of Cyrus or Cambyses. How should this be understood? The first option is to see 2Isa as dating to the reign of Cyrus or Cambyses. In this scenario, 2Isa would either be related to Cyrus's use of creation in his ideology, perhaps disseminated in relation to the *paradise* system.[110] Alternately, the two uses of creation would just be a remarkable coincidence.

The second option would be a date in the reign of Darius I, in which case a connection with official royal ideology would be hard to avoid. This apparent difficulty would be solved, however, by taking the implications of the genre of 2Isa as an oral dictated rhetorical poem seriously. This genre means that the material here would represent a poetic tradition which had been performed over a period of time, though the textualized version only represents one instantiation of it. What this would mean, then, is that the received text of 2Isa represents a version of this poetic tradition which was recorded in the reign of Darius, but had its roots in the reign of Cyrus. This does not mean redaction, or verbatim repetition, but rather a series of unique performances in a tradition that nonetheless was developing. In this scenario, the use of creation in 2Isa would have developed alongside its development in use in the Achaemenid royal presentation. If such were the case, it means the Achaemenid Creation prologue was indeed contemporary with the version of the poetry recorded in 2Isa and thus is very relevant.

In previous studies, the present author posited six criteria for discussing influence as preserved in texts.[111] These were (1) prior dating; (2) plausible historical context; (3) better structural sense; (4) a "hook" for the new material; (5) discrete particulars; (6) interpretive change. To recap the above in these categories: (1) dating is uncertain, though accepting the transcription in the reign of Darius solves it. (2) The social and historical

---

110. On the Persian *paradise*, see Dandamaev 1984; Stronach 1989, 1990; Tuplin 1996: 80–131; Hultgård 2000; Briant 2002: 442–4; Henkelman 2008: 427–41; Silverman 2016c; Morvillez 2014.

111. Silverman 2010: 7–8; 2012: 35–7; cf. Silverman 2013a: 219.

context of Babylon is a very plausible location for both interaction with Babylonians and Persians, and with royal concepts. There is no reason to posit visual inspection of OP inscriptions. Indeed, the ubiquity of the Achaemenid creation prologue and its potential links to earlier forms of creation discourse in the physical form of the *paradise* suggests the idea was widely disseminated in various media. (3) The formulation of the Achaemenid creation prologue is tightly structured, focusing on the legitimacy of the king and his empire. The use of creation in 2Isa is not so focused, though it is also used to justify the servant of YHWH. The positive, humanistic valence of creation, however, is much more "at home" in the Iranian tradition than in the Judaean one. The fact that 2Isa must belabor the point of goodness is sufficient evidence of this. (4) The suitability of creation as a theme from within the Judaean tradition requires little justification. (5) The parallels in usage have been presented several times: ordered manner, feature of divinity, benevolence, function of justification, lack of temple focus, lack of violence in process. (6) The interpretative change in 2Isa's use of creation is huge. YHWH in 2Isa's vision has started on a path of *teleological* creation. His purposes are no longer restricted to the local kingdoms which worship him, nor to response in the historical moment: he has created with a view to his servants. These servants—Yahwists and the Great King—function in this context. Moreover, YHWH is now attached to a beneficent understanding of reality and not just one predicated on superior power. He also has become a creator in a manner which 2Isa develops as a foil to Marduk but an implicitly comparable one to Ahuramazda. In light of this, it is reasonable to conclude that 2Isa is one of the earliest evidences of Iranian influence on the Judaeans, in the form of creation theology. This is not a matter of textual dependence or of religious conversion, but it is an instance of significant change. It is, in fact, perhaps best understood as an instance of *double* influence: first, of deliberate, negative influence in relation to Babylonian creation, and second, of a deliberate (though perhaps subconscious), positive influence in relation to Achaemenid creation.[112]

Creation does not exhaust the relevance of the early Persian setting for 2Isa. 2Isa's discussion of the concept of servanthood is also strongly informative of the way this discourse interacts with the early Persian Empire. The importance of the *variety* in service cannot be overemphasized. Though the use of a term such as "democratization" would be hyperbolic and anachronistic, there is a sense in which the idea of a "servant more equal than others" is elided by 2Isa. Attachment to YHWH

112. Utilizing the four modes of influence as described in Silverman 2010: 2–3, 6; 2012: 30–1, 33.

can take many forms. The particulars not only explicitly justify the founder of the empire, they also are quite conducive to life in a "cosmopolitan" setting. The nations are indeed to be impressed by the Yahwistic nature of Jacob/Israel, but they do so in a variety of ways. It would be tempting to see this line of reasoning as rather useful within a provincial setting, whereby local subjects could interact with the broader empire and be in contact with compatriots and foreigners in other provinces—a mission rather compatible to being subjects of a great empire.

Cyrus as servant and messiah is noteworthy in this regard (44:28; 45:1). Much has been made of the apparent elision of Davidic rights in 2Isa (55:3–5), but it is typically understood to mean that Israel inherits David's covenant, therefore representing a new a-monarchical view. Yet as Blenkinsopp has commented, this elision happens so that Israel might summon "a nation [they] did not know," which most likely refers to Persia.[113] The transferred covenant therefore functions as insurance that Israel would be viewed favorably by the Persian imperial elite. In her classic study of Achaemenid iconography, Root characterized the entire program as designed to "convey the aura of a sacral covenant between king and subjects," by which she means in particular the sense of voluntary cooperation depicted through the peoples holding the Persian throne aloft.[114] In this respect, it is worth recalling Isa 42:6, in which the servant of YHWH (inclusive of Cyrus) is given as "a covenant for people/light for nations" (לברית עם/לאור גוים). Already noted above, this expands the notion of covenant beyond just Israel. Read together with ch. 55, the concept of covenant becomes quite conducive to supporting Cyrus. Though there is no dynastic claim towards Cyrus's heirs, there is an implication towards Israel supporting the empire: they are to support YHWH's servant and to be attractive to the nations. This explicitly includes Cyrus, and there is no hint of excluding Darius (and Cyrus remained important for Darius's own construction of legitimacy). The international legal order (which is perhaps a better way of rendering *berit* than "covenant")[115] under the Persians is quite different from the vassal–suzerainty structure so much discussed in relation to Deuteronomy.[116]

---

113. Blenkinsopp 2013: 60.

114. Root 1979: 131, cf. 189. Accepted by Ehrenberg 2012: 108.

115. Cf. Davies 1990: 333–4, cf. 322–3. On the political analogues more generally, see Edelman et al. 2011: 8–9, 147–52.

116. E.g., McCarthy 1978; Crouch 2014; perhaps hinted at by Kitchen and Lawrence 2012: 3:264. This does not imply any comment on Deuteronomy's date, a question on which the present author is agnostic.

The relation between nations is now underneath a larger umbrella, not so much a question of which nation owes allegiance to which.

Cyrus and the nations might be unwitting, but the overall discourse of 2Isa with its creation context would not seem to make these appear as particularly negative. This urbane depiction of service allows for failed servants and thus provides within itself the tools for critique of service and particular servants. However, it fails to establish criteria for determining servant status in the future. The famous Isa 53 rather dramatically raises the specter of servants being ignored and unrecognized, but there is no authority (beyond YHWH) to which the decision can be deferred. Moreover, the radical acceptance of Cyrus raises real questions for the continuity of his form of service.[117] Does it end with the punishment of Babylon and the restoration of the Jerusalem temple? Or does the hereditary principle mean his heirs also receive the anointed status? (Of course, a similar problem attended visions of the Davidic dynasty too.) The strong parallels between creation and service noted above probably means that this discourse on servanthood is also strongly informed by Persian ideas of service to Ahuramazda and service to the Great King. In this context, to say that Cyrus is merely the representation of 2Isa's "will to power" fails to take into account the complex treatment of servanthood in this discourse.[118]

The context of newly Persian Babylon also provides an interesting lens for 2Isa's view of religion, i.e., the YHWH cult. The "exile" is often described as a period in which religion (usually called "monotheism") played an important role in forming social cohesion and identity for the Judaeans. There surely is some truth to this, as the experience of minority communities and descendants of migrants is one in which particular received cultural elements become significant social markers. In 2Isa, attachment to YHWH is the most distinctive feature which is predicated for the audience. What is interesting, however, is the way this is done. For the most part, the relationship with YHWH is envisioned in terms of praise/worship, remembering, telling, and teaching. Cult is seen as a reward for attachment rather than the key mode thereof. The social distinction is thus rather narrow and flexible (at least in this discourse). Perhaps this is a sign of (attempted?) broad appeal: YHWH was one aspect of received Judaean traditions with which the audience could be

---

117. Berges's denial of Cyrus's servant status (Berges 2014: 170) means he too easily sees Cyrus as replaced by Israel in 55:3 (p. 175); 2Isa's vision of servanthood is more complex than that.

118. Contra Linville 2010: 285; McKinlay 2013: 90.

expected to agree. The side effect of this emphasis, unintentional no doubt, is a great portability and flexibility. Return to Yehud and a restored cult are nice ideas, but unessential. They function as "home" does in "diaspora" discourse: a locus for placing concerns and longing more than an actual intended destination. This creates a particular "evangelical" tone: the audience is to tell of YHWH, but also, implicitly to tell of the one he sent, i.e., Cyrus! This makes the audience missionaries of YHWH as well as *de facto* highly mobile missionaries for the Persian crown (Isa 40:20–22). If some Judaeans did indeed view Yehud as a convenient place for organizing Judaean life in concert with Persian concerns, then 2Isa was a powerful justification for this.[119] Certainly, individual temples and shrines could also be desired and accommodated within this scheme, but so would broader, imperial service, without compromising on social identity and distinctiveness.

A further aspect of this approach to religion is the way the idol polemic functions. It expands the distinctive features of the YHWH community vis-à-vis their Babylonian neighbors, but it leaves a wide, silent space for the Persians. In this respect, it is worth considering the old problem of Persian worship practices—i.e., the lack of temples and lack of known cult statues. The fact that the 2Isa polemic is focused largely on *statues* and not on *idolatry per se* may mean it is crafted in such a way as to accommodate this, or, at the very least, it is congenial to the situation.[120] It is possible, therefore, to see in 2Isa's discourse an attitude which saw the new regime as a useful ally against the more immediate threat of the host culture. Assimilation not needed, but "postcolonial" "hidden transcripts" would seem to be missing the point, at least for 2Isa.

Finally, there is consideration of the way 2Isa directly deals with Cyrus himself. Certainly, he is discussed on Judaean terms: he brings YHWH glory, and he is the means by which Judah will gain some of its rewards. The significance of this, however, must not be overplayed. All dealings with others are always in some manner predicated on one's own needs

---

119. These are issues which this study will raise and address elsewhere. However, on the idea that "return" to Yehud may not have been voluntary, see, Davies 1992: 81–2; 1995: 221. For the idea that Yehud was envisioned as a colony of Babylonian Judaeans, see Kessler 2006.

120. Davies (1995: 222–3) has also seen this relation, though the idea that it evinces an assimilation between YHWH and Ahuramazda seems to be going too far. In respect to the question of cult statues, it is difficult to assess the significance of sacrifice being given to a statue of Darius I in Sippar during the reign of Xerxes, as attested in a tablet published by Waerzeggers (2014b). In any case, this is likely after the period represented by the discourse in 2Isa.

and concerns. Some points bear mentioning. Cyrus is viewed as a fully legitimate king, with all the key Judaean and ANE terms for legitimate, divinely approved rule.[121] Indeed, 48:14 even has YHWH declare he loves Cyrus—a strong political claim.[122] Certainly, this was surprising for some of the implied audience, perhaps even offensive. But the discourse here preserved does not question it. Moreover, this legitimacy is a *positive* legitimacy. Unlike Nebuchadnezzar, who is also called by YHWH elsewhere, there is no condemnation of Cyrus's conquests or their attendant violence. Indeed, 2Isa views the conquests as Israel's opportunity as well as the awaited judgment against the nations and Babylon, without any hint of hubris on Cyrus's part. The present form of the text also depicts Cyrus in glowing, idealistic terms (e.g., 42:1–7). Moreover, in 42:6 Cyrus is instigating the new "cosmopolitan" way of dealing with the nations already discussed. It is hard not to see 2Isa as about pro-Cyrus as any non-Persian could have been expected to be. Certainly the received text is partly responsible for the good press Cyrus still popularly enjoys.[123]

The context posited for 2Isa makes this pro-Cyrus stance even more remarkable—the legitimacy and usefulness of Jehoiachin's family and the remnants of their court are completely bypassed in silence. 2Isa does not posit their return to power, either as vassals or even as communal representatives; the "native" kingship has totally been dispensed with. Displaced communities restructure themselves, and exiled monarchs must struggle for recognition of their legitimacy. It would seem that, for 2Isa, Judaean society was no longer in need of the Davidides at all. No doubt this was behind some of the implied resistance to 2Isa's new things. It seems unlikely that this perspective, however, was a "sectarian" one. Indeed, if this is an oral dictated poem, this discourse represents a "communal opinion" over time of a culturally influential constituency within Babylon, and its redaction into the book of Isaiah means it was considered to be still important. Calling 2Isa and its broader first audience "pro-Teispid" in this context is no overstatement.

Nevertheless, this should not be understood as mere "collaboration," with all the negative valuations that word implies. Rather, the transfer of royal prerogatives to the royal Persian court would seem to function in the context of a restructuring of Judaean society and competition with

---

121. As rightly stated by Fried 2002: 380; cf. Wilson 2015.

122. As in the narrative of David and Jonathan (1 Sam 20:1 [Jonathan], 16 [Israel]).

123. E.g., the British Museum's touring exhibit of the Cyrus Cylinder, which was still touting it as the first declaration of human rights. See in particular the associated 2013 issue of *Fezana*.

the Babylonians. The elite of the Babylonian Judaean society saw the Persians as a means to improve their own status—and potentially the status of other Yahwists. This is certainly an "interested" view of Cyrus, but it need not be taken as negative or even merely pragmatic (at least at first), as Linsville understands it. The focus on Cyrus rather than on Darius or Cambyses is interesting in this regard. It functions like typical social memory, however. Firsts are always the most memorable. His cooption into the Achaemenid Dynasty by Darius also made him a still relevant figure for imperial discourse. Whether or not such a perspective meant that later Judaeans would become strongly disillusioned is a separate issue, though the possibility is most certainly there, and something that deserves consideration in future studies.

Another consequence of 2Isa's discourse around kingship and religion is the implicit separation of royal and priestly functions. Though the text expects Cyrus to rebuild the temple, the fact that it is explicitly recognized that Cyrus does not know YHWH means his relationship to YHWH's temple cannot be the same that Judaean tradition desired of the Davidic kings or even that of the Neo-Babylonian kings to the Mesopotamian temples. Priesthood plays very little explicit role in 2Isa, however, and not much can be said on the matter until the next section. The implicit separation, however, will become important later on. For now, it appears that the circles that appreciated 2Isa's poetry were primed to accept a "cosmopolitan" situation, with a cult rebuilt by a distant king.

A ritual focus is also missing for the cult itself. The primary way 2Isa appeals to the cult is *torah*, here primarily in the sense of teaching (as opposed to a particular legal tradition or text, 51:4; 54:13). The link between the cult and scholarship could be a reflection of the cultural role of the massive temple complexes in Mesopotamia and/or a result of the community's limited access to a cultic site. In either case, it would be a convenient emphasis for a group that was seeking to be involved in the Persian imperial apparatus to have. As noted in the Introduction, the Persians made significant use of Aramaic bureaucracy, and Judaean Aramaic scribes are known. Could 2Isa, therefore, be an early indication that there was already an emphasis on education or scribal scholarship developing in urban Babylonia among the Judaeans there? As there are parallel instances in migrant communities and in communities subjected to forced labor,[124] this is a topic to which it is worth returning later.

The first level of analysis of 2Isa can conclude by restating the implications for any Davidic court-in-exile. 2Isa's poet, and presumably a large

---

124. Cf. Silverman 2015b.

portion of his audience, see no continued social or political relevance for them. They are not even granted a new role, political or religious, and there is no eschatologizing of the Davidic promises. Israel remains, but it is a community functioning within a Persian world, spreading the word of YHWH's works and servants to the other nations. If Cyrus, Cambyses, or Darius wanted to appeal to Babylonian Judaean sensibilities, choosing a Davidic governor for Yehud would not appear to be necessary—unless there were other groups within Babylonia more enthralled with the court-in-exile. If the urban elite wanted to choose their own representative, either to the Persian court or to Yehud, a Davidide would not seem to have been their own likely choice, at least not due to genealogy.

These observations are at odds with common depictions of the Judaean diaspora in Babylon. It is now time to turn to the next major literary source, 1Zech.

Part II

Chapter 4

FIRST ZECHARIAH, THE TEMPLE,
AND THE GREAT KING

> Anything can happen in the woods.
>
> —James Lapine and Stephen Sondheim, *Into the Woods* (1987)

The book of Zechariah is notoriously difficult; it contains a series of complicated visions and oracles, compounded by difficult syntax and *hapax legomena*.[1] Further, the situation is more complicated than with 2Isa, as the Greek versions of Zechariah do evince some significant differences from the MT and there has been some textual corruption.[2] Nevertheless, at least the first eight chapters (1Zech) explicitly address the situation of early Persian-period Yehud and the key theological and ideological issues of kingship and temple, and thus it is a direct source for at least some of the debates over these matters in the period. As with 2Isa, the analysis begins with a close reading of the text as it survives. However, because unlike 2Isa the surviving text includes explicit dates, analysis can begin by assessing their relevance for a historical reading.

As with the previous section, only a portion of a book is taken as the unit of analysis (chs. 1–8). This is justified by the clear delineation into sections by headings and by the clear change in genre in ch. 9. This

---

1. For an amusing discussion of this, see Pyper 2005. For a collection representing some of the recent debates, see Boda and Floyd 2008.

2. For a convenient list of pluses and minuses, see Eidsvåg 2016: 61–8. This is not to say that it is the most difficult MT text. Both Meyers and Meyers 2004: lxviii and Petersen 1984: 225 call it "relatively free" of problems, though both commentaries emend the text at various places.

distinction is widely accepted. For the moment, the origins, relationship, and unity of chs. 1–8 with chs. 9–14 are left undecided.[3]

The Dating Formulae

The central question in attempting to date 1Zech (as well as Haggai) is the reliability of the dating formulae, in the second and fourth years of Darius (usually presumed to be the first).[4] Scholars have varied views on the reliability of the dates, though many accept them with little comment on their accuracy.[5] For instance, Meyers and Meyers think the dates in Haggai and Zechariah 1–8 were designed to highlight the date of the re-founding of the temple (in Hag 2:10, 20) and deployed with a "7 + 1" pattern discernible, though they accept the dates as historically relevant nonetheless.[6] Ackroyd thinks the precision in the dating means they require independent verification, but also thinks the burden of proof rests on those who dispute the dates.[7]

Nevertheless, if the dates are part of an editorial addition as many accept, this raises the question of whether they are reliably indicative for the visions and/or oracles or not. If the dates are later fabrications, then one must find a plausible reason for why the specific dates were chosen (VII/Darius 2; 24/XII/Darius 2; 4/XI/Darius 4). Moseman thinks the dates were added later on analogue with Ezekiel's use of dates.[8] This seems like an unlikely inspiration for the dates, given that the dates neither replicate any dates in Ezekiel—raising the question why these specific dates—and

---

3. The collection of material in 9–14 could either pre- or post-date that in chs. 1–8, a matter on which the present author is undecided, though the possibility that it pre-dates 1Zech has been under-considered in recent scholarship. The unity of chs. 1–8 with 9–14 is, however, rather overrated in his opinion. This question is of import for later (and modern) understanding, but not necessarily for what 1Zech says for its earliest contexts. It is also assumed it was originally separate from Haggai.

4. The given Julian dates are (27) October 520, 15 February 519, and 6 December 518, calculated using Parker and Dubberstein 1956. Other authors give somewhat variant dates. An identification with Darius II would move the dates forward a century.

5. E.g., Mitchell, Smith, and Bewer 1912: 98, cf. 109, 116; McComiskey 2009: 1008; Willi-Plein 2007: 11–16, 22, 53, 57; Coggins 1996: 11; Smith 1984: 169; Berquist 1995: 70; Gerstenberger 2011: 196–7; Petersen 1984: 20; Deissler 1988: 265, 270; cf. Blenkinsopp 2013: 75, 83; Boda 2016: 31–2.

6. Meyers and Meyers 2004: xlvii–xlviii.

7. Ackroyd 1951: 171–3; Gerstenberger 2015: 128 thinks the precision makes them likely to be secondary.

8. Moseman 2009: 581, 584.

that the standard ANE reporting of prophecy in administrative contexts could include noting the date of a prophecy.[9] If the dates were fabricated on an analogue, surely modelling on the real social praxis of prophetic reports is a more likely intention than such an indistinct reference to Ezekiel. Hallaschka argues that the dates in 1Zech were modelled on those in Haggai.[10] Given the closeness in the dates of the two texts (indeed, overlap), one wonders why the dates would be plausible for Haggai but not for 1Zech—would administrative practices around prophecy have differed so much for one prophet from the other?

Jonker rejects the dates on the assumption that the text was written in Jerusalem and that there was no one in Jerusalem at the time capable of writing.[11] Both of these assertions are uncertain (and the complete lack of writing in the province is untenable, given Achaemenid administrative practices). Moreover, these objections do not provide a rationale for the specific dates that are chosen.

Edelman argues at length that the dates in Haggai-Zechariah were added secondarily (and that they are therefore historically unreliable).[12] In her view, the seventy years of Zech 7:4 provides the rationale for the years, while the days and months relate to the attested Mesopotamian traditions of propitious and inauspicious days. Though, as she notes, year 2 of Darius is very nearly 70 years from Jerusalem's destruction, it seems highly unlikely that later Judaean scribes were sufficiently aware of chronology to enable such a calculation, given the frequent shortening of the Persian period in Second Temple chronologies. Moreover, 70 was a typical, vague number in the ANE for a "long time" and thus need not have had any relation to real time nor to a specific text such as Jeremiah.[13] The likelihood that considerations of inauspicious or auspicious moments would have been made by those deciding temple-building is high—preserved letters to the Neo-Assyrian king asking for an order to begin building note the favorability of the month.[14] Nevertheless, these do not provide any *post facto* rationale for the choice of the particular dates in

---

9. See the collection in Nissinen 2003. There are recorded dates in SAA 9 no. 9 (Parpola 1997: 40–1 ‖ Nissinen 2003: 130–1) and in Nissinen nos. 18, 54, 58 (pp. 42, 84, 87). Key factors to remember are the sporadic nature of the reports, as well as the genre. Administrative rather than epistolary contexts seem to have increased the frequency of the use of a date.

10. Hallaschka 2012: 188.

11. Jonker 2015: 202.

12. Edelman 2005: 80–150.

13. E.g., Bedford 2001: 165–6; Grabbe 2009: 118–19.

14. E.g., Cole and Machinist 1998: no. 161. This will be addressed further below.

Haggai-Zechariah. In any case, in at least one Neo-Assyrian text, only the 21st and 24th are favorable for extispicy, but not the 4th.[15] The potential favorability of the dates is a better reason to see them as explaining why prophecy may have occurred on those dates rather than as having been added much later.

If one wishes to assert that the dates were a redactional addition, then a plausible reason for the *post facto* choice of specific dates needs to be found; otherwise, the most logical reason for the specificity of the dates is that the scribe used dates which he found recorded in the source reports when compiling the cycle. The dates given do not correspond with any attested festival dates in Judaism or Zoroastrianism, except for Hag 2:1 on the last day of Sukkot. Despite much looking, the present author has been unable to find any other events corresponding to the dates given in the text. The only possible exception is Zech 1:1, if the idiosyncratic Syriac version is correct in supplying day 1, placing the oracle on the new moon.

There were no solar or lunar eclipses visible in the Near East corresponding to any of the given dates.[16] The closest potentially relevant eclipse is a very partial lunar eclipse that occurred on 8 November 520 (=13/VII/Darius 2),[17] which was in the same month as the first date in Zechariah (which, however, only gives the month and not the day). This would have appeared in the west, which in the Mesopotamian tradition would have been a bad omen for Syria-Palestine.[18]

As is well known, the best ANE comparators for oracle collections come from the Neo-Assyrian Empire, where oracles from separate, named prophets were grouped by common theme.[19] At least one appears to be for cultic purposes (Collection 3, "the covenant of Aššur").[20] Individual oracle reports are known to have on occasion included the name and location of the prophet as well as the date.[21]

---

15. KAR 151 (Koch 2015: 44, 295–6), though the relevance is debatable, given the variability in dates between various attestations.

16. As calculated in Espenak and Meeus 2006 and 2009. Note that to convert the negative numbers to BCE dates, one must add 1, so that -519 = 520 BCE.

17. Espenak and Meeus 2009: Plate 180; however, this eclipse is not attested in the published lists of Babylonian lunar observations in Hunger, Sachs, and Steele 2001 nor in the canon of eclipses by Steele and Stephenson 1998.

18. BM 22696, trans in Koch 2015: 159; Rochberg 2004: 68–9.

19. Parpola 1997.

20. Parpola 1997: no. 3.

21. E.g., Parpola 1997: no. 9 (lines 4–8, "By the mouth of the woman Dunnaša-amur of Arbela, Nisan 18, eponymy of Bel-šadû'a") = Nissinen 2003 no. 94.

Given that there are no apparent ideological or theological reasons for a later redactor to choose the specific dates and that oracle reports could indeed include the precise date, it seems prudent to accept their historical validity in (Haggai and) 1Zech.[22] Moreover, Kessler argues that the format of the dates is consistent with a transition from the monarchic-era Judaean practice of year/month/day to the Persian-period practice of day/month/year as attested in period formulae.[23] For sure, there is at least a two-year delay between the initial visions and their shaping into a corpus, but it is reasonable to accept that the dates have their basis in real performances in the second year of Darius and the oracles in chs. 7–8 in the fourth year of Darius—however much they have been shaped for the book of Zechariah. The first redaction of the vision cycle, then, cannot be earlier than 518, but there is little reason to see it as much later.[24] In terms of the political situation for Yehud, the difference between Darius 2 and 4 is small enough to provide a place to begin. For present purposes, then, a setting in the early years of Darius is considered to be highly likely. A more thorough discussion of the implications of the date of 1Zech will follow analysis of the rhetoric and meaning.

The Rhetoric and Meaning of First Zechariah

That a major concern of 1Zech is Yehud and its temple, including its rebuilding and legitimacy, is clear. As with 2Isa, the analysis will begin with a reading of the current form of the text, independently from chs. 9–14. This reading will precede consideration of the structural/diachronic elements in the formation of the text, although, unlike 2Isa, the initial reading of the message of the text is informed by the above arguments that 1Zech belongs in the early years of Darius I. The discussion will proceed by vision, followed by an overview of themes, before returning to the issue of genre and historical setting. Since the text explicitly deals with

---

22. As is the reasoning of Kessler 2002: 50–1. Ristau 2016: 140 rather thinks this lack of significance makes the dates "secondary to the core interests of the texts" and sees it as a technique to interrelate 1Zech with Haggai. Surely a vague date as appears in other minor prophets (i.e., "in the days of Darius") would have served such a function just as well.

23. Kessler 2002: 41–51; cf. Kessler 1992.

24. Boda 2016: 33 accepts the dates for the initial experience of the prophet Zechariah, but not for the book itself, though he also sees little reason for 1Zech to postdate them extensively; cf. Floyd 2000: 313, 518–16.

visions, it is important to consider the hermeneutics of images. This can be approached in at least two ways: in terms of "iconographic exegesis" or in terms of the phenomenology of visions.

"Iconographic exegesis" is a term recently championed to argue that an adequate understanding of a text's historical context must include consideration of preserved visual material.[25] De Hulster delimits a seven-step process;[26] in short, this can be summed up as treating the text and the images within it as part of a broader cultural imagination, one that included visual images as well as words and concepts. Specific images can therefore be of great assistance to the modern historian attempting to understand the world of the text. Where possible, historical analogues are sought below for the individual images which appear in 1Zech.

Another way to consider the import of the visual is to take seriously the phenomenology of dreams and visions, as the ancients most certainly did. In a very stimulating study, Tiemeyer argues for the exegetical impact of taking the reality of visions seriously.[27] As she points out, dreams and visions are prominent in the HB and the ANE, where their significance was widely entertained. Moreover, she points to psychological studies that show that visions contain material familiar to the visionary,[28] meaning that "intertextuality" in and of itself cannot be considered decisive for positing a purely literary origin. The formal shape of chs. 1–8 at first glance appears to be a vision report with the addition of introductory and concluding oracular material. Since 1Zech presents itself as a vision report, taking this phenomenology seriously has important generic ramifications. This means the question must be carefully considered before proffering an historical analysis; this is offered in the next chapter, after an overview of the text. The basic form of a dream report, however, will offer a useful starting orientation for the exploration of the text.

Visions and Oracles, Contents and Meaning

For ease of discussion, the text of 1Zech will be discussed through its eleven major sections (Introduction, 1:1–6; eight visions: 1:7–17; 2:1–4 [Eng. 1:18–21]; 2:5–17 [Eng. 2:1–13]; 3:1–10*; 4:1–14*; 5:1–4; 5:5–11; 6:1–8; a sign act, 6:9–15; inquiry concerning fasts and oracles of prosperity, 7:1–8:23). Discussion of the literary structure and formation

---

25. E.g., Hulster and LeMon 2014; Hulster and Strawn 2015. For theory, see Hulster 2009: 23–104.
26. Hulster 2009: 103.
27. Tiemeyer 2015.
28. Tiemeyer 2015: 37–40.

will follow below. Many of these passages contain notoriously difficult cruxes; rather than a comprehensive commentary, this discussion attempts to focus on elements that are useful for understanding the basic communicative and social aspects of the text as well as its overall meaning, so that it can then be used to discuss the early Persian context.

Introduction (1:1–6)

The first six verses of 1Zech are almost universally considered to function as an introduction to the current collection.[29] It reports the oracle of a prophet (נביא) Zechariah ben Berechiah ben Iddo, in VIII/Darius 2 (if Darius I then October/November 520 BCE). Zechariah is a very common name, with several different individuals with said name attested in Ezra-Nehemiah and Chronicles, even several seeming to have lived in Persian Yehud.[30] Not as many individuals are attested with the name Berechiah.[31] At least two Iddos are attested in the corpus.[32] The threefold name is atypical for biblical genealogies,[33] but it could be argued that here "Iddo" is a family or clan name, similar to the contemporary priestly practice in Babylonia.[34] Morever, Albertz and Schmitt think that Achaemenids supported nuclear families.[35] Besides the unusual nature of the addition of a grandfather, the reference in Neh 12:4 is to Iddo as a clan chief and twelve verses later (Neh 12:16) Iddo is listed as a clan (headed by a Zechariah). Indeed, understanding it as a clan name would easily explain why Ezra 5:1 and 6:14 call the prophet Zechariah son of Iddo.

---

29. Petersen 1984: 110; Floyd 2000: 308; Meyers and Meyers 2004: 98; Boda 2016: 38; cf. Wenzel 2011.

30. E.g., Ezra 10:26; Neh 11:4, 5; 1 Chr 5:7; 27:21; 2 Chr 17:7; 20:14; 35:8. It is also attested in Babylonia (Pearce and Wunsch 2014: 92 [cf. nos. 34, 45, 51]) and Elephantine (Porten 2011: 275). A link with 1Isa as argued by Sweeney 2003: 337; 2015: 155 is tenuous and unnecessary.

31. 1 Chr 6:24; 15:17; 2 Chr 28:12; Neh 3:30; 6:18. At least one individual in the Āl-Yāhūdu community also bore the name (publication forthcoming, see Pearce and Wunsch 2014: 43), as well as several in Elephantine (Porten 2011: 267–8).

32. 1 Kgs 4:14; Neh 12:4.

33. Of 126 verses in the Latter Prophets which use patronyms, 169 occurrences include just the father, with only 15 including three or more generations—including Zech 1:1, 7. Of these, six are Gedaliah (Jer 39:14; 40:5, 9, 11; 41:2; 43:6).

34. On Neo-Babylonian naming practices, see Jursa 2015a; Waerzeggers 2015b: 9, on family names being a prerogative of the aristocratic families. For priestly families, see Jursa 2013; Waerzeggers 2010b: 77–90.

35. Albertz and Schmitt 2012: 476.

Otherwise, however, nothing would be known of this clan. On the other hand, Ackroyd sees Iddo as Zechariah's father, while Edelman sees Iddo as Zechariah's grandfather.[36]

The lack of a day number in the dating formula contrasts with the other two dates in 1Zech (and those in Haggai). One could see this either as an accidental omission either from an initial report or in the course of the manuscript tradition, or as implying the first day of the month, as appears in the Syriac (and which would equal the 27 October 520).[37] One could also see it as intentionally referencing just the month itself, perhaps due to a conflation of several oracles in the chapter. The deliberate omission of the day number to fit a chronological scheme for Haggai–Zech 1–8 seems an ineffective strategy.[38] No data exist to clarify the issue, but a simple lack of recording the day number is the simplest suggestion.

In an assertion familiar from 2Isa, the section affirms that YHWH punished the audience's ancestors, and that they had been unsuccessfully warned (orally) by prophets.[39] The oracle uses this as a proof of the validity of YHWH's words and as an invitation to return (שוב) to YHWH. As a unit, the rhetoric is rather straightforward. To use the terminology of Fisher introduced in the previous part, the oracle uses the fact of previous successful prophecies and the consistency of their Neo-Babylonian experiences as judgment to argue for a return to YHWH now. What such a return entails is left unspecified, but it is coupled with the promise of a concomitant return of YHWH (v. 3). The effect is an audience expectation to hear of what this return consists, both for the Judaeans and for YHWH.

---

36. Ackroyd 1968: 148; Edelman 2005: 17–18. Boda 2016: 66–8 implies he was just an ancestor. Floyd 2000: 321 thinks it emphasizes descent from the two previous generations (but, who does not?). Sweeney 2003: 341–3's claim of a redactional link to Isa is primarily predicated on later Jewish exegesis and not the likely historical situation of 1Zech.

37. Most commentators do not follow the Syriac.

38. Meyers and Meyers 2004: 90–1 suggest the day was left out to make it appear less like the dates overlap and to highlight its central position in the scheme of seven dates. But since it neither eliminates the overlap nor makes it appear more central, this would be a poor strategy to affect either goal.

39. The most natural way to understand קראו־אליהם הנביאים הראשנים is a reference to the memory of oral prophets around the time of the Egyptian and Babylonian crises rather than to the corpus of prophetic literature which is extant today, despite the typical scholarly proclivity to read it as an intertextual allusion. E.g., contra Reventlow 1993: 38; Floyd 2000: 324; Stead 2009: 11–15; cf. Elliger 1964: 101–2; Redditt 2015: 276–7 mentions Stead, but does not comment.

This section also introduces 1Zech's favorite name for YHWH, יהוה צבאות (4×, vv. 3–4). The etymology of the epithet itself has martial implications, whether one understands the "hosts" in question to be heavenly or human.[40] This was a favorite term of 1Isa (and to a lesser extent, 2Isa).[41] Two ostraca from Elephantine attest to the use of the epithet in the Judaean military colony there as well.[42] A Greek magical papyrus addresses Sebaoth along with three archangels, in a request for dream divination.[43] This is a later text from a decidedly different context, but it suggests associations with power and divination. Whether this epithet primes the audience for a military or kingly return of YHWH is debatable, however, as it might also have more Jerusalemite connotations.[44] Davies has argued that there was a shift from a cult of YHWH Sebaoth to YHWH God of Israel, predicated largely on the former being a localized manifestation.[45] In the present context of 1Zech, the Jerusalemite connotation is no doubt significant.

Historically, one might wonder if YHWH Sebaoth was not the result of the assimilation of a local god of Jerusalem (צדק, שלם?) with YHWH, the patron of the Davidic dynasty (cf. the names Solomon and Absalom).[46] Even if this were true, it would no doubt have been long forgotten by the sixth century, other than the implication that other, less localized forms of YHWH may have been known. In any case, it is highly likely that the audience could have known of other manifestations of YHWH. The repetition of the origin of the oracular word also implies that other sources could have been the source—whether these were other deities or other manifestations of YHWH.

In sum, this section calls for the Judaeans to return to YHWH Sebaoth, with the promise that he will also return to Jerusalem and to Yehud.

Vision of Multicolored Horses (1:7–17)

The vision cycle opens with the same prophetic attributions and a date three months later (24/XI/Darius 2, i.e., 15 February 519). Although this

---

40. Scholars often see a martial connotation, e.g., Garbini 1988: 89; Kessler 2002: 122; Fox 2015: 83; Boda 2016: 133; Byrne 2006: 48–56, 167–90 emphasizes the military and kingship connotations of the term.
41. Byrne 2006.
42. Clermont-Ganneau nos. 167, 175 (Lozachmeur 2006: 1: 316–18, 324–5); cf. Lemaire 2011: 379.
43. PGM VII.1009–1016 (Betz 1986: 145); cf. Dodson 2009: 25.
44. Cf. Kessler 2002: 122.
45. Davies 2015: 206; 2016: 31.
46. E.g., Ringgren 1947: 79; Keel 2007: 211–14, 391–3.

section bristles with interpretive cruxes, the overall meaning is quite clear: the return of YHWH involves his return to a rebuilt temple in Jerusalem and a repopulated Yehud (vv. 16–17).

Though the extant syntax of the opening in v. 8 is perplexing (with "night" lacking either a preposition or accusative particle, probably indicating "last night"),[47] the following is clearly presented as a dream or vision—the distinction, though perhaps phenomenologically real, is unimportant, as both are attested in the ANE, were taken seriously as divine communicative media, and involve visual experience.[48] A location for this vision is not explicitly stated. Attested dream reports would suggest a palace or temple as plausible locations, though in principle it could have been anywhere.

The vision opens with a man riding a red horse, standing between the myrtles (החדסים) beside the pool (במצלה), in front of multiple horses of three colors. All of these details are obscure and have provoked debate: the significance of the myrtles (or whether the LXX's "mountains" should be preferred), the significance of the pool, and the significance of the three colors.

Myrtles (החדסים). A major scholarly debate has been whether the myrtles carry any symbolic significance, and, if so, what that might be.[49] Those who posit symbolic significance hold a wide array of opinions. A recurrent view holds that they represent the location as the entrance to the divine abode.[50] Several see it as a sign of favor for Israel.[51] Meyers and Meyers think they provide the hiddenness that is "the proper function of a system of intelligence."[52] Bič saw it as related to the New Year

---

47. Rignell 1950: 23 notes the differences between the versions, and prefers it indicating that all happened on the same night. Translated as "in the night" by Meyers and Meyers 2004: 109–10; "this past night" by Boda 2016: 115; and as "last night" by Petersen 1984: 136–8, who notes it is literally "this night"; Floyd 2000: 349 and Tiemeyer 2015: 61.

48. I.e., a dream is essentially a vision that happened at night while asleep. Cf. the view of Tiemeyer 2015: 17–22 and the phenomenology section below. For other attestations of "night visions," cf. Aeschylus, *Prometheus* 645; Livy 8.6.11 (LCL: 515).

49. For a handy overview, see Tiemeyer 2015: 71–6.

50. E.g., Reventlow 1993: 41; Tigchelaar 1996: 66; Keel 2007: 1012 (the gate of the sun); Tiemeyer 2015: 76; Boda 2016: 124. Hanhart 1998: 69–71 thinks it represents a combination of the Garden of Eden and Chaos traditions, making it YHWH's abode.

51. Rignell 1950: 24; Mason 1977: 36–7.

52. Meyers and Meyers 2004: 111.

enthronement festival,⁵³ while Petersen merely saw them emphasize "well-watered, luxuriant growth."⁵⁴

Turning to the attested uses of the myrtle in the ANE, however, leads to no clear set of associations. While the myrtle briefly makes an appearance in the Gilgameš epic (in V.154 Humbaba promises to guard some myrtle trees, and in XI.160 Utanapištim uses some myrtle wood on the sacrificial fire),⁵⁵ the mythologically significant trees appear to be the cedars. Otherwise, most attestations of the myrtle in the cuneiform record are related to the use of its oil, wood, and berries in aromatics and medicine.⁵⁶

According to Pliny the Elder, each species of tree was associated with a divinity, and he assigns the myrtle to Venus.⁵⁷ He also claims the tree held a "prophetic" association and was used in triumphs.⁵⁸ There is no guarantee, however, that these later Roman traditions have any relevance earlier or farther east. Herodotus mentions Persian use of myrtles in a few contexts. He claims the wreaths that were worn during animal sacrifices were typically of myrtle (I.132) and that the roads were strewn with myrtle branches for Xerxes to cross Hellespont (VII.54) and in Susa when Athens was occupied (VIII.99.1).⁵⁹ These kinds of practices are rather similar to the uses of myrtle as an aromatic in the cuneiform sources, and shed little light on any potential symbolic significance for the tree.

Though all HB occurrences of the myrtle appear to be Persian period (Zech 1:8, 10, 11; Isa 41:19; 55:13; Neh 8:15), the plant was native to the Levant, only requiring significant water resources to grow.⁶⁰ (See figs. 4.1a and 4.1b.) Specific connotations of "paradise" or heaven appear in much later texts (e.g., *Alphabet Midrash* and *Sefer Hahezyanot* 17),⁶¹ but this likely derives from exegesis of Isaiah rather than functioning as evidence for earlier ANE associations.

53. Bič 1964: 11.
54. Petersen 1984: 140.
55. George 1999: 42, 94; note that the new tablet of the series (Al-Rawi and George 2014) does not.
56. See CAD A2: 343; Thompson 1949: 300–302. Cf. SAA 07 146, line 4 (an administrative list of wood-types, Fales and Postgate 1992: 151), and a Hellenistic-era Zodiac which associates the tree with Sagittarius (Pabilsag), Eanna, and chalcedony (TCL 06, 12+, available in Oracc).
57. *Natural History* 12.2, cf. 15.38 (Pliny 1960: 5, 373).
58. For both details see *Natural History* 15.36 (Pliny 1960: 369–71).
59. Herodotus 2002: 173; 2000: 369; 2006: 97, respectively.
60. Löw 1924: 257–74; Zohary 1982: 119.
61. For the former see Wünsche 1967: 196; latter Faierstein 1999: 49 (on being a seventh-century Kabbalistic text, p. 9).

Figure 4.1a. *Myrtle Berries*

Figure 4.1b. *Myrtle Bush*

Iconographical sources also provide little illumination. While plants appear on many media, it is nearly impossible to specifically identify any of them with a myrtle.[62] In any case, the widespread "tree of life" motif is

---

62. And, in any case, nothing is labeled as such in the BODO database, either. For "twig" imagery generally (albeit not myrtles *per se*), see Staubli 2015a. Thanks

never depicted as resembling a myrtle. Prudence therefore suggests that a more prosaic interpretation of their significance is warranted. Indeed, Niditch notes that the myrtles are not interpreted in the text and seem to function more as props for the setting.[63] Mitchell et al. long ago suggested that the myrtles merely connote presence in a garden, such as the "King's Garden" in the Kidron Valley.[64] The new palynological analysis of the discoveries at Ramat Raḥel, however, suggest that such a geographical referent might be better understood as there.[65] As Christine Mitchell suggests, the myrtles can be understood as merely the real myrtles attested as being in this garden.[66] In this garden's context, the myrtles are significant for denoting the landscape's artificial supply of sufficient water. But in the visionary context, the import can just be understood as marking the location in the gubernatorial garden in Ramat Raḥel.

By the Pool (במצלה). Closely related to the issue and interpretation of the myrtles is their stated location—במצלה. Commentators and translators have been divided over its meaning. The MT can be derived from צלל, "to be dark," or צול, "deep." Rudolph has suggested emending the MT to "place of prayer," but he is rarely followed.[67] The former derivation has the support of the LXX, and this is favored by Meyers and Meyers.[68] Tiemeyer also follows this root, but understands it rather as a temporal "at dusk."[69] Given that the vision is already given a setting at night (הלילה), this reading is a bit peculiar. The majority of commentators prefer to derive it from the second root option. This receives support from poetic texts in the HB where מצלה appears in parallel to "the sea" or "the abyss" (תהום) to indicate either the cosmic ocean/chaos or the underworld (Pss 68:23; 69:3, 16; 88:7; Jonah 2:4; Mic 7:19) and by extension the exodus as a defeat of the same (Exod 15:5; Neh 9:11). Scholars who wish to see this vision as

---

to Izaak de Hulster for this reference. Staubli's appeal to Zech 4 for two later coins (pp. 338–9) seems unnecessary to me, though the relevance for the state seal is more apropos (344).

63. Niditch 1980: 144.
64. Mitchell, Smith, and Bewer 1912: 119.
65. Langgut et al. 2013.
66. Mitchell 2016: 92.
67. Rudolph 1976: 71–2. The Targums replace במצלה with בבבל "in Babylon," clearly an emendation based on lack of understanding of what the difficult term meant. Rignell 1950: 24 pointed to Arabic for a meaning "tent," which has also not been followed.
68. Meyers and Meyers 2004: 110–11.
69. Tiemeyer 2015: 73.

set at the divine abode favor this reading.[70] Indeed, Ugaritic material does place 'El's abode at the origins of the deep. In the Ba'al Cycle 'El is said to live at the "springs of the Rivers, streams of the Deep,"[71] though it uses the cognate of תהום rather than מצלה. The Sefire Treaty might use מצלה as one of the divine witnesses along with the springs,[72] but here the word must be reconstructed and Fitzmyer's reconstruction appealed to Zech 1:8 as justification. In neither case, however, do trees appear in conjunction with the deep, which is indeed a peculiar place for them. Because of this incongruity, many scholars opt for a less specific usage from the deep to something that is deep, i.e., a valley, ravine, or hollow.[73] Although a meaning of "hollow" or "valley" seems more apropos than one related to "shadow," the word seems to have a specifically water-related connotation, even if the depths of the ocean are inappropriate in this context. Christine Mitchell suggests that its meaning here could just be "pool" or "basin."[74] There is some slim support for this in much later literature. Two times in Rabbinic literature the phrase "like a מצולה in which there are fish" appears (b. Ber. 9b; b. Pes. 119a), and Jastrow thinks the word refers to fishponds in each location, though an understanding as the deeps of the ocean is still possible.[75] Lastly, a German consul reported on a 1.125 m³ basin which was used in late nineteenth-century Syria called a *miṣwal*, which he compared to Hebrew מצולה.[76] If one grants the possibility of the meaning "pool" here, then one would have good grounds for understanding the phrase to mean a particular set of myrtles which were known to be beside a pool.

The Horses' Colors. Another interpretive crux is the identity, number, and significance of the colors given for the horses. The versions give variant readings—the MT, Targums, and Latin have three colors, the LXX, Syriac, and Ethiopic have four.[77] It seems that the LXX has been influenced by the four in chapter 6, and thus it is preferable to retain three as in the MT.[78]

---

70. Petersen 1984: 139–40; Clifford 2010: 48–51; Boda 2016: 125. Cf. Bič 1964: 11; Floyd 2000: 347.

71. 4 IV 20–22; 6 I 32–4 = Parker 1997: 127, 153.

72. A, lines 11–12 = Fitzmyer 1967: 12–13, cf. 38.

73. Gesenius 1846: 452; Mitchell, Smith, and Bewer 1912: 119; Niditch 1980: 129; *DCH* 5:449.

74. Mitchell 2016: 92.

75. Goldschmidt 1929–36: 1:36, 11:677; cf. Jastrow 1950: 824.

76. See Socin and Wetzstein 1891: 3. Cf. Koehler and Baumgartner 2001: 2:623.

77. For a handy overview, see Rignell 1950: 28–34.

78. Cf. Petersen 1984: 143; Tiemeyer 2015: 65–6.

This leaves two forms of red and white.⁷⁹ While Mitchell et al. thought the colors divided the horses into troops,⁸⁰ and the Meyers thought the colors were appropriate camouflage for seasonal vegetation,⁸¹ Petersen's argument that they are just three of the five possible natural horse colors is convincing.⁸² In this case, there are just an unspecified number of horses of three normal horse colors. As an aside, it is perhaps worth noting that Achaemenid buildings also used two forms of red and white in their coloration.⁸³

Following the attractive proposal of Christine Mitchell⁸⁴—to be discussed more thoroughly below—it is possible to understand the myrtles and "the deep" as a location in the *paradise* at the gubernatorial residence in Ramat Raḥel. Indeed, the ruined state of Jerusalem at this point in time makes it an unlikely setting. If this is the case, then neither image holds any further mythological significance. The significance of the colors is uncertain, though in similar fashion to the myrtles and pool, they could have been inspired by the colors on the wall paintings at the palace. Painted features could be expected at Ramat Raḥel, and the Persian palaces were all originally painted as well.⁸⁵ The significance and identity of the horses is commonly agreed by commenters to be YHWH's imperial spies, modelled on the Persian (and Neo-Assyrian) system known as the King's Eyes (vv. 10–11).⁸⁶

---

79. Though Rignell 1950: 33–4 thought this meant just two colors.
80. Mitchell, Smith, and Bewer 1912: 119; cf. Boda 2016: 120.
81. Meyers and Meyers 2004: 113.
82. Petersen 1984: 141–2; cf. Mason 1977: 37; Niditch 1980: 143–4; Tiemeyer 2015: 64–5; Abernethy 2017.
83. Aloiz, Douglas, and Nagel 2016; cf. Nagel 2013; Ladiray 2013: 155 with an image of a red plaster floor from Susa.
84. Mitchell 2016. The author is grateful to Mitchell for forwarding her article before publication.
85. Also at Gerizim (Gudme 2013: 77). Similar colors are attested in the Achaemenid palaces. See Ladiray 2013: 155 with an image of a red plaster floor from Susa; Roaf 1983: 8 on traces of red, green, blue, yellow, and evidence of gold attachments at Persepolis; Aloiz, Douglas, and Nagel 2016, including blue, green, red, and grey colors. Cf. Albenda 1999 for Assyria.
86. With various emphases, e.g., Meyers and Meyers 2004: 111; Mathys 2010: 275; Silverman 2012: 171–4; Blenkinsopp 2013: 92 n. 40; Silverman 2014a: 3–5; Tiemeyer 2015: 158; Boda 2016: 130. Ackroyd 1968: 176, however, preferred to see only the heavenly court tradition here; Keel 2007: 1013 only "Persian messengers."

The (riderless?) horses have returned from roaming the earth to report that they have found the inhabitants secure (ישבת ושקטת)—an idiom for peace and prosperity due to security.[87] This prompts the Angel of YHWH to *ask* when YHWH would have mercy on Jerusalem and Judah. The force of this response (ענה) is often colored as a complaint,[88] but it is used repeatedly, so can better be seen as just a question determining the appropriate time (cf. Haggai).[89] The Lord responds with words of good and comfort (טובים, נחמים), surprisingly to the interpretive angel ("the angel who talked with me") rather than to the Angel of the Lord who had asked the question. In fact, the exact number of characters in this scene is unclear, and there is a series of separate dialogues within the vision itself. The confusion does not impact the overall message, but it does perhaps evoke a dream-like narrative style (see below). The content of these words is then given in vv. 14–17, although the answer is unrelated to the timing, rather affirming YHWH's anger at the "nations at ease" for overdoing the punishment and affirming his return to the Jerusalem temple. The nations at ease are presumably primarily Assyria and Babylonia, being the typical prophetic carriers of wrath and those primarily responsible for the diaspora (the significance in relation to Darius I will be discussed below). It is worth noting that, although the oracle given in response to the Angel of YHWH's question is not answered temporally, it does explicitly answer the request for רחם (v. 12) in v. 16, by identifying it with YHWH's return to Jerusalem. The rebuilding of the temple and the repopulation of Yehud follow from this return, which is, of course, standard ANE temple theology.[90]

87. Compare the Akkadian idiom *šubtu nēhtu ašābu*, "to live in security," which is common in omen literature as a favorable apodosis. See van der Spek 2003: 320; CAD A2:386 and N2: 151. ישב is cognate of *ašābu* in this phrase (see von Soden 1985: 1480). Thanks to Sebastian Fink for discussing this with me. Boda 2016: 132 sees it as a reference to Isa 14.

88. E.g., JPS translation; Ackroyd 1968: 176; Hanhart 1998: 81; Floyd 2000: 351, a "reproachful complaint"; Blenkinsopp 2013: 84; Boda 2016: 133, where he calls it a "lament." Bedford 2001: 165 calls it a lament as well, but he notes that that is merely part of a standard procedure for temple rebuilding.

89. Cf. Floyd 2000: 256.

90. I.e., the god's presence in the temple is necessary for a land's prosperity—closely linked to the topics of divine abandonment and resultant distress in the land. See, e.g., *Babylon Prism A* (Leichty 2011: no. 104, esp. i 34–ii 9 [p. 196]; including an intention to abandon for 70 years), *Babylon Prism D* (ibid, no. 114, esp. i 19–ii 11 [p. 236]), *Babylon Prism B* (ibid., no. 116 [pp. 244–5]), *Seed of Kingship* (Frame 1995: 23–28, Nabonidus's *Harran Stele* as well as his mother's (Schaudig 2001: 496–513); the *Marduk Prophecy* (Neujahr 2012: 27–41). Cf. Cogan 1974: 11–21.

The force of this section, then, is clearly the renewed cultic importance of Jerusalem. It gives more detail to what YHWH's return means. Given the ruined state of Jerusalem and the administrative loci, this assertion is more surprising than it appears in hindsight. Indeed, if the setting is the governor's complex at Ramat Raḥel, one might have expected a focus on Bethel, Mizpah, or Ramat Raḥel itself, instead.

Vision of Four Horns (2:1–4 [Eng 1:18–21])

In this vision, Zechariah sees four horns, which are identified as "the horns that tossed Judah, Israel, and Jerusalem." Though the precise form of the horns has occasioned debate,[91] the lack of clarity in form is rather suitable for a dream-reporting context. In any case, their significance is clear. Horns are a well-worn ANE symbol of strength and power, particularly military and divine power, attested across space and time on the helmets of gods and kings, altars, bulls, and in literary metaphors.[92] Whether envisioned as floating unattached, on some sort of stand, or attached to an animal, the metaphor for raw (and potentially oppressive) power remains. For a province still within a satrapy essentially identical to the Neo-Babylonian Empire, the implications are quite clear: the power structure is changing. The agents of this change are no doubt the Persians, even if the image of craftsmen depends on an older, heavenly tradition.[93]

The horns are followed by four craftsmen,[94] said to come to "terrify" these horns (להחריד). Interestingly, Zechariah does not ask the latter's identity, merely what they have come to do. This presumably means he knew who these figures were, perhaps drawing on a tradition of divine craftsmen.[95] Though the syntax of v. 4 is clunky, the message is clear—

---

91. Niditch 1980: 124; Petersen 1984: 162, 165; Tiemeyer 2015: 57–95; Boda 2016: 158–60.

92. For some handy overviews, see Süring 1980, 1984; Keel 1999: 221–3, 2013: 123–34; Niditch 1980: 121–6; for the relevant imagery, see also Staubli 2015b, though his interpretation of Zech 4 is far-fetched in this author's opinion. The author is grateful to Izaak de Hulster for discussing this.

93. Boda 2016: 156 sees the force as either Persia or divine, but on 165 sees the focus to be Persia.

94. The translation of חרש in this context is debated, with some favoring some sort of artisan and some favoring ploughmen. See the overviews in Tiemeyer 2015: 96–9; Boda 2016: 163–4.

95. E.g., Kotar-wa-Hasis (Handy 1994: 132–5, 144–7; Tiemeyer 2015: 99); Hephaestus (e.g., Aeschylus, *Prometheus Bound* lines 1–80; Hesiod, *Theogony* line 925); Tvastr (West 2010: 155–7); Weland (*Beowulf* 455); Kāva the Blacksmith (*Shahnameh*, Omidsalar 2013).

the punishment of the nations which persecuted Judah and Israel is being effected. In the present context, this answers the previous vision's notice that they had overdone Judah and Israel's punishment. This again probably primarily has Babylonia in view.[96]

Overall, this vision is closely tied to the previous one, providing "comfort" in the form of the *Schadenfreude* missing from the previous vision.

Vision of a Measuring Line (2:5–17 [Eng. 2:1–13])

The next vision takes up the image of a measuring rope (חבל מדה). The use of rope for measurement within construction is widely attested in Mesopotamia and Egypt, though its precise iconographical depiction is debatable. Ezekiel's temple vision depicts a heavenly figure with a linen cord and measuring rod (Ezek 40:3), and Horowitz has argued that both this Zechariah vision and Ezekiel's are examples of the use of rope within building contexts, even though they use different terminology.[97] Depictions of measuring ropes are extant from Egyptian tomb reliefs, both as stretched and coiled.[98] Depiction within the Mesopotamian tradition is more uncertain. Several scholars aver that the widespread iconography of a king or deity holding a ring and rod represents a coiled measuring rope and cubit rod.[99] However, the most certain cases are Sumerian.[100] Later depictions are more ring-like, and thus may not represent the same thing (see fig. 4.2).[101] However one interprets it, it is a symbol closely associated with temple building and divine approval. Here it is applied to the proper foundation of the city of Jerusalem.[102]

The narrative pattern of Zechariah and the interpretive angel's queries is altered here. Zechariah directly speaks to and receives an answer from the man holding the measuring line.

---

96. Boda 2016: 26 has a similar view. Ackroyd 1968: 178 rather thinks it is less specifically "the totality of the hostile nations of the world."

97. Hurowitz 1992: 326–7. Stead 2009: 109 claims this is an "unmistakable allusion"—which is itself mistaken.

98. Paulson 2005: 4.

99. Kuhrt 1995: 1:111; Jackobsen 1987: 4; Slanski 2007 sees it as also representing a peg and line (47, 51).

100. Depiction on the stele of Ur-Nammu (Pritchard 1954: 98 [no. 306]) and in the Sumerian version of the *Descent of Inanna*, line 19 (Pritchard 1969: 53).

101. Abram 2011: 24; cf. Pritchard 1954: 175, 178.

102. Floyd 2000: 364 thinks rather that it refers to the progression of the work on the temple.

Figure 4.2. *Rod and Ring on the Stele of Hammurabi*

It is almost as if the mediating angel did not want to disclose information to Zechariah, and has to be prodded (vv. 7–8). An extra angel appears in the scene as well, with no necessary purpose (v. 7). This is followed by a lengthy set of oracles (vv. 8–17). The oracles expound the return of YHWH in terms of security. The security will be such that Jerusalem will not require physical walls (vv. 8–9)—indeed, it will be safer than Babylonia (vv. 10–13) and attractive to the nations (vv. 14–15). The latter is phrased very inclusively, with the nations becoming part of YHWH's people (והיו לי לעם). The use of the measuring line imagery links this to royal preparations for city-building; divine permission was necessary for the success of city building projects, just as it was for temples.

YHWH promises to inherit Judah as his portion "on the holy ground" (על אדמת הקדש). This phrasing is very curious—the only other collocation of קדש with אדמה (rather than with ארץ) in the HB is for the location of the burning bush in Exodus (Exod 3:5). In Exodus this phrase highlights the presence of the divine; in practical terms, one wonders what it might mean—temple property? In any case, despite the lack of xenophobia in v. 15, a special relationship exists between YHWH and Judah, Jerusalem in particular. The key factor here is decidedly the temple, as emphasized by the concluding use of "his holy habitation" in v. 17 (מְעוֹן קָדְשׁוֹ). The current order of the oracles is not the most logical rhetorically. Placing vv. 14–16 between vv. 9 and 10 would make it flow more naturally. In any case, the current text has the interpreting angel reporting a twofold message that answers the concerns in the first vision: restoration of Jerusalem and the punishment of Babylon. There are two surprising aspects to this restoration. The first is a focus on Jerusalem itself over the land as a whole or the temple. The second is that despite the urban focus, no walls are deemed necessary.

An unclear verse (v. 12) complicates an understanding of how Babylon's punishment is depicted, perhaps as the result of some textual corruption.[103] The crux is the phrase אחר כבוד, "after glory." It is possible to see it as referring to the habitation of the temple by YHWH (cf. Hag 2:7). It is also possible to wonder if there is a connection between the use of "glory" here and the Achaemenid use of the concept of *farnah* (*xᵛarənah*), the divine glory that manifests itself in victory and prosperity.[104] Perhaps it is best to see it as another outcome of standard temple theology: there are positive results for a land when a deity is happily inhabiting a temple (and thus negative ones for its enemies).

This vision, then, makes a very strong case for the cultic and national importance of Jerusalem, making its rebuilding a sign of divine approval.

The Vetting of Joshua (3:1–10, 4:6b–10a)[105]

The form of this chapter is distinct from the other visions, lacking the typical visionary formula at the beginning. Moreover, it seems the oracular pronouncements at the end have somehow been displaced into the middle of the subsequent vision. This discussion will treat the vision as consisting of ch. 3 plus 4:6b–10a.[106]

---

103. The JPS translation favors emendation; Petersen 1984: 173, 177 n. d expresses dissatisfaction with all proposals for understanding it; Hanhart 1998: 118 offers several options; Boda 2016: 201–2 lists various options offered for understanding the phrase.

104. On the issue of *farnah*, see Silverman 2012: 73–5; 2016c: 176–8.

105. This section draws on the author's previous arguments in Silverman 2014a.

106. Since Wellhausen 1893: 41–2, 177, 4:6b–10a are often seen as a secondary intrusion into ch. 4, e.g., Ackroyd 1968: 173; Butterworth 1992: 68, 79, 236; Meyers

Verses 6b–10a have been a crux since Wellhausen, with most scholars agreeing that it is intrusive to its current setting in ch. 4, though there is no consensus on its origins. Wellhausen placed it at the end of ch. 4, but provided no reasons for doing so.[107] Halpern posits that a scribal error transposed it from ch. 3 to ch. 4, due to the repetition of "seven eyes."[108] The NEB translation of 1970 also rearranged the text of chs. 3–4, but more dramatically, with 4:1–3, 11–14 preceding 3:1 and 4:4–10 afterwards. Here it is treated as belonging after 3:10, since it reads more smoothly. Moving 4:6b–10a not only clarifies ch 4, but it also places all the "stone" oracles together. Halpern's suggestion of a scribal error seems reasonable.

This is the first section to address particular, named individuals, mentioning Joshua and (with the addition from ch. 4) Zerubbabel by name. The scene is one of a confirmation hearing for Joshua as "Great Priest" for the temple in Jerusalem. He stands before the Angel of YHWH as before a satrap, with an administrative adversary, the satan, paralleling likely Achaemenid structures.[109] He is given signs of honor (elite [not priestly!] robes, diadems),[110] and is granted the right to "rule"[111] the temple, its courts, and to have access to the attendants of YHWH (i.e.,

and Meyers 2004: 267; Floyd 2000: 328, 381; O'Kennedy 2003: 375–6; Blenkinsopp 2013: 91–2, 96; Boda 2016: 264–5, though some scholars periodically argue for the unity of ch. 4 (e.g., Tigchelaar 1996: 24; Bruehler 2001).

107. Wellhausen 1893: 177.

108. Halpern 1978: 169–70 nn. 11 and 13.

109. See the arguments in Silverman 2014a, e.g., 24: "the Satan in Zech 3 corresponds to the satrap's officers who leveled legal objections against official nominees within the satrapal administration, when one combines the picture of the mechanisms portrayed in Tiribazus's trial with the logistical necessities implied by Pheredates and the hints of such offices in the Bactrian archives. Joshua is depicted as receiving royal favor predicated on loyalty, but does so before YHWH's royal proxy, the Angel of YHWH, paralleling the satrap as the Great King's proxy. The demonstration of loyalty likely involved some sort of loyalty oath and possibly even a specific ceremony."

110. As argued in Silverman 2014a, robes and jewelry are well attested signs of Achaemenid royal favor (Briant 2002: 302–38; Brosius 2007: 39, 54–7). Since the language in ch. 3 does *not* match that in the priestly legislation of the Pentateuch (and the terms appear in Isa 3:18–23 and Job 29:14 in elite contexts), it is better to see the significance here elite status rather than priestly status *per se*. Contra such scholars as VanderKam 2004: 27; Fried 2004: 203. Subsequently, Wöhrle 2016: 185–6 has also rightly noted that the clothing is not priestly, though his assertion that it is therefore royal is mistaken, predicated more on an idea that priestly rule develops in Yehud than in the text itself. For the social implications, see Allen 2005: 87–96.

111. "Rule" is actually דין, "judge, advocate for," and is paired with שמר, "guard."

the heavenly court). The particular occasion for this decision appears to be a preparation for the temple building rituals—the ceremonial use of an object variously referred to as "a stone with seven eyes" (3:9), "excellent stone" (4:7), and "stone of distinction" (4:10). It is most likely—whatever the exact ritual correspondences one finds—that these verses relate to the numerous rituals around temple construction in the ANE.[112]

A key element in this is the declaration of divine support for the project in 4:6b–7: the work will proceed by divine effort and not by human military might, which is quite a departure from pre-exilic theophany traditions, associated with Davidic kingship as they are.[113] This is particularly striking given the heavy resonances the text so far has had with Zion traditions. The choice of this temple site is not due to military victory.

Similarly, these oracles to Zerubbabel also appear to happen in the context of a sign act or perhaps a ritual, implying an origin in "cultic prophecy" or at least the re-use of prophecy in a ritual context.

A major crux is the meaning of this sign act—the bringing of "my servant, growth" (צמח, 3:8).[114] The majority of commentators point to Jeremiah and see this as a "messianic" promise, whether with a capital or small "m."[115] However, the primary usage of the root צמח in the HB is one of prosperity, not rulership, and 3:10 is explicitly about prosperity.[116] Moreover, the context of the sign act is in the confirmation of the high priest and the rituals within temple rebuilding. This is a peculiar place to promise a king—in fact, temple building typically *required* a king, rather than being an occasion to call for one. What would be needed, therefore, was authorization of Zerubbabel to fulfill this kingly function, despite not being one.

The key observation for the moment is that YHWH *is bringing* (participle) the Growth, and that this assures that Zerubbabel will be able to fulfill the kingly duty of temple construction. This is clear without

---

112. Bruehler 2001: 436; Ellis 1968: 177; Petersen 1984; Halpern 1978: 170–7; Laato 1994; 1997: 198–200; Floyd 2000: 381; Blenkinsopp 2013: 93–4; Tiemeyer 2015: 172; Boda 2016: 266–9; see Ambos 2013a.

113. On the complex of ideas around holy war, the divine warrior, and theophany, see von Rad 1959; Weiss 1966; Cross 1973: 91–111. This is quite unlike Haggai (e.g., Sauer 1967; Kessler 2002: 173–86). Already, Pomykala has noted the tenuousness of the Davidic links in Haggai and 1Zech (Pomykala 1995: 45–60).

114. Cf. Rose 2000: chapter 3 (esp. p. 106) on the root not meaning "branch."

115. Jer 23:5; 33:15. Ackroyd 1968: 190–1; Petersen 1984: 210; Laato 1997: 202; Rose 2000: chapter 3 on a future referent; Meyers and Meyers 2004: 202–4; Tiemeyer 2003: 2; Redditt 2008: 61; Blenkinsopp 2013: 91; Boda 2016: 245–5.

116. Cf. Floyd 2000: 375; Rose 2000: 106.

the need to import meanings from other texts. Therefore the sign act is promising that צמח will authorize the placement of the stone during the temple's construction, thereby authorizing it. What is it that is being brought? Typically commentators think that Growth is a person, whether Zerubbabel or a messianic Davidide. However, it could also simply be the personification of a metaphor for prosperity. The identity of צמח will be discussed further below.

Overall, however, this section concerns the suitability and legitimacy of the re-founded priesthood and temple administration, as well as of the process itself. It is a vision which uses ANE law and structures as they were adapted by the Achaemenids to ensure and maintain loyalty throughout their large realm. Originally "the satan" was not "demonic" at all, merely a functionary designed to ensure local officials were unlikely to commit treason against their overlords. This was a separate function from the informers known as the "King's Eye," though, of course, their jobs were related and perhaps sometimes combined in particular individuals. In Zech 3 (and Job 1–2) this political and administrative role was combined with the previous heavenly council tradition and translated into a heavenly realm.[117] It projects the Achaemenid system into the heavens, and justifies the people involved in the temple's construction, despite the provincial status of Yehud. Moreover, it promises that non-kingly Zerubbabel will indeed be able to complete a task that required a king—temple building.

Vision of Lampstand and Olive Trees (4:1–14*)[118]

Rare or unique vocabulary and syntax have made this vision a matter of considerable debate over what exactly the envisioned objects were.[119] The appeals of North and of Petersen to archaeological finds of seven-spouted clay oil lamps provides a logical basis for understanding the image.[120] It is worth noting that the description here does not seem to match the well-known (though considerably later) depiction of the temple menorah on the arch of Titus (see fig. 4.3). However one decides the exact form of the lampstand envisioned, it is key to note with Tiemeyer that it is different from the descriptions of the cultic lampstands in both Exod 25 and 1 Kgs 7. She favors the idea that the vision here follows

---

117. Silverman 2014a: 26.
118. Many commentators accept the intrusiveness of vv. 6b–10b. See n. 106 above.
119. Discussed in North 1970.
120. Petersen 1984: 219–23; Niditch 1980: 91–3; North 1970; Sussman 2016 catalogues one Bronze Age, three Iron Age, and one Persian-era seven-spouted lamp (295, 385, 393), nos. 836, 1145–7, and 1501.

no previous model.¹²¹ The vision depicts a golden lampstand holding seven lamps, each with seven pinches for wicks, with two olive trees flanking it, apparently directly providing oil to the lamps through two gold tubes with human oil pressers (v. 12).¹²² Though opaque for modern readers, the first person narrator does not find the description at all odd; rather, he only questions the significance of the image (v. 4). The two identifications given by the angel are, however, also opaque. The first is the identification of the lampstand with "the seven eyes of the Lord ranging over the whole earth" (v. 10b). The second is the trees as the two "sons of oil."

Figure 4.3. *Panel from the Arch of Titus*

The eyes of the Lord are presumably another way of referring to YHWH's all-knowing capacity, in a different guise from the first vision. Lamps as a symbol for sight/vision is a readily understandable association. One might compare such usage to the Mesopotamian lamps for Nusku, who watches in the night.¹²³ This interpretation is shared by many

---

121. Tiemeyer 2015: 153.
122. Following the reading of Wolters 2012.
123. Ehrenberg 2002: 59; Hageneuer 2008; Lenzi 2011: 179–88; Nusku was also associated with the elimination of nightmares, Butler 1998: 188–90.

scholars.[124] Such an understanding is not dependent on the lampstand representing the temple menorah, since it is simply based on the associations of lamps and light.[125]

The "sons of oil" have garnered much less consensus. A common misdirection in interpretation is caused by the translation of this phrase as "anointed ones," fueling the messianic speculations of biblical theological wont. However, as commonly recognized, the word for oil here is the wrong type of oil for anointing, יצהר rather than שמן.[126] Rather, the use of oil clearly refers both to the olive trees and their provision of oil to the lamps.[127] But what does this mean? Lecanomancy is briefly alluded to in Gen 44 (esp. vv. 4, 15). This could be one way to understand the "sons of oil," since Akkadian uses a similar term "lords of oil" for lecanomancees.[128] If one opted for this interpretation, it would likely relate the passage to the process for determining the proper (auspicious) times for the various stages of temple building.[129] This is not a very attractive option, since timing is not the issue within this vision.

Moreover, they are called "attendants of the Lord of the earth" (אדון כל־הארץ). Surprisingly, given the basic nature of the words, the exact phrase "lord of all the earth" is quite rare in the HB, only occurring six times, twice in 1Zech. In each case the context implies YHWH as king, judging multiple peoples. In Josh 3:11, 13, it is in the crossing of the Jordan, as a sign of the upcoming dispossession of the seven Canaanite peoples. In Mic 4:13 it is in the context of crushing many peoples and extracting their wealth. In Ps 97:5 it praises YHWH as king who will melt the mountains.

---

124. E.g., Oppenheim 1968: 175–6; Silverman 2012: 172–3; Tiemeyer 2015: 158. Floyd 2000: 382 rather calls it "the sacramental representation of YHWH's influential involvement in human affairs." This of course depends on the identification of this lampstand with the one in the temple; Sweeney 2000: 612–13 sees it as "divine presence" that sees the whole world.

125. Keel 2007: 1018–20 has appealed to seals of moon symbols flanked by branches, but as the moon is not here, this seems infelicitous, and is based anyway on the cycle being set at "Himmelstor."

126. Van der Woude 1974: 264–5; Petersen 1984: 230–1; Tigchelaar 1996: 40; Rose 2000: 188–95; Boda 2016: 314–17.

127. Also emphasized by Strand 1982: 258; Tiemeyer 2015: 160.

128. *Bel-šamnim* is used for the customer, see Pettinato 1966: 1:40.

129. On lecanomancy, see Koch 2015: 134–8. It is attested for kings, patients, and endeavors, but always in conjunction with extispicy. She cites KAR 151, BBR 79–82, and an inscription of Sargon. A dubious passage in Strabo (XVI.2.39) mentions lecanomancy and hydromancy among the Persians. Cf. Pettinato 1966; Koch 2005: 39–45, 293–5.

In the other occurrence in 1Zech (6:5) it is in the context of imperial surveillance (and judgment of the north). The term would therefore seem to carry an imperial connotation.[130]

Attendants had previously appeared in ch. 3 for the members of YHWH's courts, to which Joshua would have access. Thus the two olive trees with their figures and branches would appear to symbolize two heavenly figures in YHWH's courts—the multiplicity of images is consonant with dream experience. These two attendants are intimately responsible for the enabling of the lamp's functioning, or YHWH's spy network.[131] These sound like two "right hand men" of YHWH—like viziers or spymasters. That such an image is built on the Persian Empire is highly likely given the unusual phrasing (see below). Therefore, the import of the vision overall would seem to be the imperial power of YHWH, one which enables close surveillance of his realm. This power, however, is intimately supported by two, as yet mysterious, figures. The relation of this to the temple is actually not as straightforward as the typical translation of the lampstand as *menorah* implies. If it does recall the temple at all, it takes a temple symbol and uses it as a sign of YHWH's solid imperial control. The implication is the supreme importance of this particular temple, since it would seem to mirror the mechanisms whereby YHWH remained abreast of his dominions. Thus, the nuance of control is noteworthy.

In this regard, two imperial contexts are worth recalling. First, the two trees are reminiscent of the garden or paradise setting. Beyond the setting of the governor's court (as argued above and below), in the Achaemenid context, this has very strong royal links.[132] Moreover, the use of יצהר for oil highlights a concern with prosperity, as did the use of צמח above.[133] Second, temples in Mesopotamia and Egypt played an important role within the administration of those satrapies.[134] The link between YHWH's eyes and the lampstand—if linked to the temple—would, therefore, imply

---

130. Note there are a few similar but not identical epithets in Gen 42:30; Isa 28:33; 54:5; and Jer 46:10.

131. Opinions on the purpose (and identity) of the two figures are quite varied. While Ackroyd 1968: 193 thought that their identity as Joshua and Zerubbabel "could not be doubted," it has indeed been doubted, cf. the overview in Tiemeyer 2015: 159–65 (her own opinion of two unspecified divine assembly members, pp. 163–5). Fried 2004: 205 suggested they were two seraphim in YHWH's court; Tigchelaar 1996: 45 thinks they ensure the presence of YHWH; Boda 2016: 314 fertility and plenty; Hanhart 1998: 253–4, 295–302; Curtis 2006: 137.

132. E.g., Tuplin 1996: 80–131; Brown 2001: chapter 21; Henkelman 2008: 427–41; Morvillez 2014; Silverman 2015a: 432–4; Silverman 2016c: 178–83.

133. Petersen 1984: 230.

134. See the overview in chapter 6.

a similar function for the Jerusalem temple vis-à-vis YHWH as subject temples for the Great King. It is an institution both for the production of prosperity as well as a site for administrative control. More important is the structure of control and resulting prosperity.

Vision of Flying Scroll (5:1–4)

In an image that immediately recalls Ezekiel (Ezek 2:9–3:3), Zechariah next sees a flying scroll. It is of massive proportions (20 × 10 cubits, c. 10.5 m × 5.25 m), the same dimensions as the previous temple portico (1 Kgs 6:3[135]). The similarity in size, however, may just be coincidental.[136] As if making up for the excessive number of questions in the previous vision, the angel offers an interpretation without being asked. The scroll itself is said to be a curse going out over the entire land against thieves and liars. The function of a written scroll as a curse like this is very reminiscent of magical practice in the ANE (cf. Num 5), where the writing itself was effective.[137] The use of numinous writing is more likely in the residually oral culture of early Persian Yehud than an appeal to a later idea of (sacred) scripture.[138] This scroll will, however, consume the perpetrators' homes rather than the people themselves. The most immediate image this brings to mind is the threat imputed to Darius in Ezra 6:11, though that also includes impalement. The vision appears to be making a declaration about the contemporary social structure, declaring it to be one for the thriving of lawfulness, more than having individual delinquents in view. The identities of these offenders are unspecified, and it is uncertain whether this ought to be directly relatable to contemporary social conflict. The fact that the curse is made against homes could make one think that it reflects battles over houses between returnees and remainees in the land.[139] Nevertheless, there is no evidence of large numbers of returnees to Yehud, and the relatively sparse population should have made such problems easily solvable.[140] Therefore, this is an unlikely reading.

135. Which Ezek 40:49 gives as 20 × 11 cubits.

136. Cf. Tiemeyer 2015: 192. Nonetheless this observation does not require following Friedman's suggestion that the dimensions reference a text column, as she does. Tiemeyer is right, however, to note that the temple link is unnecessary here, and that in a visionary context not all details are necessarily meaningful.

137. E.g., PGM VII.703–26, 740–55, two rituals using writing of incantations as part of the ritual (Betz 1986: 138–9). Cf. Tigchelaar 1996: 56; Niditch 1980: 84.

138. Contra Floyd 2000: 389; Meyers and Meyers 2004: 285; Curtis 2006: 140.

139. As Keel 2007: 1016 thinks.

140. Contra, e.g., Kessler 2006: 137; he bases his overall view on the narrative in Ezra, which is the main prompt to read Zech 5 in this manner.

Instead, the vision would seem to address the appropriateness of the timing for the return of YHWH, cleansing the land to make it suitable. The two specific offenses, theft and lying, are of course condemned elsewhere in the HB.[141] They appear as a pair as well (Lev 19:11), but appearing as the chief cause for concern is noteworthy. Curtis suggests the two offenses are meant to invoke the entirety of the Ten Commandments.[142] This is unlikely and unnecessary, given that both are common concerns.

The meaning in v. 3 is unclear, perhaps corrupt, though within the context it would seem to indicate that written prohibitions are visible on both sides of the scroll (with מזה...מזה as an idiom for this).[143] However, despite Boda and Tiemeyer, it is hard to understand how a curse could indicate something positive and yet be used negatively (against perpetrators). It seems best therefore to read נקה as a niphal and thus as "purged." Thus the curse is another way of stating that the time of YHWH's anger is over and the time of his return is at hand.[144]

Overall, this vision re-establishes the necessary moral order within the land, one suitable for the renewed presence of YHWH. Perhaps the two offenses chosen are indicative of contemporary social strife, but they could equally be metonyms for proper social order.

Vision of 'Ephah (5:5–11)

This vision is particularly obscure.[145] Zechariah sees a moving *'ephah*— presumably a container of said size (c. 19–21 liters).[146] Accepting the LXX reading (which only requires emending the MT's י to ו, and thus easily just a scribal copying error),[147] the angel declares it to be the iniquity in the land. This *'ephah* contains a woman, identified as wickedness, and she is

---

141. Theft: Exod 21:37–22:12; Lev 19:11, 13; Deut 5:17; lying: Lev 19:11; Prov 12:22; 14:25; 17:7.

142. Curtis 2006: 140; cf. Floyd 2000: 389; Boda 2016: 324.

143. See the useful discussions in Tiemeyer 2015: 195–9; Boda 2016: 332–3.

144. Supposedly this is treated by Craz 2016, but I have not been able to access it.

145. However, Assis 2010's attempt to read it as an anti-Samaritan polemic imports anachronistic concerns into the vision.

146. A wide variety of correspondences for this are given (cf. Boda 2016: 343). The calculation of 19–21 liters comes from a jar in Lachish with an inscription "1 bath" and the claim in Ezek 45:11 that 1 *'ephah* = 1 bath. See Kletter 2014: 29, 31. Thanks to Raz for discussing this matter with me. According to Ezek 43:13, this is equivalent to six days of wheat offerings. Uehlinger 1994: 94–6 prefers 32 l based on a "sackformigen, vier-henklingen Pithos" from Mizpah.

147. Floyd 1996: 55; 2000: 391, however, emphasizes that the LXX is not conclusive, given the readings of the Latin and Targums. Ackroyd 1968: 204 favors

sealed into the *'ephah* by the angel. Two females with stork wings carry it off to build a temple for it in "the land of Shinar."

It is hard not to see some sort of anti-goddess polemic in this vision, since it involves the removal and worship of a small female figure and given the strong HB antipathy to goddess worship. This is a common opinion.[148] The specific cause and meaning remains elusive, however. The reason for the *'ephah* as the vessel is not apparent, nor the reason for the use of the archaic "land of Shinar" instead of Babylon. The building of a Judaean temple in Babylonia—whether for YHWH alone or YHWH and Asherah or Anat—is not in itself implausible. It should be remembered in this context that the temple at Elephantine certainly venerated at least one goddess alongside YHWH: Anat, attested in two forms.[149] If this vision was addressing a specific contemporary context, then the building of a diasporic temple is a plausible cause—and clearly this text disapproves. The connection between this and a supposed religious revolution in Yehud[150] is highly uncertain, however.

An alternate explanation is that the woman represents an anti-Queen Mother or royal consort polemic. In the pre-exilic kingdoms of Israel and Judah it appears that royal women could be significant powerbrokers.[151] Given the nature of royal exile, the Davidic queens and princesses could have played important roles.[152] Nevertheless, the lack of royal language or imagery in this vision makes this interpretation unlikely.

Another potential explanation, if one keeps the MT's "eye" in v. 6, is that the passage refers to the removal of something cultic that the Neo-Babylonians had placed in Yehud as part of their administrative surveillance efforts. However, as there is no extant evidence to this effect, this interpretation also appears unlikely. Alternately, a similar line of interpretation could be that the vision is the removal of a Babylonian

---

the LXX; Boda 2016: 345 prefers the MT, as being more difficult; Tiemeyer 2015: 213–19 for various options for understanding this (she also ultimately favors the MT).

148. E.g., Ackroyd 1968: 205; Uehlinger 1994: esp. 94; Floyd 1996; Edelman 2003. Knowles 2006: 25, thinks the point is geographic rather than the object of worship. While there is a geographic aspect, the calling of the object "wickedness" implies a critique of said object.

149. Anat-Yahu: AP 44 (TAD B7.3); Anatbethel: AP 22 (TAD C3.15). Further, van der Toorn has recently argued that Amherst Papyrus 63 shows that at Elephantine Yaho was identified with Bethel, making the consort nature of Anat even clearer. See van der Toorn 2016.

150. On this issue, see Frevel, Pyschny, and Cornelius 2014; Hulster 2017.

151. Smith 1998.

152. See chapter 2; Osborne 2011; Hughes and Sanders 2011.

cult statue from Jerusalem to Babylon. If the figure had been placed there by Nebuchadnezzar like Zeus would be by Antiochus IV, then its removal would be necessary and welcome by the Judaeans. Its return to Babylon could also be welcomed by the Babylonians (cf. the *Cyrus Cylinder*). Nevertheless, this is only speculation, as there is no evidence for Neo-Babylonian imposition of cult statues or images on subjects, or of one being in Jerusalem. Alternately, one could speculate that a statue of the Queen of Heaven had been set up on the site by Judaeans, as implied in Jer 44. The vision would then wish to see it removed (and thus a more specific cause of an anti-goddess polemic as suggested above).

Figure 4.4. *Astarte Throne with Mischwesen (Sphinx), Beirut (DGA 20567)*

The *'ephah* is carried away by two women with stork-like wings (v. 9). At present, this is the only extant ANE text with a *Mischwesen* with stork wings, thus the imagery here is obscure. The significance of the stork reference itself is also unclear. The Hebrew name (חסידה) suggests a positive connotation for the creature, and one would suspect popular etymologies would have connected it with חסד, whether or not the word had any real historical relationship. Although only sporadically appearing in the HB,[153] the stork seems to have been a well-known bird

---

153. Lev 11:19; Deut 14:18; Ps 104:17; Job 39:13; Jer 8:7.

in the ANE.[154] Both kinds of stork which can be found in the ANE (white and black) are only present as migrants in spring and fall (see figs. 4.5a and 4.5b).[155] Interestingly, the vision cycle is dated to February, which is the beginning of the season in which storks fly north over Israel on their return to their European nesting grounds. The bird was known in Babylonia as *laqlaqqu*; one might wonder if this name suggests a cultural association with women, since the word referred both to the bird and to female genitals;[156] the Hebrew word itself was also grammatically feminine. Although the stork is classed as an unclean animal (Lev 11:19; Deut 14:18), this has no significance for the divine realm;[157] Isaiah saw winged serpents serving in heaven (Isa 6:2) despite the prohibition on snakes (Lev 11:42). Bryan argues that the use of *Mischwesen* in apocalyptic literature is designed to evoke chaos by crossing such boundaries,[158] but given the widespread use of such creatures in the ANE, in the Persian Empire, and in the HB (particularly the cherubs and seraphs), such a resonance is inappropriate for 1Zech (see fig. 4.4).[159] In his dream interpretation handbook Artemidorus claims that single storks signify good travel and children, but that groups of them signify partnerships, banditry, or enemies.[160] He gives no thought to a pair nor to *Mischwesen*. Given a lack of mythological significance, the mention of stork-like wings may only be due to the timing of the vision during

154. According to Alvarez-Mon, they might be depicted in the fourth register of the Arjan Bowl (from Neo-Elamite Elam, Álvarez-Mon 2004: 220), and they might be mentioned in a list of birds a lacunose section of the Deir 'Alla inscription (Combination 1, line 10, but the word itself is broken, Hallo 2000: 143 [2.27]).

155. Collins 2002: 60; Hancock, Kushlan, and Kahl 2001: 69–75, 97–102; Elphick 2007. This is the feature of interest to Jer 8:7.

156. Older form was *raqraqqu*; supposedly referencing the stork's call. See Black and Al-Rawi 1987: 122, 125; Oppenheim, Reiner, and Biggs 1973: 102.

157. Petersen 1984: 260 thinks the uncleanness of storks makes them appropriate for this task, but his example of eagles being equally unclean undercuts the force of this argument. The same is also true for their status as *Mischwesen*, since both seraphim and cherubim were also *Mischwesen* (contra Floyd 2000: 394). As a side note, storks were not forbidden in Mesopotamia, even if they were not typical table fare. See the note in Joannès 2009: 432.

158. He primarily intends the creatures in Dan 7, though he also discusses the bull with eagle wings in *T. Naph.* 5:6. See Bryan 1995.

159. Cf. Jeremias 1977, 199 (also nn. 18–19), who also thinks *Mischwesen* are normal ANE imagery. Cf. Pritchard 1954: nos. 644–71 (pp. 212–18). For convenient overviews of the iconography behind these, see Schmitt 2014; Hulster 2015, esp. 147–59.

160. *Oneirocritica* II.20 and IV.56, respectively (Harris-McCoy 2012: 189, 349).

a time when they would have been visible in Israel very high in the sky and heading north, just as the *'ephah* in the vision was heading northwards (to Shinar).[161] If one accepts real visionary origination, such an element corresponds well with the psychological functioning of image processing.[162]

Figure 4.5a. *Stork in Flight*

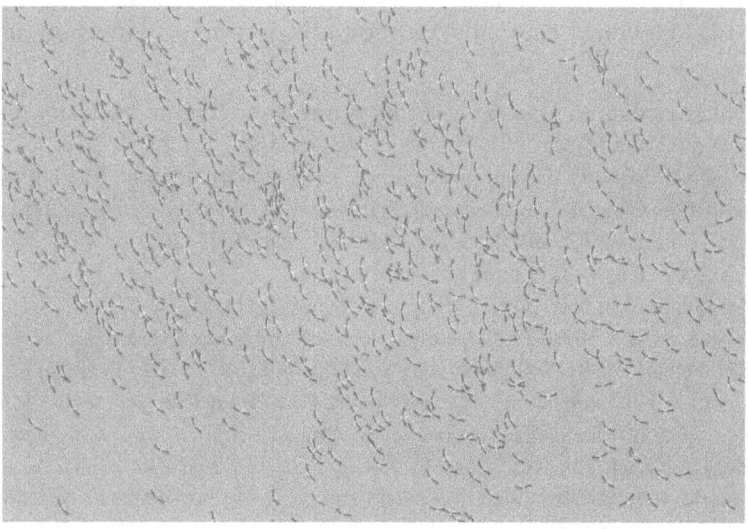

Figure 4.5b. *Flock of Migrating Storks (over Israel)*

161. This is the significance favored by Meyers and Meyers 2004: 307. Jeremias 1977: 200 rather favored their ability to fly long distances, but in principle not such a different sort of interpretation.

162. See below.

Tigchelaar in passing has picked up on a comment by Wright that this vision in Zechariah resembles an ANE phenomenon whereby evil is sealed in containers and disposed of, sometimes in enemy territory.[163] The logic behind this is simultaneously to remove evil as far away as possible as well as to harm an enemy. Wright has adduced a Hittite and a Mesopotamian ritual text in which evil is transferred specifically in the form of a figurine.[164] Whatever the specific nuances of the *'ephah*, the woman, and the storks, this provides an attractive overall meaning for the vision, one that answers a running concern of the vision cycle—the suitability of the land for YHWH's return. Moreover, it picks up a recurrent thread of *Schadenfreude* for Babylon. The fact that the figurine is set up in a shrine rather than buried or dropped into a river suggests that cultic polemic remains a likely element nevertheless.

Overall, following the previous visions, this vision again reinforces the importance of the Jerusalem site for a Yahwistic temple, and one seemingly without some element of worship that had previously been included, most probably a consort. This might be viewed as either a justification of present reality (i.e., a cult was presently being re-established in such a manner) or as programmatic (the prophetic instruction on how it should be done). This is a matter which requires further consideration.

Vision of Four Horsemen (6:1–8)

The last vision in the cycle returns to the idea of YHWH's control over the heavenly imperium, though the symbolism varies slightly in the details. It is best to see it, with Tiemeyer, as an independent vision rather than an inferior copy of the first one.[165] It plays an important rhetorical role in wrapping up the message of the vision cycle. Zechariah sees four chariots exiting the entrance of the divine abode, here delineated by two copper mountains.[166] The horses of the four chariots are again of different colors—though precisely which ones is decidedly unclear (possibly red, black, white, and spotted/grey).[167] They report to "the lord of the whole

---

163. Tigchelaar 1996: 61; Wright 1987: 254–6, 273 n. 150.

164. Wright 1987: 44 (Mulli ii 16'–25') and 69–72 (Namburbi, Caplice OR 36 1–8), though both rituals are more elaborate, including several more steps (such as bread).

165. Petersen 1984: 269; Tiemeyer 2015: 242.

166. E.g., Meyers and Meyers 2004: 319–20; Floyd 2000: 400; Boda 2016: 365–7. Curtis 2006: 143, rather, thinks they are two bronze pillars. Cf. Pritchard 1954: nos. 683, 685 (p. 220).

167. There are two lists of colors, in vv. 2 and 6, which do not match exactly. Moreover, the colors also vary in all the extant versions; for a helpful list with

earth" (as above) and each appears to be assigned to one of the four cardinal points. (Verses 6–7 are clearly corrupt and ought to be emended to finish the four directions and have the אדמים assigned to the east.¹⁶⁸) The trope of the four winds is well-known in Mesopotamia.¹⁶⁹ Thus this represents different imagery from the first vision, utilizing mythological imagery rather than contemporary reality. The point here comes in v. 8, where the chariot of the north is said to have הניחו את־רוחי. Boda sees this idiom as word-play, sound-play, and a reference to the previous vision, with רוח replacing חמא as in Ezekiel.¹⁷⁰ He cites Judg 8:3, Prov 16:32 and 29:11 for "spirit" as a synonym for anger. In these instances, however, רוח is more comprehensive than just anger, including both purpose and desire. Thus "satisfy my purposes" might be a better way to render the idiom.¹⁷¹ This directly answers the question in the first vision: the earth is indeed the way YHWH wants it, and the current status of Babylonia is in line with the divine will. The Judaean audience is likely to interpret this as having been or shortly to be punished. Nevertheless, in its current position it functions as a powerful support or justification of the political *status quo*. The punishment cycle ("the exile") is now finished. Though there is no formal marking, this is the last reported vision.

Sign Act in Temple (6:9–15)

Chapter 6 closes with an oracle commanding a sign act. According to Friebel's "rhetorical nonverbal communication" analysis,¹⁷² sign acts have three functions (informative, communicative, and interactive) and can be encoded as intrinsic, symbolic, or iconic.¹⁷³ For him, this analysis is necessary because sociological analyses miss the content and intentions

---

discussion, see Rignell 1950: 200–206. He raises the possibility of אמץ being related to חמוץ, "bright red," as in Isa 63:1. ברד would appear to mean "spotted" (Gen 31:10, 12); cf. Abernethy 2017.

168. Following Petersen 1984: 263–4 and Meyers and Meyers 2004: 325, contra Floyd 2000: 397, 400.

169. E.g., they appear in the *Enūma Eliš* I.r19'–21' (Oracc P338317) and the incantation SpTU 2, 013 r ii 26–7 (Oracc P348618). Cf. Dan 7:2 and the chariots depicted in Pritchard 1954: nos. 11, 172, 689 (p. 5, 53, 221); Neumann 1977; Niditch 1980: 148; Horowitz 1998: 91, 196–8, 298–9; Hulster 2015: 160, fig 7.22 (seal).

170. Boda 2016: 379–80. Ackroyd 1968: 182–3 entertains both "cause to rest" and "give satisfaction," but makes no clear decision.

171. Cf. Preuß 1998: 278; Koehler and Baumgartner 2001: 679. Cf. Qoh 7:9, 10:4. Cf. Floyd 2000: 397.

172. Friebel 2001. This is distinct from Searle's Sign-Act Theory.

173. Friebel 2001: 35–6, 38.

of such events, while a focus on "magical" or efficacious understandings misses the rhetorical or audience-influencing aspects. His paradigm does not deal with why a prophet would utilize a sign act instead of just an oracle, or indeed, in the context of 1Zech, a vision report. His categories should be useful for the analyses of the sign-act itself; however, this needs to be placed into its larger setting, which is the dedication and use of temple donations—the sign act itself is only one part of this scenario.

The oracle tells Zechariah to accept gifts of silver and gold from Judaeans who have arrived from Babylon, fashion them into crowns, perform a sign act with Joshua the priest by placing them on his head, issue a declaration, and store the crowns as memorials inside the temple. Four individuals are mentioned by name in v. 10 as donors, with a different list in v. 14. Demsky has suggested a title has been substituted in v. 14 ("treasurer," חן) for the fourth name[174]—if correct, this highlights the envisioned temple donation setting. It also implies a temple staff was already established, one which included a treasurer in addition to the great priest in ch. 3. (The remaining change from חלדי to חלם can possibly be accounted for as different forms of the same name or by textual corruption.[175])

An *unnamed number* of crowns are to be made, placed on Joshua's head, and left in the temple—a reasonable supposition would be four, one as a votive for each of the named donators. Otherwise, perhaps the number was merely to be based on the unspecified quantity of metals. Neither the number nor design of the crowns is mentioned, other than the use of silver and gold.[176] Use of silver with gold inlay or other elements for jewelry and utensils is attested within and around the Achaemenid Empire.[177]

174. Demsky 1981.
175. Boda 2016: 391 offers both of these options without making a decision either way. The assertion of Wöhrle that the difference between the two lists is due to a secondary hand raises the question why the second author was unable to copy the first list accurately, and thus is not explanatory at all (Wöhrle 2016: 182 n. 32).
176. If the MT is not emended, the passage merely mentions plural crowns. *Contra* most debate over this passage, there is no reason why the plural needs to be understood as two, which is then sometimes taken as evidence of a cover-up. If one accepts the plural reading, all that means is more than one is involved. For examples of scholars assuming plural means two, see Berquist 1995: 73; Boda 2016: 388 n. i, 394; Cook 1995: 135; Fried 2004: 204; Meyers and Meyers 2004: 349–51; Curtis 2006: 145, 147; Blenkinsopp 2013: 99–103; Ristau 2016: 158 n. 54.
177. E.g., a silver pin with gold pomegranate from Pasargadae (Stronach 1978: 178, pl. 160a); silver bowls with gold sheet (Curtis and Tallis 2005: 118 [no. 111]); silver rhytons with gold elements (Curtis and Tallis 2005: 122 [nos. 119, 120]); silver amphora handles with gold gilding (Curtis and Tallis 2005: 125 [nos. 127, 128]);

What significance or connotations do the crowns hold? As noted above, jewelry was a mark of royal favor and social standing within the empire. Though the evidence for the use of crowns within the empire is terminologically complicated, Henkelman has argued that for the Persians it was crenellations rather than a metal band around the head that was the distinguishing *royal* element.[178] Another use for crowns is attested by Arrian, in which they signify recognition of (Alexander's) military triumph.[179] The gift of a gold crown as a votive offering is also attested in Appian.[180] Within the enumeration of the names of Marduk in tablet VII of the *Enūma Eliš*, the name *Asaralimnunna* is interpreted as indicating "whose tiara increases abundance for the land," indicating a link to prosperity and wealth.[181]

From the biblical perspective, עטרת is not restricted to royal usage or connotation. First, it is worth noting that Est 8:15 has Mordecai given one by the Persian king as a sign of honor, in line with the above argument for elite robes in Zech 3. More generally, Ps 8:5 [Heb v. 6] uses it for YHWH's conferral of dignity on all humankind; Isa 28:1, 3 for the wealth of the "drunkards of Ephraim"; Ezek 23:42 on adulterous women and 16:12 in a list of elite clothing; Job 19:9 as a symbol of lost wealth, and Prov 4:9 as given by wisdom. *None of these uses imply royalty*, but rather wealth and elite status. This is similar to the nuance of the robe in ch. 3.

Donations to temples and votive offerings are well-attested in the ANE; perhaps most closely related in time and space is the temple at Gerizim.[182]

---

silver jar with gold wire (Treister 2010: 241]); silver statuettes with gold headgear from the Oxus Treasure (Dalton 2010: 75, 77 [nos. 1, 4]); a silver goose with gold eyes (p. 81, no. 5); a silver disk with plates of gold (87–9, no. 24), etc.

178. The crown prince and some courtiers are depicted on royal reliefs as wearing the same crown as the king. (Calmeyer 1993: §2; Roaf 1983: 131–3; note plate XXXV, with a noble wearing a dentate crown; Henkelman 1995/6: 276.) For a discussion of the complicated and variegated Greek terminology, see Tuplin 2007. He notes that the word in Esth 1:11, 2:17 is the same word as the Greek *kidaris*, possibly being the official Aramaic term.

179. Arrian, *Anabasis* I.24 (Arrian 1976: 105). Cf. Briant 2002: 855.

180. Appian, *Civil Wars* I.97 (on the basis of a dream; Appian 1913: 181; noted by Renburg 2003: 59).

181. Lines 5–8. Noted by Waerzeggers 2015a: 189; translation in Foster 1993: 1:391; Lambert 2008: 55–6; transliteration in Langdon 1923: 190–1. The epithet is also applied to Babylon in *Tintir* I, line 29, and refers to the usurpation of Marduk (see George 1992: 41, commentary 258–9). The significance here, however, is not the Sumerian epithet itself, but the commentary linking Marduk's tiara to prosperity.

182. Magen, Misgav, and Tsfania 2004. The problem with the inscriptions is the lack of context due to destruction and later building. However, they amply

Finds in the Persepolis Treasury evince a variety of (confiscated) gifts besides inscriptions, including such diverse objects as beads, cylinders, and plaques, that had perhaps adorned the statues of gods in their original temple settings.[183] Gudme has argued that such gifts can come in many forms, and be used for many different purposes.[184]

Figure 4.6. *Example Votive Inscription, Beirut (DGA 13201)*

The oracle tells what to use the offerings for, and thus the offerings are accepted as legitimate. Within biblical tradition, such gifts are often given for temple building or repairing;[185] v. 12 implies the building was yet to happen or at least to be completed. Indeed, a person named "growth" would build it, repeating the curious phrasing from ch. 3. This figure shall rule, and a priest (either by his right side or by his throne, MT/LXX)

demonstrate the custom of donations (and memorials) left in temples. Cf. Albertz and Schmitt 2012: 481; Frevel 2008; Gudme 2013. On inscriptions more broadly (related to dreams), see Renburg 2003.
183. Schmidt 1957: 56–65.
184. Gudme 2013; cf. Frevel 2008: 30.
185. Gudme 2013: 37–51.

will have "counsel of peace" (עצת שלום) with him. Moreover, men from afar will come to build (v. 15). This section has often been read either as an aborted messianic attempt (on the behalf of Zerubbabel) and/or as the usurpation of the kingship by the priesthood—neither, however, are actually in the text. Taking the sign-act and votive offerings seriously (see below) provides a more textually based understanding. Thus, the reading of this passage as a failed prophecy for Zerubbabel's coronation is little more than a figment of scholarly imagination—neither based in an extant text nor any external historical evidence that such an event occurred.[186]

The meaning of this sign act in its textual remnant turns on the identity of צמח and on the nature of עצת שלום. Skipping the issue of identity for the moment, the person is clearly a secular figure—a ruler whose job is to build the temple. Often translated "shoot," צמח connotations might be better displayed as "growth," given the root's use in contexts of prosperity and growth.[187] The use of משל is consonant with either kingship or lower forms of governance.[188] Further, this ruler's legitimacy is to be supported by the priest, who participates in the עצת שלום, a term which appears only here. Opposite sorts of constructs are attested in Ezek 11:2 (רע) and Ps 1:1 (רשעים). Given the broad connotations of שלום as the general state of proper, natural order, this phrase most likely denotes the general maintenance of society.[189]

The sign act itself consists of placing the unnumbered crowns on Joshua's head and saying an oracle to him. This is part of a much longer sequence of actions, since it is preceded by the fabrication of crowns and followed by their deposition in the temple as a memorial.

Using Friebel's categories, the function of the sign act is communicative and interactive: the message it conveys is that a ruler will build and rule the temple and its priesthood in harmony, and that this is divinely acceptable. The message is reinforced through the placing of them on Joshua's head and leaving them as memorials in the temple. For the former, this is like the Archbishop of Canterbury placing the crown on the English

---

186. *Contra* scholars such as Blenkinsopp 2013: 99–103. The idea that this text covers up a civil war over Zerubbabel's attempt for the throne is fanciful in the extreme (Sacchi 2004: 65–7).

187. See above.

188. See, *DCH* 5:531–7.

189. Petersen 1984: 278 thinks this is a subtle subordination of the priest, since advice is usually given by an inferior to a superior. But priests had always been subordinate to kings and governors. Meyers and Meyers 2004: 362 see it as both leaders being "divinely inspired." Boda 2016: 406–7 sees it as "positive council which promotes prosperity," similar to the view here, though he sees it in the context of investiture.

monarch's head as a sign of divine right of rule. The placing on Joshua's head therefore emphasizes the priesthood's duties to support this ruler in their position (rather than being the rulers, given that the priest is on the ruler's right-hand side). The latter is like any memorial. The intended response is obedience to the priest and to the "Growth." The encoding is iconic (or metonymic), with crowns functioning to signify divine approval and prosperity. The context of the sign-act is also informative socio-politically: the votive offerings come from the community in Babylon as well as from the temple staff (Hen). These appear to be a vanguard of sorts, given the proclamation in v. 15. This strongly implies an institutional context beyond just individual desires or prophetic urge. In other words, the Babylonian diaspora is in favor of the actions of "Growth" towards the temple and the priest.

Afterwards, the crowns are to be placed as a memorial in the temple (לזכרון בהיכל). If one observes the nearly contemporaneous practice at Gerizim, the votive inscriptions were placed on the wall just at the side of the presumed sacred area, where worshippers would be able to see them.[190] The bronze serpent on a pole (Nechushtan) in Num 21:8–9 and 2 Kgs 18:4 was also apparently a cult object within view of the people. Thus it seems these crowns were likely intended to be used as continual visual reminders for visitors to the temple, both for these four specific donators and for the overall message.

This may be deliberately intended to contrast the Mesopotamian practice whereby statues of the gods were adorned with clothes and jewelry,[191] be a practical outcome of a lack of cult statue on which to place the crowns, and/or simply be typical votive practice.[192] As Gudme has phrased it, by being placed in a publicly visible space, a memorial creates both vertical and horizontal social capital.[193]

Rather than messianic implications, the rhetorical force is temple-centric, but in the way common to the ANE: as part of the necessary fabric of the cosmos and of society, in which the temple supports and is supported by the social order. This is also one clearly seen as supported

---

190. Magen, Misgav, and Tsfania 2004: 14, most not *in situ*. Also note the mention of a satrap (no. 26, pp. 68–9).

191. For the clothing of divine statues, see especially Zawadzki 2006; cf. Waerzeggers 2010b: 137–9.

192. On votive practices, see Frevel 2008; Gudme 2012 and 2013. Gudme even notes the special association of votive offerings with temple construction or repair (48–9). Thus 1Zech seems to be saving gifts for a specific, non-constructive purpose in a context in which construction contributions were quite normal.

193. Gudme 2012: 12–13; cf. Frevel 2008: 26; he calls this "communicative."

by the Judaeans in Babylonia, whether the mentioned men are return migrants or just emissaries from the diaspora communities. However, an important aspect here is the use of gold and silver. The trade of gold in the Neo-Babylonian Empire was a professional prerogative, and in the Persian Empire, while local mints could coin silver and bronze, gold was reserved to the Great King.[194] In a province such as Yehud, large amounts of either would no doubt have had some form of imperial relation, as there would have been precious little bullion not intended either for taxes, payment of mercenaries, or as a gift from the state. Indeed, at present, no coins from the early Persian period are as yet attested in Yehud.[195] If this section is viewed as based on a real event of votive offerings from the diaspora, then it would likely have involved imperial approval, if only as permission for tax exemptions. One might speculate on royal support—but this is an issue for another context. For the present purpose, this pericope highlights and justifies the temple's position in the socio-political system: its role vis-à-vis the current regime and its relations with the Judaeans from Babylon. It also makes a strong claim for the validity of the temple beyond its local confines, since the Babylon diaspora are preemptively making votive offerings, despite the specter of their own polluted institution in ch. 5. (The identity of "Growth" will be discussed below).

In sum, this sign act places the temple within an important set of positive relations. It is divinely approved, approved by a ruler, approved by the Babylonian community, and in harmony with the reestablished priesthood. The sign act also arranges for a continual reminder of these relations to be visible to visitors to the site.

194. Alstola 2014: trade in gold restricted to professional merchants (though not necessarily only royal merchants). On royal merchants, see Dandamaev 1995. On Persian coins, Gariboldi has suggested that only the Great King was allowed to mint in gold (Gariboldi 2014: 131). In any case, local issues are all attested in silver. See Meadows 2005: 187–8, 200–208. It seems all the local Palestinian mints were only using silver or silver-plated bronze (Meshorer and Qedar 1999: 32; Lemaire 2015: 93; Farhi 2016: 64 n. 31). According to Farhi, even at Ramat Raḥel no coins prior to the third century have been found (in Lipschits, Gadot, and Freud 2016: 2:615).

195. The earliest attested local coins are in the fourth century. While Jursa (2014a: 123) suggests coins may have been used in Babylonia already by 545 BCE, Briant sees no Persian coinage before Darius I, with the earliest attestation being an imprint of the Daric in 500 BCE (Briant 2002: 408). Meshorer is of the opinion that minting began in Samaria only in 371 BCE (Meshorer and Qedar 1991: 66; 1999: 71). Cf. Schaper 2000: 153–61 (although I do not endorse his contention that the temple had its own mint). Recent excavations at Khirbet Qeiyafa evinced Cypriot coins from the sixth century, but Farhi thinks they arrived there only in the fourth century due to the stratigraphy and local coinages (Farhi 2016: 19).

An Inquiry Concerning Fasts (7:1–14) and Oracles of Prosperity (8:1–23)

This section is dated two years later (4/XI/Darius 4, 6 December 518). The occasion is an oracle inquiring of the priest of the house of YHWH and the prophets. Together with ch. 8 it addresses the themes raised in the introduction in ch. 1, as well as the proper conduct now that a temple (or functioning altar) exists (or is in process) again in Jerusalem.[196]

The issue of who made the inquiry is susceptible to several interpretations (MT and LXX disagree). Already suggested by Wellhausen,[197] it makes most grammatical sense to see the sender as Bethel-sar-ezer, presumably a local Neo-Babylonian official. "Bethel" is attested as a deity,[198] and -šar-uṣur is a common element in the names of royal officials.[199] Indeed, a Judaean in [Al-]Yāhūdu is attested with it (as Yahu-šar-uṣur in no. 4 and Bel-šar-uṣur in nos. 2 and 3),[200] besides being behind the new name given to Daniel (1.6). The delegation would appear to be Regem-melech and his men, with Regem-melech potentially being either a name or a title.[201] Therefore, it seems unwise to see a polemic against Bethel here, since it is likely just a theophoric name element. If Regem-melech is indeed a title, then this would imply that there is another level of imperial entanglement. However, the present author is unaware of any evidence that the Persians used the Neo-Assyrian title of Rab-Mag.[202]

The enquiry itself concerns the suitability of continued fasts for the destruction of the first temple in several months (Vth in 7:3; Vth and VIIth in v. 5; IVth, Vth, VIIth, and Xth in 8:19), though it is given a date in the XIth month. Since the fasts in 7:3 relate to the destruction, the trope of punishment is recalled, as well as previous failure to head it. The

---

196. This seems to be the implication, even though Ezra 6:15 claims the temple was not completed until 3/XII/Darius 6 (12 March 515). The reliability of Ezra's date, however, is open to doubt.

197. Wellhausen 1893: 180.

198. E.g., SAA 2 005 iv 6; acknowledged at Elephantine in two forms, in B7.2 and C3.15.

199. Stamm 1939: 118–21, 315–17 describes the phenomenon of Beamtennamen, which includes forms ending in -šar-uṣur; Baker 2002: 4–5 (in Babylonia but not in Assyria); Jursa 2011b: 165–6; Bloch 2014: 135–7. This agrees with Ackroyd 1968: 208, but *contra* Meyers and Meyers 2004: 383.

200. Pearce and Wunsch 2014: 103, 100–102.

201. Meyers and Meyers 2004: 383; Ackroyd 1968: 206, 209 favor it as Rab Mag. Petersen 1984: 281 reads both as the subject (even though the verb is singular as well as the possessive suffix on "men"). Boda 2016: 431 n. c favors it as a title.

202. Mankowski 2000: 134–5 rejects this as being the Rab Mag. HAL 1187–8 gives various options for understanding Regem-melek.

focus, however, is future. The future now envisioned is rosier. Most of the themes of prosperity return: the need to obey YHWH, social justice, return of population, attraction of nations. The extant text, however, fails to answer directly the question which had been asked. 8:19 implies that the dates will cease to be fasts, but this is part of a promise of future prosperity rather than a command for praxis. The mocking of the existing fasts, however, implies that Zechariah thought they were never legitimate. Overall, chs. 7–8 pick up on themes from 1–6 (such as perjury, 8:17; truth and peace, 8:19) and strongly emphasize the ideal of social justice. The newest element (to be discussed below) is a focus on Jerusalem as a pilgrimage site, both for Judaeans and for the nations (8:20–23). This closes the book with a hopeful note, one with Jerusalem functioning in a rather cosmopolitan and prosperous setting.

Summary of First Zechariah's Contents

The report is introduced with a call to return to YHWH, just shortly after the old autumnal New Year, in the second year of Darius. It sets up an expectation for what YHWH's return will entail. Next the vision report begins. It evokes Persian relations with surveillance to assert that YHWH is in control of the situation and returning to Jerusalem, which will again be cultically important. The second vision affirms judgment and *Schadenfreude* over the Babylonians, with the concomitant shifts in power relations. The third vision reinforced this message by linking the rebuilding of the temple with security for Judah, prestige among the nations, and the punishment of Babylon. The fourth vision affirms the suitability of the renewed priesthood in the person of Joshua, based on the Persian system of vetting, and authorizes Zerubbabel as a temple builder despite his non-kingly status. The fifth vision points to YHWH as cosmic emperor, with two close associates ensuring his knowledge and control over a well-functioning imperium. It moreover obliquely ties the temple into this system of administration. The sixth vision restores the proper moral order of the province, with the removal and punishment of theft and false testimony. The curse is over and proper order is to resume. The seventh vision justifies an altered cult for the new temple, most probably the removal of a consort. It reaffirms the suitability of the land for divine presence, with the evil being removed far away. The eighth vision closes the cycle by affirming YHWH's strong control over the cosmos and his pleasure with its current situation.

The cycle of visions introduced a number of (divine) characters, multi-colored horses, myrtles in a garden, four horns, a measuring line, a confirmation hearing, a lampstand, two olive trees, a flying scroll, a flying *'ephah* with stork-*Mischwesen*, and four chariots. Unusual sizes and motions notwithstanding, all of these images are explicable within the lifeworld of Persian Yehud.

The vision sequence is followed by Zechariah performing a sign act with votive gifts for the new temple. These symbolize the promise to have the temple built, the harmony of the priesthood with the ruler, and the participation of the Babylonian Judaean community.

The collection closes with a series of oracles prompted by a question concerning fasts for the Babylonian destructions. The themes from the previous sections return, and the temple appears as a locus for pilgrimage, a focus for unity, and to be conditional on the practice of social justice.

Rhetoric

The largest section of 1Zech presents itself as a vision report. Therefore, in order to assess the rhetoric of the text, it behooves the historian first to assess the phenomenology of dreams and visions. With this phenomenology it will then be possible to return to how this relates to the text's rhetoric. To anticipate the following argument, dreams and visions are investigated as cognate phenomena, with "night visions" (Zech 1:8) being functionally equivalent to "night dreams."

Chapter 5

THE PHENOMENOLOGY OF
DREAMS AND VISIONS*

Dreaming is a universal human phenomenon (and one likely shared with other animals).[1] Humans dream for a large proportion of time asleep.[2] While the functions and purpose of dreaming are still controversial, psychologists have discovered numerous neurological correlates that indicate that key (if still poorly understood) processes of consciousness are shaped while sleeping.[3] Dreams are, in fact, an area where common human neurophysiology, individual psychology, and cultural patterns interact in a dramatic way.[4] An adequate phenomenology can no more dispense with the general psychological aspects than it can with an understanding of the culture in which a dream occurs or with the dreamer's position within it. Given the inherent subjectivity of the topic of dreams, such considerations provide some objective controls for the discussion.

---

* From the perspectives of subjective experience and of literary report, a distinction between a vision at night and a lucid dream at night is probably impossible to make, thus they are treated as similar phenomena here. In any case, 1Zech is set at night.

1. On universality, see Bulkeley 2008: 3; Mageo 2003: 23. On dreaming in other animals—still somewhat controversial—see Tranquillo 2014: 77, 143–8; Bulkeley 2008: 14.

2. Dreaming was once correlated with REM sleep, though it is now known that dreams occur both in REM and NREM sleep (Moffitt, Kramer, and Hoffmann 1993b: 6–7; Tranquillo 2014: 44; Koulack 1993: 321; Wittmann and Schredl 2004; Domhoff 2003: 10, 18–23; Kramer 2015: 6–7; cf. Butler 1998: 11).

3. Purcell, Moffitt, and Hoffmann 1993; Kahan and LaBerge 1996; Spoormaker, Czisch, and Dresler 2010; Winckelman 2011: 29; Tranquillo 2014; Bayne, Hohwy, and Owen, in Press.

4. E.g., the critique of their sequestering in Tedlock 1989a: 22; phrased differently in Fine and Leighton 1993: 98–9.

Laboratory studies provide a basic framework for understanding the formal process.[5] Dreams occur throughout the night, after a period of about 90 minutes. They run in series, with the likelihood of "bizarreness" increasing through the REM stages. Important yet mundane preoccupations of the day recur in dreams, though delays of up to 9 days have been reported.[6] The experiences are variably affective and vivid. Subsequent waking recall is highly dependent upon the level of affect (i.e., retained emotion upon waking) and personal inclinations, and multiple studies have demonstrated that women (in the West) generally have higher recall rates than men.[7] Laboratory studies have also demonstrated the occasional ability of individuals to be lucid while dreaming (awareness of dreaming while dreaming).[8] The vast majority of dreams are forgotten upon waking.[9] "Impactful" dreams (i.e., dreams with strong affect) tend to be recalled and remembered more than other dreams. Kuiken and his colleagues have distinguished between three types of "impactful" dreams, which they call nightmares, existential dreams, and transcendent dreams, and they have adduced some evidence of the continued effect of such dreams on subsequent waking life.[10]

Both laboratory and anthropological studies demonstrate the highly contextual nature of dream contents.[11] This is true not only in terms of what types of objects or activities are dreamt of (driving a car, hunting), but also in terms of social patterns. This can be seen particularly in terms of gender roles—where statistical probability demonstrates wide scale content patterns between men and women in their dreams that reproduce their respective cultural role stereotypes.[12] Thus it is clear that whatever

---

5. The references the present author found most useful for understanding this were Moffitt, Kramer, and Hoffmann 1993a; Tranquillo 2014; Kramer and Gluckson 2015.

6. Tranquillo 2014: 71; Schredl 2015: 29–30.

7. Domhoff 2003: 21–2, 26; Krippner 2015.

8. Domhoff 2003: 17–18; Tranquillo 2014: 26; LaBerge 2015. Husser 1999: 25, is even certain that lucid dreams lay behind some ancient dream reports.

9. E.g., Domhoff 2003: 40.

10. See Kuiken and Sikora 1993; Kuiken et al. 2006; Kuiken 2015. Cf. Kahan 2016. Domhoff 2003: 42 problematizes this, but then supports it in 77–9.

11. The standard references for this are Grunebaum and Caillois 1966; Tedlock 1989b. More recently, see Moffitt, Kramer, and Hoffmann 1993a; Fine and Leighton 1993; Bulkeley 2008. I found the more recent study of Obeyesekere 2012 to be less helpful.

12. Table in Domhoff 2003: 73; Kramer 2015: 3–4; Krippner 2015; Kahan 2016: 160.

universal content patterns that may or may not exist trans-temporally and culturally (i.e., certain basic motifs regularly recur such as being chased, flying, dead relatives, etc.)[13] these appear within particular dreams in a way that is highly culturally structured and attuned to precise historical and individual circumstances. Moreover, laboratory psychologists have had some success in deliberately having items integrated into subjects' dreams.[14]

However, it must be emphasized that there is no first-hand knowledge of a dream available beyond the dreamer—even for the empirical psychologist; *access is always mediated by a dream report*.[15] This report is structured on a situationally appropriate basis, one that can either be *ad hoc* or formally determined in advance. In other words, the situation in which a report is composed (sleep laboratory, dialogue, temple incubation) will determine the formal structure of the report as much, as if not more than, the dream experience itself. Moreover, each culture has (or avoids) forms for such reports.[16] Further, a cultural selection process beyond the natural limit of human recall determines which dreams are reported at all.

For a historical exploration of the phenomenon of a dream, therefore, the nature of the *dream report* is pivotal, even more than any supposed actual dream experience, as this is itself forever beyond access.[17] An understanding the dream report as a phenomenon involves the following questions:

1. What patterns and types of content would one expect in the given context?
2. What is the relevant, cultural dream theory at work?
3. What is the typology of the extant dream reports at this time?
4. Whose dreams were recognized as important dreams, and who was an important dreamer and/or interpreter at this time?
5. What forms of intentionality and related phenomena are known?

Only after these questions are answered is it possible to determine the meaning of a given dream report in its historical context.

---

13. Bulkeley has called these "prototypical" (2008: 19).
14. Though Domhoff 2003: 19 emphasized the rarity of this (5 percent); Schredl 2015: 28.
15. Widely recognized, e.g., Domhoff 2003: 39; Kirtsoglou 2010: 322; Kramer 2015: 1–2.
16. What Fine and Leighton 1993 call "presented narration" (98–9).
17. Also emphasized by Husser 1999: 17.

The question of whether a dream report derives from an actual dream experience or is a literary creation is theoretically relevant for assessing the text's coherence, literary growth, and original sociological-historical setting, but it might be impossible to determine this with any certainty. Studies have generally shown an inability to discern between "real" and "fabricated" dream reports by modern psychologists,[18] so the likelihood of being able to do so at an historical distance seems low. The real, phenomenological question is perhaps whether it was first *received* as a real dream report or was merely fabricated upon the existing model of one—or, perhaps better, whether it derives from a situation involving the performance of a presumed report or was a creation mimicking such a performance in the scriptorium. This may still prove impossible to determine. What one can do is ask the above five questions, assess how they inform a report in question, and then use these answers in one's assessment of arguments around a particular report's phenomenology/ authenticity. A review of proposed criteria for assessing the authenticity of dream/visionary experience reports follows below.

Dream Reports in the Ancient Near East and the Persian Empire[19]

After the above general sketch of the human phenomenology of dreams, it is time to place this within the ANE broadly and the Persian Empire more specifically, then to try to sketch how that might relate to Yehud. This will then provide a way for assessing 1Zech and whether or not it fits this context as a dream report. This will provide some criteria for the generic decision and thus the historical interpretations one can make of the extant text.

In the ANE broadly, three basic types of dreams appear to have been recognized: (1) meaningless, psycho-somatic dreams; (2) demonic attacks; (3) divine signs.[20] Oppenheim sees four underlying dream theories.[21] Statements towards skepticism can be found in Greece, Israel, and

18. E.g., Carswell and Webb 1985: 655; Cavallero and Natale 1988: 20–2; cf. Kahan and LaBerge 1996.
19. This overview is heavily informed by Oppenheim 1956; Harris 2009. See also Butler 1998 and the overviews in Dodson 2009: 12–133; Flannery-Dailey 2004: 17–110; Koch 2015: 296–311. For a handy introduction, see Husser 1999. Access to Zgoll 2006 was only acquired after the bulk of this overview was already written.
20. Oppenheim 1956: 184 called these slightly differently; Butler 1998 as well.
21. Oppenheim 1956: 226–7. Butler 1998: 15 divides dreams merely into "prognostic" and "symptomatic."

Mesopotamia.[22] However, nightmares or dreams considered ill-omened required apotropaic actions.[23] In this, they were treated similarly to other omens. Thus these fall into the various systems for divination that are current across the ANE. Oppenheim distinguished between a class of "message" dreams (requiring no interpretation), and "symbolic" dreams (which did), though the latter are only preserved with their interpretations, making the distinction not so necessary—indeed, Butler sees the latter as a subclass of the previous.[24] Though the extant material spans several millennia, it is very sporadic and considerably less rich than that associated with hepatoscopy, extispicy, or astrology. The evidence has been conveniently assembled by Oppenheim and Butler for Mesopotamia and Harris for the Greco-Roman world. The earliest attested in the ANE is from the Gudea Cylinder A (Oppenheim's no 1: 245–6) and the last Artaxerxes II (no. 12: 250). However, relevant for present purposes is the mention by Arrian of several officers incubating dreams on behalf of the dying Alexander, though they seem to have been Macedonians.[25] In relation to dreams of the mantic sort, remains of an Assyrian dream book, several Egyptian dream books, and a late Greek one survive.[26] To fit this disparate material into a useable frame, the discussion follows the five questions posed above. Though the overview is heavily indebted to Oppenheim and Harris, an attempt is made to pay special attention to the Persian (and Neo-Babylonian) period where possible.

1) *What Patterns and Content Can be Expected in a Dream Report?*

Eschewing the theories of Freud or Jung,[27] it appears that certain very basic patterns recur in human dreams through time and across cultures.

---

22. Some examples: Greece: Herod. VII.16b.2; Israel: Qoh 5:3; Mesopotamia: ARM 26 229 (Nissinen 2003: no. 36). More broadly, especially for the Greco-Roman world, see Harris 2009. Sadly, at present I am unaware of any pre-Islamic native Persian source on this question.

23. See especially Butler 1998.

24. Oppenheim 1956: 206; Butler 1998: 5. Husser 1999: 24, also finds the distinction not always useful, though his subsequent analysis of material makes use of it fairly heavily.

25. Arrian, *Anabasis* VII.26.2 (Arrian 1983: 293). Noted by Oppenheim 1956: 188; Harris 2009: 160. Bivar 1988: 14 has attempted to associate this with an Iranian Sarapis, a god he associates with Mithra.

26. See Oppenheim 1956; Butler 1998; Harris-McCoy 2012; Volten 1942; Zauzich 1980; Ritner 2000; Betz 1986.

27. Both of which lack empirical support and should largely be discarded, despite their lingering use in the humanities. Bulkeley 1999: 59–66; Ropp 2000: §2; Domhoff 2003: 135–47; Tranquillo 2014: 37, 55, 72, 243; contra Lu 2016: 50–1.

Dreams relating to biological needs or limitations—such as falling and flying, being chased, sex, and dead relatives—are recurrent. The specific content, however, is much more determined by cultural context. For example, Brazilian Kagwahiv dream of tapir hunting, ancient Egyptians of ibises, and contemporary Americans of driving cars.[28] An interesting example of cultural change manifesting in dream content is the Asabano of Papua New Guinea, who reported seeing Jesus and the Holy Spirit in their dreams after the arrival of Christianity, with them functioning within these dream reports in the same manner that the indigenous spirits had previously.[29] Important, and deserving investigation, is the apparently highly gendered nature of dreaming. Several studies in the United States have consistently shown that men have more aggressive dreams and dream of more men than do women, who have fewer aggressive dreams and dream of equal numbers of men and women.[30] Cross-cultural studies show that these patterns are different in other places, patterned in ways that replicate in sleep waking cultural behavioral gender roles.[31] Beyond this display of cultural correlates, the specific dream content of a given night appears to be closely related to whatever is of immediate, emotional concern to the dreamer.[32] Certain dreamers, however, are able to exert *some* control over this process, by deliberately trying to answer a question in their dreams.[33] This latter effect is most pronounced if there is a deep emotional concern driving the question, or if the dreamer is practiced at it.

Though there is much discussion of bizarreness as a feature of dreams, "bizarreness" as an analytical concept raises a host of nearly intractable issues.[34] Beyond the subjectivity of the term (what one person sees as bizarre another might not), the largest portion of dreams appears to be

28. Kagwahiv, Kracke 1989; Egyptians, Shushan 2006; Americans: Hollan 2003: 70.
29. See Lohmann 2010.
30. Krippner 2015; Domhoff 2003: 21–2, 26; Kahan 2016: 160.
31. Krippner 2015.
32. Kramer 2015: 7; cf. Koulack 1993; Barrett 2015; Ruyneau de Saint George 2016.
33. Moffitt, Kramer, and Hoffmann 1993b: 7; Delaney 2015; Schredl 2015: 29–30.
34. According to a study of Esposito, regardless of how one defines "bizarreness" it evinces variation through the various stages of sleep, ranging from 28–65 percent. This means that it cannot be considered a decisive factor for "dreamlike" quality. Esposito et al. 2007 (on p. 384 he estimates only 16 percent of dreams in study had bizarre elements). On the issues around analyzing bizarreness more generally, see States 1993: 10–46; Montangero, Pasche, and Willequet 1996: 139–40; Bulkeley 2008: 17; Harris 2009: 17–19, 65–6; Schredl 2010a: 69–71; Hobson et al. 2011: 8; Tranquillo 2014: 16, 19, 132.

relatively verisimilitudinous. In many ways, the dream experience is analogous to the film-watching experience: the dreamer undergoes a "suspension of disbelief,"[35] much of which is reasonably true to life and the departures from which follow from the specific frame of reference, ones which may appear bizarre in retrospect. Moreover, the "bizarre" features that recur are also often cultural postulates—Hopis dream of mythological snakes and some Westerners of UFOs.[36] Perhaps more accurate is a sense of narrative that persists despite (dis)junctions in phenomenal space, time, and/or causality.[37]

Contents and Patterns in the Ancient Near East. It is difficult to find any specific patterns across the time, spatial, and generic divisions in the evidence, and the body of evidence is both voluminous and sparse. As Koch has noted,

> Dream divination spanned all categories. A dream could be a sign to be interpreted (artificial), or a theophany (natural), and both artificial and natural forms of dreams divination could be based on either spontaneous dreams (omen) or dreams induced by incubation rituals (oracle).[38]

The following selections are chosen with the assessment of 1Zech in mind, with an emphasis on material relevant for the Persian era. There is no attempt at being comprehensive.

In terms of content, two basic features are very common. First, the appearance of a supernatural figure, whether deity, messenger, or deceased relative is widespread. In the Greek world, they were often described as standing at the dreamer's head. Second, many of the extant dreams have to deal with temple-themes: building, repairing, and dedicating to them. In the Greek world, healing was a major topic.

Reports often come with a frame describing the setting and date of the dream, along with its contents, which may or may not include their interpretation.[39] Oppenheim's proposed type-distinction rests on the presence or absence of an interpretation. Butler prefers to see the type which include an interpretation as a subtype of the ones that do not.[40] In literary contexts, the "fulfillment" is often included as well.

---

35. Cf. States 1993: 31; Münsterberg 1970: 47, 95.
36. Hopis, Eggan 1966; a search found eleven dreams involving UFOs in the database at DreamBank (Schneider and Domhoff).
37. E.g., States 1993.
38. Koch 2015: 16.
39. Oppenheim 1956: 186.
40. Butler 1998: 15.

Several examples of dream reports which include dates are extant from Neo-Babylonian and Persian Babylonia. Šumukin reported to King Nabonidus two dreams of astronomical phenomena that he had seen, and the report contains the dates of both dreams (15/X/Nab 07 and 17/X; YOS 1:39).[41] They are very short, and contain an extremely brief interpretation ("for favor"). Another report by a Bēl-ittanu derives from the reign of an Artaxerxes (RT 19).[42] This contains a series of five dreams from a period of three months, with each date mentioned (4/XII/year 14, 13/I/year 15, 13/I/year 15, 14/II/year 15, ?/II/year 15). It is interesting that both reports are of astronomical omens appearing within dreams.

As mentioned above, Oppenheim has famously distinguished between "message dreams" which require no interpretation and "symbolic dreams" which did.[43] Similarly, Harris has insisted on the importance of what he calls the "epiphany" dream, which is essentially a message dream.[44] However, given the typically overwhelmingly visual nature of dream experiences and the tendency of reports to include interpretation within them, the suspicion arises that these dream reports are merely simplified reports that have sacrificed visual and narrative detail to service the relaying of the perceived interpretation. One could understand this as an example of culture shaping the formal dream report more than of the dream experiences *per se*.

A number of mentions of dreams or dream reports are extant in letters, mostly from Mari (see Nissinen nos. 35, 36, 37, 38, 39, 41, 42, 117 = SAA 16 61).[45] The contents of these are quite varied, though they mostly relate to either royal or temple matters. They include images, dialogues, commands, and in the one Neo-Assyrian example (no. 117), a date.

The surviving inscriptions of Nabonidus claim several dreams.[46] These are highly significant for present purposes, dating as they do to the cusp of the Persian conquest.

The Eḫulḫul Cylinder from Harran reports a dream of Nabonidus in which Marduk orders him to rebuild the temple in Harran, and predicts the successful campaign of Cyrus against Astyages.[47] This fits the literary trope of fulfillment. More dreams are associated with this temple in two steles.

---

41. Clay 1915: 55–6 = Oppenheim 1956: 205.
42. Pinches 1897: 101–4 = Weidner 1921–3: 297–9. Stolper 1999: 594 argued that the named scribe dates this to the reign of Artaxerxes II.
43. Oppenheim 1956: 184.
44. Harris 2009: 23.
45. Nissinen 2003.
46. Cited according to Schaudig 2001.
47. 2.12 (trans. Schaudig 2001: 436–8).

The first, by Nabonidus, mentions two dreams, including one ordering the building and one which confused the dream interpreters.[48] This appears to be duplicated on another stele.[49] His mother, Adad-Guppi, also erected a stele claiming she received a dream from Sin confirming that her son would conquer Harran and rebuild the temple.[50] It is interesting that this temple for Sin is so associated with dreams, since it is Šamaš rather than Sin who is normally associated with dreams (and divination in general).[51] Two more temple building inscriptions of Nabonidus claim to have been ordered in dreams (Larsa and Sippar).[52]

A stele of Nabonidus from Babylon depicts a dream in which Nebuchadnezzar appears to Nabonidus to interpret astrological signs.[53] What is interesting about this report is the inclusion of a dialogue between Nebuchadnezzar and a man in a chariot, as well as between Nebuchadnezzar and Nabonidus, the latter concerning the interpretation of another dream. This particular stele seems rather concerned with legitimacy (unsurprising given Nabonidus's status as a usurper), and the dream report clearly functions to provide divine legitimacy. Husser, however, thinks the non-visible nature of many of these royal inscriptions (albeit not this stele) means that they reflect the personal inclinations/piety of Nabonidus as much if not more than the purposes of propaganda.[54]

Lastly, a bead bears an inscription claiming it is from a votive sword that Sin had demanded of Nabonidus in a dream.[55] This recalls the common Greek votive inscriptions that appeal to dreams.[56] It is difficult to know if the predominance of dreams in Nabonidus's oeuvre reflects his personal inclinations or a general late Neo-Babylonian association of temple-building with dreams. In either case, however, it likely indicates that within the contemporary Babylonian culture dreams were considered a suitable medium for divining the gods' opinions on sacred matters. This is true even if such was the outcome of this king's personal predilections.

48. 3.1, columns I and III (trans. Schaudig 2001: 496–9).
49. 3.5 (trans. Schaudig 2001: 534).
50. 3.2. column II (trans. Schaudig 2001: 510–13).
51. E.g., Butler 1998: 73–8; cf. Husser 1999: 29.
52. 2.14 (trans. Schaudig 2001: 462–3, 465–6).
53. 3.3, columns VI and VII (trans. Schaudig 2001: 523–9) = Oppenheim 1956 no. 13.
54. Husser 1999: 39.
55. 4.1 (trans. Schaudig 2001: 545) = Oppenheim 1956: 192.
56. Renburg 2003 lists 1300 inscriptions potentially related to dreams.

5. The Phenomenology of Dreams and Visions

While to the present author's knowledge there are no surviving Iranian dream reports before the Sasanian era,[57] there are several literary dream reports of Persian dreams in Classical sources.

Herodotus recounts seven dreams of Iranians in his tales. A clear pattern in these dream reports is that they appear at important decision points and transitions of power.[58] In his long narrative of the rise of Cyrus, Herodotus presents a dream of Astyages, its two interpretations by the Magi, and its fulfillments (I.107.1, 108.1–122.3, 128.2).[59] The symbolic dream's contents do have parallels in various dream books.[60] Herodotus also has Cyrus receive a dream on his crossing of the Araxes River, shortly before his death (I.209.1–5).[61] Though portending his death, Cyrus misinterprets it as indicating a planned coup by Darius. A dream plays a crucial role in Herodotus's depiction of Cambyses's madness and downfall as well, with his murder of his brother Smerdis being motivated by a dream (III.30.2–3, 63.1–66.3).[62] In passing, a dream is said to be part of Otanes's motives for resettling the island of Samos (III.149.1).[63] Dreams also play a pivotal role in Herodotus's depiction of Xerxes's Hellenic campaign. The same (lying) dream ordering the attack is said to appear twice to Xerxes and once to Artabanus (complete with a nightmare of hot pokers; VII.12.1–13.4, VII.47).[64] Slightly later, Xerxes has another, symbolic dream which the Magi interpret as presaging his victory (VII.19.1–3).[65] As Hollman notes, this dream sounds "suspiciously Greek."[66] Lastly, Herodotus suggests that a potential reason that Xerxes ordered a sacrifice to be made on the Acropolis after his burning of it was due to a dream (VIII.54).[67] Though there is little likelihood of any of these dreams being based on authentic dream reports, it is interesting that Herodotus uses a mix of auditory and visionary dreams, that he frequently associates their interpretation with the Magi, and sees them as typically misinterpreted. Is the association

---

57. For an overview of Sasanian and later Shi'ite dreams, see Ziai 1995.
58. On the rhetorical functions of these, see Hollmann 2011. The conjunction with power transitions noted on p. 76. Cf. Harris 2009: 147.
59. Herodotus 2002: 139, 139–61, 167.
60. E.g., Artemidorus, *Oneirocritica* I.45; III.46; IV.11 (Harris-McCoy 2012: 99, 283, 315); Oppenheim 1956: 265.
61. Herodotus 2002: 263–5.
62. Herodotus 2000: 39–41, 81–7.
63. Herodotus 2000: 185.
64. Herodotus 2006: 325, 361–3.
65. Herodotus 2006: 333.
66. Hollmann 2011: 84.
67. Herodotus 2001: 51.

with the Magi an indication of a real function of the Magi, or merely a Greek projection onto them? Such a function would not be unthinkable in the ANE. Given the lack of native Iranian astrology or extispicy, it is not impossible that the Magi's divinatory method of choice was oneiromancy. A total lack of divination within the culture would be surprising.

Other classical literary sources continue to associate dreams with Iranian kings and with the Magi. Philostratus describes the dream of a Parthian king who supposedly told it to the Magi and then to Apollonius.[68] He dreamed of changing into Artaxerxes (I). Plutarch tells a story of Darius III's Magi misinterpreting a dream of his that portended his defeat by Alexander.[69] In his discussion of the lost *Oracle of Hystaspes*, Lactantius describes the nature of this work as "an extraordinary dream as interpreted by a boy prophesying."[70] It is unclear from the description whether the supposed dream was King Hystaspes's own, or just recorded by him. Whether this has any real relevance to the Iranian world, however, is doubtful. Lastly, one can mention that, much later, in a story that mixes Daniel and Revelation, Moses of Khoren recounts a dream of the Iranian mythological king Aždahak (Aži Dāhaka) that is interpreted as the successful rise of King Tigran of Armenia.[71] There is clearly a strong, literary association between dreams, kings, and transitions of power. Whether this trope has any relation to real Iranian praxis is harder to gauge.

Many of the dream materials above certainly qualify as pertaining to important issues of the supposed dreamers, though many of them one might suspect are purely literary. Nevertheless, the few isolated examples which were not literary or inscriptional included both dates and interpretations. And many, including the literary ones, dealt with matters of state and temple.

The only extant Judaean dream report at present comes from a fifth-century ostracon from Elephantine (TAD D7.17).[72] The beginning of the letter mentions a dream (חלם), but it is uncertain if it includes a (very brief) report of the contents, since Porten and Yardeni disagree with Levine on how to separate the words. Levine sees the letter as mentioning a very brief description of the dream contents, while TAD's translation does not mention the contents at all. The brief mention, however, would

---

68. Philostratus, *Life of Apollonius* I.29 (Philostratus 2005: 105).
69. Plutarch, *Alexander* 18.4–5 (Plutarch 1986: 275).
70. Lactantius, *Divine Institutes* 15.19 (Lactantius 2003: 423).
71. Moses of Khoren, *History of the Armenians* I.24–30 (Khorenats'i 1978: 114–21).
72. Porten and Yardeni 1986–99: 4:169; cf. Levine 1964.

seem to confirm that dreams could be taken seriously as the basis for personal actions.

For a dream report from Persian Yehud, therefore, one could expect it would reflect the contemporary state and temple world as well as the individual's emotional preoccupations. We could also expect a narrative that (on waking reflection) could be disjointed in time or space, but shaped with a clear interpretation already present. More details are impossible to predict, given the wide range of images in the extant reports. Perhaps the most likely expected feature is some sort of supernatural figure, whether deity or messenger.

2) *What Is the Relevant Cultural Dream Theory?*

Whether, how, and which dreams are reported is largely determined by a culture's "dream theory." By dream theory is meant what a culture understands a dream to be.[73] Lohmann's typology is a useful way to think about this, ranging from purely individual, neurological nonsense (as in much of the modern West) to revelations from supernatural deities. It is important that within any given culture more than one dream theory is likely to coexist, depending on the individual and/or the type of dream. It is this theory that forms the basis for who tells whom what dreams, when they do so, and what significance is placed upon them. It also determines the types of interpretation a dream report could involve. In modern laboratory studies, dreamers and psychologists relate the dream to the preoccupations of the dreamer. Egyptian and Greek dream manuals related dreams to the future of the dreamer.[74] Confucian texts dismiss dreams as superstitious nonsense.[75] Accordingly, the latter avoid interpreting dreams at all, while the dream manuals that see a prognostic feature seek to determine the predicted future by means of culturally specific codes. The theory itself, however, pre-exists any given dream experience or its report.

As already noted, there were several different dream theories in operation simultaneously within the ANE and Mediterranean. Broadly speaking, the potential divine origin of a dream was upheld, though skepticism seems to have been fairly high—or, the elite, at least, preferred other forms of divination. Oracles in Egypt, prophecy in the HB, and oracles/extispicy were favored in Greece. Already noted above was the

---

73. E.g., Lohmann 2010: 230–2; Dentan and McClusky 1993: 491–3; Tedlock 1989a: 25.

74. For Egyptian sources, see Ritner 2000; Volten 1942; Zauzich 1980; Betz 1986; Shushan 2006. For the Greek, see Harris-McCoy 2012; Flannery-Dailey 2004: 57–110; Harris 2009.

75. Dentan and McClusky 1993; cf. Bulkeley 2008: 73.

recognition of "psycho-somatic" dreams. They also double checked the veracity of dreams via these other forms of divination. The exceptions to this were "ominous" dreams or nightmares, which required apotropaic actions. The divine nature of dreams seems generally to have been the supernatural agent coming to the dreamer rather than the result of a wandering soul.[76] Oppenheim has noted some hints of links between the realm of dreams and the realm of the dead, but these links are all very allusive and uncertain.[77] This might only be relevant for those dreams that involved the visit of the deceased.

Interesting is the idea of false or lying dreams—where the dream is divinely sent but intended to deceive the recipient. Most of these appear in literary contexts (e.g., *Iliad* II; Herod. VII.12.1–13.4; Deut 13:1–3), but the idea fits with the broader social recognition that while the pantheons were to be respected, they were also dangerous and not necessarily benevolent. The phenomenon of double-checking dream reports makes ample sense in this context. A similar anxiety is apparent in the divinatory requests for a truthful answer.[78]

The closest explicit discussion of dream theory available occurs in the idiosyncratic and Hellenistic theories of Philo. In his treatise *On Dreams*, he affirms that there are dreams sent from heaven, dreams resulting from the enlightened mind moving beyond itself, and dreams from the self, in descending order of clarity (I.1–2; II.1–4). However, his theory is unlikely to reflect directly any theory current in Persian Period Yehud, given Philo's idiosyncrasies, later date, and location in Egypt. However, it is noteworthy that the basic recognition that some dreams are psycho-somatic and other divine remains.

In his satires, Juvenal mocks Jewish (female!) dream interpreters and Chaldean astrologers (*Satires* II.6.542–559), but these seem to reflect orientalist stereotypes more than being particularly accurate (and for a later period anyway).

Therefore, determining the operative dream theory/ies in Persian Yehud is difficult, given the current lack of documentary evidence in the form of dream manuals, votive inscriptions, or letters, as exists for psychologists, anthropologists, Egyptologists, or Assyriologists. Certainly, biblical texts are familiar with the phenomenon of dreaming, and with theories that affirm supernatural connections to them. Besides the oft-discussed

---

76. Oppenheim 1956: 234; Butler 1998: 23.

77. Oppenheim 1956: 223, 234; Cf. Butler 1998: 59–72; Flannery-Dailey 2004: 27–8.

78. E.g., a prayer to Šamaš and Adad, Lenzi 2011: 100–1 (refrain *kittam šuknam*, ll. 13, 18, 33, 41, 53, 57, 66). Cf. Husser 1999: 50.

narrative accounts of the dream(-interpretations) of Joseph and Daniel, Genesis has several characters receive messages in dreams (Abimelech [Gen 19]; Pharaoh [Gen 20]; Jacob [Gen 28; 31]; Laban [Gen 31]). The Torah otherwise affirms the divine origins of some dreams, and includes some of the criteria by which they could be classified. Numbers 12:6 affirms that YHWH appears to prophets in visions and dreams. Although this is in the context of affirming the superiority of Moses, who could speak to YHWH in person, it nevertheless affirms the medium, and seems to limit the relevance of dreams to specific functionaries (i.e., prophets, נביא). Deuteronomy (13:2–6 [Eng. vv. 1–5]) adds legislative ruling to this: only (prophecy and) dreams which do not encourage the worship of other divinities are to be heeded as true dreams, regardless of whether they are predictively accurate or not. This provides criteria, while still affirming the medium. Moreover, v. 4 [Eng. v. 3] claims that even these dreams are from YHWH himself, though sent as a test of obedience—thus affirming the ability of YHWH to lie in a dream, much like Zeus in the first-attested dream in Greek literature.[79] It is worth noting that Deut 18:9–14 does not include dreams in a list of banned (divinatory) practices. The affirmation recurs in the famous story of Saul's recourse to the Necromancer at Endor, as it is prefaced by the failure of previous divinatory attempts, including dreams (1 Sam 28:6, 15), and again with Solomon (1 Kgs 3:4–15). Both are, of course, instances of elite (kingly) dreams. Joel 3:1 [Eng. 2:28] and Job 33:14–16 also affirm the revelatory status of dreams. However, biblical literature also recognizes meaningless dreams (Isa 29:8; Ps 73:20; Qoh 5:2, 6 [Eng. vv. 3, 7]).

The idea sometimes asserted by scholars that the Hebrew prophets disapproved of dreams is mistaken.[80] While the book of Jeremiah has an invective against prophetic dreams (23; 27:9–11; 29:8–9), the point is that they are lying dreams not sent by YHWH (23:32). Whether such dreams not sent by YHWH are understood to be from demonic sources, other deities, or not authentic dream experiences is not specified. Yet, the general telling of dreams is permitted (23:38). The same assumption lays behind the denunciation in 2Zech (10:2, וחלמות השוא ידברו).

The extant biblical literature therefore affirms at least two dream theories: one of nonsense and one of divine revelation, though even these latter ones could be either true or misleading. This is a combination that

---

79. *Iliad* II.1–34. Noted by Bulkeley 2008: 141; Dodson 2009: 65; Harris 2009: 24; Hollmann 2011: 75.

80. E.g., Lindblom 1968: 26; Husser 1999: 143; Bulkeley 2008: 134–5, 167, who emphasize prophetic distrust of dreams, but the prophetic assumption of their potential is rightly noted by Flannery-Dailey 2004: 50; Dodson 2009: 18.

obviously raises the need to determine into which category a dream fell and requires a system for interpreting it accordingly. Further, the extant dream theories appear to lack a meaningful distinction between visions and dreams (e.g., Job 7:14; 20:8; 33:15; Dan 7:1; *1 En.* 13:8).[81] Whether the biblical picture portrays the same landscape of dream theories that existed in Persian Yehud or is just a selection from them is at present unknowable. All this noted, however, the potential of divine communication occurring through the dream of a specialist seems a likely theory to have been current for the period of 1Zech.

3) *Typology of Dream Reports*

The form of a dream report depends on the context which occasioned its creation. Many dream reports are no doubt oral and informal. Yet they are always shaped for the audience. For an illuminating example of this, see the Sambia of New Guinea, where three registers of oral dream reports are observable, wholly dependent on the audience.[82] The same is true for modern laboratory reports, in which the format is conditioned by guidelines provided by the psychologist.[83] The same is true for dream diaries, whether for one's own reflection or the secondary edification of others. The form which the report takes is intimately related to the relevant dream theory. A dream may not be told until after its predictions have come true, in order not to lose the relevant good fortune it is believed to portend, or told immediately to dispel the bad fortune.[84] They can be cited very precisely, complete with date, in a formal report—whether to king or other official.[85] They frequently come intertwined with the interpretation, whether this is told dialogically,[86] on the basis of the dreamer's own

---

81. Cf. Lindblom 1968: 28, 33; Dodson 2009: 57, 72; also the conclusion of Tiemeyer 2015: 19. Stökl 2012: 79–81, 98, 223, however, argues that there are important philological distinctions. While a linguistic distinction is observable, it cannot be closely correlated with any meaningful phenomenological or sociological distinction—analogous to how legal distinctions do not equate to social distinctions (e.g., the legal slave–free dichotomy does not equal social status or liability to forced labor in the ANE). Therefore the fact that different terms exist does not mean their investigation must be kept apart.

82. Herdt 1989.

83. Kahan 2016: 162–3 gives participants guidelines to avoid interpretations; see Delaney 2015 on how to instruct clients.

84. E.g., Kracke 1989: 33; Tedlock 1989a: 25.

85. E.g., Kaivola-Bregenhøj 2015: 186; Weidner 1921–3; Oppenheim 1956: nos. 12, 23, 24; Bulkeley 2008: 96, 97.

86. Homiak 1989; Merrill 1989: 205–6.

thoughts,[87] or by the aid of a professional interpreter. The more practiced a dreamer is at reporting, the more detailed a dream report is likely to be.[88]

Dream reports also differ in time and repetition. Some are told once, some many times, some upon waking, some with many years' delay. Studies show that the more a report is repeated, the more narratively coherent it will become, as well as increasing the assimilation of it to culturally recognized dream forms.[89] The latter can be hard to detect, however, as the influence works in both directions—one dreams culturally patterned dreams, but also reports dreams in line with cultural patterns.

Beyond the dream interpretation manuals, dream reports from the ANE are extant in a number of disparate genres and media. The interest in these reports is often not the dream itself, but the actions which should or did result from the dream. In Greece, many reports take the form of votive and healing inscriptions at temples. These were often placed in or near sanctuaries in response to a dream, or to a cure that took place in a dream.[90] Harris has distinguished between "incubation" dreams and "epiphany" dreams,[91] but this could be merely a function of these genres, which were focused on the resultant acts and outcomes from the dream rather than the dream itself. Otherwise, reports come embedded in literary contexts. As seen above, these were often concerned with the trope of fulfillment. The extant Mesopotamian reports are royal inscriptions (often concerning temple building), reports within letters, and within literature. The motivations behind these, however, are not so different from the Greek ones—they are also largely concerned with the actions which did or should result (whether this be temple building, or precautions to protect the king). The immediately apparent difference is the concern with public or royal matters rather than more private concerns. In all, the interpretation holds a key position, sometimes to the point of occluding description of the dream imagery itself.

---

87. Kracke 1993: 482; Purcell, Moffitt, and Hoffmann 1993: 225; Montangero, Pasche, and Willequet 1996: 144; Ropp 2000: §5; Kirtsoglou 2010: 322; Krippner 2015: 60; Kahan 2016: 163 (implying that they normally add them).

88. Purcell, Moffitt, and Hoffmann 1993: 237; Schredl, Stumbrys, and Erlacher 2016; cf. Montangero, Pasche, and Willequet 1996; Krippner 2015: 64.

89. Herdt 1989: 64; Montangero, Pasche, and Willequet 1996: 133–4.

90. Renburg 2003 lists 1300 votive inscriptions potentially related to dreams or visions; Dodson 2009: 37; Harris 2009: 108. For archives from Ptolemaic Egypt, see Shushan 2006.

91. Harris 2009: 39.

In general, dream report typology varies from an informal, oral, anecdotal type on one extreme, to a formal, written report to an authority on the other. The extant textual reports are all, of course, closer to the formal end of this spectrum. At either extreme the report will likely include some sort of time reference (last night, before the war, March 15), the narrative of the dream itself, and an interpretation or result. The forms to be expected in Persian Yehud therefore depend on the context in which a dream would begin and be recorded.

4) *Who Can Dream "Important" Dreams?*

Since the majority of dreams are ignored, either due to forgetfulness or disregard, the minority which are reported must be so due to criteria for their importance or relevance. Outside the artificial conditions of an empirical psychological study, such reporting is due to the dream theory at play. Some cultures hold that all dreams are potentially significant, and requiring of action.[92] Others reserve them to specialists (such as shamans), or to rulers (such as kings). Nightmares often require apotropaic rituals, regardless of to whom they occur.[93] Just as any given society may have multiple conflicting dream theories, it may have different attitudes to whose dreams are important or meaningful. A good example is Han China, where the ruling elite has traditionally viewed only the emperor's dreams as potentially relevant, while lower classes and especially women often viewed them as prognostic.[94] In this, the matter of whose and which dreams are significant closely parallels the status of divination or divine communication in general.[95]

While it is clear that in theory anyone could dream (and at Mari, at least, they were considered important enough to verify by other means), some dreams were more important than others, at least on a social level. While ominous dreams and nightmares seem to have been universally held as dangerous (as evidenced by the apotropaic rituals for them extant from Egypt, Mesopotamia, and Greece), other dreams seem to have been less likely to be taken seriously unless they occurred to kings or religious

92. E.g., Tedlock 1989a: 120; Merrill 1989: 194.
93. E.g., Tedlock 1989a: 118; Butler 1998: 115–17; Szpakowska 2003: chapter 6 (n.p.).
94. Dentan and McClusky 1993.
95. Thus, it falls into a broader consideration of divination, which is the context in which it is explored by Cryer 1994 and Oppenheim 1956. It is worth noting that Nissinen 2003: 14 also sees no "fundamental" difference between prophecy (itself a form of divination) and dreams in terms of contents, though this in itself is not necessarily relevant for whose dreams matter.

specialists, whether these be priests or prophets, whether intentionally or not. One might suspect that a situation similar to the one evinced for Confucian China prevailed: some people, particularly of lower statuses, took dreams very seriously, while only exceptional dreams were considered important by the elites, largely due to their preference for more technical (i.e., elite) forms of divination. The biblical material briefly outlined above seems to follow a pattern of kings and specialists, typically described as prophets. If the Greek depictions of Iranian dreams were representative at all, then a similar pattern (elites and Magi) might have been true for the Persians as well.

5) *Intentionality and Related Phenomena*

Dreams occur without conscious intentionality in human (and animal) sleep.[96] Nevertheless, certain dreamers—especially with practice—are able to learn to exert some control over their dreams (often associated with lucid dreaming), though the majority of their dreams remain involuntary. However, dreams share certain features with other "alternate states of consciousness" (ASC), such as waking visions, hallucinations, and trances, which are more easily induced intentionally. The phenomena of sought/induced experiences via various techniques by those seeking knowledge are typically assimilated in the dream theories of such practitioners. The chemical state of the brain is apparently quite different between the "alternate states of consciousness" and dreams,[97] and a lack of rigorous scientific research into this topic leaves it hard to assess.[98] Nevertheless, phenomenologically the results of visions in the two states are often very similar, and they are reported by participants in a similar manner, regardless of whether they make a conceptual differentiation between them or not.[99]

For present purposes, the key points are threefold: (1) since the report is so similar between dreams and ASC, the neurological distinctions are (at least in the present state of research) irrelevant for historical

---

96. Kahan and LaBerge 1996: 242–3; Purcell, Moffitt, and Hoffmann 1993; Tranquillo 2014: 60; Braun 2014: 95–100.

97. Schredl 2010b: 47 (different); Winckelman 2011; Kellogg 2016. For an attempt to theorize this in anthropological terms, see Leistle 2014.

98. A couple of studies in this area are methodologically suspicious, e.g., Krippp ner 1994; Obeyesekere 2012. As noted already, some terms such as "night visions" imply a phenomenological overlap anyway. Cf. Renburg 2003: 43, 56 on the term in Aeschylus and Livy.

99. Brown 1989: 158; Bourguignon 2003: 136; Domhoff 2003: 20, on dream-like experiences in awake subjects.

research—so it is legitimate to treat them as related phenomena; (2) the ASC highlight the element of intentionality, or better, incubation. Just as various locations, mantras, or drugs are used to seek ASC, the same is true for dreams, even if the psychological mechanism at work in dreams is merely auto-suggestion.[100] Individuals seeking to have important dreams will often go to specific, sacred sites and conduct particular rituals in the hopes of receiving a significant dream.[101] In certain cases, such as at Asclepeia, people will stay at the site until one arrives.[102] In addition to the argumentation of Tiemeyer,[103] this justifies treating visions and dreams as analogous; (3) some individuals are more inclined than others to receive/be receptive to and/or to seek such experiences. Modern psychologists note individual variances in potential to lucid dreaming and in rates of dream recall.[104] A comparative historical overview of religions seems to show a similar pattern across religions.[105]

Evidence for incubation exists in Egypt and Greece for personal concerns. Some graffiti, possibly from the late fifth century, might suggest Greek mercenaries in Abydos appealed to Bes for dreams, but the relevant graffiti are all very fragmentary.[106] Given the wide popularity of Bes in the Achaemenid Empire, this might be suggestive for garrisons elsewhere. One can see incubation behind the story of Solomon at Gibeon, and the condemnation of dreaming in Jer 29:8 uses the causative—implying intentionality.[107] There are also occasional hints in Mesopotamia for it, including an inscription by Nabonidus. Scholarship has periodically considered the possibility that the later Judaean apocalyptic and mystical texts implied practices of intentionality. It is therefore certainly a possibility that dreams could have been deliberately sought in Persian Yehud, though there is no external evidence either way at present.

100. Cf. Bulkeley 2008: 138.
101. Known as incubation. See, e.g., Meier 1966; Oppenheim 1956: 187–8, 190, 223–4; Butler 1998: 217–40; Husser 1999: 46–50; Bulkeley 2008: 31, 95, 100, 146, 206, 278; Dodson 2009: 34; Flannery-Dailey 2004: 34, 261–2; Harris 2009: 39, 75; Delaney 2015; Barrett 2015: 81.
102. Cf. Stephens 2013. See more, below.
103. Tiemeyer 2015: especially chapters 1 and 2 (12–36). However, Stökl 2012: 79–81, 98 argues on philological grounds that dreams, visions (and prophecy) were distinct phenomena in the ANE.
104. Purcell, Moffitt, and Hoffmann 1993: 205; Tranquillo 2014: 26; Schredl, Stumbrys, and Erlacher 2016.
105. Most usefully, Bulkeley 2008.
106. Husser 1999: 69; Perdrizet and Lefebvre 1919: 86–9.
107. MT Jer 29:8: אל חלמתיכם אשר אתם מחלמים, "to your dreams which you cause to be dreamed."

Assessing the Authenticity of an Historical Dream Report

Several scholars have asked whether it is possible to assess the authenticity of historical dream reports, or, phrased differently, whether one can determine if a report has a basis in a dream experience or is a purely literary construct.

In a short article based on 90 (English-language) dream reports, Shanon and Eiferman conclude that dream discourse deviates formally from other types of discourse.[108] While linguistic rules of the relevant language still apply, albeit with some irregular features, they see a higher level of circumlocutions, vagueness, and incoherence than would be typical in conversation.[109] They think this relates both to the nature of dream-content itself, as well as its complete subjectivity.[110] It is hard to derive rules for authenticity from this, however, other than a negative one: normal narrative rules or patterns do not necessarily apply.[111] Nevertheless, given the phenomenon of culture pattern dreams, plus the fact that some dream reporting happens in more formal contexts beyond those utilized by the authors (modern university classroom), one can expect that the patterns they found need not apply in the same manner to all kinds of dream discourse.

Lindblom posits eight criteria for assessing "religiös-ekstatischen Visionen" for their basis in actual experience.[112] All of his criteria, however, are problematic in view of the phenomenology sketched above. His first criterion of *spontaneity* is contradicted by the evidence of deliberate incubation and inducement of visions. His second criterion of *concision* contradicts the variability in dream report lengths from short to long, depending on the recall of the dreamer. His third criterion of *dreamlike quality* ignores the significant evidence of mundane dreams. His fourth criterion of *freshness* is both subjective and ignores culture pattern dreams. His fifth criterion of *otherworldliness* again ignores the mundane character of many real dreams, as well as their relation to the emotional concerns of the dreamer. His sixth criterion of *ineffability*, or difficulty in expression, is sometimes attested, but not always.[113] His seventh criterion, *affect*, is a significant element, or can be, at least for "impactful dreams." (Kuiken and colleagues' category of "impactful dreams" include

---

108. Shanon and Eiferman 1984. I am grateful to Helen Dixon for acquiring this article for me.
109. Shanon and Eiferman 1984: 377.
110. Shanon and Eiferman 1984: 369–70.
111. Shanon and Eiferman 1984: 375.
112. Lindblom 1968: 219.
113. Cf. Shanon and Eiferman 1984: 372–3.

nightmares, "transcendental," and "existential" dreams.[114]) His last criterion, *date and place*, is sometimes included in certain types of reports, but they are not universal. Flannery-Dailey rightly rejects these (but for the wrong reasons).[115] Rowland largely accepted them (with the proviso that incubation and mundane objects are attested), and appended four questions of his own: (1) Does it revise older imagery in a new way? (2) Is it free of exegetical activity? (3) Does it contain "spurious" (un-interpreted) material? (4) Does it contain complicated images dictated by the needs of subsequent interpretation?[116] Since the nature of dreaming is creative re-use of cognitive (both experiential and cultural) material and is culturally patterned, the first is not so useful. Since dream-interpretation was a learned activity, neither is the second. The last two, however, do appear to be useful criteria: not all aspects of real dreams are interpreted, and they rarely conform exactly to what one would want, since their interpretation is by necessity *post-hoc*.

Harris presents six reasons he believes give cause for doubting the authenticity of a dream report:[117] (1) if it is a second-hand account; (2) if the dream serves the narrator's purpose; (3) if it is a fully coherent story; (4) if it lacks dreamlike bizarreness; (5) if it predicts an event; (6) if it is dreamed on demand. However, not all of these are valid. As noted earlier, not all dreams are bizarre, autosuggestion and incubation are attested, and *post-hoc* interpretations are the rule. Most things in a well-written text serve the narrators' purpose or they would be left out. Coherence might be a valid criterion, but again, reporting is always selective and likely to increase the coherence of the actual dream experience, whether this is done consciously or not.[118] To these reasons for doubt, he adds three things which he thinks support a report's authenticity: (1) if it makes the narrator look bad; (2) if it is written immediately after waking; (3) or if the dreamer admits to faulty memory. While the first one would make a report appear more authentic, the second one is probably normally impossible to determine, and the last one can itself be a narrative trope (e.g., the dream of Nebuchadnezzar in Daniel).

114. Kuiken and Sikora 1993; Kuiken et al. 2006; Kuiken 2015.
115. Flannery-Dailey 2004: 253. She rejects these criteria because she thinks they apply to all ancient literary dreams, without noticing that the criteria actually do not tally with the phenomena. However, her real point is that the dream itself is inaccessible, which is of course true; this has already been emphasized above.
116. Rowland 1982: 235–7.
117. Harris 2009: 105–6.
118. Though Shanon and Eiferman 1984: 375–6 emphasize the potential for incoherence.

From these considerations, it is probably wise to be dubious of reports that too neatly fit their interpretations, or are overly virtuosic in their construction. One would also be suspicious of an ANE account without either supernatural element(s) or interpretation. One might also expect some level of affect, but no real rules seem to be available. Strict formal criteria, however, are likely to be misleading. With this overview, it is now possible to assess the likelihood that 1Zech might appropriately be classed as a dream report.

First Zechariah as a Dream Report in Persian Yehud?

Given the foregoing discussion of the phenomenology of dreams and visions, can one plausibly describe 1Zech's genre as a dream/vision report? (Although Husser argues that 1Zech is strictly a set of visions as distinct from dreams,[119] as discussed above this distinction does not appear to be overly phenomenologically significant insofar as reports go.) The introduction to the dream report proper (1:7) very clearly marks it as one, and the inclusion of a specific date for such reports does have parallels. This would place it on the more formal end of the report spectrum (see above). The reports surveyed in the ANE are all embedded within other contexts (building inscriptions, letters, and epics), and 1Zech is also embedded in a larger frame.

The report embeds interpretation within it. Sometimes this is explicitly said to be part of the action within the vision itself by one of the characters, and sometimes it is unclear whether it continues the dialogue or is an additional comment (e.g., the frequent נאם יהוה phrases). It was argued above that most dream reports embed their own interpretations within themselves, whether these are part of the original telling or a secondary interpretation. Therefore, this element fits the genre—and this remains true regardless of whether all or some of these are considered part of an original report or redactional additions. In terms of interpretive "fit," it is worth noting that while elements of each vision are given an interpretation, each also has elements which are not explicitly taken up (e.g., myrtles, colors, certain characters, the scene in ch. 3, golden tubes, stork *Mischwesen*, etc). The interpretations appear to be more appropriate as *post hoc* rather than "literary" interpretations (in terms of images having been selected for their interpretive suitability in advance).

---

119. Husser 1999: 151. Cf. Stökl 2012. Zgoll 2006: 164 tentatively suggests a distinction between them while noting their similarities. She points to 1Zech as a comparable situation.

In terms of content, the visions of course contain a major supernatural figure in the person of the "discursive angel" (or interpretive angel). As noted above, this is in line with parallel ANE reports, which typically include a figure such as this within them. Other than flying or abnormally sized objects, the overall character of most visual objects (horses, *'ephah*, lampstand) are objects from the daily life-world of Yehud, and are unsurprising in that context. Though attempts are frequently made to see deep mythological significance in these elements, the majority still remain mundane, daily objects. A dreamer from Yehud could be expected to have seen similar such items within the previous nine days.

Unlike reports in apocalypses (e.g., Dan 8:17), there is no explicit indication of affect (retained emotion) in 1Zech. However, not all reports explicitly mention emotion, even when one could surmise it was involved in the reasons for waking recall. In Kuiken and colleagues' concept of the "transcendent" type of impactful dreams,[120] such dreams include senses of "renewal, liberation, and awe" and "unbounded sense of life in all things."[121] Moreover, they emphasize that these do not need to include "dramatic pathos, terror, or ecstasy."[122] With the declarations of the return of YHWH and the end of punishment for Yehud, these visions could qualify for the positive state of affect which they apply to this type. There is no explicit record of the affect on the dreamer, so this level is impossible to verify more "existentially."

Dreams are paradoxical in the sense of preserving a semblance of narrative despite "disjunctions in time and space." 1Zech does indeed preserve a semblance of narrative throughout most of the report, and certainly also has many disjunctures—characters and objects appearing and disappearing in turn. A thematic coherence remains. The frequent appearance of both visual elements and embedded dialogue has parallels in other dreams, perhaps most notably those of Nabonidus. The flow between the two is inconsistent, such as one might expect in an actual experience. The visual is more emphasized than in many of the extant ANE parallels, but the episodic nature is similar to Kuiken's depictions of impactful dreams.

"Dreamlike" character is a slippery and fuzzy term for analytical use (like its frequent partner, bizarreness), but it can function as shorthand for arational changes and ambiguities as are experienced in dreams. 1Zech certainly contains these. Perhaps the most readily noticeable example is

---

120. Kuiken et al. 2006: 272–3; cf. Kuiken and Sikora 1993; Kuiken 2015.
121. Kuiken et al. 2006: 272, 273, respectively.
122. Kuiken et al. 2006: 273.

the frequent uncertainty over how many characters are present in a vision, with individuals coming, going, and speaking in ways that commentators argue to untangle. Similarly, certain mundane elements appear in partially non-mundane guises—horns in unspecified positions in space, giant flying scrolls—all of which are quite explicable within the general phenomenology.

In light of these above considerations, it seems plausible to identify the genre of 1Zech as a vision report. As argued by Tiemeyer on more textual grounds,[123] this perspective explains the features of the text in a phenomenologically plausible manner, even though it cannot be historically proven. One cannot exclude the possibility that a scribe wished to imitate a dream report, yet given the above similarities there is no real compelling reason to argue for this at present. Therefore, this study deems the genre of the vision report an appropriate description. The question of its writing and current form raises the question of the coherence and formation of the text, to which the discussion can now turn.

Coherence and Formation of the Text

Given the acceptance of 1Zech beginning as a vision report, this still does not answer the question of how it developed into the extant form of the text. There is no shortage of opinions on this matter.[124] From the dating formula alone, one must understand at least a two-year, two-stage process. Despite the appearance of a continual report from 1:7–6:8, there is no real way to know if all were reported at the same time or were collected over a period of days or even years. Collections of series of dreams are attested within Mesopotamia,[125] so this is not implausible. Moreover, these appear to have occurred over several subsequent months, which matches the lapse between 1:1 and 1:7. There are no apparent criteria for making such decisions, however.

It is tempting to see the eight visions to have been arranged (and selected?) deliberately, as there is a progression in theme, and several scholars have posited several different ways to see this arrangement as

123. Tiemeyer 2015.
124. E.g., Sinclair 1975 gives four redactions; Petersen 1984: 124–5 thinks more than one redaction, but declines to give a number; Wöhrle 2006a: 356–65 gives seven stages, while Wöhrle 2006b: 6–8 gives four stages; Hallaschka 2010: 293–313, 322–3 gives nine stages. Boda 2016: 17–23 seems to think there are two stages (visions and oracle redaction). Tiemeyer 2016: 248–53 posits a gradual growth of at least five stages from around 520 onwards.
125. YOS 1:39, RT 19; Schaudig 3.1 (see above).

chiastic.[126] The chiastic structure must be deliberate and probably unlikely to represent the progression of a single dream. However, dreams can also occur episodically and progressively, so again the distinction is of little help.

As already noted, at the very least, the vision report has been provided an introduction and concluding frame, one including a sign act and a series of oracles. One could understand this material to have been added at once (from one or more sources) or over several stages of additions. One might also postulate that some or all of the oracular material within the visions themselves were added at the same time or subsequently.

Dream and vision reports typically include their interpretation within the reporting format. A combination of visual image and interpretation is attested in Assyria.[127] Therefore, while one could theoretically add oracles to a pre-existing report in order to interpret it, one could also include them within the first form of the report. Thus, despite the assertion of some recent scholars,[128] the interpretive feature of the oracles is not a sufficient criterion for excising them or seeing them as redactional, if by redactional is meant that they are foreign to the report itself rather than from the visionary experience itself (the latter of which is, in any case, unknowable). It is possible, perhaps even likely, in chs. 7–8. The break between 7:4 and 8:18 perhaps indicates expansion, but there is no way of knowing whether this was done by the first scribe or a later one. For historical purposes, in the absence of any better alternative, a two-stage formation is here accepted—a collection of visions and sign acts, and either/or a collation/redaction with an introduction and conclusions—all within the first four years of Darius I. The relation of 1Zech to Haggai or the remainder of Zechariah is beyond the present scope.

Edelman has already argued that Haggai–1Zech each (and in combination) represent ANE temple building narratives.[129] She utilizes six thematic categories proposed by Hurowitz.[130] That the themes reflected in

---

126. Butterworth 1992: 236–7, 299–300; Meyers and Meyers 2004: liv–lvi; Hallaschka 2014: 137. Sweeney 2003: 348–50 rather sees a structure from chs. 1–14; Keel 2007: 1010–11.

127. Parpola 1997: no. 8. Cf. no. 11, which, although fragmentary, appears to contain elements of both oracles and visions.

128. E.g., Petersen 1984: 120–2; Hallaschka 2014: esp. 139–41; Tiemeyer 2016: 27, 248–53. Boda 2016: 18–19 thinks some oracles earlier and some later. Others, however, reject separating them; see, e.g., Meyers and Meyers 2004: lix; Stead 2014.

129. Edelman 2005: 131–46.

130. See Edelman 2005: 131–2; however, Hurowitz 1992: 56 gave eight elements to royal inscriptions.

these two texts are themes to be expected in a temple report holds true, regardless of whether one accepts her thesis that the dates are a secondary element designed to redact the two books together or not (and this study does not).[131] The idea of temple-building requiring a report, however, is intriguing (see below).

Achaemenids and Temple-Building in the Empire

With the above situation in mind, it is necessary to reconsider the status and function of temples within the broader Achaemenid system. What is known about how the Persians dealt with existing temples and the founding of new ones?

Lycia offers a famous inscription for the foundation of a new cult in the Persian Empire, the so-called Xanthos Trilingual Inscription. This text commemorates the foundation of a new cult for the gods Khntawati and Arkazuma/Kaunios and Arkesimas in Lycian, Greek, and Aramaic, in ?/III/Artaxerxes IV (337 BCE).[132] It was found at the foot of the cliff below the Sanctuary of Leto, roughly halfway between Xanthos and the sea.[133] The text describes a decision to found a cult (no elaboration on why or how), the establishment of a dynastic priest(hood), devotion of dedicated property, regulations for regular sacrifice, and an oath to abide by the decision. The Aramaic version is much shorter, but confirms the decision by the satrap (Pixodarus, Satrap of Caria and Lycia). The Aramaic also adds an Iranian deity to the list of gods protecting the oath (*Hšaθrapati*, presumably an Aramaic reflex of a manifestation, an epithet, or companion of Mithra).[134] In the Greek version, the newly built structure appears to be just an altar (lines 6–7, ιδρυσασθαι βωμον, "d'élever un autel"),[135] presumably in or near the sanctuary of Leto. The reason for the satrap's interest would appear to be the financial and

---

131. This view of the dates is widely held; e.g., recently Ristau 2016: 140.

132. Briant 1998: 305–6; Fried 2004: 140–54; also Lee 2011: 136–52.

133. Metzger 1979b: 21, plates XII–XIV, XVI–XVIII; Fried 2004: 140; Courtils 2009.

134. Bivar 1988; Jong 1997: 33; Bryce 1986: 185 suggested it was an epithet for Mithras [*sic*]. Fried 2004: 148 thinks it means both Apollo and Mithra. Schwartz 2005 thinks it references a Median equivalent of Negal (he strongly critiques Bivar's analysis).

135. Metzger 1979a: 32–3; the meaning of the loanword in Aramaic (KRP') and the Lycian word (*kumaziye*) are less certain. See, in the same volume, Dupont-Sommer 1979: 144–5 and Mayrhofer 1979 183; Bryce 1986: 92, 131 translated the Lycian as "altar" as well.

administrative ramifications: the priest's exemptions from taxation and the land dedicated to the cult.[136]

Scholarly understandings of the implications of the satrap's Aramaic endorsement have varied. Bryce was willing to entertain a relation to previous Lycian involvement in the Satraps' Revolt since the two deities appear to be Carian, but he does not see it as a radical departure from local norms in any case.[137] Recently, Fitzpatrick-McKinley emphasizes the "light touch" of the Persians in this matter,[138] and she is reacting against Fried, who suggests that the inscription evinces Pixodarus tightening his control over Lycia and for the benefit of new Carian mercenaries in the *birta* at Xanthus.[139] In a somewhat more moderate position, Briant thinks it demonstrates the satraps' protection of the cult, as well as a concern with the financial aspects.[140] Kuhrt follows Briant's lead, seeing the satrap as merely holding the archival copy of the decision, should there be legal disputes concerning it in the future.[141]

For present purposes, this shows a Persian interest in at least the financial aspects of cultic affairs. However, it cannot be a complete pattern for temples, since this does not seem to concern a new structure *per se*. Moreover, it is a written inscription with a narrative concerning founding. As such, it is not a parallel for the genre of 1Zech. It does show, however, *that there could be parallel and yet non-identical official representations for cultic establishments*—a more local one and an official (Aramaic) one.

As is well known, temple-building in the ANE required divine authorization and usually also required a royal builder.[142] Moreover, the process itself required multiple rituals to ensure the gods' pleasure, as well as double checking the timing for key aspects of the building process.[143] Any attempt to build a temple in Jerusalem, therefore, can be expected to have involved either the spontaneous demand by a prophet to build the temple

---

136. Briant 1986: 436. Economic interest in temples can be seen in Mesopotamia in different forms. Kozuh 2006: 262–70 discusses Achaemenid continuation of NB economic utilization of temples; Waerzeggers and Jursa 2008: 19 sees taxation on priesthoods functioning as a form of control; Waerzeggers 2010b: 348, 352–3 discusses new taxes introduced by Darius.

137. Bryce 1986: 193.

138. Fitzpatrick-McKinley 2015: 105.

139. Fried 2004: 153–4.

140. Briant 1986: 436 and 2002: 957.

141. Kuhrt 2007: 133–4.

142. Ellis 1968: 20; Linssen 2004: 101–3, 106, 108, 283–305; Fried 2010: 316, 325–6; Schaudig 2010: 142–3.

143. Ambos 2010 and 2013a; cf. Ambos 2013b.

5. *The Phenomenology of Dreams and Visions* 191

and/or a process to discern the divine will concerning such a project. It could also be expected to seek a proper patron for the temple.

It is not always clear what royal attribution might mean in practice, however. A troop commander at Seyene left an inscription at Aswan to commemorate his *brazmādānā* (shrine) to a undeciphered god (incorporating *farnah*? ופדנחתי or ופרנחתי) in the reign of Artaxerxes (I).[144] For the present purposes this inscription is significant, since it is a Persian-period inscription for a sacred site. Russell thinks the *brazmādānā* was a Zoroastrian temple,[145] but the word merely means "place of worship," making speculation as to what exactly the commander was commemorating risky. In any case, the inscription is a near-contemporary example of another official commemorating their own work and of the mention of the relevant king, who does not appear to have been directly involved. This facet has been argued at length by Lloyd, who has argued that, at least in Egypt, behind attribution to a king can lie a variety of levels of kingly responsibility, from total to merely a shorthand for dating.[146] Kings are routinely mentioned in inscriptions, but the particular implications in each case must be weighed carefully. In this case, though, it appears the inscription is by a foreigner for a foreign deity and for something smaller than a complete temple complex. One might suspect that larger temple projects for native Egyptian deities would have still required more direct royal involvement, if only by proxy (i.e., the satrap).

The building of a temple required money for labor and materials. Moreover, a temple was useless without some sort of maintenance of the cult, requiring further resources for the priesthood and sacrifices. In an area as rural as early Persian Yehud, such an outlay of expenses would likely require imperial approval, since it would likely require or involve the abrogation of tax obligations, at least temporarily, if only to free the labor necessary for building. Moreover, one might wonder about the ability to effect labor mobilization for such an effort outside the imperial administrative structures. The oft-discussed "Passover Papyrus" is most likely related to this labor aspect, i.e., royal permission for the troops not to work.[147] Monetary outlays required confirmation and reports.

---

144. Porten and Yardeni 1986–99: 4:234–6 (D17.1); Hallo 2000: 163 (2.41).
145. Russell 2002: 5.
146. Lloyd 2007: 107–10.
147. TAD A4.1 (Porten and Yardeni 1986–99: 1:54; Lindenberger 2003: 65); Briant 2002: 586; Kuhrt 2009: 854–5 n. 1.

Additionally, the appointment of a priest most likely required vetting by the responsible satrap.[148] This satrapal process could produce several kinds of written reflexes, mostly attested as letters (e.g., Pherendates correspondence).

From the above, it is plausible to expect that around the time period of Darius's accession, in order for the process of (re)building a temple in Jerusalem to happen, it would require (1) some form of divination; (2) some form of (royal) builder; and (3) Persian authorization of the project's finances and priesthood. As was seen above in discussion of the Xanthos Trilingual Inscription, inscriptions describing part of this process could have different versions for the local and imperial audiences.

One of the most abundant of genres in the ANE is the omen literature.[149] The omen literature represents one of the main repositories of Mesopotamian scholarly energy, both providing guidance in divinatory matters and serving as a large body of collected knowledge. Dreams and visions were a (relatively minor) part of this collection.[150] This collection no doubt was a vital source for decision making in Neo-Babylonian Empire, would have been consulted to interpret dreams, and would have been important during the temple-building process. However, there is no equivalent to the omen literature from southern Palestine. For Yehud, it would seem that the unparalleled phenomenon of the (biblical) prophetic books eventually came to serve this function for the Judaeans.[151] When this began and how long it lasted, and when it became "authoritative" are heavily debated questions, and beyond the present scope. Nevertheless, the early Persian period is probably only the very beginning of this process, and a less text-centric divinatory process (one potentially including dreams and visions) is quite likely.

Since dreams and visions were one possible method for both spontaneous and deliberate divination in the ANE, it is plausible to see a vision report as having been part of the process of temple building. *It is here suggested, therefore, that 1Zech was a vision report that was collated as the local version of an official report concerning the establishment of the temple, thus justifying both the temple itself and the Yehud elite's participation therewith.* 1Zech would, therefore, be analogous to the reflexes in Herodotus as discussed in the introduction and the Lycian and Greek versions of the Xanthos Trilingual. From there, it became part of the

---

148. See Silverman 2014a; and above.
149. E.g., Leichty 1970; Koch 2015.
150. Oppenheim 1956: 242.
151. Not controversial at all… see, e.g., Ben Zvi and Floyd 2000. See Silverman 2019, where the present author expands on this idea.

Yehud scribes' equivalent of ANE omen literature. Perhaps the collection of oracles in chs. 7–8 was inspired by and/or incorporated older oracle archives found within the ruins of the temple in the process of preparing the site for construction. In this context specifically, just as for dream and vision reports generally, it is the *interpretations of the imagery* and not the imagery itself that was considered key. Without a clear meaning, the recording of the visions would not have been useful to explain or justify the temple or the social structure—in fact, doing so would simply have required seeking additional interpretation.

Above it was argued that the setting behind the vision cycle should be seen as the gubernatorial seat at Ramat Raḥel, as posited by Christine Mitchell.[152] With no reason to see any administrative or cultic apparatus extant in Jerusalem at the accession of Darius—with these presumably at Ramat Raḥel, Mizpah, and perhaps Bethel—the gubernatorial seat is a reasonable place for divinatory procedures to take place, or at least to be reported. This comes at a time in the early Persian period when Darius was beginning to reorganize the administration of the empire, and after he had defeated a wide number of opponents to his accession. The proper ordering of the province, then, would have been of concern to the governor, satrap, and emperor—and something worthy of note to the administration.

While Haggai explicitly calls for the building of the temple, 1Zech is more concerned with justifying the resultant social-political situation, or, in other words, with the new Yehud elite and their engagements with the Persians. One can easily see the creation of Haggai and 1Zech as historically related, though Haggai is more concerned with beginning stages of the process (temple) and 1Zech with later ones (provincial).[153]

First Zechariah in an Early Persian Context

Visions, Vision Reports, Divination, Temple Building, and the State

Above, it was argued that 1Zech is a vision report from the first four years of Darius I's Yehud, with some framing oracular material. What does this say about the context of the presumed visions and their recording? First, a note on the location of the reporting, and then towards the question of why

---

152. Mitchell 2016.
153. Marinkovic 1994 argues that the temple is of no concern to 1Zech, which pushes this issue too far. Marinkovic is right to emphasize the text's concerns with social structure and the nature of society, but this image includes a new temple. Thus, Edelman 2005: 137 goes too far in making the concerns of 1Zech similar to those of Haggai.

the text was recorded and preserved. In the discussion of the first vision, Mitchell's suggestion that the setting for said vision was in the gubernatorial garden at Ramat Raḥel, rather than in Jerusalem, was accepted. This would likely place both the visionary experience and its recording in the provincial administrative sphere, with the governor and his scribes (rather than the priests and temple staff). We know that the Persian administration used a wide number of Aramaic scribes for its purposes, so this is a plausible location for a literate amanuensis. It also provided straightforward interpretations for the myrtles, the mysterious "deep," and the appearance of Persian riders in the vision. Indeed, the governor's residence is a likely location for frequent imperial messengers coming and going.[154] Above, and in a previous article, the present author also argued that the vision in ch. 3 presented a satrapal confirmation hearing (whether at the satrapal or gubernatorial court was not discussed). The cycle gives no clear indication of a shift in location between the various visions. The likely ruined state of Jerusalem and lack of a temple or administration there to have had much of a bureaucracy means that Ramat Raḥel can plausibly be posited as the location for the entire vision report, and potentially for its redaction into chs. 1–8. Yet, why was it recorded, stored, and transmitted? This is the million-dollar question for most HB texts, but it is worth hazarding speculation on the matter here.

Chapter 2 argued that 2Isa began life as an oral-dictated poem, drawn from the elite culture of the urban Babylonian diaspora. In the case of 1Zech the text is more concerned with justifying the resultant sociopolitical situation, or, in other words, with the new Yehud elite and their engagements with the Persians.

The first consideration is the dates in Haggai and Zechariah. Though the chronology of the events around the accession of Darius are problematic and debated, the basic timeline is reasonably reconstructable.[155] The dates which appear in Haggai and Zechariah appear to fall into a lacuna in the fighting, after the last enumerated battle with the liar-kings and between the hostilities in the second and third year mentioned in Column V of DB (see Appendix I). In other words, all of the dates are given as times when Darius would have appeared as fully in control of a pacified empire. Moreover, the revolts in Babylonian and Assyrian territory were already crushed.[156]

154. On this issue, Fox 2015 is unfortunately lacking in knowledge of this context, despite the intriguing thesis.

155. For detailed discussions of the problems and evidence, see, e.g., Balcer 1987; Zawadzki 1994; Briant 2002: 97–127; Lorenz 2008; Kuhrt 2009: 135–57.

156. Also emphasized by Kessler 1992, but for Haggai.

Zechariah's vision cycle opens with YHWH's anger at the "nations at ease" (1:14–17) and the enlistment of divine craftsmen to strike terror into their military apparatus (2:1–4). Similarly, the cycle concluded with YHWH's purposes being satisfied "in the north" (6:8). These visions are dated to 24/XI/Darius 2 (15 February 519), or in comparative political terms a little over two years past the defeat of Nebuchadnezzar III (29/IX/Darius 0, 16 December 522) and 15 months after the execution of Nebuchadnezzar IV (22/VII/Darius 1, 27 November 521). Darius's apology describes two battles against Nadintu-Bel (Nebuchadnezzar III) and his execution in Babylon (DB I§§16, 18; II§20) as well as the defeat and impaling of Arkha (Nebuchadnezzar IV) and his followers at Babylon (III§50).

It was also most likely a year before Darius marched through the Levant towards Egypt (in early 518).[157] This time frame was one in which Darius was consolidating his hold over Babylonia, suppressing a last revolt in Elam, and campaigning against the Scythians. He was also building. Boucharlat thinks that the planning and foundations for the Persepolis and Susa platforms had begun as early as 519.[158] Perrot suggests the work at Susa began between 520/519–517/16, though Briant emphasizes the uncertainty of the date.[159] However, the building works at Susa utilized extensive forced labor from Babylonia, and the earliest dated Babylonian workgang dates to Darius 6 and of businessmen traveling to the king in Susa to Darius 5.[160] These trips continued through Darius's reign, occurring at the end of the year (months XI–XII–I).[161] It is also likely that the main route to Susa from Mesopotamia, the Nār-Kabari,[162] was worked on—whether built or upgraded. In any case, this involved the extensive mobilization of labor taxes from Babylonia.[163] Overall, this seems to have affected a significant ramping up of tax obligations on the Babylonian elites.[164] Or, as Waerzeggers has described this situation,

---

157. Kessler 1992: 72 doubts Darius passed through Palestine, but this is based on lack of direct mention in the HB rather than a political or military understanding.
158. Boucharlat 2013b: 412.
159. Perrot 2013: 455–6; Briant 2013: 8; 2002: 166, 908. He calls 520 the "high date."
160. Waerzeggers 2010a: 792 (CT 56, 762), 796 (Dar 437).
161. Waerzeggers 2010a: 801–2.
162. Waerzeggers 2010a: 790, 804.
163. Waerzeggers 2010a: 805–7; Jursa 2007b: 87–8.
164. Jursa 2007b: 89.

In short, Darius' conscription of priestly delegations as corvée gangs in his Elamite building project was nothing short of the slap in the face of the privileged people – one of the very sins that any rightful king was eager to deny during the ritual of confirmation at the New Year festival.[165]

The first vision in 1Zech appears to be aware of the success of Darius in Babylon, with the entire world at peace. Though the exact nature of the final vision is debatable (four cardinal directions as implied by the four winds of heaven, or just north and south as favored by Floyd and Boda),[166] the point is clear. The land of the north has been pacified and YHWH is satisfied. If the audience were expecting more drastic repercussions (as in Habakkuk), they were disappointed. (If the theory of two directions is accepted, then the land of the South must mean Egypt, and Darius's coming campaign there, rather than Edom as suggested by Boda.[167]) Rather than positing an eschatological hope or promising extensive punitive measures, the efforts of Darius are accepted as sufficient. The vision cycle thus closes with the divine imperium at rest in Babylon, though perhaps preparing for its extension to Egypt. A politically astute dreamer in this time frame could have been expected to have had such subconscious thoughts. Moreover, it is possible that Judaeans from Nippur or Āl-Yāhūdu were involved in the construction efforts in Susa, or that their Babylonian neighbors were.

With this context in mind, it does not make sense to see these oracles as part of a "nationalistic" fervor hoping to make use of the widespread disturbances of 522–1. Rather, they would seem to be quite the opposite: reactions to the securing of power by Darius and his decisive moves to shift the imperial center eastwards. They are thus in an appropriate position chronologically to be part of the (re-)negotiations of local power with imperial power. That the oracles address both the governor and the high priest would also indicate that a social and religious dynamic is involved. A starting place for assessing the function of Haggai and Zechariah (the presumed original prophets rather than the books of those names) should be this situation of renewed Persian consolidation rather than one of "messianic ferment" as periodically appears in biblical scholarship.[168]

---

165. Waerzeggers 2015a: 200.
166. Floyd 2000: 399; Boda 2016: 375–6.
167. Contra Boda 2016: 376.
168. E.g., Seybold 1972: 71; Sweeney 2001: 320; Albertz 2003c: 7–9; Finitsis 2011: 122–4.

To begin, consider again Zechariah's first vision (1:7–17). The core is the vision of four horses, returned from roaming the earth, having found it quiet (v. 11). This parallels in action the work and function of the King's Eye system,[169] and if the date (24/XI/Darius 2, i.e., 15 February 519 [Julian]) be accepted, also a generally accurate depiction so far as we know for the imperium. At the very least, the regions of seeming concern to the text (Assyria and Babylon) were no longer in revolt (though Egypt was). The text takes this situation to declare YHWH's anger at these nations and declares his return to the Jerusalem temple. Though these two declarations are perfectly explicable from within the Judaean traditions, they *also* serve a function in this context not often mentioned. They agree and justify Darius's success in subduing these countries and authorize retaliations against them, and they justify the establishment of Jerusalem as a central(?) cult site, something of potentially administrative use to the Persians. This means then that this vision can be seen to do double-duty, as suggested in chapter 1: it provides continuity with local traditions while enabling a way to cooperate with Darius on certain policies. The next vision, in 2:1–17, expands on this function.[170] This declares the complete elimination of threat against Judah—so much so that Jerusalem will be protected without a wall (vv. 8–9). Again, assuming the same historical context, it might be worth noting that the text expects further reprisals against these countries, and calls for a return migration. Neither of these happened (immediately at least), but that does not affect the resulting function of the general support for the regime which it gives (if one accepts that the temple was actually rebuilt under Darius, and given that such a rebuilding would have happened in a city without walls and without a military garrison). The vision gives a theological significance to this—safety is so secured because YHWH himself is the wall. From the Persian perspective, safety is secured because their order is so complete and their administration is centered elsewhere. Moreover, v. 15 even sees this situation as justifying proselytes, something no doubt of use to the Persian organization of the province of Yehud and its new temple—a unifying factor.

The so-called sixth vision (5:1–4) can similarly be read in this manner.[171] The flying scroll serves to guarantee social justice. Such a concern (here specified as theft and oath-breaking) is a common trope for jurists, ethicists, and kings the ANE over. However, the iteration of this theme by

---

169. See Silverman 2012: 171–4, 192; 2014a: 3–5.
170. Cf. Tiemeyer 2015: 85–105.
171. Cf. Tiemeyer 2015: 181–202.

Darius on his tomb and disseminated throughout the empire also deserves mention in this context.[172] In his claim to be a just king, Darius here insists that he does not allow the weak to harm the strong, nor for false accusations to be believed. Surely stealing is one of the few ways the weak can harm the strong, and Darius's overall rhetoric is very much concerned with falsehood ("the lie"). It is therefore tempting to read this vision as one which could potentially justify the Achaemenids as arbiters of the law, which is here sent by YHWH (v. 4).

In addition to this, there are the practicalities around acquiring divine approval for temple building. This is something to which Haggai can probably be attached, yet 1Zech is relevant as well. A temple in the ANE required divine approval for building.[173] Typically this would be ascertained via a variety of forms of divination. In Mesopotamia the preferred method was extispicy, though the use of other forms is also attested.[174] A cheaper method was libanomancy, the observing of incense smoke. Though there is no direct evidence of the use of this in Persian Yehud, it would have been a method potentially available to the populace. It is, at any rate, a potential function for the known finds stone altars which is not often considered.[175] More directly, oneiromancy is claimed by Nabonidus for divine temple fiats, and the Hebrew tradition affirms its potential viability in general.

If the above is accepted, then 1Zech could be posited as kept in the gubernatorial archive, to be used potentially for a votive inscription in the completed temple, or just for administrative records. The view just presented is a complete contrast to that of Sweeney, who argues that 1Zech is a reaction to disillusion from 2Isa.[176] Beyond the difficulties this involves in closeness of dating and transmission between Babylon and Yehud, it is too overly text-centric and dependent upon canonical thinking. Moreover, it does not take into consideration the differences in the social implications of their respective genres (before their integration into the HB corpus).

---

172. DNb, parts of which were found at Elephantine with a version of DB. See especially §§2–6 (Schmitt 2009: 106–8); given as §8b–e by Kent 1961: 140.

173. Hurowitz 1992: 135–63; cf. Hurowitz 1993; Bedford 2001: 174–7; Ambos 2010. Ambos 2013a argues this is the reason for the large number of rituals.

174. Koch 2015; cf. Cryer 1994; Rochberg 2004; Nissinen 2003.

175. On stone altars in southern Levant, see, e.g., Dion and Daviau 2000; Daviau 2007; Frevel and Pyschny 2014. Thanks to Raz Kletter for discussing the Persian period altars.

176. Especially, Sweeney 2003.

Thus, this study hazards the hypothesis that 1Zech was written as part of the gubernatorial process of receiving divine and royal authorization for a new temple, and was presumably stored in the archives there. How the text later came to be redacted into the book of Zechariah and the so-called Book of the Twelve is a question beyond the present scope. It must be emphasized, however, that 1Zech was, in the understanding presented here, *not* first recorded in order to be "scripture."

Two Attendants in Chapter 4 and the Persian Empire

The two attendants of the Lord of the Earth in ch. 4—more commonly discussed as "sons of oil"—are a major *crux interpretum*. Instead of focusing on the aspect of oil, taking the other elements in the depiction as clues provides new light in the Persian context. To recap from the previous discussion of this vision above, the rare phrase "Lord of all the Earth" appears to carry an imperial connotation. Moreover, the two characters so described are enablers for the prime element of the vision, the lampstand. Thus, these two figures are like two "right hand men," instrumental in maintaining the proper function of the lampstand. Given the echoes of the stand with the Persian spy network, this implicates these two attendants in similar imperial structures. But on what might they be modelled?

The aforementioned case of the Xanthos cult inscription provides a clue. In a discussion of the Achaemenid imposition of loyalty on local dynasts, Briant notes that the Satrap of Caria and Lycia, Pixodarus, had installed in Xanthos a governor and two commissioners who represented his interests.[177] (The inscription names these as Iera [Heiron] and Natrbbiyemi [Apollodotus], "commissioners for the Lycians."[178]) The Lycian text calls them *pddenehmmis* and the Greek *archons*, the latter being a very vague term used for a variety of positions.[179] These two are separate from the governor of the *birta'*. Similarly, two inspectors representing the Satrap of Babylonia, Gobryas, appear in a Babylonian receipt (AnOr 8 61).[180]

---

177. Briant 1998: 309, 334 and 2002: 767.
178. Line 4 of the Lycian and lines 3–4 of the Greek; see Bryce 1986: 92; Metzger 1979a: 32. These names do not appear in the Aramaic version.
179. E.g., Herod. V.33 uses it for a ship captain, and Aeschylus, *Persians* 73 uses it for Xerxes himself.
180. See Wells, Magdalene, and Wunsch 2010: 23–7; Kozuh 2006: 256; Stolper 2003: 266 cites the text, but does not offer a translation.

Nehemiah also mentions analogous sorts of figures in Jerusalem. An overseer (פקיד) of the Levites (who has a royal order, מצות־מלך) and an advisor to the king (ליד־מלך) appear in Neh 11:22–24. The latter, "at the hand of the king" sounds like an appropriate phrase for an attendant. Both of these figures are associated with the king himself, with a royal order and an attendant, respectively. This in fact makes ample sense in light of the Persian kings' attempts to minimize satraps' independence of power. For example, Xenophon describes how Cyrus ensured that individual officials were directly responsible to himself.[181] The two satrapal officials in Xanthos can be seen therefore as functioning in a similar manner: two representatives besides the governor to ensure that the satrap's will is done.[182]

A NB document mentions the visit of a royal commissioner to the Eanna in Uruk in 29/VI/Cambyses 3, requesting to see all of the stelae and inscriptions of ancient kings belonging to the complex.[183] While Tolini emphasizes that the royal mission in this document could be interpreted in several different ways,[184] for present purposes it is noteworthy that the *šatammu* mentions both a royal commissioner and the governor of Babylon, but not the satrap. Thus, this is potentially another instance in which two officials are given responsibility to see that royal will is done. Also similar is the more general administrative practice of having multiple people aware of commands in administrative letters, even if the precise details around this are confusing. As Naveh and Shaked discuss in relation to the Bactria archive, letters mention a person who knows the order (ידע טעמא זנה) or is the "master of the order" (בעל טעם), in addition to the scribe and the letter's recipient (though sometimes the scribe also serves one of these functions).[185] For instance, document A2 has an order issued to the governor by the satrap, with both a scribe and a separate בעל טעם.[186] Though this again is not a system of two separate representatives, it shares a concern to make sure that orders are not ignored by keeping multiple parties involved. Already, Naveh and Shaked have noted that Ezra shows

---

181. Xen., *Cyr.* 8.i.16–20, ii.26–28; *Oec.* 4.9–11. Cf. Silverman 2014a. Briant 2002: 340–2 is more reticent over the usability of Xenophon's perspectives in this respect.

182. Since satraps modelled themselves on the Great King.

183. BM 113249: Kleber 2008: no. 33 (pp. 270–1) = Jursa 2007b: 78; Tolini 2011: 134.

184. Tolini 2011: 134–5.

185. Naveh and Shaked 2012: 23–4, 50.

186. Naveh and Shaked 2012: 80–1.

a similar administrative structure in scribal practices.[187] Similarly, an apparently *ad hoc* arrangement of Cambyses had two royal officials in the temple in Uruk.[188]

This does not mean that it was standard practice for the Persians to install two officials to represent royal (or satrapal) interests, merely that it is attested as an occasional strategy that paralleled the bureaucratic tendency towards checks on the power of individual officials. What is the implication of reading the two attendants in ch. 4 as two such officials? One can posit that the two figures in Zech 4 represent two officials appointed either by Darius or his satrap, whose jobs were to ensure the new temple participated in the imperial designs for it. Therefore, instead of being a declaration of diarchy in Yehud, ch. 4's vision can be read as both modelling YHWH's heavens on the Achaemenid Empire as well as an instance of elite justification for their involvement with Persian policies. This would imply that even were the initial designs for the temple based on local elite wishes, it was a project that was approved— and overseen—for being useful to imperial ends.

Pilgrimage and the Imperial Context

Twice 1Zech expects pilgrimage of the nations to Jerusalem (2:15; 8:20–23), a motif this text shares with other Judaean texts of similar and later times.[189] A number of studies of pilgrimage and religious travel highlight how pilgrimage can foster a sense of communal identity across various social boundaries (though the Turners' idea of a liminal *communitas* is widely considered to be discredited on the basis of empirical studies).[190] Pilgrimage sites are often marginal.[191] The establishment of a tradition of pilgrimage has the potential either to override existing

---

187. Ezra 4:8–9, 17; Naveh and Shaked 2012: 24 n. 14; cf. Steiner 2006: 645–6, 648.

188. Kleber 2008: 30.

189. Knowles 2006; for Jewish sacred travel in later periods, see Hezser 2011; Goodman 2007; Kelner 2010.

190. In Tweed 1997's analysis, festivals and pilgrimages to Our Lady of Charity in Miami played an important role in "diaspora nationalism" among exiled Cubans; McCorriston 2011 thinks that pilgrimage played a socially formative role on a meta-structural level in ancient Arabia; Haładewicz-Grzelak and Lubos-Koziel 2014 argue modern Lichen in Poland is creating a cohesive Polish-Catholic heritage; MacLean 2008 argues pilgrimage to Allahabad in India was formative for Indian nationalism.

191. E.g., Morinis 1992: 19.

social divisions,[192] or to reinforce them.[193] Several clear examples do exist of pilgrimage functioning to tie religion to nationalism in some form.[194] Nevertheless, it is also clear that common pilgrimage sites can be contested between groups without creating a shared community.[195] MacLean argues pilgrimages are equally able to be used by governments for control as they are by the marginalized for resistance.[196] For Iranian Jewish women in the early twentieth century, pilgrimage to the tombs of Esther and Mordecai (as well as to Zechariah and Habakkuk) provided opportunities to pray, to sacrifice, and to learn about Torah outside normal channels of authority.[197] The significance of pilgrimage sites can also alter with generational changes.[198] The key for present purposes is that pilgrimage can have significant social and economic ramifications, and these have unpredictable results. Whether a pilgrimage results from elite encouragement or "bottom up" religious inclinations, the ramifications are not easily predictable or controllable. In this light, it may be worth considering the role of Sukkot as a "pilgrimage" festival, and whether or not it was reshaped in Persian Yehud by elites in an attempt to foster Jerusalem as a pilgrimage site.[199] Knowles argues that pilgrimage is a better way than "exodus" to understand a number of texts she sees as Persian period.[200] In particular, she reads Zech 6 as a method of collecting taxes from the diaspora. Similarly, Edelman sees the temple as being involved in taxes-in-kind.[201] Though any link between pilgrimage and taxation was apt to be indirect, the temple was most likely involved in taxation, if only in the form of obligations. Therefore, the economic implication of gifts from pilgrims deserves consideration, and is something ancient elites could have considered as well.

The surprising aspect to 1Zech's two uses of pilgrimage is that they are *not* primarily diasporic in nature (the travel of Judaeans only being implied in 8:23). Rather, the text expects the widespread pilgrimage of

---

192. E.g., Younger 1992.
193. E.g., the Parsis and Iranis, Stausberg 2011: 47–51.
194. See n. 190 above.
195. E.g., Howlett 2013; the denominational competition at the Church of the Holy Sepulcher might be the most famous example.
196. MacLean 2008: compare 9, 14, 59, 85, etc.
197. Soomekh 2009: 70.
198. E.g., Tweed 1997: 94–5.
199. E.g., Ulfgard 1998: 144, 213, 241.
200. Knowles 2006: esp. 81–4.
201. Edelman 2012: 353.

external groups (גוים רבים, 2:15; עמים רבים וגוים, 8:20; עמים וישבי ערים רבות, עצומים, 8:23) to Jerusalem. What does this mean? Is it merely hyperbole to show the renewed prestige of the Judaean people and/or their god? Is it the wishful thinking of an oppressed people seeking metaphorical dominance? Or is it a prophetic extrapolation from long-standing Semitic pilgrimages (as argued by McCorriston)?

The imperial situation might provide an alternative or additional reading to these rhetorical options. 1Zech, as argued above, has emphasized YHWH as an emperor over the nations. The vision cycle concludes with YHWH expressing satisfaction with the arrangement of his imperium. This closely parallels Darius's reconsolidation of the empire, as well as being nearly contemporaneous. Things which would be necessary for wide-scale pilgrimage to a remote site include secure road networks, and systems for housing pilgrims—something well served by stable imperial hegemony. Indeed, the Greeks were impressed by the Persian road network. Yet it is clear that the use of the imperial system of roads and hostelries required an official permit (*miyatukkaš/halmi*),[202] and one might be inclined to wonder how often this was granted for non-imperial purposes. Other travel—for business or religious reason—was less facilitated, unless it was for official purposes (the semi-official business networks of the Egibis and Murašu being good examples).

Pilgrims provide cash, and being a prestigious pilgrimage site brings significant economic impact.[203] For a location such as Jerusalem—not on a major imperial network, nor directly controlling substantial natural resources nor large populations—other avenues for imperial attention are necessary. One potential is labor manipulation (e.g., for oil and wine production). Labor control requires administration and record-keeping. One option for the suitable apparatus, following the Egyptian and Mesopotamian models, is temples. Could an attempt to make Jerusalem a pilgrimage site be an attempt to make it financially viable and worthy of imperial permission, concessions, and/or patronage, and thus an organizer of labor? These are issues taken up in the next chapter.

---

202. Hallock 1969: 40–1, cf. the index on pp. 688, 733–4; Henkelman 2008: 143; Kuhrt 2009: 224, 730–41; on some travels of a likely satrap using this system, see Henkelman 2010: 704–13.

203. Edelman 2012: 352–6 includes the revenues from sacrifices and pilgrimages as among the functions of a new temple for the province (though she argues this is later, under Artaxerxes I).

From the perspective of network analysis,[204] placement between two or more networks is structurally advantageous. If administrators and elites in Yehud could succeed in making Jerusalem a pilgrimage site for both Judaeans and other subject peoples, the elites and priests of the Jerusalem temple would find themselves at a nexus between Judaeans, "gentiles," and the Persians—a relatively powerful, and potentially lucrative position. This would be advantageous to the empire, and it would also contribute to any aspirations of holding a diaspora together by creating a network with financial repercussions. It could also have been understood as a way of unifying a province that included Judaeans and other ethnic groups (including other Yahwists). That they may have been able to understand as such could be implied by the Arabian traders passing through Idumea to Gaza, for whom pilgrimage had long played a structural role.[205]

Alternatively (or additionally), the idea of Jerusalem as a pilgrimage center, rather than as a political center, could be seen as an adaptation of an Achaemenid trope. Indeed this has been argued for other appearances of pilgrimage in the HB. Brent Strawn has argued this for the oracle in Isa 60, claiming it ought to be seen as an appropriation and subversion of the image of *Pax Persica* as depicted on the Apadana reliefs.[206] For Strawn, the combination of solar elements and voluntary and peaceful tribute procession make the oracle similar in tenor to the depiction of the *Pax Persica* as depicted at Persepolis. While the relevance of solar imagery for Persepolis is mistaken,[207] the emphasis on the novelty of the peaceful and voluntary nature of the pilgrimage of the nations to Jerusalem is an important point. Jones argues even more forcibly that this oracle subverts the Persian imperial one by replacing Persepolis with Jerusalem as the center. However, his argument is largely based on the idea that 2Isa prophesied the return and rebuilding, and that the residents of Jerusalem at the time of 3Isa would have been disappointed by unfulfilled promises.[208] That 2Isa was functioning as "authoritative scripture" at this time and in such

---

204. For an inspiring, pioneer study in this for the ANE, see Waerzeggers 2015b.
205. According to McCorriston 2011.
206. Strawn 2007; Hulster and Strawn 2015. Basically reiterated by Jones 2014. More generally on the *Pax Persica*, see the Introduction and Silverman forthcoming a.
207. He identifies the ubiquitous winged disk both as a sun disk, and as Ahuramazda. While the origins of the symbol were a solar disk, there is no clear indication it still had that connotation for the Achaemenids. Moreover, the identification with Ahuramazda is based on nothing substantial. One need not make such appeals to understand light imagery in Hebrew tradition, anyway.
208. Jones 2014: 621.

a manner cannot in fact be assumed. Nor can it be assumed to be relevant for the matrix (dreamer–scribe) responsible for 1Zech. Is the application of the same concept to Jerusalem collusion or subversion or something else? One can of course read the oracle as subversive, and perhaps some would have heard it that way. But when one takes seriously the rhetorical emphasis on voluntcerism within both images, they appear compatible. The Great King imagined his rule as fostering collective prosperity and engagement, and Isa 60 takes this to benefit Jerusalem. Indeed, it should be remembered that in the Persian view the center was the king, not a physical capital.[209] Moreover, the vision in Isa 60 is strictly religious rather than political: gifts and pilgrims come to Jerusalem, but here is no mention of independent rule. While the implication that the validity of foreign kings was dependent on their support of Jerusalem is no doubt one no other kings would accept, the idea that their positions were based on proper behavior before the gods was of wide currency. The apolitical and religious nature of the imagined pilgrimage is the same for the appearances in 1Zech. This is potentially appealing to the imperial masters for three reasons: *by being apolitical in the strict sense, by being ecumenical in a social sense, and by being potentially lucrative.* An appeal for a cult center presented in such a manner may indeed have appealed to a Darius seeking to consolidate his rule and to secure Egypt, or to his satrap in Damascus. It is to be doubted that the Persians were interested in fostering any forms of ethnic exclusivity. On the contrary, their vision of cosmopolitan voluntcerism is suited to the inclusive pilgrimage language visible in 1Zech (and 3Isa). Perhaps, then, pilgrimage was a suitable way to foster closer Yehud–diaspora ties, social cohesion within Yehud, and bring local prestige while not challenging the imperial order. That this could have been expected to produce economic benefits is also pertinent.

The Identity of "Growth" (צמח, Zech 3:8; 6:12)[210]

As indicated in passing above, there is much debate over who the figure called צמח was, whether the present Davidide (Zerubbabel) or a "messianic" figure.[211] Most of these discussions proceed from the observation that צמח is used in Jer 23:5 and 33:15. This assumes that the relevant Jeremian passages pre-date the writing of this text, were available

---

209. There were royal palaces, often called capitals, at Persepolis, Pasargadae, Susa, Ecbatana, and Babylon.

210. A modified form of this section was presented at the annual SBL meeting in Boston, November 2017, in the "Book of the Twelve" section.

211. E.g., Kashow 2016; cf. the discussions of chapters 3 and 6 above.

to the author(s), and were important to the dreamer/scribe. It also assumes that the expected audience would also know them. These assumptions are in fact insecure. Moreover, if the intention were to recall these two verses, why is the distinctive word pair used in Jeremiah (used with root צדק)[212] not used in Zechariah? Rather than such a narrow textual referent, one should recall that the root, however, usually occurs in contexts related to plant growth, typically as a metaphor for prosperity. For example, Qohelet, in his description of his *paradise* (2:5–6), notes how he used water to cause tree growth (צומח עצים). Genesis 2 uses it for the scrubs and grasses (v. 5) and Eden's trees (v. 9). Sirach 40:22 plausibly uses it for a wife that produces prosperity. It is therefore surprising scholarly discourse has not more extensively considered whether צמח here is merely functioning as a metaphor for prosperity, rather than a particular person. Surely this makes much more sense than an anachronistic "messianic" figure. Nevertheless, there are good grounds for seeing that it represents a particular individual who was expected to bring prosperity in a metonymic sense.

In both passages in 1Zech, צמח appears in a sign act's oral pronouncement. In the first, the figure will come in a context of prosperity (vines and fig trees)[213] as well as one in which Zerubbabel completes the temple. In the second, he will "grow out," build the temple, and rule. This figure is clearly fulfilling traditional ANE kingship roles: prosperity in the land and temple-building. Yet this figure is neither Joshua nor Zerubbabel. Moreover, there is no hint that this figure has *any* connection to the Davidic line. Not only is he not described as in the putative source in Jeremiah,[214] the figure comes from a vague "from his place" (מהחתיו), implying an unknown distance. Despite the scholarly wont to speak of Yehud as "the kingless age," there is in fact a king of Yehud: the Persian Great King. Therefore, in the second year of Darius, the only logical candidate for this role is Darius himself. Not only is Darius in fact the reigning king, he takes up the ANE trope of the royal gardener and expands the system of *paradises*, including one in Yehud itself. Further, if one seeks a verbal

212. Jeremiah has צמח צדקה and צמח צדיק, respectively.

213. "Vines and figs" are a standard shorthand for prosperity; see, e.g., Deut 8:8; 1 Kgs 4:25; 2 Kgs 18:31∥Isa 36:16; 1 Macc 14:12 or the inversions in Isa 24:4; Jer 5:17; Ps 105:33. Thus it is not eschatological, as stated by Ackroyd 1968: 191.

214. צמח צדיק, usually understood to be a quasi-technical term for "legitimate heir," on the basis of a parallel in a Ptolemaic inscription (*KAI* 43; text available in Gibson 1982; 234–7 [line 4]; Dixon 2013: 225–7). Rose 2000: 110–14 disputes that this carries this meaning in all attested occurrences, but he still acknowledges it in some instances. It seems to be the meaning for Jeremiah. If this were the intended meaning in 1Zech, surely the entire term would be used.

echo, Darius makes a concerted effort to explain that he re-established things "in their places" in his famous apology (§14, *[adamšim] gāθavā avāstāyam*, 3×).[215]

Important for this context is understanding the situation in Egypt. Egypt is glaringly absent from Darius's Behistun narrative (only appearing in passing in a list in the Elamite version of Column II§21).[216] New evidence from the Dakhla Oasis, however, shows that the subjection of Egypt by Cambyses had likely been incomplete, and that Darius and his satrap had to work several years to defeat the Egyptian Petubastis IV.[217] Though this period remains uncertainly understood,[218] it is generally thought that Darius himself arrived in Egypt to finish the pacification of the country and/or replace the satrap Aryandes with Pherendates in 518.[219] A Babylonian receipt discussed by Tolini shows that the Ebabbar temple of Sippar provided cavalry for Egypt in 22/XI/Darius 4 (21 February 517).[220] This likely means Darius's efforts were either beginning or ongoing at this time. Nearly 80 years ago Parker already suggested that the last oracle in 1Zech is connected to Darius having marched through Palestine.[221] Whether the sign act is so immediately connected is debatable, but it is true that Darius would have passed through Palestine twice, either in 518 or 517, both of which are after the dates of chs. 3 and 6 (519).

The travels of the king involved extensive preparations by the local communities, as evidenced by the demands of the royal table.[222] Therefore, intimations of royal passage through the Levant would likely have been known among the various provinces, as they made preparations for the king and his troops to pass through on their way to defeat Petubasis IV. A prophetic expectation that the king (or his representative, a satrap) would personally intervene in Yehud would therefore not have been politically inastute. Berquist has already suggested that 1Zech related to the Persian march through Palestine, though suggesting that the visions were countering a fear that the Persians would destroy Jerusalem.[223] However, Jerusalem was presumably still in ruins at this point in time, and there is

215. Schmitt 2009: 45–6.
216. Schmitt 2009: 51.
217. Kaper 2015.
218. See Ray 1988; Cruz-Uribe 2003: 54–7; Klotz 2015: 4–7.
219. Klotz 2015: 7, this remains uncertain.
220. Dar 141; Tolini 2011: 246–7.
221. Parker 1941: 374.
222. For a reconstruction of Cyrus and Cambyses in Babylonia, see Tolini 2011: 147–75; more generally, see Briant 2002: 186–9, 200–203.
223. Berquist 1995: 70–2.

no hint of Yehudian rebellion, so such a worry would seem historically misplaced. The appeal to the military situation of the invasion of Egypt, however, is astute.

This military situation in mind, as well as both dynasties' use of the prosperity motif,[224] means the best candidate for the individual called "Growth" is Darius himself. As far as the present author can tell, this has not been suggested previously.[225] This means that rather than negotiating the relative positions of Davidide and priest, 1Zech is concerned with the relationship between a renewed temple in Yehud and the Persian emperor. The Yehudite expectations for the Persian king were much like the expectations for the role of Cyrus on the behalf on Babylonian priests as described by Waerzeggers: to fulfill the necessary roles of patron and defender of the cult.[226]

To defend this historical view within the text, it is necessary to reconsider what the phrase "behold, a man whose name is growth" (הנה איש צמח שמו)[227] in 6:12 means in the context of a sign act's oracle said to Joshua the High Priest. The simplest understanding is to see it as a reference to the sign act in ch. 3, i.e. specifying it as the same man spoken of previously, of whom Joshua and his colleagues were already functioning as signs. The statement itself is a metonymical statement, in which the crowns represent the absent but coming "Growth," rather than identifying Joshua (or a redacted out Zerubbabel) as the "Growth." This sign act affirms the previous prediction, while also affirming that Joshua will remain in office, within the individual's good graces ("at his right hand," following the LXX of v. 13, ἐκ δεξιῶν αὐτοῦ). The use of "Growth" therefore can be seen to take up the idea that proper kingship and proper service of the gods creates prosperity in the land. The coming of the Achaemenid emperor to the Levant was an occasion for the Yehud

---

224. In addition, one may point to at least a broader Iranian use for royal names: the name of the shadowy Median king, Cyaxares (OP *hu-vaxštra*) can be analyzed as containing the OP root *vaxš*, "growth" (so Kent 1961: 177), "good growth." The Median pretender in DB II claims to be a relative of Cyaxares (lines 15–16, *uvaxštrahyā taumāyā*; Schmitt 2009 §24, p. 52). Analogously, in the religious sphere, *Yasna* 10 (part of the *Hom Yašt*) claims that praise causes Haoma to grow on the mountains (Y. 10:3, 6, also using *vaxš*-).

225. E.g., not considered in Rignell 1950; Garbini 1988; Floyd 2000; Rose 2000; Meyers and Meyers 2004; Jauhiainen 2005; Mowinckel 2005: 19; Petterson 2009 and 2015; Tiemeyer 2015; Boda 2016.

226. Waerzeggers 2015a.

227. Joüon and Muraoka 1991 §154, 158 could read this as either a relative clause or a nominal clause.

elite to increase their prosperity, rather than an occasion for "nationalist" or eschatological malcontent or a relative power-struggle between supporters of the Davidic dynasty and the priesthood.²²⁸ This reading aligns with the other readings of the visionary scenes above, as one rather strongly justifying cooperation with the imperial scenario. One might still wonder whether the temple was something which the local elites wanted and therefore were seeking imperial approval for, was an imperial project with which they sought to justify their cooperation, or a combination of the two. Moreover, the sign act appears to demonstrate close cooperate in the building of the temple between Judaean leaders in Yehud and in Babylonia. Though the text sees the arrival of the Babylonians as post-dating local concern for rebuilding, it does welcome their participation in the process, to the point of establishing permanent memorials to them.

Safety and No Walls

Defensive structures and their construction are a matter of obvious interest to the empire. A recognition of this can be seen in the accusations Nehemiah's enemies level against his efforts to build a wall, regardless of one's opinion on their historicity. With a sprawling territory including a huge variety of terrains, the Persians had to be strategic about where defenses could be placed, and where they should be tolerated. The variety of existing local structures aside, the Persians used *birah/birta'*—fortified, garrisoned settlements, *paradises* (walled orchards), and unwalled estates and villages.²²⁹ It is probably no accident that all HB reflexes of *birta'* are

---

228. Contra, most recently, Wöhrle 2016: 180, 183–4.

229. On *birah*, see Lemaire and Lozachmeur 1987; Will 1987; Edelman 2005: 333; 2007: 52, 63. For meanings in both OP and Elamite reflexes for more than just "fortress," see Rossi 2010. For examples of other Persian *birta'*, see, e.g., Elephantine (TAD B2.2/AP 6, line 3, Porten and Yardeni 1986–99: 20–1); possibly Ammon (P.Cairo Zen 1 59.003, understood by Edelman as *birah* in Ammon, but Edgar 1919: 166, Bagnall and Deraw 2004: 237, and Pfeiffer 2010: 248 all see it as a place name); Xanthos (Metzger 1979a: 136, line 3); Samaria (WDSP 1, line 1, Gropp et al. 2001: 34). Tuplin's analysis of Xenophon (Tuplin 1987b and 1988) shows that while Xenophon's schema is not clearly borne out, clearly defensive structures are relatively rare. For some surveys in Iran, see Wright, Neely, and Carter 2010; Chaverdi et al. 2010; Boucharlat 2013a: 538–40; Henkelman 2013: 538–40. Even the heartland is not really characterized by cities (e.g., Boucharlat 2007). Several scholars have seen this pattern in Yehud as well (Hoglund 1991: 57–60; 2002: 18; Carter 1999: 185–248 [though focused on population numbers]; Edelman 2007).

arguably no earlier than the reign of Artaxerxes I,[230] when it would seem Jerusalem was rewalled for the first time. Edelman argues that Nehemiah turned Jerusalem into a *birah*,[231] which would have occurred later than 1Zech according to the dating argued above.

The third vision's claim that YHWH's return to Jerusalem would not require physical walls (2:8–9) should therefore be seen within this light. The renewed attention to Jerusalem in 1Zech is not to be taken militarily, and not necessarily even as a return to being a provincial capital. The vision gives this a theological interpretation, but the positive nature of the vision as a whole implies a political expectation: that the Persians will maintain order well enough that walls will be unnecessary to protect the new sanctuary. Not until the reign of his grandson do imperial views of Jerusalem appear to shift.

Such a perspective on Jerusalem is perhaps more important than it appears at first glance. Though there is a hyperbolic expectation of growth and prosperity, the vision distinctly lacks any monarchic or imperial pretences: Jerusalem will be significant for its cultic site alone. The nearly contemporaneous and also likely unwalled Yahwistic cultic site at Gerizim should be remembered. Maybe the elite in both Yehud and Samerina thought new pilgrimage sites were effective ways to appeal to the administration's needs while retaining a claim on the ever-growing Yahwistic diaspora.

Vision 6, Darius, and Falsehood

Given the direct concern over falsehood in Vision 6, it would be remiss to neglect another contemporary concern with falsehood. This is, of course, Darius's apology at Behistun: four times "the Lie" appears within the narrative (*Drauga*), while the act of insurrection is several times described as "he lied" (*adurujiya*).[232] In fact, Darius appeals to the fact that he was "not a Liar" (*nai draujana āham*, IV §63) as reason for Ahuramazda's assistance. Darius's usage of this language strikes many as pushing beyond a typical concern for honesty.[233] Side-stepping the question of Iranian religious developments for the moment, one can nevertheless notice that this sentiment matches well the concern of the curse in vision 6.

---

230. For Susa: Neh 1:1; Esth 1:2; 9:12; Dan 8:2; in Judah, 1 Chr 29:1, 19; 2 Chr 17:12, 27:4; Neh 2:8, 7:2.

231. Edelman 2005, especially 333, 344–8.

232. As a substantive: I §10; IV §§54–6, 63–4; as the act of insurrection: I § 16; III § 49; IV § 52. For a critical edition of the OP inscription, see Schmitt 2009.

233. As well as being ironic considering the dubious nature of his narrative, but that is a separate matter.

The concern with theft is also implicit in Darius's inscriptions. On his tomb (DNb) Darius boasts that he prevents the weak from harming the strong (§2),[234] and theft is one of the few ways the weak can harm the strong. Of course, this is in parallel with its opposite and is intended to express comprehensive impartiality. An emphasis on justice is unremarkable in the context of ANE kingship. A specific appeal to Achaemenid ideals in the flying scroll would therefore seem to be over-reaching. Nevertheless, it is an interesting point of connection.

For a later period, however, a connection could most definitely have been made. A version of DB with DNb has been found at Elephantine, meaning that at least 100 years later some Judaeans had direct access to Darius's conception of kingship.

Though deliberate appeal to Darius's conceptions of proper order would seem rash, it remains true that an explicit appeal to Torah (or the Ten Commandments) as a *written text* let alone scripture is here anachronistic and inappropriate as well. Instead, a better way to conceptualize the subconscious concerns of the visionary is to see an interest in proper order, this ultimately being seen as consonant with Darius's victory rather than hampered thereby.

Summary for First Zechariah

Overall, the first level of analysis of 1Zech questioned some of the statements concerning Yehud often made based upon it. From a phenomenological perspective, 1Zech has many features consonant with a dream or vision report. Since no compelling reason exists for excising the precise dates, the vision report appears to belong to the period leading up to Darius's final pacification of Egypt. It was located in the gubernatorial complex at Ramat Raḥel rather than Jerusalem itself. The vision justifies the social structures in Yehud: temple, governor, and priesthood, arguing for the renewed importance of Jerusalem. Joshua is accepted as high priest, YHWH's control of the cosmos is tied to imperial structures, and Yehud is purged of unethical behaviors of untruth and theft. Importantly, the new temple is closely linked to the Babylonian diaspora via votive offerings, and it is predicated as a central pilgrimage site for Judaeans and the nations. Having now analyzed the two main literary sources, it is now possible to consider them both in a broader Persian and Judaean context, and move to consider what this means for Achaemenid self-presentations.

234. Schmitt 2009: 106.

Part III

Chapter 6

THE GREAT KING, LOCAL ELITES, TEMPLES,
AND PRIESTS IN THE EARLY EMPIRE

Having closely analyzed two Hebrew texts, it is time to take a broader view of sources discussing the relations between the Great King, his subjects, and their religious institutions. This chapter will discuss three topics: the local relations of the Teispid dynasty, the Persian utilization of temples, and a brief excursus on Josephus's stories concerning the priesthood at the end of the empire.

*Initial Negotiations and Imperial Narratives:
The Teispid Foundation*

It is well-known, and unfortunate, that the surviving self-presentations of Cyrus and his sons Cambyses and Bardiya are rather limited. This study, however, cannot escape analyzing two issues which provide occasions for assessing the interplays between newly subjected elites and their new, Persian masters: the issues of Cyrus's and Cambyses's engagement with Babylon and its *Akītu* festival, and Cambyses's behavior in Egypt.

Cyrus, Cambyses, Babylon, and the Akītu *Festival*

The *Akītu* festival was already discussed in relation to 2Isa and the city of Babylon in Part I. As is well known, the Babylonian version of the festival and its associated epic, the *Enūma Eliš*, played an important role in the performance of Neo-Babylonian kingship.[1] As such, the way that Cyrus interacted with the tradition can shed some light on the early ways in which the Teispid conquerors negotiated with local elites, at least in

---

1. Kuhrt 1987; Pongratz-Leisten 1994: 93–112; Bidmead 2002: 2; Waerzeggers 2015a.

important centers. The key texts for this are the Nabonidus Chronicle (BM 34381), the Cyrus Cylinder, and the *Verse Account* of Nabonidus.[2] Their interpretation is not so straight-forward, however, as the first is unfortunately lacunose,[3] and the latter two are decidedly interested.

Nabonidus Chronicle. After Cyrus's general Gubaru had arranged a peaceful entrance into the city for him and Nabonidus was captured (3/VIII/Cyrus 0; III.15–20), the chronicle claims that Gubaru appointed officers and then promptly died (11/VIII).[4] The remainder of the year saw the return of Mesopotamian cult statues to their home cities (III.21–22).[5] Sometime before 27/XII Cyrus's wife died and mourning was announced (lines 22–24). Unfortunately, the remainder of the tablet is quite broken (lines 24–28), and this is the section in which Cambyses appears to participate in the events associated with the *Akītu*.

Technically, the *Akītu* is not mentioned. However, the day in which Cambyses is said to go to an official of Nabu is the 4th of Nisannu (4/I/Cyrus 1, III.24). This is the day in the *Akītu* festival in which the king was supposed to go into the shrine of Nabu and then travel to Borsippa.[6] Moreover, the text mentions the E-ningidar-kalamma-summa (the Nabu temple in Babylon),[7] an official of Nabu, the hand of Nabu, a trip of Nabu to Esangil, and Bel, all of which would be expected for

---

2. Nabonidus Chronicle (Grayson's Chronicle 7): Grayson 1975: 104–11; Glassner 2004: 232–9; a new collation of the last lines (24–28) appears in George 1996: 379–80, along with some discussion on their significance (pp. 380–4); trans. in Kuhrt 2009: 50–3.

Cyrus Cylinder: the most recent transliteration and translation is Finkel 2013b: 129–35 (translit.), 4–7 (trans.); for other translations, see Hallo 2000: 314–16; Kuhrt 2009: 70–4.

Verse Account (a.k.a. *Strophengedicht*): Pritchard 1969: 312–15; Schaudig 2001: 563–78; Kuhrt 2009: 75–80.

3. Rightly stressed by Kuhrt 1987: 51; 1988: 122.

4. Vanderhooft 2006: 362 has suggested this might be a way to treat Gubaru as a royal substitute for Cyrus, absorbing divine punishment for invading Babylon, though he is careful to note that that would merely be by implication than by direct statement of the Chronicler.

5. In this respect, it is worth noting that Nabonidus had transferred a number of cult statues to Babylon, to protect them from capture by Cyrus. This has been demonstrated by a collection of boat-rental contracts convincingly argued to be for that purpose. See Beaulieu 1993; Zawadzki 2012; Sandowicz 2015.

6. Bidmead 2002: 60–2; Zgoll 2006: 24.

7. George 1992: 24–5, 59, 310–12; 1996: 378; Waerzeggers 2011b: 732–3 (on uncertainty and day 5).

that day's events in the festival. While the date and locations match those of the *Akītu*, what precisely is being narrated is unclear, for three reasons. First, the breaks in the tablet make the exact actions unclear; even the identity of all the actors is uncertain. The identity of the person in Elamite clothing in line 25 is not extant, and scholars have understood this person variously as Cambyses or Cyrus himself.[8] Second, the E-ningidar-kalamma-summa temple was associated with royal investitures that were timed to correspond with the New Year festival, but may not have been technically part of it.[9] Moreover, since the identity of the person in line 25 is uncertain, it impossible to know whether the scepter was being given to Cyrus (and thus a formal investiture) or to Cambyses (and thus establishing his status as crown prince). George has pointed to the example of Nabonidus for the former, and Nebuchadnezzar II for the latter.[10] Noting the peculiarities around the double-titles of Cambyses and Cyrus attested in various documentary sources, Tolini has argued that Cyrus was away from Babylon and that Cambyses fulfilled the king's role at the last minute. Thus this unexpected substitution confused some northern Babylonian scribes into considering Cambyses to be the king of Babylon.[11] Third, the significance of the Elamite garment, whether on Cyrus or on Cambyses, is uncertain. One might suspect that it merely means the ceremonial court dress as visible either on the mysterious "genius" at Pasargadae or on the Persian nobles and the Great King in the Persepolis reliefs.[12] Yet the fact that the chronicler appears to find this unusual or surprising is hard to assess. Was it a deliberate snub (as argued by Oppenheim),[13] an assertion of Persian (Anšanite?) domi-

---

8. E.g., Cyrus: George 1996: 380; Kuhrt 2009: 51 (though tentatively); Sekunda 2010: 264; Cambyses: Oppenheim 1985: 555–6; Bidmead 2002: 140; Brosius 2004: 180; Waerzeggers 2015a: 201.

9. Oppenheim 1985: 555–8; George 1996: 382–3; Kessler has tied the earlier event in line 16 with royal ritual and the New Year, but that is dated several months earlier and thus does not solve the issue for these lines (Kessler 2002).

10. George 1996: 383.

11. See Tolini 2011: 135–45. On the phenomenon of the brief appearance of Cambyses as king of Babylon during Cyrus's first year, see Zawadzki 1996.

12. Álvarez-Mon 2009: 26–7 argues it is precisely the fringed garment worn by the Pasargadae genius and by the Neo-Elamite king Te'umman in Neo-Assyrian reliefs; Sekunda rather argues it is the style found at Persepolis (Sekunda 2010: 264). Henkelman 2003b: 83–5 saw a distinction between regular Elamite and royal, fringed garments, but still sees the significance in the Chronicler's note one merely of foreignness (especially n. 35).

13. Oppenheim 1985: 557–8. I have been unable to access Oppenheim 1974.

nance (as argued by Kuhrt),[14] or simply a prosaic statement (as argued by Álvarez-Mon)[15]? In addition to these problems, Zawadzki and more recently Waerzeggers have questioned how disinterested and reliable the account itself is (though from very different angles).[16] In light of these difficulties, one should be careful in using this text for any sweeping conclusions concerning Teispid policy. Nevertheless, Tolini's arguments that it represents an emergency solution are attractive. They would highlight both the inevitably experimental nature of the early years of the empire (unprecedented for the kings of Anšan) as well as the apparent desire both to accommodate some local forms of legitimation, while still retaining some level of distinctive identity (the "Elamite" garment, whatever one decides that means in the end).

Cyrus Cylinder. This text has received scholarly commentary almost rivaling that lavished on biblical texts. As has been long noted, the inscription closely follows the Mesopotamian tradition of foundation deposits, particularly those of the Assyrian kings of Babylon.[17] Moreover, recent fragment discoveries at the British Museum have shown that in addition to the buried foundation deposit, the text also existed in at least one library copy.[18]

The text has two main parts: a third-person narration of the sins of Nabonidus, and a first-person narration by Cyrus of his pious deeds in the city.[19] The first section describes the conquests of Cyrus as the result of Marduk having pity on the land and rescuing it from the impious Nabonidus. The pattern of divine anger–abandonment–suffering–divine return should be familiar from other ANE texts as well as the HB. Somewhat ironically, the cylinder's claim that Marduk gave Gutium and Media to Cyrus (line 13) was preceded by Nabonidus's similar claim in his Harran Cylinder (lines 24–29) that Marduk gave the King of Media, Astyages, into Cyrus's hands.[20] Also of note is this section's concern to disparage Nabonidus's heir, Belshazzar, a feature revealed in one of

---

14. I have been unable to access Kuhrt 1997: 300–302.
15. Álvarez-Mon 2009: 31.
16. Zawadzki 2010; Waerzeggers 2015b.
17. E.g., Harmatta 1971; Kuhrt 1983. For a contextualization of the objects, including their provenance, see Finkel 2013b.
18. Finkel 2013a: 18–22; 2013b: 2.
19. Finkel 2013a: 24 rather sees three sections, and sees them as independent compositions.
20. Schaudig 2001: 2.12 (trans. pp. 436–7). Cf. His mother's stele, Col. II (3.2, pp. 500–513).

the new fragments (line 3).[21] The second section directly contrasts the impieties listed in the first section with Cyrus's concern to seek after Marduk, restore Mesopotamian cults, and strengthen Babylon's urban architecture. Also notable is a strong concern to establish Cambyses as rightful heir (lines 27 and 35).

The disparaging of Nabonidus in this text is an interesting contrast to the depiction of the conquered Croesus, noted in chapter 1. While the Greek tradition had managed to justify Cyrus's rule while still respecting Croesus, this text denies all legitimacy to the former ruler. This is all the more striking when one considers the fate of Nabonidus and his son: while this text is silent barring mentioning his capture (line 17), several other traditions claim that Cyrus spared his life and exiled him to Iran.[22] One might suspect that the reason for this strong delegitimation was merely a standard Near Eastern *post hoc* explanation for regime change: the gods had clearly abandoned Nabonidus, so therefore he must have

---

21. Finkel 2013a: 4, 18–22; 2013b: 130. Perhaps relevant to this is that Cambyses seems to have taken over the estates of Belshazzar; cf. Wunsch 2000b: 103–4. The institution of the estate of the crown prince is attested at least until Artaxerxes I. See Stolper 1985: 54–5.

22. Berossus claims that Cyrus exiled Nabonidus to Carmania (Burstein 1978: 28, §4; De Breuker 2010: BNJ 680 F 9a). The so-called *Dynastic Prophecy* (BM 40623, ii.20–21) also claims he was exiled to an unnamed place (for transliteration, translation, and notes, see van der Spek 2003: 311–24; cf. Kuhrt 2009: 80–1). It should be noted, however, that both of these are Hellenistic period texts, and thus it is difficult to assess their reliability, though several historians, e.g., Beaulieu 1989: 231 and Waters 2010: 67, have found it credible. Herodotus describes the Germanii as an agricultural tribe of the Persians (I.125; Herodotus 2002: 164–5), and these are usually understood to be the Carmanians (Asheri, Lloyd, and Corcella 2007: 164). Strabo does describe the islands of the Persian Gulf south of Carmania as a site of exile (XVI.3.5 and 7; Strabo 1930: 302–5; Kuhrt 2009: 876; cf. Pliny VI.26.98, Pliny 1961: 413). Strabo mentions Chaldaean exiles in Gerrha, though this appears to be on the Arabian side of the gulf. As a side note, it is worth mentioning that Ctesias claimed that the gods forced Cyrus to be lenient to Croesus, exiling him near Ecbatana (F9.5 from Photius; see Stronk 2010: 315; no sections from the conquest of Babylon are extant). The fact that the two Babylonian pretenders under Darius I claimed Nabonidus as their father probably has no bearing on whether or not Cyrus had had Nabonidus executed or exiled, though maybe the fact they did not claim to be or descend from Belshazzar is significant. It is hard to know whether an exiled monarch or a martyred one would have been considered more dangerous to a conqueror. It is probably best to admit the evidence does not allow a decision on this matter.

been impious. One certainly does not need to posit a general, pre-existing dissatisfaction with Nabonidus's rule to explain either the conquest or the Cyrus Cylinder's (or the *Verse Account*'s) disparagement of Nabonidus.[23] A clear take-away from this piece of royal self-presentation, however, is how willing Cyrus was to frame his legitimacy within native terms, at least for elites of major, pre-existing entities. (Though, while Cyrus claims to take special care of Marduk, there is no mention of the *Akītu*—yet the focus on the early days of conquest could explain this.) Whether or not his own self-understanding was already deeply impacted by earlier experience of Neo-Assyrian imperialism is impossible to say from this document, the (fortuitous?) appeal to Ashurbanipal (line 43) notwithstanding.[24]

The Verse Account. The lacunose nature of this text makes it challenging to use, but nonetheless its lopsided perspective shines clearly through the gaps: like the above-discussed Cyrus Cylinder, this text portrays Nabonidus as an impious failure and Cyrus as his pious successor. There are a number of specific parallels between these two texts. Nabonidus has an unorthodox fascination with the moon cult (i.23ff.); the *Akītu* is neglected (ii.11); the king establishes a rival capital in Arabia (ii.27); there is a critique of Belshazzar (ii.18–20). Like the Cyrus Cylinder this text

---

23. There is a surprisingly persistent trend within historiography to accept the criticisms of Nabonidus in the Cyrus Cylinder and *Verse Account* uncritically, and to posit an undue devotion to Sin by Nabonidus. The evidence for an undue focus on Sin is primarily the inscriptions concerning the temple at Harran, where a focus on Sin is to be expected, and the *Verse Account*, which is *post facto* and tendentious. To claim that Nabonidus was more focused on Sin than was normal—and that this was thought at the time to be problematic—would require other pieces of evidence to that effect. See, e.g., Vanderhooft 1999: 52–6, who notes these problems but accepts it as probable anyway. For a more recent example, see Razmjou 2013. Even Finn 2017, who discusses the various texts discussed here, finds the *Verse Account* to be "a reliable historical source" (p. 189). Van der Spek is more careful, noting that there are comparators for the invitation of conquerors by quarrelling internal parties (van der Spek 2014: 245–6). He appeals mostly to Roman examples; one could also think of the Anglo-Norman invasion of Ireland. While this is of course possible, the structure of Mesopotamian theological thinking (the defeated king is by definition out of divine favor) makes it an unnecessary hypothesis without evidence to that effect. Several scholars have of course made similar cautionary comments in these respects (e.g., Kuhrt 1990; Moukarzel 2014).

24. Stronach 1997a: 47 and Stronach 2002 has seen Assyrian influence in Persian iconography, seeing it evoke imperialism for a "home" audience.

was clearly drafted with sophistication and subtlety—it is not merely the transcription of foreign ideology in Babylonian idiom.[25]

Waerzeggers has proposed a compelling new understanding of col. V of this text.[26] Noting that the two officials in lines 23'–24', Zēria and Rīmūt, retain their offices well into the reign of Cyrus and that Cyrus is already ruler in line 4, she reads the scene as a dramatization of Cyrus restoring the Marduk cult after Nabonidus's sacrileges rather than the usual reading of priestly complicity in Nabonidus's schemes. If this re-reading is correct, it tells us at least three key things about the Teispid legitimation efforts. First, it shows the efforts of high-level Neo-Babylonian officials to facilitate the transition of power. Not only do Zēria and Rīmūt retain their positions (after presumably swearing fealty), they participate in public displays of Cyrus's cultic competence (approving of his removal of Sin's crescent). Perhaps one could appeal to the example of Udjahorresnet in Egypt for a similarly effective local collaborator (see below). This echoes the sophistication taken in drafting these documents. Second, the entire scenario hints at the breadth of efforts undertaken to affirm the right of conquest.[27] Not only is the entire composition a peculiar piece of poetry, this scene is one that could be performed for a popular audience. The text times this during the *Akītu* festival (11th of Nisan, v. 28'), a festival that involved public processions and merriment; a potent time for ideological dissemination in a largely oral society. Was this text, then, intended for a wider dissemination in Babylonian circles via performative means? Third, there is an uncertain hint of Iranian innovations in marking allegiance: in line 26' Zēria and Rīmūt bare their heads during their oath; Waerzeggers finds this unusual in Babylonian practice.[28] This is a very intriguing

---

25. Machinist and Tadmor 1993 have shown how v. 12' can be seen to construct a very subtle and learned critique of Nabonidus as a pretentious wannabe scholar, which took up and twisted elements of Nabondius's own self-presentation. A more extensive effort was made in this regard by Beaulieu 2007. However, contrary to their claims (Machinist and Tadmor 1993: 150 n. 34; Beaulieu 2007: 150–9) this does not require positing pre-existing tensions or oppositions before Cyrus; all it proves is the sophistication of Cyrus's propaganda efforts. Indeed, it is the nature of propaganda to twist the truth—it is the small grain of truth that makes it so effective. The links between the accusations against Nabonidus and Nabonidus's own inscriptions should therefore be understood as masterful tendentiousness, not as evidence of pre-conquest opposition.

26. Waerzeggers 2012.

27. Finn 2017: 179 oddly calls Cyrus a usurper rather than a conqueror. The issues of legitimation are rather different in the two scenarios.

28. Waerzeggers 2012: 319.

suggestion, but it is difficult to verify. While Persian and Babylonian males are typically depicted wearing various sorts of headgear—and this has been much studied[29]—the social significance of putting them on or taking them off is much less clear, in either Iranian or Mesopotamian traditions, so far as the present author can ascertain.[30]

---

29. On Persian headgear, see Thompson 1965: 125–6; Shahbazi 1992: 724–9. He divides them into two main types, court and cavalry; Benda-Weber 2014; for post-Islamic Iran, see Algar 1989.

On Babylonian headgear, see Boehmer 1980–83: 203–10; Magen 1986 (royal Assyrian).

30. Waerzeggers 2012 does not comment on the basis for the claim of abnormality. It is true that headgear does not feature in the discussions around gestures of submission, these typically being a variety of hand gestures and prostration (Frye 1972; Choksy 2002; cf. the vast literature on *proskynesis*). Waerzeggers (personal communication) indicated that she had consulted CAD. Roth 2005's entry for *patāru* 1 includes "to bare the head" in both the contexts of mourning and oaths, but its examples are the *Cyrus Cylinder* and the *Verse Account* (p. 290). The only other instance it gives is in an incantation text as an action the lamentation priest does before the incantation (KAR 60, line 17–18, translated in Linssen 2004: 274). In his *Reallexicon* article on headgear Waetzoldt does suggest religious importance to the wearing or not of headgear, but none of the examples are clearly relevant for the issue at hand (Waetzoldt 1980–83: 197; thanks to Sebastian Fink for pointing out this reference). The most interesting is a ritual text for lunar eclipses, which requires all people to remove their headgear for the duration of the eclipse—although they are also to cover their heads with their clothing (Clay 1923: 12–17 [no. 6, see lines 21 and 44]). The primary significance would appear to be a negative situation that requires the covering of the head with a garment, the removal of the headgear being incidental to this requirement (cf. the reading of an older text by Sjöberg [1973: 30–1, 41], who explicitly appeals to this eclipse ritual as a parallel). Other instances also appear to be irrelevant. The omen series *Šumma Izbu* includes an omen for the anomalous appearance of an infant wearing headgear (Leichty 1970: 115 [Tablet IX, line 16']). Removal of headgear also appears as a punishment for criminal priests in an Assyrian letter (Parpola 1993: 73–4 [no. 96]) and in an instance of rebellion (Reynolds 2003: 151–2 [no. 183]). Several other scholars have kindly indicated to the present author that they are unaware of any relevant instances of baring the head (Jack Sasson, Pauline Abenda, and Irene Winter, personal communications). While it would seem therefore that the action is not particularly typical within Babylonian practice in this context, it also is not at present visible within Achaemenid Persian traditions either. The audience scenes at Persepolis show the subjects before the king with their traditional headgear on. Khaleghi-Motlagh 1998: 45–6 cites the ninth century CE *Shahnameh* for a tradition of removing one's hat in deference to social superiors (vv. 780 and 2470, but the present author has been unable to access any English translation

Be that as it may, the depiction of Nabonidus as a "Mad King" was remarkably successful. In this respect it is worth noting both the book of Daniel, where the motif was transferred to Nebuchadnezzar,[31] and the more direct reflex *4QPrayer of Nabonidus*, of which four fragments are extant.[32] Though the function of Judaean literature in which Babylonian kings are forced to accept Yahweh is well-rehearsed, it has not typically been considered as part of successful Teispid ideology.[33] Beaulieu saw the theme relate to Nabonidus's own self-presentations and to pre-conquest opposition to him.[34] Henze, rather, argues the differences between Nabonidus's inscriptions, Dan 4, and *4QPrayer* are due to being reflexes of differing oral traditions around the same historical event.[35] Newsom has speculated that the depiction of Nabonidus accepting YHWH means that *Prayer* derives from Judaean groups ideologically opposed to the pro-Cyrus Judaeans behind 2Isa.[36] However, as noted above, it is dangerous to posit pre-Cyrus opposition to Nabonidus in Babylon. Moreover, Newsom's claim that Judaeans had direct knowledge of Nabonidus's Haran inscription is surprising—even accepting the thesis that inscriptions were disseminated orally, why would the Haran inscription have been read aloud outside of Haran?[37]

There are two better contexts in which to consider *4QPrayer of Nabonidus* and the Danielic stories: (1) either a folkloric reflex of Cyrus's anti-Nabonidus propaganda; or (2) Hellenistic scholarly debates over kingship, as posited by Waerzeggers.[38] Since the Dead Sea Scrolls

that marks the verse numbers; Professor Dick Davies has kindly taken a look at the cited passages and indicated that he does not see them as unequivocally indicating such a practice, personal communication).

31. Cf. Beaulieu 2007: 137. A connection between Dan 4 and Nabonidus was first suggested in 1899 (Reissler 1899, cited by Beaulieu; the present author has not had access to this).

32. Collins 1996; Henze 1999: 64–73; Newsom 2010 and 2013.

33. Indeed, Finn has called the anti-Nabonidus tradition as "anti-establishment" despite the fact it clearly was pro-Cyrus, i.e., pro-new-establishment (Finn 2017: 185).

34. Beaulieu 1989: 214–19; Beaulieu 2007: esp. 159–63. See the critique in the footnotes above.

35. Henze 1999: 73.

36. Newsom 2010: 70–2; 2013: 273–4.

37. Newsom 2013: 278–9. Unless one posited that the adapted versions in the Babylon Stele and in Larsa were read out; see Beaulieu 2007: 148, cf. 155.

38. Waerzeggers 2015d: 109–19. Indeed, she adduces *4QPrayer* as parallel, later literature showing an interest in the period of transition from NB to Persian rule.

include numerous esoteric links to Mesopotamian knowledge, such an understanding is not without merit. Yet, given the thematic nature of the links and over-all folkloristic hue, in this case it seems more probable that *4QPrayer* relates to folkloric traditions around Nabonidus.[39] For present purposes, positing a folkloric tradition around Nabonidus in the sixth century onwards suggests that Cyrus's propaganda efforts were more extensive than only sophisticated literature aimed at the traditional Babylonian elites (as is the case for the *Verse Account* and *Cyrus Cylinder*). A similar sort of effort by Cyrus has previously been posited by Kuhrt, on the basis of similarities between Herodotus's and Ctesias's narratives of Cyrus's childhood and the legends of Sargon of Agade.[40] This of course makes eminent sense; in a world in which the majority of potential subjects are oral, one should find ways to impart one's claim to rule to them. Subsequent inversion of such stories is the natural result.[41] One can therefore understand the sophisticated literature of Herodotus, the Danielic authors, and the Qumran scribes as higher-class reflexes of this broader Teispid ideological agenda, refracted through the ages. One may wonder at the remarkable success of this narrative (so much so that it is essentially repeated by historians to this day). Is this mere happenstance, or did Cyrus merely employ incredibly effective Babylonian spin-doctors?[42] In either case, it seems wise to understand the Teispid ideological efforts in Babylonia to have been much more extensive than a few sophisticated inscriptions for a rarified audience.

39. As already argued by Bickerman 1967: 73–7 (*4QPrayer* on p. 76). In this respect it is interesting to note that Kvanvig posited that stories concerning Nabonidus influenced the various stories that circulated around the Iranian king Kay Kāvus (Kvanvig 1988, 476, though she does not elaborate). Several different versions of Kay Kāvus (Av. Kauui Usan)'s madness survive (caused by madness, *Bundahisn* 33.8 [Anklesaria 1956: 272–5]; caused by the demon Aēšma "wrath," *Denkard* 9.22.5–12 [West 1988: 221–3]; tempted by Eblis ["Satan"], *Shahnameh* [Davis 2006: 184–6]). Given the fact that the figure of Kay Kāvus has Indo-Iranian roots and that the parallels to Nabonidus are vague at best, the parallel serves more to show the popularity of such types of stories within folklore more generally. On Kay Kāvus, see Skjærvø 2013. More recently, Greenstein has argued that Nabonidus's Haran Stele is itself based on an Eastern Mediterranean story pattern he calls the "Fugitive Hero Pattern" (Greenstein 2015, esp. 30–5). This could perhaps help explain how Nabonidus is taken up into folkloric traditions and survive.

40. Kuhrt 2003; cf. Briant 2002: 14–16. On Herodotus's uses of oral sources (albeit not folklore *per se*) see now David 2017.

41. And this is, of course, the realm in which Scott's famous "hidden transcripts" comes to play: in the oral culture of the peasants.

42. This brings to mind the effective damning of Richard III by Shakespeare.

Cambyses in Egypt

Another key moment for assessing Teispid engagements with subjects is the conquest and pacification of Egypt, started by Cambyses (and completed by Darius). This has attracted no shortage of scholarly attention, largely due to Herodotus's depiction of Cambyses as unhinged.[43] For present purposes, it can be argued that Cambyses's policy towards Egypt was rather similar to his father's towards Babylonia. Three topics highlight this: (1) hints of the manner in which Cambyses may have justified his conquest; (2) evidence that Cambyses endeavored to be depicted as a proper pharaoh; and (3) the apparently incomplete nature of Cambyses's conquest. These will be covered in turn.

A couple of Greek stories give hints at what may have been a justification used by Cambyses for invading Egypt. Herodotus claims that the Egyptians say Cambyses's mother was the daughter of the antepenultimate pharaoh, Apries (Herod. III.2; Herodotus discounts the story).[44] A fragment from Ctesias suggests a similar tradition, in which Cambyses invades Egypt to avenge the murder of his father-in-law, Apries, after hearing the story from his wife (Herodotus says the woman in question was his mother, while Ctesias makes her his wife).[45] While the implication that the invasion was conducted on a whim for family pride is not credible, it is believable that Cambyses would have depicted the campaign as revenge for the murder of Apries.[46] The pharaoh during the preparations for invasion was Amasis, who had murdered his predecessor in a coup.[47] Campaigning in Apries's name, therefore, would have been a useful way to depict the event as a restoration of proper Egyptian order. Indeed, an episode in Herodotus's depiction of Cambyses's madness in fact suggests a concerted effort to damn the memory of Amasis—analogous to the efforts made against Nabonidus. In III.16, Herodotus describes

---

43. Essentially all of book three, but especially Herod. III.25–38 (Herodotus 2000: 32–51). For some studies, see, e.g., Hofmann and Vorbichler 1980; Brown 1982; Lloyd 1988; Briant 2002: 50–61; Cruz-Uribe 2003; Rollinger 2003; Ruzicka 2012: ch. 2. For Egyptian sources, see the useful overview in Vittman 2011: especially 377–82; also Kuhrt 2009: 107–27.

44. Herodotus 2000: 4–5.

45. Fragment 13a (Stronk 2010: 336–7; Kuhrt 2009: 109).

46. Atkinson 1956: 171–7 rather sees the same stories (with the Addition of Xenophon's *Cyropedia*) as evidence that Cambyses depicted the rule of Egypt belonging properly to his father Cyrus already, as a dowry from Apries, and thus Cambyses was punishing Amasis as a usurper.

47. This also appears in Herod. II.161–9 (Herodotus 2002: 474–83) and in the cited fragment of Ctesias.

Cambyses's desecration and burning of Amasis's corpse (Amasis died just months before the invasion, leaving his son, Psemmetichus/Psamtik III as pharaoh).⁴⁸ As Kuhrt comments, this sounds like a deliberate attempt to efface Amasis's memory in a very Egyptian way.⁴⁹

Moreover, marriage alliances and claimed descent are time-honored methods for asserting claims of legitimate rule over areas—so whether or not one is inclined to believe that either Cyrus or Cambyses had Egyptian wives, such a claim would have been a useful way to depict the Great King as an Egyptian ruler. It is quite clear that Cambyses (and after him, Darius) attempted to portray himself as a legitimate pharaoh. The campaigns against the Libyans and the Ethiopians, described by Herodotus as signs of hubris and madness, are in fact actions expected of a proper pharaoh.⁵⁰ As is well-known, the claim that Cambyses murdered the sacred Apis bull in a fit of rage is contradicted by archaeology: the bull appears to have died of natural causes and was buried with all traditional rites by Cambyses.⁵¹ The famous statue of Udjahorresnet also demonstrates that Cambyses received the proper titles and names for a pharaoh.⁵² One might also consider the fact that the later Egyptian historian Manetho included the Persians in his list of dynasties as minor evidence that they were accepted as legitimate pharaohs by some.⁵³ After Cambyses, Darius appears to have taken his role as pharaoh very seriously, building temples, canals, and adopting Egyptian architectural motifs. Wasmuth has even argued that Darius integrated Egyptian kingship into his own, Achaemenid kingship.⁵⁴

Nevertheless, in contrast to his father Cyrus and successor Darius, Cambyses was remembered badly. One factor in this might be the propaganda of Darius, though, as Kuhrt notes, his apology at Behistun is remarkably neutral towards Cambyses (and Darius did provide care

---

48. Herodotus 2000: 22–3.
49. Kuhrt 2009: 130 n. 3; cf. the comment of Briant 2002: 59; 1982: 393.
50. For the campaigns, see Herod. III.17–26 (Herodotus 2000: 24–37). For this being proper pharaonic activity, cf. Cruz-Uribe 2003: 34–5.
51. Brosius 2000: 17–18 (epitaph, inscription and image of stele); Kuhrt 2009: 122–4; cf. Cruz-Uribe 2003: 43–5; Colburn 2014: 122–9. For the story in Herodotus, see III.29 (Herodotus 2000: 38–9).
52. Brosius 2000: 15–17 (trans.); Kuhrt 2009: 117–22; cf. Lloyd 1982; Cruz-Uribe 2003: 10–13; Colburn 2014: 278–90.
53. Though, like Berossus, Manetho's fragmentary survival makes utilizing it difficult. For an extract and references, see Kuhrt 2009: 390–1.
54. Wasmuth 2015: 204–24.

for Cambyses's tomb).⁵⁵ Another, more important factor in this is likely the third topic, the apparent incompleteness of Cambyses's conquest. As Kaper has demonstrated from recent excavations in the Dakhla Oasis, a rival pharaoh, Petubasis IV, controlled portions of Egypt, including the western Oasis, during Cambyses's reign and had to be defeated by Darius.⁵⁶ In Kaper's analysis, Petubasis IV's control of the oasis actually explains the story of Cambyses's disappearing army in Herodotus (III.25.3): the story represents (successful) propaganda from Cambyses hiding the defeat of the army he sent to take control of the oases.⁵⁷ The resistance of Petubasis IV, when taken into consideration with the revived efforts of Psammetichus III and the relatively short period until Cambyses's mysterious death (only about three years), suggests that Cambyses never had the time to consolidate properly his rule over Egypt or to establish completely his credentials as pharaoh. Perhaps the incompleteness of the conquest explains Darius's silence concerning Egypt at Behistun.⁵⁸ Since Darius was able to complete the conquest, he was also able to depict himself as pharaoh successfully—and thus history remembered his rule over Egypt more favorably than Cambyses's.

Overall, the general outlines of Cambyses's approach to Egypt follow those from Babylonia: sophisticated attempts to be depicted in terms acceptable within local tradition, without surrendering the imperial identity. As mentioned above, Wasmuth argues that Egyptian kingship was very important for Darius I's own enactment of kingship.⁵⁹ This may have been a step further than the Teispids would have been willing to go, but that is, of course, unknowable.⁶⁰

---

55. Kuhrt 2009: 106 n. 5; on the tomb, see Henkelman 2003a: esp. 110–11, 144; also maybe a wife of Cambyses, pp. 147–8.

56. Kaper 2015.

57. Kaper 2015: 141–2. For Herodotus, see III.26 (Herodotus 2000: 34–7); this is therefore to be preferred to the explanation in Cruz-Uribe 2003: 35–7.

58. No Egyptian liar-kings are included in the narrative, despite the fact that Darius indeed had to travel to Egypt himself to pacify it. If he did not consider Egypt fully conquered, then its kings would not be "liars."

59. Wasmuth 2015: 204–24.

60. At the SBL meeting in Boston in 2017, Vanderhooft took up Chaverdi et al. 2014's analysis of a gate with Babylonian style art work on it in Fars as signs of strong acceptance of Babylon by Cyrus. However, it must be emphasized that the dating of the gate is quite uncertain, let alone any inferences for self-depiction.

The brief overviews of Cyrus in Babylonia and Cambyses and Darius in Egypt highlight one important aspect of the early kings' engagements with local traditions: the marshalling of local experts to craft their ideology. That this sophistication is due to the efforts of local elites who participated in the imperial project is without doubt. No one would deny that the scribes responsible for the Cyrus Cylinder were Babylonian, or that Udjahorresnet was Egyptian. Nevertheless, that they did this at the behest of their new masters is suggested by several texts. In an unprovenanced tablet translated by Kleber and Jursa (BM 113249), Cambyses and his governor of Babylon explicitly ask the Eanna temple's administrators for all royal steles in their possession.[61] This request suggests that the construction of appropriate local ideology was not left solely to the imaginations of the local scribes, but that it was crafted as part of a more intentional and dialogic process. A similar interpretation can be suggested for Darius's famous request for Egyptian laws related to the temples (on the verso of the Demotic Chronicle, section b).[62] Though the text is lacunose and late, it clearly specifies that material concerning temples and other matters were collated and put into Aramaic and Demotic. Briant is no doubt right to reject this passage as evidence of a Persian "law code."[63] Rather, such a collection would be very practical for informing locally appropriate engagements, just like the royal steles in BM 113249.

These observations do not mean that there was unanimous acceptance of the Persians. The history of revolts in Babylonia and Egypt is sufficient to prove otherwise. Nonetheless, that the Great Kings were keen to get sophisticated participation from (some of) their subjects is as important as (some of) their subjects' willingness to provide it.

Teispid and Achaemenid Relations with Temples:
A Synthetic Overview and Assessment[64]

In both of the above topics, an integral part of the historical consideration involves relations with the native temple administrations and their

---

61. Kleber 2008: no. 33 (pp. 270–1); translated in Jursa 2007b: 78 and Tolini 2011: 134. It is dated to 29/VI/ Cambyses 3. According to the British Museum online catalogue the object was bought in 1919 from a person named Alfred B. W. Holland (from whom 876 items were purchased).

62. Trans. Kuhrt 2009: 124–7.

63. Briant 2002: 510–11, cf. 956–7.

64. This section was originally presented in the "Persian Period" section at the International SBL meeting in Berlin, August 2017. A version of it is forthcoming in a volume edited by Jill Middlemas and Katherine Smith.

priesthoods, and the documents that derive therefrom. This chapter will therefore now turn to the question of Persian relations with temples as institutions.

Temples loom large in the discourse over imperial relations in ANE empires. This is partly because a large number of sources at our disposal are either concerned with or derive from temples. While there is a danger that the importance of temples and their priesthoods can therefore be overestimated in relation to other institutions and power brokers,[65] nevertheless it is very clear that they *were* important. The temples from which survive the densest documentation, from Mesopotamia, show close integration into the state apparatus. Extant documentation is not evenly distributed, however. Thus one must understand whether all temples were equally important, equally integrated into the functioning of the state, and therefore as equally important in the dialectics of elite engagement with or resistance to empires. This might appear to be almost self-evident, but the implications are not always clearly borne out in debate over Achaemenid treatment of local cults.

This section briefly summarizes the function of temples in state relations in Mesopotamia, Egypt, and Fars in the first millennium on the basis of several scholars' work, and the relative roles of mutual legitimation between temples and kings. This overview can then provide a basis for sketching an outline questioning whether smaller temples had the same function as the major ones, and lastly—the key interest of this exploration—whether the sanctuaries of more marginal provinces provided the same functions and impacts as the older, more central ones.

State Functions of Temples in NB and Persian Empires

Mesopotamia. In a very handy overview, Kleber has summarized the NB and early Persian temple as a state institution, performing important functions for the administration of labor and taxes, in addition to cultic, ideological, and local identity functions.[66] Her key institutions for this overview are the Eanna in Uruk and the Ebabbar in Sippar, the largest temples in their respective cities, as well as the temples providing the largest surviving cuneiform collections. Though the precise positions

---

65. E.g., Jursa 2013. On strong internal ranking, see Waerzeggers 2011a: 64; on different levels of social embedding in small and large cities, see p. 69.

66. Kleber 2013; cf. Kleber 2008: 102–32 (building projects), 198–236 (military duties). This should supersede the discussion of Schaper 2000: 141–50. He appears to misunderstand the nature of Babylonian tithing, and misses the role of labor obligations in taxation. See also the notes below.

varied through time, both temples had at least a royal official (the *qīpu*) heading up the temple administration, and who was, accordingly, subject to royal approval—and there were typically several other royally beholden officials.[67] Moreover, royal Aramaic scribes were obligatory in temples in the Persian era.[68]

The main difference Kleber notes between the Babylonian and Persian administrations is the disappearance of royal gifts from the record.[69] Although in general Jursa has stressed the continuity between the NB and early Persian rule in Babylonia,[70] he sees a gradual intensification of labor and taxation obligations through the reign of Darius.[71] Thus one can justifiably still consider the major Babylonian temples as integrated in Persian imperial policy, even if the ideological connection had been broken. Indeed, Waerzeggars has argued that the priests, at least, experienced Persian kingship as both more alienated and more controlling than NB kingship—with corvée labor demands inflicting both ideological and financial repercussions.[72] Lastly, one can note that the Eanna's priesthood was removed by Xerxes, in the wake of its involvement in the revolts against Persian rule in 484.[73]

One can summarize the function of the major Babylonian temples in the Persian Empire as important loci for (increased) administrative control and economic exploitation for the empire, but with a simultaneous distancing from royal ideology and patronage.

Egypt. Egypt was another ancient civilization with major temple institutions. In Pharaonic Egypt, the major temples had similar administrative and economic activities as in Mesopotamia. Perdu emphasizes the Saite dynasty's care and attention to temples throughout Egypt.[74] The major temples were perhaps even more integrated into the administration of Egypt than the temples in Mesopotamia, and they served similarly important and wide-ranging economic functions.[75] The pharaohs' patronage of the temples was a key aspect of Egyptian royal ideology, much like

67. E.g., Jursa 2007b: 76–7.
68. Jursa 2012 (thanks to Tero Alstola); Jursa 2015a: 599. For the heartland, see Tavernier 2008.
69. Kleber 2013: 175.
70. E.g., Jursa 2007b: 79–83.
71. Jursa 2007b: 86–9.
72. Waerzeggers 2015a: 192–200.
73. Waerzeggers 2003/2004; Kessler 2004; Kuhrt 2010; cf. George 2010.
74. Perdu 2014.
75. Spencer 2014, also with close links to the palace, Lloyd 1983: 325.

that of the NB kings, only in the Egyptian case, the pharaoh was a deity and priest rather than just a devotee.[76] It is clear, however, that below the major, royally sponsored temples, there were a wide array of sacred sites utilized by the populace but without such strong institutional integration.[77]

The attitudes of the Persian kings towards the temples is controversial, given the negative portrayal of Cambyses in Herodotus.[78] While there is no doubt that the picture of gross impiety is undeserved, Cambyses may not have been inclined to serve as patron to as many temples as the Saite pharaohs had. This might, instead, just be a result of the limited time Cambyses had before his death, and the incompleteness of his conquest.[79] Darius did, nonetheless, build or complete a number of temples, particularly in the western oases.[80] Nevertheless, Lloyd denies that Darius I was involved in temple construction beyond authorizing royal cartouches.[81] This seems unlikely, given that Darius I, at least, fully accepted the traditional Egyptian portrayal of himself as a god, as part of his efforts to be a legitimate pharaoh,[82] though evidence that any later Persian kings also did so is less forthcoming.[83] While Darius, and Cambyses to a lesser extent, fulfilled at least some of the Pharaonic temple duties, royal largess would seem to have dissipated, and taxes and oversight increased, much as in Babylonia.[84] Further, it seems it was the satrap who fulfilled the older pharaonic duties of confirming priestly appointments in place of the Great King himself.[85] The picture for the large temples in Egypt thus appears to be fairly similar to that in Babylonia, with Darius seeming to treat the Egyptian tradition in an analogous way to how Cyrus treated Babylonia.

76. Lloyd 1983.
77. Szpakowska 2014.
78. E.g., Lloyd 1988; cf. above.
79. See Kaper 2015; cf. above.
80. Perdu 2014: 151.
81. Lloyd 2007: 110.
82. Wasmuth 2015; cf. Fried 2004: 67.
83. There is also an obscure occurrence of a cult to a statue of Darius (I) in Sippar under Xerxes, and Waerzeggers sees the prebendary system as the same as the standard cult system, though it might have involved outsiders. What this means for deification is unclear. See Waerzeggers 2014b.
84. Fried 2004: 106; Agut-Labordére 2005.
85. This is most evident in the so-called Pherendates Correspondence (Martin 2011: 289–95) and especially P-Rylands 9 (Vittmann 1998: 1:115–203).

Fars. The view from Fars is predictably different, in at least two ways. First, it has traditionally been understood that the Persians did not use temples. This understanding derives both from the statement of Herodotus to that effect, as well as the lack of any excavated Achaemenid-era temples in Fars.[86] Recently Razmjou, independently and in collaboration with Roaf, has challenged this view, arguing that a number of installations traditionally understood to be palaces should rather be understood to be temples, as well as pointing to a number of likely outdoor sanctuaries.[87] While they are correct that there were sacred spaces, the evidence for large, household-style institutions as in Mesopotamia or the Susa plain is lacking in Fars. One cannot posit that the sacred spaces and their priesthoods had similar estates and economic activities on the basis of current information.[88]

Nevertheless, the Persepolis Tablets do contain periodic mentions of priests and sacred spaces, the most extensive exploration of which is by Henkelman.[89] For the present purposes, the key datum to note is that the PFT explicitly document state support for cults in the form of material for offerings. These are given to priests designated both by Iranian (*magus*) and Elamite (*šatin*) titles, as well as to deities with names from both linguistic traditions (with the largest quantities attested surprisingly for Humban). Henkelman also argues that the Achaemenids had a similar ideology of beneficence as the NB kings, though in this case it is not just through patronage of priestly rites but includes feasts for the wider populace (at least in Fars).[90]

Temples as Sources of Labor

An aspect of the Achaemenid use of the major temples in both Mesopotamia and Egypt is their usefulness in administering and providing for labor, particularly for building works. This is a function of their pre-Achaemenid landholdings and integrations with the palaces. As Jursa has discussed, the Achaemenids were even more interested in labor than cash.[91] Various papyri from Egypt (Verso of the Demotic Chronicle; cf.

---

86. See generally, Canepa 2013.
87. Razmjou 2010; Razmjou and Roaf 2013.
88. The continued existence of older, Elamite *ziyan*, with their ziggurats and temple complexes, seems to be confirmed by occasional mentions in the PFT, but whether these institutions were viewed as "Persian" or not is unclear.
89. Henkelman 2008.
90. Henkelman 2008: 242–6; Henkelman 2011b.
91. Jursa 2011a, 2015b.

P.Berlin 13582),⁹² show Cambyses and Darius were interested in the economic usefulness of the major Egyptian temples as well. Considering the temples' integration into the state in both provinces, this was a pragmatic strategy for the Persians, saving them considerable effort in organizing sparse labor resources.

The picture in Fars is a bit different. There is no evidence of the participation of local sanctuaries in organizing labor resources. However, a massive (forced) labor system (called the *kurtaš* system) operated in Fars, particularly under Darius, and the structure of the work force in Susa must have been similar.⁹³ The Babylonian temples were utilized to provide labor for the work in Susa.⁹⁴ This aspect of temple use within the Persian Empire has not been sufficiently stressed.

Legitimation between Temple and King

Traditionally in the ANE, the temples and the kings had mutually reinforcing ties for legitimation. In NA, Egypt, and ancient Israel, kings were understood as the priest of the gods, who typically delegated their priestly functions to a high priest.⁹⁵ In NB and Persia, there was a distinction between priestly and kingly service, though in all temple-building was a kingly prerogative.⁹⁶ In both Egypt and Babylonia, the kings retained the theoretical right to appoint priests, though over time this became hereditary. Still, in Babylonia, only kings had the right to grant a prebend.⁹⁷ Of course, this was a mutually beneficial relationship: the kings gained the support of the priesthoods and the institutions of the temples, the temples received protection and financial support,⁹⁸ and all were united in the service of the gods.

---

92. Trans. of Cambyses' decree, see Kuhrt 2009: 125–6; Trans. of P.Berlin 13582: Martin 2011: 373–4; cf. Agut-Labordére 2005; Kuhrt 2007: 126–7. For a discussion of a priest who served Darius as labor organizer, see Yoyette 2013: 252–4.

93. On the *kurtaš* sustem, see Silverman 2015b and sources cited there.

94. Waerzeggers 2010a.

95. Ahlström 1982; Rooke 2000.

96. E.g., Kapelrud 1963; Schaudig 2010. For Persia the evidence for temple-building would technically be from the earlier Elamite states, otherwise the archaeology is lacking. In Iranian perspective, however, there was a distinction between kings and priests. See Silverman 2015a for references.

97. Waerzeggers 2010b: 37; 2011a: 68; 2011b: 742–4.

98. Waerzeggers 2011b: 726–9 emphasizes royal Babylonian rhetoric of cultic munificence.

Though Cyrus, Darius, and Xerxes all make occasional claims to restore sacred sites—in the Cyrus Cylinder, in the apology at Behistun (DB), and in the Daiva inscription (XPh)—temples do not function in OP inscriptions like in the previously mentioned traditions (though admittedly we do not possess enough of Cyrus's inscriptions to assess his self-portrayal adequately). Election by and service to Ahuramazda fulfills that function. In the present author's opinion this is most likely because the Persian religious tradition would appear to have been originally based in open-air sanctuaries (including "paradises") rather than in temple complexes of the sort known in these ancient urban societies. This accords with the traditional view that the Iranian tribes, before and during the time that they infiltrated Fars, were a pastoral society.[99] Thus a strong temple-institutional appeal would have made little sense to their native constituencies. Within other contexts, however, as seen above, at least at main sanctuaries and at certain points in time, the Great Kings were willing to play the role of temple-patron. This appears to have been primarily a product of the formative years of the empire (though the notorious lack of sources for later periods makes such a statement uncertain).

Integration and Importance of Smaller Sanctuaries

So far the discussion has overviewed the major sanctuaries in some important provinces. It must be stressed, however, that these institutions were not the only temples or shrines even in these provinces. A wide array of smaller temples, street shrines, and even local numinous spaces no doubt populated all localities.[100] Even in pre-Achaemenid eras it is clear that these smaller sanctuaries were not as royally supported. Waerzeggers notes that the generous NB kings gave much more to the major cults than minor ones.[101] Szpakowska shows how the less elite populace was able to have both built and natural sacred spaces in Egypt, without the same level of administration and hierarchy as prevailed at major sites.[102] On the other hand, city size also made a difference. In her overview, Kleber found that in smaller Babylonian cities, the main temples' administration doubled as the city's administration.[103]

---

99. On pastoral and semi-pastoral elements in Persia, see, e.g., Henkelman 2011a. Alizadeh 2009 has argued for a longer-term relevance of pastoralism to the region, but the import for Persian culture is beyond the present scope.

100. E.g., Baker 2011.

101. Waerzeggers 2011b: 729.

102. Szpakowska 2014: 513–4.

103. Kleber 2008, especially 5–74; 2013: 171.

It is therefore fair to say that different sorts of temples served different functions: some were essential components of the state apparatus and a key locus for the interaction of elites and kings, while others provided more of what today one might recognize as religious needs for lower classes of society. These levels played little role in administration, and presumably little role in royal legitimation.

The system in Fars itself, having a different character, is hard to compare in this respect. There were certainly officially recognized cults, and these were no doubt not the totality of cultic activities at the time, though the extent of the latter is otherwise rather unknown. Nevertheless, both the practice of royal sponsorship of feasting, with its potentially religious overtones, and the cultic activities attested within paradises, suggest that in the home territory at least,[104] the great kings' patronage of religious rites reached a wider segment of society than did the patronage of major sanctuaries. Still requiring investigation is the question of whether the Great King performed such feasts outside of Fars, as he travelled through the empire, or if it was reserved for interaction with the heartland only.

Function of Sanctuaries in Marginal Provinces

So far the above has overviewed some of the functions of temples in the major provinces and the relations they had with native kings and the Great King. Also noted in passing was their link to labor. Even in these contexts, there were sacred spaces with differing functions, and little to no state involvement. The pattern attested so far in Fars itself follows a different pattern from Egypt and Mesopotamia. What can one say about temples and the Persian relation to them in the more marginal provinces of the empire?

Brosius has offered an analysis of Achaemenid engagements around the Black Sea (Thrace, Colchis, Iberia) as examples of areas which were rich in natural resources but without extensive pre-existing political structures.[105] All these areas were added to the empire by Darius I.[106] As recent and ongoing excavations in the Caucasus are showing, Herodotus's statements about Iberia and Colchis cannot be accurate.[107] Brosius argues both Thrace and the Caucasus were integrated into other satrapies due to their lack of usable administration, and thus this integration effected significant

---

104. Henkelman 2011b.
105. Brosius 2010.
106. Cf. Brosius 2010: 30 n. 8, who dates this c. 513 BCE.
107. Brosius 2010: 31; cf. below.

local development.¹⁰⁸ She suggests that one effect of this was a lack of integration of *local* elites into the overall system, as was done in more developed satrapies—probably due to a lack of administratively suitable local elites requiring the importation of new, non-local administrators. In Thrace the result appears to have been secondary state formation, outside of the empire itself (and one might see the Bosporan Kingdom as a similarly secondary state formation, though for different reasons).¹⁰⁹ For present purposes, the Caucasus is more interesting, as it remained within the empire until Alexander.

Here one can only mention in passing the situation of the Caucasus (Iberia, Colchis, Armenia, and Azerbaijan). Suffice it to say recent excavations have found increasing numbers of clearly Achaemenid structures, and these include administrative buildings, a complex described as a paradise, and several buildings excavators have argued to be "temples" (cf. figs. 6.1a, 6.1b).¹¹⁰ Of particular interest is the tower found at Samadlo, Georgia, that echoes the mysterious Zendan-i Sulaiman and Kabah-i Zardusht from the heartland.¹¹¹ However one interprets this mysterious structure, its presence in Georgia clearly demonstrates some sort of direct link with the heartland. Without going into the archaeological details of any of these sites, it is obvious that the administrative architecture is directly related to imperial needs. Moreover, temples also appear conterminously. Without written evidence it is hard to say where the impetus for the temples came from—imported imperial elites, elites from the satrapy of Armenia, or local elites who wished to copy other elites from around the empire. Further research could perhaps illuminate this issue, however. Given the novelty and clearly Persian architecture of the administrative sites, one would suspect the temples' appearance was related.

---

108. Brosius 2010: 32.

109. In general for the Achaemenids in the Black Sea region, see Nieling and Rehm 2010. For a recent study of Thrace (and Macedonia), see Vasilev 2015.

110. See the overviews in Knauß 2005, 2006; Knauß, Gagošidse, and Babaev 2013; Khatchadourian 2016. So far I have failed to access excavation reports for any of the sites that have been posited as Achaemenid-era temples in Georgia, so I cannot analyze them. The temple at Grakliani Gora was covered at the time of site visit.

111. Knauß 2001: 130; Ter-Martirossov 2001: 160; Knauß 2005: 203; 2006: 89.

6. The Great King, Local Elites, Temples, and Priests

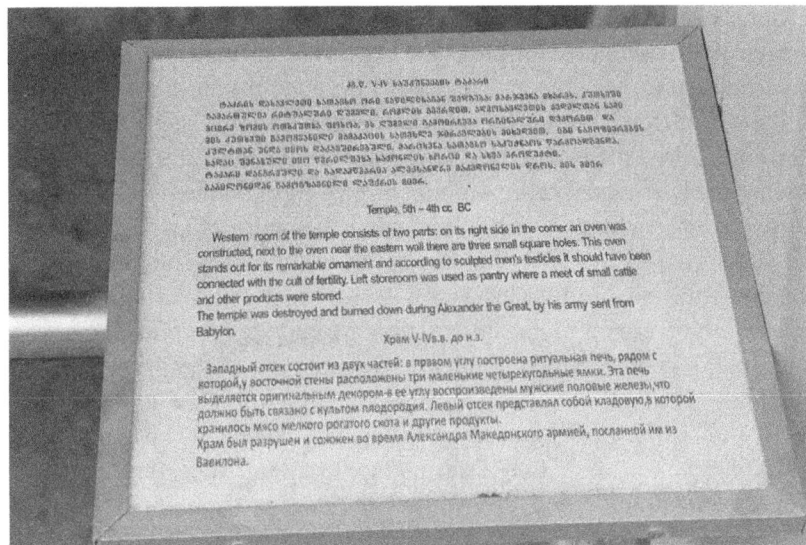

Figure 6.1a. *Public Sign Claiming Achaemenid-Era Temple, Grakliani Gora, Georgia*

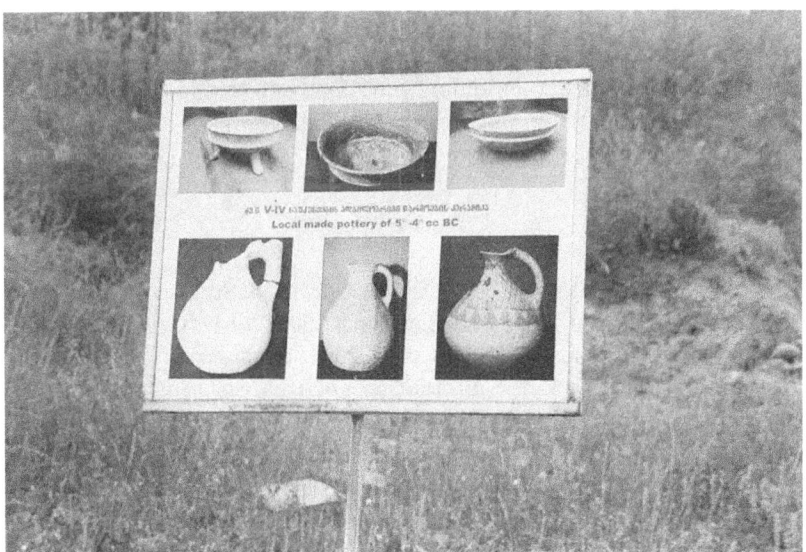

Figure 6.1b. *Public Sign Showing Achaemenid-Era Pottery, Grakliani Gora, Georgia*

A number of sites in the east have structures that have been identified by their excavators as temples.[112] These vary in date and type.[113] The most interesting for present purposes might be the building at Dahān-i Ghulāmān, Sistan, which was built roughly in the reign of Darius I (late sixth/early fifth century), was built along with a settlement, and which closely resembles the architecture of Pasargadae.[114] Though there is no written evidence from this site (the excavation reports being still incomplete), the fact that the temple appeared concomitant with a settlement, and used architectural styles from the heartland suggests imperial involvement in its construction. Moreover, the three altars which were found inside the precinct are reminiscent of other Achaemenid depictions of altars. Genito believes this site should be identified with the city of Zaris, mentioned by Ctesias.[115] This would appear, then, to be a construction of an imperial satrapal capital, in a region with no prior urbanization,[116] and this capital included a sacred site, plausibly connected with Iranian religion.[117] This could be seen to bear out Brosius's comments concerning the effects on areas without pre-existing administrative structures: they had to be created *de novo*, and thus could sometimes have more impact than in previously imperial regions like Mesopotamia and Egypt. For the present purposes one should note that this included a temple, not just a sacred enclosure.

In contrast to Iberia and Drangiana, one can mention again the oft-cited case of late-Achaemenid Xanthos. As discussed in Part II, Xanthos evinces the famous trilingual inscription that commemorates the establishment of a new cult.[118] The stele records both local and satrapal

---

112. Shenkar 2007: 175–7.

113. From Shenkar 2007: 175–7. Dahān-i Ghulāmān, Sistan, appears to be end of sixth century (Shenkar 2007: 175; Boucharlat 2005: 268–9; Genito 2010b: 103); Tash-K'irman-tepe, Chorasmia (Helms et al. 2002, fourth century); cultic terraces at Pachmak-tepe and Pshak-tepe, Bactria and Kok-tepa, Sogdiana (Francfort 2005, perhaps late).

114. Boucharlat 2005: 268–9; Genito 2010b: 103; 2010a: 81–3; 2012. Thanks to Rick Bonnie and Carly Crouch for accessing the studies of Genito.

115. Genito claims Ctesias stated Zaris was the capital of Drangiana (= OP Zranka), Genito 2014: 173; Book 18, frag. 15 §56 (Llewellyn-Jones and Robson 2010: 195 || Stronk 2010: 353), though it is not entirely clear from this passage that it is in Zranka much less the capital.

116. Genito 2014.

117. Genito 2014: 174 calls it Zoroastrianism; Gnoli 1993 contests this.

118. Teixidor 1978; Metzger 1979; Bryce 1986: 91–3, 191–3; Briant 1986: 434–7; 1998.

approval of cultic arrangements for Carian deities in Lycia, though the impetus seemingly comes from below rather than from above.[119] This inscription was found near a pre-existing sanctuary (to Leto), though it records the establishment of a *krp'*,[120] a domain, a set of regular offerings, and a priesthood. Though on first glance it would seem like the satrap's interest in this cultic affair was merely a financial and administrative one,[121] the location in a *birta*, relations with Caria (now part of the same satrapy), and obscure Iranian links,[122] combine to suggest that more is going on than meets the eye. Fried argues that this new establishment was part of the new satrap's attempt to assert control over the region as well as to benefit new Carian soldiers; she also points to examples of landowners depicting top-down decisions as if they were bottom-up.[123] One might tentatively suggest that the Achaemenids were willing to establish and/or patronize new cultic institutions in order to capitalize on their organizational potential where they deemed this useful. Indeed, Dusinberre argues that slightly north the Achaemenids had found the (preexisting) Ephesian Artemis useful for just these reasons.[124] Despite the tendency in some debates over Achaemenid temple policy to make a strong demarcation between "religious" concerns and administrative or fiscal ones, one can argue that the finances and administration of a cultic site are rather important aspects of its practical, daily functioning—as well as part of how it functioned more ideologically. Thus, a very cursory look at these three marginal areas would suggest that imperial administrative development in the margins also involved developments in the cultic sphere at times.

This leads to the famous, post-Darius I instance of royal involvement in cultic matters. This is, of course, Berossus's claim that Artaxerxes II established statues to Anāhitā in several satrapal capitals (§III.5.2/BNJ

119. Though this is a highly debatable point. Both Briant and Kuhrt emphasize the cursory role of the satrap here. Fried 2004: 154 has rather pointed to later examples of royal decisions being glossed as if they had been local decisions.

120. This word is uncertain. Teixidor 1978: 183 n. 13 follows Mayrhofer in seeing it as Iranian **karpa*, "cult." In Metzgar, however, Mayrhofer related it *karapan*, "priest" (p. 183). Dupont-Sommer 1979 translated it as "sanctuaire?" (p. 145) though he notes the Greek version has βωμον ("altar") and the Lycian has *kumaziye* ("altar"). Briant emphasizes the meaning is uncertain (1998: 316, n. 40).

121. Briant 1986: 436; Tuplin 2015: 84–5.

122. E.g., Mayrhofer 1979; Bivar 1988, the use of *karpa'*, etc.

123. Fried 2004: 154.

124. Dusinberre 2013: 218, suggesting that "Megabyzus" was a hereditary office deriving from Persian attempts to martial its resources.

680 F11).¹²⁵ This claim is sometimes seen to be supported by the fact that Artaxerxes II is the only king to appeal to Mithra and Anāhitā in addition to Ahuramazda in his inscriptions.¹²⁶ Berossus is difficult to use, however, given the fact that extant access is only through several layers of filtering.¹²⁷ Nevertheless, Kuhrt accepts the event as reliable, and understands it to be part of an effort to unify the Iranian diaspora.¹²⁸ In this, she follows Briant.¹²⁹ However, Briant's argument is based on the idea that Anāhitā was especially related to royal investiture, and this idea itself is only based on Plutarch's uncertainly identified goddess in his famous investiture passage (*Artaxerxes* 3.1–3). The earliest clear association of Anāhitā with royal investiture is in fact Sasanian, so this is not a reliable basis.¹³⁰ The idea that it had imperial-marginal functions is not dependent on this argument. One can, however, safely take this as a corroborating piece of evidence that the Persian kings were not afraid to marshal cultic means for imperial ends, when they deemed it fit to do so (even though, in this case, the relevant imperial ends are unclear).

Conclusions for Marginal Temples and Implications for Gerizim and Jerusalem

What does the foregoing survey say about temples in the Persian Empire? On one hand, Allen has characterized Persian policy towards temples as fostering "positive but removed relationship[s]."¹³¹ From another angle, in a well-known article, Kuhrt has argued that the Persians had no "religious policy."¹³² Her primary target is the old shibboleth that the Persians were uniquely tolerant, due to their enlightened ethical monotheism, with the implicit idea that this entailed evangelistic tendencies. The present author could not agree more with her in rejecting this model. Further, one can also agree with a number of her readings emphasizing the fiscal and administrative elements of Persian dealing in cults. However, her denial of any interest in cultic intervention pushes the matter too far, or is based on a too strict dichotomy between cult and its administration. Insofar as one means

---

125. Burstein 1978: 29; De Breuker 2010.
126. Indeed, Boyce 1982 used primarily these two data to weave an inventive narrative of royal "unorthodoxy"—devotion to Anāhitā and the introduction of temple based rites—by Artaxerxes and his mother (pp. 216–31).
127. For essays detailing such issues, see Haubold et al. 2013.
128. Kuhrt 2007: 124; cf. Waters 2014: 183–4.
129. Briant 1986: 431.
130. For these reservations, and further bibliography, see Silverman 2016c: 183.
131. Allen 2005: 126.
132. Kuhrt 2007. Scare quotes hers.

the Persians were not interested in micromanaging their subjects' theology or ritual, this must be correct. But leaving it at this seems to disparage the real, practical import of "safeguarding administrative and fiscal interests, or manipulating local religious structures to help underpin the reality and legitimacy of their claims" as she phrased it.[133] Further, as it relates to the concerns of this chapter, one can argue that the impact of this pragmatic Persian approach actually had the potential to be more pronounced in marginal areas of the empire. If one grants that on occasion the establishment of Achaemenid administrative structures *de novo* in marginal regions could entail the establishment of temple cults—and that this likely was due to their experience of temples' utility as such in the larger, more urbanized provinces—then there are a number of real cultic consequences for which the Persians are directly responsible. First, there is the institution itself, which presumably would not have existed otherwise. Second, there are the cultic personnel, however chosen, whose positions would also otherwise not have existed. Third, there are the administrative ramifications: scribes/administrators, taxes, and forced labor, all of which would interact with and be facilitated by the new institutions. Lastly, there are the ramifications for local elite culture and lifeways, now interacting with the new cult and its officials, either in cooperation and/or competition. These are four significant impacts on cult.

To bring this discussion around to the Judaeans, one can note that both Yehud and Samerina built new temples, probably in the reign of Darius I. Both of these provinces were relatively marginal within the empire. The establishment of both of these temples—whether as a result of Judaean/Samarian requests for them, or part of a more centrally mandated development of the two *medinat*—can safely be said to have experienced the four impacts listed above: the presence of a new institution, the presence of new cultic personnel, presence of administrators, taxes, and labor, and the resultant interactions with pre-existing local elites. At a very minimum, this would likely mean further administrative integration. At a maximum, this could mean a substantial shift in elite culture as well as in patterns of peasant labor. It is probable that the impact would have been different for Yehud and Samerina, since the former was more marginal and under-developed than Samerina. If one considers the appeals to international pilgrimage discussed above in connection with 1Zech, one might consider the possibility that some Yehudian elites saw a new temple as presenting an opportunity for the acquisition of both prestige and wealth, through the establishment of networks throughout the empire—both with other Yahwists and with imperial elites.

133. Kuhrt 2007: 136.

Excursus:
Josephus and the Tale of Rising Priestly Power[134]

A number of accounts of Yehud in the "Persian period" see it as a time slot in which priests usurped the power that had been held by the Davidic kings.[135] This narrative derives from the exegesis of a number of biblical passages, as well as the common (mis-)conception that there was no king of Yehud during this period—the lack of a local dynast does not mean there was no king. Another source often appealed to, however, comes from Josephus's narrative of the period.

The end of Book 11 of Josephus's *Antiquities* (from 11.7.1 = 11.297 onwards)[136] contains several stories about the late Persian Empire and the conquest of Alexander that are sometimes taken to indicate that the high priests had become the rulers of Yehud during the Persian period. Despite the fact that some scholars take these narratives to be basically historical,[137] these stories are best understood as retrojecting the recent Hasmonean and Roman past into the more remote past of the beginning of the Hellenistic era. Therefore, they should not be taken to imply that a "diarchy" or "theocracy" prevailed in Persian Yehud. First, some basic objections to the historicity of these accounts will be noted. The point here is not a comprehensive explanation of Josephus or his sources (nor an attempt to assess the evidence for the late Persian Empire in Palestine), but to demonstrate the narrative's dubiousness for understanding Persian Yehud. After dismissing Josephus's historical usefulness for the late Persian Empire, some features which contradict a thesis of priestly rule will be highlighted.

The first story is a story of fratricide in the temple. Josephus describes the high priest Johannan's murder of his brother Joshua in the temple. This angers Bagoses, who enters the temple and imposes taxes on the daily offerings. The second story interweaves three different sub-plots. The first subplot consists of Johannan's son, Jaddua, defying Alexander out of loyalty to Darius III; the second is a narrative of Alexander's passage through Palestine, including his obeisance to the High Priest,

---

134. This section was originally presented in the "Literature and History of the Persian Period" section at the Annual SBL Meeting in Boston, 2017.

135. A trope repeated in many forms. E.g., Laato 1997; VanderKam 2004: 23, 83–4; Honingman 2011. The approach of Rooke 2000 and Cataldo 2009: 176 is to be preferred.

136. Recently translated with commentary Spilsbury and Seeman 2017: 102–44.

137. E.g., Marcus's appendix B, pp. 498–511 in his Loeb edition; VanderKam 2004: 58–63; Albertz 2011; Becking 2011b; Kasher 2011; Mor 2011. Even Schwartz 1990, who is very careful in trying to delimit Josephus's sources, takes his credibility for granted with just the possibility that his chronology was off. Much more sober is Grabbe; Grabbe's assessment of the Bagoses episode is ambivalent towards its historicity (Grabbe 1987: 235–6), though he rejects the stories of Manasseh and Alexander (236–43); cf. Grabbe 2008: 71–4.

and the third subplot consists of the schemes of Sanballat to gain the loyalty of some Jerusalemite priests and to get favors from Alexander.[138]

First, despite frequent attempts, the characters in the first story (*Ant.* 11.7.1) cannot be easily equated with individuals from the Elephantine papyri. All of the names are, in fact, quite common:[139] Artaxerxes (four reigning monarchs), Bagoses/*Bagāvahyā (common Persian name),[140] Joshua, Jaddua, and Yoḥanan (all common Judaean names). For the post-Persian period Ilan lists four instances of Yadduas, 103 Joshuas/Jesuses, and 129 Yoḥanans.[141] One could almost say these names count as narratological equivalents of Tom, Dick, and Harry. Given that all of these names have multiple potential referents, historically known and unknown, it is unwise to try to connect them to a particular historical set of characters, despite the fact that a few of them appear in the Elephantine correspondence.[142] This is especially true for a priest named Yoḥanan, given its popularity.[143] The occurrence of Yoḥanan on a coin does nothing to improve this situation, as the relevant coin is unprovenanced and could as easily be Hellenistic as Persian.[144] Even more speculative is the connection of this story with the mysterious "one whom they have pierced" in Zech 12:10—a passage with an entirely unknown date or referent.[145] For this reason it is dangerous to connect this story with either the figures known from Elephantine or additional hypothesized individuals. Moreover, even if the identity of these characters could be secured, this would do nothing towards verifying the material's historicity any more than identifying the king in Esther as Xerxes makes that novella historical.

---

138. For a very useful table separating these subplots, see Spilsbury and Seeman 2017: 90–1; divided differently by Cohen 1983.

139. Noted already Williamson 1977: 55; cf. Frevel 2016: 322.

140. Meaning "better through Baga (god)"; see Tavernier 2007: 141. The fact that a governor of Yehud is attested with this name in the Elephantine papyri therefore is not particularly telling; as their recent commentary notes, Josephus and his intended Roman audience would not have known this or associated the name with this governor in any case (Spilsbury and Seeman 2017: 100).

141. See Ilan 2001: 112 (Yadua), 125–33 (Joshua/Jesus), 134–43 (Yoḥanan).

142. Contra Grabbe 1992.

143. Ilan 2001: 134–43.

144. Mildenberg 1979: 192 claims his coins "allegedly come from the recent Hebron hoard," for which he gives no information; the description on p. 194 says the coin is in an unnamed private collection in Zurich (thanks to Victoria Valdes for the article); typically this lack of provenance is not mentioned by scholars. Neither Barag 1985; 1986–7; Schaper 2000: 157; Meshorer 2001; 14 n. 199, pl. 13; Fried 2003b, nor Lemaire 2015: 95 mention the coin's lack of provenance; the coin mentioning a Yaddua is also apparently unprovenanced (Meshorer and Qedar 1999: 90 no. 39); Farhi 2016: 28 argues the famous "Hezekiah the Governor" coin to which the Yoḥanan the Priest coin is similar is actually Hellenistic, making this coin likely Hellenistic as well.

145. Recently attached by Redditt 2016: 166 n. 16, 168.

Second, the motifs of the story are suspiciously convenient for Josephus. The motifs of sibling rivalry for the high priesthood and imperial manipulations of them echo similar episodes from the priestly families of the Ptolemaic to the Roman eras (for example, Aristobulos and Hyrcanus).[146] That it is a Judaean who commits the crime is neither here nor there, since the deed is closely tied into Josephus's theology of Providence.[147] Especially the motif of the defiling of the temple would seem to play on a late STJ concern, one framed by Antiochus IV and the destruction of 70 CE. Spilsbury and Seeman's recent commentary has also compared Josephus's picture of Bagoses with his portrait of Pompey.[148] Moreover, it points out that there was a Greco-Roman fascination with the character of Artaxerxes III's murderer, Bagoses, a situation ripe for narrative development.[149] All of these elements combine to cast serious doubt on the value of Josephus's first story for anything but Hasmonean propaganda and/or folklore.

Even with these objections to using the narrative historically, there is little reason to see the stories as claiming priestly rule within the Persian Empire. Rooke has already rightly pointed out that the character in the first story with executive power is Bagoses, not the high priest.[150] Control over the appointment of the high priesthood is implied by his ability to promise the priesthood to a non-incumbent. Moreover, the expenses for the daily sacrifice were paid by the public treasury, which implies imperial fiscal control over the cult. Thus, even if one were to ignore the dubiousness of the story and read it as historical, it cannot serve as a foundation for increased priestly control in the Persian Empire. Indeed, the situation depicted in the letters from the Elephantine garrison with which this story is often compared also highlight the significance of gubernatorial control, both in Yehud and Samerina: the governors respond to the request.

Fewer scholars accept the Alexander narrative as reliable.[151] Kasher's argument that the high priest would have had to meet Alexander since he was the leader is merely being overly credulous.[152] For the stories around Alexander, it should be sufficient to note the parallels to the Alexander Romance traditions and the lack of any evidence that Alexander paused between the siege of Gaza and the invasion of Egypt.[153] Moreover, the entire basis of Josephus's narrative in Samaritan duplicity

146. On sibling rivalry among the Tobiads and Oniads, see Nongri 2005: 89–96. On Oniads and Hasmoneans, see Scolnic 2008: 91–144, and 145–94 (though he takes it in a moral direction).

147. Contra: Grabbe 1992: 50. The theology is convincingly shown by Spilsbury and Seeman 2017: 93.

148. Spilsbury and Seeman 2017: 102; cf. the comments on p. 104 n. 983 and 105 n. 998.

149. Spilsbury and Seeman 2017: 100–101.

150. Rooke 2000: 224.

151. E.g., Frevel 2016: 329.

152. Kasher 2011.

153. Momigliano 1979; Cohen 1983. On the Alexander Romance traditions, see the appendix by Ory Amitay in Spilsbury and Seeman 2017: 128–47.

and rivalry is anachronistic and tendentious.[154] The dating of the Gerizim temple to post-Alexandrian times is disconfirmed by the archaeology of the site—at most it might be a vague recollection of the Hellenistic period augmentation.[155] Moreover, the exemptions which both the Judaean and Samarian temples seek in 11.5 sound suspiciously like those sought from the Seleucids.[156] For the second story, given the echoes with concerns over temple defilement, sibling rivalry, negotiations with foreign powers, and the destruction of Gerizim, it is more likely that this material derives from Hasmonean justifications for their secular rule.[157] Indeed, Amitay offers a Hasmonean date for these legends.[158] By claiming that the high priest met Alexander as a ruler of the people as well as priest, a very nice, Hellenistic justification for their (later) rule results. The entire narrative is therefore not to be trusted for depicting the late Persian period or transition to the Hellenistic period.

Instead of focusing on features that mark the entire end of Book 11 as irrelevant for the Persian Empire, much scholarship has rather concerned itself with the putative sources utilized by Josephus. This typically seems to be based on a general assumption of the material's reliability unless proven otherwise. So, for example, Williamson argues that Josephus uses a paraphrase of sources, and these are therefore independent and likely reliable.[159] Schwartz uses the premise that Josephus used sources to explain how Josephus could have confused stories about multiple protagonists—but therefore assumes the data are reliable even if Josephus was confused.[160] Even if one thinks it is possible to conclude that Josephus had had a variety of sources which he used, this in and of itself says nothing about their reliability. Indeed, the above objections suggest that any such sources were later, priestly ideology rather than any reliable documentation from the late Persian period.

Thus, rather than a demonstration that the power structure had evolved from "secular" to "theocratic" or from kingly to priestly in the Persian Empire, these narratives reflect Josephus's experience of and apology for the Hasmonean family.[161]

154. Knoppers 2013: 102; Spilsbury and Seeman 2017: 93–4; cf. Pummer 2016: 86. *Contra* Mor 2011.

155. Magen 2008: 103, 167 dated the Persian-period sanctuary to the first half of the fifth century, well before Josephus's dating of it; Dušek 2012: 65 says mid-fifth century; cf. Knoppers 2013: 124–30. Mor's attempt to refute the dating of the temple seems to be predicated on excessive belief in Josephus's reliability rather than the archaeological evidence itself (Mor 2011: 182–7).

156. Spilsbury and Seeman 2017: 123 n. 1164 also notes that the wish to be granted one's own laws recurs in 11.281 and 12.150.

157. Höffken 2008 also argued Josephus deliberately parallels Cyrus and Alexander.

158. Spilsbury and Seeman 2017: 140–1. Cohen 1983: 66, however, thought it would be more useful in a pre-Maccabean setting.

159. Williamson 1977.

160. Schwartz 1990.

161. For a more thorough treatment of Josephus as a priest, see Gussman 2008.

If these two narratives are discarded, are there any reasons remaining to claim priestly elites gained power at the expense of more secular elites under Persian rule? The evidence currently does not provide any indication in that direction. The rights and privileges enjoyed by temples and their priesthoods seem to have diminished under the Persians in both Mesopotamia and Egypt.[162] The satraps maintained various levels of oversight over priests, in various ways.[163] Within Yehud, the names of several governors are attested, but there is no clear evidence of any of them being priests. Indeed, the fact that the official response to the Elephantine community came from the governors of both Yehud and Samerina would suggest that in both provinces the governors retained administrative superiority.[164] Despite arguments from Zechariah, it also does not call for any priestly rule.[165] The present study very much disagrees with attempts to read a diarchy in either Zech 4 or 6.[166] The former is in the context of supporting YHWH's imperial surveillance, and the latter is definitely not a coronation of Joshua or Zerubbabel. Moreover, the idea that Zech 6 was redacted to eliminate a coronation of Zerubbabel in support of a desired hierocracy is an argument constructed merely from silence.[167] The recurrent idea that Zerubbabel was executed for insurrection well over-interprets the available lack of evidence, and is based on a hypothesis of redacted out material—never a strong argument.[168] Similarly, Ezra is very likely a later tendentious document, probably from the Hellenistic period, and cannot be used to argue for priestly rule.

Therefore, neither Josephus nor older evidence justifies appealing to priests as the primary, ruling elites in Yehud during Persian rule. This does not mean that priests are irrelevant to understanding elite Yehudian (or Samarian) interactions with the Persians, but it does mean that the relevant category is a broader one of "elites," both "secular" and "religious." The next chapter will move to discuss the interaction of the Teispid and Achaemenid kings with local elites.

162. E.g., Waerzeggers 2011b: 744; cf. above.
163. Cf. Silverman 2014.
164. See AP 30–2 (TAD A4.7–9; Porten and Yardeni 1986–99: 1:68–77).
165. See Part II.
166. E.g., recently, Wöhrle 2016: 180, 183–4.
167. Contra, again most recently, Wöhrle 2016: 185.
168. Contra, again most recently, Wöhrle 2016: 187.

Chapter 7

THE GREAT KING AND LOCAL ELITES IN EARLY
PERSIAN PERIOD DISCOURSE

So far this study has analyzed two primary sources for elite Judaean engagements with the early Persian Empire and provided some very basic contexts for Teispid and Achaemenid attempts to justify their rule and to engage with local traditions in furtherance of their aims. The material discussed has mostly concerned the relations between the Great King, temples, governors, and priesthoods. It is now necessary to attempt to interrelate the results of the discussions of 2Isa and 1Zech, bring this into dialogue with the previous chapter, and to attempt to bring all of this into dialogue with discussions concerning early Persian self-representations and elite negotiations.

A major desidcratum for this discussion is the definition and understanding of "elites" in the ancient world—a concept often taken for granted (including by this study) but for which the implications are not always so clear. This chapter will engage with some past and recent scholarship dealing with elites in the Persian Empire in an attempt to understand these dynamics better. Sadly, due to time and space constraints, a more thorough attempt to understand social hierarchy in the ANE must await future work.[1]

First, this chapter recaps the major arguments advanced so far during the course of the study. Second, the two primary texts will be compared, and the implications for Judaean elites analyzed. This will then provide a basis for discussing Judaean elites in relation to the Achaemenids.

---

1. The present author is preparing a couple of research projects dealing more directly with the theoretical aspects of the understanding of ancient elites.

Breviloquent Refresher

The study began by emphasizing the variety of Judaean social locations and experiences, and raising the issues of administrative locus, cultural horizons, and literary impetus. It also raised the idea that prophecy could be one method for local elites to negotiate new political situations.

Part I argued that the key message of 2Isa is Israel should devote itself to YHWH, all other messages being subordinate to that claim. To support this message, the poet claims that creation demonstrates YHWH's power and efforts to *benefit* Israel. It also presents a sophisticated theology of what it means to serve YHWH in order to ask the audience what sort of servant the audience will be. Moreover, 2Isa is interested in the promulgation of teaching and posits that YHWH will give a restored cult as a gift to Israel, yet there is no demand for the audience to return to Yehud. The poet also posits that Cyrus is instituting a new treaty (Isa 42:6).

Further, it was argued that one should view 2Isa as dictated oral poetry, deriving from a community of Judaeans living in the city of Babylon, probably from the era of the *Akītu*'s performance, c. 545–530/484. In the context of being minority migrants, the apparent rejection of the Davidic heir (dismissal of the Judaean court in exile) was seen as significant. More thought is needed on the difference between patronage of older leaders and cultural products of migrants generally. It is possible to understand the new imperial leaders as allies in local social competition.

Importantly, it was argued that 2Isa's beneficial creator who supports the servant is an instance of double influence: negative towards Babylon and positive towards Achaemenid creation. Similarly, the poet's vision of variegated servanthood was suitable for justifying life in a cosmopolitan empire. While 2Isa transferred the divine treaty to Cyrus, it had unclear implications for Cyrus's heirs. Overall, the tone was one that created an "evangelistic" message that tied YHWH to the Persian crown, focused on statues rather than polytheism *per se*, left potential for later disillusionment, separated royal and priestly functions, and left an emphasis on teaching.

Part II argued that 1Zech visualized the gubernatorial garden at Ramat Raḥel, called for the renewed cultic importance of Jerusalem, translated the vetting of Joshua before the satrap to the heavens, showed a departure from Davidic traditions, and justified the new temple and new priesthood, both of which it linked with imperial control and prosperity. The visions saw the status of world and Babylonia according to divine will, as did the sign act. The latter emphasized the temple's position in the proper social order and the diaspora's approval of Growth's actions, and arranged for a visual reminder of this. The text closed on a cosmopolitan and prosperous note.

An extended review of dream reports served to argue that 1Zech is plausibly a real vision report, with a two-stage redaction in the first four years of Darius. It was suggested, therefore, that 1Zech was a vision report that was collated as the local version of an official report concerning the establishment of the temple, thus justifying both the temple itself and the Yehud elite's participation therewith. Thus, one can understand 1Zech to be more concerned with justifying the resultant social-political situation, or, in other words, with the new Yehud elite and their engagements with the Persians—therefore it does not make sense to see these oracles as part of a "nationalistic" fervor hoping to make use of the widespread disturbances of 522–21. It was further argued that the visions justify Darius's success in subduing these countries.

One can posit that the two figures in Zech 4 represent two officials appointed either by Darius or his satrap, whose jobs were to ensure the new temple participated in the imperial designs for it. Therefore, instead of being a declaration of diarchy in Yehud, ch. 4's vision can be read as both modelling YHWH's heavens on the Achaemenid Empire as well as an instance of elite justification for their involvement with Persian policies.

If administrators and elites in Yehud could succeed in making Jerusalem a pilgrimage site for both Judaeans and other subject peoples, the elites and priests of the Jerusalem temple would find themselves at a nexus between Judaeans, "Gentiles," and the Persians—a relatively powerful, and potentially lucrative position. This would be advantageous to the empire, and it would also contribute to any aspirations of holding a diaspora together by creating a network with financial repercussions.

The section also argued that the figure called "Growth" should be identified with Darius I. This means that rather than negotiating the relative positions of Davidide and priest, 1Zech is concerned with the relationship between the Persian emperor and Yehud. The Yehudite expectations for the Persian king were much like the expectations for the role of Cyrus on the behalf on Babylonian priests as described by Waerzeggers: to fulfill the necessary roles of patron and defender of the cult. Though expectations of growth and prosperity are hyperbolic, the vision distinctly lacks any monarchical or imperial pretenses: Jerusalem will be significant for its cultic site alone. A better way to conceptualize the subconscious concerns of the visionary is to see an interest in proper order, this ultimately being seen as consonant with Darius's victory rather than hampered thereby.

So far in Part III it was argued that both Babylonia and Egypt demonstrate the aid the Great Kings received from sophisticated local partners. The possibility that they also utilized more popular/folkloric efforts was raised. The incomplete nature of Cambyses's conquest of Egypt was posited as a reason for his poor memory. An overview of the role of temples in all of this emphasized the varying impact on temples, while suggesting that more marginal areas sometimes experienced a greater impact than more central ones. Lastly, Josephus was rejected as evidence of increased priestly power under the Persians.

Elite Judaean Discourses Concerning the Early Persian Kings: Comparison between Second Isaiah and First Zechariah

The above material argued that while 2Isa and 1Zech represent discourses in very different genres (dictated oral poetry versus a vision report from the establishment of a cultic site) from different locations (the city of Babylon and the gubernatorial site at Ramat Raḥel), both derive from elite Judaean discourses, in the early years of the empire. Therefore, a comparison between them ought to help flesh out some of the ways the changed political and social situations were negotiated.

Given the above arguments concerning these two texts, it is perhaps unsurprising that the present author does not agree with Sweeney in seeing Zechariah as intended to update Isaiah and call for the overthrow of the Persians.[2] Not only does the present study read these sources separately from their later canonical contexts, the fact that much later sources (*Targum Jonathan* and the Talmud) read the canonical books in conjunction is irrelevant for the early Persian Empire.[3] Moreover, his connections between the texts are all very tenuous and presume an intentional, literary connection, so it is better to analyze the two sources as independent voices reacting to the early empire. How do their reactions to the new imperial situation compare?

The initial point to note appears somewhat banal at first glance: according to this study, neither source derives from Jerusalem. While both are interested in Jerusalem and its fate, this gives some pause to the generally Jerusalem-centric narratives scholars weave for literature from the Persian Empire. Even if the Tanak's eventual collation happened in Jerusalem, the materials' origins cannot have been wholly there.[4] The often-recognized probability that there were many more texts from STJ that have not survived (and thus the non-inevitability of eventual "canonical" status)

---

2. Sweeney 2003; 2015: 155–7.

3. His starting point is the fact these later texts read them together (Sweeney 2003: 341).

4. The present author suspects other literature (perhaps the Pentateuch itself) was collated elsewhere as well, though that falls outside the present scope.

must be remembered here—the Tanak was merely a selection of material. The relations of the two texts to Jerusalem is somewhat divergent, however. For 2Isa, Jerusalem functions more as a point of unity for its community. Attachment to YHWH will result in a restoration for "home." A recurrent element of "diaspora" discourses is the renegotiation and redefinition of "home" without any real intention of permanent return. It is therefore quite explicable that 2Isa never calls for the Judaeans to return to Yehud (despite scholars frequently arguing that it does).[5] For 1Zech, the city is primarily important for being the location of a renewed cult. This cult, however, is one that will support the socio-political system and bring the province prosperity. The text sees the support of the project by the Babylonian community, but there is not an attendant call for repatriation: rather, the call is for pilgrimage.

In a similar vein, there is no compelling reason to attach the writing of either text to *priests*. It was argued that 2Isa was not originally cultic at all, but the transcription of an oral poet's performance from some unknown context in Babylon. The scribal amanuensis could therefore have been any member of the literate elite; in Babylonia the likelihood was that they functioned within the administration as much if not more likely than being priests. Of course, this argument (and the inference for the amanuensis) is not provable—but then, neither would the assertion of a cultic provenance be, whether priestly or prophetic. For 1Zech, the locus was placed in a gubernatorial sphere, one negotiating the legitimate foundation of a temple. While the text credits the visions to a prophet, the context was argued to be administrative; this is also a likely place to find scribes in early Persian Yehud. In both cases, this study argues that these texts therefore evince a wider range of Judaean elites than are sometimes considered to be important—i.e., "secular" elites.

Nevertheless, one aspect which both discourses share is an apparent disregard of the Davidic dynasty. The phenomenon of exiled monarchs was raised in Part I. While it is not known for certain whether (or how long) Jehoiachin's family pursued a claim to the throne, it was argued that both of these sources do not further any such claims. 2Isa's acceptance of Cyrus as legitimate king, and positing of a new "Teispid" treaty with the nations, seems a decisive rejection of David—especially since the family's presence in Babylon was at the very minimum a living memory if not a living reality. Similarly, 1Zech's withdrawal of theophoric Zion theology from the remit of the holy warrior tradition and appeal to Darius

---

5. YHWH returns to Jerusalem for sure, but not the implied audience.

for proper kingly legitimation of the temple points to a similar rejection. Zerubbabel's Davidic pedigree is not important for 1Zech. While there may have been Judaeans who still supported the Davidides and sought their restoration as either governors or kings, these two documents are evidence that influential Judaeans in both Babylonia and Yehud were not among them. Scholars who have posited, therefore, the idea that Cyrus and/or Darius would have tried to gain Judaean cooperation by reinstalling the family as governors (or as vassal kings) must find other sources to support such a claim.[6]

Another point of contact between the analyses above was that the discourses were seen to be amenable to "cosmopolitan" life in a broad empire. For 2Isa this took the form of a call to disseminate teaching of YHWH and his servants (one of whom was Cyrus). For 1Zech this took the form of a call for pilgrimage, one open to the nations as well as to Judah. One might understand these as initial, naïve expectations at the beginning of a regime change; one might also see them as reflexes of the benefits large empires can provide for successful local elites.

Several explicit points of "Iranian influence" were also argued. For 2Isa the most important was the concept of a benevolent creator. The beginning of a firmer separation between kingly and priestly functions, however, was also seen as a result of the development of the servanthood theme. For 1Zech, it was argued that the beginnings of a modelling of YHWH's heavens on the Achaemenid Empire can be seen: in the figure of the accuser, the beginnings of increased divine transcendence (in the use of delegated angelic authority), as well as the two divine supports of prosperity. The former has large implications for the development of Judaean theology generally, and the career of the penultimate does as well. The last one seems to have been forgotten in the course of time.

The previous chapter argued that sophisticated local cooperation was deliberately utilized by the early Persian kings. In light of the above, it is reasonable to call both 2Isa and 1Zech examples of sophisticated Judaean cooperation with the new kings. Certainly, the Persians are seen to be useful allies for the furtherance of their own, Judaean goals (in Babylonia, including competition with Babylonians; in Yehud, seemingly a ploy for the greater significance of the province and its elites). While it would be rash to claim that either were "commissioned" by the Persians, the context of a pro-imperial culture of elites must be considered.

---

6. E.g., Ackroyd 1968: 190; Sacchi 2004: 62. Of course, Hoglund 1992 already rejected this idea, though primarily in reference to Ezra-Nehemiah.

Elites in the Persian Empire:
Towards a More Sophisticated Model

Already in the 1980s, drawing on both Veblen and Marx, Kautsky argued that the gulf between ruling elites ("aristocrats") and the peasants was so great that they constituted entirely separate societies.[7] However, despite this simplistic scheme, merchants and retainers of the aristocrats fall outside of it: he expands Veblen's category of the "vicarious leisure class" for those trained to serve the aristocrats in various capacities, calling them all "townspeople."[8] Despite this group's heterogeneity, Kautsky sees them as more inclined to favor the elites than the peasants, being in essence dependent upon the elites for their existence. He especially emphasizes that bureaucrats (scribes), though theoretically holding their positions on the basis of qualifications, still largely derive from traditional landholding segments as well as depend on them for their livelihood (and thus in his analysis, still likely to favor the aristocracy).[9] He does, however, make a distinction between aristocratic clergy and village priests.[10] Overall, in Kautsky's view, the ties between lower elites and imperial elites will tend to be closer and more mutually affirmative than those with other, rival elites of the same level.[11] Such a view challenges the axiom that local elites were inherently resistant to the empire, and is similar to Fitzpatrick-McKinley's emphasis on local elite rivalries (see below).

It is important to note, however, that in Kautsky's scheme, the Achaemenid Empire does not qualify as his ideal type of "traditional aristocratic empire" as it contains commercialization.[12] Nevertheless,

---

7. Kautsky 1982, esp. chapter 3 (49–78).

8. Kautsky 1982: 191, though he calls it the "derivative leisure class"; cf. Veblen 1915: 53–67, which more narrowly discusses wives and servants, but is later expanded to all the "retainers and hangers-on of the patron" (p. 77). In chapter 14 (320–340) Kautsky uses "townspeople" to emphasize their diversity and relative closeness to the aristocrats rather than the peasants (instead of "middle class"); see also the more recent discussion of Daloz 2010: ch. 6 (94–114).

9. Kautsky 1982: 136 (speaking of China), 332–3.

10. Kautsky 1982: 158–61; cf. Daloz 2010: 107.

11. Kautsky 1982: 169. This contrasts with the view of Weinberg, who thought that non-Iranian elites were a threat to Persian elites (Weinberg 1999).

12. He also sees peasant revolts as a product of monetization (Kautsky 1982: esp. 288–92), something that would seem to happen during the course of the Persian Empire. However, this raises the question of proper economic models for understanding the period, something well beyond the scope of this monograph.

Kautsky's analysis still gives reason to consider more carefully the social status of local elites and its ramifications for the political affiliations of scribes within empires. It is in fact similar to the analysis of Philip Davies, who had understood the "scribal class" as an urban upper class that was distinct from both the peasants and the aristocracy or ruling class.[13] For him this means they had "occasion for ambiguity and satire."[14]

In this respect, it is worth returning to the oft-cited framework of James C. Scott, as mentioned in the initial sylvan peripatetics. There are two aspects of his work that are infrequently acknowledged: (1) he himself explicitly states that *organized* resistance is the "preserve" of the "middle class and intelligentsia";[15] (2) his study concerns the effects of the introduction of a new system based on new technology (i.e., threshers enabling capitalism).[16] Both of these points would appear to reinforce the difficulty in directly applying Scott's model to the pieces of evidence in this study. Not only does it support Kautsky's generalizations that the scribes (as dependent on the aristocracy) will be participating in *elite* politics on behalf of its various actors in hopes of self-advancement—rather than participating in the sorts of peasant resistance described by Scott—it is manifestly describing a situation of modernization, which cannot be directly applicable to the Persian Empire. These comments are not at all intended to imply that the "derivative leisure class" (or "literati" or however one wishes to call people like scribes) cannot be agents of resistance, critique, or change, either actively or passively. They are meant, however, to provoke a more nuanced and careful assessment of their social and political position in ancient societies, and thus the manner in which one can imagine their world and their products (i.e., texts). In the above analysis, 2Isa and 1Zech were seen as products of elite contexts, and thus fall into a category of "organized" socio-political engagement. Are there better models for this than Scott's?

Of course, one way to understand this is through models of propaganda. In a recent attempt to understand some biblical literature as propaganda, Bos has argued that it is "para-epistemic institutions" that produce propaganda on behalf of the higher elite.[17] This would imply that scribes are "derivative leisure class" members, supporting the higher elites as in Kautsky's model. Bos's claim that literature was not a leisure

---

13. Davies 1998: 17–19.
14. Davies 1998: 19.
15. Scott 1985: xv.
16. Scott 1985: esp. 179–84, 305.
17. Bos 2016: 32.

activity in the ANE and that it therefore would not have been produced without some sort of utilitarian benefit is dubious in light of the way leisure can function as a status symbol.[18] Nevertheless, his link between the literate scribes and the ruling classes fits with the comments above. One can question, though, whether cultural production (propaganda being a problematic term) was just pro-imperial, self-serving, and/or something more nuanced. A decision on this calls for more thought on the place of scribes within the elite social structure.

Another perspective to be raised in this regard is the recent proposal of Khatchadourian, who sketches a model she calls the "satrapal condition."[19] By this she intends to describe the empire as dialectically co-dependent—rulers and subjects, center and margins, objects and lands as reciprocally dependent on each other. For her, this emphasizes the importance of practical necessity within the overall system and relations between its parts. While she is most interested in the material (and archaeological) implications of this, the pragmatic and relational aspect has implications for how one can think about ancient elites within empires, especially those of the "derivative leisure class." For present purposes this means the local, pre-Persian relations between the "derivative leisure class" and their social superiors, and the early Persian manipulations of them. It is well-known that the Persians left intact pre-existing structures, and even very many individual office holders in the lands they conquered. This can be seen, for example, in the Babylonian prosopography from Nabonidus to Darius.[20] This was a pragmatic position to take, one which affected the future shape of the territories and the empire (as Khatchadourian would emphasize).[21] Nevertheless, not all individuals remained in power across the regime change, and new Persian and other Iranian power brokers were established. Beyond the obvious changes in personnel, more subtle changes were also effected thereby. Waerzegger's microhistory of Marduk-rēmanni demonstrates how this man's career was dramatically impacted by his patron, Ina-Esagil-lilbur, being appointed as Šangû by Darius I as well as by priestly indebtedness possibly caused by the king's

---

18. Bos 2016: 33–4; on studies concerning non-productivity as an aristocratic value, see the above-cited studies of Veblen 1915 and Kautsky 1982, as well as Daloz 2010.

19. Khatchadourian 2016, esp. 1–24. Earlier she had offered a similar model based on Gramsci. See Khatchadourian 2013.

20. E.g., Jursa 2007b.

21. Pragmatism also emphasized, from a different angle, by Fitzpatrick-McKinley 2015: 9.

ambitious building program.²² These are both indirect impacts on the social hierarchy of the "derivative leisure classes."

For the Judaeans in Babylon, the implications of the Persian conquest were a change in their aristocratic patrons, if they still were dependents of the Babylonian court, and new patterns of patronage among the elites for the remainder. The Persians retained the palace institution within the city,²³ placing the Persians and their favorites directly within the social network of the city. A quest for employment and advancement was now a matter of competing with Babylonians for Persian favor, or at least for favor with Babylonians with Persian favor. It would therefore seem to be self-defeating to have been fomenting anti-Persian dissent.

For the Judaeans in Yehud, the pre-Persian period is less clear, since the extant materials provide no clear data for the administration of the region after the murder of Gedaliah (though basic continuity is implied by continual use of Ramat Raḥel). The present author has previously argued that the mysterious Sheshbazzar in Ezra should be understood as another example of continuity, as both the last Neo-Babylonian governor as well as the first Persian governor.²⁴ At the very least, however, the chain of command was slightly different, and one might wonder if the local elites in the southern Levant saw the new regime as an opportunity for more autonomy or prestige, or not. The fact that the majority of the old aristocracy had been exiled under the Neo-Babylonians is probably a salient factor here. The Phoenician kings appear to have accepted Persian rule as beneficial to them (and they were granted land in Palestine as a result).²⁵

Though focused on a slightly later period (that of Nehemiah), Fitzpatrick-McKinley has emphasized the importance of both patron–client relationships as well as competition between local elites.²⁶ She argues that the general dynamic of empires in the ANE (and Persia in particular) was one in which some "elite networks" increased their power, while new elites (and their networks) were created.²⁷ Her argument

---

22. See Waerzeggers 2015b on being a client of Ina-Esagil-lilbur, pp. 14, 73, 127; on priestly indebtedness perhaps related to the Susa obligations of the priests, p. 71.

23. Indeed, Gasche 2013 argues that the Persian kings continued to build palaces within the city until Artaxerxes I. At the very least, the older palaces continued in use, cf. Haerinck 1997: 28–30.

24. Silverman 2015c.

25. See the recent summary of the evidence in Lemaire 2015: 1–36; cf. Tal 2005.

26. Fitzpatrick-McKinley 2015 and 2016. On patronage, see also Boer 2015: 105–8.

27. Fitzpatrick-McKinley 2015: 21.

that empire created a more "complex, more hierarchical, and more competitive" socio-political world for the local elites[28] (in relation to control of land and trade routes in particular) is quite compelling. For this study's purposes, however, it is worth noting that within such a context of increasing elite competition, one must reckon with the status and power ramifications of being favored by the Persians. One would imagine that savvy and successful elites and their retainers would early on seek out influential patrons among the new ruling imperial class. One way of explaining the sophisticated local justifications of Teispid and Achaemenid rule noted in the previous chapters, therefore, is to see it as a deliberate policy of the court (the king and his close retainers) in seeking "promising" clients—likely to include "aristocrats" as well as "scribes."[29]

Another angle for investigating elite relations is one of (competitive) social prestige. Not to be confused with power and wealth (though of course related), social prestige is one way for elites to try to improve their situation. In an imperial context, associations with the empire are likely to carry desirable connotations in the provinces to those seeking social advancement. A very basic way to understand the well-known diffusion of elite Achaemenid items in the Persian Empire is one of prestige. Prestige in this context connotes both an attachment to the Persian regime and a weapon against local rivals—it is both an expression of the functioning of the empire as well as a pragmatic, interested decision. Other, less shiny cultural products, however, could be understood to have a proper place in this dynamic. Might the products of poet-singers who entertained the local elites also have been part of this context? Or, indeed, the development of revered cultic places? As Daloz is careful to warn, the methods and patterns of elite distinction are quite variable through time and place, and thus will require more careful consideration than this study has allowed.[30]

Though the above rapid and scattergun survey is woefully inadequate, it is sufficient to note that the elite engagements evinced in any text in the Persian Empire cannot too rapidly be assumed to align in any predetermined direction—whether this direction be labeled "nationalistic," "religious," "resistance," "collaboration," or any other similarly easy label. Elites were part of a tapestry of loyalties, obligations, and interests,

---

28. Fitzpatrick-McKinley 2015: 36.

29. Of course, as the empire consolidated its systems, scribes were trained deliberately for imperial needs. Some of these are seen within the documentation from Persepolis, e.g., rations for "boys copying texts" in PF 871 and 1137 (Hallock 1969: 252, 330, respectively), though as Hallock notes, it is not certain that these are literally boys, since the latter are receiving wine (pp. 29–30).

30. Daloz 2010; cf. 2013.

and their interactions with other elites—local and imperial—were part of that larger tapestry. Indeed, the aspect of interpersonal relationships as part and parcel of monarchic life was long ago emphasized by Elias.[31] With this very basic claim in mind, it is finally time to make some observations concerning Achaemenid–Elite interactions as 2Isa and 1Zech can inform the reconstruction. It is also time to consider how to understand scribes—potentially as members of the "derivate leisure class"—in relation to other, higher elites ("aristocrats"), as well as the place of priests.

To provide a very preliminary sketch of Judaean elites, one can borrow the various terms utilized by some scholars for this. If we borrow the terms of Kautsky, elites consisted of aristocrats and a "vicarious retainer class." Presumably the scribes belong in the latter category. Higher levels of priests probably were probably "aristocrats," while lower levels on a level with scribes. Lenski et al. have also placed "retainers" and priests in a "middle" position.[32] For Yehud, Kessler uses Nehemiah to distinguish between "nobles" and "provincial officials."[33] In his reading, the high priest essentially functions alongside the nobles,[34] while the scribes were essentially the local face of the empire—a term like "retainers" sounds appropriate. Adams also emphasizes how imperial administration provided opportunities for the elite few, but he does not clearly differentiate between administrators and other elites.[35]

In light of the above study, it is of course important to distinguish between social structures in Yehud and in the communities in Babylonia. For Yehud, 1Zech evinces efforts to establish a new element among the existing elites (a working priesthood), and to delineate how it would interact with the existing power structures (king, governors, and presumably other elites). All this took place in administrative circles. The overall context must have included some landed "aristocracy," likely what Kessler calls a new upper class that had gained land rights when the old, Davidic-era elites had been exiled.[36] For Babylonia, the situation involves largely those who had been exiled as elites—nobles, scribes, and priests—who now probably had numerous different social positions. The key for

---

31. E.g., Elias 1983.
32. Lenski, Lenski, and Nolan 1991: 196.
33. Kessler 2006: 141; cf. 2016: 135.
34. Kessler 2006: 142.
35. Adams 2014: 96–8, 142.
36. Kessler 2006: 136, though not his emphasis on conflict between the new and old elites, at least for such an early part of the era, since there is little to no evidence for a significant settlement from Babylonia at this time.

those which still held an elite status, however, was competition with the (well-established) Babylonian elite. This was one in which imperial service provided a pathway to career advancement. Further, more precise descriptions will require more work than can be done here.

Achaemenid–Elite Interactions in the Early Persian Empire

A two-layered effort on the part of the Achaemenids was raised above: a sophisticated engagement with local elites as well as a more "popular," folkloric effort. This may be a way to finesse the old trope of Achaemenid "tolerance." Rather than painting the Persians as some pre-industrial multicultural postmodernists, perhaps one can posit an effort by the Teispids and Achaemenids to redefine what it meant to be elite in the ANE. The depiction of the empire as one of harmonious cooperation among multiple peoples is well-known—and the collaboration of local elites also recognized.[37] Where this can be nuanced is what this meant for the local elites who participated in the imperial project. They had available to them a model whereby they could attempt to increase their status by identifying as imperial elites. Yet the Persians appear to have defined imperial elites as "representatives" of their local peoples, representatives who could participate in the imperial project by offering their local expertise to the Great King. This means that one way for the local elites to redefine themselves as imperial elites was to reformulate their own traditions in a manner useful to the empire. Thus, works of lyric poetry like 2Isa are both sophisticated products of local traditions while also products which further the imperial cause. Similarly, Yehudian aristocrats could seek to have their old royal chapel refurbished as a local node for the Judaeans in the empire. This is a very fine line that Teispids and early Achaemenid kings appear on the whole to have negotiated successfully. Perhaps this can be understood practically as having taken the form of patron–client relationships: the Great King, his satraps, and other Persian elites creating personal client relations with local elites. If the analysis presented above is sound, such relationships could be posited between the poet of 2Isa and the Persians in Babylon, and Zerubbabel and Joshua with the (sub-)

37. E.g., Root 1979 and 2000; in a slightly different direction, see Root 2015. Wiesehöfer called this an ideology of "mutual benefit" and elite reactions "non-committal political applause" (Wiesehöfer 2009: 86, 93, respectively). Lincoln has called this a deliberate confusion of "two conceptual models of dominion and mutuality" (Lincoln 2012a: 123). On collaborators, see Briant 2002: 347–54. Khatchadourian 2013, however, has warned that not all support can be called "calculated collaboration."

satrap of Abar-Nahara. The client elite would therefore have very personal motivations to see cultural products and engagements with their own, inherited traditions offered to their patrons.

The implications of a model such as this is that its success would largely depend on the Persians' choice of suitable elites as clients, as well as in the strength of the resulting relationship. Another implication of such a model is that strife—even violent strife—may have less to do with the Persian Empire *per se* and more with breakdowns in relationships and/or competition for them. In this, the model would be somewhat similar to the dynamics that Fitzpatrick-McKinley stressed in her work.[38] Another implication is that regional variations could also relate to the overall percentage of local elites with imperial patron relations versus those without. Regions with few elites could be expected to be more intimately tied to the overarching networks than regions with more internal elite competitions. Babylonia and Egypt must have had more indirect relations between the Great King and the majority of the elites than Yehud or Samerina, both provinces with smaller populations and thus fewer overall elites.

Thus, for the Judaean elites in Babylon, it was argued that the text of 2Isa evinces a rejection of the House of David in exile as suitable elite leaders or even as liaisons with the Persians. Servanthood of YHWH was stressed as a way of life in "diaspora," one that was consonant with service to the empire. To pick up the suggestions above, perhaps one can see the poem as presenting teaching of YHWH as a form of imperial service that Judaeans could offer to the Great King—YHWH called and predicted Cyrus, and he offers treaties with the nations under his rule. The use of an element of elite culture such as oral lyric poetry is quite explicable within a pattern of local elites using their inherited traditions but adopting them for competition with other elites. Sadly, however, 2Isa provides no specific data on the make-up of that elite or its leadership, beyond not being Davidic.

For the text of 1Zech, the governor of the province and his local aristocratic allies saw a new temple as within their interests, and presumably one method of improving their own finances and prestige within the empire. This of course required the selection of a priesthood (Joshua and his descendants), the building of a temple, and demonstrations of firm loyalty to the empire. No doubt the majority of Yehudian elites were "nouveau riche" and may have found the support of the king comforting in light of (better off?) Babylonian-Judaean elites. Kessler argues that the governor simply took over the old role of the king, with a more important

---

38. Fitzpatrick-McKinley 2015.

role in identity formation for the new priesthood.[39] Both Kessler and Adams have used the Tobiad romance as an example of how local elites could attempt to negotiate imperial realities for their benefit.[40] This would fit well with the model of 1Zech offered in this study: the governor and his allies (presumably some nobles as well as scribes) in the southern Levant saw Darius I as a method for improving their status, and the temple as one concrete element within that effort. It was also something that could be integrated into imperial interests.

In the previous chapter, it was argued that marginal provinces offered potential locales for increased impact, and Jerusalem certainly qualifies as marginal. Given that Abar-Nahara was at this time still part of the satrapy of Babylon, it could be that a temple was seen as administratively useful since the overall administration was used to temples as such in the eastern parts of the satrapy. Since the analysis of the sign act in Zech 6 suggested cooperation between Yehudian and Babylonian-Judaean elites, the Babylonian elites' incentive to see the Persians as a source of advancement is potentially a relevant factor in this.

The reading of the situation could potentially be compatible with the above patron–client model as advanced by other scholars, though this would require further consideration. As a model for the Persians to utilize explicitly, it is a model likely to work initially very well, but cause problems later on. The "dynastic" tendencies of aristocrats—and the resultant threat to the central crown—is something emphasized by Kautsky and suggested by Fitzpatrick-McKinley.[41] This, however, steps beyond the scope of this study.

A related aspect to elite–imperial engagement is of course the imperial court itself.[42] It may not be unreasonable to assume that some Judaeans in Babylon had access to outer rings of the Persian court, especially those who had been in the NB court. The Persians took over the NB palaces and royal estates, and thus a number of individuals probably became courtiers as a result, or at least minor officials with its administration. The stories in Daniel may reflect this phenomenological reality in terms of court life during regime change in this respect. Not much more can be discussed on this point from 2Isa, however. There may be implications for later satrapal decisions for the gubernatorial positions in Yehud,

---

39. Kessler 2008: 147; cf. Kessler 2016: 136.

40. Kessler 2016; Adams 2014: 21.

41. It is something that Briant 2002: 352–4 saw the Achaemenids largely negotiate successfully within the Persian aristocracy, however.

42. For theory, see Elias 1983. Briant 2002: 255–354. For largest collection studying the Achaemenid court, see Jacobs and Rollinger 2010.

however. The most famous is certainly Nehemiah, who claims to become governor from having been in the inner circles of the Persian court. Yet since the nomination of local governors probably came from the satrap, the link with the old NB court seems pertinent. For the Judaeans in Yehud, however, at least in the very early Persian period, connections with the court seem unlikely, except with the satrap of Abar-Nahara—even though the text of 1Zech evinces the expectation or hope of supportive interaction with Darius.

Consideration of the royal court provides another context to consider the deliberate Achaemenid inculcation of elite cooperation. Like ANE kings before them, the Persian kings probably kept "cabinets of curiosities" within some of their palaces. In the treasury at Persepolis, the excavators discovered a pre-Achaemenid Elamite bronze plaque as well as a variety of votive objects presumably taken from Mesopotamian temples.[43] Such might have been true for Susa as well, although the disregard for stratigraphy and mud-brick of the earliest excavators makes certainty impossible.[44] A number of well-known ANE artifacts were in fact found in Susa, including both the steles of Naram-Sin and Hammurabi (see fig 4.2). These were definitely brought there for display by earlier Elamite monarchs, but it is possible they were still visible in the Achaemenid period.[45] The Code was in fact being copied into the Persian period; BM 54795, a tablet from Sippar dated to the reign of Artaxerxes I, includes an excerpt from the stele (§53). However, it may have been copied from clay copies of the text rather than the stele itself.[46] At the very least, the "Egyptianizing" statue of Darius I was visible.[47] Perhaps relevant in this respect is the tablet already mentioned twice in this study, BM 113249, and its request for royal inscriptions, as well as the much discussed collation of Egyptian decrees. What all of these together might suggest is that in the imperial palaces imperial elites had access to a font of local traditions, and local elites with court access had a context for reshaping local traditions in a "courtly" manner. The gifts of the people as depicted

---

43. Schmidt 1957: 56–5.

44. See the description in Harper and Amiet 1992: 159–62. A quick glance at the *Mémoires de la Délégation en Perse* series shows no concern to specify where objects were found besides the particular trench; nothing clearly indicates a useful historical context.

45. Harper and Amiet 1992: 162 notes multiple instance of damage in the city and evinced on artifacts, from Assurbanipal to Shapur II.

46. Tablet mentioned in Maul 2012: nn. 1 and 29. He thinks it is unlikely copies were made via physical inspection (p. 80). Thanks to Sebastian Fink for the reference.

47. Yoyette 2013; Wasmuth 2015.

on the Apadana could therefore be imagined to include more intangible "gifts"—not just distinctive local material products, but also culturally specific forms of "elite distinctions" that the local elites transformed in their quest to become members of the imperial elite.

The second aspect of the previous chapter's analysis is the "folkloric" aspect. Such a dynamic has already been posited by Kuhrt for the Cyrus legends,[48] and has been periodically considered for its relevance to the sources of Herodotus and Ctesias.[49] However, given the ephemeral nature of folklore, it is difficult to nearly impossible to trace its developments in any detail, much less to analyze how it may have been deliberately inculcated. Isolated examples, however, such as *4QPrayer of Nabonidus*, may present themselves to such an interpretation if the possibility is kept in mind. The general significance of this, however, might be a way to consider the cultural history of the empire, with folklore being used to shape legitimation, while simultaneously shaping imperial culture.

Perhaps specific settings, such as the multi-ethnic garrisons dotted around the empire or the hostelries servicing the royal road network, serve as fruitful locations to consider the ways oral traditions and folklore could shape a shared imperial culture at lower social levels. Though attested as a manuscript, Bledsoe has offered a consideration of *Ahiqar* among the garrison in Elephantine.[50] He sees it as both inculcating loyalty to the monarchy while expressing dissatisfaction with its imperfections. Whether one agrees with his reading of the text or not, such an ambivalent function of narrative is an important part of cultural discourse generally. Both the narrative and the proverbs have claims to folkloric links, and thus its functions here may be suggestive, if not identical. It is possible that the imperial elite encouraged the dissemination of folklore with such a constitutive role in mind; it is also possible that it may simply be "popular" echoes of more elite productions. Perhaps more realistically, one should reckon with a combination of the two. In this context, it is important to emphasize that such oral traditions co-exist, and that the transcription of any of them has little to no bearing on the living oral tradition itself. Thus, even though it was argued above that 2Isa was a transcription, this has no bearing on the presumed continued oral performance of that poetic tradition. Therefore, interactions with any such oral tradition are subsequently likely to be pluriform.[51]

48. Kuhrt 2003.
49. E.g., for some debates concerning this: Shrimpton 1997: Appendix 1; Skjærvø 1998: 105; Tuplin 2005: 235–9; Evans 2014: 41–88.
50. Bledsoe 2015.
51. E.g., Silverman 2016b.

Perhaps another potential location for such would be royally sponsored feasts for (forced) work gangs (at least in the heartland). Henkelman has collated evidence for feasts, likely held in paradises, which served to depict the king's largess.[52] He has posited the potential of a feast known as *šip* for unifying pastoralists and sedentary populations.[53] The known practice of special rations to work gangs (known as *kurtaš*) suggests that a similar dynamic was true on a less-elaborate scale lower down the pecking order.[54] Feasts are often venues for oral storytelling, and thus both of these contexts are venues for the deliberate and accidental formation and transmission of folkloric elements related to the king. Alimentary remains found at Ramat Raḥel have been interpreted by the excavators as signs of elaborate feasting by the elite located there in the seventh century.[55] One would expect the Persian governors to have continued similar practices, and thus this would be a venue within Yehud for the dissemination of folklore and oral poetry. This study has not identified either of its source texts as deriving from folklore, but it remains an important factor to consider for the overall cultural context of the local (and imperial) elites.

All of the locations described above are merely suggestions for potential locations of interactions, and require further studies to determine how much data might be adduced for them. The concrete results of the two main analyses in this study at least point to locations within elite, probably administratively adjacent, circles. For 2Isa, the setting was argued to be elites within the satrapal capital, and for 1Zech to be within the gubernatorial sphere of a small province. The broad strokes images of the Persians in both placed them within well-known ANE categories of and patterns for kingship—military victors, bringers of prosperity and peace, divinely favored. An image of imperial benevolence was discernible within 2Isa. This suggests that the Great Kings attempted to depict themselves in ways local elites were able to take up and adapt in locally suitable ways. That elements of Persian kingship echo earlier ANE forms, particularly Neo-Assyrian, is also nothing new.[56] What is meant here, however, is that, despite the elements of novelty and discontinuity in the "theology" of the Persian kings,[57] it can be argued that they attempted to depict their rule

52. Henkelman 2011b.
53. Henkelman 2011b: 131.
54. The exact status of these workers is debated. See the various opinions in Dandamaev 1975; Aperghis 2000; Briant 2002: 429–39; Henkelman and Stolper 2009; Henkelman 2012; Silverman 2015b.
55. Lipschits et al. 2017: 85.
56. E.g., Root 1979; Panaino 2000.
57. E.g., Silverman 2016c.

as *functionally* appropriate to previous regimes of rule. To use language used earlier, the Achaemenids deliberately provided local elites with a "hook" whereby they could adapt their own traditions of leadership to the new imperial realities. Taking titles such as King of Babylon and Pharaoh obviously fall into this category. But even without titles, playing patron to cultic sites and supporting fecundity played into pre-existing local patterns in various regions. That all of this is manifestly practical does not speak against its ideological import for local elites.

This brings the discussion back to the idea raised in the first chapter: efforts at imperial legitimation can function simultaneously as self-justification and self-advancement on the part of local elites. In light of the presented reading of 2Isa and 1Zech this can be pushed further and claimed that the Teispids and early Achaemenids sought out talented local elites willing to do just this. Whether or not terms like "collaboration" are useful here, this is a perspective that takes the agencies of all parties involved seriously. It also provides an implicit mechanism for exploring cultural influences—in the individual elites and their relationships. This is a mechanism which will bear further scrutiny.

Chapter 8

EXIT, PURSUED BY A BEAR

ותצאנה שתים דבים מן היער ותבקענה מהם ארבעים ושני ילדים

And two (gynecomorphous) bears came from the forest and rent forty-two children in twain.

—2 Kgs 2:24b

And there was much rejoicing.

—*Monty Python and the Holy Grail* (1975)

This study has admittedly left out some crucial information that the author had originally intended to have included: analyses of other more or less contemporaneous sources (Haggai, Gerizim) or relevant later sources (Elephantine materials, Ezra-Nehemiah, and Chronicles); evaluation of the effect and reception of 2Isa and 1Zech; more in-depth theorizing of ancient elites. It is hoped, however, that the analysis presented here will still provide minor progress towards understanding the Judaeans' early relations to the Persians, and that these omissions will not come back to maul the modest findings (even if, no doubt, some reviewers will).

Moreover, departing from standard paradigms of interpretation can lead to dire consequences, and this study has offered a few discrete interpretations outside the canon of long-recurrent debates attached to both 2Isa and 1Zech, as well as to the early Persian Period. One can fully expect a few reviewers to savage the text for these reasons. This brief, ultimate chapter will attempt to pre-empt a few potential lines of attack as well as point to some directions in which future escape may be possible.

First, it is necessary to clarify that the critique mounted here of recent discussions of "resistance" (and the buzzword "hidden transcripts") on no account is meant to attack the *concept* of nor *possibility* for resistance among ancient elites. Anyone can reject and resist anything if they so wish. However, no matter what the social or political contexts of an agent are, resistance is ever only *one* option among others. It cannot, therefore, serve as a starting assumption for all interactions with other, higher elites or with empire *per se*. Even further, discussion of interaction needs to be more nuanced than a binary of acquiescence—resistance. All humans, ancients included, face situations where their motives and intentions are complicated, even conflicted, and their choices made for complex reasons. Fisher's "logic of good reasons," appealed to in chapter 2 for its import on rhetoric, also applies to social and political posturing: neither rationality nor any other single factor ever totally determines human choices.[1] Neither should a single factor (in this case, resistance) play a heroic role in modern reconstructions of the past.

Beyond this very general critique, "resistance" does not exist *an sich*. One can only resist something, something particular. Therefore to determine whether an individual scribe, a group, or a text, wishes to resist, one must define the object of their resistance first. To do so, one must first understand what was deemed natural and therefore unquestioned within their world view (what Bourdieu called *doxa*) and what was open to negotiation (and therefore resistance, or the situation that Bourdieu called *orthodoxy* and *heterodoxy*).[2] The question at hand, therefore, is first whether ancient elites were able to envision a reality other than kingship and its imperial tendencies or not; second, if they could envision another potential reality whether they objected to the orthodoxy of kingship or merely particular aspects of it (e.g., a different king); and third, if they championed a heterodox view what that meant specifically. One does not need the Bourdieusian language used above to see that the question of sociopolitical vision and allegiance is more complicated than it is sometimes indicated to be.

Scott's infamous study defined the object of peasant resistance as their elite overlords.[3] The fact that literary evidence from the ANE does not derive from peasants makes his study not a suitable match for such evidence, without some serious adaption. More importantly, it raises a question of what exactly "elites" means in the ANE. Many studies of the ANE—admittedly, this study included—use the term in a rather vague way. This terminal vagueness only increases when the roles of "scribes" are discussed. It is hoped that this study might point to the need for a more nuanced understanding of the variegation, structures, and roles of ANE elites, and what the implications of these are for how elites interacted with other elites, and with their imperial masters. In particular, the

1. Fisher 1987.
2. E.g., Bourdieu 2005: 164, 168.
3. Scott 1985: xv–xix.

social positions of scribes and priests in the overall structure of the elites of Judaean communities needs deeper consideration. The previous chapter tentatively raised the issues of prestige and patron–client relationships as avenues perhaps illuminating for such issues. Surely, the implications do not stop there.

Hand in hand with a more sophisticated understanding of "elites," therefore, this study hopes to suggest a more sophisticated understanding of the ways "local" elites interacted with other local elites and with imperial elites. This study has argued that two texts, 2Isa and 1Zech, evince local elite machinations to improve their situations by supporting the Persian Empire. Such a position is more than simply being "acolytes" in the sense of offering supporting service to a higher power, it is also a way of being creative in self-interest. Even if their historical agency had practically been quite limited, they shaped it in dramatic ways, with implications for their own traditions, and the traditions of their fellow acolytes of Yahweh. Moreover, the analysis of these two sources need not mean that all Judaean elites, or Yahwists, would have taken a similar stance. Neither does it mean that other elites who may have also serviced the Persian Empire would not have quarreled with these elites on some issues. It merely means that, at the very minimum, enough Judaeans that were Teispid and Achaemenid "acolytes" existed at the beginning of the Persian Empire for these two texts to exist, survive, and later be redacted into their present literary contexts.

Another implication of this study is to call for a recognition of the Persians' sophistication in co-opting talented local elites for their own purposes. This is one way of explaining the reputations of Cyrus and Darius in Babylon and Egypt respectively. Just as argued for the Judaean texts, this is neither groveling sycophancy on the behalf of local elites nor "going native" on the part of Persian elites. It is a situation in which the Persians were, at least sometimes, able to coopt the talents of various elites for mutually beneficial purposes (from the Persians' perspective, and from their local supporters' too). At times, this coopting could utilize local cults as a tool, as much as it could any other aspect of life. One may rightly gripe that this perspective ignores the reality of Persian latent violence and parasitical feeding off the backs of their subjects (and ultimately their subjects' peasants), but this is neither the perspective found in the texts that have been discussed here, nor is that a reality likely any different from any other "agrarian empire" in history. Moreover, just because some local elites did indeed choose to place themselves in the service of the Persian crown does not imply there were others who did not. For example, Nebuchadnezzar III, Inarus, and Šamaš-erība are sufficient evidence of this.

Though taking a more explicitly socio-political approach than my previous book, *Persepolis and Jerusalem*, this study is still compatible with the hermeneutical approach taken there. Just as the study of religious influence ought to take seriously the ways humans must continually interpret and reinterpret their world in light of changing circumstances, the study of political influences and social changes ought to as well. Political and ideological allegiances, as much as theological ones, may be positive or negative, conscious or unconscious.

For readers disappointed by the lack of heavy-going redaction criticism or exploration of "intertextuality" within this study, the present author can simply point out the differing methodological presuppositions between their expectations and this study's. For the former, one can offer little beyond the extended discussion already offered in chapter 3 of *Persepolis and Jerusalem* (which was central to the overall method and results there, though apparently that was not spelled out sufficiently for all readers).[4] For the latter, one can point to the complications with the methods often used for the biblical corpus offered elsewhere.[5]

Unfortunately, an analysis of Haggai similar to the one provided for 1Zech has not been possible here, as originally intended. However, the arguments concerning the political situation advanced for 1Zech would equally apply to Haggai, in contrast to much discussion of that book. At this point, it is worth noting that (1) there is no reason to assume that the views of the individuals behind 1Zech would necessarily have been identical to those behind Haggai—and indeed, scholars have posited differences between the two for various reasons.[6] Second, the "messianic" overtones sometimes seen in Hag 2 appear on first glance to be overblown, especially in light of the chronology of Darius's successes (as argued for 1Zech; cf. Appendix).[7] While a reading of Haggai similar to the ones

---

4. Silverman 2012: 98–129. A number of reviewers commented on a seeming disconnect between this chapter and the remainder of the study. The main driving point of that chapter remains true for this study: that the point of comparison of *texts* here is not to find *textual* links—unless stated as a quotation or allusion—but rather to explore the *cultural and social* links as evidenced by extant texts since direct access to the oral culture is of course no longer possible. A distinction is to be made between comparison for reconstruction of historical-cultural contexts and comparison for the purpose of arguing direct links (quotations, allusions, or influence).

5. Silverman 2016b. Other, more sophisticated attempts to deal with the relationships between texts do exist (such as those by Gérard Genette), but they are not the focus of this study.

6. E.g., Sauer 1967; Kessler 2008; Lux 2009: 258.

7. Cf. Kessler 2002, especially 237.

performed here is certainly relevant and would likely add nuance to the discourse of the period, it should not invalidate the readings and interpretations offered here.

In sum, this study has argued that a close reading of 2Isa and 1Zech in an early Persian context sees both as accepting the new regime and angling for it to justify renewed configurations of the their respective communities. This was taken to evince Teispid and Achaemenid efforts to engage sophisticated local elites in empire-building. The success of these efforts was suggested to be based on personal relationships and motivations, and with differing levels of impact for large and small provinces. The impact on local and imperial cultures and interactions should thus be seen in a matrix of elites seeking both mutually useful legitimation strategies as well as seeking greater prestige than their fellow local elites. The subtle shaping of inherited traditions could be the result.

Further work in the early and later periods of the empire will no doubt flesh out this picture more. Similarly, deeper consideration of the category of ancient "elites" will help to improve understanding of these inter-elite dynamics, on local and imperial levels. Moreover, future "microhistories" of local elite–imperial elite engagements should help flesh out how the long experience of the massive Achaemenid Empire shaped ANE culture in ways perhaps unintended by all the actors involved—Great King, his acolytes, and his rivals included.

Appendix:
Table of Dates*

Julian Date (BCE)	Source Date	Event		
		Imperial	Hebrew Bible	Cosmological
14 Aug. 586	7/V/Nebu. 19		Temple destroyed (2 Kgs 25:8)	
28 May 585		Median–Lydian truce[1]		Full solar eclipse
550 /549	Nab. 6	Cyrus takes Ecbatana		
10 Oct. 539	14/VII/Nab. 17	Cyrus takes Sippar		
29 Oct. 539	3/VIII/Nab. 17	Cyrus himself enters Babylon		
27 Mar. 528	4/I/Cyr. 1	Someone attends *Akītu*		
11 Mar. 522	14/XII/Camb. 7	Bardiya revolts		
1 Sep. 522	12/VI/Dar. 0	First date to Nebu. III[2]		
20 Sep. 522	1/VII/Dar. 0	Last date to Bardiya[3]		
29 Sep. 522	10/VII/Dar. 0	"Gaumata" killed[4]		
14 Dec. 522	27/IX/Dar. 0	Last date to Nebu. III[5]		
16 Dec. 522	29/IX/Dar. 0	Nebu. III's second defeat[6]		

* Dates calculated using Parker and Dubberstein 1956. Also consulted, Lorenz 2008, from which derive the early and late dates for pretenders.

1. Herod. I.74 (Herodotus 2002: 90–1).
2. ASJ 19 1.
3. ZA 4 Sm-9.
4. DB I § 13.
5. YOS 17 126.
6. DB I § 19.

8 May 521	25/I/Dar. 1	Fraortes defeated		
20 Nov. 521	15/VIII/Dar. 1	Latest date to Nebu. IV[7]		
27 Nov. 521	22/VIII/Dar. 1	Nebu. IV killed[8]		
10 Dec. 521	23/IX/Dar. 1	Frada defeated		
520?	Dar. 2	Third Elamite revolt		
520		Construction begins at Susa and Persepolis? ("high date")		
30 May 520				Annular solar eclipse
29 Aug. 520	1/VI/Dar. 2		Haggai's first oracle	
(27) Oct. 520	VII/Dar. 2		Zech.'s first oracle	
8 Nov. 520	13/VII/Dar. 2			Partial lunar eclipse
15 Feb. 519	24/XI/Dar. 2		Zech.'s first vision	
519?	Dar. 3	Scythian campaign		
518?		Egyptian campaign		
6 Dec. 518	4/IX/Dar. 4		Zech's enquiry	
516	Dar. 6	First attested Bab. workgangs in Susa[9]		
12 Mar. 515	3/XII/Dar. 6		Ezra 6:15's date for temple completion	
484	c. 4/V/Xer. 2– 29/VII/Xer. 2	Revolts of Bēl-šimânni and Šamaš-erība[10]		

7. Nbk 19.
8. DB III § 50.
9. Waerzeggers 2010: 792.
10. Waerzeggers 2003/04.

Bibliography

Adams, Samuel L. (2014), *Social and Economic Life in Second Temple Judea*, Louisville, KY: Westminster John Knox.

Abdi, Kamyar (2006), "The 'Daiva' Inscription Revisited," *Nāme-ye Irān Bāstān* 6 (1–2): 45–74.

Abdi, Kamyar (2010), "The Passing of the Throne from Xerxes to Artaxerxes I, or How an Archaeological Observation Can Be a Potential Contribution to Achaemenid Historiography," in John Curtis and St. John Simpson (eds), *The World of Achaemenid Persia: History, Art and Society in Iran and the Ancient Near East*, 275–84, London: I. B. Tauris.

Abernethy, Diana (2017), "Translation of Horse Colors in Zechariah 1:8; 6:2–3, 6 Based on Textual and Material Evidence," *JBL* 136 (3): 593–607.

Abraham, Kathleen (2004), *Business and Politics under the Persian Empire: The Financial Dealings of Marduk-nasir-apli of the House of Egibi (521–487 B.C.E.)*, Bethesda, MD: CDL.

Abram, Mary (2011), "A New Look at the Mesopotamian Rod and Ring: Emblems of Time and Eternity," *StAn* 10.1: 15–36, http://scholarsarchive.byu.edu/studiaantiqua/vol10/iss1/5.

Abu-Lughod, Lila (2009), "Shifting Politics in Bedouin Love Poetry," in Maria Damon and Ira Livingston (eds), *Poetry and Cultural Studies: A Reader*, 116–32, Champaign: University of Illinois Press.

Ackroyd, Peter R. (1951), "Studies in the Book of Haggai," *JJS* 2 (4): 163–76.

Ackroyd, Peter R. (1968), *Exile and Restoration*, London: SCM.

Adam, Jeroen (2008), "Forced Migration, Adat, and a Purified Present in Ambon, Indonesia," *Ethnology* 47 (4): 227–38.

Adams, Jim W. (2006), *The Performative Nature and Function of Isaiah 40–55*, LHBOTS 448, London: T&T Clark.

Aelian (1997), *Historical Miscellany*, trans. Nigel G. Wilson, LCL 486, Cambridge, MA: Harvard University Press.

Agosino, Biko (2000), *Theoretical and Methodological Issues in Migration Research: Interdisciplinary, Intergenerational and International Perspectives*, Aldershot: Ashgate.

Agut-Labordère, Damien (2005), "Le sens du Décret de Cambyse," *Transeuphraténe* 29:9–16.

Ahlström, Gösta W. (1982), *Royal Administration and National Religion in Ancient Palestine*, SHANE 1, Leiden: Brill.

Ahn, Gregor (1992), *Religiöse Herrscherlegitimation im achämenidischen Iran: Die Voraussetzungen und die Struktur ihrer Argumentation*, Acta Iranica 31, Leiden: Brill.

Ahn, John J. (2011), *Exile as Forced Migrations: A Sociological, Literary, and Theological Approach on the Displacement and Resettlement of the Southern Kingdom of Judah*, BZAW 417, Berlin: de Gruyter.
Albenda, Pauline (1999), "Horses of Different Colors," *N.A.B.U* (1999–13: http://www.achemenet.com/pdf/nabu/nabu1999-013.pdf.
Albertz, Rainer, and Rüdiger Schmitt (2012), *Family and Household Religion in Ancient Israel and the Levant*, Winona Lake, IN: Eisenbrauns.
Albertz, Rainer (1994), *From the Exile to the Maccabees*, A History of Israelite Religion in the Old Testament Period 2, Louisville, KY: Westminster John Knox.
Albertz, Rainer (2003a), "Darius in Place of Cyrus: The First Edition of Deutero-Isaiah (Isaiah 40.1–52.12) in 521 BCE," *JSOT* 27: 371–83.
Albertz, Rainer (2003b), *Israel in Exile: The History and Literature of the Sixth Century BCE*, trans. David Green, SBLStBL 3, Atlanta: SBL.
Albertz, Rainer (2003c), "The Thwarted Restoration," in Rainer Albertz and Bob Becking (eds), *Yahwism After the Exile: Perspectives on Israelite Religion in the Persian Era*, 1–17, Assen: Royal van Gorcum.
Albertz, Rainer (2011), "The Controversy about Judean versus Israelite Identity and the Persian Government: A New Interpretation of the Bagoses Story (*Jewish Antiquities* XI.297–301)," in Oded Lipschits, Gary N. Knoppers and Manfred Oeming (eds), *Judah and the Judeans in the Achaemenid Period: Negotiating Identity in an International Context*, 483–504, Winona Lake, IN: Eisenbrauns.
Albertz, Rainer (2014), "On the Structure and Formation of the Book of Deutero-Isaiah," in Richard J. Bautch and J. Todd Hibbard (eds), *Book of Isaiah: Enduring Questions Answered Anew*, 21–40, Grand Rapids, MI: Eerdmans.
Alizadeh, Abbas (2009), "Prehistoric Mobile Pastoralists in South-Central and Southwestern Iran," in Jeffrey Szuchman (eds), *Nomads, Tribes, and the State in the Ancient Near East: Cross-Disciplinary Perspectives*, 129–45, Oriental Institute Seminars 5, Chicago: Oriental Institute of the University of Chicago.
Algar, H. (1989), "'Amāma," *EncIr* 1 (9): 919–21, http://www.iranicaonline.org/articles/amama-or-ammama-arabic-emama-the-turban.
Allen, Lindsay (2005), *The Persian Empire: A History*, London: British Museum.
Allen, Lindsay (2013), "The Letter as Object: On the Experience of Achaemenid Letters," *BICS* 56 (2): 21–36.
Aloiz, Emily, Janet G. Douglas, and Alexander Nagel (2016), "Painted Plaster and Glazed Brick Fragments from Achaemenid Pasargadae and Persepolis, Iran," *Heritage Science* 4 (3), http://heritagesciencejournal.springeropen.com/articles/10.1186/s40494-016-0072-7.
Al-Rawi, Farouk N. H., and Andrew George (2014), "Back to the Cedar Forest: The Beginning and End of Tablet V. of the Standard Babylonian Epic of Gilgameš," *JCS* 66: 69–90.
Alstola, Tero E. (2014), "On the Road: Judean Royal Merchants in Babylonia". Paper read at SBL, in San Diego.
Alstola, Tero E. (2017a), "Judean Merchants in Babylonia and Their Participation in Long-Distance Trade," *WO* 47 (1): 25–51.
Alstola, Tero E. (2017b), "Judeans in Babylonia: A Study of Deportees in the Sixth and Fifth Centuries BCE," PhD diss., University of Helsinki.
Alstola, Tero, Jason M. Silverman, Jonathan Stökl, Caroline Waerzeggers, and Anne-Mareike Wetter (forthcoming), *Handbook of the Babylonian Exile*.

Alter, Robert (1987), "The Characteristics of Ancient Hebrew Poetry," in Robert Alter and Frank Kermode (eds), *The Literary Guide to the Bible*, 611–24, Cambridge, MA: Harvard University Press.

Álvarez-Mon, Javier (2004), "Imago Mundi: Cosmological and Ideological Aspects of the Arjan Bowl," *IrAnt* 39: 203–37.

Álvarez-Mon, Javier (2009), "Notes on the 'Elamite' Garment of Cyrus the Great," *AJ* 89: 21–33.

Ambos, Claus (2010), "Building Rituals from the First Millennium BC: The Evidence from the Ritual Texts," in Mark J. Boda and Jamie Novotny (eds), *From the Foundations to the Crenellations: Essays on Temple Building in the Ancient Near East and Hebrew Bible*, 221–38, Münster: Ugarit-Verlag.

Ambos, Claus (2013), *Der König im Gefängnis und das Neujahrsfest im Herbst. Mechanismen der Legitimation des babylonischen Herrschers im 1. Jahrtausend v. Chr. und ihre Geschichte*, Dresden: ISLET.

Ambos, Claus (2013a), "Rituale beim Abriß und Wiederaufbau eines Tempels," in Kai Kaniuth, Anne Löhnert, Jared L. Miller, Adelheid Otto, Michael Roaf and Walther Sallaberger (eds), *Tempel im Alten Orient*, 19–32, Wiesbaden: Harrassowitz.

Ambos, Claus (2013b), "Temporary Ritual Structures and Their Cosmological Symbolism in Ancient Mesopotamia," in Deena Ragavan (ed.), *Heaven on Earth: Temples, Ritual, and Cosmic Symbolism in the Ancient World*, 245–8, Chicago: University of Chicago Press.

Anderson, Bernard W. (1962), "Exodus Typology in Second Isaiah," in Bernard W. Anderson and Walter Harrelson (eds), *Israel's Prophetic Heritage*, 177–95, New York: Harper & Brothers.

Anklesaria, Behramgore T. (1956), *Zand-Ākāsīh: Iranian or Greater Bundahisn: Text and Translation*, Bombay: Rahnumae Mazdayasnan Sabha.

Aperghis, Gerassimos G. (2000), "War Captives and Economic Exploitation: Evidence from the Persepolis Fortification Tablets," in Jean Andreau, Pierre Briant and Raymond Descat (eds), *Économie Antique: La guerre dans les économies antiques*, 127–44, Saint-Bertrand-de-Comminges: Musée archéologique départemental de Saint-Bertrand-de-Comminges.

Appian (1913), 'The Civil Wars', in *Roman History III: The Civil Wars, Books 1–3.26*, trans. Horace White, LCL, Cambridge, MA: Harvard University Press.

Archdeacon, Thomas J. (1990), "Hansen's Hypothesis as a Model of Immigrant Assimilation," in Peter Kivisto and Dag Blanck (eds), *American Immigrants and Their Generations*, 42–63, Urbana, IL: University of Illinois Press.

Arnold, Bill T. (2003), "What has Nebuchadnezzar to do with David? On the Neo-Babylonian Period and Early Israel," in K. Lawson Younger and Mark W. Chavalas (eds), *Mesopotamia and the Bible: Comparative Explorations*, 330–55, London: T&T Clark.

Arrian (1976), "Anabasis Alexandri, Books I–IV," in *Arrian I*, trans. P. A. Brunt, LCL, Cambridge, MA: Harvard University Press.

Arrian (1983), "Anabasis Alexandri Books V–VII: Indica," in *Arrian II*, trans. P. A. Brunt, LCL, Cambridge, MA: Harvard University Press.

Asheri, David, Alan B. Lloyd, and Aldo Corcella (2007), *A Commentary on Herodotus, Books I–IV*, trans. Barbara Grazius, Matteo Rossetti, Carlotta Dos and Vanessa Cazzato, Oxford: Oxford University Press.

Assis, Elie (2010), "Zechariah's Vision of the Ephah (Zech. 5:5–11)," *VT* 60: 15–32.

Athenaeus (2007), "Deipnosophists," in *The Learned Banqueters II*, trans. S. Douglas Olson, LCL, Cambridge, MA: Harvard University Press.

Atkinson, K. M. T. (1956), "The Legitimacy of Cambyses and Darius as Kings of Egypt," *JAOS* 76 (3): 167–77.

Avishur, Y., and Michael Heltzer (2007), "Jehoiachin, King of Judah in Light of Biblical and Extra-Biblical Sources: His Exile and Release according to Events in the Neo-Babylonian Kingdom and the Babylonian Diaspora," *Transeuphraténe* 34: 17–36.

Bailey, Daniel P. (1998), "Concepts of *Stellvertretung* in the Interpretation of Isaiah 53," in William H. Bellinger, Jr. and William R. Farmer (eds), *Jesus and the Suffering Servant: Isaiah 53 and Christian Origins*, 231–50, Harrisburg, PA: Trinity Press International.

Bailey, H. W. (1971), *Zoroastrian Problems in the Ninth-Century Books*, rev. ed., Ratanbai Katrak Lectures, Oxford: Clarendon.

Baker, Heather D. (2002), "Approaches to Akkadian Name-Giving in First-Millennium BC Mesopotamia," in Cornelia Wunsch (ed.), *Mining the Archives: Festschrift for Christopher Walker on the Occasion of his 60th Birthday*, 1–24, Dresden: ISLET.

Baker, Heather D. (2011), "From Street Altar to Palace: Reading the Built Environment of Urban Babylonia," in Karen Radner and Eleanor Robson (eds), *Oxford Handbook of Cuneiform Culture*, 533–56, Oxford: Oxford University Press.

Baker, Heather D. (2014), "House Size and Household Structure: Qualitative Data in the Study of Babylonian Living Conditions," in Heather D. Baker and Michael Jursa (eds), *Documentary Sources in Ancient Near Eastern and Greco-Roman Economic History: Methodology and Practice*, 7–23, Oxford: Oxbow.

Baker, Heather D. (2015), "Family Structure, Household Cycle, and the Social Use of Domestic Space in Urban Babylonia," in Miriam Müller (ed.), *Household Studies in Complex Societies: (Micro) Archaeological and Textual Approaches*, 371–407, Chicago: Oriental Institute of the University of Chicago.

Baker, Heather D., and Michael Jursa, eds (2005), *Approaching the Babylonian Economy*, AOAT 330, Münster: Ugarit-Verlag.

Baker, Heather D., and Michael Jursa, eds (2014), *Documentary Sources in Ancient Near Eastern and Greco-Roman Economic History: Methodology and Practice*, Oxford: Oxbow.

Balcer, Jack M. (1987), *Herodotus and Bisitun: Problems in Ancient Persian Historiography*, Historia Einzelschriften 49, Stuttgart: Franz Steiner.

Balcer, Jack M. (1993), *A Prosopographical Study of the Ancient Persians Royal and Noble c. 550–450 B.C.*, Lewiston, NY: Edwin Mellon.

Baltzer, Klaus (2001), *Deutero-Isaiah: A Commentary on Isaiah 40–5*, Hermeneia, Minneapolis: Fortress.

Barag, Dan P. (1985), "Some Notes on a Silver Coin of Johanan the High Priest," *BA* 48 (3): 166–8.

Barag, Dan P. (1986–7), "A Silver Coin of Yoḥanan the High Priest and the Coinage of Judea in the Fourth Century B.C," *INJ* 9: 4–21.

Barrett, Deirdre (2015), "Dreams: Thinking in a Different Biochemical State," in Milton Kramer and Myron L. Gluckson (eds), *Dream Research: Contributions to Clinical Practice*, 80–94, New York: Taylor and Francis.

Barstad, Hans M. (1997), *The Babylonian Captivity of the Book of Isaiah: "Exilic" Judah and the Provenance of Isaiah 40–55*, Oslo: Institute for Comparative Research in Human Culture.

Bartholomae, Christian (1904), *Altiranisches Wörterbuch*, Strasbourg: Trübner.

Batto, Bernard Frank (2013), *In the Beginning: Essays on Creation Motifs in the Ancient Near East and the Bible*, Siphrut 9, Winona Lake, IN: Eisenbrauns.

Bayne, Tim, Jakob Hohwy, and Adrian M. Owen (In Press), "Are There Levels of Consciousness?" *Trends in Cognitive Sciences*.

Beaulieu, Paul-Alain (1989), *The Reign of Nabonidus King of Babylon 556–539 B.C.*, YNER 10, New Haven, CT: Yale University Press.

Beaulieu, Paul-Alain (1993), "An Episode in the Fall of Babylon to the Persians," *JNES* 52 (4): 241–61.

Beaulieu, Paul-Alain (2007), "Nabonidus the Mad King: A Reconsideration of His Stelas from Harran and Babylon," in Marlies Heinz and Marian H. Feldman (eds), *Representations of Political Power: Case Histories from Times of Change and Dissolving Order in the Ancient Near East*, 137–66, Winona Lake, IN: Eisenbrauns.

Becking, Bob (2011a), "Yehudite Identity in Elephantine," in Oded Lipschits, Gary N. Knoppers and Manfred Oeming (eds), *Judah and the Judeans in the Achaemenid Period: Negotiating Identity in an International Context*, 403–20, Winona Lake, IN: Eisenbrauns.

Becking, Bob (2011b), "Zedekiah, Josephus and the Dating of the Book of Chronicles," *SJOT* 25 (2): 217–33.

Bedford, Peter R. (2001), *Temple Restoration in Early Achaemenid Judah*, SJSJ 65, Leiden: Brill.

Beentjes, Pancratius C. (1989), "Relations between Ben Sira and the Book of Isaiah: Some Methodological Observations," in Jacques Vermeylen (ed.), *The Book of Isaiah/Le Livre d'Isaïe: Les Oracles et Leurs Relectures Unité et Complexité de l'ouvrage*, 155–9, Leuven: Peeters.

Bellinger, William H., Jr., and William R. Farmer, eds (1998), *Jesus and the Suffering Servant: Isaiah 53 and Christian Origins*, Harrisburg, PA: Trinity Press International.

Ben Zvi, Ehud (2004), "Observations on Prophetic Characters, Prophetic Texts, Priests of Old, Persian Period Priests and Literati," in Lester L. Grabbe and Alice Ogden Bellis (eds), *The Priests in the Prophets: The Portrayal of Priests, Prophets and Other Religious Specialists in the Latter Prophets*, 19–30, London: T&T Clark.

Ben Zvi, Ehud (2011), "On Social Memory and Identity Formation in Late Persian Yehud: A Historian's Viewpoint with a Focus on Prophetic Literature, Chronicles, and the Deuteronomistic Historical Collection," in Louis Jonker (ed.), *Texts, Contexts and Readings in Postexilic Literature: Explorations into Historiography and Identity Negotiation in Hebrew Bible and Related Texts*, 95–148, Tübingen: Mohr Siebeck.

Ben Zvi, Ehud, and Michael H. Floyd (2000), *Writings and Speech in Israelite and Ancient Near Eastern Prophecy*, Symposium, Atlanta: SBL.

Benda-Weber, Isabella (2014), "Non-Greek Headdresses in the Greek East," in Carmen Alfaro Giner, Jónatan Ortiz García and María Antón Peset (eds), *Tiarae, Diadems and Headdresses in the Ancient Mediterranean Cultures: Symbolism and Technology*, 95–113, Valencia: Sema.

Bergamini, Giovanni (2011), "Babylon in the Achaemenid and Hellenistic Period: The Changing Landscape of a Myth," *Mesopotamia* 46: 35–40.

Berges, Ulrich (2008), *Jesaja 40–48*, HThKAT, Freiburg: Herder.

Berges, Ulrich (2010), "The Literary Construction of the Servant in Isaiah 40–55: A Discussion about Individual and Collective Identities," *SJOT* 24 (1): 28–38.

Berges, Ulrich (2014), "Kingship and Servanthood in the Book of Isaiah," in Richard J. Bautch and J. Todd Hibbard (eds), *The Book of Isaiah: Enduring Questions Answered Anew: Essays Honoring Joseph Blenkinsopp and his Contribution to the Study of Isaiah*, 159–78, Grand Rapids, MI: Eerdmans.

Bergman, Jan, Helmer Ringgren, Karl-Heinz Bernhardt, and G. Johannes Botterweck (1975), "ברא bārā'," in G. Johannes Botterweck and Helmer Ringgren (eds), *Theological Dictionary of the Old Testament*, 242–9, Grand Rapids, MI: Eerdmans.

Berlin, Adele (1985), *The Dynamics of Biblical Parallelism*, Bloomington, IN: Indiana University Press.

Berquist, Jon L. (1995), *Judaism in Persia's Shadow*, Minneapolis: Fortress.

Betegh, Gábor (2004), *The Derveni Papyrus: Cosmology, Theology and Interpretation*, Cambridge: Cambridge University Press.

Betz, Hans Dieter (1986), *The Greek Magical Papyri in Translation, Including the Demotic Spells*, Chicago: University of Chicago Press.

Bianchi, Francesco (2013), "Influssi iranici nel Deutero-Isaia?" in M. Pina Scanu (ed.) *Alla Luce Delle Scritture: Studi in Onore di Giovanni Odasso*, 77–92, Brescia: Paideia Editrice.

Bič, Miloš (1964), *Die Nachtgeschichte des Sacharja: eine Auslegung von Sacharja 2–6*, BibS(N) 42, Neukirchen-Vluyn: Neukirchener Verlag.

Bickerman, Elias J. (1967), *Four Strange Books of the Bible*, New York: Schocken.

Bidmead, Julye (2002), *The Akītu Festival: Religious Continuity and Royal Legitimation in Mesopotamia*, GDNES 2, Piscataway, NJ: Gorgias.

Bitzer, Lloyd (1968), "The Rhetorical Situation," *Philosophy & Rhetoric* 1 (1): 1–14.

Bivar, A. D. H. (1988), "An Iranian Sarapis," *BAI* (NS 2): 11–17.

Black, Jeremy A., and Farouk N. H. Al-Rawi (1987), "A Contribution to the Study of Akkadian Bird Names," *ZA* 77 (1): 117–26.

Black, Jeremy, Andrew R. George, and Nicholas Postgate (2000), *A Concise Dictionary of Akkadian*, SANTAG Arbeiten und Untersuchungen zur Keilschriftkunde 5, Wiesbaden: Harrassowitz.

Bledsoe, Seth A. (2015), "Conflicting Loyalties: King and Context in the Aramaic Book of Ahiqar," in Jason M. Silverman and Caroline Waerzeggers (eds), *Political Memory in and after the Persian Empire*, ANEM 13, 239–68, Atlanta, GA: SBL.

Blenkinsopp, Joseph (1988), "Second Isaiah–Prophet of Universalism," *JSOT* 41: 83–103.

Blenkinsopp, Joseph (2001), "The Social Roles of Prophets in Early Archaemenid Judah," *JSOT* 93: 39–58.

Blenkinsopp, Joseph (2002), *Isaiah 40–55: A New Translation with Introduction and Commentary*, AB 19A, New York: Doubleday.

Blenkinsopp, Joseph (2006), *Opening the Sealed Book: Interpretations of the Book of Isaiah in Late Antiquity*, Grand Rapids, MI: Eerdmans.

Blenkinsopp, Joseph (2011), "The Cosmological and Protological Language of Deutero-Isaiah," *CBQ* 73: 493–510.

Blenkinsopp, Joseph (2013), *David Remembered: Kingship and National Identity in Ancient Israel*, Grand Rapids, MI: Eerdmans.

Bloch, Yigal (2014), "Judeans in Sippar and Susa during the First Century of the Babylonian Exile: Assimilation and Perseverance under Neo-Babylonian and Achaemenid Rule," *JNEH* 1 (2): 119–72.

Boda, Mark J. (2016), *The Book of Zechariah*, NICOT, Grand Rapids, MI: Eerdmans.

Boda, Mark J., and Michael H. Floyd, eds (2008), *Tradition in Transition: Haggai and Zechariah 1–8 in the Trajectory of Hebrew Theology*, LHBOTS 475, New York: T&T Clark.

Boehmer, R. M. (1980–83), "Kopfbeckung B," in Dietz Otto Edzard (eds), *Reallexikon der Assyriologie und Vorderasiatischen Archäologie*, 203–10, Berlin: de Gruyter.

Boer, Roland (2015), *The Sacred Economy of Ancient Israel*, LAI, Louisville, KY: Westminster John Knox.

Boiy, T. (2004), *Late Achaemenid and Hellenistic Babylon*, OLA 136, Leuven: Peeters.

Bos, James M. (2016), "Memories of Judah's Past Leaders Utilized as Propaganda in Yehud," in Diana V. Edelman and Ehud Ben Zvi (eds), *Leadership, Social Memory, and Judean Discourse in the Fifth-Second Centuries BCE*, 27–40, Sheffield: Equinox.

Boucharlat, Rémy (2005), "Iran," in Pierre Briant and Rémy Boucharlat (eds), *L'archéologie de l'empire achéménide: nouvelles recherches: actes du colloque organisé au Collège de France par le Réseau international d'études et de recherches achéménides" (GDR 2538 CNRS), 21–22 novembre 2003*, Persika 6, 221–312, Paris: De Boccard.

Boucharlat, Rémy (2007), "Achaemenid Residences and Elusive Imperial Cities," in Robert Rollinger, Andreas Luther, and Josef Wiesehöfer (eds), *Getrennte Wege? Kommunikation, Raum und Wahrnehmung in der Alten Welt*, 454–72, Oikumene Studien Zur Antiken Weltgeschichte 2. Frankfurt-am-Mein: Verlag Antike, 2007.

Boucharlat, Rémy (2013a), "Southwestern Iran in the Achaemenid Period," in Daniel T. Potts (eds), *The Oxford Handbook of Ancient Iran*, 503–27, Oxford: Oxford University Press.

Boucharlat, Rémy (2013b), "Susa in Iranian and Oriental Architecture," in Jean Perrot (ed.), *The Palace of Darius at Susa: The Great Royal Residence of Achaemenid Persia*, 408–50, London: I. B. Tauris.

Bourdieu, Pierre (2005), *Outline of a Theory of Practice*, trans. Richard Nice, 19th English printing ed., CSSCA 16, Cambridge: Cambridge University Press. Orig. pub. 1972.

Bourguignon, Erika (2003), "Dreams That Speak: Experience and Interpretation," in Jeannette Marie Mageo (ed.), *Dreaming and the Self: New Perspectives on Subjectivity, Identity, and Emotion*, 133–54, Albany, NY: SUNY Press.

Boyce, Mary (1957), "The Parthian *gōsān* and Iranian Minstrel Tradition," *JRAS* 89 (1/2): 10–45.

Boyce, Mary (1975), "On Varuna's Part in Zoroastrianism," in Françoise Bader (ed.), *Mélanges Linguistiques offerts à Émile Benveniste*, 57–66, Louvain: Peeters.

Boyce, Mary (1982), *A History of Zoroastrianism: Under the Achaemenians*. Vol. II, HdO VIII.1.2.2A.2, Leiden: Brill.

Boyce, Mary (1986), "Apąm Napāt," *EncIr* 2 (2): 148–150.

Boyce, Mary (1989), "The Poems of the Persian Sibyl and the Zand i Vahman Yasht," in Philippe Gignoux and Charles-Henri de Fouchécour (eds), *Etudes irano-aryennes offertes a Gilbert Lazard*, 59–77, Paris: Association pour l'avancement des études irannienes.

Boyce, Mary (2000), "Persian Religion in the Achaemenid Age," in W. D. Davies and L. Finkelstein (eds), *The Cambridge History of Judaism*, 279–307, Cambridge: Cambridge University Press.

Brandon, S. G. F. (1963), *Creation Legends of the Ancient Near East*, London: Hodder & Stoughton.

Braun, Allen R. (2014), "Your PET Studies Demonstrate Major Differences Between REM Sleep and Waking. How Do You Conceive of These Differences in Relation to Theories of Waking and Dreaming Consciousness?" in Nicholas Tranquillo (ed.), *Dream Consciousness: Allan Hobson's New Approach to the Brain and its Mind*, 95–100, Heidelberg: Springer.

Briant, Pierre (1986), "Polythéismes et empire unitaire (Remarques sur la politique religieuse des Achéménides)," in Pierre Lévêque and Marie-Madeleine Mactoux (eds), *Les Grandes Figures Religieuses: Fonctionnement Pratique et Symbolique dans l'antiquite*, 425–43, Paris: Les Belles Lettres.

Briant, Pierre (1998), "Cités et satrapies dans l'Empire achéménide: Xanthos et Pixôdaros," *Comptes rendus des séances de l'Académie des Inscriptions et Belles-Lettres* 142 (1): 305–47.

Briant, Pierre (2002), *From Cyrus to Alexander: A History of the Persian Empire*, trans. Peter T. Daniels, Winona Lake, IN: Eisenbrauns. Original edition Paris, 1996.

Briant, Pierre (2013), "Susa and Elam in the Achaemenid Empire," in Jean Perrot (ed.), *The Palace of Darius at Susa: The Great Royal Residence of Achaemenid Persia*, 3–28, London: I. B. Tauris.

Briant, Pierre, Wouter Henkelman, and Matthew W. Stolper, eds (2008), *L'archive des Fortifications de Persépolis: État des questions et perspectives de recherches*, Persika 12, Paris: Éditions de Boccard.

Brosius, Maria (1998), *Women in Ancient Persia (559–331 BC)*, OCM, Oxford: Clarendon.

Brosius, Maria (2000), *The Persian Empire from Cyrus II to Artaxerxes I*, London: Classical Teachers Association.

Brosius, Maria (2004), "Investiture i. Achaemenid Period," *EncIr* 13 (2): 180–8, http://www.iranicaonline.org/articles/investiture#i.

Brosius, Maria (2005), "*Pax persica*: Köningliche Ideologie und Kriegführung im Achämenidenreich," in Burkhard Meißner, Oliver Schmitt and Michael Sommer (eds), *Krieg–Gesellschaft–Institutionen: Beiträge zu einer vergleichenden Kriegsgeschichte*, 135–62, Berlin: Akademie Verlag.

Brosius, Maria (2007), "New out of Old? Court and court ceremonies in Achaemenid Persia," in A. J. S. Spawforth (eds), *The Court and Court Society in Ancient Monarchies*, 17–57, Cambridge: Cambridge University Press.

Brosius, Maria (2010), "*Pax Persica* and the Peoples of the Black Sea Region: Extent and Limits of Achaemenid Imperial Ideology," in Jens Nieling and Ellen Rehm (eds), *Achaemenid Impact in the Black Sea Communication of Powers*, 29–40, Aarhus: Aarhus University Press.

Brown, John P. (2001), *Israel and Hellas III: The Legacy of Iranian Imperialism and the Individual*, BZAW 299, Berlin: de Gruyter.

Brown, Michael F. (1989), "Ropes of Sand: Order and Imagery in Aguaruna dreams," in Barbara Tedlock (ed.), *Dreaming: Anthropological and Psychological Interpretations*, 154–70, Cambridge: Cambridge University Press.

Brown, Truesdell S. (1982), "Herodotus' Portrait of Cambyses," *Historia* 31: 387–403.

Brueggemann, Walter (1998), *Isaiah 40–66*, WestBC, Louisville, KY: Westminster John Knox.

Bruehler, Bart B. (2001), "Seeing through the עינים of Zechariah: Understanding Zechariah 4," *CBQ* 63: 430–43.

Bryan, David (1995), *Cosmos, Chaos and the Kosher Mentality*, JSPSup 12, Sheffield: Sheffield Academic.

Bryce, Trevor R. (1986), *The Lycians in Literary and Epigraphic Sources*, The Lycians I, Copenhagen: Museum Tusculanum Press.
Bulkeley, Kelly (1999), *Visions of the Night: Dreams, Religion, and Psychology*, SUNY Series in Dream Studies, Albany, NY: SUNY Press.
Bulkeley, Kelly (2008), *Dreaming in the World's Religions: A Comparative History*, New York: New York University Press.
Burke, Kenneth (1953), *Counter-Statement*. 2nd ed., Los Altos, CA: Hermes Publications. First Published 1931.
Burstein, Stanley M. (1978), *The Babyloniaca of Berossus*, SANE 1.5, Malibu: Undena.
Butler, Sally A. L. (1998), *Mesopotamian Conceptions of Dreams and Dream Rituals*, AOAT 258, Münster: Ugarit-Verlag.
Butterworth, Mike (1992), *Structure and the Book of Zechariah*, JSOTSup 130, Sheffield: Sheffield Academic.
Byrne, Máire (2006), *"My People Shall Know My Name": The Divine Designations in the Book of Isaiah as a Hermeneutical Key to the Formation of the Text in its Final Form*, PhD diss., National University of Ireland Maynooth, Maynooth, Ireland.
Calmeyer, Peter (1993), "Crown i. In the Median and Achaemenid Periods," *EncIr* 6 (4): 407–8, http://www.iranicaonline.org/articles/crown-i.
Cameron, George G. (1954–9), "The 'Daiva' Inscription of Xerxes: In Elamite," *WO* 2 (5/6): 470–6.
Canepa, Matthew P. (2013), "The Transformation of Sacred Space, Topography, and Royal Ritual in Persia and the Ancient Iranian World," in Deena Ragavan (ed.), *Heaven on Earth*, 319–72, Chicago: University of Chicago Press.
Carr, David M. (2011), "Reading into the Gap: Refractions of Trauma in Israelite Prophecy," in Brad E. Kelle, Frank Ritchel Ames and Jacob L. Wright (eds), *Interpreting Exile: Displacement and Deportation in Biblical and Modern Contexts*, 295–308, Atlanta, GA: SBL.
Carroll, Robert P. (1979), *When Prophecy Failed: Cognitive Dissonance in the Prophetic Traditions of the Old Testament*, New York: Seabury.
Carswell, C. Melody, and Wilse B. Webb (1985), "Real and Artificial Dream Episodes: Comparison of Report Structure," *Journal of Abnormal Psychology* 94 (4): 653–5.
Carter, Charles E. (1999), *The Emergence of Yehud in the Persian Period: A Social and Demographic Study*, JSOTSup 294, Sheffield: Sheffield Academic.
Carter, George William (1970), *Zoroastrianism and Judaism*, New York: AMS. Orig., 1918.
Cataldo, Jeremiah W. (2009), *A Theocratic Yehud? Issues of Government in a Persian Period*, LHBOTS 498, London: T&T Clark.
Caton, Steven C. (2009), "The Poetic Construction of Self," in Maria Damon and Ira Livingston (eds), *Poetry and Cultural Studies: A Reader*, 133–46, Urbana: University of Illinois Press.
Cavallero, C., and V. Natale (1988), "Was I Dreaming or Did It Really Happen? A Comparison between Real and Artificial Dream Reports," *Imagination, Cognition and Personality* 8 (1): 19–24.
Chavel, Simeon (2014), "Prophetic Imagination in the Light of Narratology and Disability Studies in Isaiah 40–48," *JHebS* 14 (3), http://www.jhsonline.org/Articles/article_197.pdf.

Chaverdi, Alireza Askari, Alireza Kosrowzadeh, Bernadette McCall, Cameron A. Petrie, D. T. Potts, Mojgan Seydin Roustei, Lloyd Weeks, and Mohsen Zaidi (2010), "Archaeological Evidence for Achaemenid Settlement within the Mamasani Valleys, Western Fars, Iran," in John Curtis and St. John Simpson (eds), *The World of Achaemenid Persia: History, Art and Society in Iran and the Ancient Near East*, 287–98, London: I. B. Tauris.

Chaverdi, Alireza Askari, Pierfrancesco Callieri, and Sébastien Gondet. "Tol-E Ājori, a New Monumental Building in Pārsa: Preliminary Cross Interpretations from Recent Surveys and Excavations Works around Persepolis (2005–2012)," *ARTA* 2013.006 (2014), http://www.achemenet.com/document/ARTA_2013.006-Askari-Callieri-Gondet.pdf.

Cheung, Johnny (2007), *Etymological Dictionary of the Iranian Verb*, Leiden Indo-European Etymological Dictionary Series 2, Leiden: Brill.

Childs, Brevard S. (1959), "The Enemy from the North and the Chaos Tradition," *JBL* 78: 187–98.

Childs, Brevard S. (2001), *Isaiah*, OTL, Louisville, KY: Westminster John Knox.

Choksy, Jamsheed K. (2002), "In Reverence for Deities and Submission to Kings: A Few Gestures in Ancient Near Eastern Societies," *IrAnt* 37: 7–29.

Chong, Joong Ho (1996), "Were There Yahwistic Sanctuaries in Babylonia?" *AsJT* 10 (1): 198–217.

Clay, Albert T. (1915), *Miscellaneous Inscriptions in the Yale Babylonian Collection*, YOS 1, New Haven, CT: Yale University Press.

Clay, Albert T. (1923), *Babylonian Records in the Library of J. Pierpont Morgan*, New Haven, CT: Yale University Press.

Clifford, Richard J. (1994), *Creation Accounts in the Ancient Near East and in the Bible*, CBQMS 26, Washington, DC: Catholic Biblical Association of America.

Clifford, Richard J. (2010), *The Cosmic Mountain in Canaan and the Old Testament*, Eugene, OR: Wipf & Stock. First Pub. 1972.

Clifford, Richard J., and John J. Collins (1992a), *Creation in the Biblical Traditions*, CBQMS 24, Washington, DC: Catholic Biblical Association of America.

Clifford, Richard J., and John J. Collins (1992b), "Introduction: The Theology of Creation Traditions," in Richard J. Clifford and John J. Collins (eds), *Creation in the Biblical Traditions*, 1–15, Washington, DC: Catholic Biblical Association of America.

Clines, David J. A. (1976), *I, He, We, & They: A Literary Approach to Isaiah 53*, JSOTSup 1, Sheffield: JSOT Press.

Cogan, Mordechai (2013), *Bound for Exile: Israelites and Judeans under Imperial Yoke. Documents from Assyria and Babylonia*, Jerusalem: Carta.

Cogan, Morton (1974), *Imperialism and Religion: Assyria, Judah and Israel in the Eighth and Seventh Centuries B.C.E.*, SBLMS 19, Missoula, MT: Scholars Press.

Coggins, R. J. (1996), *Haggai, Zechariah, Malachi*, OTG, Sheffield: Sheffield Academic. First pub. 1987.

Cohen, Mark E. (1993), *The Cultic Calendars of the Ancient Near East*, Bethesda, MD: CDL.

Cohen, Shaye J. D. (1983), "Alexander the Great and Jaddua the High Priest according to Josephus," *AJS Review* 7/8: 41–68.

Cohn, Norman (1995), *Cosmos, Chaos and the World to Come: The Ancient Roots of Apocalyptic Faith*, 2nd ed., New Haven: Yale University Press. First pub. 1993.

Colburn, Henry P. (2014), *The Archaeology of Achaemenid Rule in Egypt*, PhD diss., University of Michigan.

Cole, Steven W., and Peter Machinist (1998), *Letters from Priests to the Kings Esarhaddon and Assurbanipal*, SAA 13, Helsinki: Helsinki University Press.
Collins, Billie Jean (2002), *A History of the Animal World in the Ancient Near East*, HdO I.64, Leiden: Brill.
Collins, John J. (1983), "The Sibylline Oracles," in James H. Charlesworth (ed.), *The Old Testament Pseudepigrapha*, 317–472, New York: Doubleday.
Collins, John J. (1996), "4QPrayer of Nabonidus," in James C. VanderKam (ed.), *Qumran Cave 4 XVII Parabiblical Texts 3*, 83–94, Oxford: Clarendon.
Collins, John J. (1997), *Seers, Sibyls and Sages in Hellenistic-Roman Judaism*, Leiden: Brill.
Cook, Stephen L. (1995), *Prophecy and Apocalypticism: The Postexilic Social Setting*, Minneapolis, MN: Fortress.
Courtils, Jacque des (2009), "The Physical Evolution of the Sanctuary of Leto at Xanthos," in Charles Gates, Jacques Morin and Thomas (eds), *Sacred Landscapes in Anatolia and Neighboring Regions* Zimmerman, 63–7, Oxford: Archaeopress.
Cowley, A. (1967), *Aramaic Papyri of the Fifth Century B.C.*, Osnabrück: Otto Zeller. Orig. Pub 1923.
Craz, Isabel (2016), "Magic and Maledictions: Zechariah 5,1–4 in its ancient Near Eastern Context," *ZAW* 128: 404–18.
Cross, Frank Moore (1973), *Canaanite Myth and Hebrew Epic: Essays in the History of the Religion of Israel*, Cambridge, MA: Harvard University Press.
Crouch, Carly L. (2014), *Israel and the Assyrians: Deuteronomy, the Succession Treaty of Esarhaddon, and the Nature of Subversion*, ANEM 8, Atlanta, GA: SBL.
Cruz-Uribe, E. (2003), "The Invasion of Egypt by Cambyses," *Transeuphratène* 25: 9–60.
Cryer, Frederick H. (1994), *Divination in Ancient Israel and Its Near Eastern Environment: A Socio-Historical Investigation*, JSOTSup 142, Sheffield: JSOT.
Curtis, Byron G. (2006), *Up the Steep and Stony Road: The Book of Zechariah in Social Location Trajectory Analysis*, Academia Biblica 25, Atlanta, GA: SBL.
Curtis, John E., and Nigel Tallis, eds (2005), *Forgotten Empire: The World of Ancient Persia*, Berkeley, CA: University of California Press.
Dalley, Stephanie (2008), *Myths from Mesopotamia: Creation, the Flood, Gilgamesh, and Others*, OWC, Oxford: Oxford University Press.
Daloz, Jean-Pascal (2010), *The Sociology of Elite Distinction: From Theoretical to Comparative Perspectives*, Basingstoke: Palgrave Macmillan.
Daloz, Jean-Pascal (2013), *Rethinking Social Distinction*, Basingstoke: Palgrave Macmillan.
Dalton, Ormonde Maddock (2010), *The Treasure of the Oxus with Other Objects from Ancient Persia and India*, Facsimilie of 1905 edition, Whitefish, MT: Kessenger.
Dandamaev, Muhammad A. (1975), "Forced Labour in the Palace Economy of Achaemenid Iran," *Alt-Orientalische Forschungen* 2: 71–8.
Dandamaev, Muhammad A. (1984), "Royal Paradeisoi in Babylonia," in *Orientalia J. Duchesne-Guillemin Emerito Oblata*, 113–17, Leiden: Brill.
Dandamaev, Muhammad A. (1995), "The Neo-Babylonian tamkārū," in Ziony Zevit, Seymour Gitin and Michael Sokoloff (eds), *Solving Riddles and Untying Knots: Biblical, Epigraphic, and Semitic Studies in Honor of Jonas C. Greenfield*, 523–30, Winona Lake, IN: Eisenbrauns.
Darmesteter, James (1988), *The Sīrōzahs, Yasts, and Nyāyis. The Zend-Avesta, Part II*, SBE, Delhi: Motilal Banarsidass. Orig. pub. 1882.

Darmesteter, James (1992), *The Vendidad. The Zend-Avesta, Part I*, SBE, Delhi: Motilal Banarsidass. Orig. pub. 1895.
Daviau, P. M. Michèle (2007), "Stone Altars Large and Small: The Iron Age Altars from Ḫirbet el-Mudēyine (Jordan)," in Susanne Bickel, Silvia Schroer, René Schurte and Christoph Uehlinger (eds), *Bilder als Quellen/Images as Sources: Studies on Ancient Near Eastern Artefacts and the Bible Inspired by the Work of Othmar Keel*, 125–50, Göttingen: Vandenhoeck & Ruprecht.
David, Jonathan (2017), "Achaemenid Propaganda and Oral Traditions: A Reassessment of Herodotus' Early Persian *Logoi*," in Baruch Halpern and Kenneth Sacks (eds), *Cultural Contact and Appropriation in the Axial-Age Mediterranean World: A Periplos*, 60–82, CHANE 86, Leiden: Brill.
Davies, Philip R. (1990), "Do Old Testament Studies Need a Dictionary?" in David J. A. Clines, Stephen E. Fowl and Stanley E. Porter (eds), *The Bible in Three Dimensions*, 321–36, Sheffield: JSOT.
Davies, Philip R. (1992), *In Search of 'Ancient Israel'*, JSOTSup 148, Sheffield: Sheffield Academic.
Davies, Philip R. (1995), "God of Cyrus, God of Israel: Some Religio-Historical Reflections on Isaiah 40–55," in Jon Davies, Graham Harvey and Wilfred G. E. Watson (eds), *Words Remembered, Texts Renewed: Essays in Honour of John F.A. Sawyer*, 207–25, Sheffield: Sheffield Academic.
Davies, Philip R. (1998), *Scribes and Schools: The Canonization of the Hebrew Scriptures*, Louisville, KY: Westminster John Knox.
Davies, Philip R. (2000), "'Pen of Iron, Point of Diamond' (Jer 17:1): Prophecy as Writing," in Ehud Ben Zvi and Michael H. Floyd (eds), *Writings and Speech in Israelite and Ancient Near Eastern Prophecy*, 65–82, Atlanta, GA: SBL.
Davies, Philip R. (2007), *The Origins of Biblical Israel*, LHBOTS 485, London: T&T Clark.
Davies, Philip R. (2015), "Judahite Prophecy and the Achaemenids," in Anne Fitzpatrick-McKinley (eds), *Assessing Biblical and Classical Sources for the Reconstruction of Persian Influence, History and Culture*, 203–16, Wiesbaden: Harrassowitz.
Davies, Philip R. (2016), "Monotheism, Empire, and the Cult(s) of Yehud in the Persian Period," in Diana V. Edelman, Anne Fitzpatrick-McKinley and Philippe Guillaume (eds), *Religion in the Achaemenid Persian Empire*, 24–35, OLA, Tübingen: Mohr Siebeck.
Davis, Dick (2006), *Shahnameh: The Persian Book of Kings*, New York: Viking.
Day, John (1985), *God's Conflict with the Dragon and the Sea: Echoes of a Canaanite Myth in the Old Testament*, Cambridge: Cambridge University Press.
Day, John (1998), "God and Leviathan in Isaiah 27:1," *BSac* 155 (620): 423–36.
Day, John (2000), *Yahweh and the Gods and Goddesses of Canaan*, JSOTSup 265, Sheffield: Sheffield Academic.
De Breuker, Geert (2010), "Berossos of Babylon (680)," in Ian Worthington (ed.), *Brill's New Jacoby*, Leiden: Brill.
Deissler, A. (1988), *Zwölf Propheten III: Zefanja Haggai Sacharja Maleachi*, Die Neue Echter Bibel, Würzburg: Echter Verlag.
Delaney, Gayle (2015), "Dream Incubation: Targeting Dreaming to Focus on Particular Issues," in Milton Kramer and Myron L. Gluckson (eds), *Dream Research: Contributions to Clinical Practice*, 38–55, New York: Taylor & Francis.
Delitzsch, Franz (1877), *Biblical Commentary on the Prophecies of Isaiah*, trans. James Denney, 2 vols, New York: Funk & Wagnalls.

Delitzsch, Franz (1881), *Biblical Commentary on the Prophecies of Isaiah*, trans. James Martin, vol. 2, Clark's Foreign Theological Library 4/14, Edinburgh: T&T Clark.
Demsky, Aaron (1981), "The Temple Steward Josiah ben Zephaniah," *IEJ* 31 (1–2): 100–102.
Dentan, Robert Knox, and Laura J. McClusky (1993), "'Pity the Bones by Wandering River Which Still in Lovers' Dreams Appear as Men'," in Alan Moffitt, Milton Kramer and Robert Hoffmann (eds), *The Functions of Dreaming*, 489–48, Albany, NY: SUNY Press.
Dick, Michael B. (1999), "Prophetic Parodies of Making the Cult Image," in Michael B. Dick (ed.), *Born in Heaven, Made on Earth: The Creation of the Cult Image in the Ancient Near East*, 1–54, Winona Lake, IN: Eisenbrauns.
Dines, Jennifer (2004), *The Septuagint*, London: T&T Clark.
Dion, Paul E., and P. M. Michèle Daviau (2000), "An Inscribed Incense Altar of Iron Age II at Ḫirbet el-Mudēyine (Jordan)," *ZDPV* 116 (1): 1–13.
Dixon, Helen (2013), *Phoenician Mortuary Practice in the Iron Age I–III (ca. 1200–ca. 300 BCE) Levantine "Homeland"*, PhD diss., University of Michigan, Ann Arbor.
Doan, William, and Terry Giles (2005), *Prophets, Performance, and Power: Performance Criticism of the Hebrew Bible*, New York: T&T Clark.
Dobbs-Allsopp, F. W. (2015), *On Biblical Poetry*, Oxford: Oxford University Press.
Dodson, Derek S. (2009), *Reading Dreams: An Audience-Critical Approach to the Dreams in the Gospel of Matthew*, LNTS 397, London: T&T Clark.
Domhoff, G. William (2003), *The Scientific Study of Dreams: Neural Networks, Cognitive Development, and Content Analysis*, Washington, DC: American Psychological Association.
Dupont-Sommer, André (1979), "L'inscription araméenne," in Henri Metzger (ed.), *Fouilles de Xanthos VI: La Stèle Trilingue du Létôon*, 129–78, Paris: Klincksieck.
Dušek, Jan (2012), *Aramaic and Hebrew Inscriptions from Mt. Gerizim and Samaria between Antiochus III and Antiochus IV Epiphanes*, CHANE 54, Leiden: Brill.
Dusinberre, Elspeth R. M. (2013), *Empire, Authority, and Autonomy in Achaemenid Anatolia*, Cambridge: Cambridge University Press.
Eaton, John (1979), *Festal Drama in Deutero-Isaiah*, London: SPCK.
Edelman, Diana V. (2003), "Proving Yahweh Killed His Wife (Zechariah 5:5–11)," *BibInt* 11 (3–4): 335–44.
Edelman, Diana V. (2005), *The Origins of the "Second" Temple: Persian Imperial Policy and the Rebuilding of Jerusalem*, Bible World, London: Equinox.
Edelman, Diana V. (2007), "Settlement Patterns in Persian-Era Yehud," in Yigal Levin (ed.), *A Time of Change: Judah and Its Neighbors in the Persian and Early Hellenistic Periods*, 52–64, London: T&T Clark.
Edelman, Diana V. (2012), "What Can We Know about the Persian-Era Temple at Jerusalem?" in Jens Kamlah (ed.), *Temple Building and Temple Cult: Architecture and Cultic Paraphernalia of Temples in Levant (2.–1. Mill. B.C.E.)*, 343–68, Wiesbaden: Harrassowitz.
Edelman, Diana V., Philip R. Davies, Christophe Nihan, and Thomas Römer (2011), *Opening the Books of Moses*, London: Routledge.
Eggan, Dorothy (1966), "Hopi Dreams in Cultural Perspective," in Gustave Edmund von Grunebaum and Roger Caillois (eds), *The Dream and Human Societies*, 237–66, Berkeley, CA: University of California Press.

Ehrenberg, Erica (2002), "The Rooster in Mesopotamia," in Erica Ehrenberg (ed.), *Leaving No Stones Unturned: Essays on the Ancient Near East and Egypt in Honor of Donald P. Hansen*, 53–62, Winona Lake, IN: Eisenbrauns.

Ehrenberg, Erica (2012), "*Dieu et Mon Droit*: Kingship in Late Babylonian and Early Persian Times," in Nicole Brisch (ed.), *Religion and Power: Divine Kingship in the Ancient World and Beyond*, 103–32, Chicago: University of Chicago Press.

Eidevall, Göran (2014), "Propagandistic Constructions of Empires in the Book of Isaiah," in Alan Lenzi and Jonathan Stökl (eds), *Divination, Politics, and Ancient Near Eastern Empires*, 109–28, ANEM, Atlanta, GA: SBL.

Eidsvåg, Gunnar Magnus (2016), *The Old Greek Translation of Zechariah*, VTSup 170, Leiden: Brill.

Elias, Norbert (1983), *The Court Society*, trans. Edmund Jephcott, New York: Pantheon. First pub. 1969.

Elliger, Karl (1964), *Das Buch der zwölf kleinen Propheten II*, 5th ed., ATD 25, Göttingen: Vandenhoeck & Ruprecht.

Elliger, Karl (1978), *Deuterojesaja 1: Jesaja 40,1–45,7*, BKAT 11/1, Neukirchen-Vluyn: Neukirchener Verlag.

Ellis, Richard S. (1968. *Foundation Deposits in Ancient Mesopotamia*, YNER 2, New Haven, CT: Yale University Press.

Elphick, Jonathan (2007), *The Atlas of Bird Migration: Tracing the Great Journeys of the World's Birds*, London: Marshall Editions.

Espenak, Fred, and Jean Meeus (2006), "Five Millennium Canon of Solar Eclipses: -1999 to +3000," in *NASA Technical Publication TP-2006-214141*, Greenbelt, MD: NASA.

Espenak, Fred, and Jean Meeus (2009), "Five Millennium Canon of Lunar Eclipses: -1999 to +3000," in *NASA Technical Publication TP-2009-214172*, Greenbelt, MD: NASA.

Esposito, Maria José, P. C. Cicogna, M. Occhionero, and V. Natale (2007), "Bizarreness of Size and Shape in Dream Images," *Consciousness and Cognition* 16 (2): 381–90.

Evans, James Allan Stewart (2014), *Herodotus, Explorer of the Past: Three Essays*, Princeton Legacy Library: Princeton University Press.

Evelyn-White, Hugh G. (1998. *Hesiod, Homeric Hymns, Epic Cycle, Homerica*. LCL, Cambridge, MA: Harvard University Press.

Faierstein, Morris M. (1999), *Jewish Mystical Autobiographies: Book of Visions and Book of Secrets*, Classics of Western Spirituality 94, New York: Paulist.

Fales, F. M., and J. N. Postgate (1992), *Imperial Administrative Records 1*, SAA 7, Helsinki: Helsinki University Press.

Farhi, Yoav (2016), *Khirbet Qeiyafa 5: Excavation Report 2007–2013: The Numismatic Finds: Coins and Related Objects*, Jerusalem: Israel Exploration Society.

Faust, Avraham (2007), "Settlement Dynamics and Demographic Fluctuations in Judah from the Late Iron Age to the Hellenistic Period and the Archaeology of Persian-Period Yehud," in Yigal Levin (ed.), *A Time of Change: Judah and Its Neighbors in the Persian and Early Hellenistic Periods*, 3–51, London: T&T Clark.

Faust, Avraham (2012), "Social, Cultural and Demographic Changes in Judah during the Transition from the Iron Age to the Persian Period and the Nature of the Society during the Persian Period," in Johannes Unsok Ro (ed.), *From Judah to Judaea: Socio-Economic Structures and Processes in the Persian Period*, 106–32, Sheffield: Sheffield Academic.

Fine, Gary Alan, and Laura Fischer Leighton (1993), "Nocturnal Omissions: Steps Towards a Sociology of Dreams," *Symbolic Interaction* 16 (2): 95–104.

Finitsis, Antonios (2011), *Visions and Eschatology: A Socio-Historical Analysis of Zechariah 1–6*, LSTS 79, New York: T&T Clark.

Finkel, Irving L. (2013a), "The Cyrus Cylinder: The Babylonian Perspective," in Irving L. Finkel (ed.), *The Cyrus Cylinder: The King of Persia's Proclamation from Ancient Babylon*, 4–34, London: I. B. Tauris.

Finkel, Irving L. ed. (2013b), *The Cyrus Cylinder: The King of Persia's Proclamation from Ancient Babylon*, London: I. B. Tauris.

Finn, Jennifer (2017), *Much Ado about Marduk: Questioning Discourses of Royalty in First Millennium Mesopotamian Literature*, SANER 16, Berlin: de Gruyter.

Finnegan, Ruth (1992), *Oral Poetry: Its Nature, Significance, and Social Context*, 2nd ed., Bloomington, IN: Indiana University Press.

Firby, Nora Kathleen (1988), *European Travellers and their Perceptions of Zoroastrians in the 17th and 18th Centuries*, AMIE 14, Berlin: Reimer.

Fisher, Michael T., and Matthew W. Stolper (2015), "Achaemenid Elamite Administrative Tablets, 3: Fragments from Old Kandahar, Afghanistan," *ARTA* 2015.001: 1–26, http://mini-site.louvre.fr/trimestriel/achemenet/ARTA_2015.001-Fisher-Stolper.pdf.

Fisher, Walter R. (1987), *Human Communication as Narration: Toward a Philosophy of Reason, Value, and Action*, Studies in Rhetoric/Communication. Columbia, SC: University of SC Press.

Fitzmyer, Joseph A. (1967), *The Aramaic Inscriptions of Sefire*, BibOr 19, Rome: Pontifical Biblical Institute.

Fitzpatrick-McKinley, Anne (2015), *Empire, Power and Indigenous Elites: A Case Study of the Nehemiah Memoir*, JSJS 169, Leiden: Brill.

Fitzpatrick-McKinley, Anne (2016), "Models of Local Political Leadership in the Nehemiah Memoir," in Diana V. Edelman and Ehud Ben Zvi (eds), *Leadership, Social Memory, and Judean Discourse in the Fifth-Second Centuries BCE*, 165–200, Sheffield: Equinox.

Flannery-Dailey, Frances (2004), *Dreamers, Scribes, and Priests: Jewish Dreams in the Hellenistic and Roman Eras*, SJSJ 90, Leiden: Brill.

Floyd, Michael H. (1996), "The Evil in the Ephah: Reading Zechariah 5:5–11 in its Literary Context," *CBQ* 58: 56–68.

Floyd, Michael H. (2000), *Minor Prophets, Part 2*, FOTL 22, Grand Rapids, MI: Eerdmans.

Fohrer, Georg (1968), *Introduction to the Old Testament*, trans. David Green, London: SPCK.

Foley, John Miles (2002), *How to Read an Oral Poem*, Urbana, IL: University of Illinois Press.

Folmer, Margaretha (2011), "Imperial Aramaic as an Administrative Language of the Achaemenid Period," in Stefan Weninger (ed.), *The Semitic Languages: An International Handbook*, 587–97, Berlin: de Gruyter.

Foster, Benjamin R. (1993), *Before the Muses: An Anthology of Akkadian Literature*, 2 vols, Bethesda, MD: CDL.

Fox, R. Michael (2015), *A Message from the Great King: Reading Malachi in Light of Ancient Persian Royal Messenger Texts from the Time of Xerxes*, Siphrut 17, Winona Lake, IN: Eisenbrauns.

Frahm, Eckart (2010), "Hochverrat im Assur," in Stefan Maul and N. P. Heeßel (eds), *Assur-Forschungen*, 89–137, Wiesbaden: Harrassowitz.

Frame, Grant (1995), *Rulers of Babylonia: From the Second Dynasty of Isin to the End of Assyrian Domination (1157–612 BC)*, RIME 2, Toronto: University of Toronto Press.

Francfort, Henri-Paul (2005), "État de la question: les données disponibles ne permettent guère de traiter la période achéménide comme un ensemble cohérent," in Pierre Briant and Rémy Boucharlat (eds), *L'archéologie de l'empire achéménide: nouvelles recherches: actes du colloque organisé au Collège de France par le Réseau international d'études et de recherches achéménides" (GDR 2538 CNRS), 21–22 novembre 2003*, 313–52, Persika 6, Paris: De Boccard.

Frevel, Christian (2008), "Gifts to the Gods? Votives as Communication Markers in Sanctuaries and other Places in the Bronze and Iron Ages in Palestine/Israel," in Izak Cornelius and Louis Jonker (eds), *"From Ebla to Stellenbosch"; Syro-Palestinian Religions and the Hebrew Bible*, 25–48, Wiesbaden: Harrassowitz.

Frevel, Christian (2016), *Geschichte Israels*, Kohlhammer Studienbücher Theologie 2, Stuttgart: Kohlhammer.

Frevel, Christian, and Katharina Pyschny (2014), "Perserzeitliche Räucherkästchen: Zu einer wenig beachteten Fundgattung im Kontext der These Ephraim Sterns," in Christian Frevel, Katharina Pyschny and Izak Cornelius (eds), *A "Religious Revolution" in Yehûd? The Material Culture of the Persian Period as a Test Case*, 111–220, Göttingen: Vandenhoeck & Ruprecht.

Frevel, Christian, Katharina Pyschny, and Izak Cornelius (2014), *A 'Religious Revolution' in Yehud? The Material Culture of the Persian Period as a Test Case*, OBO 267, Fribourg: Academic.

Friebel, Kelvin G. (2001), "A Hermeneutical Paradigm for Interpreting Prophetic Sign-Actions," *Didaskalia* 12 (2): 25–45.

Fried, Lisbeth S. (2002), "Cyrus the Messiah? The Historical Background to Isaiah 45:1," *HTR* 95 (4): 373–93.

Fried, Lisbeth S. (2003a), "A Governor of Byblos from Sippar," *N.A.B.U* (2003–2): http://www.achemenet.com/pdf/nabu/Nabu2003-036.pdf.

Fried, Lisbeth S. (2003b), "A Silver Coin of Yohanan Hakkôhen," *Transeuphraténe* 26: 65–85.

Fried, Lisbeth S. (2004), *The Priest and the Great King: Temple-Palace Relations in the Persian Empire*, Biblical and Judaic Studies from the University of California 10, Winona Lake, IN: Eisenbrauns.

Fried, Lisbeth S. (2010), "Temple Building in Ezra 1–6," in Mark J. Boda and Jamie Novotny (eds), *From the Foundations to the Crenellations: Essays on Temple Building in the Ancient near East and Hebrew Bible*, 319–38, Münster: Ugarit-Verlag.

Friedli, Richard (2007), "Creation I. History of Religions," in Hans Dieter Betz, Don S. Browning, Bernd Janowski and Eberhard Jüngel (eds), *Religion Past & Present*, 545–6, Leiden: Brill.

Frye, Richard N. (1972), "Gestures of Deference to Royalty in Ancient Iran," *IrAnt* 9: 102–7.

Garbini, Giovanni (1988), *History and Ideology in Ancient Israel*, trans. John Bowden, London: SCM. First pub. 1986.

García Sánchez, Manel (2014), "The Second after the King and Achaemenid Bactria on Classical Sources," in Borja Antela-Bernárdez and Jordi Vidal (eds), *Central Asia in Antiquity: Interdisciplinary Approaches*, 55–63, Oxford: Archaeopress.

Gariboldi, A. (2014), "The Achaemenid Coinage: Regal and Satrapal Coins," in Touraj Daryaee, Ali Mousavi and Khodadad Rezakhani (eds), *Excavating an Empire: Achaemenid Persia in Longue Durée*, 122–32. Costa Mesa, CA: Mazda Publishers.

Garrison, Mark B. (2013), "Royal Achaemenid Iconography," in D. T. Potts (ed.), *The Oxford Handbook of Ancient Iran*, 566–97, Oxford: Oxford University Press.

Garrison, Mark B., and Margaret Cool Root (2001), *Seals on the Persepolis Fortification Tablets I: Images of Heroic Encounter*, OIP 117, Chicago: University of Chicago Press.

Gasche, Hermann (2013), "The Achaemenid Palaces of Babylon," in Jean Perrot (ed.), *The Palace of Darius at Susa: The Great Royal Residence of Achaemenid Persia*, 436–50, London: I. B. Tauris.

Gates, Charles (2011), *Ancient Cities: The Archaeology of Urban Life in the Ancient Near East and Egypt, Greece, and Rome*, 2nd ed., Abingdon: Routledge.

Genito, Bruno (2010a), "The Achaemenid Empire as Seen from its Eastern Periphery: The Case of Dahān-i Ghulāmān in Sistan: Forty Years Later, a revision of Data," in Paolo Matthiae, Frances Pinnock, Lorenzo Nigro and Nicolò Marchetti (eds), *Proceedings of the 6th International Congress of the Archaeology of the Ancient Near East*, 77–92, Wiesbaden: Harrassowitz.

Genito, Bruno (2010b), "From the Achaemenids to the Sasanians in Seistan (Iran): Dahān-i Ghulāmān and Qala-ye Tepe, Italian Archaeological Mission in Iran of Is.I.A.O: Archaeology, Settlement, and Territory," in Pierfrancesco Callieri and Luca Colliva (eds), *South Asian Archaeology 2007: Proceedings of the 19th Meeting of the European Association of South Asian Archaeology in Ravenna, Italy, July 2007*, Oxford: Archaeopress.

Genito, Bruno (2012), "An 'Achaemenid' Capital of the Imperial Periphery: Zranka/Drangiana/Sistan," in Gian Pietro Basello and Adriano V. Rossi (eds), *Dariosh Studies II: Persepolis and Its Settlements: Territorial System and Ideology in the Achaemenid State*, 365–86, Naples: Ismeo.

Genito, Bruno (2014), "Landscape, Sources, and Architecture at the Archaeological Remains of Achaemenid Sistān (East Iran): Dāhān-i Ghūlāmān," in Touraj Daryaee, Ali Mousavi and Khodadad Rezakhani (eds), *Excavating an Empire: Achaemenid Persia in Longue Durée*, 163–80, Costa Mesa, CA: Mazda Publishers.

George, Andrew R. (1992), *Babylonian Topographical Texts*, OLA 40, Leuven: Peeters.

George, Andrew R. (1996), "Studies in Cultic Topography and Ideology," *BO* 53 (3/4): 363 95.

George, Andrew R. (1999), *The Epic of Gilgamesh*, London: Penguin.

George, Andrew R. (2005/2006), "The Tower of Babel: Archaeology, Historiography, and Cuneiform Texts," *AfO* 51: 75–95.

George, Andrew R. (2010), "Xerxes and the Tower of Babel," in John Curtis and St. John Simpson (eds), *The World of Achaemenid Persia: History, Art and Society in Iran and the Ancient Near East*, 471–80, London: I. B. Tauris.

Gerschevitch, Ilya (1957), "Sissoo at Susa," *BSOAS* 19 (2): 317–20.

Gerstenberger, Erhard S. (2011), *Israel in the Persian Period: The Fifth and Fourth Centuries B.C.E.*, trans. Siegfried S. Schatzmann, BibEnc 8, Atlanta, GA: SBL.

Gerstenberger, Erhard S. (2015), "Twelve (and More) Anonyms: A Biblical Book without Authors," in Mark J. Boda, Michael H. Floyd and Colin M. Toffelmire (eds), *The Book of the Twelve and the New Form Criticism*, 119–36, Atlanta, GA: SBL.

Gesenius, D. Wilhelm (1846), *Gesenius's Hebrew and Chaldee Lexicon to the Old Testament Scriptures*, trans. Samuel P. Tregelles, London: Bagster & Sons.

Geva, Hillel (2014), "Jerusalem's Population in Antiquity: a Minimalist View," *Tel Aviv* 41: 131–60.

Gibson, John C. L. (1982), *Textbook of Syrian Semitic Inscriptions III: Phoenician Inscriptions*, Oxford: Clarendon.

Gignilliat, Mark (2004), "A Servant Follower of the Servant: Paul's Eschatological Reading of Isaiah 40–66 in 2 Corinthians 5:14–6:10," *HBT* 26 (1): 98–124.

Girard, René (1977), *Violence and the Sacred*, trans. Patrick Gregory. Baltimore, MD: Johns Hopkins University Press. First pub. 1972.
Girard, René (1982), *Le Bouc émissaire*, Paris: Grasset.
Girard, René (1988), *'To Double Business Bound': Essays on Literature, Mimesis, and Anthropology*, London: Athlone. First pub. 1978.
Gitay, Yehoshua (1980), "Deutero-Isaiah: Oral or Written?" *JBL* 99 (2): 185–97.
Glassner, Jean-Jacques (2004), *Mesopotamian Chronicles*, WAW 19, Atlanta, GA: SBL.
Gnoli, Gherardo (1989), *The Idea of Iran: An Essay on its Origin*, Serie Orientale Roma 62, Rome: Istituto Italiano per il Medio ed Estermo Oriente.
Gnoli, Gherardo (1993), "Dahan-e ḡolāmān," *EncIr* 6 (6): 582–5, http://www.iranicaonline.org/articles/dahan-e-golaman-or-according-to-walther-hinz-p.
Goldingay, John (2005), *The Message of Isaiah 40–55: A Literary-Theological Commentary*, London: T&T Clark.
Goldingay, John, and David Payne (2006), *A Critical and Exegetical Commentary on Isaiah 40–55*, 2 vols, ICC, London: T&T Clark.
Goldschmidt, Lazarus (1929–1936), *Der babylonische Talmud*, 12 vols, Berlin: Jüdischer Verlag.
Goldstein, Jonathan (2002), *Peoples of an Almighty God: Competing Religions in the Ancient World*, AB Reference Library, New York: Doubleday.
Goodblatt, David M. (1994), *The Monarchic Principle: Studies in Jewish Self-Government in Antiquity*, TSAJ 38, Tübingen: Mohr Siebeck.
Goodman, Martin (2007), "The Pilgrimage Economy of Jerusalem in the Second Temple Period," in *Judaism in the Roman World: Collected Essays*, 59–68, Leiden: Brill.
Gottwald, Norman K. (1954), *Studies in the Book of Lamentations*, SBT 14, London: SCM.
Goulder, Michael D. (2004), *Isaiah as Liturgy*, SOTSMS, Aldershot: Ashgate.
Grabbe, Lester L. (1987), "Josephus and the Reconstruction of the Judean Restoration," *JBL* 106 (2): 231–46.
Grabbe, Lester L. (1992), "Who Was the Bagoses of Josephus (*Ant.* 11.7.1, §§297–301)," *Transeuphratène* 5: 49–55.
Grabbe, Lester L. (2008), *A History of the Jews and Judaism in Second Temple Judaism 2*, LSTS 68, London: T&T Clark.
Grabbe, Lester L. (2009), "'They Shall Come Rejoicing to Zion'—or Did They? The Settlement of Yehud in the Early Persian Period," in Gary N. Knoppers, Lester L. Grabbe and Deirdre Fulton (eds), *Exile and Restoration Revisited: Essays on the Babylonian and Persian Periods in Memory of Peter R. Ackroyd*, 116–27, London: T&T Clark.
Graf, David F. (1994), "The Persian Royal Road System," in Heleen Sancisi-Weerdenburg, Amélie Kuhrt and Margaret Cool Root (eds), *Continuity and Change*, 167–89, AchHist, Leiden: NINO.
Granerød, Gard (2013), "'By the Favour of Ahuramazda I am King': On the Promulgation of a Persian Propaganda Text among Babylonians and Judaeans," *JSJ* 44: 455–80.
Granerød, Gard (2016), *Dimensions of Yahwism in the Persian Period: Studies in the Religion and Society of the Judaean Community at Elephantine*, BZAW 488, Berlin: de Gruyter.
Grayson, A. K. (1975), *Assyrian and Babylonian Chronicles*, Texts from cuneiform Sources 5, Locust Valley, NY: J.J. Augustin.
Greenfield, Jonas C., Bezalel Porten, and Ada Yardeni (1982), *The Bisitun Inscription of Darius the Great: Aramaic Version*, CII, London: Lund Humphries.

Greenstein, Edward L. (2015), "The Fugitive Hero Narrative Pattern in Mesopotamia," in John J. Collins, T. M. Lemos and Saul M. Olyan (eds), *Worship, Women, and War: Essays in Honor of Susan Niditch*, 17–35. Providence, RI: Brown University.

Gropp, Douglas M., Moshe Bernstein, Monica Brady, and James H. Charlesworth (2001), *Wadi Daliyeh II: The Samaria Papyri from Wadi Daliyeh and Qumran Cave 4 XXVIII*, DJD 28, Oxford: Clarendon.

Grunebaum, Gustave Edmund von, and Roger Caillois (1966), *The Dream and Human Societies*, Berkeley, CA: University of California Press.

Gudme, Anne Katrine de Hemmer (2010), "Modes of Religion: An Alternative to 'Popular/Official' Religion," in Emanuel Pfoh (ed.), *Anthropology and the Bible: Critical Perspectives*, 77–92, Piscataway, NJ: Gorgias.

Gudme, Anne Katrine de Hemmer (2012), "Out of Sight, Out of Mind? Dedicatory Inscriptions as Communication with the Divine," in C. L. Crouch, Jonathan Stökl and Anna Elise Zernecke (eds), *Mediating between Heaven and Earth: Communication with the Divine in the Ancient Near East*, 1–15, London: T&T Clark.

Gudme, Anne Katrine de Hemmer (2013), *Before the God in this Place for Good Remembrance: A Comparative Analysis of the Aramaic Votive Inscriptions from Mount Gerizim*, BZAW 441, Berlin: de Gruyter.

Gunkel, Hermann, and Heinrich Zimmern (2006), *Creation and Chaos in the Primeval Era and the Eschaton: A Religio-historical Study of Genesis 1 and Revelation 12*, trans. K. William Whitney, Jr., The Biblical resource series, Grand Rapids, MI: Eerdmans. Orig. pub. 1895.

Gussman, Oliver (2008), *Das Priesterverständnis des Flavius Josephus*, TSAJ 124, Tübingen: Mohr Siebeck.

Haerinck, Ernie (1997), "Babylonia under Achaemenid Rule," in John E. Curtis (ed.), *Mesopotamia and Iran in the Persian Period: Conquest and Imperialism 539–331 BC*, 26–34, London: British Museum.

Hageneuer, Sebastian (2008), "Nusku," in J. Eggler, Dominik Bonatz, Christoph Uehlinger, Susanne Bickel and Oskar Kaelin (eds), *Iconography of Deities and Demons: Electronic Pre-Publication*, http://www.religionswissenschaft.uzh.ch/idd/prepublications/e_idd_nusku.pdf. Zürich: University of Zurich.

Haładewicz-Grzelak, Małgorzata, and Joanna Lubos-Kozieł (2014), "Story-ing memory in the Licheń Pilgrimage Centre (Poland)," *European Journal of Cultural Studies* 17 (6): 647–64.

Hale, Mark (1988), "Old Persian Word Order," *Indo-Iranian Journal* 31 (1): 27–40.

Hallaschka, Martin (2010), *Haggai und Sacharja 1–8: Eine redaktionsgeschichtliche Untersuchung*, BZAW 411, Berlin: de Gruyter.

Hallaschka, Martin (2012), "From Cores to Corpus: Considering the Formation of Haggai and Zechariah 1–8," in Rainer Albertz, James D. Nogalski and Jakob Wöhrle (eds), *Perspectives on the Formation of the Book of the Twelve: Methodological Foundations, Redactional Processes, Historical Insights*, 171–90, Berlin: de Gruyter.

Hallaschka, Martin (2014), "Interpreting Zechariah's Visions: Redaction-Critical Considerations of the Night Vision Cycle (Zechariah 1.7–6.8) and its Earliest Readers," in Elizabeth R. Hayes and Lena-Sofia Tiemeyer (eds), *'I Lifted My Eyes and Saw': Reading Dream and Vision Reports in the Hebrew Bible*, 135–48, London: Bloomsbury Academic.

Hallo, William W. (1997), *The Context of Scripture*. Vol. I. *Canonical Compositions from the Biblical World*, Leiden: Brill.

Hallo, William W. (2000), *The Context of Scripture*. Vol. II. *Monumental Inscriptions from the Biblical World*, Leiden: Brill.
Hallock, Richard T. (1969), *Persepolis Fortification Tablets*, OIP 92, Chicago: Chicago University Press.
Halpern, Baruch (1978), "The Ritual Background of Zechariah's Temple Song," *CBQ* 40: 167–90.
Hancock, James A., James A. Kushlan, and M. Philip Kahl (2001), *Storks, Ibises, and Spoonbills of the World*, London: Academic.
Handy, Lowell, K. (1994), *Among the Host of Heaven: The Syro-Palestinian Pantheon as Bureaucracy*, Winona Lake, IN: Eisenbrauns.
Hanhart, Robert (1998), *Dodekapropheten 7.1 Sacharja 1–8*, BKAT 14.7.1. Neukirchener-Vluyn: Neukirchener Verlag.
Harmatta, János (1971), "The Literary Patterns of the Babylonian Edict of Cyrus," *AAASH* 19 (3/4): 217–31.
Harris, William V. (2009), *Dreams and Experience in Classical Antiquity*, Cambridge: Harvard University Press.
Harris-McCoy, Daniel E. (2012), *Artemidorus' Oneirocritica: Text, Translation, and Commentary*, Oxford: Oxford University Press.
Haubold, Johannes, Giovanni B. Lanfranchi, Robert Rollinger, and John Steele, eds (2013), *The World of Berossos*, CleO 5, Wiesbaden: Harrassowitz.
Heffelfinger, Katie (2011), *I Am Large, I Contain Multitudes: Lyric Cohesion and Conflict in Second Isaiah*, BibInt 105, Leiden: Brill.
Heinsch, Sandra, and Walter Kuntner (2011), "Herodot und die Stadtmauern Babylons: Bemerkungen zur archäologischen Befundsituation der Landmauern," in Robert Rollinger, B. Truschnegg and R. Bichler (eds), *Herodot und das Persische Weltreich*, 499–529. CleO 3, Wiesbaden: Harrassowitz.
Helms, S. W., N. Yagodin, A. V. G. Betts, Ghairat Khozhaniyazov, and M. Negus (2002), "The Krakalpak-Australian Excavations in Ancient Chorasmia: The Northern Frontier of the 'Civilised' Ancient World," *ANES* 39: 3–43.
Heltzer, Michael (1995/6), "The Flogging and Plucking of Beards in the Achaemenid Empire and the Chronology of Nehemiah," *AMIT* 28: 305–7.
Hengel, Martin, and Daniel P. Bailey (2004), "The Effective History of Isaiah 53 in the Pre-Christian Period," in Bernd Janowski and Peter Stuhlmacher (eds), *The Suffering Servant: Isaiah 53 in Jewish and Christian Sources*, 75–146, Grand Rapids, MI: Eerdmans.
Henkelman, Wouter F. M. (1995/6), "The Royal Achaemenid Crown," *AMIT* 28: 275–94.
Henkelman, Wouter F. M. (2003a), "An Elamite Memorial: the *šumar* of Cambyses and Hystaspes," in Wouter Henkelman and Amélie Kuhrt (eds), *A Persian Perspective: Essays in Memory of Heleen Sancisi-Weerdenburg*, 101–72. AchHist, Leiden: NINO.
Henkelman, Wouter F. M. (2003b), "Persians, Medes, Elamites: Acculturation in the Neo-Elamite Period," in Giovanni B. Lanfranchi, Michael Roaf and Robert Rollinger (eds), *Continuity of Empire (?): Assyria, Media, Persia*, 181–231. Padova.
Henkelman, Wouter F. M. (2007), "Ruhurater," in Michael P. Streck (ed.), *Reallexikon der Assyriologie*, 11, no. 5/6:449, Berlin: de Gruyter.
Henkelman, Wouter F. M. (2008), *The Other Gods Who Are: Studies in Elamite-Iranian Acculturation Based on the Persepolis Fortification Texts*, AchHist 14, Leiden: NINO.

Henkelman, Wouter F. M. (2010), "'Consumed before the King': The Table of Darius, that of Irdabama and Irtaštuna, and that of his Satrap, Karkiš," in Bruno Jacobs and Robert Rollinger (eds), *Der Achämenidenhof/The Achaemenid Court*, 667–776, CleO, Wiesbaden: Harrassowitz.

Henkelman, Wouter F. M. (2011a), "Of Tapyroi and Tablets, States and Tribes: The Historical Geography of Pastoralism in the Achaemenid Heartland in Greek and Elamite Sources," *BICS* 54: 1–16.

Henkelman, Wouter F. M. (2011b), "Parnakka's Feast: *šip* in Pārsa and Elam," in Javier Álvarez-Mon and Mark B. Garrison (eds), *Elam and Persia*, 89–166, Winona Lake, IN: Eisenbrauns.

Henkelman, Wouter F. M. (2012), "Elam," in Heinz Heinen, Ulrich Eigler, Peter Gröschler, Elisabeth Herrmann-Otto, Henner Von Hesberg, Hartmut Leppin, Hans-Albert Rupprecht, Winfried Schmitz, Ingomar Weiler and Bernhard Zimmermann (eds), *Handwörterbuch der Antiken Sklaverei*, np, Stuttgart: Franz Steiner Verlag.

Henkelman, Wouter F. M. (2013), "Administrative Realities: The Persepolis Archives and the Archaeology of the Achaemenid Heartland," in D. T. Potts (ed.), *The Oxford Handbook of Ancient Iran*, 528–46, Oxford: Oxford University Press.

Henkelman, Wouter F. M., and Matthew W. Stolper (2009), "Ethnic Identity and Ethnic Labelling at Persepolis: The Case of the Skudrians," in Pierre Briant and Michel Chaveau (eds), *Organisation des pouvoirs et contacts culturels dans les pays de l'empire achéménide*, 271–330, Persika 14, Paris: de Boccard.

Henze, Matthias (1999), *The Madness of King Nebuchadnezzar: The Ancient Near Eastern Origins and Early History of Interpretation of Daniel 4*, SJSJ 61, Leiden: Brill.

Herdt, Gilbert (1989), "Selfhood and Discourse in Sambia Dream Sharing," in Barbara Tedlock (ed.), *Dreaming: Anthropological and Psychological Interpretations*, 55–85, Cambridge: Cambridge University Press.

Herman, Geoffrey (2012), *A Prince without a Kingdom: The Exilarch in the Sasanian Era*, TSAJ 150, Tübingen: Mohr Siebeck.

Hermisson, Hans-Jürgen (2003), *Deuterojesaja 2: Jesaja 45,8–49,13*, BKAT 11/2, Neukirchen-Vluyn: Neukirchener Verlag.

Herodotus (2000), The Persian Wars, in *The Persian Wars, Books III–IV*, trans. A. D. Godley, LCL, Cambridge, MA: Harvard University Press.

Herodotus (2001), The Persian Wars, in *The Persian Wars, Books VIII–IX*, trans. A. D. Godley, LCL, Cambridge, MA: Harvard University Press.

Herodotus (2002), The Persian Wars, in *The Persian Wars, Books I–II*, trans. A. D. Godley, LCL, Cambridge, MA: Harvard University Press.

Herodotus (2006), The Persian Wars, in *The Persian Wars, Books V–VII*, trans. A. D. Godley, LCL, Cambridge, MA: Harvard University Press.

Herrenschmidt, Clarisse (1976), "Désignation de l'empire et concepts politiques de Darius 1er d'après ses inscriptions en vieux perse," *SIr* 5: 33–65.

Herrenschmidt, Clarisse (1977), "Les créations d'Ahuramazda," *SIr* 6: 17–58.

Herrenschmidt, Clarisse (1991), "Vieux-Perse *šiyāti*," in Jean Kellens (ed.), *La religion iranienne à l'époque achéménide*, 13–21, Ghent: IrAnt.

Herrenschmidt, Clarisse (2014), "Designation of the Empire and its Political Concepts of Darius I according to Old Persian Records," in Touraj Daryaee, Ali Mousavi and Khodadad Rezakhani (eds), *Excavating an Empire: Achaemenid Persia in Longue Durée*, 12–36, Costa Mesa, CA: Mazda. First pub (1976).

Hesiod (2006), *Theogony; Works and Days; Testimonia*, trans. Glenn W. Most, LCL 57, Cambridge, MA: Harvard University Press.

Hezser, Catherine (2011), *Jewish Travel in Antiquity*, TSAJ, Tübingen: Mohr Siebeck.
Hinnells, John R. (1976), "Zoroastrian Influence on the Judeo-Christian Tradition," *Journal of the K. R. Cama Oriental Institute* 45: 1–23.
Hinnells, John R. (2000), *Zoroastrian and Parsi Studies: Selected Works of John R. Hinnells*, Aldershot: Ashgate.
Hinnells, John R. (2002), "Bombay Parsis and the Diaspora in the 18th and 19th Centuries," in Pheroza J. Godrej and Firoza Punthakey Mistree (eds), *A Zoroastrian Tapestry: Art, Religion, and Culture*, 458–77, Ahmedabad: Mapin Publishing.
Hinnells, John R. (2015), "The Parsis," in Michael Stausberg and Yuhan Sohrab-Dinshaw Vevaina (eds), *The Wiley-Blackwell Companion to Zoroastrianism*, 157–72, Malden, MA: John Wiley & Sons.
Hintze, Almut (1994), *Zamyad-Yašt: Introduction, Translation, and Commentary*, Beiträge zur Iranistik Bd. 15, Wiesbaden: Reichert.
Hobson, J. Allan, Suchada Sangsanguan, Henry Arantes, and David Kahn (2011), "Dream Logic: The Inferential Reasoning Paradigm," *Dreaming* 21 (1): 1–15.
Höffken, Peter (2004), *Jesaja: Der Stand der Theologischen Diskussion*. Darmstadt: Wissenschaftliche Buchgesellschaft.
Höffken, Peter (2008), "Einige Beobachtungen zum Juda der Perserzeit in der Darstellung des Josephus, *Antiquitates* Buch 11," *JSJ* 39 (2): 151–69.
Hoffner, Harry A. (1998), *Hittite Myths*, WAW 2, Atlanta, GA: Scholars Press.
Hofmann, Inge, and Anton Vorbichler (1980), "Das Kambysesbild bei Herodot," *AfO* 27: 86–105.
Hoglund, Kenneth G. (1991), "The Achaemenid Context," in Philip R. Davies (ed.), *Second Temple Studies I*, 54–72, Sheffield: JSOT.
Hoglund, Kenneth G. (1992), *Achaemenid Imperial Administration in Syria-Palestine and the Missions of Ezra and Nehemiah*, ed. David L. Peterson, SBLDS, Atlanta, GA: Scholars Press.
Hoglund, Kenneth G. (2002), "The Material Culture of the Persian Period and the Sociology of the Second Temple Period," in Philip R. Davies and John M. Halligan (eds), *Second Temple Studies III*, 14–18, London: Sheffield Academic.
Hollan, Douglas (2003), "Selfscape Dreams," in Jeannette Marie Mageo (ed.), *Dreaming and the Self: New Perspectives on Subjectivity, Identity, and Emotion*, 61–74, Albany, NY: SUNY Press.
Hollmann, Alexander (2011), *The Master of Signs: Signs and Interpretation of Signs in Herodotus' Histories*, Washington, DC: Center for Hellenic Studies.
Homiak, John (1989), "The Mystic Revelation of Rasta Far-Eye: Visionary Communication in a Prophetic Movement," in Barbara Tedlock (ed.), *Dreaming: Anthropological and Psychological Interpretations*, 220–45, Cambridge: Cambridge University Press.
Honingman, Sylvie (2011), "King and Temple in *2 Maccabees*: The Case for Continuity," in Lester L. Grabbe and Oded Lipschits (eds), *Judah between East and West: The Transition from Persian to Greek Rule (ca. 400–200 BCE)*, 91–130, London: T&T Clark.
Hooker, Jay (2013), "Zion as a Theological Symbol in Isaiah: Implications for Judah, for the Nations, and for Empire," in Andrew T. Abernathy, Mark G. Brett, Tim Bulkeley and Tim Meadowcroft (eds), *Isaiah and Imperial Context: The Book of Isaiah in the Times of Empire*, 107–21, Eugene, OR: Pickwick.
Horowitz, Wayne (1998), *Mesopotamian Cosmic Geography*, MC 8, Winona Lake, IN: Eisenbrauns.

Horowitz, Wayne (2011), *Mesopotamian Cosmic Geography*. 2nd ed., MC 8, Winona Lake, IN: Eisenbrauns.
Howlett, David (2013), *Parallel Pilgrimage at Kirtland Temple: Cooperation and Contestation among Mormon Denominations, 1965–2009*, PhD diss., University of Iowa.
Hrushovski-Harshav, Benjamin (2007), "Prosody, Hebrew," in Michael Berenbaum and Fred Skolnik (eds), *Encyclopaedia Judaica*, 595–623, Detroit, MI: Macmillan Reference.
Huffmon, Herbert B. (2000), "A Company of Prophets: Mari, Assyria, Israel," in Martti Nissinen (ed.), *Prophecy in its Ancient Near Eastern Context*, 47–70, Atlanta, GA: SBL.
Hughes, Ann, and Julie Sanders (2011), "Gender, Exile and the Hague Courts of Elizabeth, Queen of Bohemia, and Mary, Princess of Orange, in the 1650s," in Peter Mansel and Torsten Riotte (eds), *Monarchs and Exile: The Politics of Legitimacy from Marie de Médicis to Wilhelm II*, 44–65, New York: Palgrave Macmillan.
Hulster, Izaak J. de (2009), *Iconographic Exegesis and Third Isaiah*, FAT 2/36, Tübingen: Mohr Siebeck.
Hulster, Izaak J. de (2015), "Of Angels and Iconography: Isaiah 6 and the Biblical Concept of Seraphs and Cherubs," in Izaak J. de Hulster, Brent A. Strawn and Ryan P. Bonfiglio (eds), *Iconographic Exegesis of the Hebrew Bible/Old Testament: An Introduction to Its Method and Practice*, 147–64, Göttingen: Vandenhoeck & Ruprecht.
Hulster, Izaak J. de (2017), *Figurines in Achaemenid Period Yehud: Jerusalem's History of Religion and Coroplastics in the Monotheism Debate*, ORA 26, Tübingen: Mohr Siebeck.
Hulster, Izaak J. de, and Brent A. Strawn (2015), "The Power of Images: Isaiah 60, Jerusalem, and Persian Imperial Propaganda," in Izaak J. de Hulster, Brent A. Strawn and Ryan P. Bonfiglio (eds), *Iconographic Exegesis of the Hebrew Bible/Old Testament: An Introduction to Its Method and Practice*, 197–216, Göttingen: Vandenhoeck & Ruprecht.
Hulster, Izaak J. de, and Joel M. LeMon, eds (2014), *Image, Text, Exegesis: Iconographic Interpretation and the Hebrew Bible*, LHBOTS 588, London: Bloomsbury T&T Clark.
Hultgård, Anders (2000), "Das Paradies: vom Park des Perserkönigs zum Ort der Seligen," in Martin Hengel, Siegfried Mittmann and Anna M. Schwemer (eds), *La Cité de Dieu/ Die Stadt Gottes. 3. Symposium Strasbourg, Tübingen, Uppsala 19.–23. September 1998 in Tübingen*, 1–43, Tübingen: Mohr Siebeck.
Hunger, Hermann, Abraham J. Sachs, and John M. Steele (2001), *Astronomical Diaries and Related Texts from Babylonia, V: Lunar and Planetary Texts*, Vienna: Verlag der Österreichischen Akademie der Wissenschaften.
Hurowitz, Victor A. (1992), *I Have Built You an Exalted House: Temple Building in the Bible in Light of Mesopotamian and Northwest Semitic Writings*, JSOTSup 115, Sheffield: JSOT.
Hurowitz, Victor A. (1993), "Temporary Temples," in A. F. Rainey (ed.), *Kinattūtu ša Dārâti: Raphael Kutscher Memorial Volume*, 37–50, Tel Aviv: Institute of Archaeology, Hebrew University.
Husser, Jean-Marie (1999), *Dreams and Dream Narratives in the Biblical World*, trans. Jill M. Munro, Biblical Seminar 63, Sheffield: Sheffield Academic.
Huyse, P. (1990), "Noch einmal zu Parallelen zwischen Achaemeniden- und Sāsānideninschriften," *AMIT* 23: 177–83.

Ilan, Tal (2001), *Lexicon of Jewish Names in Late Antiquity Part I: Palestine 300 BCE–200 CE*, TSAJ 91, Tübingen: Mohr Siebeck.
Jackobsen, Thorkild (1987), "Picture and Pictoral Language (The Burney Relief)," in M. Mindlin, M. J. Geller and J. E. Wansbrough (eds), *Figurative Language in the Ancient Near East*, 1–10, London: School of Oriental and African Studies.
Jacobs, Bruno (2015), "Achaemenid Royal Communication," *EncIr* Online: http://www.iranicaonline.org/articles/achaemenid-royal-communication.
Jacobs, Bruno, and Robert Rollinger, eds (2010), *Der Achämenidenhof/The Achaemenid Court*, CLeO 2, Wiesbaden: Harrassowitz.
Jacobson, Howard (1983), *The Exagoge of Ezekiel*, Cambridge: Cambridge University Press. Reprinted 2009.
Janowski, Bernd, and Peter Stuhlmacher, eds (2004), *The Suffering Servant: Isaiah 53 in Jewish and Christian Sources*, Grand Rapids, MI: Eerdmans. First pub. 1996.
Jastrow, Marcus (1950), *A Dictionary of the Targumim, the Talmud Babli and Yerushalmi, and the Midrashic Literature*, New York: Hendrickson.
Jauhiainen, Marko (2005), *The Use of Zechariah in Revelation*, WUNT/II 199, Tübingen: Mohr Siebeck.
Jeremias, Christian (1977), *Die Nachtgesichte des Sacharja: Untersuchungen zu ihrer Stellung im Zusammenhang der Visionsberichte im Alten Testament und zu ihrem Bildmaterial*, FRLANT 117, Göttingen: Vandenhoeck & Ruprecht.
Joannès, Francis (2009), "Préparation et consommation de la viande à l'époque néo-babylonienne," *Cahier des thèmes transversaux ArScAn* 9: 431–5.
Jones, Christopher M. (2014), "'The Wealth of Nations Shall Come to You': Light, Tribute, and Implacement in Isaiah 60," *VT* 64 (4): 611–22.
Jong, Albert de (1997), *Traditions of the Magi: Zoroastrianism in Greek and Latin Literature*, RGRW 133, Leiden: Brill.
Jong, Albert de (2010), "Ahura Mazda the Creator," in John Curtis and St. John Simpson (eds), *The World of Achaemenid Persia: History, Art and Society in Iran and the Ancient Near East*, 85–90, London: I. B. Tauris.
Jonker, Louis (2015), "Who's Speaking? On Whose Behalf? The Book of Haggai from the Perspective of Identity Formation in the Persian Period," in Ian Douglas Wilson and Diana V. Edelman (eds), *History, Memory, Hebrew Scriptures: A Festschrift for Ehud Ben Zvi*, 197–214, Winona Lake, IN: Eisenbrauns.
Joüon, Paul, and T. Muraoka (1991), *A Grammar of Biblical Hebrew*, 2 vols, Rome: Pontifical Biblical Institute.
Jursa, Michael (2001), "Kollationen," *N.A.B.U* 2001-4: 98–100.
Jursa, Michael (2004), "Grundzüge der Wirtschaftsformen Babyloniens im ersten Jahrtausend v. Chr.," in Robert Rollinger and Christoph Ulf (eds), *Commerce and Monetary Systems in the Ancient World: Means of Transmission and Cultural Interaction*, 115–36, Munich: Franz Steiner Verlag.
Jursa, Michael (2005), *Neo-Babylonian Legal and Administrative Documents: Typology, Contents, and Archives*, Guides to Mesopotamian Text Record 1, Münster: Ugarit-Verlag.
Jursa, Michael (2007a), "Eine Familie von Königskaufleuten judäischer Herkunft," *N.A.B.U* 2007-22: 23.
Jursa, Michael (2007b), "The Transition of Babylonia from the Neo-Babylonian Empire to the Achaemenid Rule," in Harriet Crawford (ed.), *Regime Change in the Ancient Near East and Egypt: from Sargon of Agade to Saddam Hussein*, 73–94, Oxford: Oxford University Press.

Jursa, Michael (2010), *Aspects of the Economic History of Babylonia in the First Millennium BC: Economic Geography, Economic Mentalities, Agriculture, the Use of Money, and the Problem of Economic Growth*, Veröffentlichungen zur Wirtschaftsgeschichte Babyloniens im 1. Jahrtausend v. Chr. 4, AOAT 377, Münster: Ugarit-Verlag.

Jursa, Michael (2011a), "Taxation and Service Obligations in Babylonia from Nebuchadnezzar to Darius and the Evidence for Darius' Tax Reform," in Robert Rollinger, Brigitte Truschnegg and Reinhold Bichler (eds), *Herodot und das Persische Weltreich*, 431–48, CleO, Wiesbaden: Harrassowitz.

Jursa, Michael (2011b), "'Höflinge' (ša rēši, ša rēš šarri, ustarbaru) in babylonischen Quellen des ersten Jahrtausends," in Robert Rollinger and Giovanni B. Lanfranchi (eds), *Ktesias' Welt/Ctesias' World* Joseph Wiesehöfer, 159–74, CleO, Wiesbaden: Harrassowitz.

Jursa, Michael (2012), "Ein Beamter flucht auf Aramäisch: Alphabetschreiber in der spätbabylonischen Epistolographie und die Rolle des Aramäischen in der babylonischen Verwaltung des sechsten Jahrhunderts v. Chr," in Giovanni B. Lanfranchi (ed.), *Leggo!: Studies Presented to Frederick Mario Fales on the Occasion of his 65th Birthday*, 379–97, Wiesbaden: Harrassowitz.

Jursa, Michael (2013), "Die babylonische Priesterschaft im ersten Jahrtausend v. Chr," in Kai Kaniuth, Anne Löhnert, Jared L. Miller, Adelheid Otto, Michael Roaf and Walther Sallaberger (eds), *Tempel im Alten Orient*, 151–66, Wiesbaden: Harrassowitz.

Jursa, Michael (2014a), "Economic Development in Babylonia from the Late 7th to the Late 4th Century BC: Economic Growth and Economic Crises in Imperial Contexts," in Heather D. Baker and Michael Jursa (eds), *Documentary Sources in Ancient Near Eastern and Greco-Roman Economic History: Methodology and Practice*, 113–38, Oxford: Oxbow.

Jursa, Michael (2014b), "Factor Markets in Babylonia from the Late Seventh to the Third Century BCE," *JESHO* 57 (2): 173–202.

Jursa, Michael (2015a), "Families, Officialdom, and Families of Royal Officials in Chaldean and Achaemenid Babylonia," in Alfonso Archi (ed.), *Tradition and Innovation in the Ancient Near East: Proceedings of the 57th Rencontre Assyriologique Internationale at Rome, 4–8 July 2011*, 597–606, Winona Lake, IN: Eisenbrauns.

Jursa, Michael (2015b), "Labor in Babylonia in the First Millennium BC," in Piotr Steinkeller and Michael Hudson (eds), *Labor in the Ancient World*, 345–96, Dresden: ISLET.

Jursa, Michael, and Caroline Waerzeggers (2009), "On Aspects of Taxation in Achaemenid Babylonia: New Evidence from Borsippa," in Pierre Briant and Michel Chaveau (eds), *Organisation des pouvoirs et contacts culturels dans les pays de l'empire achéménidé*, 237–69, Persika 14, Paris: de Boccard.

Kahan, Tracey L. (2016), "Phenomenological Features of Dreams: Results from Dream Log Studies Using the Subjective Experiences Rating Scales," *Consciousness and Cognition* 41 (1): 159–76.

Kahan, Tracey L., and Stephen LaBerge (1996), "Cognition and Metacognition in Dreaming and Waking," *Dreaming* 6 (4): 235–49.

Kaivola-Bregenhøj, Annikki (2015), "Dreams of the Second World War," in Wojciech Owczarski and Zofia Ziemann (eds), *Dreams, Phantasms and Memories*, 179–90, Gdansk: Wydawnictwo Uniwersytety Gdanskiego.

Kaminsky, Joel (2006), "God of All the World: Universalism and Developing Monotheism in Isaiah 40–66," *HTR* 99 (2): 139–63.

Kapelrud, Arvid S. (1963), "Temple Building, a Task for Gods and Kings," *Orientalia* 32: 56–62.

Kapelrud, Arvid S. (1982), "The Main Concern of Second Isaiah," *VT* 32: 50–8.

Kaper, Olaf E. (2015), "Petubastis IV in the Dakhla Oasis: New Evidence about an Early Rebellion against Persian Rule and its Suppression in Political Memory," in Jason M. Silverman and Caroline Waerzeggers (eds), *Political Memory in and after the Persian Empire*, 125–50, ANEM 13, Atlanta, GA: SBL.

Kasher, Aryeh (2011), "Further Revised Thoughts on Josephus' Report of Alexander's Campaign to Palestine (Ant. 11.304–347)," in Lester L. Grabbe and Oded Lipschits (eds), *Judah between East and West: The Transition from Persian to Greek Rule (ca. 400–200 BCE)*, 131–57, London: T&T Clark.

Kashow, Robert C. (2016), "Two Philological Notes on Zechariah 6, 12–13 Relevant for the Identification of Ṣemaḥ," *ZAW* 128: 472–7.

Kautsky, John H. (1982), *The Politics of Aristocratic Empires*, Chapel Hill, NC: University of North Carolina Press.

Keel, Othmar (1999), "Powerful Symbols of Victory: The Parts Stay the Same, the Actors Change," *Journal of Northwest Semitic Languages* 25 (2): 205–50.

Keel, Othmar (2007), *Die Geschichte Jerusalems und die Entstehung des Monotheismus*, 2 vols, Orte und Landschaften der Bibel IV/1, Göttingen: Vandenhoeck & Ruprecht.

Keel, Othmar (2013), *Wirkmächtige Siegeszeichen im Alten Testament. Ikonographische Studien zu Jos 8,12–26; Ex 17,8–13; 2 Kön 13,14–19 und 1 Kön 22,11*, OBO 5, Fribourg: Academic Press.

Kellens, Jean, and Eric Pirart (1988, 1990, 1991), *Les Textes Vieil-Avestiques*, Wiesbaden: Reichert.

Kellens, Jean (1989), "Ahura Mazdā n'est pas un dieu créateur," in C.-H. de Fouchécour and Philippe Gignoux (eds), *Études irano-aryennes offertes à Gilbert Lazard*, 217–28, Paris: Association pour l'avancement des études iraniennes.

Kellens, Jean (1995a) [1989], "L'âme entre le cadavre et le paradis," *JA* 283 (1): 19–56.

Kellens, Jean (1995b), *List du Verbe Avestique: avec un appendice sur l'orthographe des racines avestiques par Eric Pirart*, Wiesbaden: Reichert.

Kellogg, Ed (2016), "Out-of-Body Experiences and Lucid Dreams: A Phenomenological Approach," in Alexander De Foe (ed.), *Consciousness Beyond the Body: Evidence and Reflections*, 43–55, Melbourne: Melbourne Centre for Exceptional Human Potential.

Kelner, Shaul (2010), *Tours that Bind: Diaspora, Pilgrimage, and Israeli Birthright Tourism*, New York: New York University Press.

Kent, Roland Grubb (1961), *Old Persian: Grammar, Texts, Lexicon*. 2nd ed., New Haven, CT: American Oriental Society.

Kessler, John (1992), "The Second Year of Darius and the Prophet Haggai," *Transeuphraténe* 5: 63–84.

Kessler, John (2002), *The Book of Haggai: Prophecy and Society in Early Persian Yehud*, VTSup 91, Leiden: Brill.

Kessler, John (2006), "Persia's Loyal Yahwists: Power Identity and Ethnicity in Achaemenid Yehud," in Oded Lipschits and Manfred Oeming (eds), *Judah and the Judeans in the Persian Period*, 91–122, Winona Lake, IN: Eisenbrauns.

Kessler, John (2008), "Tradition, Continuity and Covenant in the Book of Haggai: An Alternative Voice from Early Persian Yehud," in Mark J. Boda and Michael H. Floyd (eds), *Tradition in Transition: Haggai and Zechariah 1–8 in the Trajectory of Hebrew Theology*, 1–39, New York: T&T Clark.

Kessler, Karlheinz (2002), "Harinê—Zur einer problematischen Passage der Nabonid-Chronik," in Werner Arnold and Hartmut Bobzin (eds), *'Sprich doch mit deinen Knechten aramäisch, wir verstehen es!' 60 Beiträge zur Semitistik Festschrift für Otto Jastrow zum 60. Geburtstag*, 389–93, Wiesbaden: Harrassowitz.

Kessler, Karlheinz (2004), "Urukäische Familien versus babylonische Familien: Die Namengebung in Uruk, die Degradierung der Kulte von Eanna und der Aufsteig des Gottes Anu," *AoF* 31 (2): 237–62.

Kessler, Rainer (2008), *The Social History of Ancient Israel: An Introduction*, trans. Linda M. Maloney, Minneapolis: Fortress, 2008. First pub. 2006.

Kessler, Rainer (2016), "Political Elites in Ancient Judah: Continuity and Change," in Rainer Kessler, Walter Sommerfeld and Leslie Tramontini (eds), *State Formation and State Decline in the Near and Middle East*, 135–44, Wiesbaden: Harrassowitz.

Khaleghi-Motlagh, Djalal (1998), "Etiquette i. Etiquette in the Sassanian Period," *EncIr* 9 (1): 45–8, http://www.iranicaonline.org/articles/etiquette.

Khatchadourian, Lori (2013), "An Archaeology of Hegemony: The Achaemenid Empire and the Remaking of the Fortress in the Armenian Highlands," in Gregory E. Areshian (ed.), *Empires and Diversity: On the Crossroads of Archaeology, Anthropology, and History*, 108–45, Ideas, Debates, and Perspectives 7, Los Angeles, CA: Cotsen Institute of Archaeology.

Khatchadourian, Lori (2016), *Imperial Matter: Ancient Persia and the Archaeology of Empires*, Luminos 13, Oakland, CA: University of California Press.

Khorenats'i, Moses (1978), History of the Armenians. In *History of the Armenians: Translation and Commentary*, trans. Robert W. Thomson, Cambridge, MA: Harvard University Press.

King, Philip J., and Lawrence E. Stager (2001), *Life in Biblical Israel*, LAI, Louisville, KY: Westminster John Knox.

Kingsley, Peter (1995), "Meetings with Magi: Iranian Themes among the Greeks, from Xanthus of Lydia to Plato's Academy," *JRAS* 5 (2): 173–209.

Kirtsoglou, Elisabeth (2010), "Dreaming the Self: A Unified Approach towards Dreams, Subjectivity and the Radical Imagination," *History and Anthropology* 21 (3): 321–35.

Kiste, Robert C. (1974), *The Bikinians: A Study in Forced Migration*, Kiste-Ogan Social Change Series in Anthropology, Menlo Park, CA: Cummings.

Kitchen, Kenneth A., and Paul J. N. Lawrence (2012), *Treaty, Law, and Covenant in the Ancient Near East*, 3 vols, Wiesbaden: Harrassowitz.

Kittel, R. (1898), "Cyrus und Deuterojesaja," *ZAW* 18: 149–62.

Kivisto, Peter, and Dag Blanck (1990), *American Immigrants and Their Generations*, Urbana, IL: University of Illinois Press.

Kleber, Kristin (2008), *Tempel und Palast: die Beziehungen zwischen dem König und dem Eanna-Tempel im spätbabylonischen Uruk*, AOAT 358, Münster: Ugarit-Verlag.

Kleber, Kristin (2013), "The Late Babylonian Temple: Economy, Politics and Cult," in Kai Kaniuth, Anne Löhnert, Jared L. Miller, Adelheid Otto, Michael Roaf and Walther Sallaberger (eds), *Tempel im Alten Orient*, 167–78, Wiesbaden: Harrassowitz.

Kletter, Raz (2014), "Vessels and Measures: The Biblical Liquid Capacity System," *IEJ* 64 (1): 22–37.

Klotz, David (2015), "Persian Period," in Wolfram Grajetzki and Willeke Wendrich (eds), *UCLA Encyclopedia of Egyptology*, Los Angeles, CA: University of California Press, http://digital2.library.ucla.edu/viewItem.do?ark=21198/zz002k45rq.

Knäpper, Katharina (2011), *Die Religion der frühen Achaimeniden in ihrem Verhältnis zum Avesta*, Quellen und Forschungen zur Antiken Welt, Munich: Herbert Utz Verlag.

Knauß, Florian S. (2001), "Persian Rule in the North: Achaemenid Palace on the Periphery of the Empire," in Inge Nielsen (ed.), *The Royal Palace Institution in the First Millennium BC: Regional Development and Cultural Interchange between East and West*, 125–44, Athens: Danish Institute at Athens.

Knauß, Florian S. (2005), "Caucasus," in Pierre Briant and Rémy Boucharlat (eds), *L'archéologie de L'empire achéménide: Nouvelles Recherches: Actes du colloque organisé au Collège de France par le réseau international d'études et de Recherches achéménides" (Gdr 2538 Cnrs), 21–22 Novembre 2003*, 197–220, Persika 6, Paris: De Boccard.

Knauß, Florian S. (2006), "Ancient Persia and the Caucasus," *IrAnt* 41: 79–118.

Knauß, Florian S., Iolon Gagošidse, and Illyas Babaev (2013), "Karačamirli: Ein persisches Paradies," *ARTA* 2013.004: http://www.achemenet.com/document/ARTA_2013.004-Knauss-Gagosidse-Babaev.pdf.

Knoppers, Gary N. (2013), *Jews and Samaritans: The Origins and History of their Early Relations*, Oxford: Oxford University Press.

Knowles, Melody D. (2006), *Centrality Practiced: Jerusalem in the Religious Practice of Yehud and the Diaspora in the Persian Period*, ABS 16, Atlanta, GA: SBL.

Koch, Heidemarie (2002), "Iranische Religion in achaimenidischen Zeitalter," in Reinhard G. Kratz (ed.), *Religion und Religionskontakte im Zeitalter der Achämeniden*, 11–26. Gütersloh: Chr Kaiser.

Koch, Klaus (2007), "Ugaritic Polytheism and Hebrew Monotheism in Isaiah 40–55," in Robert P. Gordon (ed.), *The God of Israel*, 205–28, Cambridge: Cambridge University Press.

Koch, Ulla Susanne (2005), *Secrets of Extispicy: The Chapter Multābiltu of the Babylonian Extispicy Series and Niṣirti bārûti Texts mainly from Aššurbanipal's Library*, AOAT 326, Münster: Ugarit-Verlag.

Koch, Ulla Susanne (2015), *Mesopotamian Divination Texts: Conversing with the Gods: Sources from the First Millennium BCE*, Guides to the Mesopotamian Textual Record 7, Münster: Ugarit-Verlag.

Koehler, Ludwig, and Walter Baumgartner (2001), *The Hebrew and Aramaic Lexicon of the Old Testament*, trans. M. E. J. Richardson, Study ed., 2 vols, Leiden: Brill.

Koldeway, Robert (1913), *Das Wieder Erstehende Babylon*, Leipzig: J. C. Hinrichs'sche Buchhandlung.

Kolyada, Yelena (2009), *A Compendium of Musical Instruments and Instrumental Terminology in the Bible*, Bible World, London: Equinox.

Koole, Jan L. (1997), *Isaiah III.1/Isaiah 40–48*, trans. Antony P. Runia, HCOT, Kampen: Kok Pharos. First pub. 1985.

Koole, Jan L. (1998), *Isaiah III.2/Isaiah 49–55*, trans. Antony P. Runia, HCOT, Leuven: Peeters. First pub. 1990.

Korpel, Marjo C. A., and Johannes C. de Moor (1998), *The Structure of Classical Hebrew Poetry: Isaiah 40–55*, Oudtestamentische Studiën 51, Leiden: Brill.

Koulack, David (1993), "Dreams and Adaptation to Contemporary Stress," in Alan Moffitt, Milton Kramer and Robert Hoffmann (eds), *The Functions of Dreaming*, 321–40, Albany, NY: SUNY Press.

Kouremenos, Theokritos, George M. Parássoglou, and Kyriakos Tsantsanoglou (2006), *The Derveni Papyrus: Edited with Introduction and Commentary*, Studi e testi per il corpus dei papiri filosofici Greci e Latini 13, Florence: Leo S. Olschki Editore.

Kozuh, Michael (2006), *The Sacrificial Economy: On the Management of Sacrificial Sheep and Goats at the Neo-Babylonian/Achaemenid Eanna Temple of Uruk (c. 625–520 BC)*, PhD, Department of Near Eastern Languages and Civilizations, University of Chicago.

Kracke, Waud (1989), "Myths in Dreams, Thought in Images: An Amazonian Contribution to the Psychoanalytic Theory of Primary Process," in Barbara Tedlock (ed.), *Dreaming: Anthropological and Psychological Interpretations*, 31–54, Cambridge: Cambridge University Press.

Kracke, Waud (1993), "Reasons for Oneiromancy: Some Psychological Functions of Conventional Dream Interpretation," in Alan Moffitt, Milton Kramer and Karl Hoffman (eds), *The Functions of Dreaming*, 477–88, Albany, NY: SUNY Press.

Kramer, Milton (2015), "Establishing the Meaning of a Dream," in Milton Kramer and Myron L. Gluckson (eds), *Dream Research: Contributions to Clinical Practice*, 1–13, New York: Taylor & Francis.

Kramer, Milton, and Myron L. Gluckson, eds (2015), *Dream Research: Contributions to Clinical Practice*, New York: Taylor & Francis.

Kratz, Reinhard G. (1991), *Kyros im Deuterojesaja-Buch: Rekationsgeschichtliche Untersuchungen zu Entstehung und Theologie von Jes 40–55*, FAT 1, Tübingen: Mohr Siebeck.

Krippner, Stanley (1994), "Waking Life, Dream Life and the Construction of Reality," *Anthropology of Consciousness* 5 (3): 17–23.

Krippner, Stanley (2015), "Finding Gender Differences in Dream Reports," in Milton Kramer and Myron L. Gluckson (eds), *Dream Research: Contributions to Clinical Practice*, 56–66, New York: Taylor & Francis.

Kroll, Stephen, Claudia Gruber, Ursula Hellwag, Michael Roaf, and Paul E. Zimansky, eds (2012), *Biainili-Urartu: The Proceedings of the Symposium held in Munich 12–14 October 2007*, Acta Iranica 51, Leuven: Peeters.

Kuhrt, Amélie (1983), "The Cyrus Cylinder and Achaemenid Imperial Policy," *JSOT* 25: 83–97.

Kuhrt, Amélie (1987), "Usurpation, Conquest, and Ceremonial: From Babylon to Persia," in David Cannadine and Simon Price (eds), *Rituals of Royalty: Power and Ceremonial in Traditional Societies*, 20–55, Cambridge: Cambridge University Press.

Kuhrt, Amélie (1988), "Babylonia from Cyrus to Xerxes," in John Boardman, N. G. L. Hammond, D. M. Lewis and M. Ostwald (eds), *Cambridge Ancient History*, 112–38, Cambridge: Cambridge University Press.

Kuhrt, Amélie (1990), "Nabonidus and the Babylonian Priesthood," in Mary Beard and John North (eds), *Pagan Priests: Religion and Power in the Ancient World*, 117–56, London: Duckworth.

Kuhrt, Amélie (1995), *The Ancient Near East c. 3000–330 BC*, 2 vols, Routledge History of the Ancient World, London: Routledge.

Kuhrt, Amélie (1997), "Some Thoughts on P. Briant, *Histoire de l'Empire perse*," in *Topoi Supplément 1: Recherches récentes sur l'Empire achéménide*, 299–304, Paris: De Boccard.

Kuhrt, Amélie (2003), "Making History: Sargon of Agade and Cyrus the Great of Persia," in Wouter Henkelman and Amélie Kuhrt (eds), *A Persian Perspective: Essays in Memory of Heleen Sancisi-Weerdenburg*, 347–61, AchHist, Leiden: NINO.

Kuhrt, Amélie (2007), "The Problem of Achaemenid 'Religious Policy'," in Brigitte Groneberg and Hermann Spieckermann (eds), *Die Welt der Götterbilder*, 117–42, Berlin: de Gruyter.

Kuhrt, Amélie (2009), *The Persian Empire: A Corpus of Sources from the Achaemenid Period*, London: Routledge. Orig. pub. 2007.
Kuhrt, Amélie (2010), "Xerxes and the Babylonian Temples: A Restatement of the Case," in John Curtis and St. John Simpson (eds), *The World of Achaemenid Persia: History, Art and Society in Iran and the Ancient Near East*, 491–4, London: I. B. Tauris.
Kuhrt, Amélie (2014), "Reassessing the Reign of Xerxes in the Light of New Evidence," in Michael Kozuh, Wouter F. M. Henkelman, Charles E. Jones and Christopher Woods (eds), *Extraction and Control: Studies in Honor of Matthew E. Stolper*, 163–70, Chicago: University of Chicago Press.
Kuhrt, Amélie, and Susan Sherwin-White (1987), "Xerxes' Destruction of Babylonian Temples," in Heleen Sancisi-Weerdenburg and Amélie Kuhrt (eds), *Greek Sources*, 69–78, AchHist 2, Leiden: NINO.
Kuiken, Don, and Shelley Sikora (1993), "The Impact of Dreams on Waking Thoughts and Feelings," in Alan Moffitt, Milton Kramer and Robert Hoffmann (eds), *The Functions of Dreaming*, 419–76, Albany, NY: SUNY Press.
Kuiken, Don, Ming-Ni Lee, Tracy Eng, and Terry Singh (2006), "The Influence of Impactful Dreams on Self-perceptual Depth and Spiritual Transformation," *Dreaming* 16 (4): 258–79.
Kuiken, Don (2015), "The Contrasting Effects of Nightmares, Existential Dreams, and Transcendent Dreams," in Milton Kramer and Myron Gluckson (eds), *Dream Research: Contributions to Clinical Practice*, 174–87, New York: Routledge.
Kvanvig, Helge S. (1988), *Roots of Apocalyptic: The Mesopotamian Background of the Enoch Figure and the Son of Man*, WMANT 61, Neukirchen-Vluyn: Neukirchener Verlag.
Laato, Antti (1994), "Zachariah 4,6b–10a and the Akkadian Royal Building Inscriptions," *ZAW* 106: 53–69.
Laato, Antti (1997), *A Star is Rising: The Historical Development of the Old Testament Royal Ideology and the Rise of Jewish Messianic Expectations*, University of South Florida International Studies in Formative Christianity and Judaism 5, Atlanta, GA: Scholars Press.
LaBerge, Stephen (2015), "Lucid Dreaming: Metaconsciousness During Paradoxical Sleep," in Milton Kramer and Myron L. Gluckson (eds), *Dream Research: Contributions to Clinical Practice*, 198–214, New York: Taylor & Francis.
Lactantius, Caeculius (2003), "Divine Institutes," in *The Divine Institutes of Lactantius*, trans. Anthony Bowen and Peter Garnsey, Liverpool: Liverpool University Press.
Ladiray, Daniel (2013), "The Archaeological Results," in Jean Perrot (ed.), *The Palace of Darius at Susa: The Great Royal Residence of Achaemenid Persia*, 138–75, London: I. B. Tauris.
Lambert, Wilfred G. (2008), "Mesopotamian Creation Stories," in Markham J. Geller and Mineke Schipper (eds), *Imagining Creation*, 15–60, Leiden: Brill.
Lambert, Wilfred G. (2013), *Babylonian Creation Myths*, Mesopotamian Civilizations 16, Winona Lake, IN: Eisenbrauns.
Langdon, S. (1923), *The Babylonian Epic of Creation*, Oxford: Clarendon.
Langgut, Dafna, Yuval Gadot, Naomi Porat, and Oded Lipschits (2013), "Fossil Pollen Reveals the Secrets of Royal Persian Garden at Ramat Rahel (Jerusalem)," *Palynology* 37 (1): 1–15.
Law, David R. (2012), *The Historical-Critical Method: A Guide for the Perplexed*, T&T Clark Guides for the Perplexed, London: T&T Clark.

Lecoq, Pierre (1997), *Les inscriptions de la Perse achéménide: Traduit du vieux perse, de l'élamite, du babylonien et de l'araméen*, Paris: Éditions Gallimard.

Lee, Kyong-Jin (2011), *The Authority and Authorization of Torah in the Persian Period*, Contributions to Biblical Exegesis and Theology 64, Leuven: Peeters, 2011.

Leichty, Erle (1970), *The Omen Series Šumma Izbu*, Texts from Cuneiform Sources 6, Locust Valley, NY: Augustin.

Leichty, Erle (2011), *The Royal Inscriptions of Esarhaddon, King of Assyria (680–669 BC)*, RIMA 4, Winona Lake, IN: Eisenbrauns.

Leistle, Bernhard (2014), "From the Alien to the Other: Steps toward a Phenomenological Theory of Spirit Possession," *Anthropology of Consciousness* 25 (1): 53–90.

Lemaire, André (2003), "Nabonidus in Arabia and Judah in the Neo-Babylonian Period," in Oded Lipschits and Joseph Blenkinsopp (eds), *Judah and the Judeans in the Neo-Babylonian Period*, 285–300, Winona Lake, IN: Eisenbrauns.

Lemaire, André (2011), "Judean Identity in Elephantine: Everyday Life according to the Ostraca," in Oded Lipschits, Gary N. Knoppers and Manfred Oeming (eds), *Judah and the Judeans in the Achaemenid Period: Negotiating Identity in an International Context*, 365–74, Winona Lake, IN: Eisenbrauns.

Lemaire, André (2015), *Levantine Epigraphy and History in the Achaemenid Period (539–332 BCE)*, The Schweich Lectures of the British Academy 2013, Oxford: Oxford University Press.

Lemaire, André, and Hélène Lozachmeur (1987), "Bīrāh/birtā' en araméen," *Syria* 64 (3–4): 261–6.

Lemos, T. M. (2012), "'They Have Become Women': Judean Diaspora and Postcolonial Theories of Gender and Migration," in Saul M. Olyan (ed.), *Social Theory and the Study of Israelite Religion: Essays in Retrospect and Prospect*, 81–110, Atlanta, GA: SBL.

Lenski, Gerhard, Jean Lenski, and Patrick Nolan (1991), *Human Societies: An Introduction to Macrosociology*, 6th ed., New York: McGraw-Hill.

Lenzi, Alan, and Jonathan Stökl, eds (2014), *Divination, Politics, and Ancient Near Eastern Empires*, ANEM 7, Atlanta, GA: SBL.

Lenzi, Alan (2011), *Reading Akkadian Prayers and Hymns: An Introduction*, ANEM, Atlanta, GA: SBL.

Lenzi, Alan (2012), "The Curious Case of Failed Revelation in *Ludlul Bēl Nēmeqi*: A New Suggestion for the Poem's Scholarly Purpose," in C. L. Crouch, Jonathan Stökl and Anna Elise Zernecke (eds), *Mediating between Heaven and Earth*, 36–66, London: T&T Clark.

Levine, Baruch A. (1964), "Notes on an Aramaic Dream Text from Egypt," *JAOS* 84 (1): 18–22.

Lewis, David M. (1994), "The Persepolis Tablets: Speech, Seal and Script," in A. K. Bowman and Greg Woolf (eds), *Literacy and Power in the Ancient World*, 17–32, Cambridge: Cambridge University Press.

Light, Timothy (2000), "Orthosyncretism: An Account of Melding in Religion," *Method and Theory in the Study of Religion* 12 (1): 162–85.

Lightfoot, J. L. (2007), *The Sibylline Oracles with Introduction, Translation and Commentary on the First Two Books*, Oxford: Oxford University Press.

Lincoln, Bruce (1975), "The Indo-European Myth of Creation," *History of Religions* 15 (2): 121–45.

Lincoln, Bruce (1986), *Myth, Cosmos, and Society: Indo-European Themes of Creation and Destruction*, Cambridge, MA: Harvard University Press.

Lincoln, Bruce (1997), "Pahlavi *kirrēnīdan*: Traces of Iranian Creation Mythology," *JAOS* 117 (4): 681–5.
Lincoln, Bruce (2007), *Religion, Empire and Torture: The Case of Achaemenian Persia with a Postscript on Abu Ghraib*, Chicago: University of Chicago Press.
Lincoln, Bruce (2012a), *'Happiness for Mankind': Achaemenian Religion and the Imperial Project*, Acta Iranica 53, Leuven: Peeters.
Lincoln, Bruce (2012b), "The One and the Many in Iranian Creation Myths: Rethinking 'Nostalgia for Paradise'," *Archiv für Religionsgeschichte* 13 (1): 15–30.
Lindblom, Johannes (1968), *Gesichte und Offenbarungen: Vorstellungen von göttlichen Weisungen und übernatürlichen Erscheinungen im ältesten Christentum*, Humanistiska vetenskapssamfundet i Lund 65, Lund: Gleerup.
Lindenberger, James M. (2003), *Ancient Aramaic and Hebrew Letters*, 2nd ed., WAW 14, Atlanta, GA: SBL.
Lindhagen, Curt (1950), *The Servant Motif in the Old Testament*, Uppsala: Lundequistika Bokhandeln.
Linssen, Marc J. H. (2004), *The Cults of Uruk and Babylon: The Temple Ritual Texts as Evidence for Hellenistic Cult*, CM 25, Leiden: Brill.
Linville, James R. (2010), "Playing with Mapes of Exile: Displacement, Utopia, and Disjunction," in Ehud Ben Zvi and Christoph Levin (eds), *The Concept of Exile in Ancient Israel and its Historical Contexts*, 275–93, Berlin: de Gruyter.
Lippolis, Carlo, Bruno Monopoli, and Paolo Baggio (2011), "Babylon's Urban Layout and Territory from Above," *Mesopotamia* 46: 1–8.
Lipschits, Oded, Manfred Oeming, Yuval Gadot, and Benjamin Arubas (2009), "The 2006 and 2007 Excavation Seasons at Ramat Rahel: Preliminary Report," *IEJ* 59 (1): 1–20.
Lipschits, Oded, Yuval Gadot, and Dafna Langgut (2012), "The Riddle of Ramat Raḥel: The Archaeology of a Royal Persian Period Edifice," *Transeuphratène* 41: 57–80.
Lipschits, Oded, Yuval Gadot, and Liora Freud (2016), *Ramat Raḥel III*, 2 vols, Tel Aviv Sonia and Marco Nadler Institute of Archaeology Monograph Series 35, Winona Lake, IN: Eisenbrauns.
Lipschits, Oded, Yuval Gadot, Benjamin Arubas, and Manfred Oeming (2017), *What are the Stones Whispering? Ramat Raḥel: 3000 Years of Forgotten History*, Winona Lake, IN: Eisenbrauns.
Liss, Hanna, and Manfred Oeming, eds (2010), *Literary Construction of Identity in the Ancient World*, Winona Lake, IN: Eisenbrauns.
Lloyd, Alan B. (1982), "The Inscription of Udjahorresnet, a Collaborator's Testament," *Journal of Egyptian Archaeology* 68: 166–80.
Lloyd, Alan B. (1983), "The Late Period," in Bruce G. Trigger (ed.), *Ancient Egypt: A Social History*, 279–348, Cambridge: Cambridge University Press.
Lloyd, Alan B. (1988), "Herodotus on Cambyses," in Amélie Kuhrt and Heleen Sancisi-Weerdenburg (eds), *Theory and Method*, 55–66, AchHist, Leiden: NINO.
Lloyd, Alan B. (2007), "Darius I in Egypt: Suez and Hibis," in Christopher Tuplin (ed.), *Persian Responses: Political and Cultural Interaction with(in) the Achaemenid Empire*, 99–116, Swansea: Classical Press of Wales.
Lohmann, Roger Ivar (2010), "How Evaluating Dreams Makes History: Asabano Examples," *History and Anthropology* 21 (3): 227–49.
Long, Charles H. (1987), "Cosmogony," in Mircea Eliade (ed.), *Encyclopedia of Religion*, 94–100, New York: Macmillan.
López-Ruiz, Carolina (2014), *Gods, Heroes, and Monsters: A Sourcebook of Greek, Roman and Near Eastern Myths in Translation*, Oxford: Oxford University Press.

Lord, Albert B. (2000), *The Singer of Tales*, 2nd ed., Cambridge, MA: Harvard University Press. Orig. pub. 1960.
Lorenz, Jürgen (2008), *Nebukadnezar III/IV: Die politischen Wirren nach dem Tod des Kambyses im Spiegel der Keilscrifttexte*, Dresden: ISLET.
Löw, Immanuel (1924), *Die Flora der Juden. 2, Iridaceae-Papilionaceae*, Veröffentlichungen der Alexander Kohut memorial foundation 2, Vienna: Löwit.
Lozachmeur, Hélène (2006), *La collection Clermont-Ganneau: ostraca, épigraphes sur jarre, étiquettes de bois*, 2 vols, Mémoires de l'Académie des inscriptions et belles-lettres, Nouvelle série 35, Paris: De Boccard.
Lu, Yong (2016), "A Theological, Ancient Hellenistic, and Psychological Look at the dream of Pharaoh's Chief Cupbearer and Chief Baker (Genesis 40:5–13, 16–18)," *International Journal of Dream Research* 9 (1): 46–57.
Lundblom, Jack R. (2013), *Deuteronomy: A Commentary*, Grand Rapids, MI: Eerdmans.
Luukko, Mikko, and Grata Van Buylaere (2002), *The Political Correspondence of Esarhaddon*, SAA 16, Helsinki: Neo-Assyrian Text Corpus Project.
Lux, Rüdiger (2009), "'Wir wollen mit euch gehen…' Überlegungen zur Völkertheologie Haggais und Sacharjas," in Rüdiger Lux (ed.), *Prophetie und Zweiter Tempel. Studien zu Haggai und Sacharja*, 241–65, Tübingen: Mohr Siebeck.
Machinist, Peter, and Hayim Tadmor (1993), "Heavenly Wisdom," in Mark E. Cohen, Daniel C. Snell and David B. Weisberg (eds), *The Tablet and the Scroll: Near Eastern Studies in Honor of William W. Hallo*, 146–51, Bethesda, MD: CDL.
MacLean, Kama (2008), *Pilgrimage and Power: The Kumbh Mela in Allahabad, 1765–1954*, New York: Oxford University Press.
MacPherson, Sonia (2001), "A Genre to Remember: Tibetan Popular Poetry and Song as Remembrance," *Language and Literacy* 3 (2): 1–19, http://ejournals.library.ualberta.ca/index.php/langandlit/article/view/17652/14009.
Magen, Ursala (1986), *Assyrische Königsdarstellungen: Aspekte der Herrschaft: eine Typologie*, Baghdafer Forschungen 9, Mainz am Rhein: Zabern.
Magen, Yitzhak, Haggai Misgav, and Levana Tsfania (2004), *Mount Gerizim Excavations I: The Aramaic, Hebrew, and Samaritan Inscriptions*, Judea and Samaria Publications 2, Jerusalem: Israel Antiquities Authority.
Magen, Yitzhak (2008), *Mount Gerizim Excavations II: A Temple City*, Judea and Samaria Publications 8, Jerusalem: Israel Antiquities Authority.
Mageo, Jeannette Marie (2003), "Subjectivity and Identity in Dreams," in Jeannette Marie Mageo (ed.), *Dreaming and the Self: New Perspectives on Subjectivity, Identity, and Emotion*, 23–42, Albany, NY: SUNY Press.
Malandra, William W. (1977), *The Fravaši Yašt: Introduction, Text, Translation and Commentary*, London: University Microfilms, PhD, University of Pennsylvania, 1971.
Malandra, William W. (1983), *An Introduction to Ancient Iranian Religion*, Minnesota Publications in the Humanities 2, Minneapolis: University of Minnesota Press.
Malkki, Liisa H. (1995), *Purity and Exile: Violence, Memory, and National Cosmology among Hutu Refugees in Tanzania*, Chicago: University of Chicago Press.
Mankowski, Paul V. (2000), *Akkadian Loanwords in Biblical Hebrew*, HSS 47, Winona Lake, IN: Eisenbrauns.
Mansel, Peter, and Torsten Riotte (2011a), "Introduction: Monarchical Exile," in Peter Mansel and Torsten Riotte (eds), *Monarchs and Exile: The Politics of Legitimacy from Marie de Médicis to Wilhelm II*, 1–16, New York: Palgrave.
Mansel, Peter, and Torsten Riotte, eds (2011b), *Monarchs and Exile: The Politics of Legitimacy from Marie de Médicis to Wilhelm II*, New York: Palgrave MacMillan.

Marinkovic, P. (1994), "What Does Zechariah 1–8 Tell us about the Second Temple?" in Tamara C. Eskenazi and Kent H. Richards (eds), *Second Temple Studies 2: Temple and Community in the Persian Period*, 88–103, Sheffield: JSOT Press.

Martin, Cary J. (2011), "The Demotic Texts," in Bezalel Porten (ed.), *The Elephantine Papyri in English: Three Millennia of Cross-Cultural Change*, 277–384, Atlanta, GA: SBL.

Mason, Rex (1977), *Books of Haggai, Zechariah, and Malachi*, CBC, Cambridge: Cambridge University Press.

Mathys, Hans-Peter (2010), "Der Achämenidenhof im Alten Testament," in Bruno Jacobs and Robert Rollinger (eds), *Der Achämenidenhof/the Achaemenid Court*, 231–310, CleO 2, Wiesbaden: Harrassowitz.

Maul, Stefan M. (2012), "Tontafelabschriften des ‚Kodex Hammurapi' in Altbabylonischer Monumentalschrift," *ZA* 102: 76–99.

Mayrhofer, Manfred (1979), "Die iransichen Elemente im aramäischen Text," in Henri Metzger (ed.), *Fouilles de Xanthos VI: La Stèle Trilingue du Létôon*, 179–85, Paris: Klincksieck.

McCarthy, Dennis J. (1978), *Treaty and Covenant*, new rev. ed., Analecta Biblica 21a, Rome: Biblical Institute.

McComiskey, Thomas Edward (2009), "Zechariah," in Thomas Edward McComiskey (ed.), *The Minor Prophets*, 1003–244, Grand Rapids, MI: Baker. Original edition, 1992.

McCorriston, Joy (2011), *Pilgrimage and Household in the Ancient Near East*, Cambridge: Cambridge University Press.

McGinnis, Claire Mathews, and Patricia K. Tull (2006), *'As Those Who are Taught': The Interpretation of Isaiah from the LXX to the SBL*, Symposium 27, Atlanta, GA: SBL.

McKenzie, John L. (1968), *Second Isaiah*, AB, New York: Doubleday.

McKinlay, Judith E. (2013), "The Usefulness of a Daughter," in Andrew T. Abernathy, Mark G. Brett, Tim Bulkeley and Tim Meadowcroft (eds), *Isaiah and Imperial Context: The Book of Isaiah in the Times of Empire*, 85–106, Eugene, OR: Pickwick.

McSpadden, Lucia Ann (1999), "Negotiating Masculinity in the Reconstruction of Social Place: Eritrean and Ethiopian Refugees in the United States and Sweden," in Doreen Indra (ed.), *Engendering Forced Migration: Theory and Practice*, 242–60, New York: Berghahn Books.

Meadows, Andrew R. (2005), "The Administration of the Achaemenid Empire," in John Curtis and Nigel Tallis (eds), *Forgotten Empire*, 181–209, London: British Museum.

Meier, Carl Alfred (1966), "The Dream in Ancient Greece and its Use in Temple Cures (Incubation)," in Gustave Edmund von Grunebaum and Roger Caillois (eds), *The Dream and Human Societies*, 303–20, Berkeley, CA: University of California Press.

Mein, Andrew (2001), *Ezekiel and the Ethics of Exile*, OTM, Oxford: Oxford University Press.

Melugin, Roy F. (1976), *The Formation of Isaiah 40–55*, BZAW 141, Berlin: de Gruyter.

Merkt, Andreas, Walther Sallaberger, Heinz Felber, Martin Heimgartner, Elisabeth Hollander, and Isabel Toral-Niehoff (2002), "Weltschöpfung," in Hubert Cancik and Helmuth Schneider (eds), *Der Neue Pauly*, 463–74, Stuttgart: J. B. Metzler.

Merrill, Eugene H. (1987a), "The Literary Character of Isaiah 40–55, Pt 1: Survey of a Century of Studies," *BSac* 144 (573): 24–53.

Merrill, Eugene H. (1987b), "Literary Genres in Isaiah 40–55 (Literary Character of Isaiah 40–55 Part 2)," *BSac* 144 (574): 144–56.

Merrill, William (1989), "The Raramuri Stereotype of Dreams," in Barbara Tedlock (ed.), *Dreaming: Anthropological and Psychological Interpretations*, 194–219, Cambridge: Cambridge University Press.

Meshorer, Ya'akov, and Shraga Qedar (1991), *The Coinage of Samaria in the Fourth Century BCE*, Beverly Hills, CA: Numismatic Fine Arts International.

Meshorer, Ya'akov, and Shraga Qedar (1999), *Samarian Coinage*, Numismatic Studies and Researches 9, Jerusalem: Israel Numismatic Society.

Meshorer, Ya'akov (2001), *A Treasury of Jewish Coins: From the Persian Period to Bar Kokhba*, Jerusalem: Yad Ben-Zvi Press.

Metzger, Henri, ed. (1979a), *Fouilles de Xanthos VI: La stèle trilingue du Létôon*, Paris: Klincksieck.

Metzger, Henri (1979b), "Le sanctuaire de Léto," in Henri Metzger (ed.), *Fouilles de Xanthos VI: La Stèle Trilingue du Létôon*, 5–28, Paris: Klincksieck.

Meyers, Carol L., and Eric M. Meyers (2004), *Haggai, Zechariah 1–8*, AB 25B. Hartford, CT: Yale University Press. First pub. 1987.

Michel, Diethelm (1981), "Deuterojesaja," in Gerhard Krause and Gerhard Müller (eds), *Theologische Realenzyklopädie Vol. 8*, 510–30, Berlin: de Gruyter.

Michelini, Ann M. (1982), *Tradition and Dramatic Form in the Persians of Aeschylus*, Cincinnati Classical Studies NS 4, Leiden: Brill.

Middlemas, Jill (2007), *The Templeless Age*, Louisville, KY: Westminster John Knox.

Mieroop, Marc van de (2003), "Reading Babylon," *American Journal of Archaeology* 107 (2): 257–75.

Mieroop, Marc van de (2004), *The Ancient Mesopotamian City*, Oxford: Oxford University Press. First pub. 1997.

Milbank, John (1992), "'I Will Gasp and Pant': Deutero-Isaiah and the Birth of the Suffering Subject," *Semeia* 59: 59–71.

Mildenberg, Leo (1979), "Yehud: A Preliminary Study of the Provincial Coinage of Judaea," in Otto Mørkholm and Nancy M. Waggoner (eds), *Greek Numismatics and Archaeology: Essays in Honor of Margaret Thompson*, 183–96 + Pl. 21–2, Wetteren: Éditions NR.

Mills, Lawrence H. (1905–6), *Zarathuštra, Philo, the Achaemenids, and Israel*, Leipzig: Brockhaus.

Mills, Lawrence H., trans (1988), *The Yasna, Visparad, Āfrīnagān, Gāhs, and Miscellaneous Fragments. The Zend-Avesta, Part III: SBE*, Delhi: Motilal Banarsidass. Orig. pub. 1887.

Mitchell, Christine (2014), "A Note on the Creation Formula in Zechariah 12:1–8; Isaiah 42:5–6; and Old Persian Inscriptions," *JBL* 133 (2): 305–8.

Mitchell, Christine (2015), "The Testament of Darius (DNa/DNb) and Constructions of Kings and Kingship in 1–2 Chronicles," in Jason M. Silverman and Caroline Waerzeggers (eds), *Political Memory in and after the Persian Empire*, ANEM 13, Atlanta, GA: SBL.

Mitchell, Christine (2016), "A Paradise at Ramat Rahel and the Setting of Zechariah," *Transeuphratène* 48: 81–95.

Mitchell, Christine (2017), "Berlin Papyrus P. 13447 and the Library of the Yehudite Colony at Elephantine," *JNES* 76 (1): 139–47.

Mitchell, Hinckley G., John Merlin Powis Smith, and Julius A. Bewer (1912), *A Critical and Exegetical Commentary on Haggai, Zechariah, Malachi and Jonah*, ICC, Edinburgh: T&T Clark.

Moffitt, Alan, Milton Kramer, and Robert Hoffmann, eds (1993a), *The Functions of Dreaming*, SUNY Series in Dream Studies, Albany, NY: SUNY Press.
Moffitt, Alan, Milton Kramer, and Robert Hoffmann (1993b), "Introduction," in Alan Moffitt, Milton Kramer and Robert Hoffmann (eds), *The Functions of Dreaming*, 1–11, Albany, NY: SUNY Press.
Momigliano, A. (1979), "Flavius Josephus and Alexander's Visit to Jerusalem," *Athenaeum* 57: 442–8.
Montangero, Jacques, Pascale Pasche, and Pierre Willequet (1996), "Remembering and Communicating the Dream Experience: What Does a Complementary Morning Report add to the Night Report?" *Dreaming* 6 (2): 131–5.
Mor, Menachem (2011), "The Samaritans in Transition from the Persian to the Greek Period," in Lester L. Grabbe and Oded Lipschits (eds), *Judah between East and West: The Transition from Persian to Greek Rule (ca. 400–200 BCE)*, 176–98, London: T&T Clark.
Morinis, Alan (1992), "Introduction," in Alan Morinis (ed.), *Sacred Journeys: The Anthropology of Pilgrimage*, 1–30, Westport, CT: Greenwood.
Morrow, William (2004), "Post-Traumatic Stress Disorder and Vicarious Atonement in the Second Isaiah," in J. Harold Ellens and Wayne G. Rollins (eds), *Psychology and the Bible: A New Way to Read the Scriptures 1, From Freud to Kohut*, 167–84. Westport, CA: Praeger.
Morvillez, Éric, ed. (2014), *Paradeisos: Genèse et métamorphose de la notion de paradis dans l'Antiquité*, Orient & Méditerranéé archéologie 15, Paris: De Boccard.
Moseman, R. David (2009), "The Date Formulae in the Book of Zechariah: An Important Key for Interpreting Zechariah," *Review and Expositor* 106 (4): 575–89.
Moukarzel, Kabalan (2014), "The Religious Reform of Nabonidus: A Sceptical View," in Markham J. Geller (ed.), *Melammu: The Ancient World in an Age of Globalization*, 157–90, Berlin: Edition Open Access.
Mowinckel, Sigmund (2002), *The Spirit and the Word: Prophecy and Tradition in Ancient Israel*, Fortress Classics in Biblical Studies, Minneapolis, MN: Augsburg Fortress.
Mowinckel, Sigmund (2005), *He That Cometh*, trans. G.W. Anderson, Grand Rapids, MI: Eerdmans. Orig. pub. 1951.
Münsterberg, Hugo (1970), *The Film: A Psychological Study*, Mineola, NY: Dover Publications. Orig. pub. 1916.
Nagel, Alexander (2013), "Color and Gilding in Achaemenid Architecture and Sculpture," in Daniel T. Potts (ed.), *The Oxford Handbook of Ancient Iran*, 596–621, Oxford: Oxford University Press.
Nasrabadi, Behzad Mofidi (2005), "Eine Steininschrift des Amar-Suena aus Tappeh Bormi (Iran)," *Zeitschrift für Assyriologie und Vorderasiatische Archäologie* 95 (2): 161–71, https://doi.org/10.1515/zava.2005.95.2.161.
Naveh, Joseph, and Shaul Shaked (2012), *Aramaic Documents from Ancient Bactria from the Khalili Collections*, London: Khalili Family Trust.
Neujahr, Matthew (2012), *Predicting the Past in the Ancient Near East: Mantic Historiography in Ancient Mesopotamia, Judah, and the Mediterranean World*, Providence, RI: SBL.
Neumann, J. (1977), "The Winds in the World of the Ancient Mesopotamian Civilizations," *Bulletin of the American Meteorological Society* 58 (10): 1050–5.

Newsom, Carol A. (2010), "Why Nabonidus? Excavating Traditions from Qumran, the Hebrew Bible, and Neo-Babylonian Sources," in Sarianna Metso, Hindy Najman and Eileen Schuller (eds), *The Dead Sea Scrolls: Transmission of Traditions and Production of Texts*, 57–79, Leiden: Brill.

Newsom, Carol A. (2013), "Now You See Him, Now You Don't: Nabonidus in Jewish Memory," in Diana V. Edelman and Ehud Ben Zvi (eds), *Remembering Biblical Figures in the Late Persian and Early Hellenistic Periods: Social Memory and Imagination*, 270–82, Oxford: Oxford University Press.

Niditch, Susan (1980), *The Symbolic Vision in Biblical Tradition*, Harvard Semitic Monographs 30, Chico, CA: Scholars Press.

Niditch, Susan (1996), *Oral World and Written Word: Ancient Israelite Literature*, Louisville, KY: Westminster John Knox.

Niditch, Susan, and Robert Doran (1977), "The Success Story of the Wise Courtier: A Formal Approach," *JBL* 96 (2): 179–93.

Nieling, Jens, and Ellen Rehm, eds (2010), *Achaemenid Impact in the Black Sea: Communication of Powers*, Black Sea Studies 11, Aarhus: Aarhus University Press.

Nilsen, Tina Dykesteen (2008), "The Creation of Darkness and Evil (Isaiah 45:6c–7)," *RB* 115: 5–25.

Nilsen, Tina Dykesteen (2013), "Creation in Collision? Isaiah 40–48 and Zoroastrianism, Babylonian Religion and Genesis 1," *JHebS* 13 (8), http://www.jhsonline.org/Articles/article_188.pdf.

Nissinen, Martti (1998), *References to Prophecy in Neo-Assyrian Sources*, SAA 7, Helsinki: The Neo-Assyrian Text Corpus Project.

Nissinen, Martti (2000a), *Prophecy in its Ancient Near Eastern Context*, Symposium, Atlanta: SBL.

Nissinen, Martti (2000b), "Spoken, Written, Quoted, and Invented: Orality and Writtenness in Ancient Near Eastern Prophecy," in Ehud Ben Zvi and Michael H. Floyd (eds), *Writings and Speech in Israelite and Ancient Near Eastern Prophecy*, 235–72, Atlanta, GA: SBL.

Nissinen, Martti (2003), *Prophets and Prophecy in the Ancient Near East*, Writings from the Ancient World, Atlanta: SBL.

Nissinen, Martti (2005), "How Prophecy became Literature," *SJOT* 19 (2): 153–75.

Nissinen, Martti (2008), "Das Problem der Prophetenschüler," in Juha Pakkala and Martti Nissinen (eds), *Houses Full of All Good Things: Essays in Memory of Timo Veijola*, 337–53, Göttingen: Vandenhoeck & Ruprecht.

Nissinen, Martti (2014), "Since When Do Prophets Write?" In *In the Footsteps of Sherlock Holmes* Kristin de Troyer, T. Michael Law and Markette Liljeström, 585–606, Leuven: Peeters.

Nongri, Brent (2005), "The Motivations of the Maccabees and Judean Rhetoric of Ancestral Traditions," in Carol Bakhos (ed.), *Ancient Judaism in its Hellenistic Context*, 85–111, Leiden: Brill.

North, Christopher R. (1956), *The Suffering Servant in Deutero-Isaiah: An Historical and Critical Study*. 2nd ed., London: Oxford University Press. First pub. 1948.

North, Robert (1970), "Zechariah's Seven-spout Lampstand," *Bib* 51: 183–206.

O'Kennedy, Daniël François (2003), "Zechariah 3–4: Core of Proto-Zechariah," *OTE* 16 (2): 370–88.

Obeyesekere, Gananath (2012), *The Awakened Ones: The Phenomenology of Visionary Experience*, New York: Columbia University Press.

Oded, Bustenay (1995), "Observations on the Israelite/Judaean Exiles in Mesopotamia During the Eighth–Sixth Centuries BCE," in Karel van Lerberghe and Antoon Schoors (eds), *Immigration and Emigration within the Ancient Near East*, 205–12, Leuven: Peeters.
Olden, Anthony (1999), "Somali Refugees in London: Oral Culture in a Western Information Environment," *Libri* 49: 212–24.
Olszewska, Zuzanna (2007), "'A Desolate Voice': Poetry and Identity among Young Afghan Refugees in Iran," *Iranian Studies* 40 (2): 203–24.
Omidsalar, Mahmud (2013), "Kāva," *EncIr* 16 (2): 130–2, http://www.iranicaonline.org/articles/kava-hero.
Oppenheim, A. Leo (1956), *The Interpretation of Dreams in the Ancient Near East with a Translation of an Assyrian Dream-Book*, Transactions of the American Philosophical Society 46/3, Philadelphia: American Philosophical Society.
Oppenheim, A. Leo (1968), "The Eyes of the Lord," *JAOS* 88 (1): 173–80.
Oppenheim, A. Leo (1974), "A New Cambyses Incident," in Jay Gluck (ed.), *A Survey of Persian Art from Prehistoric Times to the Present XV*, 3497–502. Tokyo: Asia Institute.
Oppenheim, A. Leo (1985), "The Babylonian Evidence of Achaemenian Rule in Mesopotamia," in Ilya Gershevitch (ed.), *The Cambridge History of Iran*, 529–87, Cambridge: Cambridge University Press.
Oppenheim, A. Leo, Erica Reiner, and Robert D. Biggs (1973), *The Assyrian Dictionary of the University of Chicago*, Vol. 9 (L), Chicago: The Oriental Institute of the University of Chicago.
Orlinsky, Harry M. (1964), *The So-Called 'Suffering Servant' in Isaiah 53*, The Goldenson Lecture of 1964, Cincinnati, OH: Hebrew Union College Press.
Osborne, Tony (2011), "A Queen Mother in Exile: Marie de Médicis in the Spanish Netherlands and England," in Peter Mansel and Torsten Riotte (eds), *Monarchs and Exile: The Politics of Legitimacy from Marie de Médicis to Wilhelm II*, 17–43, New York: Palgrave Macmillan.
Otzen, Benedikt (1990), "יצר yāṣar," in G. Johannes Botterweck and Helmer Ringgren (eds), *Theological Dictionary of the Old Testament*, 257–65, Grand Rapids, MI: Eerdmans.
Overholt, Thomas W. (1986), *Prophecy in Cross-Cultural Perspective*, SBLSBS 17, Atlanta: Scholars Press.
Overholt, Thomas W. (1989), *Channels of Prophecy: The Social Dynamics of Prophetic Activity*, Minneapolis: Fortress.
Panaino, Antonio (2000), "The Mesopotamian Heritage of Achaemenian Kingship," in Sanno Aro and R. M. Whiting (eds), *The Heirs of Assyria: Proceedings of the Opening Symposium of the Assyrian and Babylonian Intellectual Heritage Project. Tvärminne, Finland, October 8–11, 1998*, 35–49, Helsinki: Neo-Assyrian Text Corpus Project.
Parke, H. W. (1988), *Sibyls and Sibylline Prophecy in Classical Antiquity*, ed. Brian C. McGing, Croom Helm Classical Studies, London: Routledge.
Parker, Richard A. (1941), "Darius and his Egyptian Campaign," *American Journal of Semitic Languages* 58 (4): 373–7.
Parker, Richard A., and Waldo H. Dubberstein (1956), *Babylonian Chronology 626 B.C.–A.D. 75*, Brown University Studies 19, Providence, RI: Brown University Press.
Parker, Simon B. (1997), *Ugaritic Narrative Poetry*, WAW 9, Atlanta, GA: Scholars Press.
Parpola, Simo (1993), *Letters from Assyrian and Babylonian Scholars*, SAA 10, Helsinki: Helsinki University Press.
Parpola, Simo (1997), *Assyrian Prophecies*, SAA 9, Helsinki: Helsinki University Press.

Paul, Shalom M. (2012), *Isaiah 40–66: Translation and Commentary*, Eerdmans Critical Commentary, Grand Rapids: Eerdmans.
Paulson, Joel F. (2005), "Surveying in Ancient Egypt," in *From Pharaohs to Geoinformatics: Semiramis Inter-continental Cairo, Egypt 16–21 April 2005 Proceedings* 1–12, https://www.fig.net/resources/proceedings/fig_proceedings/cairo/papers/wshs_02/wshs02_02_paulson.pdf. Online.
Pearce, Laurie E. (2015), "Identifying Judeans and Judean Identity in the Babylonian Evidence," in Caroline Waerzeggers and Jonathan Stökl (eds), *Exile and Return: The Babylonian Context*, 7–32, BZAW 478, Berlin: de Gruyter.
Pearce, Laurie E. (2016), "Looking for Judeans in Babylonia's Core and Periphery," in Ehud Ben Zvi and Christoph Levin (eds), *Centres and Peripheries in the Early Second Temple Period*, 43–65, Tübingen: Mohr Siebeck.
Pearce, Laurie E., and Cornelia Wunsch (2014), *Documents of Judean Exiles and West Semites in Babylonia in the Collection of David Sofer*, Cornell University Studies in Assyriology and Sumerology 28, Bethesda, MD: CDL.
Pedersén, Olof, Paul J. J. Sinclair, Irmgard Hein, and Jakob Andersson (2010), "Cities and Urban Landscapes in the Ancient Near East and Egypt with a Special Focus on the City of Babylon," in Paul J. J. Sinclair, Gullög Nordqvist, Frands Herschend and Christian Isendahl (eds), *The Urban Mind: Cultural and Environmental Dynamics*, 113–47. Uppsala: Uppsala University.
Pedersén, Olof (2005), "Foreign Professionals in Babylon: Evidence from the Archive in the Palace of Nebuchadnezzar II," in W. H. van Soldt (ed.), *Ethnicity in Ancient Mesopotamia: Papers Read at the 48th RAI*, 267–72, Leiden: NINO.
Pedersén, Olof (2011), "Work on a Digital Model of Babylon using Archaeological and Textual Evidence," *Mesopotamia* 46: 9–22.
Pedersén, Olof (2014), "Waters at Babylon," in Terje Tvedt and Terje Oestigaard (eds), *Waters and Urbanization*, 107–29, London: I. B. Tauris.
Perdrizet, Paul, and Gustave Lefebvre (1919), *Les Graffites Grecs du Memnonion d'Abydos*, Inscriptiones Graecae Aegypti III: Inscriptiones Memnonii Sive Besae Oraculi ad Abydum Thebaidis, Chicago: Ares.
Perdu, Olivier (2014), "Saites and Persians," in Alan B. Lloyd (ed.), *A Companion to Ancient Egypt*, 40–58. Malden, MA: Wiley Blackwell.
Perrot, André (1961), *The Arts of Assyria*, trans. Stuart Gilbert and James Emmons, New York: Golden Press.
Perrot, Jean (2013), "Darius in his Time," in Jean Perrot (ed.), *The Palace of Darius at Susa: The Great Royal Residence of Achaemenid Persia*, 453–74, London: I. B. Tauris.
Petersen, David L. (1984), *Haggai and Zechariah 1–8: A Commentary*, OTL: Westminster John Knox.
Petersen, David L. (1997), "The Nature of Prophetic Literature," in Yehoshua Gitay (ed.), *Prophecy and Prophets: The Diversity of Contemporary Issues in Scholarship*, 23–40, Atlanta, GA: Scholars Press.
Petersen, David L. (2000), "Defining Prophecy and Prophetic Literature," in Martti Nissinen (ed.), *Prophecy in its Ancient Near Eastern Context*, 33–44, Atlanta: SBL.
Petterson, Anthony R. (2009), *Behold Your King: The Hope for the House of David in the Book of Zechariah*, LHBOTS 513, London: T&T Clark.
Petterson, Anthony R. (2015), "A New Form-Critical Approach to Zechariah's Crowning of High Priest Joshua and the Identity of 'Shoot' (Zechariah 6:9–15)," in Mark J. Boda, Michael H. Floyd and Colin M. Toffelmire (eds), *The Book of the Twelve and the New Form Criticism*, 285–304, Atlanta, GA: SBL.

Pettinato, Giovanni (1966), *Die Ölwahrsagung bei den Babyloniern*, 2 vols, Studi Semitici 21, Rome: Istituto di Studi del Vicino Oriente.
Philostratus (2005), "The Life of Apollonius of Tyana," in *Apollonius of Tyana I*, trans. Christopher P. Jones, LCL, Cambridge, MA: Harvard University Press.
Pinches, Theophilus G. (1897), "Some Late-Babylonian Texts in the British Museum," *Recueil de travaux relatifs à la philologie et à l'archéologie égyptiennes et assyriennes* 19: 101–4.
Pliny (1960), "Natural History," in *Pliny IV: Libri XII–XVI*, trans. H. Rackham, LCL, Cambridge, MA: Heinemann.
Pliny (1961), "Natural History," in *Natural History II, Libri III–VII*, trans. H. Rackham, LCL, London: Heinemann.
Plutarch (1931), "Regum et imperatorum apophthegmata," in *Moralia III*, 3–153, trans. Frank Cole Babbitt, LCL, London: William Heinemann.
Plutarch (1986), *Alexander*. In *Plutarch's Lives VII*, trans. Bernadotte Perrin, LCL, Cambridge, MA: Harvard University Press.
Pompeo, Flavia (2012), "Some Syntactic and Semantic Remarks on XPl 30–31," in Gian Pietro Basello and Adriano V. Rossi (eds), *Dariosh Studies II: Persepolis and its Settlements: Territorial System and Ideology in the Achaemenid State*, 155–82, Naples: Ismeo.
Pomykala, Kenneth E. (1995), *The Davidic Dynasty Tradition in Early Judaism: Its History and Significance for Messianism*, EJL 7, Atlanta, GA: Scholars.
Pongratz-Leisten, Beate (1994), *Ina šulmi īrub: die kulttopographische und ideologische Programmatik der akītu-Prozession in Babylonien und Assyrien im 1. Jahrtausend v. Chr.*, Baghdader Forschungen 16, Mainz am Rhein: Von Zabern.
Porten, Bezalel (2011), *The Elephantine Papyri in English: Three Millennia of Cross-Cultural Continuity and Change*, 2nd rev. ed., Atlanta, GA: SBL.
Porten, Bezalel, and Ada Yardeni (1986–99), *Textbook of Aramaic Documents from Ancient Egypt*, 6 vols, Jerusalem: Hebrew University.
Porten, Bezalel, and Jerome Alan Lund (2002), *Aramaic Documents from Egypt: A Key-Word-in-Context Concordance*, CAL Project Texts and Studies 1, Winona Lake, IN: Eisenbrauns.
Portes, Alehandro, and Min Zhou (1993), "The New Second Generation: Segmented Assimilation and Its Variants," *The Annals of the American Academy of Political and Social Science* 530: 74–96.
Portier-Young, Anathea (2011), *Apocalypse against Empire: Theologies of Resistance in Early Judaism*, Grand Rapids, MI: Eerdmans.
Potts, Daniel T. (1997), *Mesopotamian Civilization: The Material Foundations*, Athlone Publications in Egyptology and Ancient Near Eastern Studies, London: Athlone.
Preuß, Horst Dietrich (1976), *Deuterojesaja: Eine Einführung in seine Botschaft*, Neukirchen-Vluyn: Neukirchener Verlag.
Preuß, Horst Dietrich (1998), "רוח *ruaḥ*," in G. Johannes Botterweck, Helmer Ringgren and Heinze-Josef Fabry (eds), *Theological Dictionary of the Old Testament*, 277–85, Winona Lake, IN: Eerdmans.
Pritchard, James B. (1954), *Ancient Near Eastern Pictures related to the Old Testament*, Princeton, NJ: Princeton University Press.
Pritchard, James B. (1969), *Ancient Near Eastern Texts Relating to the Old Testament*, 3rd ed., Princeton: Princeton University Press.
Pummer, Reinhard (2016), *The Samaritans: A Profile*, Grand Rapids, MI: Eerdmans.

Purcell, Sheila, Alan Moffitt, and Robert Hoffmann (1993), "Waking, Dreaming, and Self-Regulation," in Alan Moffitt, Milton Kramer and Robert Hoffmann (eds), *The Functions of Dreaming*, 197–260, Albany, NY: SUNY Press.
Pyper, Hugh S. (2005), "Reading in the Dark: Zechariah, Daniel and the Difficulty of Scripture," *JSOT* 29: 485–504.
Rad, Gerhard von (1959), "The Origin of the Concept of the Day of Yahweh," *JSS* 4 (2): 97–108.
Ray, J. D. (1988), "Egypt 525–404 BC," in John Boardman, N. G. L. Hammond, D. M. Lewis and M. Ostwald (eds), *The Cambridge Ancient History*, 254–86, Cambridge: Cambridge University Press.
Razmjou, Shahrokh (2010), "Persepolis: A Reinterpretation of Palaces and Their Function," in John Curtis and St. John Simpson (eds), *The World of Achaemenid Persia: History, Art and Society in Iran and the Ancient Near East*, 231–46, London: I. B. Tauris.
Razmjou, Shahrokh (2013), "The Cyrus Cylinder: A Persian Perspective," in Irving L. Finkel (ed.), *The Cyrus Cylinder: The King of Persia's Proclamation from Ancient Babylon*, 104–26, London: I. B. Tauris.
Razmjou, Shahrokh, and Michael Roaf (2013), "Temples and Sacred Places in Persepolis," in Kai Kaniuth, Anne Löhnert, Jared L. Miller, Adelheid Otto, Michael Roaf and Walther Sallaberger (eds), *Tempel im Alten Orient*, 407–26, Wiesbaden: Harrassowitz.
Redditt, Paul L. (2008), "The King in Haggai-Zechariah 1–8 and the Book of the Twelve," in Mark J. Boda and Michael H. Floyd (eds), *Tradition in Transition: Haggai and Zechariah 1–8 in the Trajectory of Hebrew Theology*, 56–82, New York: T&T Clark.
Redditt, Paul L. (2015), "Form Criticism in Haggai, Zechariah, and Malachi: From Oral Sayings to Literature," in Mark J. Boda, Michael H. Floyd and Colin M. Toffelmire (eds), *The Book of the Twelve and the New Form Criticism*, 265–84, Atlanta, GA: SBL.
Redditt, Paul L. (2016), "King, Priest, and Temple in Haggai-Zechariah-Malachi and Ezra-Nehemiah," in Lena-Sofia Tiemeyer (ed.), *Priests and Cults in the Book of the Twelve*, 157–72, Atlanta, GA: SBL.
Reissler, P. (1899), *Das Buch Daniel*, Kurzgefasster wissenschaftlicher Kommentar zu den Heiligen Schriften des Alten Testaments 3/3/2, Stuttgart: Roth.
Renburg, Gil Haviv (2003), *'Commanded by the Gods': An Epigraphical Study of Dreams and Visions in Greek and Roman Religious Life*, 2 vols, PhD diss., Duke University.
Reventlow, Henning Graf (1993), *Das Propheten Haggai, Sacharja, und Maleachi*, ATD 25/3, Göttingen: Vandenhoeck & Ruprecht.
Reynolds, Frances (2003), *The Babylonian Correspondence of Esarhaddon*, SAA 18, Helsinki: Helsinki University Press.
Rignell, Lars Gösta (1950), *Die Nachtsgesichte des Sacharja*, Lund: Gleerup.
Rignell, Lars Gösta (1956), *A Study of Isaiah Ch. 40–55*, Lunds Universitets Årsskrift NF 1.52.5. Lund: Gleerup.
Ringgren, Helmer (1947), *Word and Wisdom: Studies in the Hypostatization of Divine Qualities and Functions in the Ancient Near East*, Lund: Hakan Ohlssons Boktryckeri.
Ringgren, Helmer (2001), "עשה 'āśâ," in G. Johannes Botterweck, Helmer Ringgren and Heinz-Josef Fabry (eds), *Theological Dictionary of the Old Testament*, 387–403, Grand Rapids, MI: Eerdmans.
Ringgren, Helmer, and B. Johnson (2003), "צדק," in (eds), *Theological Dictionary of the Old Testament* G. Johannes Botterweck, Helmer Ringgren and Heinze-Josef Fabry, 239–63, Grand Rapids, MI: Eerdmans.
Ristau, Kenneth A. (2016), *Reconstructing Jerusalem: Persian-Period Prophetic Perspectives*, Winona Lake, IN: Eisenbrauns.

Ritner, Robert K. (2000), "Dream Oracles (P. Chester Beatty III, P. BM 10683)," in William W. Hallo and K. Lawson Younger (eds), *Contexts of Scripture I*, 52–4, Leiden: Brill.
Roaf, Michael (1983), "Sculptures and Sculptors at Persepolis," *Iran* 21: 1–164.
Rochberg, Francesca (2004), *The Heavenly Writing: Divination, Horoscopy, and Astronomy in Mesopotamian Culture*, Cambridge: Cambridge University Press.
Rohrmoser, Angela (2014), *Götter, Tempel und Kult der Judäo-Aramäer von Elephantine: archäologische und schriftliche Zeugnisse aus dem perserzeitlichen Ägypten*, AOAT 396, Münster: Ugarit-Verlag.
Rollinger, Robert (2003), "Herodotus v. Cambyses According to Herodotus," *EncIr* 12 (3): 262–4, http://www.iranicaonline.org/articles/herodotus-v.
Rom-Shiloni, Dalit (2013), *Exclusive Inclusivity: Identity Conflicts between the Exiles and the People who Remained (6th–5th Centuries BCE)*, LHBOTS 543, New York: T&T Clark.
Rooke, Deborah W. (2000), *Zadok's Heirs: The Role and Development of the High Priesthood in Ancient Israel*, OTM, Oxford: Oxford University Press.
Root, Margaret Cool (1979), *The King and Kingship in Achaemenid Art: Essays on the Creation of an Iconography of Empire*, Acta Iranica 19, Leiden: Brill.
Root, Margaret Cool (2000), "Imperial Ideology in the Achaemenid Persian Art: Transforming the Mesopotamian Legacy," *Bulletin of the Canadian Society for Mesopotamian Studies* 35: 19–27.
Root, Margaret Cool (2010), "Palace to Temple-King to Cosmos: Achaemenid Foundation Texts in Iran," in Mark J. Boda and Jamie Novotny (eds), *From the Foundations to the Crenellations: Essays on Temple Building in the Ancient Near East and Hebrew Bible*, 165–210, Münster: Ugarit-Verlag.
Root, Margaret Cool (2013), "Defining the Divine in Achaemenid Persian Kingship: The View from Bisitun," in Lynette Mitchell and Charles Melville (eds), *Every Inch a King: Comparative Studies on Kings and Kingship in the Ancient and Medieval Worlds*, 23–66, Leiden: Brill.
Root, Margaret Cool (2015), "Achaemenid Imperial Architecture: Performative Porticoes of Persepolis," in Sussan Babaie and Talinn Grigor (eds), *Persian Kingship and Architecture: Strategies of Power in Iran from the Achaemenids to the Pahlavis*, 1–64, London: I. B. Tauris.
Ropp, Cyd C. (2000), "A Hermeneutic and Rhetoric of Dreams," *Janus Head* 3 (1): np, http://www.janushead.org/3-1/cropp.cfm.
Rose, Wolter H. (2000), *Zemah and Zerubbabel: Messianic Expectations in the Early Postexilic Period*, JSOTSup 304, Sheffield: Sheffield Academic.
Rösel, Martin (2003), "Inscriptional Evidence and the Question of Genre," in Marvin A. Sweeney and Ehud Ben Zvi (eds), *The Changing Face of Form Criticism for the Twenty-First Century*, 107–21, Grand Rapids, MI: Eerdmans.
Rosenmeyer, Thomas G. (1982), *The Art of Aeschylus*, Berkeley, CA: University of California Press.
Rossi, Adriano V. (2010), "Elamite *halmarris*—vieux-Perse *dida*—est-elle vraiment une forteresse? (I)," in Maria Macuch, Dieter Weber and Desmond Durkin-Meisererernst (eds), *Ancient and Middle Iranian Studies: Proceedings of the 6th European Conference of Iranian Studies, Held in Vienna, 18–22 September 2007*, 205–18, Wiesbaden: Harrassowitz.
Roth, Martha (2005), *The Assyrian Dictionary of the University of Chicago*, Vol. 12 (P), Chicago: University of Chicago Press.

Rowland, Christopher (1982), *The Open Heaven: A Study of Apocalyptic in Judaism and Early Christianity*, London: SPCK.
Rubanovich, Julia, ed. (2015), *Orality and Textuality in the Iranian World: Patterns of Interaction across the Centuries*, Jerusalem Studies in Religion and Culture 19, Leiden: Brill.
Rudolph, Wilhelm (1976), *Haggai–Sacharja 1–8–Sacharja 9–14–Maleachi*, Kommentar zum Alten Testament XIII/4, Gütersloh: Gütersloher Verlagshaus.
Russell, James R. (2002), "Zoroastrian Notes," *Iran and the Cacasus* 6 (1/2): 1–10.
Ruyneau de Saint George, Pierre (2016), "Regarding Affects and Imagery in Dreams," *International Journal of Dream Research* 9 (1): 93–5.
Ruzicka, Stephen (2012), *Trouble in the West: Egypt and the Persian Empire 525–332 BCE*, Oxford: Oxford University Press.
Sacchi, Paolo (2004), *History of the Second Temple Period*, London: T&T Clark. First pub. 2000.
Sachs, Abraham J., and Hermann Hunger (1996), *Astronomical Diaries and Related Texts from Babylonia 3, Diaries from 164 B. C. to 61 B. C.*, Vienna: Verlag der Österreichischen Akademie der Wissenschaften.
Sack, Ronald H. (1972), *Amēl-Marduk 562–560 B.C.: A Study Based on Cuneiform, Old Testament, Greek, Latin, and Rabbinical Sources*, AOATS 4, Neukirchen-Vluyn: Neukirchener Verlag.
Sandowicz, Małgorzata (2015), "More on the End of the Neo-Babylonian Empire," *JNES* 74 (2): 197–210.
Sauer, Georg (1967), "Serubbabel in der Sicht Haggais und Sacharjas," in Fritz Maass (ed.), *Das ferne und nahe Wort. Festschrift Leonhard Rost zur vollendung seines 70. Lebensjahres am 30. November 1966 gewidmet*, 199–207, Berlin: Töpelmann.
Sawyer, John F. A. (1996), *The Fifth Gospel: Isaiah in the History of Christianity*, Cambridge: Cambridge University Press.
Schaper, Joachim (2000), *Priester und Leviten im achämenidischen Juda: Studien zur Kult- und Sozialgeschichte Israels in persischer Zeit*, FAT 31, Tübingen: Mohr Siebeck.
Schaudig, Hanspeter (2001), *Die Inschriften Nabonids von Babylon und Kyros' des Grossen samt den in ihrem Umfeld entstandenen Tendenzschriften: Textausgabe und Grammatik*, AOAT 256, Münster: Ugarit-Verlag.
Schaudig, Hanspeter (2008), "'Bēl Bows, Nabû Stoops!' The Prophecy of Isaiah xlvi 1–2 as a Reflection of Babylonian 'Processional Omens'," *VT* 58: 557–72.
Schaudig, Hanspeter (2010), "The Restoration of Temples in the Neo- and Late Babylonian Periods: A Royal Prerogative as the Setting for Political Argument," in Mark J. Boda and Jamie Novotny (eds), *From the Foundations to the Crenellations: Essays on Temple Building in the Ancient Near East and Hebrew Bible*, 141–64, Münster: Ugarit-Verlag.
Scheil, Vincent (1929), *Inscriptions des Achéménides a Suse*, Mémoires de la Mission Archéologique de Perse 21, Paris: Librairie Ernest Leroux.
Scheil, Vincent (1930), *Actes Juridiques Susiens, No 1 à No 165*, Mémoires de la Délégation Archeologique en Perse 22, Paris: Ernest Leroux.
Scheuer, Blaženka (2008), *The Return of YHWH: The Tension between Deliverance and Repentance in Isaiah 40–55*, BZAW 377, Berlin: de Gruyter.
Schipper, Jeremy (2013), "Interpreting the Lamb Imagery in Isaiah 53," *JBL* 132 (2): 315–25.
Schmidt, Erich F. (1953), *Persepolis I: Structures, Reliefs, Inscriptions*, OIP 68, Chicago: University of Chicago Press.

Schmidt, Erich F. (1957), *Persepolis II: Contents of the Treasury and Other Discoveries*, OIP 69, Chicago: University of Chicago Press.

Schmidt, Erich F. (1970), *Persepolis III: The Royal Tombs and Other Monuments*, OIP 70, Chicago: University of Chicago Press.

Schmitt, Rüdiger (2000), *The Old Persian Inscriptions of Naqsh-i Rustam and Persepolis*, CII I.1.2, London: SOAS.

Schmitt, Rüdiger (2005), "Personal Names, Iranian iii: Achaemenid Period," *EncIr* Online edition: http://www.iranica.com/articles/personal-names-iranian-iii-achaemenid.

Schmitt, Rüdiger (2009), *Die altpersischen Inschriften der Achaimeniden: editio minor mit Deutscher Übersetzung*, Wiesbaden: Reichert.

Schmitt, Rüdiger (2014), "Mixed Creatures and the Assyrian Influence on the West Semitic Glyptic Repertoire," in Izaak J. de Hulster and Joel M. LeMon (eds), *Image, Text, Exegesis: Iconographic Interpretation and the Hebrew Bible*, 19–28, LHBOTS, London: Bloomsbury Academic.

Schneider, Adam, and G. William Domhoff, *DreamBank*, University of California, Santa Cruz, http://dreambank.net/.

Schökel, Louis Alonso (1987), "Isaiah," in Robert Alter and Frank Kermode (eds), *Literary Guide to the Bible*, 165–84, Cambridge, MA: Harvard University Press.

Schredl, Michael (2010a), "Dream Content Analysis: Basic Principles," *International Journal of Dream Research* 3 (1): 65–73.

Schredl, Michael (2010b), "Dreaming and Waking: Phenomenological and Biological Differences," *International Journal of Dream Research* 3 (1): 46–8.

Schredl, Michael (2015), "The Continuity between Waking and Dreaming: Empirical Research and Clinical Implications," in Milton Kramer and Myron L. Gluckson (eds), *Dream Research: Contributions to Clinical Practice*, 27–37, New York: Taylor & Francis.

Schredl, Michael, Tadas Stumbrys, and Daniel Erlacher (2016), "Dream Recall, Nightmare Frequency, and Spirituality," *Dreaming* 26 (1): 1–9.

Schwartz, Daniel R. (1990), "On Some Papyri and Josephus' Sources and Chronology for the Persian Period," *JSJ* 21 (2): 175–99.

Schwartz, Martin (2005), "Apollo and Khshathrapati, the Median Nergal, at Xanthos," *BAI* 19: 145–50.

Scolnic, Benjamin Edidin (2008), *Thy Brother's Blood: The Maccabees and Dynastic Morality in the Hellenistic World*, Studies in Judaism, Lanham, MD: University Press of America.

Scott, James C. (1985), *Weapons of the Weak: Everyday Forms of Peasant Resistance*, New Haven, CT: Yale University Press.

Scudder, Thayer, and Elizabeth Colson (1982), "From Welfare to Development: A Conceptual Framework for the analysis of a Dislocated People," in Art Hanson and Anthony Oliver-Smith (eds), *Involuntary Migration and Resettlement: The Problems and Responses of Dislocated People*, 267–88, Boulder, CO: Westview.

Scurlock, JoAnn, and Richard H. Beal (2013), *Creation and Chaos: A Reconsideration of Herman Gunkel's Chaoskampf Hypothesis*, Winona Lake, IN: Eisenbrauns.

Seeligmann, Isac Leo (1948), *The Septuagint Version of Isaiah: A Discussion of its Problems*, Leiden: Brill. Reprinted (pp. 119–294) by Mohr Siebeck in 2004.

Seitz, Christopher R. (1991), *Zion's Final Destiny: The Development of the Book of Isaiah: A Reassessment of Isaiah 36–39*, Minneapolis: Fortress.

Seitz, Christopher R. (1996), "How Is the Prophet Isaiah Present in the Latter Half of the Book? The Logic of Chapters 40–66 within the Book of Isaiah," *JBL* 115 (2): 219–40.

Sekunda, N. V. (2010), "Changes in Achaemenid Royal Dress," in John Curtis and St. John Simpson (eds), *The World of Achaemenid Persia: History, Art and Society in Iran and the Ancient Near East*, 255–74, London: I. B. Tauris.

Seri, Andrea (2012), "The Role of Creation in *Enūma eliš*," *JANER* 12 (1): 4–29.

Seybold, Klaus (1972), "Die Königserwartung bei den Propheten Haggai und Sacharja," *Judaica* 28 (2): 69–78.

Shahbazi, A. Shapur (1992), "Clothing ii. In the Median and Achaemenid Periods," *EncIr* 5 (7): 723–37, http://www.iranicaonline.org/articles/clothing-ii.

Shanon, Benny, and Rivka Eiferman (1984), "Dream-Reporting Discourse," *Text: An Interdisciplinary Journal for the Study of Discourse* 4 (4): 369–79.

Sharma, R. S. (1993), "The Aryan Problem and the Horse," *Social Scientist* 21 (7/8): 3–16.

Sharp, Carolyn J. (2009), "(Re)Inscribing Power through Torah Teaching: Rhetorical Pedagogy in the Servant Songs of Deutero-Isaiah," in Stephen L. Cook and John J. Ahn (eds), *Thus Says the Lord: Essays on the Former and Latter Prophets in Honor of Robert R. Wilson*, 167–78, London: T&T Clark.

Shayegan, M. Rahim (2012), *Aspects of History and Epic in Ancient Iran: From Gaumāta to Wahnām*, Hellenic Studies 52, Cambridge, MA: Center for Hellenic Studies.

Shenkar, Michael (2007), "Temple Architecture in the Iranian World before the Macedonian Conquest," *Iran and the Caucasus* 11 (2): 169–94.

Sherwin, Simon J. (2003), "In Search of Trees: Isaiah XLIV 14 and its Implications," *VT* 53: 514–29.

Shrimpton, Gordon S. (1997), *History and Memory in Ancient Greece*, Montreal: McGill-Queen's University Press.

Shushan, Gregory (2006), "Greek and Egyptian Dreams in Two Ptolemaic Archives: Individual and Cultural Layers of Meaning," *Dreaming* 16 (2): 129–42.

Siddiq, Muhammad (1995), "On Ropes of Memory: Narrating the Palestinian Refugees," in E. Valentine Daniel and John Chr. Knudsen (eds), *Mistrusting Refugees*, 87–101, Berkeley, CA: University of California Press.

Siljanen, Esko (2017), *Judeans of Egypt in the Persian period (539–332 BCE) in Light of the Aramaic Documents*, PhD diss., University of Helsinki.

Silver, Edward (2014), "Performing Domination/Theorizing Power: Israelite Prophecy as a Political Discourse beyond the Conflict Model," *JANER* 14 (2): 186–216.

Silverman, Jason M. (2010), "On Cultural and Religious Influence," in Jason M. Silverman (ed.), *A Land Like Your Own: Traditions of Israel and Their Reception*, 1–12, Eugene, OR: Pickwick.

Silverman, Jason M. (2011), "Iranian Influence on Judaism," *Bible and Interpretation Website*, http://www.bibleinterp.com/articles/sil358017.shtml.

Silverman, Jason M. (2012), *Persepolis and Jerusalem: Iranian Influence on the Apocalyptic Hermeneutic*, LHBOTS 558, London: T&T Clark.

Silverman, Jason M. (2013a), "It's a Craft! It's a Cavern! It's a Castle! Yima's *Vara*, Iranian Flood Myths, and Jewish Apocalyptic Traditions," in Jason M. Silverman (ed.), *Opening Heaven's Floodgates: The Genesis Flood Narrative, Its Contexts and Reception*, 191–230, Piscataway, NJ: Gorgias.

Silverman, Jason M. (2013b), "Noah's Flood as Myth and Reception: An Introduction," in Jason M. Silverman (ed.), *Opening Heaven's Floodgates*, 1–29, Piscataway, NJ: Gorgias.

Silverman, Jason M. (2014a), "Vetting the Priest in Zech 3: The Satan between Divine and Achaemenid Administrations," *JHebS* 14 (6): 1–27, http://www.jhsonline.org/Articles/article_200.pdf.

Silverman, Jason M. (2014b), "Yes We Can (Hyperbolize)! Ideals, Rhetoric, and Tradition Transmission," *Journal of the Bible and its Reception* 1 (2): 263–84.

Silverman, Jason M. (2015a), "From Remembering to Expecting the 'Messiah': Achaemenid Kingship as (Re)formulating Apocalyptic Expectations of David," in Jason M. Silverman and Caroline Waerzeggers (eds), *Political Memory in and after the Persian Empire*, 419–46, Atlanta. GA: SBL.

Silverman, Jason M. (2015b), "Judaeans under Persian Forced Labor and Migration Policies," *Anabasis* 6: 14–34.

Silverman, Jason M. (2015c), "Sheshbazzar, a Judaean or a Babylonian? A Note on His Identity," in Jonathan Stökl and Caroline Waerzeggers (eds), *Exile and Return: The Babylonian Context*, 308–21, BZAW 478, Berlin: de Gruyter.

Silverman, Jason M. (2016a), "*Pax persica* ja juudealaiset," in Niko Huttunen and Nina Nikki (eds), *Sota, Rauha ja Raamattu*, 115–42, Helsinki: Suomen Eksegeettinen Seura.

Silverman, Jason M. (2016b), "'We May Be Through with the Past…': *Magnolia*, the Exodus Plague Narrative, and Tradition History," *Religion and the Arts* 20 (4): 459–90.

Silverman, Jason M. (2016c), "Was There an Achamenid 'Theology' of Kingship?" in Diana V. Edelman, Anne Fitzpatrick-McKinley and Philippe Guillaume (eds) *Religion in the Persian Period: Emerging Trends Judaisms and Other Trends*, 160–85, ORA 17, Tübingen: Mohr Siebeck.

Silverman, Jason M. (2017), "Achamenid Creation and Second Isaiah," *Journal of Persianate Studies* 10 (1): 26–48.

Silverman, Jason M. (2018), "Achaemenid Sources and the Problem of Genre," in Sebastian Fink and Robert Rollinger (eds), *Conceptualizing Past, Present, and Future*, 261–78, Münster: Ugarit-Verlag.

Silverman, Jason M. (2019), "Are the Concepts of 'Torah' and 'the Prophets' Texts or Something Else? Educational, Media, and Elite Contexts from the Persian Empire Onwards," in Raimo Hakola, Jessi Orpana, and Paavo Huotari (eds), *Scriptures in the Making: Texts and Their Transmission in Late Second Temple Judaism*, Leuven: Peeters.

Silverman, Jason M. (forthcoming a), "The *Pax Persica* and the Judaeans."

Silverman, Jason M. (forthcoming b), "Social Scientific Approaches to Exile," in Tero Alstola, Jonathan Stökl, Jason M. Silverman, Caroline Waerzeggers and Anne-Mareike Wetter, *Handbook of the Babylonian Exile*.

Simcox, Carroll E. (1937), "The Role of Cyrus in Deutero-Isaiah," *JAOS* 57 (2): 158–71.

Sims-Williams, Nicholas (1981), "The Final Paragraph of the Tomb-Inscription of Darius I (DNb, 50–60): The Old Persian Text in the Light of the Aramaic Version," *BSOAS* 44: 1–7.

Sinclair, Lawrence A. (1975), "Redaction of Zechariah 1–8," *BR* 20: 36–47.

Sjöberg, Åke W. (1973), "Nungal in the Ekur," *AfO* 24: 19–46.

Skehan, Patrick W., and Eugene Ulrich (1997), "Isaiah," in Eugene Ulrich, Frank Moore Cross, Russell E. Fuller, Judith E. Sanderson, Patrick W. Skehan and Emmanuel Tov (eds), *Qumran Cave 4.X: The Prophets*, 1–144, Oxford: Clarendon.

Skjærvø, Prods Oktor (1994), "Achaemenid **Vispašiyātiš*, Sasanian *Wispšād*," *SIr* 23 (1): 79–80.

Skjærvø, Prods Oktor (1998), "Royalty in Early Iranian Literature," in Nicholas Sims-Williams (ed.), *Proceedings of the Third European Conference of Iranian Studies, Cambridge, 11–15 September 1995*, 99–108, Wiesbaden: Reichert.

Skjærvø, Prods Oktor (1999), "Avestan Quotations in Old Persian? Literary Sources of the Old Persian Inscriptions," in Shaul Shaked and Amnon Netzer (eds), *Irano-Judaica IV*, 1–64, Jerusalem: Ben Zvi Institute.

Skjærvø, Prods Oktor (2002), *An Introduction to Old Persian*, rev. and exp. 2nd ed., https://www.fas.harvard.edu/~iranian/OldPersian/ (cited by permission).

Skjærvø, Prods Oktor (2005), "The Achaemenids and the Avesta," in Vesta Sarkhosh Curtis and Sarah Stewart (eds), *Birth of the Persian Empire: The Idea of Iran I*, 52–84, London: I. B. Tauris.

Skjærvø, Prods Oktor (2005–2006), "The Importance of Orality for the Study of Old Iranian Literature and Myth," *Nāme-ye Irān Bāstān* 5 (1–2): 9–31.

Skjærvø, Prods Oktor (2009), "Old Iranian: Avestan and Old Persian," in Gernot Windfuhr (ed.), *The Iranian Languages*, 43–195, London: Routledge.

Skjærvø, Prods Oktor (2013), "Kayāniān v. Kauui Usan, Kay-Us, Kay Kāvus," *EncIr*, http://www.iranicaonline.org/articles/kayanian-v.

Skjærvø, Prods Oktor (2014), "Achaemenid Religion," *Religion Compass* 8 (6): 175–87.

Slanski, Kathryn (2007), "The Mesopotamian 'Rod and Ring': Icon of Righteous Kingship and Balance of Power between Palace and Temple," in Harriet Crawford (ed.), *Regime Change in the Ancient Near East and Egypt from Sargon of Agade to Saddam Hussein*, 37–59, Oxford: Oxford University Press.

Slings, S. R. (1990–2), "Orality and the Poet's Profession," *AAASH* 33: 9–14.

Smith, Carol (1998), "'Queenship' in Israel? The Cases of Bathsheba, Jezebel and Athaliah," in John Day (ed.), *King and Messiah in Israel and the Ancient Near East*, 142–63, Sheffield: Sheffield Academic.

Smith, Mark S. (1997), *Ugaritic Narrative Poetry*, WAW 9, Atlanta, GA: Scholars Press.

Smith, Mark S. (2001), *The Origins of Biblical Monotheism: Israel's Polytheistic Background and the Ugaritic Texts*, Oxford: Oxford University Press.

Smith, Morton (1963), "II Isaiah and the Persians," *JAOS* 83: 415–21.

Smith, Morton (1990), "Bible II: Persian Elements in the Bible," *EncIr* 4: 200–203.

Smith, Ralph L. (1984), *Micah–Malachi*, WBC 32, Waco, TX: Word.

Smith[-Christopher], Daniel L. (1989), *The Religion of the Landless*, Bloomington, IN: Meyer-Stone Books.

Smith[-Christopher], Daniel L. (1997), "Reassessing the Historical and Sociological Impact of the Babylonian Exile (597/587–539 BCE)," in James M. Scott (ed.), *Exile: Old Testament, Jewish, and Christian Conceptions*, 7–36, Leiden: Brill.

Smith[-Christopher], Daniel L. (2002), *A Biblical Theology of Exile*, Overtures to Biblical Theology, Minneapolis: Fortress.

Smith[-Christopher], Daniel L. (2011), "Reading War and Trauma: Suggestions Toward a Social-Psychological Exegesis of Exile and War in Biblical Texts," in Brad E. Kelle, Frank Ritchel Ames and Jacob L. Wright (eds), *Interpreting Exile: Displacement and Deportation in Biblical and Modern Contexts*, 253–74, Atlanta, GA: SBL.

Smith[-Christopher], Daniel L. (2012), "Reading Exile Then: Reconsidering the methodological Debates for Biblical Analysis in Dialogue with Sociological and Literary Analysis," in John J. Ahn and Jill Middlemas (eds), *By the Irrigation Canals of Babylon: Approaches to the Study of the Exile*, 139–57, New York: T&T Clark.

Snyman, Gerrie (2011), "Why Asa was not Deemed Good Enough: A Decolonial Reading of 2 Chronicles 14–16," in Louis Jonker (ed.), *Texts, Contexts and Readings in Postexilic Literature: Explorations into Historiography and Identity Negotiation in Hebrew Bible and Related Texts*, 241–68, Tübingen: Mohr Siebeck.

Socin, A., and Consul Wetzstein. 1891), "Über die Siebe in Syrien," *ZDPV* 14: 1–7.

Soden, Wolfram von (1985), *Akkadisches Handwörterbuch*, 3 vols, Wiesbaden: Harrassowitz.
Sommer, Benjamin D. (1998), *A Prophet Reads Scripture: Allusion in Isaiah 40–66*, Contraversions, Jews and other Differences, Stanford, CA: Stanford University Press.
Sonik, Karen (2013), "From Hesiod's Abyss to Ovid's *rudis indigestaque moles*: Chaos and Cosmos in the Babylonian 'Epic of Creation'," in JoAnn Scurlock (ed.), *Creation and Cosmos*, 1–25, Winona Lake, IN: Eisenbrauns.
Soomekh, Saba (2009), "Iranian Jewish Women: Domesticating Religion and Appropriating Zoroastrian Religion in Ritual Life," *Nashim* 18: 13–38.
Southwood, Katherine E. (2015), "The Impact of the Second and Third Generation Returnees as a Model for Understanding the Post-Exilic Context," in Caroline Waerzeggers and Jonathan Stökl (eds), *Exile and Return*, BZAW 478, Berlin: de Gruyter.
Spek, Robartus J. van der (2003), "Darius III, Alexander the Great and Babylonian Scholarship," in Wouter Henkelman and Amélie Kuhrt (eds), *A Persian Perspective: Essays in Memory of Heleen Sancisi-Weerdenburg*, 289–302, AchHist, Leiden: NINO.
Spek, Robartus J. van der (2014), "Cyrus the Great, Exiles and Foreign Gods: A Comparison of Assyrian and Persian Policies on Subject Nations," in Wouter Henkelman, Charles E. Jones, Michael Kozuh and Christopher Woods (eds), *Extraction and Control: Studies in Honor of Matthew Stolper*, 233–64, Chicago: University of Chicago Press.
Spencer, Bradley J. (2000), "The 'New Deal' for Post-exilic Judah in Isaiah 41:17–20," *ZAW* 112: 583–97.
Spencer, Neal (2014), "Priests and Temples: Pharaonic," in Alan B. Lloyd (ed.), *A Companion to Ancient Egypt*, 255–73, Malden, MA: Wiley Blackwell.
Spieckermann, Hermann (2004), "The Conception and Prehistory of the Idea of Vicarious Suffering in the Old Testament," in Bernd Janowski and Peter Stuhlmacher (eds), *The Suffering Servant: Isaiah 53 in Jewish and Christian Sources*, 1–15, Grand Rapids, MI: Eerdmans.
Spilsbury, Paul, and Chris Seeman (2017), *Judean Antiquities 11*, Flavius Josephus Translation and Commentary 6a, Leiden: Brill.
Spoormaker, V. I., M. Czisch, and M. Dresler (2010), "Lucid and Non-lucid Dreaming: Thinking in Networks," *International Journal of Dream Research* 3 (1): 49–51.
Stamm, Johann Jakob (1939), *Akkadische Namengebung*, MVÄG 44, Leipzig: Hinrichs.
States, Bert O. (1993), *Dreaming and Storytelling*, Ithaca, NY: Cornell University Press.
Staubli, Thomas (2015a), "Judith's Victory Celebration and the Iconography of Twigs in Judith 15:12–13," in Izaak J. de Hulster, Brent A. Strawn and Ryan P. Bonfiglio (eds), *Iconographic Exegesis of the Hebrew Bible/Old Testament: An Introduction to its Method and Practice*, 329–47, Göttingen: Vandenhoeck & Ruprecht.
Staubli, Thomas (2015b), "What Do You See? Reading Zechariah's YHWH-Vision (4:1–14) in Light of Southern Levantine Lunar Iconography," in Izaak J. de Hulster, Brent A. Strawn and Ryan P. Bonfiglio (eds), *Iconographic Exegesis of the Hebrew Bible/Old Testament: An Introduction to Its Method and Practice*, 217–26, Göttingen: Vandenhoeck & Ruprecht.
Stausberg, Michael (2002–2004), *Die Religion Zarathushtras: Geschichte–Gegenwart– Rituale*, 3 vols, Stuttgart: Kohlhammer.
Stausberg, Michael (2011), *Religion and Tourism: Crossroads, Destinations and Encounters*, London: Routledge.
Stead, Michael R. (2009), *The Intertextuality of Zechariah 1–8*, LHBOTS 506, London: T&T Clark.

Stead, Michael R. (2014), "The Interrelationship between Vision and Oracle in Zechariah 1–6," in Elizabeth R. Hayes and Lena-Sofia Tiemeyer (eds), *'I Lifted My Eyes and Saw': Reading Dream and Vision Reports in the Hebrew Bible*, 148–68, London: Bloomsbury Academic.

Steele, John M., and F. R. Stephenson (1998), "Canon of Solar and Lunar Eclipses for Babylon: 750 BC–AD 1," *AfO* 44–45: 195–209.

Steen, Eveline van der (2011), "Empires and Farmers," in Lester L. Grabbe and Oded Lipschits (eds), *Judah between East and West: The Transition from Persian to Greek Rule (ca. 400–200 BCE)*, 210–24, London: T&T Clark.

Steiner, Richard C. (2006), "Bishlam's Archival Search Report in Nehemiah's Archive: Multiple Introductions and Reverse Chronological Order as Clues to the Origin of the Aramaic Letters in Ezra 4–6," *JBL* 125 (4): 641–85.

Stephens, John (2013), *The Dreams and Visions of Aelius Aristides: A Case-Study in the History of Religions*, Perspectives on Philosophy and Religious Thought 10, Piscataway, NJ: Gorgias.

Steve, M.-J (1967), *Tchoga Zanbil (Dur-Untash) III: Textes élamites et eccadiens de Tchoga Zanbil*, Mémoires de la Délégation Archeologique en Iran 41, Paris: Paul Geuthner.

Stock, Fremke (2010), "Home and Memory," in Kim Knott and Seán McLoughlan (eds), *Diasporas: Concepts, Intersections, Identities*, 24–8, London: Zed Books.

Stökl, Jonathan (2012), *Prophecy in the Ancient Near East: A Philological and Sociological Comparison*, CHANE 56, Leiden: Brill.

Stolper, Matthew W. (1985), *Entrepreneurs and Empire: The Murašû Archive, the Murašû firm, and Persian Rule in Babylonia*, Uitgaven van het Nederlands Historisch-Archaeologisch Institute te Istanbul 54, Istanbul: Nederlands historisch-archaeologisch Institute te Istanbul.

Stolper, Matthew W. (1989), "The Governor of Babylon and Across-the-River in 486 B.C.," *JNES* 48 (4): 283–305.

Stolper, Matthew W. (1999), "Iurindu the Maiden, Bēl-ittannu the Dreamer, and Artaritassu the King," in Barbara Böck, Eva Cancik-Kirschbaum and Thomas Richter (eds), *Munuscula Mesopotamica. Festschrift für Johannes Renger*, 591–8, Münster: Ugarit-Verlag.

Stolper, Matthew W. (2003), "'No-one has Exact Information Except for You': Communication between Babylon and Uruk in the First Achaemenid Reigns," in Wouter Henkelman and Amélie Kuhrt (eds), *A Persian Perspective: Essays in Memory of Heleen Sancisi-Weerdenburg*, 265–87, AchHist, Leiden: NINO.

Stolper, Matthew W. (2006), "Parysatis in Babylon," in Ann K. Guinan, Maria deJ. Ellis, A. J. Ferrara, Sally M. Freedman, Matthew T. Rutz, Leonhard Sassmannshausen, Steve Tinney and Matthew W. Waters (eds), *'If a Man Builds a Joyful House': Assyriological Studies in Honor of Erle Verdun Leichty*, 463–72, Leiden: Brill.

Strabo (1930), *Geography* XV–XVI, in *The Geography of Strabo, VII*, trans. Horace Leonard Jones, LCL, London: Heinemann.

Strand, Kenneth A. (1982), "The Two Olive Trees of Zechariah 4 and Revelation 11," *AUSS* 20 (3): 257–61, http://digitalcommons.andrews.edu/auss/vol20/iss3/5.

Strawn, Brent A. (2007), "'A World Under Control': Isaiah 60 and the Apadana Reliefs from Persepolis," in Jon L. Berquist (ed.), *Approaching Yehud: New Approaches to the Study of the Persian Period*, 85–116, Leiden: Brill.

Stronach, David (1978), *Pasargadae: A Report on the Excavations*, Oxford: Clarendon.

Stronach, David (1989), "The Royal Garden at Pasargadae: Evolution and Legacy," in L. de Meyer and Ernie Haerinck (eds), *Archaeologia Iranica et Orientalis: Miscellanea in honorem Louis Vanden Berghe*, 475–502, Ghent: Peeters.

Stronach, David (1990), "The Garden as a Political Statement: Some Case Studies from the Near East in the First Millennium B.C," *BAI* (NS 4): 171–82.

Stronach, David (1997a), "Anshan and Parsa: Early Achaemenid History, Art and Architecture on the Iranian Plateau," in John E. Curtis (ed.), *Mesopotamia and Iran in the Persian Period: Conquest and Imperialism 539–331 BC. Proceedings of a Seminar in Memory of Vladimir G. Lukonin*, 35–53, London: British Museum.

Stronach, David (1997b), "Darius at Pasargadae: A Neglected Source for the History of Early Persia," in Marie-Françoise Boussac (ed.), *Recherches récentes sur l'Empire achéménide*, 351–63, Lyon: Société des Amis de la Bibliothèque Salomon Reinach.

Stronach, David (2002), "Icons of Dominion: Review Scenes at Til Barip and Persepolis," *IrAnt* 37: 373–402.

Stronach, David (2003), "Early Achaemenid Iran: New Considerations," in William G. Dever and Seymour Gitin (eds), *Symbiosis, Symbolism, and the Power of the Past: Canaan, Ancient Israel, and Their Neighbors from the Late Bronze Age Through Roman Palestina*, 133–44, Winona Lake, IN: Eisenbrauns.

Stronk, Jan P. (2010), *Ctesias' Persian History Part I: Introduction, Text, Translation*, Reihe Geschichte 2, Düsseldorf: Wellem Verlag.

Süring, Margit L. (1980), *Horn-Motifs in the Hebrew Bible and Related Ancient Near Eastern Literature and Iconography*, Berrien Springs: Andrews University Press.

Süring, Margit L. (1984), "The Horn-Motifs of the Bible and the Ancient Near East," *AUSS* 22 (3): 327–40.

Sussman, Varda (2016), *Oil-lamps in the Holy Land: Saucer Lamps: From the beginning to the Hellenistic Period: Collections of the Israel Antiquities Authority*, BAR International Series 1598, Oxford: BAR. Orig. pub. 2007.

Sweeney, Marvin A. (2000), *The Twelve Prophets*, Berit Olam, Collegeville, MN: Liturgical Press.

Sweeney, Marvin A. (2001), *King Josiah of Judah: The Lost Messiah of Israel*, Oxford: Oxford University Press.

Sweeney, Marvin A. (2003), "Zechariah's Debate with Isaiah," in Marvin A. Sweeney and Ehud Ben Zvi (eds), *The Changing Face of Form Criticism for the Twenty-First Century*, 335–50, Grand Rapids, MI: Eerdmans.

Sweeney, Marvin A. (2015), "Form and Eschatology in the Book of the Twelve Prophets," in Mark J. Boda, Michael H. Floyd and Colin M. Toffelmire (eds), *The Book of the Twelve and the New Form Criticism*, 137–62, Atlanta, GA: SBL.

Szpakowska, Kasia (2003), *Behind Closed Eyes: Dreams and Nightmares in Ancient Egypt*, Swansea: Classical Press of Wales.

Szpakowska, Kasia (2014), "Religion in Society: Pharaonic," in Alan B. Lloyd (ed.), *A Companion to Ancient Egypt*, 507–25, Malden, MA: Wiley Blackwell.

Tainter, Joseph A. (1994), *The Collapse of Complex Societies*, New Studies in Archaeology, Cambridge: Cambridge University Press. First pub. 1988.

Tal, Oren (2005), "Some Remarks on the Coastal Plain of Palestine under Achaemenid Rule—an Archaeological Synopsis," in Pierre Briant and Rémy Boucharlat (eds), *L'archéologie de l'empire achémémenide: nouvelles recherches*, 71–96, Persika 6, Paris: De Boccard.

Talon, Philippe (2005), *The Standard Babylonian Creation Myth Enūma Eliš*, SAA CT 4, Helsinki: The Neo-Assyrian Text Corpus Project.

Tavernier, Jan (2007), *Iranica in the Achaemenid Period (ca. 550–330 B.C.): Lexicon of Old Iranian Proper Names and Loanwords, Attested in Non-Iranian Texts*, OLA 158, Leuven: Peeters.

Tavernier, Jan (2008), "Multilingualism in the Fortification and Treasury Archives," in Pierre Briant, Wouter F. M. Henkelman and Matthew W. Stolper (eds), *L'archive des Fortifications de Persépolis: État des questions et perspectives de recherches*, 59–86, Paris: Éditions de Boccard.

Taylor, Helen (2013), "Refugees, the State and the Concept of Home," *Refugee Survey Quarterly* 32 (2): 130–52.

Tedlock, Barbara (1989a), "Dreaming and Dream Research," in Barbara Tedlock (ed.), *Dreaming: Anthropological and Psychological Interpretations*, 1–30, Cambridge: Cambridge University Press.

Tedlock, Barbara, ed. (1989b), *Dreaming: Anthropological and Psychological Interpretations*, Schools of American Research Advanced Seminar Series, Cambridge: Cambridge University Press.

Teixidor, Javier (1978), "The Aramaic Text in the Trilingual Stele from Xanthus," *JNES* 37 (2): 181–5.

Ter-Martirossov, Felix I (2001), "The Typology of the Columnar Structures of Armenia in the Achaemenid Period," in Inge Nielsen (ed.), *The Royal Palace Institution in the First Millennium BC: Regional Development and Cultural Interchange between East and West*, 155–64, Athens: Danish Institute at Athens.

Thompson, Georgina (1965), "Iranian Dress in the Achaemenian Period: Problems concerning the Kandys and Other Garments," *Iran* 3: 121–6.

Thompson, R. Campbell (1949), *A Dictionary of Assyrian Botany*, London: The British Academy.

Thompson, Stith (1955–58), *Motif-Index of Folk-Literature*, rev. ed., 6 vols, Bloomington, IN: Indiana University Press.

Tiemeyer, Lena-Sofia (2003), "The Guilty Priesthood (Zech 3)," in Christopher Tuckett (ed.), *The Book of Zechariah and Its Influence*, 1–20, Aldershot: Ashgate.

Tiemeyer, Lena-Sofia (2011a), *For the Comfort of Zion: The Geographical and Theological Location of Isaiah 40–55*, VTSup 139, Leiden: Brill.

Tiemeyer, Lena-Sofia (2011b), "Lamentations in Isaiah 40–55," in R. A. Parry and Heath A. Thomas (eds), *Great is Thy Faithfulness? Reading Lamentations as Sacred Scripture*, 55–63, Eugene, OR: Pickwick Press.

Tiemeyer, Lena-Sofia (2015), *Zechariah and His Visions: An Exegetical Study of Zechariah's Vision Report*, LHBOTS 605, London: T&T Clark.

Tiemeyer, Lena-Sofia (2016), *Zechariah's Vision Report and Its Earliest Interpreters: A Redaction-Critical Study of Zechariah 1–8*, LHBOTS 626, London: Bloomsbury T&T Clark.

Tigchelaar, Eibert J. C. (1996), *The Prophets of Old and the Day of the End: Zechariah, the Book of Watchers, and Apocalyptic*, Leiden: Brill.

Tilia, Ann Britt (1972–78), *Studies and Restorations at Persepolis and Other Sites of Fars*, 2 vols, Rome: Istituto Italiano per il Medio ed Estermo Oriente.

Tolini, Gauthier (2011), *La Babylonie et l'Iran: Les Relations d'Une Province avec le coeur de l'Empire Achéménide*, PhD diss., École doctorale d'Histoire, Sorbonne, Paris.

Toorn, Karel van der (2000), "Mesopotamian Prophecy between Immanence and Transcendence: a Comparison of Old Babylonian and Neo-Assyrian Prophecy," in Martti Nissinen (ed.), *Prophecy in its Ancient Near Eastern Context*, 71–87, Atlanta, GA: SBL.

Toorn, Karel van der (2016), "Eshem-Bethel and Herem-Bethel: New Evidence from Amherst Papyrus 63," *ZAW* 128 (4): 668–80.

Tranquillo, Nicholas, ed. (2014), *Dream Consciousness: Allan Hobson's New Approach to the Brain and Its Mind*, Vienna Circle Institute Yearbook 3, Heidelberg: Springer.

Treister, Mikail (2010), "'Achaemenid' and 'Achaemenid-inspired' Goldware and Silverware, Jewellery and Arms and their Imitations to the North of the Achaemenid Empire," in Jens Nieling and Ellen Rehm (eds), *Achaemenid Impact in the Black Sea Communication of Powers*, 223–79, Aarhus: Aarhus University Press.

Tuplin, Christopher (1987a), "The Administration of the Achaemenid Empire," in Ian Carradice (ed.), *Coinage and Administration in the Athenian and Persian Empires: The Ninth Oxford Symposium on Coinage and Monetary History [held St. Hilda's College in April 1986]*, 109–58, Oxford: BAR.

Tuplin, Christopher (1987b), "Xenophon and the Garrisons of the Achaemenid Empire," *AMIT* 20: 167–245.

Tuplin, Christopher (1988), "Persian Garrisons in Xenophon and Other Sources," in Amélie Kuhrt and Heleen Sancisi-Weerdenburg (eds), *Method and Theory*, 67–70, AchHist 3, Leiden: NINO.

Tuplin, Christopher (1991), "Darius' Suez Canal and Persian Imperialism," in Heleen Sancisi-Weerdenburg and Amélie Kuhrt (eds), *Achaemenid History VI*, 237–83, Leiden: NINO.

Tuplin, Christopher (1996), *Achaemenid Studies*, Historia 99, Stuttgart: Franz Steiner.

Tuplin, Christopher (2005), "Darius' Accession in (the) Media," in Christopher Mee and Elizabeth Slater (eds), *Writing and Ancient Near Eastern Society* Piotr Bienkowski, 217–44, London: T&T Clark.

Tuplin, Christopher (2007), "Treacherous Hearts and Upright Tiaras: the Achaemenid King's Head-Dress," in Christopher Tuplin (ed.), *Persian Responses: Political and Cultural Interaction with(in) the Achaemenid Empire*, 67–97, Swansea: Classical Press of Wales.

Tuplin, Christopher (2015), "The Justice of Darius: Reflections on the Achaemenid Empire as a Rule-Bound Environment," in Anne Fitzpatrick-McKinley (ed.), *Assessing Biblical and Classical Sources for the Reconstruction of Persian Influence, History and Culture*, 73–126, CleO 10, Wiesbaden: Harrassowitz.

Tweed, Thomas A. (1997), *Our Lady of the Exile: Diasporic Religion at a Cuban Catholic Shrine in Miami*, Religion in America, Oxford: Oxford University Press.

Uehlinger, Christoph (1994), "Die Frau im Efa (Sach 5,5–11): Eine Programmvision von der Abschiebung der Göttin," *Bibel und Kirche* 49 (2): 93–103.

Ulfgard, Håkan (1998), *The Story of Sukkot: The Setting, Shaping, and Sequel of the Biblical Feast of Tabernacles*, Beiträge zur Geschichte der biblischen Exegese 34, Tübingen: Mohr Siebeck.

Ulrich, Eugene, and Peter W. Flint (2010), *Qumran Cave 1.II: The Isaiah Scrolls*, 2 vols, DJD 32, Oxford: Clarendon.

Utas, Mats (1997), *Assiduous Exile: Liberian Refugees in Danane, Ivory Coast*, Working Papers in Cultural Anthropology 6, Uppsala: Uppsala University Department of Cultural Anthropology.

Valkama, Kirsi (2013), *Judah in the Mid-Sixth Century BCE: Archaeological Evidence for a Post-Collapse Society*, PhD diss., University of Helsinki.

Vallat, François (1997), "La caractère funéraire de la *ziggurat* en Elam," *N.A.B.U* 1997-1: 36–7.

Vallat, François (1998), "Elam vi. Elamite Religion," *EncIr* 8 (3–4): 335–42, http://www.iranicaonline.org/articles/elam-vi.
Vallat, François (2013a), "Darius: The Great King," in Jean Perrot (ed.), *The Palace of Darius at Susa: The Great Royal Residence of Achaemenid Persia*, 29–52, London: I. B. Tauris.
Vallat, François (2013b), "The Main Achaemenid Inscriptions of Susa," in Jean Perrot (ed.), *The Palace of Darius at Susa: The Great Royal Residence of Achaemenid Persia*, 281–95, London: I. B. Tauris.
Vanderhooft, David (1999), *The Neo-Babylonian Empire and Babylon in the Latter Prophets*, HSM 59, Atlanta, GA: Scholars Press.
Vanderhooft, David (2006), "Cyrus II, Liberator or Conqueror? Ancient Historiography concerning Cyrus in Babylon," in Oded Lipschits and Manfred Oeming (eds), *Judah and the Judeans in the Persian Period*, 351–72, Winona Lake, IN: Eisenbrauns.
Vanderkam, James C. (2004), *From Joshua to Caiaphas: High Priests After the Exile*, Minneapolis: Fortress.
Veblen, Thorstein (1915), *The Leisure Class: An Economic Study of Institutions*, 2nd ed., New York: MacMillan. First pub. 1899.
Vittmann, Günter (1998), *Der Demotische Papyrus Rylands 9*, 2 vols, Ägypten und Altes Testament 38, Wiesbaden: Harrassowitz.
Vittmann, Günter (2011), "Ägypten zur Zeit der Perserherrschaft," in Robert Rollinger, Brigitte Truschnegg and Reinhold Bichler (eds), *Herodot und das Persische Weltreich*, 373–430, CleO, Wiesbaden: Harrassowitz.
Vogelsang, W. J. (1992), *The Rise and Organization of the Achaemenid Empire: The Eastern Iranian Evidence*, Leiden: Brill.
Volten, Aksel (1942), *Demotische Traumdeutung: (Pap. Carlsberg XIII und XIV verso)*, Analecta Aegyptiaca 3, Copenhagen: Munksgaard.
Vorländer, Hermann (1981), "Der Monotheismus Israels als Antwort auf die Krise des Exils," in Berhard Lang (ed.), *Der einzige Gott: Die Geburt des biblischen Monotheismus*, 84–114, Munich: Kösel-Verlag.
Waerzeggers, Caroline (2003/2004), "The Babylonian Revolts against Xerxes and the 'End of Archives'," *AfO* 50: 150–73.
Waerzeggers, Caroline (2010a), "Babylonians in Susa: The Travels of Babylonian Businessmen to Susa Revisited," in Bruno Jacobs and Robert Rollinger (eds), *Der Achämenidenhof/The Achaemenid Court*, 777–813, CleO, Wiesbaden: Harrassowitz.
Waerzeggers, Caroline (2010b), *The Ezida Temple of Borsippa: Priesthood, Cult, Archives*, AchHist 15, Leiden: NINO.
Waerzeggers, Caroline (2011a), "The Babylonian Priesthood in the Long Sixth Century BC," *BICS* 54 (2): 59–70.
Waerzeggers, Caroline (2011b), "The Pious King: Royal Patronage of Temples in the Neo-Babylonian Period," in Karen Radner and Elenor Robson (eds), *Oxford Handbook of Cuneiform Cultures*, 725–51, Oxford: Oxford University Press.
Waerzeggers, Caroline (2012), "Very Cordially Hated in Babylonia? Zēria and Rēmūt in the Verse Account," *AoF* 39 (2): 316–20.
Waerzeggers, Caroline (2014a), "Locating Contact in the Babylonian Exile: Some Reflections on Tracing Judean-Babylonian Encounters in Cuneiform Texts," in Uri Gabbay and Shai Secunda (eds), *Encounters by the Rivers of Babylon: Scholarly Conversations between Jews, Iranians, and Babylonians in Antiquity*, 131–46, Tübingen: Mohr Siebeck.

Waerzeggers, Caroline (2014b), "A Statue of Darius in the Ebabbar Temple of Sippar," in Michael Kozuh, Wouter F. M. Henkelman, Charles E. Jones and Christopher Woods (eds), *Extraction and Control*, 323–9, Chicago: University of Chicago Press.

Waerzeggers, Caroline (2015a), "Babylonian Kingship in the Persian Period: Performance and Reception," in Jonathan Stökl and Caroline Waerzeggers (eds), *Exile and Return*, 181–222, Berlin: de Gruyter.

Waerzeggers, Caroline (2015b), *Marduk-remanni. Local Networks and Imperial Politics in Achaemenid Babylonia*, OLA 233, Leuven: Peeters.

Waerzeggers, Caroline (2015c), "Review Article: Laurie E. Pearce and Cornelia Wunsch, Documents of Judean Exiles and West Semites in Babylonia in the Collection of David Sofer," *STRATA: Bulletin of the Anglo-Israel Archaeological Society* 33: 179–94.

Waerzeggers, Caroline (2015d), "Facts, Propaganda, or History? Shaping Political Memory in the Nabonidus Chronicle," in Jason M. Silverman and Caroline Waerzeggers (eds), *Political Memory in and after the Persian Empire*, 95–124, ANEM 13, Atlanta, GA: SBL.

Waerzeggers, Caroline, and Michael Jursa (2008), "On the Initiation of Babylonian Priests," *Zeitschrift für Altorientalische und Biblische Rechtsgeschichte* 14: 1–23.

Waerzeggers, Caroline, and Maarja Seire, eds (2019), *Xerxes and Babylonia: The Cuneiform Evidence*, OLA 277, Leuven: Peeters 2019.

Waetzoldt, H. (1980–83), "Kopfbeckung A," in Dietz Otto Edzard (ed.), *Reallexikon Der Assyriologie und Vorderasiatischen Archäologie*, 197–203, Berlin: de Gruyter.

Walde, Christine (2001), "Sibylle (Σίβυλλα), lat. Sibylla," in Hubert Cancik and Helmuth Schneider (eds), *Der Neue Pauly Enzyklopädie der Antike*, 499–501, Stuttgart: Metzler.

Walton, John H. (2003), "The Imagery of the Substitute King Ritual in Isaiah's Fourth Servant Song," *JBL* 122 (4): 734–43.

Wasmuth, Melanie (2015), "Political Memory in the Achaemenid Empire: The Integration of Egyptian Kingship into Persian Royal Display," in Jason M. Silverman and Caroline Waerzeggers (eds), *Political Memory in and after the Persian Empire*, 203–38, ANEM 13, Atlanta, GA: SBL.

Waters, Matt (2004), "Cyrus and the Achaemenids," *Iran* 42: 91–102.

Waters, Matt (2010), "Cyrus and the Medes," in John Curtis and St. John Simpson (eds), *The World of Achaemenid Persia: History, Art and Society in Iran and the Ancient Near East*, 63–74, London: I. B. Tauris.

Waters, Matt (2014), *Ancient Persia: A Concise History of the Achaemenid Empire 550–330 BCE*, Cambridge: Cambridge University Press.

Watson, Rebecca S. (2005), *Chaos Uncreated: A Reassessment of the Theme of 'Chaos' in the Hebrew Bible*, BZAW 341, Berlin: de Gruyter.

Watson, Wilfred G. E. (1984), *Classical Hebrew Poetry: A Guide to Its Techniques*, JSOTSup 26, Sheffield: JSOT Press.

Watson, Wilfred G. E. (2005), *Classical Hebrew Poetry: A Guide to Its Techniques*, London: T&T Clark.

Watts, John D. W. (2005), *Isaiah 34–66*, rev. ed., WBC 25, Nashville, TN: Nelson.

Watts, Rikki E. (1997), *Isaiah's New Exodus and Mark*, WUNT 2/88, Tübingen: Mohr Siebeck.

Weidner, Ernst F. (1921–3), "Studien zur babylonischen Himmelskinde," *Rivista degli Studi Orientali* 9: 287–300.

Weidner, Ernst F. (1939), "Jojachin, König von Juda, in Babylonischen Keilschrifttexten," in *Mélanges Syriens offerts à M. René Dussaud II*, 923–35, Paris: Geuthner.

Weinberg, Joel (1999), "The International Elite of the Achaemenid Empire: Reality and Fiction," *ZAW* 111: 583–608.
Weippert, Manfred (2001), "'Ich bin Jahwe'—'Ich bin Ištar von Arbela': Deuterojesaja im Lichte der neuassyrischen Prophetie," in Beat Huwyler, Hans-Peter Mathys and Beat Weber (eds), *Prophetie und Psalmen: Festschrift für Klaus Seybold*, 31–60, Münster: Ugarit-Verlag.
Weiss, Meir (1966), "The Origin of the 'Day of the Lord'—Reconsidered," *Hebrew Union College Annual* 37: 29–60.
Weissbach, F. H. (1911), *Die Keilinschriften der Achämeniden*, Voderasiatische Bibliotek 3, Leipzig: J. C. Hinrichs.
Wellhausen, Julius (1893), *Skizzen und Vorarbeiten, Fünftes Heft: die Kleinen Propheten übersetzt, mit notes*, Berlin: Reimer.
Wells, Bruce, F. Rachel Magdalene, and Cornelia Wunsch (2010), "The Assertory Oath in Neo-Babylonian and Persian Administrative Texts," *Revue Internationale des droits de l'Antiquité* 57: 13–29.
Wenzel, Heiko (2011), *Reading Zechariah with Zechariah 1:1–6 as the Introduction to the Entire Book*, Contributions to Biblical Exegesis and Theology 59, Leuven: Peeters.
West, E. W., trans. (1988), *Contents of the Nasks*, in *Pahlavi Texts, Part IV*, SBE, Delhi: Motilal Banarsidass. Orig. pub. 1892.
West, M. L. (1997), *The East Face of Helicon: West Asiatic Elements in Greek Poetry and Myth*, Oxford: Clarendon.
West, M. L. (2010), *Indo-European Poetry and Myth*, Oxford: Oxford University Press. First pub. 2007.
West, M. L. (2011), *Old Avestan Syntax and Stylistics: With an Edition of the Texts*, Abhandlungen der Akademie der Wissenschaften zu Göttingen: Neue Folge 13, Berlin: de Gruyter.
Westermann, Claus (1969), *Isaiah 40–66*, trans. David M. G. Stalker, OTL, Philadelphia: Westminster. First pub. 1966.
Whitley, C. F. (1972), "Deutero-Isaiah's Interpretation of Ṣedeq," *VT* 22: 469–75.
Whybray, R. N. (1978), *Thanksgiving for a Liberated Prophet: An Interpretation of Isaiah Chapter 53*, JSOTSup 4, Sheffield: JSOT Press.
Whybray, R. N. (1983), *The Second Isaiah*, OTG, Sheffield: JSOT Press.
Wiesehöfer, Josef (2009), "The Achaemenid Empire," in Ian Morris and Walter Scheidel (eds), *The Dynamics of Ancient Empires: State Power from Assyria to Byzantium*, 66–98, Oxford: Oxford University Press.
Wilcox, Peter, and David Paton-Williams (1988), "The Servant Songs in Deutero-Isaiah," *JSOT* 42: 79–102.
Wilks, John G. F. (2003), "The Prophet as Incompetent Dramatist," *VT* 53: 530–43.
Will, Ernest (1987), "Qu'est-ce qu'une *baris*?" *Syria* 64 (3–4): 253–60.
Willey, Patricia Tull (1997), *Remember the Former Things: The Recollection of Previous Texts in Isaiah 40–55*, Atlanta, GA: SBL.
Williamson, H. G. M. (1977), "The Historical Value of Josephus' *Jewish Antiquities* XI.297-301," *JTS* 28 (1): 48–67.
Williamson, H. G. M. (1994), *The Book Called Isaiah: Deutero-Isaiah's Role in Composition and Redaction*, Oxford: Clarendon.
Williamson, H. G. M. (1998), *Variations on a Theme: King, Messiah and Servant in the Book of Isaiah*, The Didsbury Lectures 1997, Carlisle: Paternoster.

Williamson, H. G. M. (2015), "The Setting of Deutero-Isaiah: Some Linguistic Considerations," in Jonathan Stökl and Caroline Waerzeggers (eds), *Exile and Return*, 253–67. BZAW 478, Berlin: de Gruyter.

Willi-Plein, Ina (2007), *Haggai, Sacharja, Maleachi*, Zürcher Bibel Kommentare. Zürich: Teologischer Verlag Zürich.

Wilson, Andrew (1986), *The Nations in Deutero-Isaiah: A Study in Composition and Structure*, ANETS 1, Lewiston, NY: Edwin Mellen.

Wilson, Ian Douglas (2015), "Yahweh's Anointed: Cyrus, Deuteronomy's Law of the King, and Yehudite Identity," in Jason M. Silverman and Caroline Waerzeggers (eds), *Political Memory in and after the Persian Empire*, 325–62, ANEM 13, Atlanta, GA: SBL.

Wilson, Ian Douglas (2017), *Kingship and Memory in Ancient Judah*, Oxford: Oxford University Press.

Wilson, Robert R. (1980), *Prophecy and Society in Ancient Israel*. Philadelphia: Fortress.

Wilson, Robert R. (1988), "The Community of Second Isaiah," in Christopher R. Seitz (ed.), *Reading and Preaching the Book of Isaiah*, 53–70. Philadelphia: Fortress.

Wilson, Robert R. (2012), "The Persian Period and the Shaping of Prophetic Literature," in Jon L. Berquist and Alice Hunt (eds), *Focusing Biblical Studies: The Crucial Nature of the Persian and Hellenistic Periods*, 107–20, London: T&T Clark.

Winckelman, Michael J. (2011), "A Paradigm for Understanding Altered Consciousness: The Integrative Mode of Consciousness," in Etzel Cardeña and Michael J. Winckelman (eds), *Altering Consciousness: Multidisciplinary Perspectives*, 23–41, Santa Barbara, CA: Praeger.

Wittmann, L., and Michael Schredl (2004), "Does the Mind Sleep? An Answer to 'What is a Dream Generator?'," *Sleep and Hypnosis* 6: 177–8.

Wöhrle, Jakob (2006a), *Die frühen Sammlungen des Zwölfprophetenbuches: Entstehung und Komposition*, BZAW 360, Berlin: de Gruyter.

Wöhrle, Jakob (2006b), "The Formation and Intention of the Haggai-Zechariah Corpus," *JHebS* 6 (10): 1–14.

Wöhrle, Jakob (2016), "On the Way to Hierocracy: Secular and Priestly Rule in the Books of Haggai and Zechariah," in Lena-Sofia Tiemeyer (ed.), *Priests and Cults in the Book of the Twelve*, 173–90, ANEM, Atlanta, GA: SBL.

Wolters, Al (2012), "The Meaning of Ṣantĕrôt (Zech 4:12)," *JHebS* 12 (1): 1–15.

Woodard, Roger D. (2007), "Hesiod and Greek Myth," in Roger D. Woodard (ed.), *The Cambridge Companion to Greek Mythology*, 84–165, Cambridge: Cambridge University Press.

Woude, A. S. van der (1974), "Die Beiden Söhne des Öls (Sach. 4:14): Messianische Gestalten?" in M. S. H. G. Heerma van Voss, Ph. H. J. Houwink ten Cate and N. A. Van Uchelen (eds), *Travels in the World of the Old Testament: Studies presented to Professor M. A. Beek on the Occasion of his 65th Birthday*, 262–8, Assen: Van Gorcum.

Woude, A. S. van der (2005), "'Hearing Voices While Reading': Isaiah 40–55 as a Drama," in Patrick Chatelion Counet and Ulrich Berges (eds), *One Text, a Thousand Methods: Studies in Memory of Sjef van Tilborg*, 149–75, Leiden: Brill.

Wright, David P. (1987), *The Disposal of Impurity: Elimination Rites in the Bible and in Hittite and Mesopotamian Literature*, SBLDS 101, Atlanta, GA: Scholars Press.

Wright, Henry T., James A. Neely, and Elizabeth Carter (2010), *Elamite and Achaemenid Settlement on the Deh Lurān Plain: Towns and Villages of the Early Empires in Southwestern Iran*, Memoirs of the Museum of Anthropology, University of Michigan 47, Ann Arbor, MI: University of Michigan Press.

Wunsch, Cornelia (2000a), *Das Egibiarchiv I: Die Felder und Gärten*, 2 vols, CM 20a–b, Groningen: Styx.
Wunsch, Cornelia (2000b), "Neubabylonische Geschäftsleute und ihre Beziehungen zu Palast- und Tempelverwaltungen: Das Beispiel de Familie Egibi," in A. C. V. M. Bongenaar (ed.), *Interdependency of Institutions and Private Entrepreneurs*, 95–118, Istanbul: Nederlands Historisch-Archaeologisch Instituut te Istanbul.
Wunsch, Cornelia (2013), "Glimpses on the Loves of Deportees in Rural Babylonia," in A. Berlejung and M. P. Streck (eds), *Arameans, Chaldeans and Arabs in Mesopotamia and Palestine*, 247–60, Wiesbaden: Harrassowitz.
Wunsch, Cornelia (forthcoming), *Judeans by the Waters of Babylon: New Historical Evidence in Cuneiform Sources from Rural Babylonia*, Babylonische Archive 6, Dresden: ISLET.
Wunsch, Cornelia, and F. Rachel Magdalene (2012), "A Slave is Not Supposed to Wear Such a Garment," *Kaskal* 9: 99–120.
Wünsche, August (1967), *Aus Israels Lehrhallen*, vol. 4, Hildesheim: Georg Olms Verlafsbuchhandlung.
Wüst, Walther (1966), *Altpersische Studien: Sprach- und Kulturgeschichtliche Beiträge zum Glossar der Achämeniden-Inschriften*, Munich: Kitzinger.
Wyatt, Nicolas (2007), "Religion in Ancient Ugarit," in John R. Hinnells (ed.), *A Handbook of Ancient Religions*, 105–60, Cambridge: Cambridge University Press.
Yarbro Collins, Adela (2001), *The Combat Myth in the Book of Revelation*, Eugene, OR: Wipf & Stock. First pub. 1976.
Younger, Paul (1992), "Velankanni Calling: Hindu Patterns of Pilgrimage at a Christian Shrine," in Alan Morinis (ed.), *Sacred Journeys: The Anthropology of Pilgrimage*, 89–100, Westport, CT: Greenwood.
Yoyette, Jean (2013), "The Egyptian Statue of Darius," in Jean Perrot (ed.), *The Palace of Darius at Susa: The Great Royal Residence of Achaemenid Persia*, 240–71, London: I. B. Tauris.
Zadok, Ran (2002), *The Earliest Diaspora: Israelites and Judeans in Pre-Hellenistic Mesopotamia*, Publications of the Diaspora Research Institute 151, Tel Aviv: Tel Aviv University.
Zadok, Ran (2014), "Judeans in Babylonia—Updating the Dossier," in Uri Gabbay and Shai Secunda (eds), *Encounters by the Rivers of Babylon: Scholarly Conversations between Jews, Iranians, and Babylonians in Antiquity*, 109–130, Tübingen: Mohr Siebeck.
Zapff, B. M. (2001), *Jesaja 40–55*, Die Neue Echter Bibel, Würzburg: Echter Verlag.
Zauzich, Karl-Theodor (1980), "Aus zwei demotischen Traumbüchern," *Archiv für Papyrusforschung* 27: 91–8.
Zawadzki, Stefan (1994), "Bardiya, Darius and Babylonian Usurpers in the Light of the Bisitun Inscription and Babylonian Sources," *AMIT* 27: 127–45.
Zawadzki, Stefan (1996), "Cyrus-Cambyses Coregency," *RA* 90 (2): 171–83.
Zawadzki, Stefan (2006), *Garments of the Gods: Studies on the Textile Industry and the Pantheon of Sippar according to the Texts from the Ebabbar Archive*, OBO 218, Fribourg: Academic Press.
Zawadzki, Stefan (2010), "The Portrait of Nabonidus and Cyrus in Their (?) Chronicle. When and Why the Present Version was Composed," in Petr Charvát and Petra Maříková Vlčková (eds), *Who was King? Who was not King?*, 142–54, Prague: Institute of Archaeology of the Academy of Sciences of the Czech Republic.

Zawadzki, Stefan (2012), "The End of the Neo-Babylonian Empire: New Data Concerning Nabonidus's Order to Send the Statues of Gods to Babylon," *JNES* 71 (1): 47–52.

Zgoll, Annette (2006), "Königslauf und Götterrat: Struktur und Deutung des babylonischen Neujahrsfestes," in Erhard Blum and Rüdiger Lux (eds), *Festtraditionen in Israel und im Alten Orient*, 11–80, Gütersloh: Gütersloher Verlagshaus.

Zgoll, Annette (2006), *Traum und Welterleben im antiken Mesopotamien: Traumtheorie und Traumpraxis im 3.–1. Jahrtausend v. Chr. als Horizont einer Kulturgeschichte des Träumens*, AOAT 333, Münster: Ugarit-Verlag.

Zhou, Min (1997), "Segmented Assimilation: Issues, Controversies, and Recent Research on the New Second Generation," *International Migration Review* 31 (4): 975–1008.

Ziai, Hossein (1995), "Dreams and Dream Interpretation in the Persian Tradition," *EncIr* 7 (4): 549–51, http://www.iranicaonline.org/articles/dreams-and-dream-interpretation.

Ziegler, Nele (2011), "Music, the Work of Professionals," in Karen Radner and Eleanor Robson (eds), *The Oxford Handbook of Cuneiform Culture*, 288–312, Oxford: Oxford University Press.

Zohary, Michael (1982), *Plants of the Bible*, Cambridge: Cambridge University Press.

Zumthor, P. (1990), *Oral Poetry: An Introduction*, trans. Kathryn Murphy-Judy, Theory and History of Literature 70, Minneapolis, MN: University of Minnesota Press.

Index of Sources

HEBREW BIBLE/
OLD TESTAMENT

Genesis
2	206
2:5	206
2:9	206
19	177
20	177
28	177
31	177
31:10	154
31:12	154
42:30	146
44	145
44:4	145
44:15	145

Exodus
3:5	140
15.5	133
21:37–22:12	148
25	143
32	43

Leviticus
11:19	150, 151
11:22	37
11:42	151
16	43
19:11	148
19:13	148

Numbers
5	147
12:6	177
21:8–9	159

Deuteronomy
5:17	148
8:8	206
11	46
13:1–5 Eng.	177
13:1–3	176
13:2–6	177
13:3 Eng.	177
13:4	177
14:18	150, 151
18:9–14	177
21	43
28	46

Joshua
3:11	145
3:13	145

Judges
8:3	154

1 Samuel
28:6	177
28:15	177

2 Samuel
6	4

1 Kings
3:4–15	177
4:14	127
4:25	206
6–7	4
6:3	147
7	143

2 Kings
2:24	266
18:4	159
18:31	206
24:8	6
25	76
25:8	271
25:27–30	6

1 Chronicles
5:7	127
6:24	127
15:17	127
27:21	127
29:1	210
29:19	210

2 Chronicles
7:13	37
17:7	127
17:12	210
20:14	127
27:4	210
28:12	127
35:8	127

Ezra
4:8–9	201
4:17	201
5:1	127
6:11	147
6:14	127
6:15	161, 272
8:17	69
10:26	127

Nehemiah
1:1	210
2:8	210
3:30	127
6:7	21
6:10–14	21

Nehemiah (cont.)

6:18	127
7:2	210
8:15	131
9:11	133
11:4	127
11:5	127
11:22–24	200
12:4	127
12:16	127

Esther

1:2	210
1:11	156
2:17	156
8:15	156
9:12	210

Job

1–2	143
2:10	39
7:14	178
19:9	156
20:8	178
26:13	64
29:14	141
33:14–16	177
33:15	178
39:13	150

Psalms

1:1	158
8:5	156
8:6 MT	156
68:23	133
69:3	133
69:16	133
73:20	177
88:7	133
97:5	145
104:17	150
105:33	206

Proverbs

4:9	156
12:22	148
14:25	148
16:32	154
17:7	148
29:11	154

Ecclesiastes

2:5–6	206
5:2	177
5:3	168
5:3 Eng.	177
5:6	177
5:7 Eng.	177
7:9	154
10:4	154

Isaiah

1–39	28, 49
3:18–23	141
6:2	151
13	49
20:1	115
21	49
24:4	206
27:1	64
28:1	156
28:3	156
28:33	146
29:8	177
36:16	206
40–48	36, 47, 48, 52, 53
40:1–11	29, 52
40:1–2	51
40:1	35
40:2	29, 34, 39
40:9	51
40:12–31	37
40:12–17	29
40:12–16	36
40:12	36, 37
40:13–14	37
40:15–17	37
40:18–20	29, 35, 37, 47
40:20–22	46, 114
40:20	65
40:21–22	29, 36, 37
40:21	36
40:23–24	30, 37
40:25–31	30, 36
40:25–26	37
40:27–31	37
40:27	34, 39, 51
41:1–5	21, 48
41:1–4	30
41:2	35, 37
41:4	36, 37
41:5–7	30, 47
41:6–7	65
41:8–20	30
41:8	34, 41, 51
41:9	41
41:10	35
41:14	51
41:17–19	70
41:17	47
41:19	131
41:21–24	30, 47
41:25–29	30
41:25–27	48
41:25–26	49
41:25	35
42:1–9	30
42:1–7	44, 48, 49, 115
42:1–4	38, 43
42:1	41, 42, 50
42:2	50
42:3	50
42:4	50
42:5–7	37, 109
42:5–6	36
42:6–7	43, 50
42:6	50, 112, 115, 248
42:8	47
42:9	34
42:10–12	30, 44
42:11–12	69
42:13–17	30
42:18–25	30, 38
42:18–21	42
42:21	35
42:22–25	70
42:24–25	39

Index of Sources

42:49	42	44:25	47, 66	47:11	63
43	38	44:26–45:13	44	47:13	66
43:1–8	30	44:26–28	38, 44, 46, 50	47:14	63
43:1	36, 38, 51			47:15	70
43:2	38, 45	44:26	34, 35, 44, 51	48:1–16	30
43:3–8	35			48:2	44, 45, 51
43:3	69	44:28	34, 35, 44, 48, 51, 112	48:3–5	34
43:5–8	46			48:5–6	47
43:7	36, 38	45:1–8	30, 48, 50	48:7	36, 40
43:9–13	30	45:1–2	44	48:8	36
43:9	42	45:1	43, 48, 112	48:12–13	36, 40
43:10–13	36	45:3–4	44	48:12	43, 51
43:10	38, 67	45:4–5	42	48:14–16	21, 44, 48, 51
43:14–15	30	45:4	50, 51		
43:14	38, 62, 64	45:5	50	48:14–15	41
43:15	36, 38, 67	45:6	44	48:14	51, 62, 63, 115
43:16–21	30	45:7–12	36, 44		
43:16–17	34	45:7	38, 40	48:16	36, 40, 51
43:21–28	44, 45	45:8	43, 44	48:17–19	30
43:21	36, 38, 41, 42	45:9–13	30	48:18	35
		45:9–12	40	48:20–22	30
43:22–44:5	30	45:13	41, 44, 46, 48, 51	48:20–21	46
43:22–28	69			48:20	51
43:22–26	34	45:14–17	30, 35, 40	49–55	53
43:22–24	34	45:14–15	45	49–54	52
43:22	51	45:14	69	49	70
43:26	45	45:16	47	49:1–6	30
43:27	34	45:17	51	49:5	42, 43, 51
43:28	51	45:18–19	30	49:6–7	35
44	38	45:18	36, 40	49:6	42, 45, 51
44:1	51	45:20–25	30, 47	49:7–13	30
44:2	36, 41, 51	45:20	66	49:8–23	46
44:3–4	43	45:23–25	32, 45	49:8	36, 40
44:5	43, 45, 51, 52	45:28	69	49:12	69
		46:1–10	47	49:14–21	30
44:6–20	35, 47	46:1–4	30	49:14–18	44
44:6–8	30	46:1–2	63, 64, 66	49:14	39, 51
44:9–20	30	46:4	36, 40	49:18–23	35
44:14	65	46:5–13	30	49:19–23	35
44:16	43	46:11–13	48	49:22–26	30
44:20	66	46:13	51	49:22–23	35
44:21–23	30	47	33, 47, 63	50	42
44:21–22	42	47:1–15	30	50:1–3	30
44:21	36, 45, 51	47:8	47, 70	50:1	34
44:23	51	47:9	63	50:4–11	30
44:24–28	30	47:10	47	50:6	68
44:24	36, 38	47:11–13	50	50:11	47

Isaiah (cont.)		55:5	35	7:2	154
51	40, 46	55:9–13	31	8:2	210
51:1–11	30	55:12–13	46	8:17	186
51:2	34	55:13	45, 131		
51:3	34, 46, 51	56–66	28	*Joel*	
51:4	45, 116	60	204	2:28 Eng.	177
51:9–10	34	63	42	3:1	177
51:11	46	63:1	154		
51:12	30			*Amos*	
51:13–14	70	*Jeremiah*		5:18–20	39
51:13	36, 40	5:17	206		
51:16–17	51	8:7	150, 151	*Jonah*	
51:16	36, 40, 42	23	177	2:4	133
51:17–23	34	23:5	142, 205		
51:20–23	70	23:32	177	*Micah*	
51:22–23	63	23:38	177	4:13	145
52:1–12	34	27:9–11	177	7:19	133
52:1–2	44, 69	29:8–9	177		
52:1	51	29:8	182	*Nahum*	
52:2	51	33:15	142, 205	2:1	62
52:4–5	63	39:14	127		
52:6	30, 45	40:5	127	*Haggai*	
52:7–12	31, 46	40:9	127	2	269
52:7	51, 62	40:11	127	2:1	124
52:8	51	41:2	127	2:7	140
52:9	51	43:6	127	2:10	122
52:10	35	44	150	2:20	122
52:11–12	44, 63	46:10	146		
52:11	73	52	76	*Zechariah*	
52:12	46			1–8	121, 122, 126, 128, 194
52:13–53:12	31, 42, 53	*Ezekiel*			
53	41, 43, 113	2:9–3:3	147		
54	35	11:2	158	1–6	162
54:1–17	31, 46	11:16	69	1	161
54:5	146	16:12	156	1:1–6	127
54:9	34	23:42	156	1:1	124, 127, 187
54:13	45, 116	40:3	138		
54:14	45	40:49	147	1:3–4	129
54:16	36, 40	43:13	148	1:3	128
55	112	45:11	148	1:7–6:8	187
55:1–13	52			1:7–17	126, 129, 197
55:1–8	31, 32	*Daniel*			
55:3–5	112	1–6	77	1:7	127, 185, 187
55:3–4	34	1:6	161		
55:3	113	4	223	1:8	130, 131, 134, 163
		7:1	178		

1:10–11	135	4:4–10	141	9–14	122, 125
1:10	131	4:4	144	10:2	177
1:11	131, 197	4:6–10	140, 143	12:10	243
1:12	136	4:6–7	142		
1:14–17	136, 195	4:7	142	**APOCRYPHA**	
1:16–17	130	4:10	142, 144	*Ecclesiasticus*	
1:16	136	4:11–14	141	40:22	206
1:18–21 Eng.	126, 137	4:12	144	48:23–25	62
2:1–17	197	5	147, 160		
2:1–13 Eng.	126, 138	5:1–4	126, 147, 197	*1 Maccabees*	
2:1–4	126, 137, 195	5:3	148	14:12	206
2:4	137	5:4	198		
2:5–17	126, 138	5:5–11	69, 126, 148	**PSEUDEPIGRAPHA**	
2:7–8	139	5:6	149	*1 Enoch*	
2:8–17	139	5:9	150	13:8	178
2:8–9	139, 197, 210	6	134, 154, 202, 207, 246	*Testament of Naphtali*	
2:9	140			5:6	151
2:10–13	139	6:1–8	126, 153	**DEAD SEA SCROLLS**	
2:10	140	6:2	153	1QIsa^a	
2:12	140	6:5	146	39:7	51
2:14–16	140	6:6–7	154		
2:14–15	139	6:6	153	4QIsa^h	50
2:15	140, 197, 201, 203	6:8	154, 195	4QPrayer of Nabonidus	223, 224, 263
		6:9–15	126, 154		
2:17	140	6:10	155		
3–4	141	6:12	157, 205, 208	**BABYLONIAN TALMUD**	
3	140, 141, 143, 146, 155–57, 185, 207, 208	6:13	208	*Berakhot*	
		6:14	155	9b	134
		6:15	158, 159		
		7–8	162, 188, 193	*Pesaḥim*	
3:1–10	126, 140	7:1–8:23	126	119a	134
3:1	141	7:1–14	161		
3:6–10	141	7:3	161	**OTHER RABBINIC WORKS**	
3:8	142, 205	7:4	123, 188	*Alphabet Midrash*	
3:9	142	7:5	161		131
3:10	141, 142	8	161		
4	133, 137, 140, 141, 199, 201, 246, 249	8:1–23	161	*Sefer Hahezyanot*	
		8:17	162	17	131
		8:18	188		
		8:19	161, 162	*Targum Jonathan*	
4:1–14	126, 143	8:20–23	162, 201		250
4:1–3	141	8:23	202, 203		

Index of Sources

GREEK AND LATIN
LITERATURE
Aelian
Varia Historia
XII.43

Aeschylus
Persians
73   199

Prometheus Bound
645   130
lines 1–80   137

Appian
Civil Wars
I.97   156

Arrian
Anabasis
I.24   156
VII.26.2   168

Artemidorus
Oneirocritica
I.45   173
II.20   151
III.46   173
IV.11   173
IV.56   151

Aristophanes
Knights
61   60

Athenaeus
IV.145d   55

Berossus
BNJ
680 F 9a   219
680 F 11   239, 240

Ctesias
Frag. 9.5   219
Frag. 13a   225

Frag. 15§56   238
§27   19

Diodorus Sicculus
Library   7

Ezekiel
Exagoge   58

Herodotus
I.50–6   17
I.74   271
I.78   18
I.91   17
I.107.1   173
I.108.1–122.3   173
I.125   219
I.127–30   61
I.128.2   173
I.132   131
I.158–9   18
I.174   18
I.209.1–5   173
II.161–69   225
III.2   225
III.16   225
III.17–26   226
III.25–38   225
III.25.3   227
III.29   226
III.30.2–3   173
III.63.1–66.3   173
III.139   7
III.149.1   173
V.33   199
VII.12.1–13.4   173, 176
VII.16b.2   168
VII.19.1–3   173
VII.47   173
VII.54   131
VIII.54   173
VIII.99.1   131

Hesiod
Theogony
lines 925   137

Homer
Iliad
II   176
II.1–34   177

Odyssey   60

Josephus
Jewish Antiquities
11.5   245
11.7.1   242, 243
11.281   245
11.297   242
12.150   245

Juvenal
Satires
II.6.542–559   176

Lactantius
Divine Institutes
15.19   174

Livy
8.6.11   130

Manetho   226

Oracle of Hystaspes   174

Pausanius
VIII.46.3   19

Philo
On Dreams
I.1–2   176
II.1–4   176

Philostratus
Life of Apollonius
I.29   174

Plato
Phaedrus
244   60

Index of Sources

Theages
124d   60

Pliny the Elder
Natural History
12.2   131
15.36   131
15.38   131

Plutarch
Regum et imperatorum apophthegmata
173d   69

Alexander
18.4–5   174

Artaxerxes
3.1–3   240

Strabo
14.1.5   19
16.2.39   20, 145
16.3.5   219
16.3.7   219
17.1.5   7

Sibylline Oracles
    60

Xenophon
Cyropaedia
8.i.16–20   200
8.ii.26–28   200

OTHER LITERATURE
Beowulf
455   137

ANCIENT NEAR EASTERN AND IRANIAN TEXTS
Astronomical Diary
-132   20

Ahiqar
    13, 49, 263

Akītu Chronicle
(ABC 16)   67

Akītu liturgy
    50

Amherst Papyrus
    63

AnOr
8   61

Arjan Bowl
Register 4   151

ARM
26.229   168

ASJ
19.1   271

Atraḫasīs
    103

Baʻal Cycle
4 IV 20–22   134
6 I 32–34   134

Babylon Prism A
    136

Babylon Prism B
    136

Babylon Prism D
    136

Babylon Stele of Nabonidus
(Schaudig 3.3)
    172

Babylonian lunar observations
    124

Bactria   200

BBR 79–82
    145

BM 22696
(Koch 2015)
    124

BM 54795
    262

BM 72747
(Waerzeggers 2014b)
    231

BM
113249   200, 228

Bundahišn
33.8   224

Cambyses
276   68

Chronicle 8
    67

Chronicle 9
    75

Chronicle 13a
    67

Clermont-Ganneau
no. 167   129
no. 175   129

CT
56, 762   195

CUSAS 28
Nos. 2–3   77, 161
nos. 2–4   10
no. 4   161
no. 34   127
no. 45   76, 127
no. 51   127
no. 61   76

Index of Sources

Cyrus Cylinder
line 3   219
line 12 50
line 13 218
line 17 219
line 27 219
line 35 219
line 43 220

DAR 141
         207

DAR 437
         195

Deir 'Alla
Combination 1,
  line 10 151

Dēnkard
9.22.5–12   224

Derveni Papyrus
         105

Descent of Inanna
Line 19   138

Dynastic Prophecy
ii.20–21 219

Egibi Archive
         76

Enki and Ninmaḫ
         103

Enūma Eliš
Lines 5–8   156
I.r19–21   154
VII   156

Gilgamesh Epic
V.154   131
XI.160   160

Gudea Cylinder A
         168

*Harran Eḫulḫul
Cylinder of Nabonidus
(Schaudig 2.12)*
         171, 218

*Harran Stele of Adad-
Guppi (Schaudig 3.2)*
         172, 218

Ilias Archive
         76

K 1292 rev. 6'–7'
         57

KAI 43   206

KAR 60
lines 17–18 222

KAR 151   124, 145

*Larsa cylinder of
Nabonidus*
         172

Ludlul Bēl Nēmeqi
         40

*Marduk Prophecy
MDP 22*
Nos. 52, 71–6, 81,
132, 162   104

MDP 41
Nos. 19, 20, 39
         104

Moses of Khoren
History of the Armenians
I.24–30   174

Mulli
ii 16'–25'   153

Murašu archive
         76
CBS 5213 68

*Nabonidus Chronicle
(ABC 7, BM 34381)*
         67, 216
II.1–4   61
III.15–20 216
III.21–22 216
III.22–24 216
III.24   216
III.24–28 216
III.25   217

*Namburbi,
Caplice OR*
36 1–8   153

Nbk
19   272

Nissinen 2003
Nos 18, 54, 58
          123
Nos 35, 36, 37,
38, 39, 41, 42,
117   171
Nos. 115–117
          20

P. Berlin
13582   233

P. Cairo Zen.
1 29.3   209

P. Rylands
9   231

*Persepolis Fortification
Tables*
PF
871   257
1137   257

Index of Sources

PGM
VII.703–26   147
VII.740–55   147
VII.1009–1016
                129

Pherendates
correspondance 192,
                231

Prayer to Šamaš and
Adad
Lines 13, 18,
33, 41, 53, 57,
66   176

Religious Chronicle
(ABC 17)   67

RT
19   171, 187

SAA 2
005 iv 6   161

SAA 7
146 l. 4   131

SAA 9
no. 3, col. II
  27–32   57
no. 8   188
no. 9   123
no. 9, 4–8 123

SAA 16
nos. 59–61 = Nissinen
2003 no. 115–17
            20
no. 61   171
K 1292 rev. 6'–7'
            57

Sefire Treaty
A, lines 11–12 134

Shahburāgān
            93

Shahnameh
            137, 224
780   222
2470   222

Šumma Izbu
IX line 16' 222

Sippar Cylinder of
Nabonidus
(Schaudig 2.14)
            172

Song of the Hoe 103

SpTU 2
013 r ii 26–7   154

Stele of Naram-Sin
            262

Stele of Hammurabi
            139, 262

Stele of Ur Nammu
            138

Tablets mentioning
Judaeans in Babylon
Dar 310   76
BM 26553   76
BM 74554   76
PBS 2/1 005   76
Zadok 2014
  nos. 1 and 5 76

Tablets mentioning
Judaeans in Sippar
BM 65149   76
BM 68921   76

TAD
A4.1   191

A4.7/8
 (AP 30/31)   22,
                69, 246
A4.9
 (AP 32)   22
B2.2
 (AP 6)   209
B7.2   161
B7.3
 (AP 44)   149
C3.15
 (AP 22)   149, 161
D7.17   174
D17.1   191

Tale of Ḥor
            13

TCL
06 12+   131

Theogony of Dunnu
            103

Tintir
I, l. 29   156
IV   80

Vidēvdad
3:1   95
7:3   95

Verse Account of
Nabonidus 67, 216,
             220, 222,
             224
i.23ff   220
ii.9   50
ii.11   220
ii.18–20   220
ii.27   220
iv.26–7   50
v.18   50
v.23'–24'   221
v.26'   221
v.28'   221

Verso of the Demotic Chronicle   228, 232

Votive Bead of Nabonidus (Schaudig 4.1)   172

WDSP
l. 1   209

Weidner texts (Babylon 28122; 28178; 28186; 28232)   10, 75, 171, 178

Xanthos Trilingual Inscription   189, 192, 199, 209, 238, 239
Greek, lines 3–4   199
Greek, lines 6–7   189
Lycian, line 4   199
Aramaic, line 3   209

Yasna
10   208
10:3   208
10:6   208
19:19   93
30:7–9   96
44   89
51:8   95
71:29   95

Yašt
13:153   95
19:11   96

YOS
1:39   171, 187
17 126   271

PERSIAN ROYAL INSCRIPTIONS
AmH   99
AsH   99
A2Hc   90, 91
A3Pa   90, 91
D2Ha   90
DB   198, 211, 234
I § 10   210
I § 13   271
I § 16   195
I § 18   195
I § 19   271
II § 15–16   208
II § 20   195
III § 49   210
III § 50   195, 272
IV § 52   210
IV § 54–6   210
IV § 63–4   210
IV § 63   210
V   194

DB_e
II.21   207

DB Aramaic   90

DEa   90

DNa   90, 91, 96

DNa_e 91

DNb   13, 90, 94, 95, 96, 198, 211
§1   96
§§2–6   198
§2   211
§3   94

DPd   90, 97, 100
DPg_a 94, 97
DSab   90, 94
DSe   90, 91
DSf   90, 96
DSi   90, 96
DSs   90, 95, 97
DSt   90, 91
DZc   90, 91
XEa   90
XPa   90, 91
XPb   90, 91
XPc   90
XPd   90, 91
XPf   90, 91
XPh   90, 91, 94, 234
§6   94
XPh_e
2   90
§1   96

XVa   90

Index of Sources

ARCHAEOLOGICAL DATA
Achaemenid palaces
  65, 75, 205, 256
Apis stele 226
Arch of Titus
  143, 144
Ay-ibūr-šabû
  80

Dahān-i Ghulāmān
  238
Depictions of four wind chariots (Pritchard 1954: nos. 11, 172, 689) 154

"Egyptianizing" Statue of Darius I
  262
Esagila 79, 80

Gerizim temple 69, 135, 156, 159, 210, 245

Ištar Gate 78, 80

Jar from Lachish
  148

Kabah-i Zardušt
  236

Merkes Quarter
  65, 79

Naqš-ī Rustam
  90

Objects in the Persepolis Treasury
  157, 262

Palace of Babylon
  10, 78, 79, 256
Paleo-botany 65, 66, 73, 133
Persepolis reliefs
  156, 204, 217

Royal road 13, 203, 263

Samadlo, Georgia
  236
Seven-spouted lamps
  143
Ship models of the Merkes Quarter
  65
Silver amphora handles with gold gilding
  155
Silver bowl with gold sheet 155
Silver disk with gold plates 156
Silver goose with gold eyes 156
Silver jar with gold wire
  156
Silver pin with gold pomegranate 155

Silver rhytons with gold elements 155
Silver statuettes with gold headgear 156
Site of Ramat Raḥel
  9, 57, 59, 133, 135, 137, 160, 193, 194, 211, 250, 256, 264
Statue of Udjahorresnet
  226
Sun God between two mountains (Pritchard 1954: nos. 683, 685)
  153
Susa construction
  65, 70, 96, 135, 195, 196, 233, 256, 262, 272

Walls of Babylon
  78, 79, 80, 81

Yaddua coin
  243
Yoḥanan coin
  243

Ziggurat of Babylon
  79

Index of Authors

Abdi, K. 94
Abernethy, D. 135, 154
Abraham, K. 76
Abram, M. 138
Abu-Lughod, L. 55
Ackroyd, P. R. 46, 122, 128, 135, 136, 138, 140, 142, 146, 148, 149, 154, 161, 206, 252
Adam, J. 82, 85
Adams, S. L. 32, 60, 258, 261
Agosino, B. 85
Agut-Labordere, D. 231, 233
Ahlström, G. W. 233
Ahn, G. 93, 94, 98
Ahn, J. J. 85, 87
Al-Rawi, F. N. H. 151
Albenda, P. 135
Albertz, R. 39, 50, 53, 56, 61, 69, 71, 72, 127, 157, 196, 242
Algar, H. 222
Alizadeh, A. 234
Allen, L. 9, 141, 240
Aloiz, E. 135
Alstola, T. E. 6, 76, 77, 82, 160
Alter, R. 33
Álvarez-Mon, J. 151, 217, 218
Ambos, C. 58, 64, 142, 190, 198
Anderson, B. W. 46
Andersson, J. 78, 81
Anklesaria, B. T. 224
Aperghis, G. G. 264
Archdeacon, T. J. 87
Arnold, B. T. 62
Arubas, B. 9, 264
Asheri, D. 219
Assis, E. 148
Atkinson, K. M. T. 225
Avishur, Y. 75, 76

Babaev, I. 236
Baggio, P. 78

Bailey, D. P. 42, 43
Bailey, H. W. 94, 96
Baker, H. D. 78–81, 161, 234
Balcer, J. M. 5, 93, 194
Baltzer, K. 28, 29, 31, 39, 51, 53, 56, 64, 71
Barag, D. P. 244
Barrett, D. 169, 182
Barstad, H. M. 31, 39, 72
Bartholomae, C. 92, 95
Batto, B. F. 101, 103
Baumgartner, W. 134, 154
Bayne, T. 164
Beal, R. H. 101
Beaulieu, P.-A. 216, 219, 221, 223
Becking, B. 74, 242
Bedford, P. R. 123, 136, 198
Beentjes, P. C. 62
Bellinger, W. H., Jr. 41
Ben Zvi, E. 14, 22, 192
Benda-Weber, I. 222
Bergamini, G. 78
Berges, U. 29, 41, 113
Bergman, J. 39, 92
Berlin, A. 33
Bernhardt, K.-H. 39, 92
Berquist, J. L. 72, 74, 122, 155, 207
Betegh, G. 105
Betts, A. V. G. 238
Betz, H. D. 129, 147, 175
Bewer, J. A. 122, 133–5
Bianchi, F. 89
Bič, M. 131, 134
Bickerman, E. J. 224
Bidmead, J. 50, 58, 64–7, 215–17
Biggs, R. D. 151
Bitzer, L. 34
Bivar, A. D. H. 93, 168, 189, 239
Black, J. 65, 151
Blanck, D. 87
Bledsoe, S. A. 263

Blenkinsopp, J. 21, 28, 31, 39, 41, 42, 49–51, 61, 64–6, 72, 85, 89, 112, 122, 135, 136, 141, 142, 155, 158
Bloch, Y. 6, 76, 161
Boda, M. J. 121, 122, 125, 127–30, 134–8, 140–2, 145, 146, 148, 149, 153–5, 158, 161, 187, 188, 196, 208
Boehmer, R. M. 222
Boer, R. 13, 70, 256
Boiy, T. 78–80
Bos, J. M. 254, 255
Botterweck, G. J. 39, 92
Boucharlat, R. 195, 209, 238
Bourdieu, P. 266
Bourguignon, E. 181
Boyce, M. 8, 20, 39, 55, 94, 95, 98, 99, 240
Brandon, S. G. F. 101
Braun, A. R. 181
Briant, P. 5, 18, 19, 55, 69, 91, 94, 110, 141, 156, 160, 189–91, 194, 195, 199, 200, 207, 224–6, 228, 238–40, 259, 261, 264
Brosius, M. 7, 11, 93, 141, 217, 226, 235, 236
Brown, J. P. 68, 146
Brown, M. F. 181
Brown, T. S. 225
Brueggemann, W. 31, 39, 51, 64
Bruehler, B. B. 141, 142
Bryan, D. 151
Bryce, T. R. 189, 190, 199, 238
Bulkeley, K. 164–6, 168, 169, 175, 177, 178, 182
Burke, K. 32–4
Burstein, S. M. 102, 219, 240
Butler, S. A. L. 144, 164, 167, 168, 170, 172, 176, 180, 182
Butterworth, M. 140, 188
Byrne, M. 35, 38, 52, 129

Caillois, R. 165
Callieri, P. 227
Calmeyer, P. 156
Cameron, G. G. 95
Canepa, M. P. 232
Carr, D. M. 19, 45
Carroll, R. P. 28, 39
Carswell, C. M. 167
Carter, C. E. 209

Carter, E. 209
Carter, G. W. 39
Cataldo, J. W. 242
Caton, S. C. 55
Cavallero, C. 167
Chavel, S. 45, 53, 72
Chaverdi, A. A. 209
Cheung, J. 96
Childs, B. S. 49, 53, 64
Choksy, J. K. 222
Chong, J. H. 69
Cicogna, P. C. 169
Clay, A. T. 171, 222
Clifford, R. J. 101–4, 106, 134
Clines, D. J. A. 41
Cogan, M. 75
Cogan, Mort. 136
Coggins, R. J. 122
Cohen, M. E. 58, 64
Cohen, S. J. D. 243–45
Cohn, N. 98
Colburn, H. P. 226
Cole, S. W. 123
Collins, B. J. 151
Collins, J. J. 60, 101, 106, 223
Colson, E. 82
Cook, S. L. 155
Corcella, A. 219
Cornelius, I. 149
Courtils, J. des 189
Cowley, A. 69
Craz, I. 148
Cross, F. M. 106, 142
Crouch, C. L. 112
Cruz-Uribe, E. 207, 225–7
Cryer, F. H. 180, 198
Curtis, B. G. 146–8, 153
Curtis, J. E. 155
Czisch, M. 164

Dalley, S. 101–3
Daloz, J.-P. 253, 255, 257
Dalton, O. M. 156
Dandamaev, M. A. 77, 110, 160, 264
Darmesteter, J. 95
Daviau, P. M. M. 198
David, J. 224
Davies, P. R. 16, 28, 52, 72, 108, 112, 114, 129, 254
Davis, D. 224

Day, J. 64, 106
De Breuker, G. 219, 240
Deissler, A. 122
Delaney, G. 169, 178, 182
Delitzsch, F. 39, 45, 69
Demsky, A. 155
Dentan, R. K. 175, 180
Dick, M. B. 65, 67, 77
Dines, J. 61
Dion, P. E. 198
Dixon, H. 206
Doan, W. 28
Dobbs-Allsopp, F. W. 54, 55, 60
Dodson, D. S. 129, 167, 177–9, 182
Domhoff, G. W. 164–6, 168, 169, 181
Doran, R. 33
Douglas, J. G. 135
Dresler, M. 164
Dubberstein, W. H. 122, 271
Dupont-Summer, A. 189, 239
Dušek, J. 245
Dusinberre, E. R. M. 11, 19, 239

Eaton, J. 29
Edelman, D. V. 112, 123, 128, 149, 188, 193, 202, 203, 209, 210
Eggan, D. 170
Ehrenberg, E. 112, 144
Eidevall, G. 19
Eidsvåg, G. M. 121
Eiferman, R. 183, 184
Elias, N. 258, 261
Elliger, K. 39, 64, 128
Ellis, R. S. 142, 190
Elphick, J. 151
Eng, T. 165, 184, 186
Erlacher, D. 179, 182
Espenak, F. 124
Esposito, M. J. 169
Evans, J. A. S. 263
Evelyn-White, H. G. 104

Faierstein, M. M. 131
Fales, F. M. 131
Farhi, Y. 160, 244
Farmer, W. R. 41
Faust, A. 14
Felber, H. 101
Fine, G. A. 164–6
Finitsis, A. 196

Finkel, I. L. 216, 218, 219
Finn, J. 19, 220, 221, 223
Finnegan, R. 61
Firby, N. K. 86
Fisher, M. T. 9, 266
Fisher, W. R. 32–4
Fitzmyer, J. A. 134
Fitzpatrick-McKinley, A. 12, 73, 190, 255, 256, 260
Flannery-Dailey, F. 167, 175–7, 182, 184
Flint, P. W. 53, 61, 69
Floyd, M. H. 121, 125, 127, 128, 130, 134, 136, 138, 141, 142, 145, 147–9, 151, 153, 154, 192, 196, 208
Fohrer, G. 41, 46
Foley, J. M. 61, 83
Folmer, M. 9
Foster, B. R. 101, 102
Fox, R. M. 129, 194
Frahm, E. 20
Frame, G. 136
Francfort, H.-P. 238
Freud, L. 160
Frevel, C. 149, 157, 159, 243, 245
Friebel, K. G. 154
Fried, L. S. 68, 115, 141, 146, 155, 189, 190, 231, 239, 244
Friedli, R. 101
Frye, R. N. 222

Gadot, Y. 9, 133, 160, 264
Gagošidse, I. 236
Garbini, G. 68, 129, 208
García Sánchez, M. 12
Gariboldi, A. 160
Garrison, M. B. 11, 90
Gasche, H. 78, 256
Gates, C. 78
Genito, B. 238
George, A. 65, 68, 78, 80, 131, 156, 216, 217, 230
Gerschevitch, I. 65
Gerstenberger, E. S. 122
Gesenius, D. W. 134
Geva, H. 79
Gibson, J. C. L. 206
Gignilliat, M. 41
Giles, T. 28
Girard, R. 43
Gitay, Y. 29

Glassner, J.-J. 61, 67, 75, 216
Gluckson, M. L. 165
Gnoli, G. 91, 94, 95
Goldingay, J. 31, 32, 39, 46, 65
Goldschmidt, L. 134
Goldstein, J. 49
Gondet, S. 227
Goodblatt, D. M. 83
Goodman, M. 201
Gottwald, N. K. 34
Goulder, M. D. 29
Grabbe, L. L. 123, 242–5
Graf, D. F. 13
Granerød, G. 7, 13, 90
Grayson, A. K. 67, 75, 216
Greenfield, J. C. 90
Greenstein, E. L. 224
Gropp, D. M. 209
Gruber, C. 105
Grunebaum, G. E. von 165
Gudme, A. K. de H. 45, 77, 135, 157, 159
Gunkel, H. 101
Gussman, O. 208

Haerinck, E. 256
Hageneuer, S. 144
Haładewicz-Grzelak, M. 201
Hale, M. 92
Hallaschka, M. 123, 187, 188
Hallo, W. W. 101, 103, 151, 191, 216
Hallock, R. T. 203, 257
Halpern, B. 141, 142
Hancock, J. A. 151
Handy, L. K. 137
Hanhart, R. 130, 136, 140, 146
Harmatta, J. 218
Harris, W. V. 167–9, 171, 173, 175, 177, 179, 182, 184
Harris-McCoy, D. E. 151, 168, 173, 175
Haubold, J. 240
Heffelfinger, K. 28, 29, 31, 32, 39, 54
Heimgartner, M. 101
Hein, I. 78, 81
Heinsch, S. 79
Hellwag, U. 105
Helms, S. W. 238
Heltzer, M. 68, 75, 76
Hengel, M. 43

Henkelman, W. 5, 7, 9, 13, 94, 95, 104, 110, 146, 156, 203, 209, 217, 227, 232, 234, 235, 264
Henze, M. 223
Herdt, G. 178, 179
Herman, G. 83
Hermisson, H.-J. 51, 69
Herrenschmidt, C. 12, 90–3, 96, 98–100
Hezser, C. 201
Hinnells, J. R. 2, 8, 86
Hintze, A. 96
Hobson, J. A. 169
Höffken, P. 53, 61
Hoffmann, R. 164, 165, 169, 179, 181, 182
Hoffner, H. A. 104
Hofmann, I. 225
Hoglund, K. G. 209, 252
Hohwy, J. 164
Hollan, D. 169
Hollander, E. 101
Hollmann, A. 173
Homiak, J. 178
Honingman, S. 242
Hooker, J. 106
Horowitz, W. 102, 103, 154
Howlett, D. 202
Hrushovski-Harshav, B. 33
Huffmon, H. B. 57
Hughes, A. 149
Hulster, I. J. de 126, 149, 151, 154, 204
Hultgård, A. 110
Hunger, H. 20, 124
Hurowitz, V. A. 138, 188, 198
Husser, J.-M. 165–8, 172, 176, 177, 182, 185
Huyse, P. 8

Ilan, T. 244

Jacobs, B. 9, 261
Jacobson, H. 58
Jakobsen, T. 138
Janowski, B. 41
Jastrow, M. 134
Jauhianen, M. 208
Jeremias, C. 151, 152
Joannès, F. 151
Johnson, B. 35
Jones, C. M. 204

Jong, A. de 90, 100, 189
Jonker, L. 123
Joüon, P. 208
Jursa, M. 7, 68, 70, 76–8, 80, 81, 127, 160, 161, 190, 195, 200, 229, 230, 232, 255

Kahan, T. L. 164, 165, 167, 169, 178, 179, 181
Kahl, M. P. 151
Kaivola-Bregenhøj, A. 178
Kaminsky, J. 85
Kapelrud, A. S. 31, 233
Kaper, O. E. 207, 227, 231
Kasher, A. 242, 245
Kashow, R. C. 205
Kautsky, J. H. 253, 255
Keel, O. 129, 130, 135, 137, 145, 147, 188
Kellens, J. 92, 95, 96
Kellogg, E. 181
Kelner, S. 201
Kent, R. G. 89, 92, 93, 95, 198, 208
Kessler, J. 81, 82, 114, 147, 194, 195, 258, 261
Kessler, K. 125, 129, 142, 217, 230, 269
Khaleghi-Motlagh, D. 222
Khatchadourian, L. 236, 255
Khorenats'i, M. 106, 174
Khozhaniyazov, G. 238
King, P. J. 55
Kingsley, P. 18
Kirtsoglou, E. 166, 179
Kiste, R. C. 82
Kitchen, K. A. 112
Kittel, R. 50
Kivisto, P. 87
Kleber, K. 200, 201, 228–30, 234
Kletter, R. 148
Klotz, D. 207
Knäpper, K. 94, 98
Knauß, F. S. 236
Knoppers, G. N. 246
Knowles, M. D. 149, 201, 202
Koch, H. 98
Koch, K. 92, 105
Koch, U. S. 124, 145, 167, 170, 192, 198
Koehler, L. 134, 154
Koldeway, Y. 65, 78, 79
Kolyada, Y. 55

Koole, J. L. 29, 39, 51, 53, 64, 69
Korpel, M. C. A. 28, 33, 51, 53, 55, 56, 64
Kosrowzadeh, A. 209
Koulack, D. 164, 169
Kouremenos, T. 105
Kozuh, M. 190, 199
Kracke, W. H. 169, 178, 179
Kramer, M. 164–6
Kratz, R. G. 53, 61
Krippner, S. 165, 169, 179, 181
Kroll, S. 105
Kuhrt, A. 7, 18, 50, 61, 65, 67, 68, 94, 97, 138, 190, 191, 194, 203, 215–20, 224–8, 230, 233, 240, 241, 263
Kuiken, D. 165, 184, 186
Kuntner, W. 79
Kushlan, J. A. 151
Kvanvig, H. S. 224

LaBerge, S. 164, 165, 167, 181
Laato, A. 142, 242
Ladiray, D. 135
Lambert, W. G. 102, 103, 156
Lanfranchi, G. B. 240
Langdon, S. 156
Langgut, D. 9, 133
Law, D. R. 53
Lawrence, P. J. N. 112
LeMon, J. M. 126
Lecoq, P. 89, 91, 96, 97
Lee, K.-J. 189
Lee, M.-L. 165, 184, 186
Lefebvre, G. 182
Leichty, E. 136, 192, 222
Leighton, L. F. 164–6
Leistle, B. 181
Lemaire, A. 62, 129, 160, 209, 244, 256
Lemos, T. M. 82
Lenski, G. 258
Lenski, J. 258
Lenzi, A. 40, 144, 176
Levine, B. A. 174
Lewis, D. M. 8
Light, T. 2
Lightfoot, J. L. 60
Lincoln, B. 11, 90, 92–4, 96, 97, 99, 106, 259
Lindblom, J. 177, 178, 183
Lindenberger, J. M. 22, 69, 191

Lindhagen, C. 41
Linssen, M. J. H. 190, 222
Linville, J. R. 113
Lippolis, C. 78
Lipschits, O. 9, 133, 160, 264
Liss, H. 14
Lloyd, A. B. 191, 219, 225, 226, 230, 231
Lohmann, R. I. 169, 175
Long, C. H. 101
López-Ruiz, C. 104, 105
Lord, A. B. 54–6
Lorenz, J. 194
Löw, I. 131
Lozachmeur, H. 129, 209
Lu, Y. 168
Lubos-Kozieł, J. 201
Lundblom, J. R. 46
Luukko, M. 20
Lux, R. 269

MacLean, K. 201, 202
MacPherson, S. 61, 83
Machinist, P. 123, 221
Magdalene, R. 6, 199
Magen, U. 222
Magen, Y. 159
Mageo, J. M. 164
Malandra, W. W. 95
Malkki, L. H. 82, 84
Mankowski, P. V. 161
Mansel, P. 82, 83
Marinkovic, P. 193
Martin, C. J. 231, 233
Mason, R. 130, 135
Mathys, H.-P. 135
Maul, S. M. 262
Mayrhofer, M. 189, 239
McCall, B. 209
McCarthy, D. J. 112
McClusky, L. J. 175, 180
McComiskey, T. E. 122
McCorriston, J. 201, 204
McGinnis, C. M. 41
McKenzie, J. L. 41, 43
McKinlay, J. E. 19, 45, 113
McSpadden, L. A. 82
Meadows, A. R. 160
Meeus, J. 124
Meier, C. A. 182
Mein, A. 19, 82

Melugin, R. F. 53
Merkt, A. 101
Merrill, E. H. 31
Merrill, W. 178, 180
Meshorer, Y. 160, 244
Metzger, H. 189, 199, 209, 238
Meyers, C. L. 121, 122, 127, 128, 130, 133, 140, 142, 147, 152–5, 158, 161, 188, 208
Meyers, E. M. 121, 122, 127, 128, 130, 133, 140–2, 147, 152–5, 158, 161, 188, 208
Michel, D. 56
Michelini, A. M. 58
Middlemas, J. 45, 72
Mieroop, M. van de 78–81
Milbank, J. 85
Mildenberg, L. 244
Mills, L. H. 39, 95, 96
Misgav, H. 159
Mitchell, C. 13, 89, 90, 122, 193
Mitchell, H. G. 122, 133–5
Moffitt, A. 164, 165, 169, 179, 181, 182
Momigliano, A. 245
Monopoli, B. 78
Montangero, J. 169, 179
Moor, J. C. de 28, 33, 51, 53, 55, 56, 64
Mor, M. 242
Morinis, A. 201
Morrow, W. 43
Morvillez, E. 110, 146
Moseman, R. D. 122
Moukarzel, K. 220
Mowinckel, S. 56, 208
Münsterberg, H. 170
Muraoka, T. 208

Nagel, A. 135
Nasrabadi, B. M. 104
Natale, V. 167, 169
Naveh, J. 9, 200, 201
Neely, J. A. 209
Negus, M. 238
Neujahr, M. 136
Neumann, J. 154
Newsom, C. A. 223
Niditch, S. 13, 33, 55, 133–5, 137, 143, 147, 154
Nieling, J. 236
Nihan, C. 112

Nilsen, T. D. 39, 108
Nissinen, M. 13, 16, 20, 28, 43, 57, 123, 168, 171, 180, 198
Nolan, P. 258
Nongri, B. 245
North, C. R. 41
North, R. 143

O'Kennedy, D. F. 141
Obeyesekere, G. 165, 181
Occhionero, M. 169
Oded, B. 75
Oeming, M. 9, 14, 264
Olden, A. 61, 83
Olszewska, Z. 61, 83, 84
Omidsalar, M. 137
Oppenheim, A. L. 145, 151, 167, 168, 170–3, 176, 178, 180, 182, 192, 217
Orlinsky, H. M. 42
Osborne, T. 149
Otzen, B. 39, 92
Overholt, T. W. 16, 19, 28
Owen, A. M. 164

Panaino, A. 264
Parássoglou, G. M. 105
Parke, H. W. 60
Parker, R. A. 122, 207, 271
Parker, S. B. 134
Parpola, S. 57, 123, 188, 222
Pasche, P. 169, 179
Paton-Williams, D. 41
Paul, S. M. 34, 39, 41, 46, 49, 51, 61, 64
Paulson, J. F. 138
Payne, D. 31, 65
Pearce, L. E. 10, 76, 77, 127, 161
Pedersén, O. 75, 78–81
Perdrizet, P. 182
Perdu, O. 230, 231
Perrot, A. 55
Perrot, J. 195
Petersen, D. L. 28, 121, 122, 127, 130, 131, 134, 135, 137, 140, 142, 143, 145, 146, 151, 153, 154, 158, 161, 187, 188
Petrie, C. A. 209
Petterson, A. R. 208
Pettinato, G. 145
Pinches, T. G. 171
Pirart, E. 95, 96
Pompeo, F. 92, 97

Pomykala, K. E. 142
Pongratz-Leisten, B. 50, 58, 64, 65, 215
Porat, N. 9, 133
Porten, B. 9, 13, 22, 69, 90, 127, 174, 191, 209, 246
Portes, A. 87
Portier-Young, A. 19
Postgate, N. 65
Potts, D. T. 66, 73, 78, 209
Preuß, H. D. 35, 154
Pritchard, J. B. 138, 151, 153, 154, 216
Pummer, R. 245
Purcell, S. 164, 179, 181, 182
Pyper, H. S. 121
Pyschny, K. 149

Qedar, S. 160, 244

Rad, G. von 142
Ray, J. D. 207
Razmjou, S. 96, 220, 232
Redditt, P. L. 128, 142, 244
Rehm, E. 236
Reiner, E. 151
Reissler, P. 223
Renburg, G. H. 156, 172, 179, 181
Reventlow, H. G. 128, 130
Reynolds, F. 222
Rignell, L. G. 29, 43, 64, 130, 133–5, 208
Ringgren, H. 35, 39, 92, 129
Riotte, T. 82, 83
Ristau, K. A. 125, 155, 189
Ritner, R. K. 168, 175
Roaf, M. 96, 105, 135, 156, 232
Rochberg, F. 124, 198
Rohrmoser, A. 7
Rollinger, R. 225, 240, 261
Römer, T. 112
Rom-Shiloni, D. 72
Rooke, D. W. 233, 242, 245
Root, M. C. 11, 90, 100, 107, 112, 259, 264
Ropp, C. C. 168, 179
Rose, W. H. 142, 145, 206, 208
Rösel, M. 57
Rosenmeyer, T. G. 58
Rossi, A. V. 209
Roth, M. 222
Roustei, M. S. 209
Rowland, C. 184

Rubanovich, J. 8
Rudolph, W. 133
Russell, J. R. 191
Ruyneau de St. G., P. 169
Ruzicka, S. 225

Sacchi, P. 158, 252
Sachs, A. J. 20, 124
Sack, R. H. 6, 76
Sallaberger, W. 101
Sanders, J. 149
Sandowicz, M. 216
Sauer, G. 142, 269
Sawyer, J. F. A. 41
Schaper, J. 160, 229, 244
Schaudig, H. 50, 61, 65, 66, 136, 171, 172, 190, 216, 218, 233
Scheil, V. 97, 104
Scheuer, B. 35
Schipper, J. 43
Schmidt, E. F. 90, 94, 96, 157, 262
Schmitt, R. 89, 93–5, 97, 127, 151, 157, 198, 207, 208, 210, 211
Schneider, A. 170
Schökel, L. A. 33
Schredl, M. 164–6, 169, 179, 181, 182
Schwartz, D. R. 242
Schwartz, M. 189
Scolnic, B. E. 245
Scott, J. C. 254, 266
Scudder, T. 82
Scurlock, J. 101
Seeligmann, I. L. 61, 69
Seeman, C. 242, 243, 245
Seire, M. 68
Seitz, C. R. 28, 34, 49, 72
Sekunda, N. V. 217
Seri, A. 102
Seybold, K. 196
Shahbazi, A. S. 222
Shaked, S. 9, 200, 201
Shanon, B. 183, 184
Sharma, R. S. 91
Sharp, C. J. 41
Shayegan, M. R. 5
Shenkar, M. 238
Sherwin, S. J. 65, 66, 73
Sherwin-White, S. 68
Shrimpton, G. S. 263
Shushan, G. 169, 175, 179

Siddiq, M. 61, 83
Sikora, S. 165, 186
Siljanen, E. 7
Silver, E. 18
Silverman, J. M. 2, 3, 5, 6, 9, 11, 17, 22, 23, 27, 31, 36, 46, 49, 52, 54, 82, 93, 101, 110, 111, 116, 135, 140, 141, 143, 145, 146, 192, 197, 200, 204, 233, 240, 246, 256, 257, 263, 264, 269
Simcox, C. E. 39
Sims-Williams, N. 13, 90, 94
Sinclair, L. A. 187
Sinclair, P. J. J. 78, 81
Singh, T. 165, 184, 186
Sjöberg, A. W. 222
Skehan, P. W. 50
Skjaervø, P. O. 8, 89, 92, 94–6, 100, 224, 263
Slanski, K. 138
Slings, S. R. 61
Smith, C. 149
Smith, J. M. P. 122, 133–5
Smith, M. 39, 89, 50, 109
Smith, M. S. 105
Smith, R. L. 122
Smith-Christopher, D. L. 19, 31, 77, 82
Snyman, G. 72
Socin, A. 134
Soden, W. von 136
Sommer, B. D. 34, 62
Sonik, K. 104
Soomekh, S. 202
Southwood, K. E. 85
Spek, R. J. van der 67, 136, 219, 220
Spencer, B. J. 46, 71
Spencer, N. 230
Spieckermann, H. 42
Spilsbury, P. 242, 243, 245
Spoormaker, V. I. 164
Stager, L. E. 55
Stamm, J. J. 161
States, B. O. 169, 170
Staubli, T. 132, 133, 137
Stausberg, M. 86, 202
Stead, M. R. 128, 138, 188
Steele, J. 124, 240
Steen, E. van der 13
Steiner, R. C. 201
Stephens, J. 182
Stephenson, F. R. 124

Steve, M.-J. 104
Stökl, J. 16, 17, 20, 28, 82, 178, 182, 185
Stock, F. 85
Stolper, M. W. 7, 9, 76, 93, 171, 199, 219, 264
Strand, K. A. 145
Strawn, B. A. 204
Stronach, D. 5, 110, 155, 220
Stronk, J. P. 219, 225, 238
Stuhlmacher, P. 41
Stumbrys, T. 179, 182
Süring, M. L. 137
Sussman, V. 143
Sweeney, M. A. 127, 145, 188, 196, 198, 250
Szpakowska, K. 180, 231, 234

Tadmor, H. 221
Tainter, J. A. 14
Tal, O. 256
Tallis, N. 155
Talon, P. 102
Tavernier, J. 8, 9, 93, 230, 243
Taylor, H. 85
Tedlock, B. 164, 165, 175, 178, 180
Teixidor, J. 238, 239
Ter-Martirossov, F. I. 236
Thompson, G. 222
Thompson, R. C. 131
Thompson, S. 101
Tiemeyer, L.-S. 29, 34, 39, 46, 52, 67, 72, 126, 130, 133–5, 137, 142, 144–9, 153, 178, 182, 187, 188, 197, 208
Tigchelaar, E. J. C. 130, 141, 145–7, 153
Tilia, A. B. 96
Tolini, G. 67, 68, 200, 207, 217, 228
Toorn, K. van der 57, 149
Toral-Niehoff, I. 101
Tranquillo, N. 164, 165, 168, 169, 181, 182
Treister, M. 156
Tsantsanoglou, K. 105
Tsfania, L. 159
Tull, P. K. 41
Tuplin, C. 5, 7, 110, 146, 156, 209, 239, 263
Tweed, T. A. 82, 201, 202

Uehlinger, C. 148, 149
Ulfgard, H. 202

Ulrich, E. 50, 53, 61, 69
Utas, M. 85

Valkama, K. 14
Vallat, F. 94, 95, 104
Van Buylaere, G. 20
VanderKam, J. C. 141, 242
Vanderhooft, D. 64, 65, 72, 77, 216, 220
Vasilev, M. 236
Veblen, T. 253, 255
Vittmann, G. 225, 231
Vogelsang, W. J. 12
Volten, A. 168, 175
Vorbichler, A. 225
Vorländer, H. 85

Waerzeggers, C. 7, 8, 10, 64, 67, 68, 70, 76, 80–82, 114, 127, 156, 159, 190, 195, 196, 204, 208, 215–18, 221–3, 229–31, 233, 234, 246, 256, 272
Waetzoldt, H. 222
Walde, C. 60
Walton, J. H. 43
Wasmuth, M. 226, 227, 231, 262
Waters, M. 5, 219, 240
Watson, R. S. 106
Watson, W. G. E. 33, 55
Watts, J. D. W. 53, 71
Watts, R. E. 46
Webb, W. B. 167
Weeks, L. 209
Weidner, E. F. 10, 75, 171, 178
Weinberg, J. 253
Weippert, M. 59
Weiss, M. 142
Weissbach, F. H. 97
Wellhausen, J. 140, 141, 161
Wells, B. 199
Wenzel, H. 127
West, E. W. 224
West, M. L. 96, 104, 137
Westermann, C. 31, 39, 53, 56, 64, 69
Wetter, A.-M. 82
Wetzstein, C. 134
Whitley, C. F. 35
Whybray, R. N. 31, 42
Wiesehöfer, J. 259
Wilcox, P. 41
Wilks, J. G. F. 59
Will, E. 209

Willequet, P. 169, 179
Willey, P. T. 34, 62
Willi-Plein, I. 122
Williamson, H. G. M. 28, 41, 53, 66, 74, 243
Wilson, A. 31
Wilson, I. D. 22, 115
Wilson, R. R. 14, 16, 19, 28, 56
Winckelman, M. J. 164, 181
Wittman, L. 164
Wöhrle, J. 141, 155, 187, 209, 246
Wolters, A. 144
Woodard, R. D. 104
Woude, A. S. van der 29, 145
Wright, D. P. 153
Wright, H. T. 209
Wunsch, C. 6, 10, 76, 77, 81, 127, 161, 199, 219
Wünsche, A. 131
Wüst, W. 94, 96
Wyatt, N. 105

Yagodin, N. 238
Yarbro Collins, A. 106
Yardeni, A. 9, 13, 22, 69, 90, 174, 191, 209, 246
Younger, P. 202
Yoyette, J. 233, 262

Zadok, R. 76
Zaidi, M. 209
Zapff, B. M. 53
Zauzich, K.-T. 168, 175
Zawadzki, S. 5, 159, 194, 216–18
Zgoll, A. 58, 64–7, 167, 185, 216
Zhou, M. 87
Ziai, H. 173
Ziegler, N. 55
Zimansky, P. E. 105
Zimmern, H. 101
Zohary, M. 131
Zumthor, P. 61